basic histology

Original Portuguese title: *Histologia Basica,* 2nd ed. © 1971 by Editôra Guanabara Koogan S.A., Rio de Janeiro, Brazil

Basic Histology was translated from the Second Portuguese Edition by the original authors and revised and reedited by Dr. Alexander N. Contopoulos with the assistance of the editorial staff of Lange Medical Publications and Lange Medical Publications International.

Many of the illustrations in this book were prepared with financial aid from the Fundação de Amparo à Pesquisa do Estado de São Paulo.

basic
histology

LUIS C. JUNQUEIRA, MD

Professor of Histology and Embryology
Institute of Biomedical Science
University of São Paulo, Brazil

JOSÉ CARNEIRO, MD

Professor and Chairman of
Histology and Embryology
Institute of Biomedical Science
University of São Paulo, Brazil

ALEXANDER N. CONTOPOULOS, PhD, MD

Associate Professor of Anatomy
University of California School of Medicine
San Francisco, California

Los Altos, California   **LANGE Medical Publications**

International Standard Book Number: *0–87041–200–0*
Library of Congress Catalogue Card Number: *74–84747*

A Concise Medical Library for Practitioner and Student

Basic Histology $11.00

Lithographed in USA

Table of Contents

Foreword

We are pleased to publish the first edition in English of *Basic Histology,* originally written in Portuguese by our Brazilian colleagues, Drs L. Carlos Junqueira and José Carneiro. In its Portuguese version, published by Guanabara Koogan, the book has gone through two editions and has become accepted as the standard histology text in the medical schools in Brazil. It has also appeared in a well-received Spanish edition.

When we evaluated the original Portuguese edition, we recognized that it could be translated and adapted to fit the needs of American medical students. As the acquisition of ever greater quantities of knowledge becomes an increasing burden to medical students in this country, the need for textbooks that are at the same time concise and comprehensive has grown correspondingly. The original edition of this book seemed to us an excellent point of departure for the preparation of a text in English on the subject of histology.

Drs Junqueira and Carneiro themselves undertook the initial translation into English. Dr Alexander N. Contopoulos of the Department of Anatomy, University of California School of Medicine, San Francisco, adapted the translation to the demands of American usage and practices and continued the processes of revision and updating. The result, we believe, will be useful both to medical students and to postgraduate students of histology.

Drs Junqueira and Carneiro are Professors of Histology and Embryology at the Institute of Biomedical Science, University of São Paulo, Brazil, and both have had experience in teaching and research in medical schools in North America. Dr Junqueira was Research Associate at the University of Chicago Medical School and holds an honorary degree in biology from Harvard University. Professor Carneiro has taught in the Departments of Anatomy at McGill University Medical School in Montreal and at the University of Virginia Medical School in Charlottesville.

We hope that the book prepared by these academicians will prove as useful to medical students as our other publications have been.

Jack D. Lange, MD

Preface

This book represents the effort of the authors to produce a compact text with the relevant information necessary for students in the biomedical and biologic fields. A strong emphasis has been placed on the biology of the cells as a basis for a better understanding of tissue physiology.

New editions of this book will be produced periodically. Our readers' comments on any aspects of the presentation or content will be gratefully received.

We are greatly indebted to all of the men and women who have given so generously of their talents and skills in providing additional data and much useful criticism and advice. Particular thanks are due to Drs P.A. Abrahamsohn, D. Andreucci, C. Baros, E. Barras, T. deBrito, F. Fava de Moraes, S. Drouva, E. Erhardt, L.L. George, H. Kirkman, E.C. Mesquita, M.P. Monteiro, I. Motta, W.S. Sasso, A.M.S. Toledo, S. Yoneda, and D. Zago, and to Mesdames G.C. Fernandes, E. Andrade, and V. Rigonatti.

Most especially, however, we wish to welcome our American colleague and co-author, Dr Alexander N. Contopoulos, of the University of California School of Medicine in San Francisco, whose extensive revisions have made this book—we sincerely believe—the most carefully organized and up to date textbook of histology the student can find today.

—LCJ
—JC

August 1975

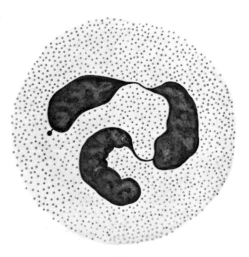

Neutrophilic granulocyte

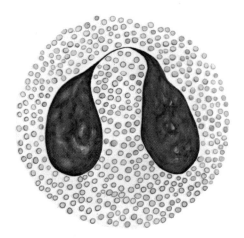

Eosinophilic granulocyte

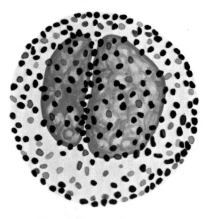

Basophilic granulocyte

Lymphocyte

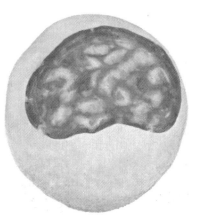

Monocyte

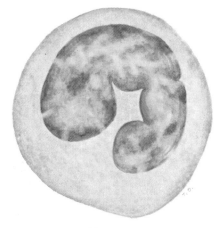

Monocyte

The 5 Types of Human Leukocytes. (See Fig 13–5.)

Proerythroblast

Hemocytoblast

Basophilic erythroblast

Neutrophilic promyelocyte

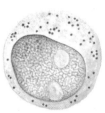

Myeloblast

Basophilic promyelocyte

Polychromatophilic erythroblast

Neutrophilic myelocyte

Eosinophilic promyelocyte

Normoblast

Neutrophilic metamyelocyte

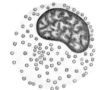

Eosinophilic myelocyte

Basophilic myelocyte

Reticulocyte

Neutrophil with
band-shaped nucleus

Eosinophilic
metamyelocyte

Erythrocyte

Mature neutrophil

Mature eosinophil

Mature basophil

Stages of Development of Erythrocytes and Granulocytes. (See Fig 14—5.)

1...
Methods of Study

Familiarity with the tools and methods of any branch of science is essential for proper understanding of the subject. Some of the more common methods used to study cells and tissues and the principles involved in these methods will be reviewed here: units of measurement, preparation of tissues for examination, optical microscopy, phase contrast microscopy, polarizing microscopy, electron microscopy, radioautography, examination of living cells and tissues, differential centrifugation, and problems in interpretation of tissue sections.

The most important units of measurement used in histology are given in Table 1–1. At a recent international conference, it was recommended that the *Ångström unit* (Å; 10^{-10} meter) be abandoned in favor of the *nanometer* (nm, 10^{-9} meter) and that the nanometer be used in place of the *millimicron* (mμ, 10^{-9} meter). In this book, the nanometer will be used in place of the Ångström unit (1 nm = 10 Å). The *micron* (μ) is now called a *micrometer* (μm), with the value (10^{-6} meter) unchanged.

parent membranes of living animals (eg, the mesentery, the tail of a tadpole, the wall of a hamster's cheek pouch) can be observed in the microscope. In such instances, it is possible to study these structures for long periods and under varying physiologic or experimental conditions. If a permanent slide preparation is desired, small fragments of these thin structures can be fixed, spread on a glass slide, stained and mounted with resin, and examined under the microscope. In most cases, however, tissues must be sliced into thin sections before they can be examined. These sections are cut by precision fine cutting instruments called *microtomes,* and the organ or tissue must be prepared and fixed before the section is made. (See Table 1–2.)

The ideal microscope tissue preparation would of course be perfectly treated with suitable chemicals so that the tissue on the slide would have the same structure and chemical composition as it has in the body. This is sometimes possible but, as a practical matter, seldom feasible, and artifacts resulting from the preparation process are almost always present.

Table 1–1. Units of measurement used in light and electron microscopy.*

SI Unit*	Symbol and Value
Micron (micrometer)	μ (μm) = 0.001 mm, 10^{-6} m
Millimicron (nanometer)	mμ (nm) = 0.001 μm, 10^{-9} m
Ångström	Å = 0.1 nm, 10^{-10} m

*The preferred *SI (Système International)* units (in parentheses) will be used throughout this book.

PREPARATION OF TISSUES FOR MICROSCOPIC EXAMINATION

The most common procedure used in the study of tissues is the preparation of permanent histologic slides that can be studied with the aid of the optical microscope. Under the optical microscope, tissues are examined by transillumination. Since tissues and organs are usually too thick for transillumination, technics have been developed for obtaining thin, translucent sections. In some cases, very thin layers of tissues or trans-

Table 1–2. Stages through which the tissues must pass before paraffin impregnation. (The next steps are microtome sectioning, staining, and mounting.)

Stage	Purpose	Duration
1. Fixation in simple or compound fixatives (Bouin's, Zenker's formalin)	To preserve tissue morphology and chemical composition	About 12 hours, according to the fixative and the size of the piece of tissue
2. Dehydration in graded concentrated ethyl alcohol (70% up to 100% alcohol)	To remove cell water	6–24 hours
3. Clearing in benzene, xylene, or toluene	To impregnate the tissues with a paraffin solvent	1–6 hours
4. Embedding in melted paraffin at 58–60 °C	Paraffin penetrates all intercellular spaces and even into the cells, making the tissues more resistant to sectioning	½–6 hours

Fixation

In order to avoid tissue digestion by enzymes (autolysis) or bacteria and to preserve physical structure, pieces of organs should be promptly and adequately treated as soon as removed from the animal's body. This treatment—*fixation*—usually consists of submerging the tissues in chemical substances in order to preserve as much as possible of their morphologic and chemical characteristics.

The chemical substances used to fix tissues are called *fixatives.* Some fixatives (eg, mercuric chloride, picric acid) promote the precipitation or clumping of proteins. Others (eg, formalin, glutaraldehyde) promote coagulation but not coarse precipitation of proteins. All fixatives have both desirable and undesirable effects. The goal of combining the desirable effects and minimizing the undesirable ones has led to the development of several mixtures. The most commonly used mixtures are *Bouin's fluid,* composed of picric acid, formalin (a saturated solution—37% by weight of formaldehyde gas in water), acetic acid, and water; and *Zenker's formalin (Helly's fluid),* containing formaldehyde, potassium dichromate, mercuric chloride, and water. The simple fixatives most commonly used are a 10% solution of formalin in saline and a 2—6% solution of buffered glutaraldehyde.

The chemistry of the process involved in fixation is complex and not well understood. However, formaldehyde and glutaraldehyde are known to react with the amine groups (NH_2) of tissue amino acids. In the case of glutaraldehyde, the fixing action is reinforced by the fact that it is a dialdehyde and can form stabilizing bonds between protein molecules. For electron microscopic fixation, buffered glutaraldehyde is often used alone or in combination with osmium tetroxide.

Embedding

In order to be able to obtain thin sections with the microtome, tissues must be infiltrated after fixation with a substance that will impart a firm consistency necessary for cutting. This can be gelatin, celloidin, paraffin, resins, or other plastic materials.

Figure 1—1. Microtome for paraffin-embedded tissues. Rotation of the drive wheel—seen with a handle on the right side of the instrument—moves the tissue block holder up and down. The paraffin block passes through the knife edge at each up-and-down movement. Each turn of the drive wheel advances the specimen holder 3—8 μm, and the block strikes the knife edge, making the sections. The sticky paraffin sections adhere to each other, producing a ribbon which is collected and fixed on a slide. (Courtesy of American Optical Co.)

Paraffin is used routinely for light microscopy; resins of the epoxy type (Epon or Araldite) are more commonly employed for electron microscopy.

The process of embedding or tissue impregnation is usually preceded by 2 main steps: *dehydration* and *lipid clearing.* The water of the fragments to be embedded is first extracted by bathing successively in a graded series of mixtures of ethanol with water (usually from 70% to 100% ethanol). The ethanol is then replaced by a lipid solvent. (In paraffin embedding, the solvent used is xylene or benzene.) As the tissues become impregnated with the solvent, they usually become transparent in a step called *clearing.* Once the tissue is impregnated with the solvent, it is placed in melted paraffin in the oven, usually at 58–60 °C. The heat causes the solvent to evaporate, and the space becomes filled with paraffin. This is the infiltration or embedding procedure.

The small blocks of paraffin containing the tissues are then sectioned by the keen steel blade of the microtome to a thickness of 3–8 μm (Fig 1–1). The sections are then laid out in warm water and transferred to glass slides. For electron microscopy, much thinner sections are necessary (0.02–0.1 μm); embedding is therefore performed in a hard epoxy plastic. The blocks thus obtained are so hard that glass or diamond knives are usually necessary to section them.

Immersion of tissues in lipid solvents such as benzene or xylene dissolves the tissue lipids, which is an undesirable effect when these compounds are studied. To prevent this, a *freezing microtome* has been devised in which the tissues are hardened at low temperatures in order to permit sectioning. The freezing microtome—and its more elaborate and efficient successor, the *cryostat*—permit sections to be obtained quickly without going through the embedding procedure described above. They are often used in hospitals, for they allow rapid study of pathologic specimens during surgical procedures. They are also effective in the histochemical study of very sensitive enzymes or small molecules, since freezing does not inactivate enzymes and hinders the diffusion of small molecules.

Staining

With few exceptions, most tissues are colorless, so that observing them unstained in the optical microscope is difficult. Methods of staining tissues have therefore been devised that not only make various tissue components conspicuous but also permit distinctions to be made between them. This is done by using mixtures of dyes which stain tissue components more or less selectively. In histology, most dyes behave like acidic or basic compounds and have a tendency to form electrostatic (salt) linkages with ionizable radicals of the tissues. Tissue components that stain more readily with basic dyes are termed *basophilic;* those with an affinity for acid dyes are termed *acidophilic.*

Examples of basic dyes are toluidine blue and methylene blue. Hematoxylin behaves in the manner of a basic dye, ie, it stains the tissues basophilically. The main tissue components that ionize and react with basic dyes do so because of acids in their composition (nucleoproteins and acid mucopolysaccharides). Acid dyes (eg, orange G, eosin, acid fuchsin) stain mostly the basic components present in cytoplasmic proteins. The basic or acid character of a dye usually explains the staining reaction on a chemical basis, but a physical basis is sometimes also present.

Of all dyes, the combination of hematoxylin and eosin (H&E) is most commonly used. Many other dyes are used in different histologic procedures; it must be stated, however, that, although they are very useful in visualizing the different tissue components, they usually provide no insight into the chemical nature of the tissue being studied.

Besides tissue staining with dyes, impregnation with such metals as silver and gold is a much used technic, especially in the study of the nervous system.

Table 1–3 summarizes some of the staining and impregnation technics used in preparing routine microscope slides.

THE OPTICAL MICROSCOPE

With the optical microscope, stained preparations are usually examined by transillumination. The microscope is composed of both mechanical and optical

Table 1–3. Examples of staining technics commonly used in histology.

Technics	Components	Nucleus	Cytoplasm	Collagen	Elastic Fibers	Reticular Fibers
H&E	Hematoxylin and eosin	Blue	Pink	Pink	Irregular	. . .
Masson's trichrome	Iron hematoxylin, acid fuchsin, Ponceau 2R, light green	Black	Red	Green	. . .	Green
Weigert's elastic stain	Resorcin and fuchsin, HCl, hematoxylin, Ponceau's picric acid, glacial acetic acid	Gray	Yellow	Red	Black	. . .
Silver impregnation for reticular fibers	Silver salt solution	. . .	. . .	Dark brown	. . .	Black

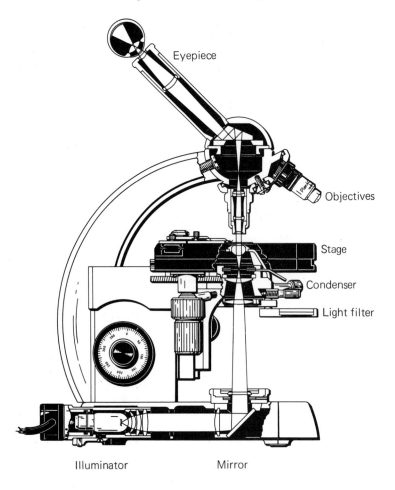

Eyepiece

Objectives

Stage

Condenser

Light filter

Illuminator   Mirror

Figure 1–2. Schematic drawing of a student's light microscope showing its main components and the pathway of light from the source (substage lamp) to the eye of the observer. (Courtesy of Carl Zeiss Co.)

parts. The mechanical components are illustrated in Fig 1–2. The optical components consist of 3 systems of lenses: condenser, objective, and ocular. The *condenser* projects a cone of light to illuminate the object to be observed. (The role of the condenser is usually underestimated because it does not contribute to the magnification; however, its proper use influences the quality of the image observed.) The *objective* lens enlarges the object and projects its image in the direction of the ocular lens. The *ocular* lens further amplifies this image and projects it onto the viewer's retina or onto a screen or photographic plate. The degree of total magnification is obtained by multiplying the magnifying power of the objective and ocular lenses.

Resolution

The critical factor in obtaining a good image with the microscope is the resolution, which is the smallest distance between 2 particles that can be distinguished from each other. For example, 2 particles will appear distinct if they are separated by a distance of 0.3 μm

and the microscope has a resolution factor of 0.2 μm. However, if the same particles are examined with a microscope that has a resolution factor of only 0.5 μm, they will appear as a single point. The resolving power of the best optical microscopes is approximately 0.2 μm.

The quality of an image—its clarity and richness in detail—depends on the microscope's resolving power. The *magnification* is independent of its resolving power and is only of value when accompanied by a high resolution capacity. The resolving power of a microscope depends mainly on its objective lens. The ocular lens only enlarges the image obtained by the objective; it does not improve resolution. Thus, high magnification with low resolution gives blurred images of little value.

Numerical Aperture

One of the main characteristics of an objective lens is its numerical aperture (NA), for resolution is a function of NA and of the light wavelength employed

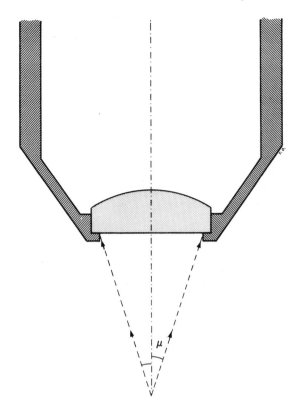

Figure 1–3. Drawing of the light beam which enters the objective lens to show the semiangle of aperture (μ) from which the numerical aperture can be calculated.

(Fig 1–3). NA can be defined as the smallest refractive index (n)* observed between the microscopic preparation and the objective multiplied by the sine of the semiangle of aperture of the lens (μ): NA = n × sine μ (Fig 1–3).

The resolution of an objective can be defined by the equation:

$$R = \frac{K \times \lambda}{NA}$$

where K is a constant of 0.61 and λ is the wavelength. Resolution is directly proportionate to the wavelength used and inversely proportionate to the NA. To calculate the resolution when working with white light, a wavelength of 0.55 μm is most often used. This corresponds to yellowish-green, a color to which the human eye is very sensitive. Fig 1–4 is an example of the importance of resolution in microscopy.

An objective lens system often has several numbers engraved on it (Fig 1–5). The first number (upper left) refers to the enlargement; to its right is the NA. The number on the left in the second line is the tube length in millimeters; the number on the right indicates the thickness (in millimeters) of the coverslip for which the objective is corrected. The thickness of the coverslip is important in dry field examination, but when oil immersion is used the oil equalizes the refractive index of the light path between the coverslip and the objective, and the thickness between the usual limits of the coverslip becomes irrelevant.

*The refractive index is a measure of the optical density of an object. A light wave traverses an object readily or otherwise depending on the object's optical density.

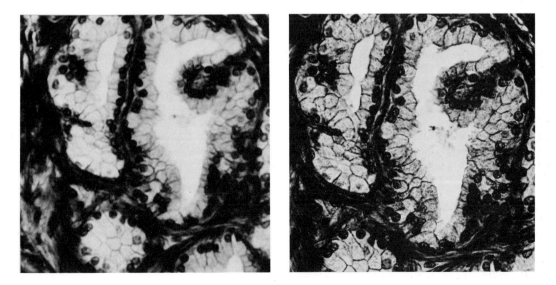

Figure 1–4. Photomicrographs of the same microscopic field at the same magnification (× 350) but with objectives of different numerical apertures (NA). The photomicrograph on the left was made with an objective of NA = 0.22; the one on the right was made with an objective of NA = 1.0. Dog prostate gland stained by Masson's trichrome stain. Observe that the picture at right (NA = 1.0) shows more detail and is sharper than the one on the left.

Figure 1–5. Drawing of an objective with the following characteristics: magnification × 25, NA = 0.45, planachromatic, corrected for 160 mm tube and for 0.17 mm coverslips.

Objective & Ocular Lenses

Objective and ocular lenses are formed by systems of lenses put together in order to achieve partial correction of their individual defects (aberrations). Although a perfect lens system has not been developed, it is possible to devise objective lenses with increasing optical perfection.

Three common aberrations are encountered in microscope lenses:

A. Chromatic Aberration: This type of aberration occurs because spherical lenses bring light of shorter wavelength into focus closer to the retina than light of longer wavelength. Consequently, several slightly separate images of the object are formed and details are blurred. In the achromatic lens system, this aberration is corrected to a large extent.

B. Spherical Aberration: In spherical aberration, the quality of the image is hindered because the optical properties of the center of a lens are somewhat different from those of its periphery. In apochromatic objective lens systems, complete correction of chromatic and spherical aberrations has been achieved.

C. Curvature of Field: Lenses with this aberration produce an image in which either the central field is in focus while the peripheral field is out of focus or vice versa.

PHASE CONTRAST MICROSCOPY

Unstained biologic specimens are usually transparent and are difficult to see in detail since all parts of the specimen have almost the same optical density. Consequently, another form of microscopy—*phase contrast microscopy*—has been developed which produces in vivo visible images from transparent objects (Fig 1–6).

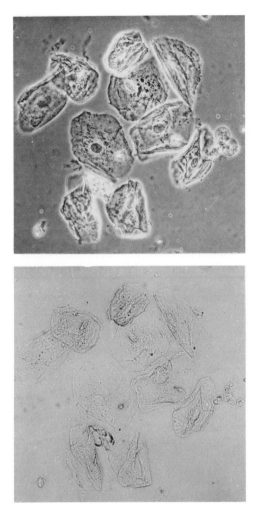

Figure 1–6. Desquamated cells from the oral mucosa. (Unstained fresh preparation.) The top photomicrograph was taken with the phase contrast microscope; the bottom photomicrograph with the standard light microscope. × 300.

Phase contrast microscopy is based on the fact that light passing through media with different refractive indexes slows down and changes direction. This forms phase differences between 2 adjoining regions. These phase differences are—by means of a special optical system—transformed into differences of light intensity so that the image becomes visible (Fig 1–6). The examination of this fresh tissue or living cells has been facilitated by the development of phase contrast microscopy.

THE POLARIZING MICROSCOPE

When light passes through certain substances or body tissues, it divides in a way that produces 2 light rays from one. This is called *polarization.* It occurs with substances whose atoms have a periodic arrangement. Whether or not this arrangement is apparent, these substances are *crystalline (birefringent)*. Substances that do not belong to the crystalline group are *amorphous (monorefringent)*.

The velocity with which light travels through amorphous substances is always the same regardless of the direction. Therefore, the substance has only one refractive index. In crystalline substances, light velocity changes according to the direction of propagation; from one light ray, 2 refracted rays result. They are polarized rectilinearly, ie, the direction of light vibration follows a determinate direction.

Crystalline calcium carbonate (calcite) is highly birefringent. The *ordinary* ray follows the law of isotropic substances (Descartes' law); the *extraordinary* ray follows slightly different laws.

In the polarizing microscope, the properties of the extraordinary ray are utilized whereas those of the ordinary ray are not. This is achieved with the use of the Nicol prism, made from calcite and balsam. The Nicol prism permits only the passage of rectilinearly polarized light; the ordinary ray is eliminated by total reflection.

Sheets of *polaroid film* are most often used at present. They contain special organic compounds so disposed that ordinary vibration is totally absorbed, resulting in a uniform field superior to that provided by the Nicol prism.

If this polarized light is transmitted to a second Nicol prism or polaroid plate similar to the first, it does not pass through when the main axes of the 2 prisms or plates are crossed. In any other position, light is transmitted with greater or lesser intensity.

Principle of the Polarizing Microscope

The polarizing microscope contains a rotating stage with 2 polarizing elements: one located under the stage—the *polarizer*—and the other located above it, adjacent to the eyepiece on the *analyzer*.

The polarizer and the analyzer are placed so that their main axes are perpendicular, thus preventing the appearance of light in the eyepiece. When the stage contains an amorphous object, there is no light because the light rays are not modified. However, when a crystalline or birefringent object is placed on the stage, light appears with greater or lesser intensity in the microscope field, depending on the orientation of the analyzer. The usual test is to rotate the specimen to find the points of maximum and minimum brightness.

With the polarizing microscope it is therefore possible to distinguish between monorefringent and birefringent substances. With birefringent substances, it is now possible to discern their internal arrangement and their orientation at the submicroscopic level.

Although the birefringence observed in biologic specimens is generally weak, such crystalline or semicrystalline substances as bone tissue, cellulose walls, structures with linear symmetry (collagen, muscle fibers, nerve fibers, cilia, flagella), and structures with radial symmetry (starch granules, lipid droplets) can be easily studied by making use of this principle.

ELECTRON MICROSCOPY

The principle upon which electron microscopy is based can be understood by referring to the following equation:

$$R = \frac{K \times \lambda}{NA}$$

where K is a constant of 0.61. The wavelength (λ) of an electron beam accelerated by 60 kV is approximately 0.005 nm, which gives a very high theoretic resolution. In practice, however, a resolution of 1—5 nm in tissue sections is considered to be quite satisfactory. This by itself permits enlargements to be obtained up to 170 times greater than those achieved with the optical microscope.

The electron microscope functions on the principle that a beam of electrons can be deflected by electromagnetic fields in a manner similar to light deflection in glass lenses. Electrons are produced by high-temperature heating of a metallic filament in a vacuum (cathode). The electrons emitted are then submitted to a difference of potential of approximately 60—100 kV between the cathode and the anode (Fig 1—7). The anode has the shape of a metallic plate with a small hole in its center. Electrons are accelerated from the cathode to the anode. Some of these particles pass the central orifice of the anode, forming a constant stream (or beam) of electrons. This beam is deflected by electromagnetic lenses in a way roughly analogous to that which occurs in the optical microscope. Thus, the condenser focuses the beam at the object plane and the objective forms an image of the object. The image obtained is further enlarged by 1—2 projecting lenses and is finally projected on a fluorescent screen or photographic plate (Figs 1—7 and 1—8).

Differences Between Electron & Optical Microscopes

In contrast to what happens in the optical microscope, the enlargement produced by the objective in the electron microscope is fixed (or unvariable). The enlargements are produced by changes in the magnetic field of the projecting "lenses," which are analogous to the "zoom" ocular lens in the optical microscope.

Because electrons are easily scattered by the object, it is necessary to use very thin sections of tissue—usually 0.02—0.1 μm. In order to obtain sections of this quality, tissues are usually fixed in glutaraldehyde and osmic acid and are then embedded in an epoxy resin (eg, Epon, Araldite). Sections are prepared in a special ultramicrotome with a glass or diamond cutting edge.

Another characteristic of the electron microscope is that the electrons are scattered by portions of the object with high molecular weight, whereas in the optical microscope light is absorbed by the aperture of the objective lens (usually a diameter of 25—100 μm). The aperture filters out the scattered electrons that consequently do not contribute to image formation. There-

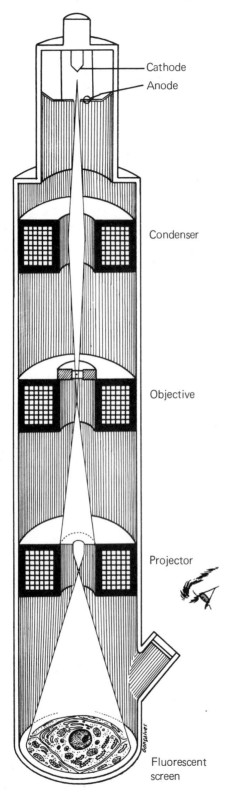

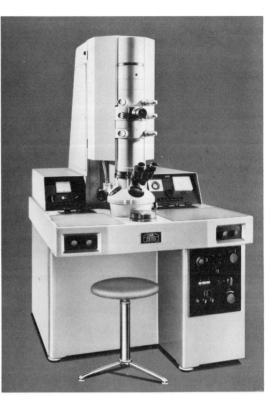

Figure 1—8. Photograph of the Zeiss model EM 9A electron microscope. (Courtesy of Carl Zeiss Co.)

fore, the structures that scatter electrons appear in the fluorescent screen as dark bodies (electron-dense regions). The capacity to scatter electrons depends on the molecular weight (and therefore the density) of a given particle. Heavy metals (eg, uranium, lead) are therefore used to impregnate tissue sections; they increase contrast and permit better images.

Limitations in the Use of the Electron Microscope

The nature of electron rays requires that work with the electron microscope be done in high vacuum with very thin sections. These conditions preclude the use of living material. Additionally, the action of an electron beam on an object can damage it and can produce unwanted changes in tissue structures. Electron microscopy is a rapidly developing field, however, and improvements are expected that will give increased resolution of biologic structures and will permit work to be done with living specimens.

SCANNING ELECTRON MICROSCOPY

A variant of electron microscopy called scanning electron microscopy, in use since 1963, permits 3-dimensional analysis of surfaces. The scanning electron microscope possesses a deflection layer between

Figure 1—7. Pathway of the electron beam in the electron microscope. The ultrathin section is placed just over the objective electromagnetic lens. The image is projected on a fluorescent screen and observed directly or through a ✕ 10 magnifying optical system.

the electromagnetic lens and the object which causes a deflection of the electron beam so that it is incident upon the object, point by point, in a sequence with determined time. The electrons do not pass through the object because of its thickness and because of a cover formed by the evaporation of heavy metal (eg, gold) on its surface. In this way, the electron beam—called the primary beam—is reflected. Secondary electrons are created and are caught by special detectors that make electrical signals which are then transferred to a television tube. The tube gives a 3-dimensional image of the object's surface.

A scanning electron micrograph illustrating the surface of the oocyte before and after fertilization and the initial stages of the formation of a morula is shown in Fig 24–14.

RADIOAUTOGRAPHY

Radioautography permits the localization of radioactive substances in cells or tissues by means of the effect of emitted radiation on photographic emulsions. Silver bromide crystals present in the emulsion act as microdectors of radioactivity. In radioautography, tissue sections obtained from animals previously treated with radioactive compounds are covered with photographic emulsion by dipping mounted specimens in a glass container filled with a warmed mixture of gelatin and silver bromide (Fig 1–9). The slide, now covered with this thin layer of emulsion, is then dried and stored in a light-proof box in a refrigerator. After different exposure times depending on the experiment and the radioactive element, the slides are developed photographically and examined. All silver bromide crystals hit by radiation are reduced to small black granules; this indicates the existence of radioactivity in the structures in contact with these granules. The location and amount of radiation are thus determined, and the quantity of silver granules is proportionate to the intensity of the radioactivity present. The tissue is then stained with regular stains and the preparation is mounted in resin and covered with a coverslip. This procedure can be employed in electron microscopy by using thin sections of resin-embedded material. In this type of radioautography, the granules usually appear as short, coiled filaments (Fig 1–10).

In light microscopy, radioautography permits distinction of radioactive particles that are 1 μm apart. It therefore has a resolving power (or resolution) of 1 μm; in electron microscopy, this resolution is increased 5–10 times.

Radioautography is often used to study important biologic phenomena. As soon as it became possible to synthesize radioactive isotopes of normal metabolites with the aid of carbon-14 (^{14}C) and tritium (^{3}H), it was possible to study not only different metabolic pathways in tissue specimens but also the speed with which metabolic processes occurred. For exam-

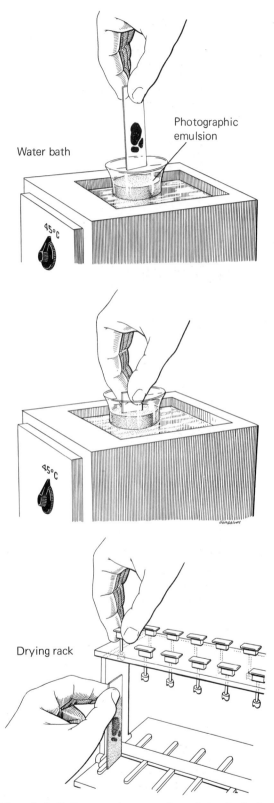

Photographic emulsion

Water bath

45° C

45° C

Drying rack

Figure 1–9. Radioautographs are usually made by dipping labeled tissues fixed on slides in photographic emulsion. All steps shown above are made in the darkroom under a dark red safelight.

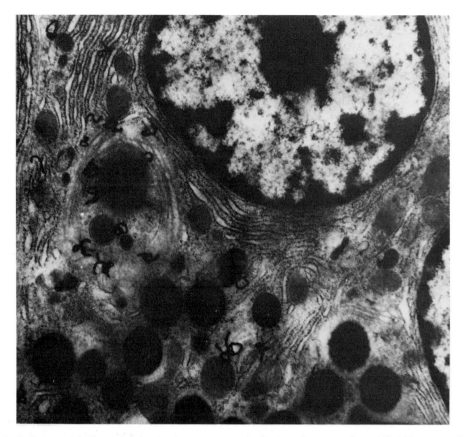

Figure 1—10. Radioautograph observed under the electron microscope. Section of pancreas of a rat killed 20 minutes after a labeled injection of ^{3}H-tryptophan. The coiled black filaments appear in the developed photograph emulsion, indicating radioactive spots in the cell. Silver deposits, which appear as dots under the light microscope, usually exhibit a coiled structure under the electron microscope. Radioactivity is mainly concentrated in the granular endoplasmic reticulum and in the secretory granules. × 5000. (Courtesy of A Sesso.)

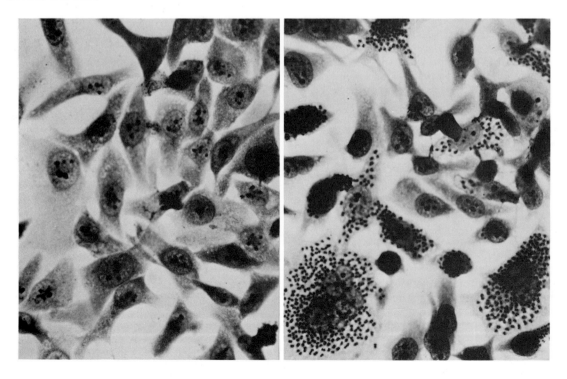

[Legend on facing page.]

ple, the metabolism of proteins and nucleic acids can be studied by injecting labeled amino acids and nucleosides in animals. In both cases, the precursors are incorporated within the tissues and cells into protein or nucleic acids and can be localized and quantitated with the aid of radioautography. If a fixed unit of time is used in the experiments, it is possible to estimate the speed of the metabolic process under study. The metabolism of proteins, carbohydrates, lipids, and nucleic acids has been localized and analyzed in this way successfully. Specific examples include localization of the site and time of DNA synthesis in the nucleus and in mitochondria as well as the sulfation of glycoproteins at the Golgi apparatus of the goblet and fibroblast cells.

EXAMINATION OF LIVING CELLS & TISSUES

Living cells from the body of an animal can be suspended fresh in an appropriate liquid (saline solution, serum) and examined for a short time under the microscope. Such cells, however, will soon die by a process known as autolysis.

Prolonged study of living cells and tissues can be achieved by culturing them in solutions that contain the necessary nutrients to keep them alive. The culture medium should be changed frequently since the nutrients become depleted and toxic products of metabolism accumulate. Rigorous aseptic technic is necessary during the process of cell cultivation in order to avoid contamination of the culture medium.

The first culture media used consisted of blood plasma and an extract from embryonic tissues, and the composition of the fluid was complicated and difficult to control. Synthetic media of rigidly defined chemical composition are now available. In preparing cultures, the cells can be dispersed mechanically by prior treatment with trypsin.

Once isolated, the cells can be cultivated in suspension and then spread out on a glass surface to which they adhere spontaneously as a single layer of cells (Fig 1–11).

Organs can also be cultured, starting from the respective embryonic rudiments. For example, a small bone can be maintained in a culture and allowed to grow. This technic permits study of the factors that influence the development of the organs in conditions much simpler than those that exist inside the living organism. However, the term organ culture means primarily the culture of fragments of organs maintained in conditions such that the architecture of the organ is kept intact.

Cultures have been used for the study of the me-

tabolism of normal and cancerous cells. This technic is most useful in experiments with viruses which proliferate only in the interior of cells. Some protozoa have also been studied in tissue culture to observe their development inside the cytoplasm (Fig 1–11).

In cytogenetic research, tissue cultures permit the study of mitoses and of chromosomes in human cells. Determination of human karyotypes (the number and morphology of an individual's chromosomes) is accomplished by the cultivation of blood cells. In examining these cells during mitotic division, one can detect anomalies in the number and morphology of the chromosomes, thus perhaps establishing the diagnosis of certain diseases caused by these anomalies.

DIFFERENTIAL CENTRIFUGATION

Differential centrifugation is the physical process by which centrifugal force is used to separate organelles and cellular inclusions as a function of the sedimentation coefficient of each one. The sedimentation coefficient of a particle depends on its size, form, and density and on the viscosity of the medium. If a cell is subjected to an adequate centrifugal force, the organelles inside the cell will be distributed in different layers (Fig 1–12). In each layer, one finds only one type of organelle, and its position inside the cell depends on its coefficient of sedimentation

By means of the technic of centrifugation, any cellular organelle can be isolated and its chemical composition and its functions determined in vitro.

Differential centrifugation is achieved by subjecting a suspension of cellular elements obtained by a process called *homogenization* to the action of different centrifugal forces (Fig 1–13).

The organ or tissue from a recently killed animal is cut into very small fragments which are then immersed in an appropriate solution. Sucrose in an 0.25 M concentration is most often used, but the density and viscosity of the medium can vary.

The fragments of the organ with the solution of sucrose are placed in a homogenizer, usually consisting of a glass cylinder within which is a rod that turns with great velocity (Fig 1–13). The fragments of the tissues are crushed by the friction of the rod on the wall of the cylinder, breaking the cell membranes and liberating the organelles and the inclusions into the solution.

After homogenization is complete, the suspension is allowed to rest for a few minutes so that the fibers of connective tissue and the intact cells can settle out. The supernatant is then centrifuged, and the more dense particles (organelles or inclusions) sediment first. The supernatant from each centrifugation is subjected again to greater centrifugal force, thus separating out

Figure 1–11 (on facing page). Photomicrographs of chicken fibroblasts grown in tissue culture. *Left:* Normal cells. *Right:* Fibroblasts infected by *Trypanosoma cruzi.* Giemsa staining was used. × 340. (Courtesy of S Yoneda.)

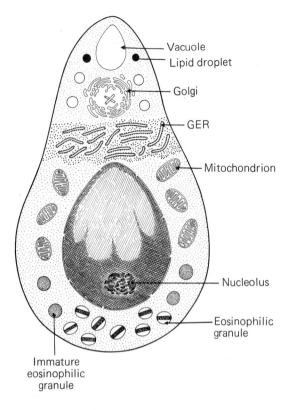

Figure 1–12. Stratification seen in an immature eosinophil after centrifugation. Cell components of higher density (eosinophilic granules, nucleus) accumulate at the bottom of the cell, whereas lighter organelles (Golgi, granular endoplasmic reticulum [GER]) are displaced to the opposite side. (Redrawn and reproduced, with permission, from Bessis in: *The Cell.* Vol 5. Brachet J, Mirsky AE [editors]. Academic Press, 1961.)

the different cellular components, in decreasing order of their density, as shown in Fig 1–13.

A recent improvement in the technic of differential centrifugation is centrifugation against a gradient, or *zonal centrifugation.* The gradient consists of a sucrose solution whose concentration is maximal at the bottom of the tube and minimal at the top, with a gradual increase in concentration from top to bottom. The homogenate is placed on top of this stabilized gradient and centrifuged. The particles penetrate the gradient, but do so when an equilibrium exists between the action of the centrifugal force and the tendency of the particle to float. This technic permits one to obtain purer fractions of organelles.

In contrast to the continuous gradient just described, one can use a discontinuous gradient, which is made up of superimposed zones whose density decreases from one zone to the other, starting from the bottom and proceeding to the top of the centrifuge tube.

All of the stages of the technics described are carried out at a temperature slightly higher than the freezing point in order to combat the action of enzyme systems that would disrupt the organelles during the separation.

Control of the purity of the fractions thus obtained is carried out with the optical microscope (for nuclei, mitochondria, and secretory granules), with the electron microscope (for ribosomes, microsomes, etc) (Fig 1–14), or with chemical methods. For example, the fraction that contains the lysosomes can be identified by the quantity of acid phosphatase, an enzyme usually found in these particles, while the fraction containing the nuclei can be identified by the quantity of DNA present in it.

The isolation of cellular components by differential centrifugation represents a great technical advance and allows the detailed study of cellular components which have been obtained in a relatively pure state, ie, nuclei, nucleoli, mitochrondria, granular endoplasmic reticulum, ribosomes, secretory granules, and pigment granules. An example of the application of this method is the study of the physiology of mitochondria; after much discussion, it was established by the isolation of these organelles and confirmed in vitro that they are responsible for the processes of liberation of energy and for storage of ATP.

PROBLEMS IN THE INTERPRETATION OF TISSUE SECTIONS

During the study and interpretation of stained tissue sections in microscope preparations, it should be remembered that the observed product is the end result of a series of processes which considerably distort the image observable in the living tissue, mainly through shrinking and retraction. As a consequence of these processes, the spaces frequently seen between the cells and other tissue components are artifacts. Furthermore, there is a tendency to think in terms of only 2 dimensions when examining thin sections, whereas in actuality the structures from which the sections are made have 3 dimensions. In order to understand the architecture of an órgan, it is therefore necessary to study sections made in different planes and to reason accordingly (Fig 1–15).

The *serial sectioning technic* is often used in the study of organ and tissue structure. In this technic, continuous serial sections of a whole organ or an organ fragment are prepared and studied. By analysis of each section in the sequence in which it was prepared, information on the architecture of the organ can be gained.

Another difficulty in the study of microscope preparations is the impossibility of differentially staining all tissue components on only one slide. It is therefore necessary to examine several preparations stained by different methods before a general idea of the composition and structure of any type of tissue can be obtained.

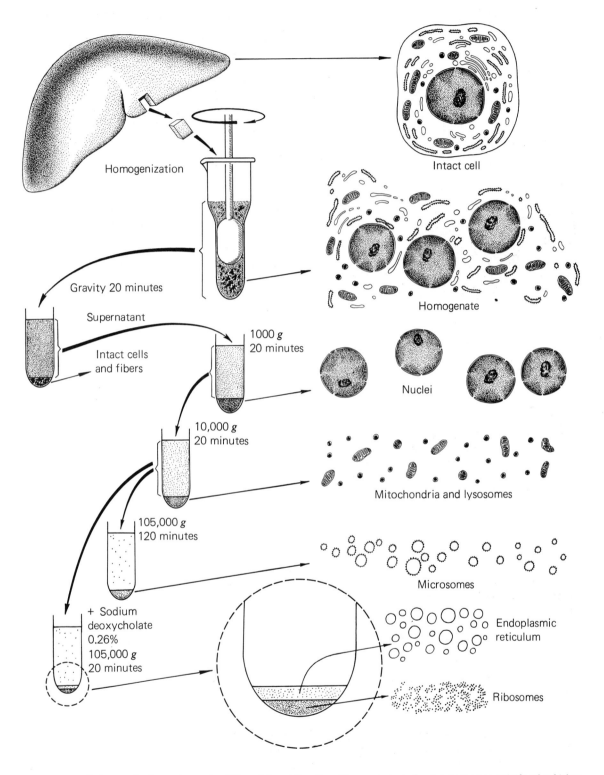

Figure 1–13. Isolation of cell constituents by differential centrifugation. The supernatant of each tube is again centrifuged at higher speeds. The drawings at right show the cellular organelles at the bottom of each tube after centrifugation. Centrifugal force is expressed by *g*, which is equivalent to the force of gravity (1000 *g* means a force 1000 times stronger than that of the gravitational field). (Redrawn and reproduced, with permission, from Bloom W, Fawcett DW: *A Textbook of Histology*, 9th ed. Saunders, 1968.)

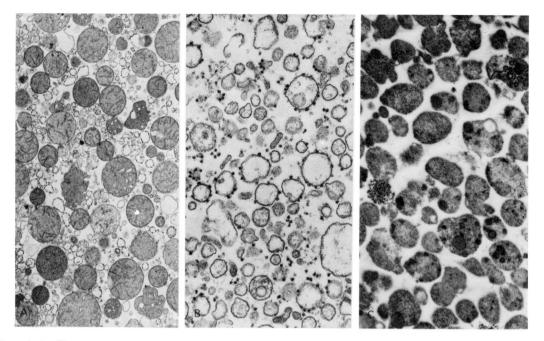

Figure 1–14. Electron micrographs of 3 cell fractions isolated by density gradient centrifugation. *A:* Mitochondrial fraction, contaminated with microsomes. × 13,000. *B:* Microsomal fraction. × 42,500. *C:* Lysosomal fraction. × 25,000. (Courtesy of P Baudhuin.)

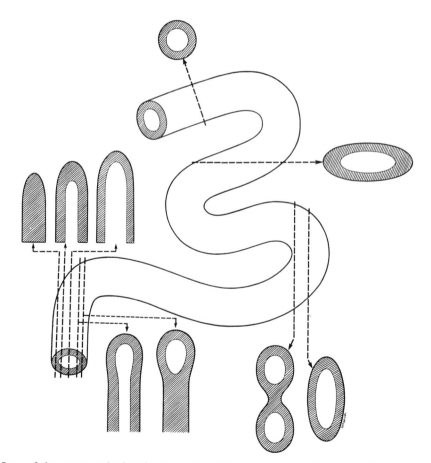

Figure 1–15. Some of the aspects a tube-shaped organ might exhibit when sectioned. The arrows indicate what is seen under the microscope in each particular section plane.

• • •

References

Allfrey V: The isolation of subcellular components. In: *The Cell.* Vol 1. Brachet J, Mirsky AE (editors). Academic Press, 1960.

Baker JR: *Cytological Technique,* 4th ed. Methuen, 1960.

Baserga R, Malamud D: *Autoradiography: Techniques and Application.* Harper, 1969.

Caro LG: High resolution autoradiography. In: *Methods in Cell Physiology.* Vol 1. Prescott DM (editor). Academic Press, 1964.

Everhart TE, Hayes TL: The scanning electron microscope. Sc Am 226:54, Jan 1972.

Hayat MA: *Principles and Techniques of Electron Microscopy.* Vol 1. Van Nostrand-Reinhold, 1970.

Humason GL: *Animal Tissue Techniques.* Freeman, 1962.

Kopac MJ: Microsurgical studies on living cells. In: *The Cell.* Vol 1. Brachet J, Mirsky AE (editors). Academic Press, 1960.

Kopriwa BM, Leblond CP: Improvements in the coating technique of radioautography. J Histochem Cytochem 10:269, 1962.

Lillie RD: *Histopathologic Technique and Practical Histochemistry,* 2nd ed. Blakiston, 1954.

McManus JFA, Mowry RW: *Staining Methods: Histologic and Histochemical.* Hoeber, 1960.

Parker RC: *Methods of Tissue Culture,* 3rd ed. Hoeber, 1961.

Salpeter MM, Bachmann L: Assessment of technical steps in electron microscope autoradiography. In: *The Use of Radioautography in Investigating Protein Synthesis.* Leblond CP, Warren KB (editors). Academic Press, 1965.

2 . . .
Histochemistry & Cytochemistry

The chemistry of tissues and cells is studied by both microscopic and chemical analytic methods. Chemical substances in tissues and cells can be identified by chemical reactions that produce insoluble colored compounds—observed with the light microscope—or electron scattering of precipitates that can be observed with the electron microscope. In Perls's reaction, for example, potassium ferrocyanide reacts with ferric ions in the tissues to produce an insoluble dark blue precipitate of ferric ferrocyanide.

In addition to the chemical reactions that take place in the tissues, other methods—chiefly physical ones—are frequently used. Examples are interference microscopy, which permits determination of the mass of cells or tissues; and microspectrophotometry, which permits, by means of ultraviolet light, localization and quantitation of DNA and RNA in the cells.

In 1936, histochemistry came into its own as a field of scientific inquiry when Lison compiled his treatise, *Histochimie Animale*. Since then; progress in histochemistry and cytochemistry is evident from the large number of specialized texts and journals presently devoted to the subject.

Histochemical and cytochemical procedures have made substantial contributions to recent progress in the fields of cytology, histophysiology, and pathology.

BASIC HISTOCHEMICAL & CYTOCHEMICAL PRINCIPLES

For a histochemical reaction to be recognized as valid and meaningful, it must fulfill the following basic requirements:

(1) **The substances being analyzed must not diffuse out of their original sites.** This problem is easily solved when macromolecules (eg, DNA, proteins) are analyzed. However, when the substance is soluble in the fixative used or in the medium in which the reaction is taking place—as in the case of urea and glycogen and of sodium, potassium, or chloride ions—special care must be exercised in the interpretation of the results. Fixatives should both preserve the structure of the cell and prevent diffusion of the compounds to be studied. For example, the fixatives used to study lipids

should not contain lipid solvents, and acid fixatives should not be used in technics for identifying calcium phosphate since calcium phosphate is soluble in an acid medium. The fixatives most commonly used are formaldehyde (formalin) for light microscopic and glutaraldehyde for electron microscopic histochemical procedures.

(2) **The product of the reaction should be insoluble and colored or electron-scattering.** Insolubility prevents diffusion of the product of the reaction into the fluid reagent or its spread to a different site in the specimen. A colored or electron-scattering product can be studied with the light or electron microscope.

(3) **The method employed should be specific for the substance or chemical groups being studied.** Obviously, it is difficult to interpret results if the reaction used is nonspecific.

In some histochemical reactions, the intensity of color produced is directly proportionate to the concentration of the substance being analyzed. In such cases, the concentration of the substance under study can be determined by *histophotometry*. This procedure is carried out in a histophotometer, a combination microscope and spectrophotometer. By measuring the light absorbed by small areas of a cell or a tissue, it is possible to quantitate chemical substances in this region. Unfortunately, though most technics permit accurate localization of substances, only a rough idea of their quantity can be obtained. Therefore, these methods usually give good qualitative results but do not provide accurate quantitative information.

SOME EXAMPLES OF HISTOCHEMICAL METHODS FOR SUBSTANCES OF BIOLOGIC INTEREST

Ions

A. Iron: When sections of tissues containing ferric ions (F^{3+}) are incubated in a mixture of potassium ferrocyanide and hydrochloric acid, the ions can be detected by the formation of a highly insoluble, dark blue precipitate of ferric ferrocyanide. This method not only allows localization in the tissues of cells that catabolize hemoglobin but also permits diagnosis of diseases in which a deposit of iron occurs in the tissues.

B. Phosphates: Phosphates are demonstrated by means of a reaction with silver nitrate. The silver phosphate formed is, in the following phase of the reaction, reduced by hydroquinone, thus forming a black precipitate of reduced silver (Fig 2–1). This reaction is frequently used to study bone and the ossification process because the only insoluble phosphate found abundantly in the body is calcium phosphate, which is present in large amounts in bone tissue.

Lipids

Lipids are best revealed with dyes that are highly soluble in fat. This is based on the fact that the dyes used are physically more soluble in lipids than in the medium in which they are dissolved.

In this process, frozen sections are immersed in alcoholic solutions saturated with the appropriate dyes. The stain then migrates from the alcohol to the cellular lipid droplets. The dyes most commonly used for this purpose are Sudan IV and Sudan black; they confer on lipids red and black colors, respectively (Fig 2–2).

Additional methods used for the localization of cholesterol and its esters, phospholipids, and glycolipids are useful in the diagnosis of metabolic diseases in which intracellular accumulations of different kinds of lipids occur.

Nucleic Acids

A. Deoxyribonucleic Acid (DNA): DNA is studied chiefly with Feulgen's reaction, a method that consists of the hydrolysis of DNA by hydrochloric acid. This process separates purine bases from sugar, promoting the formation of aldehyde groups in deoxyribose. The free aldehyde groups then react with the Schiff reagent (basic fuchsin bleached by sulfurous anhydride), giving rise to an insoluble red substance. By this method, it is possible to semiquantitate the content of DNA in the nuclei of cells.

B. Ribonucleic Acid (RNA): RNA can be identified in tissues by virtue of its great affinity for basic stains (basophilia)—eg, it stains intensely with toluidine blue or methylene blue. Since RNA is not the only basophilic substance in the tissue, it is necessary to incubate a control slide with ribonuclease (an enzyme that destroys RNA) for comparison with a slide not so treated. Any structure that loses its basophilia as a result of pretreatment with ribonuclease is considered to contain RNA.

Proteins

Reactions for nonspecific demonstration of proteins in tissues and cells are based chiefly on methods of identifying amino acids. Localization and, sometimes, quantitation of proteins in tissues can be done by means of reactions for tyrosine (Millon reaction), tryptophan (tetrazotized benzidine; Fig 2–3), and arginine (Sakaguchi reaction). The Sakaguchi reaction is

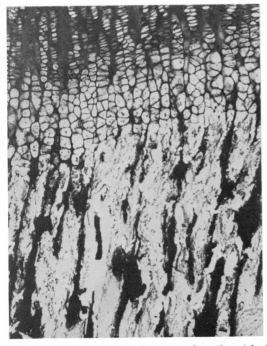

Figure 2–1. Photomicrograph of a section from the epiphysis of an undecalcified bone treated with silver nitrate and subsequently reduced by hydroquinone. The black precipitate indicates the presence of calcium phosphate. × 120.

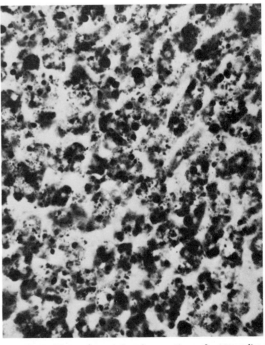

Figure 2–2. Photomicrograph of a section of puppy liver stained by Sudan black. Observe the stained intracellular lipid droplets. × 200.

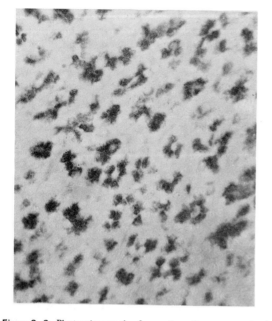

Figure 2—3. Photomicrograph of a section of pancreas stained by the tetrazotized benzidine method for proteins (tryptophan). The secretory granules stain heavily. × 400.

used frequently in the study of the distribution of basic proteins in nuclei (eg, histones and protamines, which are both rich in arginine). There are also methods for studying the abundant SH and SS groups of certain proteins such as keratin.

Polysaccharides

Polysaccharides in the body occur either in a free state or combined with proteins. In the combined state, they constitute an extremely complex heterogeneous group known generically as *glycoproteins*. The only polysaccharide in the body that is not bound to protein is *glycogen*, which can be demonstrated by the periodic acid–Schiff (PAS) reaction. The PAS reaction is based on the oxidative action of periodic acid (HIO_4) on 1,2-glycol groups present in the glucose residues, giving rise to aldehyde groups as shown in the following equation:

specificity of this reaction depends on pretreatment with a glycogenolytic enzyme. Salivary amylase is generally used. Structures that stain intensely with the PAS reaction but fail to do so after pretreatment with amylase are considered to contain glycogen. By this method, for example, glycogen is demonstrated in the normal liver and striated muscle. It also permits the diagnosis of several diseases in which abnormal intracellular accumulations of glycogen are observed.

Acid mucopolysaccharides and glycoproteins in living animals constitute an extremely varied and difficult group for study. By histochemical methods, it is possible to distinguish acid from neutral mucopolysaccharides. The former contain the carbohydrate moiety with carboxyl or SO_3H groups in their structure and are the so-called carboxylated mucopolysaccharides, eg, hyaluronic acid. The latter contain sulfated moieties, eg, heparin and chondroitin sulfates.

It is currently believed that neutral glycoproteins give a PAS-positive reaction. Acidic glycoproteins are revealed by their action with alcian blue dye (Figs 2—4 and 2—5). It is possible to differentiate between a sulfated or a carboxylated glycoprotein by using solutions of alcian blue at different pH levels. Sulfated compounds react with alcian blue both below and above pH 1.7, whereas carboxylated compounds react only above pH 1.7. Mixtures of neutral and acid mucopolysaccharides can be observed in tissues.

Catecholamines

The fact that formaldehyde reacts with catecholamines to produce fluorescent compounds makes it possible to localize epinephrine (adrenaline) and norepinephrine (noradrenaline) in tissue structures. This method is founded on the observation that ring hydroxylated phenylethylamines, indolealkylamines, and their corresponding amino acids are converted to fluorescent complexes in the presence of relatively dry formaldehyde vapor at 60–80 °C. This method has been very helpful in studying the distribution of catecholamines and their precursors in neuronal pathways, cell bodies, and nerve endings.

Enzymes

Many histochemical methods are used to reveal

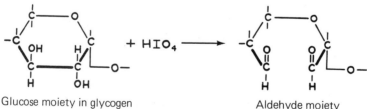

Glucose moiety in glycogen   Aldehyde moiety

As in Feulgen's reaction, these aldehyde groups react with bleached fuchsin (Schiff's reagent), producing a new complex compound having an insoluble purple or magenta color. This can be seen in the light microscope, and we call such substances PAS-positive. Since other PAS-positive substances occur in cells, the

and identify enzymes. When unstable enzymes are studied, sections of frozen, unfixed material must be used. Most enzymes withstand fixation for short periods, however, and formalin and glutaraldehyde are most often used for this purpose. Most enzymatic histochemical procedures are based on the production

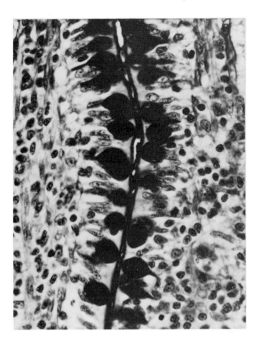

Figure 2—4. Photomicrograph of an intestinal villus stained by alcian blue. The goblet cells stain intensely because of their high content of acid mucopolysaccharides. ✕ 400.

of intensely stained or electron-dense precipitates at the site of enzymatic activity. Three enzymes that are demonstrated by either the light or the electron microscope are described below as examples.

A. Acid Phosphatase: One method of demonstrating acid phosphatase activity consists of incubating formalin-fixed tissue sections in a solution containing sodium glycerophosphate and lead nitrate buffered to pH 5.0. The enzyme hydrolyzes the glycerophosphate, liberating the phosphate ion that reacts with lead nitrate to produce an insoluble, colorless precipitate of lead phosphate at the site of the enzymatic activity. In a second step, the preparation is immersed in a solution of ammonium sulfide which reacts with the colorless precipitate to produce a black precipitate of lead sulfide. This method permits the localization of this enzyme's activity and is frequently used to demonstrate the *lysosomes,* cytoplasmic organelles that contain acid phosphatase (Figs 2—6 and 2—7).

B. Dehydrogenases: These enzymes remove hydrogen from one substrate and transfer it to another. There are many different dehydrogenases in the body; they play an important role in several metabolic processes and can be distinguished by means of the substrate on which they act. The histochemical demonstration of dehydrogenases consists of incubating nonfixed tissue sections in an adequate substrate contain-

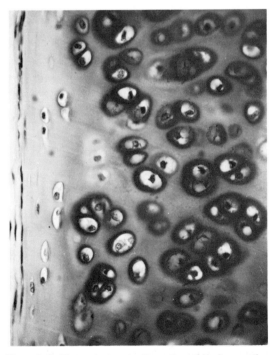

Figure 2—5. Photomicrograph of a section of hyaline cartilage, previously stained by PAS and alcian blue. The region of the matrix close to the cartilage cells contain acid mucopolysaccharides and stains blue with the alcian method, while the rest of the matrix contains neutral mucopolysaccharides and stains red by the PAS method.

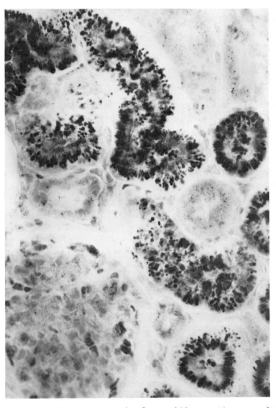

Figure 2—6. Photomicrograph of a rat kidney section treated by the lead acid phosphatase method. The lysosomes stain intensely as dark granules present in the proximal convoluted tubule cells. ✕ 400.

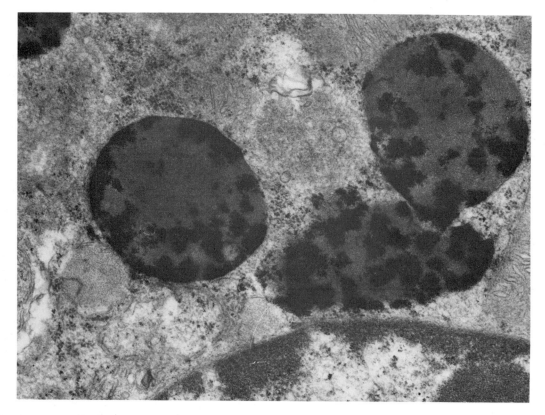

Figure 2–7. Electron micrograph of a rat kidney cell previously treated by the Gomori method for acid phosphatase. Observe the dense precipitate formed in 3 lysosomes. × 4000. (Courtesy of E Katchburian.)

ing *tetrazole,* a weakly stained, soluble, hydrogen-accepting substance. The enzyme transports hydrogen from the substrate to tetrazole and reduces it to an intensely stained insoluble compound called *formazan,* which precipitates at the site of the enzymatic activity. By this method, succinate dehydrogenase—a key enzyme in the citric acid (Krebs) cycle—can be localized in mitochondria (Fig 2–8).

C. Peroxidase: This enzyme, which is present in several types of cells, promotes the reduction of certain substrates with the transfer of hydrogen ions to hydrogen peroxide, forming molecules of water.

localization of peroxidase activity in the optical and electron microscopes. Since it is an extremely active enzyme, it produces an appreciable amount of insoluble precipitate in a short time; this is, therefore, a very sensitive method.

FLUORESCENCE MICROSCOPY

This technic is based on the fact that, when cer-

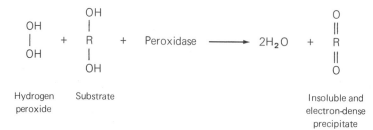

tain fluorescent substances are stimulated by light of a proper wavelength, they emit light with a longer wavelength. In microscopy, tissue is usually stimulated with ultraviolet light so that the emission is in the visible portion of the spectrum: The fluorescent substances

In this method, sections of adequately fixed tissue are incubated in a solution containing hydrogen peroxide and 3,3′-diaminoazobenzidine. In the presence of peroxidase, this compound is reduced, resulting in an insoluble colored precipitate that permits the

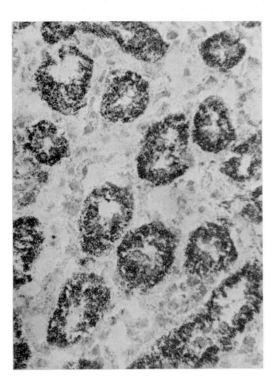

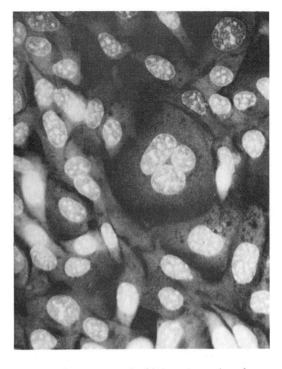

Figure 2–8. Photomicrograph of a frozen section of fresh, unfixed kidney previously incubated in succinate plus monotetrazole (MTT). The dark precipitate seen in the tubules indicates the activity of succinic dehydrogenase. ✕ 400. (Courtesy of AGE Pearse.)

Figure 2–9. Photomicrograph of kidney tissue culture from an embryonic hamster transformed by simian virus 40, stained with acridine orange and photographed with the fluorescent microscope. A green fluorescence (shown as white in photo) appears in the regions containing DNA (nucleus); a red color (shown as gray) is characteristic of the RNA-rich cytoplasm. In the center is a giant cell. Reduced from ✕ 750. (Courtesy of A Geraldes and JMV Costa.)

appear as brilliant shiny particles on a dark background. In this procedure, a microscope with a strong ultraviolet light source is used. Special filters that eliminate ultraviolet light are employed to protect the observer's eyes.

Fluorescent Compounds

Some naturally fluorescent substances are normal constituents of cells, eg, vitamin A, vitamin B_2, and porphyrins. Other fluorescent compounds that have an affinity for tissues and cells are used as fluorescent stains. Acridine orange is most widely used because it can combine with DNA and RNA. When observed in the fluorescent microscope, the DNA–acridine orange complex emits a yellowish-green light whereas the RNA–acridine orange complex emits a red light. In this way it is possible to identify and localize nucleic acids in the cells (Fig 2–9). Since cancer cells frequently contain larger amounts of RNA than normal cells, acridine orange is often used to identify them in smears obtained from patients.

Fluorescent spectroscopy is a method of analyzing the light emitted by a fluorescent compound in a spectroscope. It is used to characterize several compounds present in cells and is of particular importance in the study of catecholamines.

IMMUNOCYTOCHEMISTRY

This technic is based on the reaction of a foreign substance—an *antigen*—introduced into an organism. It usually produces a protein—*antibody*—that will react specifically and bind strongly with the antigen, neutralizing it. Antibodies are proteins of the globulin group that appear in blood plasma after antigen injection. Their production enables the organism to oppose invasion by foreign proteins, microorganisms, and certain other foreign matter. Immunocytochemistry is also based on the coupling of such proteins to tracer substances without causing loss of the biologic activity of the antigen or antibody. It is a useful technic since it permits the intracellular localization of specific proteins. Conventional cytochemical methods detect specific amino acids or reactive groups, but they do not localize specific proteins. When a solution containing an antibody labeled with a tracer is incubated with a tissue section containing the antigen, it is possible to determine the site of the antigen by the specific and firm binding of the labeled antibody to the antigen.

Three methods of labeling proteins (antigens or antibodies) are frequently used:

(1) Coupling of a protein with fluorescent com-

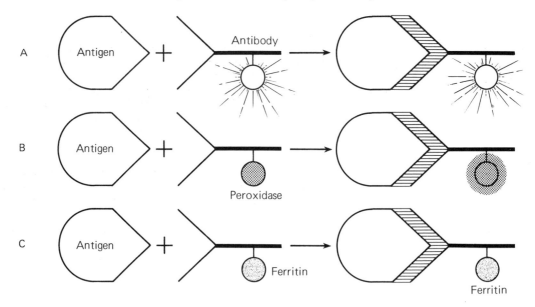

Figure 2–10. Three current methods of labeling and identifying specific proteins by immunocytochemistry. *A:* The antibody is coupled to a fluorescent compound. After incubation, the sections containing the antigen exposed to the labeled antibody solution are studied in the fluorescent microscope. *B:* The antibody is coupled to peroxidase. After the antigen-antibody reaction, the section is submitted to the histochemical method for peroxidase and studied with the light or electron microscope (see text). *C:* The antibody is coupled to ferritin. After the antigen-antibody reaction, this material is studied with the electron microscope.

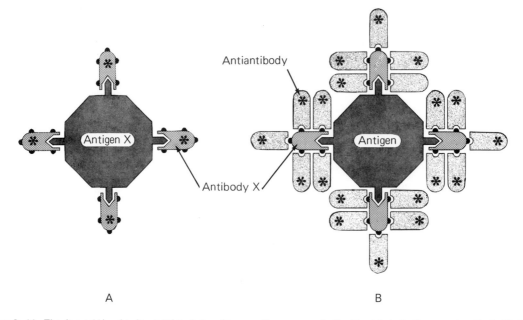

Figure 2–11. The direct *(A)* and indirect *(B)* technics of immunofluorescence. In the direct technic, fluorescent antibody binds to the antigen present in the cells. Observe that in this hypothetical case each antigen molecule binds only 4 antibody molecules. In the indirect technic, nonfluorescent antibody is first bound to the antigen, and fluorescent antiantibody (also called fluorescent gamma globulin) then binds itself to the antibody. Because each antibody molecule binds 5 molecules of fluorescent antiantibody, the indirect procedure is more sensitive, for each antigen molecule binds 20 fluorescent molecules.

pounds. It is possible to tag antigen or antibody molecules by coupling them to fluorescent compounds without loss of reactivity.

(2) Coupling of the protein molecule with an enzymatic protein. This permits detection of the labeled protein by conventional technics used in enzymatic cytochemistry. The enzyme most often used is peroxidase, which can be detected by the method described above.

(3) Coupling of the protein molecules to an electron-scattering compound that can be detected in the electron microscope. An iron-rich protein called ferritin is often used for coupling to antigens or antibodies. (See Fig 2—10.)

There are both direct and indirect immunocytochemical methods for determining the way in which the antigen-antibody reaction occurs.

(1) Direct method. Sections of a tissue whose cells contain a protein X (antigen) are incubated with a labeled prepared antibody to X. This antibody is prepared by injecting the protein X into an animal (usually a rabbit). After a certain period of time, the blood of the animal containing the antibody to X is withdrawn, purified, and coupled to a fluorescent, enzymatic, or electron-scattering compound. When a section containing the antigen is incubated in a solution of the labeled antibody, the antigen and antibody combine. The tissue section is then washed to remove the excess antibody and processed for study in the optical or electron microscope (Fig 2—11A).

(2) Indirect method. As in the direct method, the prepared nonfluorescent antibody X reacts with original antigen X in the tissue. These sections are then incubated in a solution containing a labeled antibody to the previously prepared antibody X. This technic has the advantage of increasing the sensitivity of the method considerably (Fig 2—11B).

● ● ●

References

Barka T, Anderson PJ: *Histochemistry: Theory, Practice, and Bibliography.* Hoeber, 1963.

Chayen T, Bitensky L, Butcher RG: *Practical Histochemistry.* Wiley, 1973.

Coons, AH: Fluorescent antibody methods. In: *General Cytochemical Methods.* Danielli JF (editor). Academic Press, 1958.

Fawcett DW: Electron microscopy in histology and cytology. In: *Modern Developments in Electron Microscopy.* Siegel BM (editor). Academic Press, 1963.

Glick D: *Techniques of Histo- and Cytochemistry: A Manual of Morphological and Quantitative Micromethods for Inorganic, Organic and Enzyme Constituents in Biological Materials.* Interscience, 1949.

Graumann W, Neumann K: *Handbuch der Histochimie.* Gustav Fischer, since 1959 (irregular).

Harper HA: *Review of Physiological Chemistry,* 15th ed. Lange, 1975.

Lison L: *Histochimie et Cytochimie Animale: Principles et Méthodes.* 2 vols. Gauthier-Villars, 1960.

Pearse AGE: *Histochemistry: Theoretical and Applied,* 3rd ed. Little, Brown, 1968.

Pollister AW, Ornstein L: The photometric chemical analysis of cells. In: *Analytical Cytology,* 2nd ed. Mellors RC (editor). McGraw-Hill, 1959.

Scarpelli DG, Kanczak NM: Ultrastructural cytochemistry: Principles, limitations and applications. Int Rev Exp Pathol 4:55, 1965.

3 . . .
The Cell

Mammalian tissue is made up of 3 distinct components: cells, intercellular substance, and tissue fluid. The cells comprise the greater part and are of most interest since the cell is the smallest living part of the body and its basic morphologic and functional unit.

CELLULAR FUNCTIONS & DIFFERENTIATION

During the process of evolution, the cells of metazoan organisms gradually became modified and specialized, resulting in increased efficiency of function. This phenomenon is similar to the evolution of human societies. In primitive societies, all men knew and did a little of everything—built houses, planted crops, healed the sick, hunted for food, etc. With the development of large cities, these functions were undertaken by specialists—engineers, farmers, doctors, etc. Similarly, in metazoan cells, specialization is characterized by gradual morphologic, chemical, and functional modifications of the cell. An undifferentiated primitive cell that is able to perform several functions with little efficiency is transformed into a series of differentiated cells that are collectively able to perform the same functions but with much greater efficiency. This process of cell specialization is known as *cell differentiation*.

For example, the muscle cell during its differentiation has become elongated, synthesizes fibrillary proteins, and is transformed into a spindle-shaped cell—called muscle fiber—that efficiently converts chemical energy into contractile force. Another example is the pancreatic cell, which has become specialized to secrete digestive enzymes.

Morphologic modifications during differentiation are understandably accompanied by chemical changes, and the quantitative synthesis of one or more specific proteins by each cell type characterizes this process. Examples are the synthesis of the proteins actin and myosin by the muscle cell or of several digestive enzymes by the acinar pancreatic cells. Cellular functions involving specialized cells in the body are listed in Table 3—1.

It should be borne in mind that a cell does not always have only one function; more commonly, cells are capable of performing 2 or more functions. Thus, the cells of the proximal convoluted tubules of the kidney not only transport ions but also reabsorb metabolites and digest proteins. Similarly, the intestinal epithelial cells reabsorb metabolites and synthesize digestive enzymes (proteins) such as disaccharidases and peptidases (see Chapter 16).

It will be seen that the morphology of the cell components varies according to the functions of the cell.

CELL COMPONENTS

The cell is composed of 2 basic parts: *cytoplasm* and *nucleus*. The cytoplasm is usually not clearly visible in common hematoxylin and eosin–stained preparations; the latter appears intensely stained in dark blue or black (Fig 3—1).

Table 3—1. Cellular functions in specialized cells.

Function	Specialized Cell(s)
Movement	Muscle cell
Conductivity	Nervous cell
Synthesis and accumulation of proteins	Pancreatic acinar cells
Synthesis and accumulation of mucous substances	Mucous gland cells
Synthesis and accumulation of steroids	Some cells of the adrenal gland, testis, and ovary
Ion transport	Cells of the kidney and salivary gland ducts
Intracellular digestion	Macrophages and some white blood cells
Transformation of physical and chemical stimuli into nervous impulses	Sensory cells
Metabolite absorption	Cells of the intestine, kidney, etc

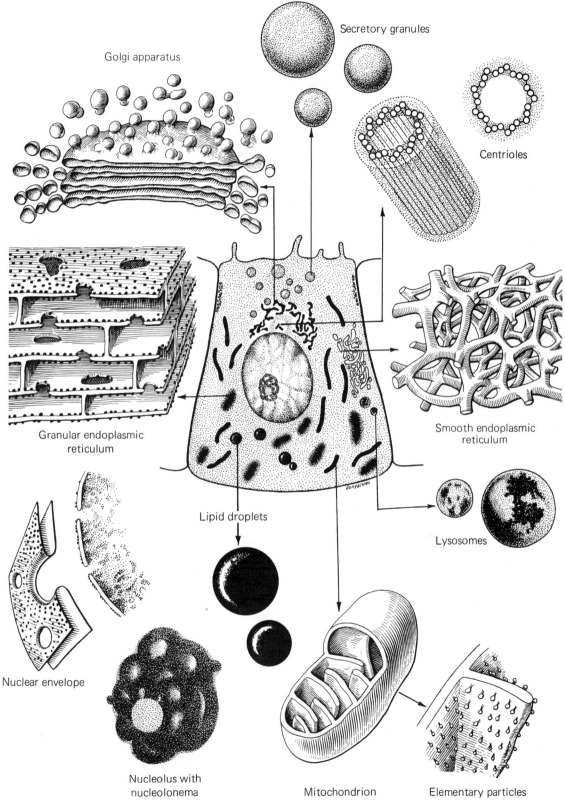

Golgi apparatus

Secretory granules

Centrioles

Granular endoplasmic
reticulum

Smooth endoplasmic
reticulum

Lipid droplets

Lysosomes

Nuclear envelope

Nucleolus with
nucleolonema

Mitochondrion

Elementary particles

Figure 3–1. Diagram showing a hypothetical cell in the center as seen by the optical microscope surrounded by its various structures as seen by the electron microscope. (Redrawn and reproduced, with permission, from Bloom A, Fawcett D: *A Textbook of Histology.* Saunders, 1968.)

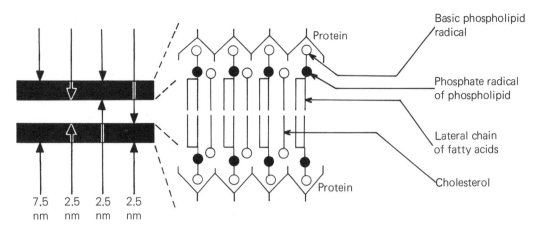

7.5 nm   2.5 nm   2.5 nm   2.5 nm

Figure 3–2. The ultrastructure *(left)* and molecular structure *(right)* of the cell membrane.

Cytoplasm

The outermost component of the cytoplasm, separating it from its extracellular environment, is the *plasma membrane.* The cytoplasm is composed of the matrix or ground substance, and embedded in it are several structures classified into 2 groups: organelles and inclusions. The structures known as *organelles* are present in almost all cells and are permanent cell components. Examples include the endoplasmic reticulum, the mitochondria, the Golgi apparatus, the centrioles, the microtubules, and the lysosomes. The *inclusions* generally are temporary components of certain cells and usually are accumulations of pigment, lipids, proteins, or carbohydrates. Many organelles are membranous structures; others are associated with membranes, and some show controlled movement.

A. Plasma Membrane: The plasma membrane is not resolved by the light microscope because its width is approximately 7.5–10 nm. As early as 1925, Gortner and Grendell proposed that the cell membrane is composed of molecular layers of lipid material. Work done by other investigators in the next decade suggested that protein was also present in the membrane, and in 1952 Davson and Danielli proposed a model formed by 2 layers of lipid covered by 2 protein layers (Fig 3–2). In the electron microscope, the membrane appears as a trilaminar structure, and at that time it was thought to consist of an internal layer of lipid 3.5 nm thick covered on either side by a layer of protein about 2 nm thick to make a total of 7.5 nm. The internal lipid layer is itself composed of 2 layers of phospholipid and cholesterol molecules whose nonpolar (hydrophobic) groups face inward. The hydrophilic polar groups of the lipid molecules face outward and are covered by the 2 layers of protein molecules which are perpendicular to them (Fig 3–3A). This type of membrane, studied mainly in myelin sheaths of nerves, was claimed by Robertson in 1959 to represent the typical *unit membrane* forming the basis of all membranous structures of cells. The unit membrane concept also lent credibility to the belief that the membrane was asymmetric; that the base protein layers

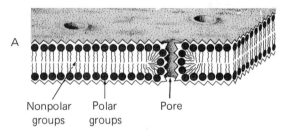

Figure 3–3. Proposed models of cell membrane ultrastructure. *A* represents a Davson-Danielli model consisting of 2 layers of lipids covered by 2 protein layers. The pores are hypothetical and might be hydrophilic channels instead of true orifices. Model *B* shows lipoprotein units bound together, with hydrophilic regions through which water-soluble substances enter the cells. Models *C* and *D* show globular proteins on the surface of the membrane and proteins between the bimolecular lipid layer.

gests the presence of globular protein micelles inserted in various positions in the membrane structure (Figs 3–3C and 3–3D). These micelles might be responsible for membrane permeability to hydrophilic substances and also might be the site of the so-called membrane "pores" (Fig 3–3B).

Recently, a new model has been proposed as an alternative to the unit membrane idea advanced by Davson and Danielli and by Robertson. In this *lipid-globular protein mosaic model* or *fluid model*, globular proteins are embedded within a matrix of lipid molecules. The nonpolar hydrocarbons of the lipid molecules and residue of proteins are found in the interior, whereas the ionic or polar groups of lipids and proteins are in contact with the environmental tissue fluid. The validity of this concept has been confirmed by the isolation of globular proteins found in membranes. These proteins are rhodopsin and cytochrome oxidase. X-ray diffraction analysis of the membrane of the surface of the cell has shown that rhodopsin (a protein formed in the rods of the retina) is distributed at random throughout the membrane, penetrating approximately half-way into the lipid matrix, whereas cytochrome oxidase (a protein found on the mitochondrial membrane) extends throughout the cell membrane lipid matrix, thus forming a mosaic in the plane of the membrane (Fig 3–4).

Although the very thin membrane is not resolved by the light microscope, the cells sometimes appear to be separated from each other by a membrane (mainly in certain epithelial tissues) (Figs 4–1 and 4–2). This is due to the existence of a layer of glycoprotein that covers or is part of the membrane and forms a visible intercellular partition (Fig 3–5). (See Glycocalyx in

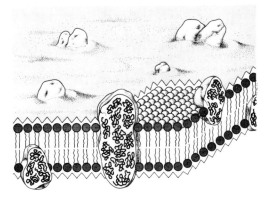

Figure 3–4. Plasma membrane structure according to a currently accepted concept. It is composed of a bimolecular lipid layer covered by fibrous proteins, with large globular proteins nested in the membrane.

(inner and outer) were not exactly the same in structure; and that the outer layer probably contained polysaccharide as well.

Although the membrane described above is typical of the structure of most plasma membranes, it does not account for such characteristics as rapid changes in membrane permeability or for the physiologic evidence that suggests the presence of pores in the membrane. There is morphologic evidence that plasma membrane probably has an unstable structure which varies according to its permeability to different substances, but little is known about what occurs within the membrane in these circumstances. Recent evidence strongly sug-

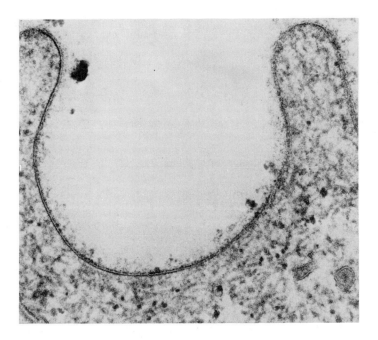

Figure 3–5. Electron micrograph of a section of the surface of an epithelial cell, showing the unit membrane with its 2 dark lines limiting a clear band. On the surface of the membrane is a depot of granular material forming the glycocalyx. × 100,000.

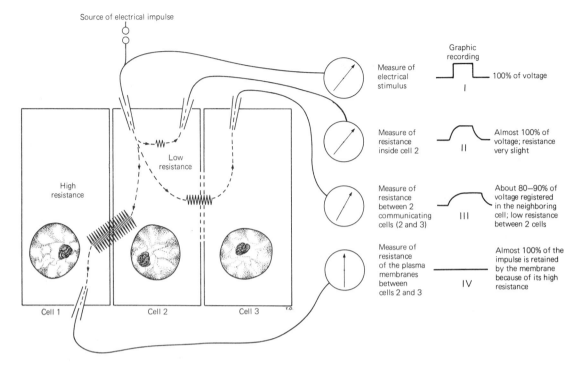

Figure 3—6. Experiments measuring the electrical conductivity between cells with or without communication. Cells 1 and 2 do not communicate, whereas cells 2 and 3 do. In cell 2, two microelectrodes were inserted. One is connected simultaneously to a stimulator (generator of electrical impulse) and to a measuring device. The other electrode is connected to a registering electrode and measures the current that crosses the cell cytoplasm. Electrodes were also inserted in cells 1 and 3 to measure the current that passes from cell 2 to cell 1 and from cell 2 to cell 3. Graphs obtained from the electrical stimulations are shown to the right of the figure. The upper graph expresses the total impulse measured by the electrode to the left of cell 2. The second graph shows only a very small lowering of the current due to the resistance of the cytoplasm. The third and fourth graphs show that most of the current (80–90%) passes from cell 2 to cell 3 while practically no current crosses the membranes that separate cell 2 from cell 1. Cells 2 and 3 have a special junction that lowers the membrane's resistance. This does not occur between cells 1 and 2.

Chapter 4.) The cellular structures that result from modification of the plasma membrane—villi, desmosomes, etc—are also discussed in Chapter 4. The structures of other membranes (nuclear envelope, endoplasmic reticulum, Golgi apparatus, secretory granules, and lysosomes)—although not identical—are similar to those of the plasma membrane. The structural and functional differences observed are at present being actively investigated. Chemical differences have been noted, and structural differences have been associated with the presence of different structural proteins, lipids, enzymes, and receptors on them.

B. Cellular Communication: It has been shown that the cells of several tissues of both vertebrates and invertebrates are not independent and isolated biologic units but have intercellular communications, permitting the free interchange of ions and larger molecules. This occurs by means of specialized regions present in the membranes of neighboring cells. This recently discovered phenomenon is being actively studied by the following technics:

1. Following the intracellular microinjection of stains or fluorescent compounds by means of micropipettes, it was observed that the injected compound gradually passed to neighboring cells and then to still

other cells.

2. By inserting microelectrodes into neighboring cells, it was shown that an electric current can pass between cells with very slight loss of voltage (Fig 3–6). The curves registered for the electrical impulse (curve I) were compared with tracings from the 3 microelectrodes (curves II, III, and IV). Analysis led to the following conclusions:

a. The electrical stimulus is transmitted with no loss of its intensity to electrode II inserted in the same cell. The cell cytoplasm is therefore a good conductor and does not hinder the flow of the stimulus.

b. When the electrical impulse is applied to cell 2, it is not registered in cell 1 (curve IV). This indicates that the plasma membranes between cells 1 and 2 offer high resistance.

c. When the electrical impulse is applied to cell 2, the stimulus registered in the electrode inserted in cell 3 is almost the same (curve III) as the one observed in the electrode of cell 2 (curve II), where the total impulse was measured initially and within the cell (curves I and II). This is due to low resistance between cells 2 and 3 and suggests communication between these cells.

Indeed, careful measurements have shown that the resistance between communicating cells can be a thousand times lower than between noncommunicating cells. The above-mentioned results are important because they clearly demonstrate that most tissues are not an aggregate of independent cells; rather, they behave as a functional unit. Because of these communications, cardiac and smooth muscle cells are not composed of independent cells; they contract synchronously to form a functional unit. (See also Chapter 11.) Cellular communication appears during the embryonic stage and is probably important in the coordination of intrauterine development.

C. Intercellular Junctions: Morphologic studies have shown that 3 types of junctions occur in cells with intercellular communication.

1. Zonula occludens (tight junction)—The zonula occludens is characterized by apposition and fusion of the outer layers of the cell membranes from 2 contiguous cells, and this occurs near the free surface of epithelial cells. Consequently, the 2 membranes originally formed by the 7 layers seen in the electron microscope

present only 5 layers because of the fusion of the outer layer of each cell's plasma membrane (Fig 3–7). These junctions usually form a continuous belt around the cell apex (Fig 4–6). In some instances, they are restricted to a limited region (spotlike area) of the membrane called the *macula occludens*. These junctions are found between cells in both vertebrates and invertebrates.

2. Gap junctions (junctions of the nexus type)—In gap junctions, the outer leaflets do not fuse but remain separated by a narrow gap (approximately 2 nm). In this space, electron-dense regions alternate periodically with less dense portions. The "gap" area of the junction is continuous with the extracellular environment and is probably limited in its penetrability only by the size of the substances that may pass through. This type of junction is common in cells of both vertebrates and invertebrates (Fig 3–7).

3. Septate junctions—Septate junctions (septate desmosomes) are characterized by a relatively large

Name	Morphology	Distribution	Probable Functions
Zonula occludens (tight junction)	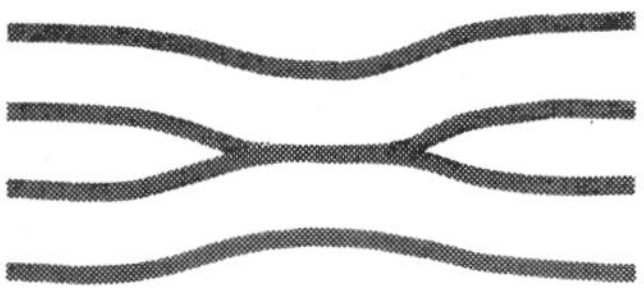	Mainly in vertebrates but has been observed in invertebrates	Sealing and regulation of transcellular permeability (epithelia)
Septate junction	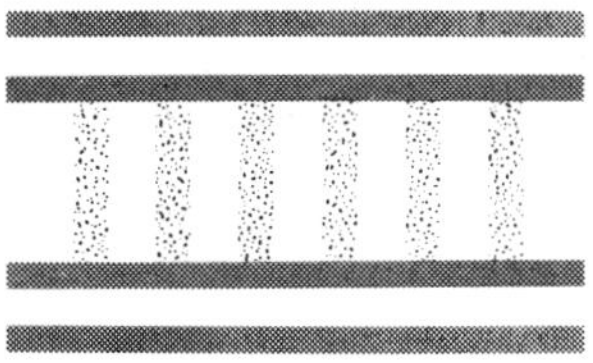	In invertebrates; septatelike junctions in vertebrates	Partial sealing, adhesion, low-resistance ionic coupling(?)
Gap junction	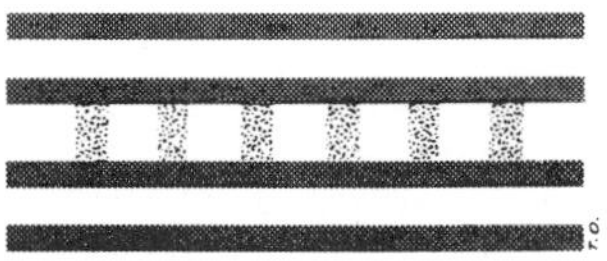	Invertebrates, vertebrates, and cells in culture. Most frequent cell junction.	Intercellular communication. No complete sealing action.

Figure 3–7. Morphology of the main known types of cell junctions. When fusion of the outer portion of the membranes occurs in the zonula occludens, the structure assumes 5 layers instead of the 7 layers resulting from two 7.5 nm thick parallel unit membranes separated by a 2–4 nm "gap" which is electron-lucent.

space between the membranes of 2 adjacent cells that are bound by columnar, electron-dense structures at right angles to the surface that alternate with less dense regions (septa) (Fig 3–7). These junctions are found in invertebrates.

The use of lanthanum salts as a tracer showed that, while gap junctions can be permeated by these compounds, zonula occludens and septate junctions are usually tight and do not permit their passage. The available data strongly suggest that the gap junctions are responsible for ionic or electronic coupling and metabolic cooperation in intercellular communication, whereas the other 2 types are probably more closely related to the sealing of intercellular spaces and to adhesions between cells. These junctions are effective barriers to the diffusion of large molecules between cells, although osmotic changes might influence the permeability of epithelial cells (transepithelial permeability). This is a subject in continuous development; more data will be needed to clarify the exact roles of these junctions.

Junctions can be formed rapidly between previ-ously isolated cells. Metabolic inhibitors—especially those blocking oxidative phosphorylation—can block the formation of junctions or undo junctions already present between cells. This suggests that the maintenance of intercellular junctions is an active process dependent on energy production. In addition, it is probable that calcium ions and a specific glycoprotein complex at the cell surface are needed to establish junctions between cells. The analysis of cellular communication between tumors shows that in several types there is no communication.

Matrix or Cytosol

Very little is known about the composition of the matrix, which is the basic component of cytoplasm. It is believed to consist mainly of large enzymatic or non-enzymatic protein molecules linked (or not linked) to carbohydrates, mineral salts, and other absorbed soluble substances.

Mitochondria

Mitochondria were observed in 1850 by Kollicker

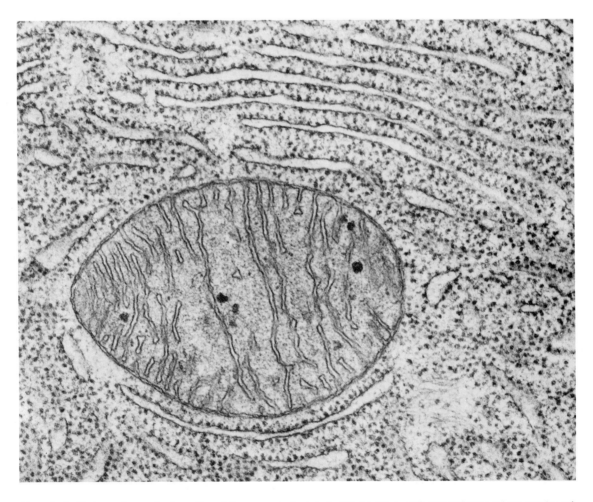

Figure 3–8. Electron micrograph of a section of the pancreas of a bat. A mitochondrion—with its membranes, cristae, matrix, and dense granules—is clearly visible. Surrounding it is typical granular endoplasmic reticulum. × 50,000. (Courtesy of KR Porter.)

in muscle cells and described in detail with the aid of the electron microscope by Palade and Sjöstrand in 1952–1955. They are present in all mammalian cells. They are organelles that transform the chemical energy of the metabolites present in cytoplasm into available energy that is easily accessible to the cell. This energy is stored in a class of unstable substances that is rich in energy. These substances, typified by adenosine triphosphate (ATP), promptly release energy when required by the cell to perform work of osmotic, mechanical, electrical, or chemical nature. The mitochondria are spherical or elongated particles 0.1–0.5 μm wide and up to 10 μm long. Their distribution in the cells varies. They tend to accumulate in parts of the cytoplasm where metabolic activity is more intense, such as at the apical ends of ciliated cells, at the middle piece of spermatozoa, or at the base of ion-transferring cells. In instances where they are not polarized, they have a tendency to be oriented along the long axis of cylindric or long cells or radially on round cells.

Cells contain great numbers of mitochondria—an estimated 2500 in one rat liver cell—but always in a characteristic number for that cell. The mitochondria are composed mainly of protein. Lipids are present to a lesser degree, along with small quantities of DNA and RNA. Like most cell components, mitochondria have a short life span and are constantly being renewed. The average half-life of mitochondria in rat liver cells is 10 days. The ultrastructure of mitochondria varies with the organ and species from which the tissue is obtained for examination.

Mitochondria generally have a characteristic structure under the electron microscope (Fig 3–8). They are composed of an external continuous membrane and an internal membrane which projects folds into the interior of the mitochondria, giving rise to the *cristae mitochondriales.* These membranes surround 2 spaces—one outer space between the 2 membranes, called the intracristal space, and one within the internal membrane, penetrated by the cristae. Most mitochondria have cristae in their interior (Figs 3–1 and 3–8); however, the cells that synthesize steroids (see Chapter 4) frequently contain tubules in addition to cristae (Fig 4–21). The cristae and tubules increase the internal surface area of the mitochondria, and it is on this surface that enzymes of the oxidative phosphorylation and electron transport systems are located. Small, rounded particles about 9.8 nm in diameter have recently been observed that are attached to the internal surface of the internal membrane of the mitochondria (Fig 3–1). These are the *elementary particles* or *oxysomes;* they contain a stem 4–5 nm long and 3–3.5 nm wide and a round head 7.5–8 nm in diameter. It is possible that they contain several of the enzymes and pigments related to the process of oxidative phosphorylation. The exact identity of enzymes located in the elementary particles is unknown. The outer membrane also shows cylindric structures perpendicular to the membrane surface.

The number of mitochondria and the number of cristae in each mitochondrion are proportionate to the rate of metabolism of the cells. Thus, cells with a high rate of metabolism (eg, cardiac muscle or kidney tubule cells) have abundant mitochondria with a large number of closely packed cristae, whereas others with low metabolism have short cristae.

Filaments of DNA in the mitochondria have been isolated and show mostly a circular structure. Although the mitochondrial DNA might represent DNA synthesized in the nucleus and transferred into the mitochondria, it is generally believed today that the nuclear DNA does not synthesize mitochondrial DNA. This is supported by the observation in vitro of the duplication of mitochondrial DNA in the presence of essential triphosphates. Particles resembling ribosomes have also been noted. Both of these observations are consistent with the protein synthesis known to occur in the mitochondria. An extranuclear genetic system related to the synthesis of part but not all of the mitochondrial proteins is apparently present. It has been suggested that mitochondria can code structural proteins such as cytochrome oxidase, whereas nuclear DNA codes most of the proteins of the matrix and of the outer membrane. It might also be involved in the duplication of these particles.

An amorphous matrix rich in protein is present between the cristae or the tubules. In a great number of cell types, the matrix presents electron-dense, rounded granules which are thought to be rich in calcium and magnesium but whose function is not completely understood. Metabolites within the cell are utilized in the mitochondria by the catalytic activity of the enzymes of the *citric acid cycle (Krebs tricarboxylic acid cycle),* and the energy liberated in this process is captured by the processes of oxidative phosphorylation. CO_2 and water are the chemical end products in addition to the high-energy compounds (ATP) concurrently produced.

The initial degradation of proteins, carbohydrates, and fats is carried out in the cytosol or matrix— that portion of the cell outside the mitochondria. The ultimate metabolic end product of these extramitochondrial metabolic pathways is acetyl-CoA, which then enters the mitochondria. Within the mitochondria, acetyl-CoA combines with oxaloacetate to form citric acid. Within the citric acid cycle, there are several reactions of decarboxylation producing CO_2, and 5 pairs of hydrogen atoms are removed by specific reactions of oxidation catalyzed by dehydrogenases. The H atoms are transferred ultimately to oxygen to form H_2O via the electron transport system. In this system, by virtue of the action of cytochromes a, b, and c and coenzyme Q, as well as cytochrome oxidase, there are mechanisms to capture released energy at 3 points by formation of ATP from ADP and phosphate. Under aerobic circumstances, the combined activity of extramitochondrial glycolysis and the citric acid cycle as well as the electron transport system gives rise to 38 molecules of ATP per mol of glucose. This is 19 times the energy obtainable under anaerobic circumstances, when only the glycolytic pathway can be utilized.

Origin & Evolution of Mitochondria

Opinion differs about the genesis and evolution of mitochondria. They have been said to derive from the nuclear membrane and from the plasma membrane or endoplasmic reticular membrane; to arise by division from existing mitochondria; or to come into existence by de novo synthesis.

Sufficient evidence has been presented to suggest that new mitochondria originate from preexisting mitochondria by accretion of material, causing growth and subsequent division of the organelle. During mitosis, an equal division of the mitochondria occurs between parent and daughter cell.

The fact that mitochondria present a circular DNA molecule and respiratory enzymes in their membranes, as in bacteria, has led to speculation regarding the evolutionary origin and history of this organelle. It has thus been proposed that mitochondria evolved from an ancestral prokaryote which became adapted to a symbiotic life within the host eukaryotic cell. The fact that the processes of protein synthesis in mitochondria are much more similar to those occurring in bacteria than in eukaryotes gives weight to this opinion. Thus, certain antibiotics such as chloramphenicol inhibit both mitochondrial and bacterial protein synthesis and do not affect cytoplasmic synthesis.

However, despite this evidence, the endosymbiont theory is not universally accepted, and other models have been proposed.

Endoplasmic Reticulum

This organelle, described originally by Garnier and later defined in the electron microscope by Porter and others in 1945, was called *ergastoplasm* by early investigators. It appears as a network of flattened, rounded, tubular vesicles that frequently anastomose with one another in a network form. The disposition of these vesicles varies considerably from cell to cell and also in different parts of one particular cell. There are 2 types of endoplasmic reticulum—granular (rough) and smooth. Endoplasmic reticulum appears very early in embryonic development and varies in appearance and size with the functional state of the cells.

The membranes of the endoplasmic reticulum are continuous with the nuclear envelope membrane and very seldom with plasma membranes. These membranes are arranged in the form of cisternae (especially in cells producing proteins) stacked in parallel and convey the impression of reservoirlike formations. Membrane-bound small or large vesicles represent the second component of this organelle. These vesicles might represent the vehicle for transfer of materials from the cisternae of endoplasmic reticulum to the Golgi apparatus, in which case they are called "transfer vesicles." Finally, tubular vesicles are seen in cross section as small circles with many tubular configurations freely anastomosing and branching.

The membranes of the *granular (rough) endoplasmic reticulum* have *ribosomes* attached to their external surfaces (Figs 3–1 and 3–8). These are small, electron-dense particles, 15–20 nm in diameter, attached to the outer surfaces of the membranes. They are composed mostly of RNA and protein and are responsible for the basophilia seen in the cytoplasm of cells. There are 2 classes of ribosomes: one type found in the prokaryotes, chloroplasts, and mitochondria and the other in the cytoplasm of eukaryotic cells. Both classes of ribosomes are composed of 2 particles of different sizes. They can appear as isolated granules free in the cytoplasm or can accumulate as spiral or rosette configurations called *polysomes.* The ribosomal material is synthesized in the nucleoli, and in mutant animals in which no nucleoli are present no ribosomes are synthesized. *Polysomes* or *polyribosomes* (Fig 3–9A) are groups of ribosomes held together by a strand of messenger RNA. Ribosomes may adhere to the surface of the endoplasmic reticulum or may exist free in the cytoplasm. In the adherent state, they form the granular endoplasmic reticulum present in cell types that produce "export proteins" which will later be extruded from the cell. This occurs in several cell types (eg, those in protein-synthesizing glands, fibroblasts, and plasma cells), wherein the synthesized proteins are released through the membrane of the endoplasmic reticulum and remain segregated in the interior of that structure (Fig 3–9B). The carbohydrate moiety of glycoproteins is bound to the proteins not only in the endoplasmic reticulum but also in the Golgi apparatus. Therefore, besides participating in protein synthesis, granular endoplasmic reticulum also has a function in the synthesis of glycoproteins.

In cell types in which proteins are produced for local use (sedentary proteins), the polysomes appear freely in the cytoplasm and are not attached to membranes of the endoplasmic reticulum. Thus, the proteins are not segregated in the endoplasmic reticulum; they can be observed permeating the cytoplasm. An example is the immature red blood cell (erythroblast) that synthesizes hemoglobin. (These concepts are summarized in Figs 3–9A and 3–9B.)

The ribosomes, which are intensely basophilic, react with such basic stains as methylene blue and toluidine blue because they contain great quantities of RNA. Thus, the sites in cytoplasm that stain with these dyes are usually rich in ribosomes. These basophilic regions in cytoplasm were described in the 19th century and were named according to the cell studied. In glandular cells, they were known as ergastoplasm; in neurons, as *Nissl bodies;* and in other cells as *basophilic bodies* or *components.* Thus, although the ribosomes per se are invisible in the light microscope, they can be revealed indirectly because of their staining characteristics.

The term *microsome* as used in cytology and biochemistry is sometimes confusing. It refers to particles resulting from fragmentation of the granular endoplasmic reticulum during the process of homogenization that precedes differential centrifugation. The fusion of membrane fragments of the ruptured endoplasmic reticulum generates small vesicles covered with ribosomes. These microsomes can then be isolated by means of differential centrifugation. It is now possible

A

B

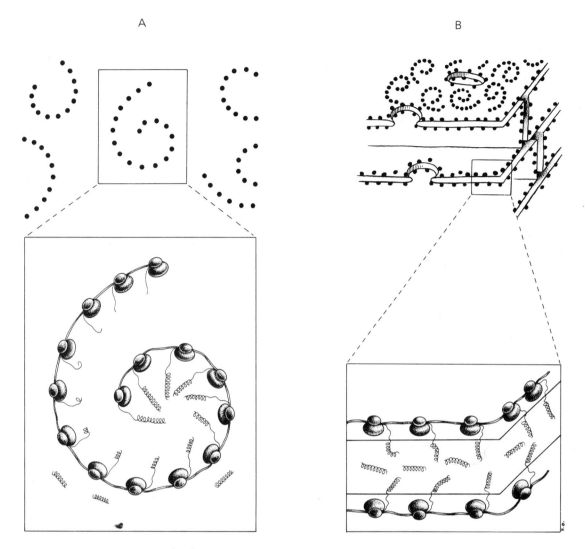

Figure 3—9. This diagram illustrates (in *A*) the concept expressed in the text that cells that synthesize proteins that stay within the cytoplasm of the cell (represented here by spirals) display polysomes nonadherent to the endoplasmic reticulum. In *B*, where the proteins are eventually extruded from the cytoplasm (exportation proteins), not only do the polysomes adhere to the membranes of granular endoplasmic reticulum but the proteins produced by them are transported to the interior of the organelle across its membrane. In this way, the proteins—especially enzymes such as ribonucleases and proteases, which could have undesirable effects on the cytoplasm—are separated from it.

to fractionate the microsomes further and separate the membranous component from the ribosomes (Figs 1–13 and 1–14).

There are no ribosomes attached to the membrane of the *smooth endoplasmic reticulum*. This organelle, originally described in the electron microscope in nerve cells, is composed entirely of membranes that generally appear as profusely anastomosing tubules (Fig 3–1). The cells with abundant smooth endoplasmic reticulum are acidophilic. Post mortem, they undergo rapid autolysis. The smooth and the granular endoplasmic reticulum intercommunicate; there are intercommunications also between smooth endoplasmic reticulum and the Golgi apparatus or the nuclear envelope; and in some cells there are apparently transi-

tional structures between them (Fig 3–10). Smooth endoplasmic reticulum is very abundant in cells that synthesize steroids (Figs 4–20 and 4–21) and is also responsible for the conjugation, oxidation, and methylation processes employed by the cell to neutralize or detoxify certain hormones and noxious substances. It is also believed that smooth endoplasmic reticulum conducts excitatory impulses in striated muscle cells where it appears in a special form called *sarcoplasmic reticulum.* It is involved in the synthesis of the glycogen in liver cells, and the enzyme glucose-6-phosphatase is found in the membranes of the smooth endoplasmic reticulum.

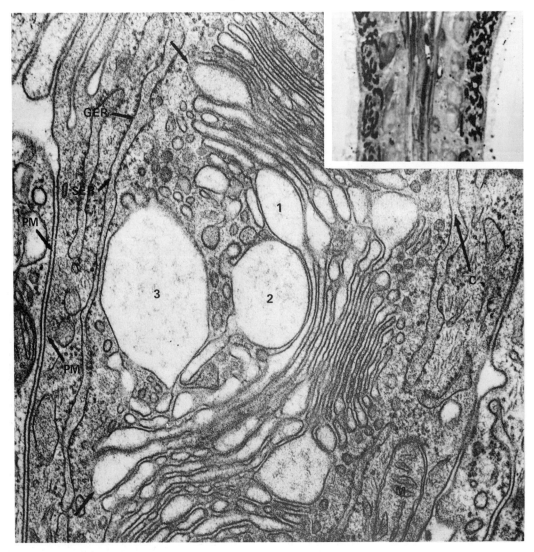

Figure 3–10. Electron micrograph of a Golgi apparatus of a goblet cell. To the right is a cisterna (C) of the granular endoplasmic reticulum containing granular material. Close to it are small vesicles containing this material. To the left are flattened and piled-up cisternae of the Golgi apparatus. At the lateral regions of these cisternae, dilatations can be observed (arrows). These dilatations gradually detach themselves from the cisternae and fuse, forming the secretory granules (1, 2, and 3). PM is the plasma membrane of 2 neighboring cells. Near the membrane is an endoplasmic reticulum with a smooth section (SER) and a granular (rough) section (GER). × 30,000. *Inset:* The aspect of the Golgi apparatus as seen in 1 μm sections of epididymis cells impregnated by silver. × 1200.

Golgi Apparatus

This organelle, which is present in all cells, appears as a group of piled-up flat vesicles with peripheral dilatations (Figs 3–1 and 3–10). The Golgi apparatus usually occupies a finite and fixed area in the cytoplasm of most cells. In protein-secreting cells and nerve or liver cells, however, it may appear in small groups scattered throughout the cytoplasm. The size and development of this organelle is variable from cell to cell and also changes with the type of activity of the cell.

It is believed that the Golgi apparatus plays a role in the process of receiving, concentrating, and storing the secretory products of most glandular cells. The proteins synthesized in granular endoplasmic reticulum are transferred to the Golgi apparatus, probably with the aid of small vesicles which bud from the endoplasmic reticulum and are called transfer vesicles. They migrate and fuse to the Golgi membranes, where they are collected and condensed into relatively large, dense particles and enclosed by a membrane to form *secretory granules.*

Radioautographic studies using sulfur-35 (^{35}S) reveal that, in cells which elaborate sulfated glycoproteins, the Golgi apparatus is the site of sulfation (Fig 5–9). Similar experiments performed with labeled galactose and glucose strongly suggest that the Golgi

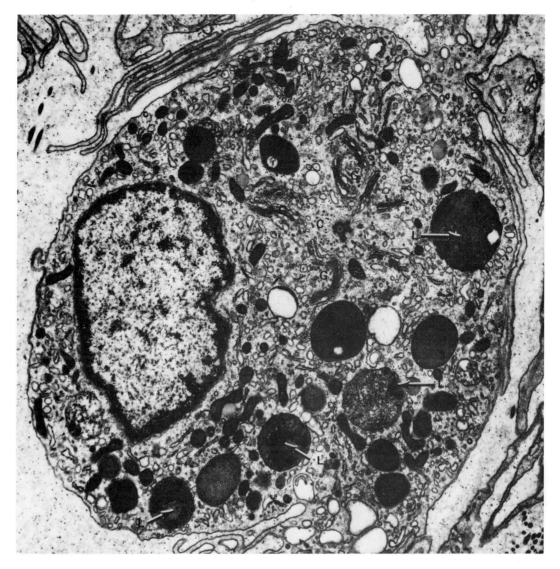

Figure 3–11. Electron micrograph of a mesenteric macrophage. Observe the presence of abundant cytoplasmic extensions. In the center is a centriole (C) surrounded by Golgi cisternae (G). Lysosomes (L) are abundant. × 15,000.

apparatus is also the site of polysaccharide synthesis.

Lysosomes

Lysosomes, discovered by de Duve (1951), are very widespread among cells and are particularly abundant where intracytoplasmic digestion occurs, eg, in macrophages and in kidney, nerve, and white blood cells. They contain a variety of lytic enzymes which are active at acid pH. The nature and activity of these enzymes varies depending on the type of cell studied, but the ones most commonly found are acid phosphatase, ribonuclease, deoxyribonuclease, cathepsin (A, B, and C), proteases, sulfatases, and β-glucuronidase (Fig 3–11).

Lysosomes are usually spherical and are enclosed by a lipoprotein membrane that separates their contents from the cytoplasm (Figs 3–12 and 3–13). This membrane plays an important part in preventing lytic enzymes contained within the lysosomes from attacking and digesting the cytoplasm.

Under the light microscope, the lysosomes of some leukocytes appear as granules. Under the electron microscope, however, they present extremely varied morphologic characteristics and are sometimes difficult to characterize (Figs 3–12 and 3–13.) There is evidence that the lysosomal enzymes are synthesized in the granular endoplasmic reticulum. It is also known that the Golgi apparatus participates in the formation of these organelles in many cell types. They appear to bud off from the maturing face of the Golgi apparatus and contain the active enzymes. It is known that the vacuoles formed by phagocytosis or pinocytosis of extracellular substances—*phagosomes*—fuse with the virgin or *primary lysosomes* so that their enzymic con-

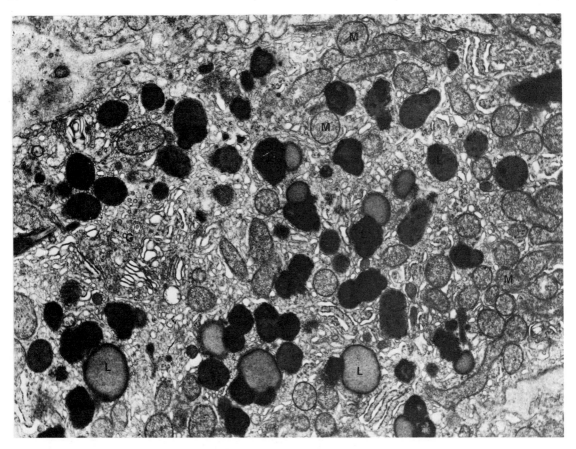

Figure 3—12. Electron micrograph of a section of human adrenal gland showing abundant polymorphic lysosomes (L). Note Golgi apparatus (G) and abundant smooth endoplasmic reticulum and mitochondria (M). × 15,000. (Courtesy of M Magalhães.)

tent contacts the engulfed particle. The phenomenon of intracellular digestion takes place within this new vacuole, which is called the *secondary lysosome* (Fig 3—14).

Another function of the lysosomes concerns cytoplasmic turnover. Under certain conditions, one or more parts of the cytoplasm become surrounded by a membrane. Lysosomes fuse to it, promoting partial lysis of a finite, thin portion of the cytoplasm, sometimes including an organelle (Fig 3—15). These lysosomes are called *autophagosomes*. The product of the hydrolysis of these vacuoles is probably used by the cell for synthesis, permitting the cell to renew, rearrange, and reconstruct part of its cytoplasm. This type of intracellular digestion is common in pituitary cells. In certain pathologic conditions, or when cellular damage or death occurs, the lysosomes may rupture and destroy the cytoplasm. This process is known as *autolysis*.

There is evidence that lysosomes can be eliminated from the cell, in which case their enzymes act in the extracellular medium. This is exemplified by the destruction of bone tissue by collagenase synthesized by certain types of cells in the bone. Enzymes present in the lysosomes are sometimes discharged to the sur-

face of cells in cases where antigen-antibody complexes cannot be ingested and are found only on the cell membranes. This type of reaction might play a very important role in the response to inflammation or injury. Several possibilities that may explain the activities of lysosomes are illustrated schematically in Fig 3—14.

Lysosomes play an important part in the metabolism of certain substances in the human body, and diseases have been ascribed to deficiencies of lysosomal enzymes. Thus, in *metachromatic leukodystrophy*, there is an intracellular accumulation of sulfated cerebrosides caused by the deficiency of sulfatase. In most of these diseases, a specific lysosomal enzyme is absent, and the elimination of certain substances (glycogen, cerebrosides, gangliosides, sphingomyelin, etc) does not occur, having as a result the accumulation of these substances and subsequent interference with the normal function of the cells.

Microbodies or Peroxisomes

Recently it has been possible to isolate a cytoplasmic particle from liver by differential centrifugation. This microbody (or peroxisome) (Figs 3—13 and 3—18) is slightly smaller than a mitochondrion, has a

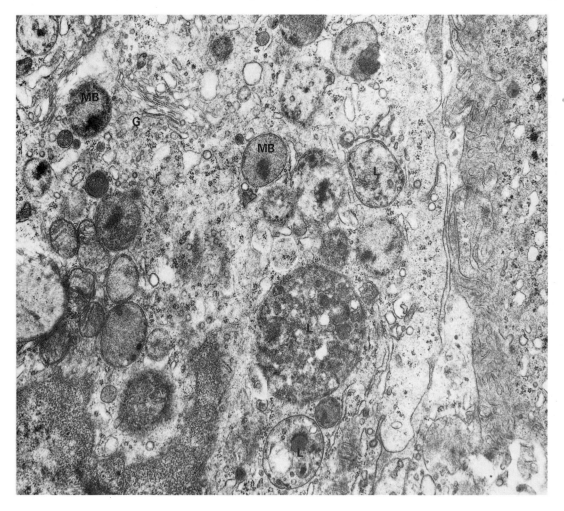

Figure 3–13. Electron micrograph of a section of a Kupffer cell from a rat submitted to experimental biliary obstruction. Lysosomes (L) are shown in different stages of development. Microbodies (MB) show dense central cores and limiting membranes. The Golgi apparatus (G) is shown. × 21,000.

single boundary membrane, and presumably contains a characteristic central core. It seems to be quite widespread in the natural world and has been identified in protozoa and in vegetable and animal cells. These particles are known to have a high catalase, urate oxidase, and D-amino acid oxidase activity. The function of these particles is being actively studied, and it seems probable that they participate in various processes similar to those of the lysosome. In vertebrates, they may be related to the oxidation of D-amino acids produced by bacteria in the digestive tract and absorbed by the body.

Centrioles

The centrioles are a pair of short, cylindric, tubular structures usually located near or within the Golgi apparatus (Fig 3–1). Under the light microscope they are visible as granules. The electron microscope reveals that they are composed of an electron-dense, circular wall composed of an amorphous substance in which 9

longitudinally placed tubular elements are immersed. Each element is in turn made up of 2 or 3 microtubules fused to one another (Fig 3–1).

The centrioles become apparent during mitosis, when they function as the points of origin and convergence for the spindle microtubules. The cilia and flagella insert themselves in the so-called basal corpuscles, which have a similar structure. It is believed that the cilia and flagella originate from structures with the morphologic aspect of centrioles.

Filaments & Tubules

Thin filaments and tubular structures are frequently encountered in the cytoplasm of some cells; their functions are being actively studied. It is believed that these structures, among others, maintain the shape of the cell, since they give the cytoplasm a certain amount of rigidity. They are probably the equivalent of the cytoskeleton whose existence was postulated many years ago (Fig 3–16). The terminal webs of the

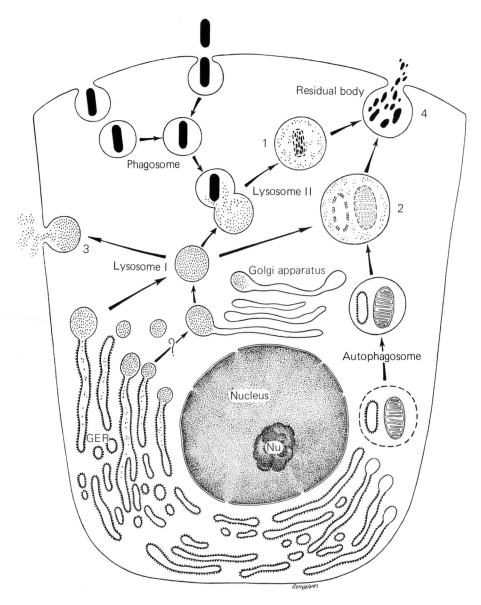

Figure 3—14. Present concepts of the functions of the lysosomes. Synthesis occurs in the granular endoplasmic reticulum (GER). Participation of the Golgi apparatus in lysosome formation is discussed in the text. *1* and *2:* Lysosome participation in intracellular digestion. *3:* Extrusion and extracellular action of lytic enzymes. *4:* The elimination of residues. Nu, nucleolus.

columnar epithelium and keratin fibers in epithelial cells (see Chapter 4) are examples of the above-mentioned functions.

It is also believed that the filaments and tubules participate in particle transport and contractile phenomena in the cytoplasm. It has been observed that the microtubules forming the mitotic spindle rays play an important part in the migration of chromosomes during anaphase. Colchicine and vinblastine alkaloids that arrest mitosis in metaphase by blocking the migration of the chromosomes act to prevent formation of the microtubules of the mitotic spindle. Microtubules usually have a diameter of 24 nm and are present in

different cell types (eg, white blood cells and neurons) (Fig 3–17).

Cytoplasmic filaments have variable diameters (4–10 nm). There is evidence that in some instances they may participate in cytoplasmic movements, eg, cell division, cytokinesis, ameboid movement, pinocytosis, cytoplasmic streaming, and transport and secretion of cellular materials. They are present in abundance in the region of the furrow of dividing cells and in neurons, glial cells, etc. Recently, a substance called *cytochalasin,* which breaks down microfilaments, has been isolated from cultures of fungi. This substance inhibits most cellular activities previously mentioned.

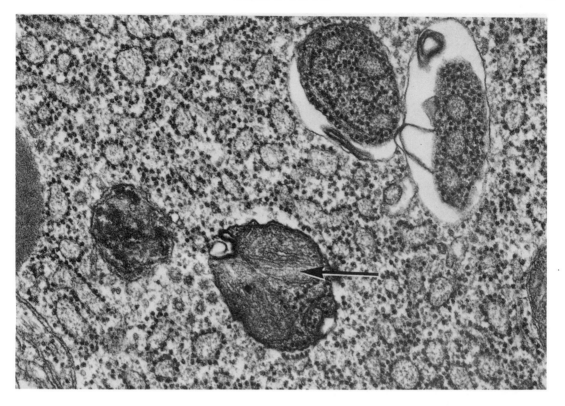

Figure 3–15. Section of a pancreatic acinar cell showing autophagosomes. *Above:* Two portions of the granular endoplasmic reticulum segregated by a membrane. *Below:* An autophagosome containing mitochondria (arrow) plus granular endoplasmic reticulum. *Left:* A probable phagosome at a late stage of digestion.

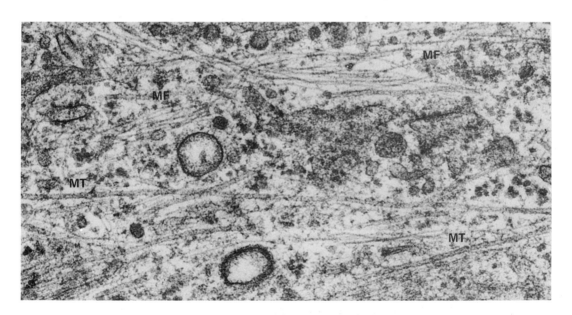

Figure 3–16. Electron micrograph of rat fibroblast cytoplasm. Observe the microfilaments (MF) and microtubules (MT). $\times$ 60,000. (Courtesy of E Katchburian.)

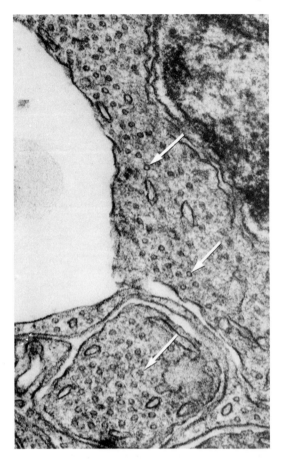

Figure 3–17 (at left). Electron micrograph of a section of a photosensitive retinal cell of a monkey. Observe the accumulation of transversely sectioned microtubules (arrows). Reduced slightly from X 80,000.

Figure 3–18 (below). Electron micrograph of a section of a liver cell showing microbodies (MB) and glycogen inclusions appearing as accumulations of electron-dense particles (arrows). X 30,000.

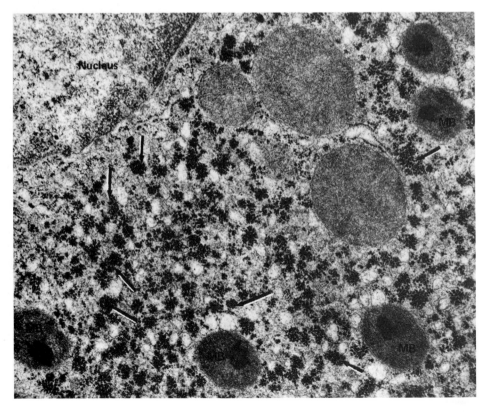

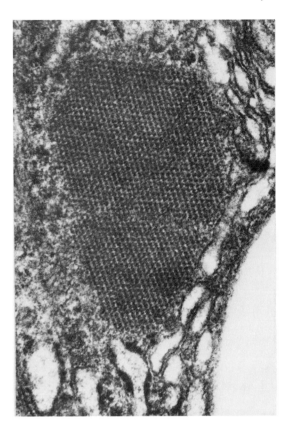

Figure 3—19 (at left). Electron micrograph of a crystalloid inclusion body from a human adrenal cell. Most of these inclusions are composed of proteins. (Courtesy of M Magalhães.)

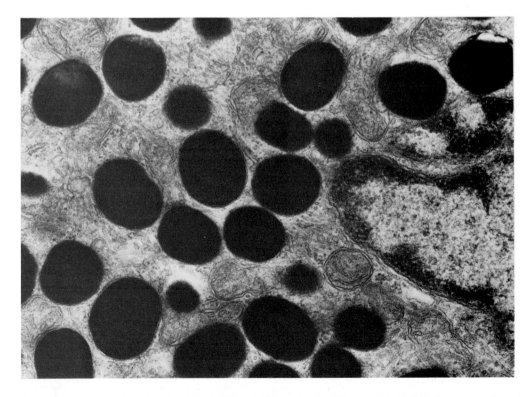

Figure 3—20. Section of a fish melanophore. The nucleus is shown at right. The cytoplasm is full of dense, membrane-bound melanin granules. Mitochondria and microtubules are also numerous. × 20,000.

Both fibrils and microtubules are made up of spherical monomers with diameters of 3–4 nm. These monomers aggregate spirally, forming the microtubules (Fig 3–17). The microfilaments apparently consist of 3 intertwined chains of these monomers.

Cytoplasmic Inclusions

These are usually transitory components of the cytoplasm, composed mainly of accumulated metabolites or deposits of varied nature. The accumulated metabolites occur in several forms, one of them being lipid droplets present in adipose tissue and liver cells. Carbohydrate accumulations are also visible in several cells in the form of glycogen. After impregnation with lead salts, this substance appears as collections of coarse, irregular, electron-dense particles (Fig 3–18). Proteins appear in glandular cells as zymogen granules; these are periodically released into the extracellular medium. In some cells, protein crystals of unknown significance have been described (Fig 3–19).

Deposits of colored substances—*pigment*—are often found in cells (Fig 3–20). They may be synthesized by the cell (eg, pigment cells) or may come from outside the body (eg, vitamin A). One of the most common pigments is *lipofuscin,* a yellowish-brown substance that increases in quantity in cells with age. Its chemical constitution is complex and little is known about its origin, but it is believed that granules of lipofuscin derive from secondary lysosomes and represent deposits of undigested substances. Another widely distributed pigment, *melanin,* is abundant in the epidermis of the skin and in the pigment layer of the retina in the form of dense, intracellular, membrane-bound granules.

THE NUCLEUS

The nucleus of the cell appears as a rounded or elongated structure, usually in the center of the cell, in hematoxylin and eosin–stained preparations. In mammalian tissues, its diameter usually varies between 5 and 10 μm. The nucleus is composed of the nuclear envelope, chromatin, the nucleolus, and nucleoplasm.

Nuclear Envelope

The nuclear envelope can be observed under the light microscope as a thin membrane surrounding the nucleus. Under the electron microscope, however, it appears as a double-layered structure consisting of 2 parallel unit membranes 40–70 nm apart, leaving a perinuclear space. What is actually seen in the light microscope as the nuclear envelope is mainly a layer of chromatin lining the internal surface (Figs 3–21 and 3–22). Ribosomes are frequently attached to its external membrane, and this portion of the nuclear envelope sometimes merges with the granular endoplasmic reticulum. The nuclear envelope has circular gaps—the

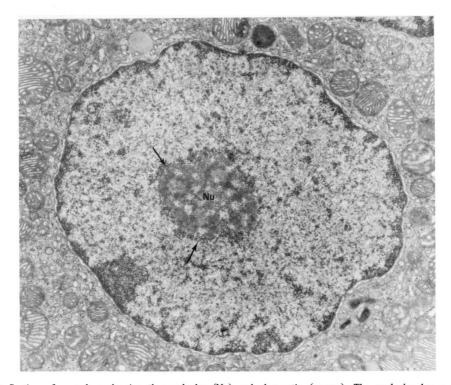

Figure 3–21. Section of a nucleus showing the nucleolus (Nu) and chromatin (arrows). The nucleolus has a thin rim of chromatin—the nucleolar-associated chromatin—and a fibrillar portion in the center surrounded by a granular portion. Reduced from X 12,500. (Courtesy of J Long.)

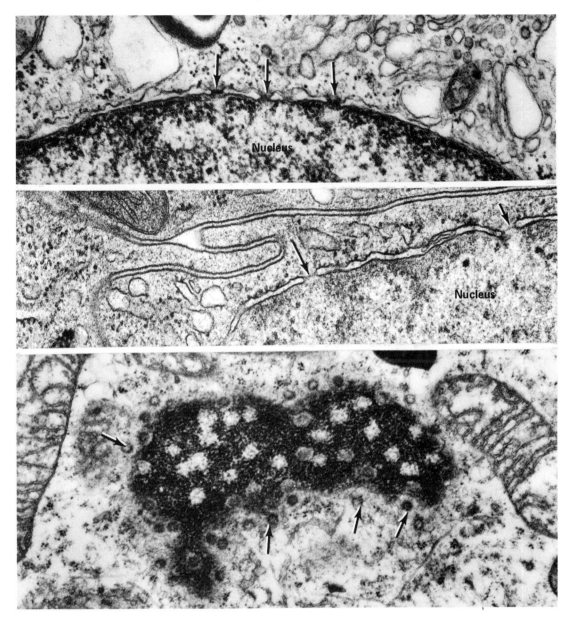

Figure 3—22. Electron micrographs of nuclei showing their envelopes composed of 2 membranes and the nuclear pores (arrows). The 2 upper pictures are of transverse sections. The lower one is of a tangential section. Observe that the pores are closed by a diaphragm that appears as dense rounded structures in the lower pictures. Chromatin, frequently condensed below the nuclear envelope, is not usually seen in the pore regions. × 80,000.

nuclear pores—which provide pathways between the nucleus and the cytoplasm. The structures of these pores vary with the cell being studied (Figs 3—22 and 3—23). The pores sometimes show electron-dense granular material or a single diaphragm closing the gap. This structure is thinner than the 2 membranes comprising the nuclear envelope. The permeability of the nucleus to molecules is also variable and is probably related to the different types of pores described above. In some instances, the membrane is permeable to macromolecules. Examples have been described in which the nuclear envelope is a barrier to the free diffusion of even such small molecules as ions.

Chromatin

Chromatin is an intensely staining substance which appears in the form of filaments, granules, or flakes irregularly dispersed within the nucleus and visible with the light microscope. The arrangement of chromatin in the nucleus is often typical of a tissue or type of cell. In most tissues, the nucleus presents a great quantity of visible chromatin; in others, however,

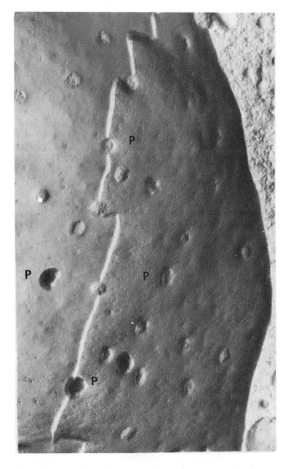

Figure 3–23. Freeze etching preparation of a mesenchymal cell nucleus. At left is seen cleavage between the membranes of the nuclear envelopes. There are numerous nuclear pores (P). X 39,000. (Courtesy of E Katchburian.)

such as the nerve cells, there is less visible chromatin. This difference in the amount of visible chromatin explains why light or dark nuclei may be observed. Since cytoplasm does not stain well with the usual methods, it is easy to understand why chromatin, which stains intensely, is frequently used to differentiate and identify different tissues and types of cells under the light microscope. Consequently, the morphology of chromatin in cell nuclei is mentioned throughout this book with respect to the study and identification of tissues and cells.

Chromatin is formed mainly of coiled strands of DNA bound to basic proteins. Chromatin DNA represents the major reservoir of DNA in the cell and carries most of its genetic information. It is in chromatin that messenger, ribosomal, and transfer ribonucleic acids (mRNA, rRNA, and tRNA) are synthesized. The darkly stained bodies seen in the nucleus under the light microscope are due to the clumping of part of the nucleoprotein caused by the fixatives. The degree of nucleoprotein coiling varies, some portions being tightly coiled whereas others are dispersed. The bodies seen

in the interphase nuclei are usually the result of clumping of tightly coiled portions of undispersed deoxyribonucleoprotein. The dimensions of the dispersed portions that do not clump readily are too small to be revealed by the light microscope. The degree of coiling permits differentiation between light and dark nuclei. The nucleoprotein of chromatin is coiled, and the degree of coiling varies during cell activity. Using the chromatin pattern of a nucleus as an index of cell activity, it can be determined that, in lightly staining nuclei (with few chromatin clumps), much DNA surface is available for the transcription of genetic information. In darkly staining nuclei, less surface is available as a result of the coiling of DNA. Thus, cells with light nuclei are more active than those with condensed, dark nuclei. It has recently become possible to separate light from dark nuclei in liver cells and to show that light nuclei synthesize mRNA more actively than dark nuclei.

Careful study of the chromatin of mammalian cell nuclei has revealed the presence of a chromatin particle frequently observed in female cells but not in male cells. This chromatin particle is the *sex chromatin*. It was first observed in nerve cells obtained from female cats and is present in cells of several other species, including humans. It is believed that this chromatin particle is one of the pair of X chromosomes that exists in female cells. It somehow remains tightly coiled and is therefore easily visible during interphase, while the other X chromosome is uncoiled and therefore not visible. The coiling of this chromosome explains why it is easily stained and can be observed by the light microscope. The male has one X chromosome and one Y chromosome as sex determinants; the X chromosome is dispersed, and therefore no sex chromatin is visible. In human epithelial cells, sex chromatin appears as a small granule attached to the nuclear membrane. The cells lining the internal surface of the cheek are frequently used to study sex chromatin. Blood smears are also often used, in which case the sex chromatin appears as a bulblike appendix to the nuclei of the neutrophilic leukocytes (Fig 3–24).

The study of sex chromatin has wide applicability

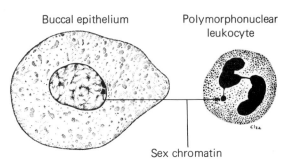

Figure 3–24. Morphology of sex chromatin in human mouth epithelium and in a polymorphonuclear leukocyte. In the epithelium, it appears as a small, dense granule adhering to the nuclear envelope. In the leukocyte, it has a drumstick shape.

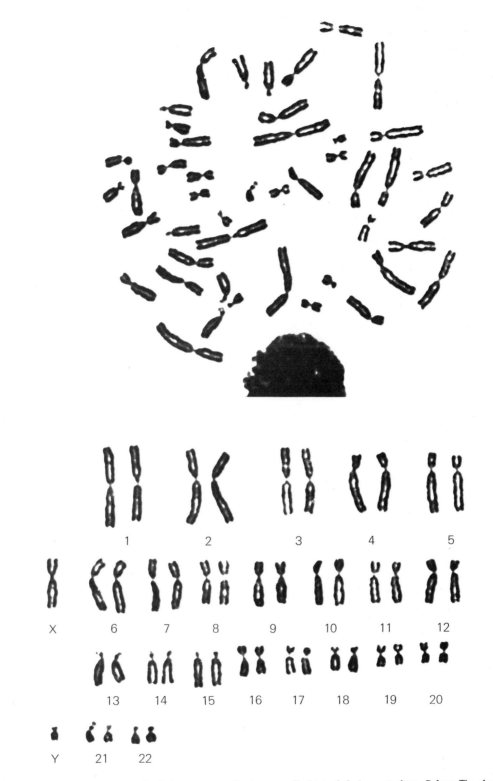

Figure 3–25. *Above:* Photomicrograph of chromosomes of a human cell obtained during metaphase. *Below:* The chromosomes grouped according to their morphologic characteristics. (Courtesy of G Gimenez-Martin.)

in medicine because it permits an accurate diagnosis of genetic sex in doubtful cases (hermaphroditism, pseudohermaphroditism). It is also useful for the study of anomalies involving the sex chromosomes—eg, Klinefelter's syndrome, in which patients present with testicular abnormalities, azoospermia, and other symptoms associated with the presence of XXY chromosomes in the cell.

The study of chromosomes of animals, and particularly of man, made considerable progress after the discovery of methods of inducing cells to divide, of arresting mitosis during metaphase, and of causing cellular rupture, thus permitting the separation and detailed observation and analysis of chromosomes. Mitosis can be induced by a protein called phytohemagglutinin and can be arrested by colchicine. Rupture of cells is brought about by initial immersion in a hypotonic solution, causing swelling, after which they are flattened and broken between a glass slide and a coverslip. The pattern obtained with a human cell after staining is illustrated in Fig 3—25. In addition to the 2 chromosomes, it is customary to group the remaining chromosomes according to their morphologic characteristics in 22 successively numbered pairs (Fig 3—25).

The number and type of chromosomes encountered in an individual is known as his or her *karyotype*. Study of karyotypes has produced interesting results and has revealed alterations associated with several types of diseases, including a form of leukemia.

Nucleolus

The nucleolus is a rounded structure, generally acidophilic and rich in RNA and basic proteins. The nucleus may contain one or more nucleoli of variable dimensions. When the nuclear chromatin is very condensed—as in lymphocytes—it becomes difficult to visualize the nucleoli within the nucleus. A dense portion of chromatin is found attached to the nucleolus and is known as *nucleolus-associated chromatin* (Fig 3—21). Dividing cells have no nucleoli, and they are formed de novo in the telophase stage of cell division.

Under the light microscope—and more easily under the electron microscope—it is possible to see in several cell types that the nucleolus resembles a spongy structure called the *nucleolonema* (Fig 3—26). The significance of this structure is unknown.

Under the electron microscope, the nucleoli, which are not membrane-bound, usually consist of 3 distinct regions. The *pars granulosa* and the *pars fibrosa* both contain mainly ribonucleoprotein composed of clearly visible subunits of future ribosomes. The dense fibrillary structures around chromatin threads are called its fibrillary center. The area between the pars granulosa and the pars fibrosa represents the maturation site of ribonucleoprotein to the subunits of the ribosomes held in place by a protein matrix. The third region—the chromosomal portion—consists of dispersed filaments of DNA that permeate the other 2 regions.

In the nucleolus, ribosomal RNA is synthesized, transformed, and deposited before being transferred to cytoplasm. Morphologically, larger nucleoli are encountered in young cells during intense reproductive activity, in cells that synthesize proteins actively, and in the majority of rapidly growing malignant tumors. Light areas of the nucleolus are seen to be continuous with the nucleoplasm.

Nucleoplasm

Nucleoplasm is an amorphous substance that fills the space between the chromatin and the nucleoli in the nucleus. It is composed mainly of proteins (some of which have enzymatic activity), metabolites, and ions.

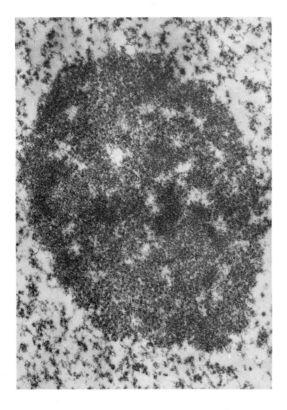

Figure 3—26. Nucleolus of a newt showing its fibrillar and granular portions. When the nucleolus consists of anastomosing coarse strands, it is called a nucleolonema. X 40,000.

CELL DIVISION

Most body tissues undergo a constant turnover because of continuous cell multiplication and death of cells. The nerve tissue cells are an exception since they do not regenerate or multiply postnatally. The turnover rate of the cells varies greatly from one tissue to another—rapid in the epithelium of the alimentary canal and the epidermis, slow in the pancreas and thyroid and in the Sertoli cells of the testis.

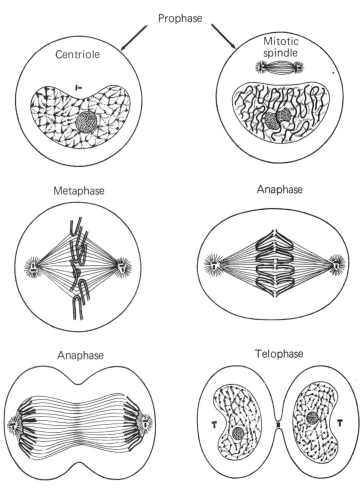

Figure 3—27. Phases of mitosis.

Cell division can be observed with the light microscope. During this process, known as *mitosis,* the mother cell divides and each of the daughter cells receives a chromosomal karyotype identical to that of the mother cell. Essentially, a longitudinal duplication of the chromosomes takes place, and they are distributed to the daughter cells. The phase during which the cell does not undergo division is called *interphase,* and the nucleus appears as it is normally observed in microscope preparations. The process of mitosis is in fact continuous but is usually subdivided into phases to facilitate study (Figs 3—27 and 3—28).

The *prophase* is characterized by the gradual coiling up of chromatin of the nucleus, giving rise to several individualized rod-shaped or hairpin-shaped bodies which stain intensely. These are the *chromosomes.* The nuclear membrane remains unaltered, and the chromosomes appear coiled in the nucleus. The centrioles separate, and a pair migrates to each pole of the cell. Simultaneously, the microtubules of the mitotic spindle appear between the 2 pairs of centrioles (Fig 3—27).

During *metaphase,* the nuclear envelope and the nucleolus disappear. The chromosomes migrate to the equatorial plane of the cell, where each divides longitudinally to form 2 chromatids. These attach to the microtubules of the mitotic spindle at a special plaque-like, electron-dense region, the *centromere (kinetochore)* (Figs 3—27, 3—28, 3—29, and 3—30).

In *anaphase,* the chromatids separate from one another and migrate toward the centrioles, following the direction of the spindle microtubules. Throughout this process the centromeres move from the center, pulling the remainder of the chromosome along (Figs 3—27 and 3—28).

Recent evidence suggests that this displacement might be due to the sliding of 2 systems of microtubules disposed in opposite directions. Hypothetically, one system consists of the microtubules inserted in the centromere while the other is composed of the tubules connecting both centrioles (Fig 3—31). The presence of attachments between the 2 systems of microtubules lends support to this hypothesis.

Telophase is characterized by the reappearance of nuclei in the daughter cells. The chromosomes revert to their semidispersed state and the nucleoli, chro-

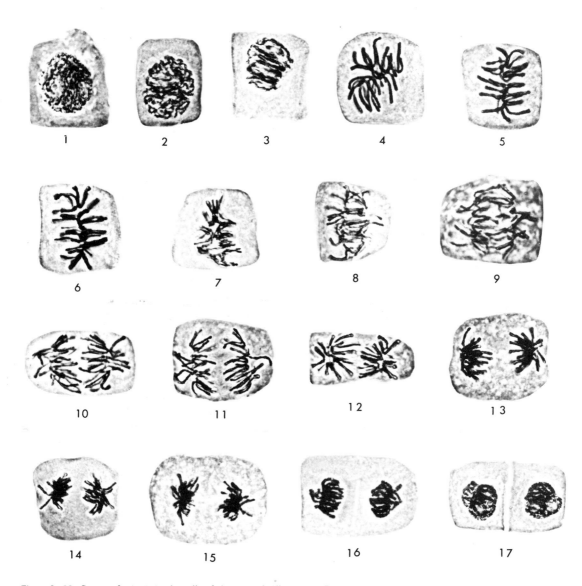

Figure 3—28. Stages of mitosis in the cells of the root of *Allium cepa*. Phase microscopy. 1–3, prophase; 4–7, metaphase; 8–13, anaphase; 17, telophase. (Courtesy of G Gimenez-Martin.)

matin, and nuclear membrane reappear. While these nuclear alterations are taking place, a constriction develops at the level of the equatorial plane of the mother cell and progresses until it divides the cytoplasm and its organelles in half (Figs 3—27 and 3—28). In different cell types, an accumulation of microfilaments occurs beneath the cell membrane in the region of mitotic constriction. This and other evidence suggests that the microfilaments participate in the cytoplasmic component of cell division.

THE CELL CYCLE

Mitosis is the visible manifestation of cell division, but there are other processes, not so easily observed by the light microscope, that play a fundamental role in cell multiplication. Principal among these is the phase in which DNA, the main chromosomal component, duplicates. This process can be analyzed by the introduction of labeled, radioactive DNA precursors and followed by biochemical and radioautographic methods. DNA duplication has been shown to occur during *interphase*, when no visible phenomena of cell division are observable in the microscope. This alternation between mitosis and DNA duplication in all tissues with

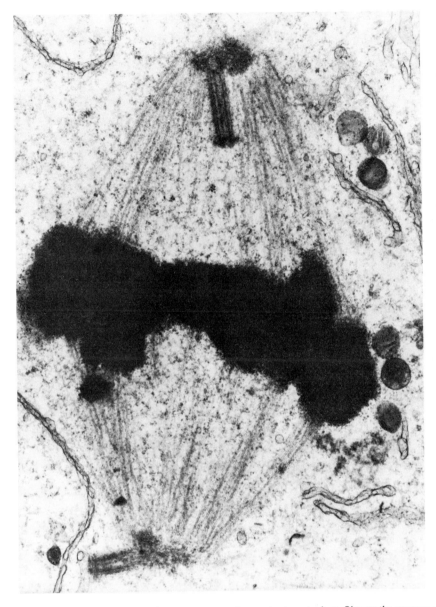

Figure 3–29. Electron micrograph of a section of a spermatocyte of a rooster in metaphase. Observe the presence of 2 centroles in each pole, the mitotic spindle formed by microtubules, and the chromosomes in the equatorial plate. Reduced from X 30,000. (Courtesy of R McIntosh.)

cellular turnover is known as the *cell cycle*. A careful study of the cell cycle reveals that it may be divided into 2 stages: mitosis, consisting of the 4 phases already described (prophase, metaphase, anaphase, and telophase) and interphase.

Interphase is itself divided into 3 phases: G_1 (preduplication), S (synthesis), and G_2 (postduplication) (Fig 3–32). Synthesis and duplication of DNA take place in the S phase. The sequence of these phases and the time involved are illustrated in Fig 3–32. The G_1 (for gap) phase is usually the phase in which the cell remains stationary during its cycle. Consequently, the duration of this phase varies. It is also the phase during which RNA and protein synthesis occur and the

cell volume, reduced to one-half by mitosis, is restored to its normal size. Duration is short in tissues with fast cell turnover and long in tissues with slow cell turnover. For example, the epithelium of the human small intestine is renewed every 2–3 days. Other tissues have a slower rate—eg, in man, the epidermis is renewed in 20 days and the sperm cells of the testicle in 74 days. Finally, some cells—eg, the neurons of nerve tissues—never reproduce in the adult animal.

Other important processes during interphase, in addition to DNA synthesis, include energy production, accumulation, and utilization during mitosis; reproduction of centrioles; and synthesis of macromolecules which assemble into microtubules during mitosis.

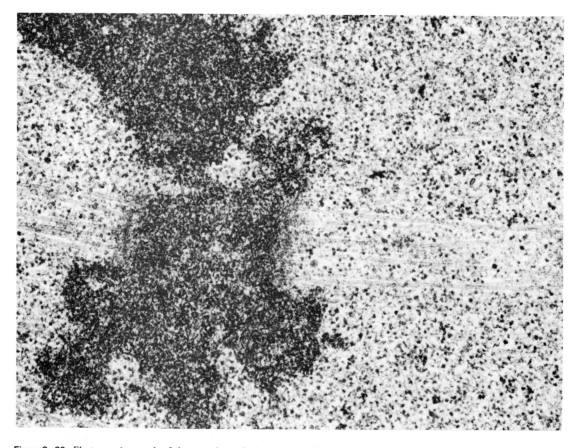

Figure 3–30. Electron micrograph of the metaphase of a human lung cell in tissue culture. Note the insertion of microtubules in the centromeres of the densely stained chromosomes. Reduced from X 50,000. (Courtesy of R McIntosh.)

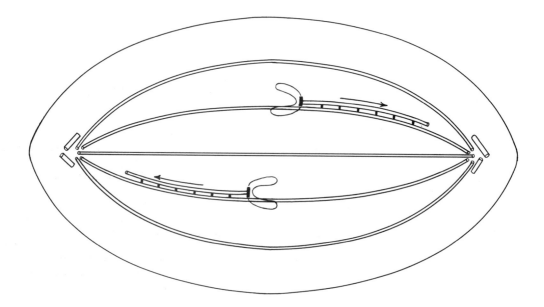

Figure 3–31. Proposed mechanism of chromosome migration during anaphase. There are 2 systems of microtubules: one from centriole to centriole and the other bound to the centromere. The sliding of the microtubules of the centromere over the centriolar microtubules (analogous to the interaction of actin and myosin in muscle) provides a tentative explanation of chromosome migration. (Based on the work of R McIntosh.)

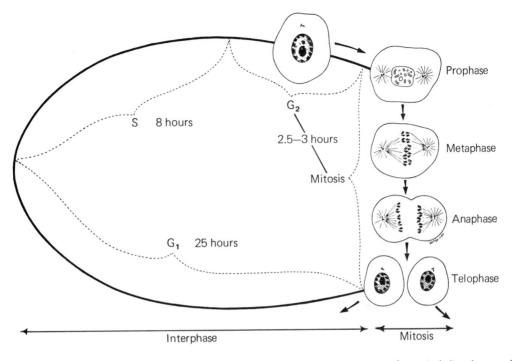

Figure 3–32. Phases of the cell cycle. G_1 (presynthetic) phase is variable and depends on many factors including the rate of cell division in the tissue. The S (DNA synthetic) phase lasts about 8 hours. The G_2 phase lasts 2–3 hours. The times are from Young in J Cell Biol 14:357, 1962.

CELL DYNAMICS

Study of the cell by means of the light or electron microscope gives the false impression that the cell is static. However, cinemicrography at accelerated rates (5–30 times normal) shows considerable activity in the cells. Thus, it has been observed that the nucleus can rotate within the cytoplasm at a speed of up to 270 rotations per minute. Mitochondria demonstrate active wriggling movements in the cytoplasm. In only a few minutes, they can be seen to become fragmented and fuse together again.

Profound cellular changes can also be observed during cell differentiation. Depending upon the function of the cell, some organelles become better developed than others and are major features of the cytoplasm. Thus, the cytoplasm in striated muscle cells is composed mainly of contractile fibrils, the myofibrils. Cells of the acinar pancreas that synthesize and accumulate protein contain cytoplasm almost completely filled with granular endoplasmic reticulum and zymogen granules. Furthermore, in an already differentiated cell, modification of the organelles can be observed according to the phase of cell activity. This depends on whether the cell is hypoactive or hyperactive. Cells that actively secrete protein have a more highly developed granular endoplasmic reticulum and Golgi apparatus than those that secrete protein in moderate or minimal amounts.

In addition to the organelles, it is known that, with the exception of DNA, chemical elements that make up the cell are constantly being actively renewed.

FREEZE FRACTURE TECHNIC & THE CELL

The cytologist must always be alert to distinguish true cell components from artifacts resulting from errors of procedure in preparing specimens for examination. Problems of this sort were much more common before the introduction of electron microscopy. A classical example is the Golgi complex, whose existence was for many years a subject of vigorous debate.

The recent introduction of the technic known as freeze etching has made it possible to avoid many steps in the procedure, thus reducing the number of artifacts to a minimum. This technic is illustrated in Fig 3–33.

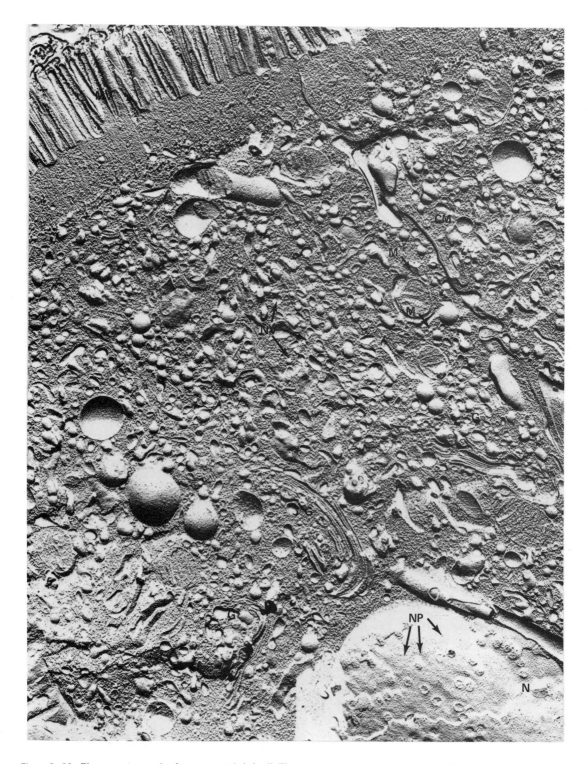

Figure 3–33. Electron micrograph of a mouse epithelial cell. This picture was obtained by a process called freeze etching. It consists of freezing a fragment of tissue to very low temperatures and fracturing it with a sharpened metal blade. The fractured surface is kept at low temperature in a vacuum environment. A portion of the water in the surface thus sublimates, giving a bas-relief effect (etching). A replica of this surface is then obtained by covering it with a layer of platinum and carbon. In this picture, one can observe in material that has not been submitted to the processes of embedding and sectioning the presence of the various cell components described by classical transmission electron microscopy, eg, microvilli (MV), cell membrane (CM), mitochondria (M), Golgi apparatus (G), nucleus (N), nuclear pores (NP), and nuclear vesicles (NV). × 24,000. (Courtesy of LS Staehelin.)

● ● ●

References

Afzelius BA: Ultrastructure of cilia and flagella. Page 1218 in: *Handbook of Molecular Biology*. Lima de Faria A (editor). North Holland Publishing Co, 1969.

Arbuzona GS & others: Investigation of diffuse and compact chromatin in the rat liver during hormonal induction. Molec Biol 2:245, 1968.

Arstila AU, Trump BF: Studies on cellular autophagocytosis: The formation of autographic vacuoles in the liver after glucagon administration. Am J Path 53:687, 1965.

Bajer A, Mole-Bajer J: Architecture and function of the mitotic spindle. Advances Molec Biol 1:213, 1971.

Baserga R, Weibel F: The cell cycle of mammalian cells. Internat Rev Exper Path 7:1, 1969.

Baud CA: Nuclear membrane and permeability. In: *Intracellular Membranous Structure*. Seno S, Cowdry EV (editors). Chugoku Press, 1965.

Baudhuin P: Liver peroxisomes: Cytology and function. Ann New York Acad Sc 168:214, 1969.

Bertalanffy FD: Tritiated thymidine vs. colchicine technique in the study of cell population cytodynamics. Lab Invest 13:871, 1964.

Blams HW, Kessel RG: The Golgi apparatus: Structure and function. Internat Rev Cytol 23:209, 1968.

Brachet J, Mirsky AE (editors): *The Cell*. Academic Press, 1959.

Bresnich E, Schwartz A: *Functional Dynamics of the Cell*. Academic Press, 1968.

Dalton AJ, Haguenau F (editors): *The Nucleus*. Academic Press, 1968.

De Duve C: The lysosome. Sc Am 208:64, May 1963.

De Duve C, Wattiaux R: Functions of lysosomes. Ann Rev Physiol 28:435, 1966.

De Pierre JW, Karnovsky ML: Plasma membranes of mammalian cells: A review of methods for their characterization and isolation. J Cell Biol 56:275, 1973.

Farquhar MG, Palade GE: Junctional complexes in various epithelia. J Cell Biol 17:375, 1963.

Favard P: The Golgi apparatus. Page 1131 in: *Handbook of Molecular Biology*. Lima de Faria A (editor). North Holland Publishing Co, 1969.

Fawcett DW: Structural and functional variations in the membranes of the cytoplasm. In: *Intracellular Membranous Structure*. Seno S, Cowdry EV (editors). Chugoku Press, 1965.

Friend DS, Gilula NB: A distinctive cell contact in the rat adrenal cortex. J Cell Biol 53:148, 1972.

Friend DS, Gilula NB: Variation in tight and gap junctions in mammalian tissues. J Cell Biol 53:758, 1972.

Gahan PB: Histochemistry of lysosomes. Int Rev Cytol 21:2, 1967.

Giese AC: *Cell Physiology*, 2nd ed. Saunders, 1966.

Gilula NB, Branton D, Satie P: The septate junction: A structural basis for intercellular coupling. Proc Nat Acad Sc 67:213, 1970.

Goodenough DA, Revel JP: A fine structural analysis of intercellular junctions in the mouse liver. J Cell Biol 45:272, 1970.

Granboulan N, Granboulan P: Cytochimie ultrastructure de nucléole. 2. Étude des sites de synthese du RNA dans le nucléole et le noyau. Exp Cell Res 38:604, 1965.

Jones AL, Fawcett DW: Hypertrophy of the agranular endoplasmic reticulum in hamster liver induced by phenobarbital. J Histochem Cytochem 14:215, 1966.

Junqueira LCU: Control of cell secretion. In: *Secretory Mechanisms of Salivary Glands*. Schneyer LH, Schneyer CA (editors). Academic Press, 1967.

Leblond CP: Classification of cell populations on the basis of their proliferative behaviours. Nat Cancer Inst Monogr 14:119, 1964.

Loewenstein WR: Intercellular communication. Sc Am 227:79, May 1970.

Mazia D: Mitosis and the physiology of cell division. In: *The Cell*. Vol 3. Brachet J, Mirsky AE (editors). Academic Press, 1961.

McNutt NS, Weinstein RS: Membrane ultrastructure at mammalian intercellular junctions. Prog Biophys Molec Biol 26:45, 1973.

McIntosh JR, Story CL: The distribution of spindle microtubules during mitosis in cultured human cells. J Cell Biol 49:468, 1974.

Monneron A, Bernhard W: Fine structural organization of the interphase nucleus in some mammalian tissues. J Ultrastruct Res 27:266, 1969.

Munn EA: Ultrastructure of mitochondria. Page 876 in: *Handbook of Molecular Biology*. Lima de Faria A (editor). North Holland Publishing Co, 1969.

Neutra M, Leblond CP: The Golgi apparatus. Sc Am 220:100, Feb 1969.

Nomura M: Ribosomes. Sc Am 221:28, Oct 1969.

Orrenius S, Ericson JLE, Ernster L: Phenobarbital-induced synthesis of the microsomal drug metabolizing enzyme system and its relationship to the proliferation of endoplasmic membranes: A morphological and biochemical study. J Cell Biol 25:627, 1965.

Paine PL, Feldhers CM: Nucleocytoplasmic exchange of macromolecules. Exp Cell Res 74:81, 1972.

Pinto da Silva P, Gilula NB: Gap junctions in normal and transformed fibroblasts in culture. Exp Cell Res 71:393, 1972.

Pitelka DR & others: Cell contacts in the mouse mammary gland. J Cell Biol 56:797, 1973.

Pollard TD, Ito S: Cytoplasmic filaments of amoeba proteins. 1. The role of filaments in consistency changes and movement. J Cell Biol 46:267, 1970.

Rabinowitz M, Swift H: Mitochondrial nucleic acids and the problem of biogenesis. Physiol Rev 50:376, 1970.

Rambourg A: Morphological and histochemical aspects of glycoproteins at the surface of animal cells. Int Rev Cytol 31:57, 1971.

Rappaport R: Cytokinesis in animal cells. Int Rev Cytol 31:301, 1972.

Remmer H, Merker HJ: Effect of drugs on the formation of smooth endoplasmic reticulum and drug metabolizing enzymes. Ann New York Acad Sc 123:79, 1965.

Resibois A & others: Lysosome and storage diseases. Int Rev Exp Pathol 9:93, 1970.

Revel JP, Karnovsky MJ: Hexagonal array of subunits in intercellular junctions of the mouse heart and liver. J Cell Biol 33:C7, 1967.

Roodyn DB: *Enzyme Cytology*. Academic Press, 1967.

Schroeder TE: The contractile ring. 1. Fine structure of dividing mammalian (HeLa) cells and the effects of cytochalasin B. Z Zellforsch Mikrosk Anat 109:431, 1970.

Siekevitz P: Biological membranes: The dynamics of their organization. Ann Rev Physiol 34:117, 1972.

Singer SJ, Nicolson GL: The fluid mosaic model of the structure of cell membrane. Science 175:720, 1972.

Spooner BS & others: Microfilaments and cell locomotion. J Cell Biol 49:595, 1971.

Structure and function of membranes. (Various authors.) Brit Med Bull 24:1, 1968.

Subak-Sharpe JH, Burk RR, Pitt JD: Metabolic cooperation between biochemically marked mammalian cells in tissue culture. J Cell Sci 4:353, 1969.

Summers KE, Gibbons IR: Adenosine triphosphate-induced sliding of tubules in trypsin-treated flagella of sea urchin sperm. Proc Nat Acad Sc 68:3092, 1971.

Vincent WS, Miller OL Jr (editors): *International Symposium on the Nucleolus: Its Structure and Function.* Monograph No. 12. National Cancer Institute, 1967.

Weiner J, Spiro D, Loewenstein WR: Ultrastructure and permeability of nuclear membranes. J Cell Biol 27:107, 1965.

Weinstein RS & others: Cell junctions. New England J Med 286:321, 1972.

Wessels NK & others: Microfilaments in cellular and developmental processes. Science 171:135, 1971.

Wilson HJ: Arms and bridges on microtubules in the mitotic apparatus. J Cell Biol 40:854, 1969.

4 . . .
Epithelial Tissue

Tissues are structures formed by collections of cells that frequently have similar morphologic characteristics and similar functions. Despite its complexity, the human body is composed of only 4 basic types of tissue: epithelial, connective, muscular, and nervous. These tissues do not exist as isolated units but rather in association one with another and in variable proportions, forming different organs and systems of the body.

Connective tissue is characterized by the abundance of intercellular material produced by its cells; muscular tissue is composed of elongated cells which have the specialized function of contraction; and nervous tissue is composed of cells with elongated processes extending from the cell body which have the specialized functions of receiving, generating, and transmitting nervous impulses.

Epithelial tissues—the subject of this chapter—are composed of closely aggregated polyhedral cells with very little intercellular substance. Adhesion of the cells is strong. Thus, cellular sheets are formed that cover the surface of the body and line its cavities.

Epithelium is derived from all 3 embryonic germ layers. Most of the epithelium covering the skin and body cavities (eg, mouth, nose, and anus) has an ectodermal origin. From the endoderm derive the lining of the digestive tract, the respiratory system, and the glands of the digestive tract such as the pancreas and the liver. Most other epithelial tissue (eg, the kidney) originates from mesoderm.

Epithelial tissues have the following principal functions: (1) covering and lining surfaces (eg, skin); (2) absorption (eg, the intestines); (3) secretion (eg, the epithelial cells of glands); and (4) sensory (eg, neuroepithelium).

The distribution of epithelial tissues in organs with different functions explains the morphologic and functional diversity of these tissues.

GENERAL CHARACTERISTICS
OF EPITHELIAL TISSUES

Although the epithelial tissues have varied morphology and function depending on their position in the body, they possess some basic common characteristics.

The Forms of Epithelial Cells

The form and dimensions of epithelial cells are varied, ranging from high columnar to low squamous cells and including all intermediate forms (Fig 4–1). Their common polyhedral form is accounted for by their juxtaposition in cellular layers or masses. A similar aspect might be observed if a large number of inflated rubber balloons were compressed into a limited

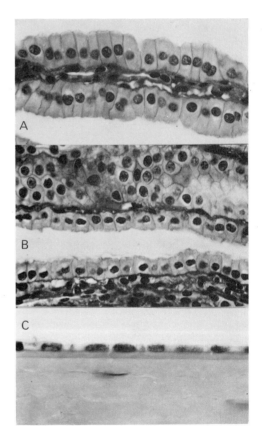

Figure 4–1. Photomicrographs of simple epithelial tissues. *A:* Simple columnar type. *B:* Simple cuboid type (from kidney). *C:* Simple squamous type (from cornea). H&E stain, × 500.

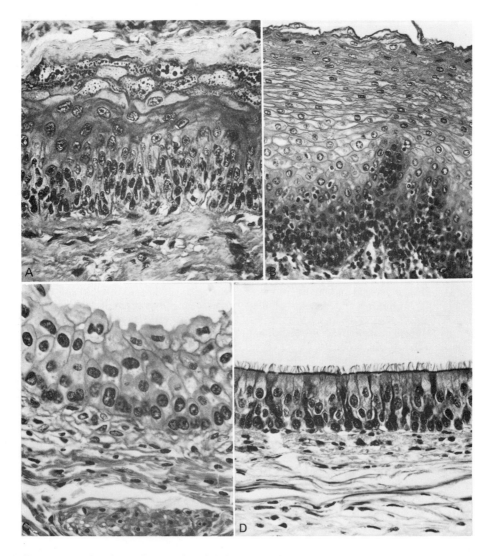

Figure 4–2. Photomicrographs of several types of epithelial tissue. *A:* Stratified squamous keratinized epithelium. *B:* Stratified nonkeratinized squamous epithelium. *C:* Transitional epithelium. *D:* Columnar ciliated pseudostratified epithelium. H&E stain, × 500.

space. In hematoxylin and eosin preparations, the cell nuclei have a distinctive appearance, varying from spherical to elongated or elliptic in shape. The cell form usually corresponds grossly to the nuclear shape; thus, cuboid cells have spherical nuclei whereas squamous cells have horizontal, elliptic nuclei. The long axis of the nucleus always lies along the main axis of the cell.

Since the limits between cells are frequently indistinguishable, observation of the form of the cell nucleus is of great importance because it is an indirect clue to the shape of the cell. This is of value not only for itself but also for determining cell disposition, whether in layers or masses, which is useful in classifying epithelial tissues (Fig 4–2).

Absence of Interstitial Substance

With the exception of a variable, usually thin layer of glycoproteins that covers the epithelial cells, no interstitial substance can be observed with the light microscope. This is in contrast to most of the other tissues in the body, in which the cells are separated by a variable amount of fibers and amphorous substance. The thin glycoprotein covering is called *glycocalyx* (Fig 4–3), which is a generic term used regardless of possible differences in its composition and thickness. Available evidence—mostly indirect—suggests that the glycocalyx participates in the adhesion of cells, in pinocytosis, in the phenomena of immunologic characterization, and other vital processes. This covering may also be seen in muscle cells and the Schwann cells that surround the nerve fibers, since glycocalyx is not an exclusive characteristic of epithelial cells.

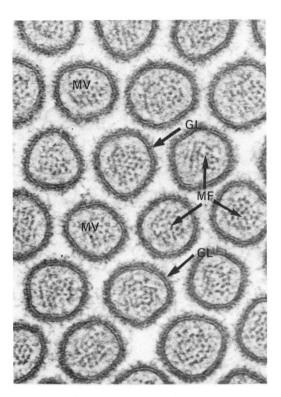

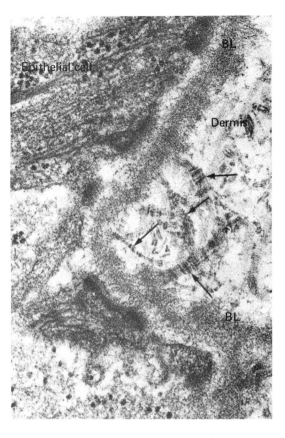

Figure 4–3. Electron micrograph of a section from the apical region of a cell from the intestinal lining showing cross-sectioned microvilli (MV). In their interiors, note the microfilaments (MF) in cross-section. The surrounding unit membrane can be clearly discerned and is covered by a layer of glycocalyx (GL). × 100,000. (Courtesy of KR Porter.)

Figure 4–4. Section of human skin showing the zone of the epithelial–connective tissue junction. Observe the anchoring fibers (arrows) that apparently insert in the basal lamina (BL). The characteristically irregular spacing of these fibers distinguishes them from common collagen fibers. × 54,000. (Courtesy of FM Guerra Rodrigo.)

Presence of a Basal Lamina

Almost all epithelial tissue has on its surface, in contact with connective tissue, a membranelike structure called the *basal lamina*. This structure, composed mainly of proteins and neutral glycoproteins (PAS-positive), is visible with the electron microscope as a thin granular deposit in which very fine fibrils may occasionally be observed (Fig 4–4).

Conflicting experimental data suggest that the basal lamina may be of either epithelial or connective tissue origin. However, results obtained with immunofluorescence, combined with the observation that basal laminas are formed in pure epithelial tissue cultures, suggest that epithelial cells are probably the main source of the basal lamina. Near the basal lamina, a number of thin reticular fibers are usually seen, and some of them appear to be anchored to the basal lamina (Fig 4–4). These fibers contribute to the staining of basal laminas with silver stains. The basal lamina, the reticular fibers, and some amorphous material just under the basal surface of the epithelial cells comprise the *basement membrane*.

Although the thickness of the basal lamina is vari-

able, it does not present a barrier to the diffusion of most substances. It might present a barrier to the flow of larger molecules (MW 50,000). Since epithelial tissues are avascular, epithelial permeability to substances is a prerequisite for proper nutrition and function.

In some types of tissue, the basal laminas have characteristic antigens which under certain conditions may induce the production of antibodies whose effect is to destroy the basal lamina and cause autoimmune diseases.

Cohesion Among Epithelial Cells

Epithelial cells are extremely adhesive, and relatively strong mechanical forces are necessary to separate them. This quality of intercellular binding is especially marked in those epithelial tissues usually subjected to traction and pressure (eg, the skin). This is due in part to the binding action of the glycoproteins of the glycocalyx. Staining of the cell surface by the PAS technic for examination with the light microscope and with special technics for electron microscopy has shown at the surface of many cells the presence of carbohydrates containing 1,2-glycol. These carbohydrates might form part of a physiologic barrier which prevents substances from reaching the cell surface. The protein moieties of the glycoproteins that make up the glycocalyx are formed in the granular endoplasmic reticulum. Some of the sugars (eg, mannose) are added here, whereas others (eg, glucose, fucose) are added at the Golgi apparatus. From here, small Golgi vesicles transported through the cytoplasm open to the exterior of the cell by exocytosis, adding their glycoprotein content to the outside of the plasma membrane. The rate at which glycoprotein is added probably varies in different cells and even on different surfaces of the same cell, and it appears that turnover in this glycocalyx coat occurs in most cells that have been examined. Loss of the glycocalyx might occur by participation in surface activities such as intercellular adhesion, pinocytosis, or phagocytosis, by contact with injurious agents, etc. The glycocalyx or cell coat and its basement membrane are probably structurally different since they have different staining characteristics.

Calcium ions are also important in maintaining cell cohesion. Thus, the chelating agent EDTA, which complexes with calcium, is known to decrease cell adhesion and is widely used in cell biology to separate epithelial cells, a necessary step in obtaining a suspension of isolated cells. Intercellular adhesiveness changes with age and responds in different ways to the presence of trypsin or deoxycholate or the removal of calcium. Probably the most important factors in cell adhesion, however, are special structures the most frequent of which are the *desmosomes,* or *maculae adherentes* (Figs 4–5 and 4–6). These are complex disk-shaped structures which are formed by the juxtaposition of 2 electron-dense regions present near the cell membranes of 2 neighboring cells but within the cytoplasm of each cell. These regions, called *attachment plaques* or *dense plates,* consist essentially of a granular electron density closely associated with the innermost surface of the cellular unit membrane. Groups of cytoplasmic fibrils *(tonofilaments)* are sometimes inserted in the intracellular region of the desmosome or make a hairpin turn and return into the cytoplasm. Between the membranes of 2 cells of a desmosome region—and therefore in the extracellular space—fibrillar and granular structures are frequently observed which are probably responsible for the intense intercellular adhesion. This material has in its center a dense line which corresponds to a central layer—thin but very dense.

In the contact zone between an epithelial cell and the basal lamina, a so-called *hemidesmosome* can often be observed. Morphologically, this structure takes the shape of half of a desmosome on the epithelial cell side only and probably binds the epithelial cell to the subjacent tissue.

The thin intracellular fibrils inserted into the desmosomes are also present at other sites in the epithelial cells. Particularly in the columnar cells of the intestinal epithelium, they may form a horizontal mat of fibrils just below the surface membrane—the *terminal web*—from which the cytoplasmic organelles are excluded (Fig 4–7). These fibrils apparently form a sort of intra-

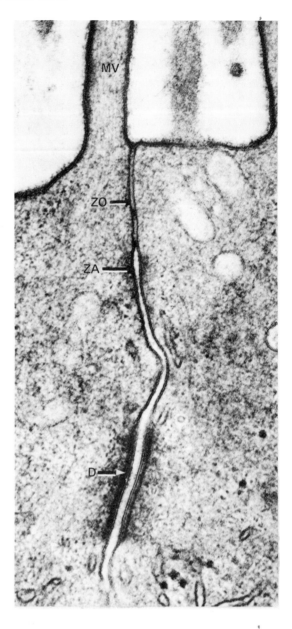

Figure 4–5. Electron micrograph of a section of epithelial cells in the large intestine showing a junctional complex with its zonula occludens (ZO), zonula adherens (ZA), and desmosome (D). Also shown is a microvillus (MV). × 80,000.

cellular skeleton (cytoskeleton) with the microtubules to maintain cell form.

Desmosomes are distributed in patches along the surface of the cell. Despite the fact that they maintain cell cohesion, they do not prevent the separation of the cell membranes in regions without desmosomes. Consequently, fluid material can circulate between epithelial cells, providing an important pathway in the physiology of epithelial tissues.

Another structure of importance in maintaining adherence is the *junctional complex* (Fig 4–8). Many

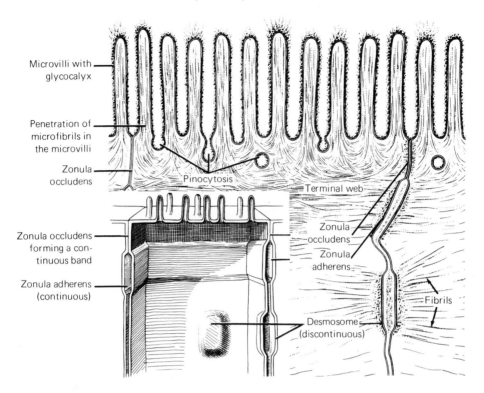

Microvilli with glycocalyx

Penetration of microfibrils in the microvilli

Zonula occludens

Pinocytosis

Terminal web

Zonula occludens

Zonula adherens

Zonula occludens forming a continuous band

Zonula adherens (continuous)

Desmosome (discontinuous)

Fibrils

Figure 4–6. Structures in the apical zone of an intestinal epithelium. Microvilli, covered with glycocalyx, are frequent. Micropinocytosis is occurring in the region between the insertion of the microvilli. Observe the junctional complex and the terminal web. Microfilaments from this region ascend to fill the microvilli. The inset at lower left shows that, while zonula occludens and zonula adherens are continuous structures surrounding the cell apex, the desmosomes are discontinuous.

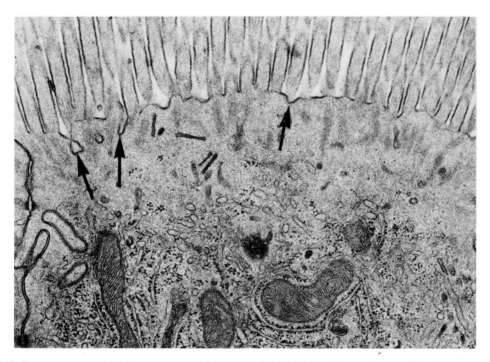

Figure 4–7. Electron micrograph of the apical region of an intestinal epithelial cell. Observe the microvilli in the upper region and, below, the terminal web from which fibrils pass into the microvilli. At upper left is shown the junctional complex structure that partly corresponds to the terminal bar as viewed in the light microscope. The arrows show regions where micropinocytosis occurs. × 10,000. (Courtesy of HI Friedman.)

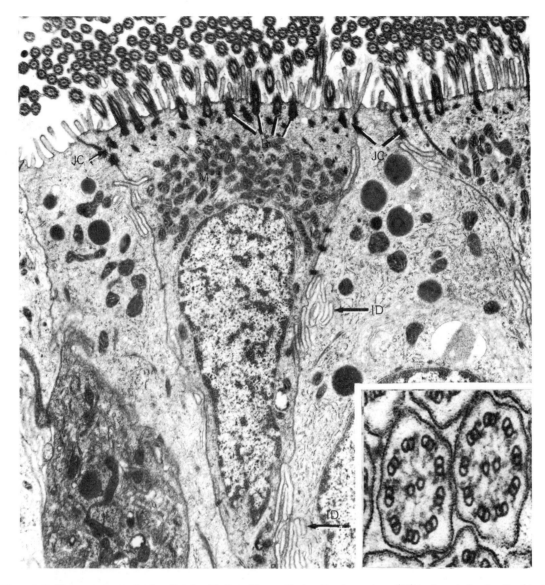

Figure 4—8. Electron micrograph of a ciliated epithelium. Observe the junctional complexes (JC) in the apical region. Basal bodies (B) are shown at the bases of cilia. Mitochondria (M) are in a supranuclear position. The presence of these organelles is probably related to the provision of energy for the movement of the cilia. Membrane interdigitations (ID) are frequent. The inset shows a transverse section of cilia with a typical microtubular pattern. × 120,000.

years ago, the presence of a dense condensation of the cell membrane was discerned by means of the light microscope. This condensation was especially evident in the apexes of tall columnar epithelial cells, and they were called *terminal bars* (Figs 4—10 and 4—11). In horizontal section, they appear as a continuous net around the polygonal perimeter of these cells. Under the electron microscope, it can be seen that this structure corresponds to some of the 3 specialized types of attachment which form a junctional complex.

From the apex of the cell to its base, there is, first, the *zonula occludens* (tight junction), a region in which the outer components of 2 adjoining cell membranes fuse into one (Figs 4—5 and 4—6). Below the

zonula occludens is the *zonula adherens,* a region characterized by separation of the cell membranes, leaving an extracellular space 20 nm wide, and moderate accumulation of dense material in the inner surface of the cell membranes. Some cytoplasmic filaments are inserted on it and blend with the terminal web. The third part of the junctional complex is composed of the desmosomes, also called *maculae adherentes.*

Interestingly, whereas the zonula occludens forms a continuous belt around the cell apex, the desmosomes are discontinuous and patchy (Fig 4—6). The zonula adherens is usually—but not always—continuous. The junctional complex is important not only in the adhesion of cells but also to the understanding (morphologically) of the barrier that epithelium usually presents to the passage of certain substances. The junctional complex explains the difference of electrical potential between the 2 surfaces of an epithelial membrane and is important in understanding absorptive processes in some organs such as the kidneys and salivary glands.

Adhesion of cells may also be enhanced by membrane interdigitation, often observed between the membranes of the lateral walls of epithelial cells (Fig 4–8). It increases the area of surface contact between the cells and, therefore, their adhesion.

Another type of junction is the *gap junction* (Figs 3–7 and 4–9) or *nexus,* which is found deep in the lateral surface of epithelial cells. It is present in the cells of the heart and between smooth muscle cells and appears to be used for the direct passage of small molecules among cells or for rapid spread of depolarization in adjacent cell membranes. Under the electron microscope, it shows structures that are embedded in the membranes of adjacent cells and which have in their center very small pores through which the communication of cells might occur.

SPECIALIZATION OF THE CELL SURFACE

Microvilli

The electron microscopic study of epithelia with absorptive functions (eg, the intestinal epithelium or certain epithelial tissues in the kidney) shows that the surface membrane presents a multitude of fingerlike evaginations called *microvilli*. These structures have a dense core of filaments similar to those present in and probably continuous with the terminal web (Fig 4–6). The glycoprotein layer which covers the epithelial cells (glycocalyx) is frequently thicker around the villi, and occasionally it can even assume a filamentous aspect at the extremity of the villi (Fig 4–6). This differential localization of the glycocalyx is important for the in-

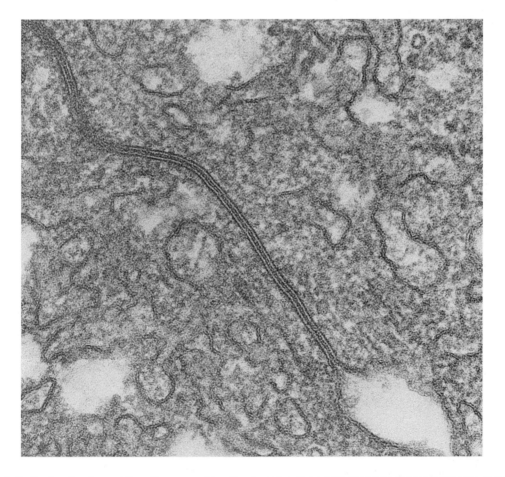

Figure 4–9. Gap junction from rat liver. Two apposed junctional membranes are separated by an electron-lucent space or gap 2–4 nm wide. X 193,000. (Courtesy of MC Williams.)

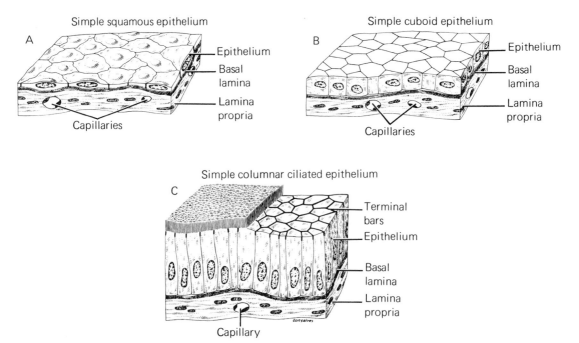

Simple squamous epithelium

A

Epithelium
Basal lamina
Lamina propria
Capillaries

Simple cuboid epithelium

B

Epithelium
Basal lamina
Lamina propria
Capillaries

Simple columnar ciliated epithelium

C

Terminal bars
Epithelium
Basal lamina
Lamina propria
Capillary

Figure 4–10. Diagrams of epithelial tissues. *A:* Simple squamous epithelium. *B:* Simple cuboid epithelium. *C:* Simple ciliated columnar epithelium. All are separated from the subjacent connective tissue by a basal lamina. Note in *C* the terminal bars, which correspond in light microscopy to the zonula occludens and zonula adherens of the junctional complex.

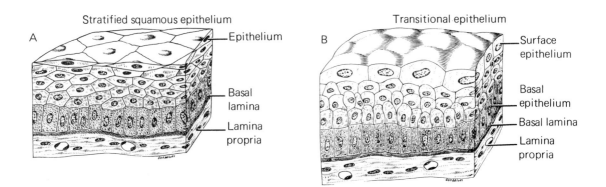

Stratified squamous epithelium

A

Epithelium
Basal lamina
Lamina propria

Transitional epithelium

B

Surface epithelium
Basal epithelium
Basal lamina
Lamina propria

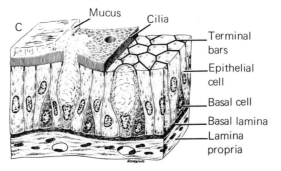

Ciliated pseudostratified epithelium

Mucus   Cilia

C

Terminal bars
Epithelial cell
Basal cell
Basal lamina
Lamina propria

Figure 4–11. Diagrams of epithelial tissue. *A:* Stratified squamous epithelium. *B:* Transitional epithelium. *C:* Ciliated pseudostratified epithelium. In *C,* the goblet cells form a continuous mucous layer over the ciliary layer.

tense pinocytotic processes occurring here, especially near the base of the microvilli. The microvilli increase considerably the efficiency of absorption and the surface area of the cell, thus enhancing the efficiency of all processes occurring in this region.

Cilia & Flagella

Cilia are numerous elongated, motile structures on the surface of epithelial cells, $5-10$ μm long and 0.2 μm in diameter—much longer and different in structure than the microvilli. Under the electron microscope in cross-section, they are surrounded by the cellular membrane and contain a central pair of microtubules and, at the periphery below the membrane, arranged in a circle, 9 more pairs of microtubules all of which run in the direction of the long axis (Fig 4-8).

The cilia are inserted on the *basal bodies,* which are dense structures present at the apical pole just below the cell membrane. They have an internal structure analogous to that of the centrioles (see Chapter 3).

In living organisms, rapid back-and-forth movement can be observed in cilia. Ciliary movement is frequently coordinated to permit a current of fluid or particulate matter to be propelled in one direction over the ciliated epithelium. ATP, which enhances this type of movement, seems to be a source of energy for it.

Dynein, a protein with ATPase activity, has been isolated from cilia. Its mode of action and its role in ciliary movement are not completely known. It is estimated that a ciliated cell of the trachea can have about 250 cilia. Flagella, present in the human body only in the spermatozoa, are similar in structure to cilia but are much longer.

Stereocilia

Sterocilia are long, nonmotile processes in the apical region of the cells lining the epididymis. Under the electron microscope, they have the appearance of elongated, flexible microvilli.

CLASSIFICATION OF EPITHELIAL CELLS

Epithelial cells are customarily classified according to their structure and function into 2 main groups: covering epithelium and glandular epithelium. This is an arbitrary division, for there are covering epithelial tissues in which all cells secrete mucus (eg, the surface epithelium of the stomach) or in which glandular cells are very sparse (eg, mucous cells in the intestine or trachea).

Covering Epithelial Tissue

Covering epithelial tissues are tissues whose cells are organized in membranous layers that cover the external surface or line the cavities of the body. They can be classified morphologically according to the number of cell layers and the form of the superficial cells (Table 4-1). Simple epithelium contains only one layer of cells, and stratified epithelium contains more than one layer (Figs 4-1, 4-10, and 4-11).

Simple epithelium can, according to cell form, be squamous, cuboid, or columnar. The endothelium lining blood vessels and the mesothelium lining certain body cavities are examples of simple squamous epithe-

Table 4-1. Common types of epithelial lining in the human body.

According to the Number of Cell Layers	According to the Form of the Cells	Distribution	Function
Simple (one layer)	Squamous	Lining of vessels (endothelium). Serous lining of cavities: pericardium, pleura, peritoneum (mesothelia).	Facilitates the movement of the viscera (mesothelium), active transport by pinocytosis.
	Cuboid	Covering the ovary, thyroid.	Covering, secretion.
	Columnar	Lining of intestine, gallbladder.	Protection, lubrication, absorption, secretion.
Pseudostratified (layers of cells with nuclei at different levels; not all cells reach surface		Lining of trachea, bronchi, nasal cavity.	Protection; transport of particles out of the air passages; secretion.
Stratified (2 or more layers)	Squamous keratinized (dry)	Skin	Protection; prevents water loss.
	Squamous non-keratinized (moist)	Mouth, esophagus, vagina, anal canal.	Protection; prevents water loss; secretion.
	Cuboid	Sweat glands, developing ovarian follicles.	Protection, secretion.
	Transitional	Bladder, ureters, renal calyces.	Protection.
	Columnar	Conjunctiva	Protection.

lium (Fig 4–10A). An example of cuboid epithelium is the surface of the ovary (Fig 4–10B), and an example of columnar epithelium is the intestinal lining (Fig 4–10C).

Stratified epithelium is classified according to the cell form of its superficial layer. These include *squamous, columnar* or *cylindric,* and *transitional* epithelium. Pseudostratified epithelium forms a separate group.

Stratified squamous epithelium is found mainly in the skin. Its cells form many layers; the cells closer to the underlying tissue are usually cuboid or columnar. In the following layers, however, toward the surface, the cells become irregular in shape and flatten progressively as they get closer to the surface, where they are thin squamous (Fig 4–11A). (For details, see Chapter 19.)

Stratified columnar epithelium is rare; it is present on the human body only in small areas such as the ocular conjunctiva and the ducts of large glands.

Transitional epithelium, which lines the urinary bladder, the ureter, and the upper part of the urethra, is characterized by the presence on its surface of globular cells that are neither squamous nor columnar (Fig 4–11B). It is known that the form of these cells changes according to the degree of distention of the bladder. This type of epithelium is discussed in detail in Chapter 20.

Pseudostratified epithelium is so called because, although nuclei are observed in various layers, all cells are attached to the basal lamina but some do not reach the surface. The best-known example of this tissue is the ciliated pseudostratified columnar epithelium present in the respiratory passage (Fig 4–11C).

Mucous membranes are the epithelial membranes that line wet cavities (eg, mouth, bladder, intestines), in contrast to the skin, whose surface is dry.

Two other types of epithelium warrant brief mention. The neuroepithelia are cells of epithelial origin with specialized sensory functions (eg, cells of taste buds and olfactory mucosa). Myoepithelial cells specialize in contraction (eg, in the sweat, mammary, and salivary glands).

Glandular Epithelia

Glandular epithelial tissues are those formed by cells specialized in producing a fluid secretion that differs in composition from blood or intercellular fluid. This process is usually accompanied by the intracellular synthesis of macromolecules. These compounds are generally stored in the cells in small droplets called secretory granules.

The nature of these macromolecules is variable; they secrete proteins (eg, pancreas), lipids (eg, adrenal and sebaceous glands), or complexes of carbohydrate and proteins (eg, salivary glands). In the mammary glands, all 3 substances—proteins, lipids, and carbohydrates—are secreted. Less common are the cells of glands which have low synthetic activity (eg, sweat glands) and in which secretion is mostly composed of substances transferred from the blood to the lumen of the gland.

In some cases, a gland may contain active synthesizing cells in association with cells specializing in ion transport. This occurs in the striated ducts of most major mammalian salivary glands (see Chapter 17).

All gland cells produce and expel to an extracellular compartment products that are not used by the cell itself but are of importance to other parts of the organism.

Types of Glandular Epithelium

The epithelial tissue that forms the glands of the body can be classified according to various criteria, eg, unicellular glands consist of isolated glandular cells and multicellular glands are composed of clusters of cells. An example of a unicellular gland is the goblet cell of the lining of the small intestine or of the respiratory tract. However, most glands are multicellular.

Glands always derive from epithelial covering membranes by means of cell proliferation and invasion of subjacent connective tissue, followed by further differentiation later. Fig 4–12 shows how this occurs. The secretion of *exocrine glands* will, by special structures called ducts, be taken to the epithelial surface from which the glands originate. The secretions of *endocrine glands* are released into blood vessels.

Multicellular glands are not merely collections of cells; they are complete organs with a definite and orderly architecture. They may have a surrounding capsule of connective tissue which emits septa that will divide it into lobules. These lobules then subdivide, and in this way the connective tissue separates and binds the glandular components. Blood vessels and nerves also penetrate and subdivide in the gland.

According to the way the secretory products leave the cell, glands may be classified as *merocrine* or *holocrine.* In merocrine glands (eg, in the pancreas), the secretory granules leave the cell with no loss of cellular material. In holocrine glands (eg, sebaceous glands), the product of secretion is shed with the whole cell—a process which involves destruction of the secretion-filled cells. In an intermediate type—the *apocrine* gland—the secretory product is discharged together with parts of the apical cytoplasm. This type of secretion is observed in certain sweat glands.

Two types of endocrine glands can be differentiated according to cell grouping. In the first type, the agglomerated cells form anastomosing cords interspersed between dilated blood capillaries (eg, adrenal gland, parathyroid, anterior lobe of the pituitary) (Fig 4–12). In the second *(vesicular)* type, the cells line a vesicle or follicle filled with noncellular material (eg, the thyroid gland) (Fig 4–12).

Exocrine glands have a *secretory portion,* which contains the cells responsible for the secretory process; and the *gland ducts,* which transport the secretion to the exterior of the gland (Fig 4–12). Simple glands have only one unbranched duct. Compound glands have ducts that branch repeatedly. The form of the secretory portion of the gland further classifies the glands. The simple glands can be tubular, coiled tubu-

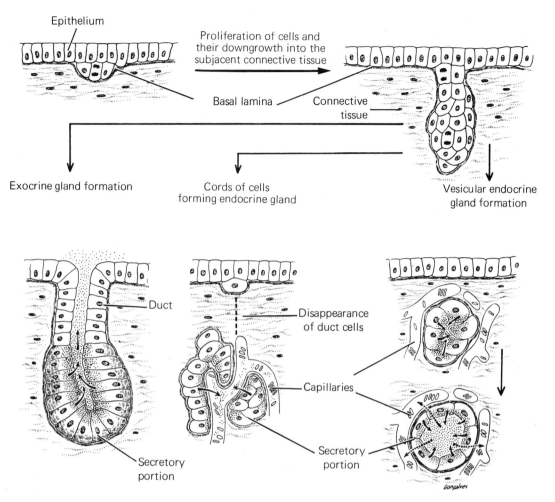

Figure 4—12. Formation of glands from covering epithelia. Epithelial cells proliferate and penetrate into connective tissue. They may or may not maintain contact with the surface. When contact is maintained, exocrine glads are formed; when contact is not maintained, endocrine glands are formed. The cells of these glands can be arranged in cords or follicles. The lumens of follicles accumulate large quantities of secretion; cells of the cords store only small quantities in their cytoplasm. (Redrawn and reproduced, with permission, from Ham AW: *Histology,* 6th ed. Lippincott, 1969.)

lar, branched tubular, and acinar. The compound glands can be tubular, acinar, or tubulo-acinar. Fig 4—13 illustrates these types of glands schematically. Some organs have both endocrine and exocrine functions, and one cell type may function both ways—eg, in the liver, where cells that secrete bile into the duct system also secrete their products into the bloodstream. In other organs, some cells are specialized in exocrine secretion whereas others are concerned exclusively with endocrine secretion. This occurs, for example, in the pancreas, where the acinar cells secrete digestive enzymes into the intestinal lumen while the islet cells secrete insulin and glucagon into the blood.

GENERAL BIOLOGY
OF EPITHELIAL TISSUES

Covering epithelial tissues are situated on a layer of connective tissue called lamina propria and separated from it by the basal lamina. The lamina propria not only serves to support the epithelium but also binds it to neighboring structures. The contact between epithelium and lamina propria is often increased by irregularities in the surface in the form of evaginations called papillae. They occur most frequently in epithelial tissues subject to strain such as the skin and the tongue.

Nutrition & Innervation

With rare exceptions, blood vessels do not penetrate to the epithelium, so that there is no direct contact between these cells and blood vessels. Epithelial

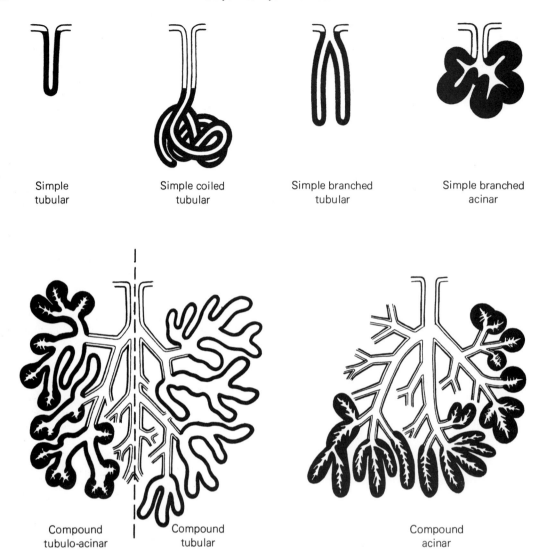

Simple tubular

Simple coiled tubular

Simple branched tubular

Simple branched acinar

Compound tubulo-acinar

Compound tubular

Compound acinar

Figure 4—13. Principal types of exocrine glands. The part of the gland formed by secretory cells is shown in black; the remainder shows the glandular ducts. The compound glands have ramified ducts.

nutrition depends, therefore, on the diffusion of metabolites through the basal lamina and, frequently, through parts of the lamina propria also. The diffusion process is probably enhanced by the papillae, which increase the area of contact between epithelium and lamina propria, and it probably limits the thickness of the epithelium. Most epithelial tissues receive nerve endings from a rich nervous network.

The Renewal of Epithelial Cells

Epithelial tissues are labile structures whose cells are constantly renewed by means of continuous mitotic activity. However, this renewal rate is variable. It can be fast in such tissues as the intestinal epithelium, which is changed every 2–3 days; or slow, as in the pancreas, where tissue renewal takes about 50 days. In stratified and pseudostratified epithelial tissues, mitosis occurs with greater frequency in the cells closest to the basal lamina.

Metaplasia

Under certain physiologic or pathologic conditions, a single type of epithelial tissue may undergo a series of transformations into another type. This process is called metaplasia. It is reversible, and the following examples illustrate this process: (1) In heavy cigarette smokers, the pseudostratified epithelium lining the bronchi can be transformed into stratified squamous epithelium. (2) In individuals with chronic vitamin A deficiency, epithelial tissues of the type found in the bronchi and urinary bladder are gradually replaced by stratified squamous epithelium.

Metaplasia is not restricted to epithelial tissue; it may also occur in connective tissue.

Easily reversible changes that cells undergo during the process of metaplasia are also called *modulation*, in contrast to the process of *differentiation*, in which the cellular changes are irreversible (see Chapter 3).

Control of Glandular Activity

The activity of a gland depends on 2 types of mechanisms: The first is genetic and is related to the presence and expression of one or more genes that promote the synthesis and secretion of specific compounds or products. During the differentiation of a glandular cell, for example, the main event is the expression of the genes that control secretion.

The second type of mechanism is exogenous. The nervous and endocrine systems are the main participants in its control. Most glands are sensitive to both nervous and endocrine control, but one is frequently more important than the other. Thus, exocrine secretion in the pancreas depends mainly on stimulation by the hormones secretin and pancreozymin. The salivary glands, on the other hand, are essentially under nervous control.

BIOLOGY OF THE MAIN TYPES OF EPITHELIAL CELLS

As cells differentiate, they gradually acquire morphologic and physiologic characteristics according to the various functions they assume. Since these differentiated cells frequently have the same functions in different tissues and organs, descriptions of the main cell types will be given.

Cells That Transport Ions

The observation that certain dyes injected into the bloodstream can be concentrated in the lumens of renal tubules and that this activity depends on the integrity of their energy-yielding metabolism led to the concept of *active transport*. Active transport is an energy-dependent process. Certain cells of the metazoa also utilize this system for ion transport, an important physiologic activity in the maintenance of ionic balance.

The most important ions for ionic balance are sodium and potassium; in the human body, several cells have mechanisms to transport these ions through cell membranes. The most conspicuous of these are the cells of the proximal and distal renal tubules and those of the striated ducts of the salivary gland. These cells are cuboid or columnar. They usually have a central nucleus, and they exhibit the following characteristics (Fig 4–14): (1) Multiple and deep invaginations of the membrane of the basal portion of the cell. These invaginations are not followed by the basal lamina, and they divide the basal pole into a series of vertical compartments, thus increasing considerably the surface of the basal area of the cell. (2) Frequent interdigitations in their lateral surfaces with similar structures of adja-

cent cells. (3) A great amount of filamentous mitochondria, with abundant cristae filling most of the compartments, near the base of the cell. (4) As expected in cells rich in mitochondria, great metabolic activity with high oxygen consumption. The cells exhibit strong histochemical reactions with succinic dehydrogenase and cytochrome oxidase, enzymes which are compatible with high energy metabolism.

Adding oxidative phosphorylation inhibitors to these cells blocks ionic transport, which suggests that this process is linked to energy metabolism. Although ionic transport occurs in certain cell types that do not have membrane invaginations and mitochondria-filled compartments, these characteristics are always present in cells in which this activity is highly developed. Studies performed on this material suggest that sodium reabsorbed by the apical pole of the cell passes in part through the mitochondria and that chloride is transported in the cytoplasm (Fig 4–14). The close contact of the mitochondria with cell membrane invagination also suggests that this organelle participates in ion transport. The mechanism of water transport through the cell is obscure; very probably, it occurs following an osmotic gradient formed by the transport of ions.

Cells That Transport by Pinocytosis

In various cells of the body, pinocytotic vesicles that form abundantly on their surfaces permit the transport of macromolecules across their membranes. This activity is clearly observed in the simple squamous epithelium lining the blood vessels (endothelia) or the body cavities (mesothelia). These cells have few organelles but abundant pincoytotic vesicles both on the cell surfaces and in the cytoplasm (Fig 4–15). These observations, in conjunction with results obtained by injection of electron-dense colloidal particles (eg, ferritin, colloidal gold, thorium) and evidence obtained by electron microscopy, indicate that the vesicles flow in both directions through the cells (Fig 4–15), transporting the injected materials.

Calculations based on these studies suggest that a pinocytotic vesicle can cross these cells in 2–3 minutes. Since the frequency of vesicle formation and vesicle volume can be measured, it has been possible to calculate the quantity of the transferred liquid through the walls of capillaries. In the case of muscle tissue, the amount transported has been estimated to be 2–3 ml/hour/1000 g of tissue.

Protein-Secreting Cells

The acinar cells of the pancreas are typical protein-secreting cells. They are polyhedral and pyramidal, with a round nucleus in the center and well-defined polarity. In the basal infranuclear region, these cells are characterized by their intense basophilia, which results from local accumulation of granular endoplasmic reticulum in the form of parallel arrays of cisternae and tubular elements (Fig 4–16).

Filamentous mitochondria are frequently interspersed in the endoplasmic reticulum. The position of the nucleus and the presence of an evident basal baso-

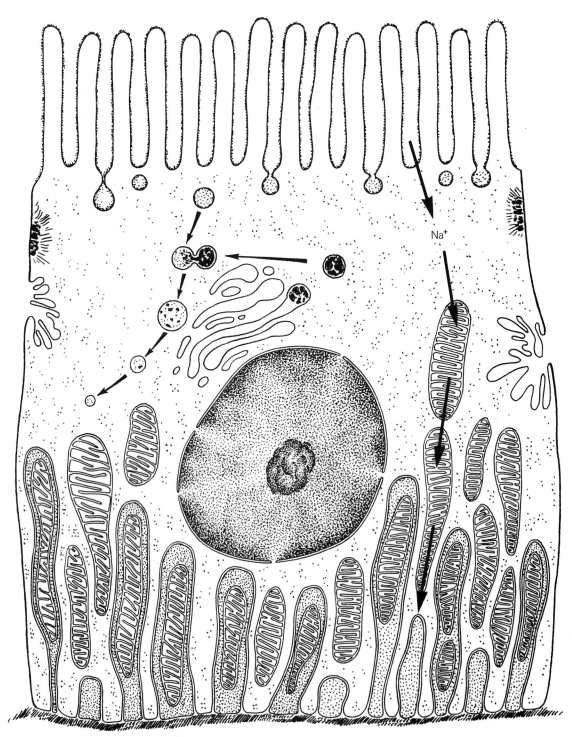

Figure 4—14. Ultrastructure of a proximal convoluted tubule cell of the kidney. Invagination of the basal cell membrane outlines regions filled with elongated mitochondria. This typical disposition is present in ion-transporting cells. Interdigitations from neighboring cells (stippled structures) interlock with those of this cell. Protein absorbed by pinocytosis and being digested by lysosomes is shown in the upper portion of the diagram. The arrows at the right indicate the path by which sodium ions presumably cross the cell. Chloride ions probably flow in the cytoplasm between the mitochondria. This is an example of a cell with more than one function, since it transports ions in addition to providing for protein digestion.

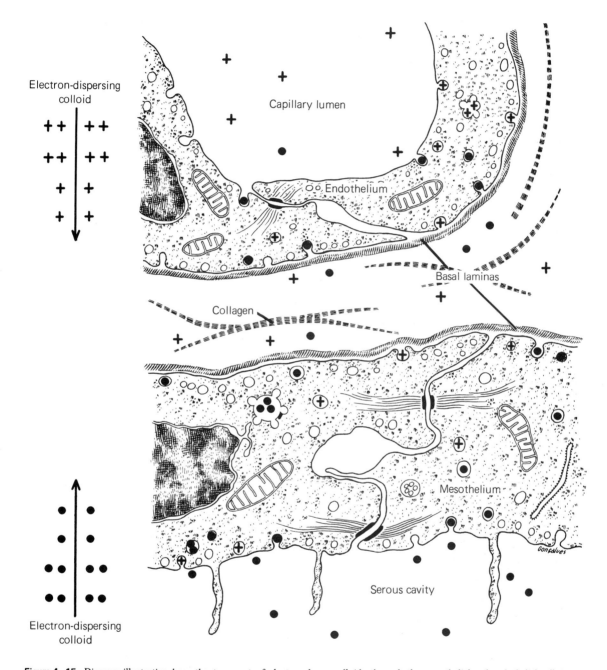

Figure 4–15. Diagram illustrating how the transport of electron-dense colloids through the mesothelial and endothelial cells was studied. Simultaneous injections of colloids that differ morphologically were made, one intravenously and the other in a serous cavity (eg, the mesentery or pericardial cavity) lined by the cells. After short periods of time (minutes), fragments of the serous membranes were fixed and studied in the electron microscope. It was observed that the transport of colloid occurred in both directions. These particles are engulfed by pinocytosis and are transported across the cells in vesicles. (Redrawn and reproduced, with permission, from Staubesand J: Zur Histophysiologie des Herzbeutels. Z Zellforsch Mikrosk Anat 58:915, 1963.)

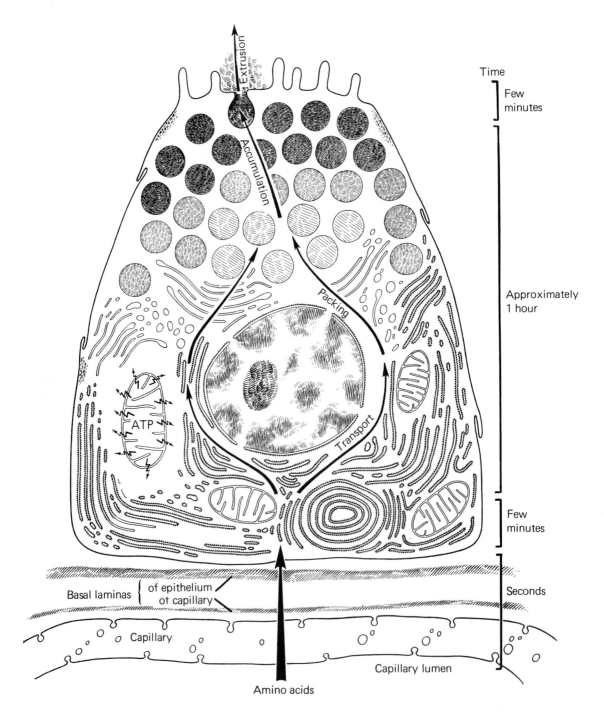

Figure 4—16. Diagram of a serous cell (pancreatic acinar). Observe its evident polarity with abundant basal granular endoplasmic reticulum (ergastoplasm). The Golgi apparatus and secretory granules are in the supranuclear region. The secretory process is described in the text. To the right is a time scale indicating the approximate time necessary for each step.

philic region in these cells are characteristic of protein-synthesizing cells and are frequently used as criteria to distinguish them from cells secreting acid mucopolysaccharides.

In the apical supranuclear region, a well-developed Golgi apparatus can be observed just above the nucleus. The rest of the cytoplasm is filled with rounded, protein-rich, membrane-bound structures called *secretory granules*. In cells that produce digestive enzymes (eg, the pancreas), these structures are called *zymogen granules* (Figs 4–16 and 4–17).

Enough evidence has been presented from biochemical and cytologic studies to define the secretory process in these cells as follows:

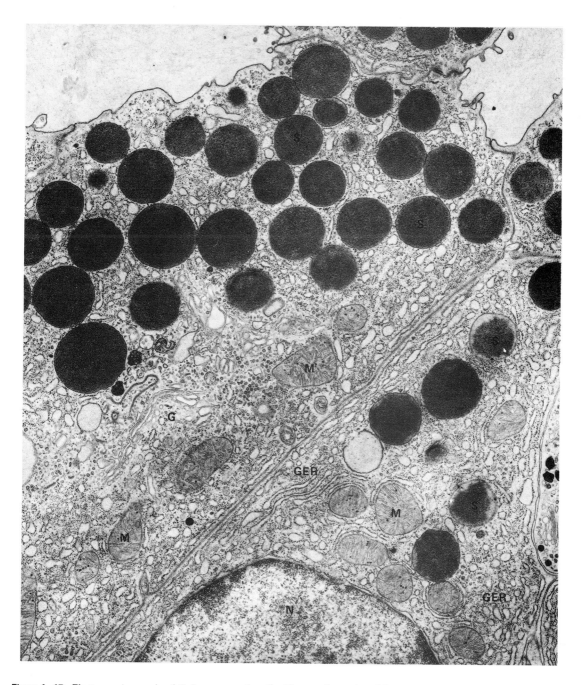

Figure 4–17. Electron micrograph of 2 frog pancreatic cells. Observe the nucleus (N), mitochondria (M), Golgi apparatus (G), secretory granules (S) in various stages of condensation, and granular endoplasmic reticulum (GER). × 13,000. (Courtesy of KR Porter.)

(1) Amino acids from the bloodstream pass through the capillary walls and their basal lamina, through the secretory cell basal lamina, and through its membrane into the cells. The entry of amino acids through the membrane is greatly accelerated by an active transport mechanism.

(2) At the level of the polysomes bound to the endoplasmic reticulum membrane, these amino acids first form filamentous protein molecules which are secreted into the endoplasmic reticulum. These proteins can often be seen as diverse intracisternal granules. In this stage, the proteins are segregated in an extracytoplasmic space—the interior of the granular endoplasmic reticulum cisternae—which is important because it avoids direct contact of the secretory product, often digestive enzymes (eg, ribonuclease and protease), with the cytoplasm.

(3) The proteins thus segregated are transported through the endoplasmic reticulum to the Golgi apparatus. The mechanism by which they reach the interior of the Golgi cisternae is still somewhat obscure; however, evidence shows that in several cell types this occurs by formation of small vesicles containing protein that bud from the endoplasmic reticulum, migrate, and fuse to the convex surface of Golgi cisternae.

(4) This material is then accumulated in the Golgi cisternae and forms bulges in the lateral dilatation in its borders. These bulges form large membrane-bound vesicles that lose contact with the Golgi cisternae to form the *secretory vesicles* or *granules* (Figs 4–16 and 4–17).

(5) The newly formed granules in turn migrate to the cell apex and in doing so become more dense. They have been designated mature granules, in contrast to the less dense, recently formed granules. They continue to accumulate for a period that varies with the type of gland until they are mobilized.

(6) When the cells extrude their secretory products, the membranes of the secretory granules fuse to the cell membrane and the granule content spills out of the cell in a process that roughly resembles (and has been called) *reverse pinocytosis*.

The energy for these processes is known to be furnished by oxidative phosphorylation at the mitochondrial level.

Glycoprotein Cells

The most typical and most thoroughly studied example of glycoprotein cells is the goblet cell of the intestines, which is characterized by the presence of abundant, large, lightly staining secretory granules filling its extensive supranuclear apical pole. The nucleus is usually flattened vertically and is localized in the cell base. This region is usually rich in granular endoplasmic reticulum (Figs 4–18 and 4–19). The Golgi apparatus located just above the nucleus is exceptionally well developed, which suggests that it has an important function in this cell. Data obtained mainly by radioautography suggest that in this cell proteins are synthesized from amino acids at the level of the endoplasmic reticulum present in the cell base. The complex, high-

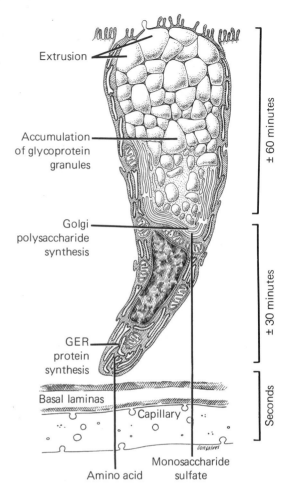

Figure 4–18. Diagram of a mucus-secreting intestinal goblet cell. Its constricted base, where the mitochondria and granular endoplasmic reticulum (GER) are located, is typical. Synthesis of the protein part of the glycoprotein complex and secretion occur in the endoplasmic reticulum. A developed Golgi apparatus, where the polysaccharides are synthesized, is present in the supranuclear region. In cells that secrete sulfated polysaccharides, the process of sulfation occurs in the Golgi complex. (Redrawn after Gordon and reproduced, with permission, from Ham AW: *Histology,* 6th ed. Lippincott, 1969.)

molecular-weight carbohydrates seem to be synthesized in the endoplasmic reticulum and in the Golgi apparatus.

Evidence also shows that in those cells that produce sulfated glycoproteins the process of sulfation of the polysaccharide moiety occurs in the region of the Golgi apparatus.

The goblet cell of the intestines is only one of several types of cells that synthesize glycoproteins. Other types—discussed later—show great variability in the chemistry of their secretion and present somewhat different morphologic characteristics.

Serous & Mucous Cells

Pancreatic cells and goblet cells are typical ex-

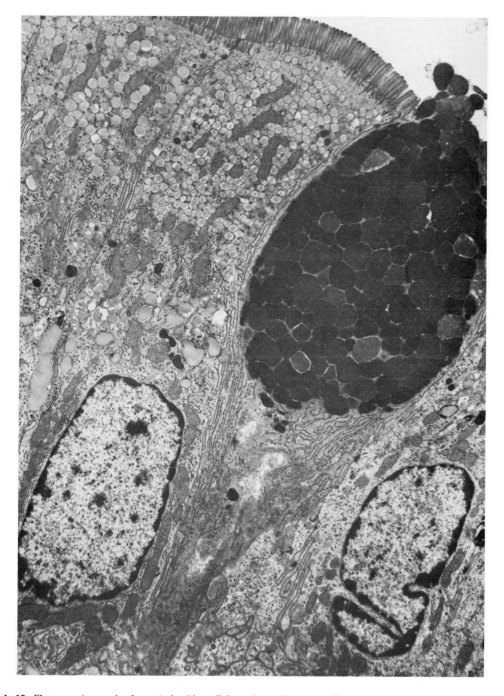

Figure 4–19. Electron micrograph of a typical goblet cell from the small intestine. The granular endoplasmic reticulum is present mainly in the cell base, while the cell apex is filled with dense secretory granules. × 5000. (Courtesy of HI Friedman.)

amples of cells called serous and mucous cells, respectively, because of the consistency and appearance of their products of secretion.

However, the differences between these 2 types of cells are not always clear, and in mammalian organisms various cell types have been described that produce variable proportions of polysaccharides and proteins. This occurs, for example, in the parotid and subman-

dibular salivary glands. Close analysis of these cell types shows that there is an almost continuous gradient from serous to mucous cells, which consequently makes it impossible to classify certain cell types as either mucous or serous. In doubtful instances, an intermediate classification of *seromucous cells* has been proposed (Fig 4–20).

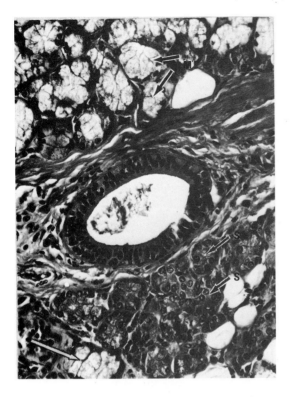

Figure 4—20. Photomicrograph of a section of tongue showing in the center a duct from a salivary gland with its cylindric stratified epithelium surrounded by connective tissue. Above, a gland made up of mucous cells (M); below, of seromucous cells (S). Some adipose cells can be seen at right. At left, an acinus of mucous cells (arrow). H&E stain, × 400.

Steroid-Secreting Cells

Cells secreting steroids are found in various structures of the body (eg, testicles, ovaries, adrenals). They are endocrine cells specialized for synthesizing and storing steroid substances with hormonal activity. They have the following characteristics (Figs 4—21 and 4—22):

(1) They are polyhedral or rounded acidophilic cells with a central nucleus and a cytoplasm that is usually but not invariably rich in lipid droplets.

(2) The cytoplasm of steroid-secreting cells presents an exceptionally rich smooth endoplasmic reticulum, which takes the form of vesicles and tubules. In properly fixed material, they appear mainly as freely anastomosing tubules. Studies performed principally with organelles of these cells obtained by differential centrifugation suggest that the endoplasmic reticulum contains the necessary enzymes to synthesize cholesterol from acetate and other substrates and to transform (mainly in the testicles and ovaries) the pregnenolone produced in the mitochondria into androgens, estrogens, and progestogens.

(3) The spherical or elongated mitochondria that are present usually contain tubular rather than lamellar cristae, which are common to mitochondria of other epithelial cells. Besides being the main site of energy

production for cell function, these organelles have the necessary enzymatic equipment not only to cleave the cholesterol side chain and produce pregnenolone but also to participate in the synthesis of the steroids of the adrenal glands.

Myoepithelial Cells

Several glands (eg, sweat, mammary, and salivary glands) commonly contain a special cell type which surrounds mainly the cells of its secretory portions. This is the star-shaped myoepithelial cell, which has a centrally located nucleus and long cytoplasmic arms bound to the secretory cells by desmosomes. Myoepithelial cells are located between the basal lamina and basal pole of the secretory cells. They embrace gland cells as an octopus would embrace a rounded boulder. The presence of filaments similar to those of smooth muscle, as well as other characteristics, suggests that these cells are contractile. They are considered to participate actively in the secretion of the glands in which they are present by pressing on its secretory portion.

Polypeptide-Secreting Cells

Recent studies suggest that, to some extent, cells synthesizing low-molecular-weight polypeptides or proteins with hormonal activity have morphologic and histochemical characteristics in common. They are endocrine cells present in several organs of vertebrates. They either concentrate ready-made biogenic amines such as epinephrine, norepinephrine, or 6-hydroxytryptamine in their cytoplasm or are capable of concentrating precursors of these amines and then synthesizing them. They also exhibit a high level of amino acid decarboxylase activity—an enzyme related to the synthesis of these amines. These characteristics explain the designation APUD (amine precursor uptake and decarboxylation) that has been given to these cells. They have low cytoplasmic basophilia—in contrast to the protein-secreting cells. Under the electron microscope, their main features are shown to be the presence of unusually small, round secretory granules (100—200 nm) accumulated in the cellular region close to the capillaries and relatively scarce granular endoplasmic

Table 4—2. APUD cells in humans.*

Cell Name	Polypeptide Produced	Cell Site
C and M of the pituitary	Adrenocorticotropin/MSH	Pars distalis
A of the Langerhans islets (a_2)	Glucagon	Pancreas
B of the Langerhans islets (β)	Insulin	Pancreas
D of the Langerhans islets (δ, a_1)	Gastrin	Pancreas
AL of the stomach (A-like)	Enteroglucagon	Stomach
G of the stomach	Gastrin	Stomach
EG of intestine	Enteroglucagon	Intestine
S of the duodenum	Secretin	Intestine
Parafollicular	Calcitonin	Thyroid

*APUD is an acronym for amine precursor uptake and decarboxylation.

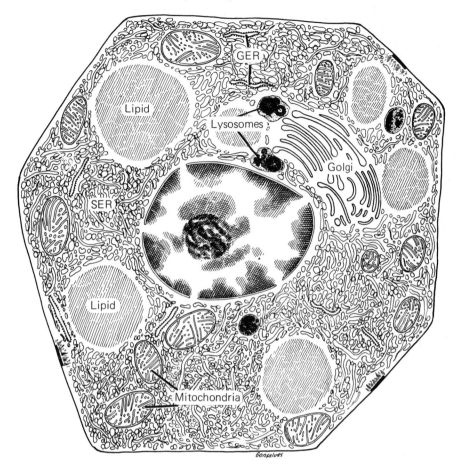

Figure 4–21. Diagram of the ultrastructure of a hypothetic steroid-secreting cell. Observe the richness of the smooth endoplasmic reticulum (SER), lipid droplets, Golgi apparatus, and lysosomes. The abundant mitochondria frequently have tubular cristae. They not only produce the energy necessary for activity of the cell but also participate in steroid synthesis. GER, granular (rough) endoplasmic reticulum.

reticulum. The Golgi apparatus is not developed.

In view of their function, which is mainly to form peptide bonds, it might be expected that these cells would present characteristics of protein-secreting cells, high basophilia, and a well-developed granular endoplasmic reticulum and Golgi apparatus. Radioautographic and physiologic studies suggest, however, that the rate of protein synthesis is low in the polypeptide-secreting cell, which explains the characteristics mentioned above. Thus, it has been calculated that the pancreatic islet beta cells secrete insulin at a rate that is about one-fiftieth the rate of protein synthesis in the exocrine acinar cells.

The characterization of polypeptides or low-molecular-weight proteins produced by these cells has been achieved mainly by the immunofluorescence method described in Chapter 2. It was thus possible to identify in humans several APUD cells (Table 4–2).

The morphology and histochemistry of these cells varies with the species studied. At present, several polypeptides with biologic activity, as well as several cells of the APUD type but with undetermined function, are known to exist. Clearly, it will be necessary to isolate sufficient quantities of polypeptides in order to produce the antibodies required to apply the immunofluorescence method to the study of APUD cells with unknown function.

Several tumors derived from the APUD cells have been described—among them, tumors of the nonbeta cells of the pancreatic islets that produce gastrin and are responsible for Zollinger-Ellison syndrome, and the calcitonin-producing tumor of the thyroid. Tumors derived from the APUD cells are called apudomas and are one of a group of tumors having their origin in cells of the neural crest.

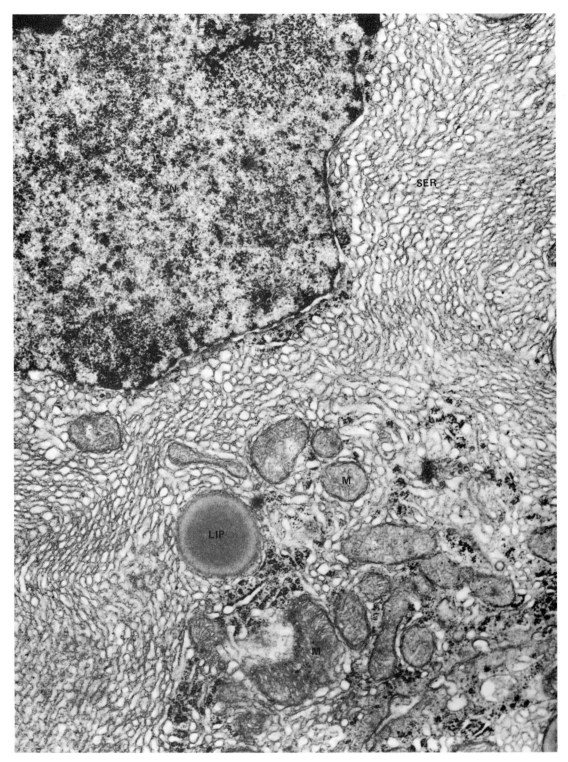

Figure 4–22. Electron micrograph of a steroid-producing cell from the corpus luteum of a pregnant guinea pig. Observe the nucleus (N), the abundance of smooth endoplasmic reticulum (SER), the lipid droplet (LIP), and the mitochondria (M). Reduced from X 30,000. (Reproduced, with permission, from Christensen & Gillim, in: *The Gonads.* McKerns KW [editor]. Appleton-Century-Crofts, 1969.)

• • •

References

Amsterdam A, Ohad I, Schramm M: Dynamic changes in the ultrastructure of the acinar cell of the rat parotid gland during the secretory cycle. J Cell Biol 41:753, 1969.

Bennett G, Leblond CP, Haddad A: Migration of glycoproteins from the Golgi apparatus to the surface of various cell types as shown by radioautography after labelled fucose injection into rats. J Cell Biol 60:258, 1974.

Botelho SY, Brooks FP, Shelley WB: *Symposium on the Exocrine Glands.* Pennsylvania Univ Press, 1969.

Bretscher MS: Some general principles of membrane structure. Page 17 in: *The Cell Surface in Development.* Moscona AA (editor). Wiley, 1974.

Christensen AK, Gillim SW: The correlation of fine structure and function in steroid-secreting cells with emphasis on those of the gonads. In: *The Gonads.* McKerns KW (editor). Appleton-Century-Crofts, 1969.

Farquhar MG, Palade GE: Junctional complexes in various epithelia. J Cell Biol 17:375, 1963.

Freeman JA: Goblet cell fine structure. Anat Rec 154:121, 1966.

Gabe M, Arvy L: Gland cells. Page 1 in: *The Cell.* Vol 5. Brachet J, Mirsky AE (editors). Academic Press, 1961.

Hughes RC: Glycoproteins as components of cellular membranes. Progr Biophys Molec Biol 26:191, 1973.

Jamieson JD, Palade GE: Intracellular transport of secretory protein in the pancreatic exocrine cell. 4. Metabolism requirements. J Cell Biol 39:589, 1968.

Junqueira LCU, Hirch GC: Cell secretion: A study of pancreas and salivary glands. Internat Rev Cytol 5:323, 1956.

Kefalides NA: Chemical properties of basement membranes. Internat Rev Exper Path 10:36, 1971.

Kelly DE: Fine structure of desmosomes, hemidesmosomes, and an adepidermal globular layer in developing newt epidermis. J Cell Biol 28:51, 1966.

Komnick H, Komnick U: Elektronenmikroskopische Untersuchungen zur funktionellen Morphologie des Ionentransportes in der Salzdrüse von *Larus argentatus.* Z Zellforsch Mikrosk Anat 60:163, 1963.

Lane N & others: On the site of sulfation in colonic goblet cells. J Cell Biol 21:339, 1964.

Leblond CP, Bennett G: Elaboration and turnover of cell coat glycoproteins. Page 29 in: *The Cell Surface in Development.* Moscona AA (editor). Wiley, 1974.

Mukherjee TM, Williams AW: A comparative study of the ultrastructure of microvilli in the epithelium of small and large intestines of mice. J Cell Biol 34:447, 1967.

Neutra M, Leblond CP: Synthesis of the carbohydrate of mucus of the Golgi complex, as shown by electron microscope radioautography of goblet cells from rats injected with glucose-H^3. J Cell Biol 30:119, 1966.

Neutra M, Leblond CP: Radioautographic comparison of the uptake of galactose-H^3 and glucose ^3H in the Golgi region of various cells secreting glycoproteins or mucopolysaccharides. J Cell Biol 30:137, 1966.

Palay SL: Morphology of secretion. Page 303 in: *Frontiers in Cytology.* Yale Univ Press, 1958.

Pearse AGE: The cytochemistry and ultrastructure of polypeptide hormone-producing cells of the APUD series and the embryologic, physiologic and pathologic implications of the concept. J Histochem Cytochem 17:303, 1969.

Pearse AGE, Polak JM: Endocrine tumours of neural crest origin: Neurolophomas, apudomas and the APUD concept. Med Biol 52:3, 1974.

Pearse AGE, Polak JM: Neural crest origin of the endocrine polypeptide (APUD) cells of the gastrointestinal tract and pancreas. Gut 12:783, 1971.

Pierce GB & others: Basement membranes. 4. Epithelial origin and immunologic cross reactions. Am J Path 45:929, 1964.

Rambourg A, Leblond CP: Electron microscope observations on the carbohydrate-rich cell coat present at the surface of cells in the rat. J Cell Biol 32:27, 1967.

Rambourg A, Neutra M, Leblond CP: Presence of a "cell coat" rich in carbohydrate at the surface of cells in the rat. Anat Record 40:41, 1966.

Tamarin A: Myoepithelium of the rat submaxillary gland. J Ultrastruct Res 16:320, 1966.

Warshawsky H, Leblond CP, Droz B: Synthesis and migration of proteins in the cells of exocrine pancreas as revealed by specific activity determination from radioautographs. J Cell Biol 16:1, 1963.

5 . . .
Connective Tissue

Connective tissue is characterized morphologically by the presence of several types of cells immersed in abundant intercellular material synthesized by these cells. Richness in intercellular material is one of the main characteristics of connective tissue. This material is composed of *fibers* which have a definite microscopic structure and of *amorphous intercellular substance (matrix)*. The cells, fibers, and amorphous substance are embedded in a small quantity of liquid, the *tissue fluid*, but the greater part of the extracellular water of connective tissue exists not in a free state but in the form of solvation water of acid mucopolysaccharide and protein complexes.

There are 3 main types of connective tissue fiber: *collagenous, elastic,* and *reticular* . Connective tissues have various functions as discussed further in the section on histophysiology (see p 100). The capsules that surround the organs of the body and the internal architecture that supports their cells are composed of connective tissue. This tissue also makes up tendons, ligaments, and the areolar tissue that fills the spaces between organs. Bone and cartilage are types of connective tissue which function to support the soft tissues of the body.

The role of connective tissue in defense of the organism is related to its content of phagocytic and antibody-producing cells. Phagocytic cells engulf inert particles and microorganisms which enter the body. Specific proteins called *antibodies,* produced by connective tissue cells, combine with foreign proteins of bacteria and viruses—or with the toxins produced by bacteria—and combat the biologic activity of these harmful agents.

The role of connective tissue in nutrition depends upon its close association with blood vessels. Thus, the nutrients carried in the blood and the metabolic wastes transported to the excretory organs diffuse through the connective tissue which surrounds the capillaries.

Connective tissue develops from an embryonic tissue, the *mesenchyme,* which is characterized by branched cells embedded in an abundant amorphous intercellular substance. The mesenchymal cells have oval nuclei with well-developed nucleoli and fine chromatin. The mesenchyme that derives from the middle layer of the embryo, the *mesoderm,* spreads throughout the fetus, surrounding the developing organs and penetrating into them. In addition to being the point of origin of all types of connective tissue, the mesenchyme develops into other types of tissues (eg, muscle, blood vessels, epithelium, and some glands).

FIBERS

Collagenous, elastic, and reticular fibers are distributed unequally among the different types of connective tissue. In many cases, the predominant fiber type is responsible for conferring certain specific properties on the tissue. Elastic tissue, with a predominance of elastic fibers, is an obvious example.

Collagenous fibers

Collagenous fibers are the most numerous fibers in connective tissue. Fresh collagenous fibers are colorless strands, but they cause the tissues in which they are present in great numbers to be white—for example, in tendons and aponeuroses. In the polarizing microscope, collagenous fibers are birefringent, and this was taken as an indication that they contain long and parallel molecules—an interpretation that was later fully confirmed by other technics.

In many parts of the body, collagenous fibers are organized in a parallel array, forming *collagenous bundles.*

Because of their long and tortuous course, the morphologic characteristics of collagenous fibers are better studied in spread preparations than in histologic sections. Mesentery is frequently used for this purpose, for, when spread on a slide, it is sufficiently thin to be stained and examined under the microscope. Mesentery is composed of a central portion of connective tissue lined on both surfaces by a simple squamous epithelium, the mesothelium. The collagenous fibers in a spread preparation appear as elongated and tortuous cylindric structures. Their endings merge with other components of the tissue and cannot be seen. The diameter of collagenous fibers varies from $1-20$ μm (Fig 5-1). These fibers are longitudinally striated and are composed of *fibrils* with a diameter of $0.2-0.5$ μm. The diameter of the fibers depends on the number of fibrils they contain.

The electron microscope also shows that each

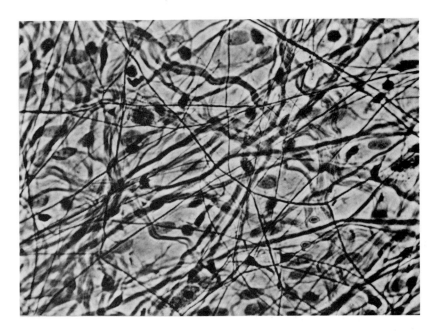

Figure 5—1. Whole mesentery spread on a microscope slide. The preparation was stained by the Weigert method for elastic fibers and photographed under the phase contrast microscope. The thin filaments are elastic fibers. Collagen fibers are the thick and wavy structures. × 200.

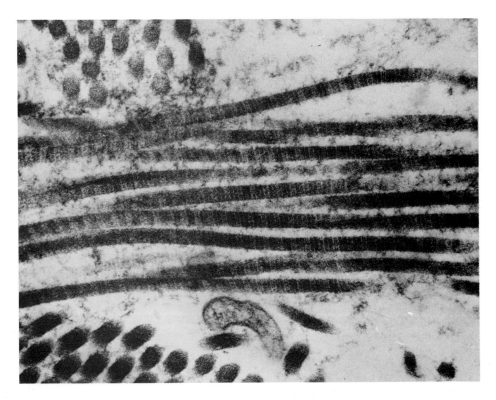

Figure 5—2. Electron micrograph of human collagen microfibrils in cross and longitudinal sections. Each microfibril consists of alternating dark and light bands, which are further divided by cross-striations. Amorphous ground substance appears in the spaces around the microfibrils. × 100,000.

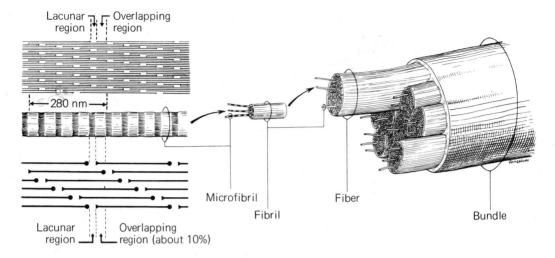

Figure 5–3. Schematic drawing of collagen microfibrils, fibrils, fibers, and bundles. In collagen shaded bundles, the fibers are bound together by a cementing substance. Under the electron microscope, the microfibrils show periodicity of dark and light bands. This periodicity is explained by the arrangement of the rodlike collagen molecules (tropocollagen), each measuring 280 nm. Lacunar regions contain more stain (uranyl acetate, phosphotungstic acid) and appear dark.

fibril is made up of finer filaments, the *microfibrils,* whose dimensions cannot be resolved by the light microscope. Collagenous microfibrils present a characteristic cross-banding with a periodicity of 64 nm (Fig 5–2). Each microfibril consists of 2 bands—one dark and one light. The dark bands retain more of the contrast materials used in electron microscopy because they have more free chemical radicals than the light bands (Fig 5–3).

Collagenous fibers are acidophilic; they stain pink with hematoxylin and eosin, blue with Mallory's trichrome stain, and green with Masson's trichrome stain. It is important to note that these are only selective staining technics and that there are still no specific histochemical methods with which to demonstrate collagen only.

Collagenous fibers are composed mainly of a scleroprotein called *collagen* whose principal amino acid composition is glycine (33.5%), proline (12%), and hydroxyproline (10%). The remainder is made up of other amino acids, although it is interesting to note that collagen is very low in sulfated amino acids and in tyrosine. It is the only protein containing an appreciable amount of hydroxyproline. (Elastin is the only other substance that contains hydroxyproline, although in very small quantities.) The amount of collagen in a tissue can therefore be determined by measurement of the hydroxyproline content. Collagen is the most abundant protein of the human body, representing 30% of total body proteins.

The protein unit that polymerizes itself to form collagenous microfibrils is an elongated molecule called *tropocollagen* which measures 280 nm in length and 1.5 nm in width. Tropocollagen consists of 3 polypeptide chains (Fig 5–4). Two of these peptide chains are alike (alpha-1) and differ from the third (alpha-2) in the formation of their amino acid sequence. The tropocollagen molecule is asymmetric, ie, each end has a different chemical composition. These molecules are the building blocks from which microfibrils are formed. The transverse striation of the collagen microfibrils is determined by the arrangement of the tropocollagen molecules (Fig 5–3).

In addition to the typical 64 nm fibrils, collagenous fibrils with a periodicity of approximately 250 nm have been observed in the connective tissue of the

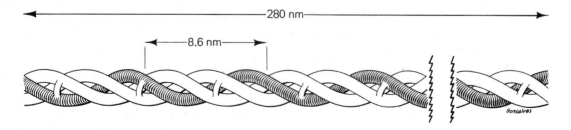

Figure 5–4. The collagen molecule (tropocollagen) is composed of 2 alpha-1 and one alpha-2 (shaded area) peptide chains, each with a molecular weight of approximately 100,000, intertwined in a helix and held together by hydrogen bonds.

eye and in the cartilage of elderly people. These fibrils are called *fibrous long space* collagen.

It is possible to extract several collagen fractions with different solubility characteristics from connective tissue that is in an active phase of fibrilogenesis (eg, in growing animals or during wound healing). The first fraction, extracted in neutral solutions, appears to contain tropocollagen molecules not yet polymerized as well as those which, at the beginning of polymerization, form only very fine microfibrils. This is the recently synthesized *neutral-soluble collagen.* For this reason, collagen that is soluble in neutral solutions is the first to become radioactive after the administration of ^{3}H-proline or ^{3}H-glycine, which are radioactive amino acid collagen precursors. If the remaining tissue is treated with sodium citrate solutions at pH 3.0, a second fraction is obtained which is called *acid-soluble collagen.*

The third fraction, *insoluble collagen,* contains the collagen not extracted by the 2 previous steps. It can only be dissolved by means of very drastic procedures. Because isotope-labeled collagen precursors appear after injection first in the fraction soluble in neutral solution, next in the acid-soluble fraction, and finally in the insoluble fraction, it is believed that these 3 fractions represent successive stages of collagen formation.

The synthesis of collagen proceeds through the following steps:

(1) The polypeptide chains of protocollagen are assembled on polyribosomes containing mRNA.

(2) Hydroxylation of proline and lysine occurs while these are present in the polypeptide precursor of collagen, the protocollagen. Free hydroxyproline and hydroxylysine are not incorporated directly into the chains. The hydroxylation begins after the peptide chain has reached a certain minimum length and is still on the ribosomes but probably continues even after the peptide is released. The 2 enzymes involved are (a) protocollagen proline hydroxylase and (b) protocollagen lysine hydroxylase.

(3) Glycosylation of hydroxylysine occurs after its hydroxylation; all collagens have variable amounts of carbohydrate in the form of galactose or glycosylgalactose linked to hydroxylysine.

(4) The newly synthesized polypeptide chains of tropocollagen are larger than the a chains. This larger form, a precursor of collagen, is called the transport form of collagen; it has been observed in the electron microscope to be 13 nm longer than the tropocollagen. This extra length probably inhibits the formation of intracellular collagen fibrils and is cleaved either intracellularly, just before release, or in the interstitial space. By removal of the peptides in the extracellular space, a transition might occur from a soluble to a fibrillar form of tropocollagen.

(5) Although early experimental data (see p 83 and Fig 5–9) pointed to reverse pinocytosis of Golgi-produced vesicles as a means of secretion from the fibroblasts, later experiments have indicated that collagen might move in the cytoplasm directly from the ribosomes and then through the plasma membrane or directly from the cisternae of the granular endoplasmic reticulum. Carbohydrate molecules linked to hydroxylysine are necessary for the release of tropocollagen. During maturation of tropocollagen macromolecules, covalent cross-links are formed between a chains; collagen microfibrils, fibrils, and fibers are composed of orderly arrangements of tropocollagen macromolecules.

Collagen microfibrils are bound first into fibrils and then into fibers by a cementing substance containing carbohydrates. This substance then binds the fibers into collagen bundles (Fig 5–3). The faint PAS-positive reaction seen in collagen fibers is due to the presence of hexose in this cementing substance.

Elastic Fibers

Elastic fibers are easily distinguished from the collagenous fibers in stretched connective tissue preparations because they are thinner and do not have longitudinal striations (Fig 5–5). They branch and unite with one another, forming an irregular network (Fig 5–1). When they are fresh and present in great quantity, elastic fibers appear characteristically yellow. Elastic fibers predominate in elastic tissue and are known as yellow fibers of connective tissue, while collagenous fibers are known as white fibers. Elastic fibers yield easily to very small traction forces but return to their original shape when these forces are relaxed. The presence of elastic fibers in blood vessels contributes to the efficiency of blood circulation and has contributed to the successful evolution of vertebrates. Elastin is an important component of the skin.

Elastic fibers stain weakly and irregularly with hematoxylin and eosin. They may stain with either agent, but normally they appear unstained with this method. Selective methods to demonstrate elastic fibers, although they are devoid of histochemical specificity, include resorcin-fuchsin, aldehyde-fuchsin, and orcein, resulting in purple or dark blue staining.

Electron microscopy has shown that elastic fibers are composed of fibrils 10 nm in width with an amorphous central part. During their formation, the fibrils appear first, followed by small droplets of amorphous electron-lucent substance attached to the fibrils. The microfibrillar arrangement is composed probably of structural glycoprotein as judged by biochemical, immunochemical, and electron microscopic technics. The proelastin molecules are globular, have a molecular weight of about 76,000, and probably correspond to the amorphous lamellar structures seen in the electron microscope. The amorphous substance becomes more abundant and ultimately predominates in the mature fiber.

The principal component of elastic fibers is a scleroprotein called *elastin,* a significantly "younger" protein than collagen and much more resistant to extracting procedures. It is produced by fibroblasts in skin and tendon and probably by smooth muscle cells in the large vessels with elastic tissue. Elastin resists boiling, dilute acids, and alkalis and is not digested by

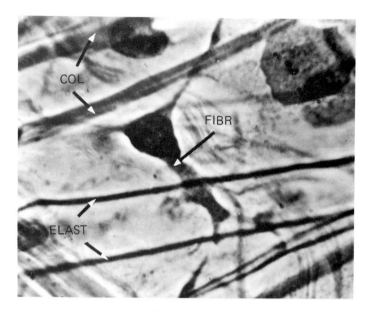

Figure 5–5. Phase contrast photomicrograph of a piece of mesentery spread on a glass slide. Shown are a fibroblast (FIBR), collagen fibers (COL), and elastic fibers (ELAST). H&E stain, × 800.

trypsin; and all of this, apparently, is due to its tertiary and quaternary structure, stabilized by hydrophobic interactions between the nonpolar peptide chains. This probably also explains the affinity of elastin for lipids. Pepsin at pH 2.0 acts very slowly upon elastin, but elastin is easily hydrolyzed by the pancreatic enzyme *elastase*. The amino acid composition of elastin is somewhat similar to that of collagen—it is rich in proline and glycine—but it contains a greater quantity of valine, alanine, desmosine, and isodesmosine. In addi-

tion to elastic fibers, elastin occurs also in the form of *fenestrated membranes* appearing in the walls of blood vessels.

Reticular Fibers

Reticular fibers are very fine, with a diameter comparable to that of collagen fibrils (Fig 5–6), and are not visible in hematoxylin and eosin preparations. Since they are strongly PAS-positive, however, they can be demonstrated by means of impregnation with

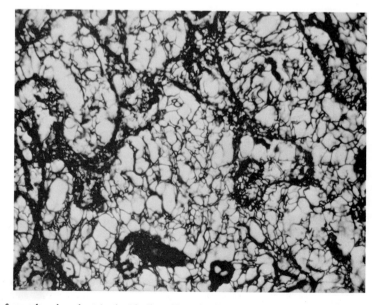

Figure 5–6. Section from a lymph node stained with silver. Note the thin black lines representing the argyrophilic reticular fibers forming an extensive network.

silver salts and by the PAS technic. These fibers are called *argyrophilic fibers* because of their affinity for silver salts. When impregnated with silver, they appear black. Reticular fibers are often continuous with collagenous fibers, which appear brown after silver impregnation. The argyrophilia and positive PAS reaction of the reticular fibers can be explained on the basis of their high content of hexoses—6–12% as opposed to 1% in collagen—and the configuration of the macromolecular architecture of glycoproteins, making available end groups to bind the dyes.

Reticular fibers are composed mainly of the protein collagen. They present a 64 nm periodicity, which is characteristic of collagenous fibers.

The reticular fiber represents a collagenous fibril which acquires a layer of carbohydrates and lipids that probably prevents the formation of more complex collagenous fibers. The difference between reticular and collagenous fibers is that the former correspond to recently formed collagenous fibrils which may continue to polymerize, forming collagenous fibers and bundles.

Reticular fibers are abundant in embryonic connective tissue and in all parts where collagenous fibers are formed. Postnatally, reticular fibers are particularly abundant in the framework of hematopoietic organs (eg, spleen, lymph nodes, red bone marrow) and constitute a network around the cells of epithelial organs (eg, liver, kidney, endocrine glands).

CELLS

Cell specialization in connective tissue has given rise to several types of cells, each having its own morphologic and functional characteristics: fibroblasts, macrophages, undifferentiated mesenchymal cells, mast cells, plasma cells, adipose cells, and leukocytes.

Fibroblasts

The fibroblast is the most common cell found in connective tissue. It is responsible for the synthesis of fibers and amorphous intercellular substance. There are 2 quite different types of fibroblasts and several with intermediate characteristics. The young cell with intense synthetic activity is morphologically distinct from the fibroblast that is found scattered among the fibers it has already synthesized. Some histologists reserve the term fibroblast for the young cell and call the mature cell a *fibrocyte* (Fig 5–7).

The young fibroblast presents abundant and irregular cytoplasmic processes; its nucleus is ovoid, large, and light, with fine chromatin and an evident nucleolus (Fig 5–7 and 5–8). The cytoplasm is rich in granular endoplasmic reticulum, and the Golgi apparatus is well developed (Figs 5–7 and 5–8).

The fibrocyte is a smaller cell. It tends to be spindle-shaped and has fewer processes than the young fibroblast. It presents a smaller—and darker—elongated nucleus and an acidophilic cytoplasm (Fig 5–7).

The electron microscope shows that the fibrocyte has a less well developed granular endoplasmic reticulum and Golgi apparatus than the young fibroblast. When it is adequately stimulated, the fibrocyte may again synthesize fibers. This occurs during wound healing, and in such instances the cell resumes the form and appearance of a young fibroblast.

The functions of the fibroblasts have been studied in radioautographs examined under the light and electron microscope. It has been demonstrated that these cells synthesize both the collagen and the acid mucopolysaccharides of the amorphous intercellular substance. Proline and glycine labeled with ^{3}H have been used in the study of collagen synthesis. The same technic has been used to study the synthesis of collagen in other polarized cells that produce collagen; these cells secrete all of their collagen at one pole. This is the case with osteoblasts and odontoblasts, polarized cells responsible for the production of the collagen of bone and dentin, respectively. The fibroblast that is present in common connective tissue (eg, in the skin) is not a polarized cell and secretes collagen over its entire surface.

Radioautographic technics have also revealed that tropocollagen synthesized by the granular endoplasmic reticulum accumulates in the cisternae of this structure. It is subsequently encountered in the Golgi apparatus and is then transported to the outside of the cell (Fig 5–9). Collagen, therefore, most probably follows the same path as other secreted proteins (see Chapter 4). Evidence has been presented, however, that in some cases part of the synthesized collagen might be secreted by the fibroblast by means of a direct communication between the endoplasmic reticulum and the cell membrane without passing through the Golgi apparatus (Fig 5–9).

The synthesis of acid mucopolysaccharides has been studied mainly by radioautography after the administration of sulfate labeled with ^{35}S, since many connective tissue acid mucopolysaccharides are sulfated. It is possible that fibroblasts synthesize collagen and acid mucopolysaccharides at the same time, although some cell culture experiments indicate that a cell that produces collagen in substantial amounts produces little acid mucopolysaccharide and vice versa. It is also possible that the rate of secretion of different molecules of connective tissue by the same cell might vary with the age of the individual or in response to hormonal influences.

Fibroblasts secrete tropocollagen molecules into the intercellular matrix, and their polymerization into microfibrils takes place outside the cytoplasm (Fig 5–9). Part of the cytoplasm of the fibroblasts, being extremely thin at the periphery of the cell and containing the formed microfibril, detaches itself from the remainder of the cell.

In adults, fibroblasts in connective tissue rarely undergo division. Mitoses are observed only when the organism requires more fibroblasts, ie, when connective tissue is damaged. In this instance, they also develop from undifferentiated mesenchymal cells.

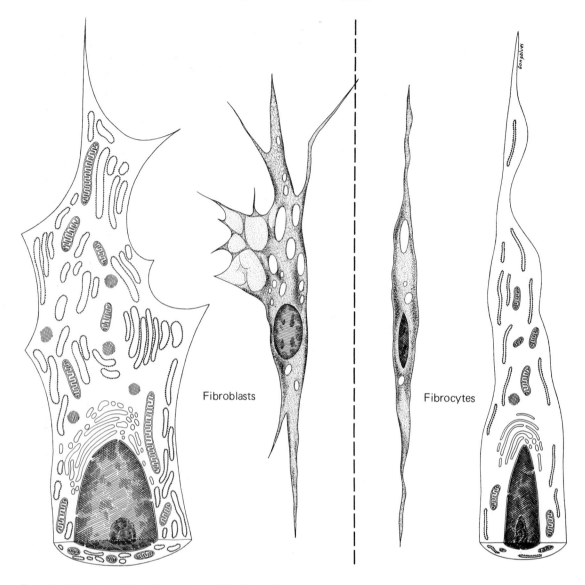

Figure 5—7. Immature *(left)* and mature *(right)* fibroblasts. External morphology and ultrastructure of each cell are shown. Immature or young fibroblasts are richer in mitochondria, lipid droplets, Golgi apparatus, and granular endoplasmic reticulum than mature fibroblasts, often called fibrocytes.

Macrophages

The macrophage is distinguished by its great capacity for pinocytosis and phagocytosis rather than by its morphologic characteristics, which vary according to its functional state and localization. Macrophages are either fixed or wandering. Fixed macrophages are also known as *histiocytes;* wandering macrophages migrate by means of ameboid movement.

The phagocytic capacity of the macrophages permits their identification. When a vital dye such as trypan blue, India ink, or lithium carmine is injected into an animal, the macrophages engulf it and accumulate it in their cytoplasm in the form of granules visible under the light microscope. Fixed macrophages are spindle-shaped or star-shaped and have an ovoid nucle-

us with condensed chromatin. In loose connective tissue, macrophages are almost as numerous as the fibroblasts and can be mistaken for them.

The wandering macrophage is more active in phagocytosis than the fixed macrophage. It migrates and phagocytoses by means of short, thick pseudopodia which cause it to have an irregular shape. The nucleus contains condensed chromatin and is usually kidney-shaped.

The electron microscope reveals that the surface of the macrophage is irregular; its plasma membrane is pleated and contains protrusions and indentations (Fig 5—10). These cells have lysosomes which spill their contents into vacuoles containing phagocytosed material, giving rise to secondary lysosomes or phagosomes

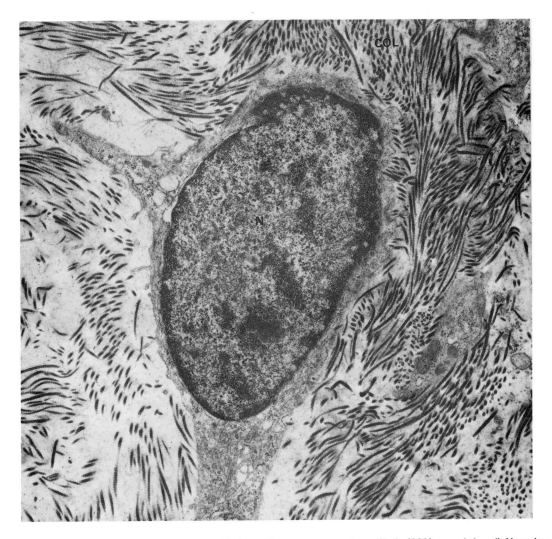

Figure 5–8. Electron micrograph of an immature fibroblast. There are many collagen fibrils (COL) around the cell. N, nucleus. × 7000.

in which digestion of the engulfed material occurs. The surface charge of the particle to be phagocytosed plays an important role in the initiation of phagocytosis. Materials with positive charge are easily engulfed; those with negative or neutral charge are seldom phagocytosed.

Fixed and wandering macrophages are different phases of the same cell, and one may transform itself into the other. It is more frequent for a fixed macrophage to be transformed into a wandering macrophage than vice versa.

Because of their capacity for locomotion and phagocytosis, the main function of macrophages is in the defense of the organism. They engulf cellular remains, altered intercellular substances, microorganisms, and inert particles that enter the body. When they encounter large foreign bodies, macrophages fuse together to form large cells with 100 or more nuclei called *foreign body giant cells* (Fig 5–11).

Undifferentiated Mesenchymal Cells

In connective tissue in adults, some cells persist with the same potentiality as embryonic mesenchymal cells, ie, the ability to give rise to any kind of connective tissue cell. When they are located in connective tissue which forms blood and lymph cells (myeloid and lymphoid tissues), these undifferentiated cells are called *primitive reticular cells.* When they are located in other types of connective tissue, they are called *adventitial cells* because they are usually found along the blood capillaries.

Morphologically, adventitial cells are quite similar to fibroblasts and macrophages, which makes their identification difficult in some instances. They are smaller than fibroblasts and possess elongated nuclei with coarse chromatin.

The primitive reticular cell is described in Chapter 15 along with the other cells of the hematopoietic tissues.

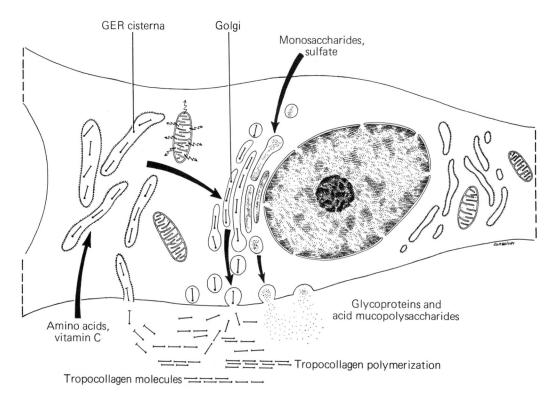

Figure 5–9. Synthesis and extrusion of collagen and glycoprotein molecules by fibroblasts. Tropocollagen molecules are segregated in the cisternae of the granular endoplasmic reticulum (GER); they move to the Golgi complex and next appear in the extracellular spaces. Much evidence points to the Golgi complex as the site of acid mucopolysaccharide synthesis. It is also in the Golgi complex that protein molecules combine with acid mucopolysaccharides to complete the proteoglycan complexes of amorphous ground substance.

Mast Cells

A mast cell is large and ovoid. Its cytoplasm is full of basophilic granules, which stain intensely (Fig 5–12). The nucleus of the mast cell is spherical and centrally situated. Because the nucleus is covered by cytoplasmic granules, it sometimes cannot be seen.

Mast cells are numerous in several types of connective tissue but are difficult to detect in hematoxylin and eosin preparations. They are easily demonstrated by toluidine blue, which stains their granules reddish purple.

The property that cells and tissues have of changing the color of a dye they are stained with is called *metachromasia.* It is believed to be due to the presence of numerous acidic groups in the structure amenable to metachromatic staining. Mast cell granules are surrounded by a unit membrane (Fig 5–13). They consist mainly of acid and neutral mucopolysaccharides in association with proteins. They are therefore PAS-positive and stain with alcian blue. Heparin, which contains sulfate, is the best known acid mucopolysaccharide of these granules.

In addition to heparin, the granules of the mast cells contain histamine. Both of these substances are synthesized by the mast cells. In some animals (but not in man), these granules also contain serotonin. The role

played by the mast cells in human physiology is still obscure, although the effects of heparin and histamine have been well studied. Heparin is an anticoagulant; histamine causes contraction of part of the smooth muscle (mainly the bronchioles) and dilates blood capillaries and increases their permeability.

Mast cells liberate heparin and histamine during *anaphylactic shock,* a potentially fatal condition which may occur when the organism comes into contact with an antigen to which it has been previously sensitized. Anaphylactic shock may occur, for example, when a person is injected with tetanus antitoxin some months after having had one or several injections of it. The process of anaphylaxis probably consists of the following events in sequence: Antibodies are formed after the first administration of antitoxin and are absorbed on the surface of the mast cells. With the second administration, the antitoxin reacts with the antibodies absorbed on the surface of the mast cells and triggers the release of mast cell granules, which contain heparin and histamine (Fig 5–14). Mast cells probably play an important part in anaphylactic shock, but they are not the only cells that do so.

Extrusion of mast cell granules is an active, energy-consuming process that may be easily observed with the light microscope. Extrusion is inhibited by

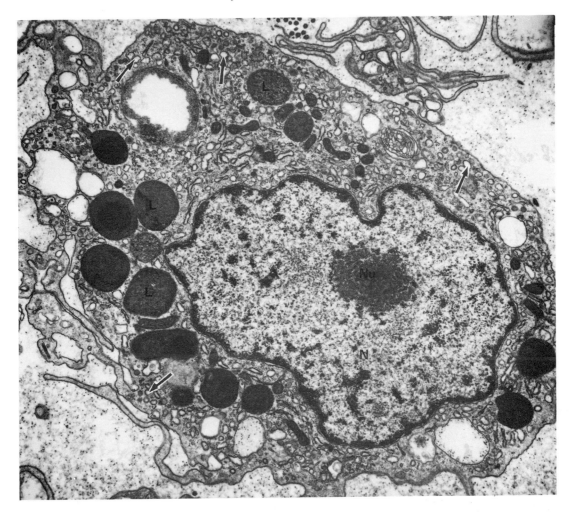

Figure 5–10. Electron micrograph of a macrophage. Note the secondary lysosomes (L), the nucleus (N), and the nucleolus (Nu). The arrows point to pinocytotic vesicles. Reduced from × 15,000.

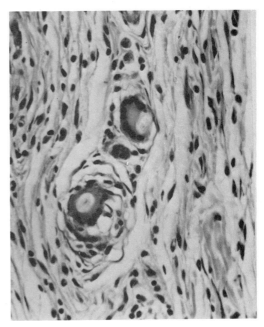

Figure 5–11 (at right). Photomicrograph of 2 foreign body giant cells. Both cells contain, in their cytoplasm, phagocytosed material which appears lightly stained. At the periphery of these cells, many nuclei can be seen. H&E stain, × 320.

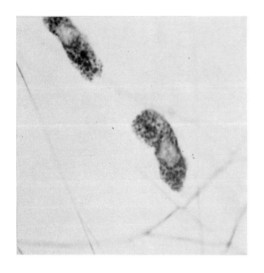

Figure 5–12. Whole mount of spread mesentery. Two mast cells appear stained by Gomori's aldehyde-fuchsin. X 400.

cytochalasin, a compound which depolymerizes microfilaments, which suggests that microfilaments participate in the release of mast cell granules.

Plasma Cells

Plasma cells usually appear infrequently in connective tissue. However, they are numerous in sites subject to the penetration of bacteria and foreign proteins (eg, intestinal mucosa) and in regions where there is chronic inflammation.

Plasma cells are ovoid and have a basophilic cytoplasm owing to their richness in granular endoplasmic reticulum. The Golgi apparatus and the centrioles are next to the nucleus, occupying a region which appears light in regular histologic preparations (Fig 5–15). The nucleus of the plasma cells is spherical, containing compact, coarse, flaky chromatin alternating with lighter areas of approximately equal size. The configuration resembles a wheel with spokes, giving the nucleus a clock-face appearance (Fig 5–15).

For a long time there were doubts about whether plasma cells synthesized antibodies. It is now known, however, that plasma cells are responsible for the

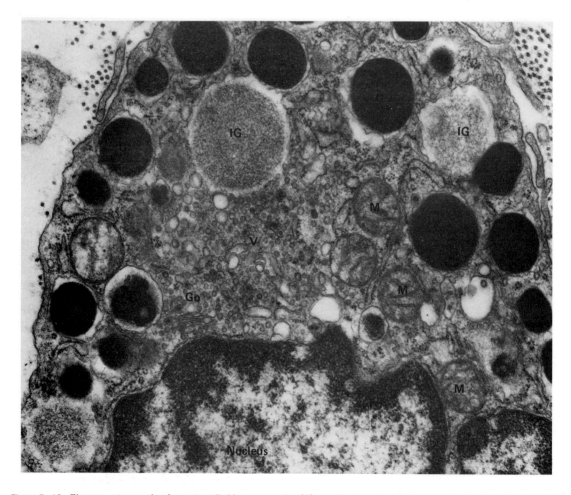

Figure 5–13. Electron micrograph of a mast cell. Mature granules (G) are electron-dense and appear darker than the immature granules (IG). M, mitochondria; Go, Golgi apparatus; V, small and large Golgi vesicles. X 36,000.

synthesis of the antibodies found in the bloodstream. Antibodies are specific gamma globulins produced by the organism in response to the penetration of antigens. Each synthesized antibody is specific for the one antigen that gave rise to its production and reacts with it. The results of the antibody-antigen reaction are variable. Its capacity to neutralize harmful effects which the antigen may cause is very important. When an antigen is bound to the plasma membrane of a cell, its reaction with an antibody present there may result in damage to and even destruction of the cell. When an antigen is a toxin (eg, tetanus, diphtheria), it may lose its capacity to do harm when it combines with its respective antibody.

By means of immunofluorescence and cytochemical technics, it has been demonstrated at the electron microscopic level that, after injection of an antigen, the corresponding antibody appears first in the cytoplasm of the plasma cell. Experiments involving injection of a vegetable protein (peroxidase) into animals as an antigen have shown that the first intracellular site in which antibodies appear is the cisternae of the granular endoplasmic reticulum. The morphology of the plasma cells also indicates intense protein synthesis, for they are very rich in granular endoplasmic reticulum (Figs 5–15 and 5–16).

Many of the antibodies synthesized by the plasma cells are specific for bacterial antigens and thus protect the body against these microorganisms. Since bacteria are never found inside plasma cells but rather are engulfed by the macrophages, it is thought that there is a mechanism by which the plasma cell "learns" about the nature of the antigens present in the bacteria. Although the process by which this information is transmitted has not been completely elucidated, it has been shown by the electron microscope that cellular contact occurs between macrophages and precursor cells of plasma (see Chapters 14 and 15). This suggests a transfer of information-bearing substances. It has also been demonstrated that extracts of macrophages that have phagocytosed certain antigens are able to induce the appearance of plasma cells which form antibodies against these antigens (Fig 5–17).

Even though it is well demonstrated experimentally that some antigens need contact with macrophages in order to produce antibody-forming plasma cells, it is also true that other antigens act directly on plasma cells. In such instances, the plasma cells synthesize antibodies without assistance from macrophages.

Adipose Cells

Adipose cells (adipocytes) are cells that have be-

Figure 5–14 (at right). Schematic drawing showing how antigens act on mast cells. Antibodies synthesized by plasma cells become attached to the surface of mast cells. A new injection of the same antigen promotes the liberation of mast cell granules through the combination of the newly injected antigen with membrane-fixed antibodies. Mast cell granules liberate histamine and heparin in the intercellular space.

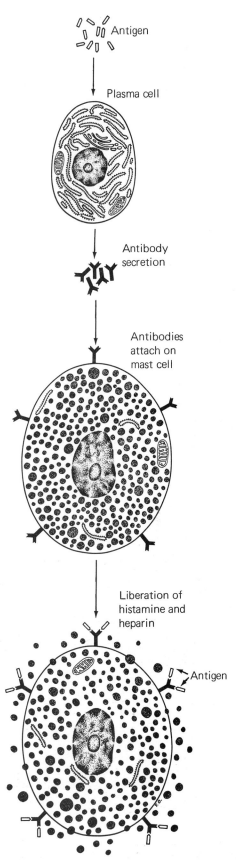

Antigen

Plasma cell

Antibody secretion

Antibodies attach on mast cell

Liberation of histamine and heparin

Antigen

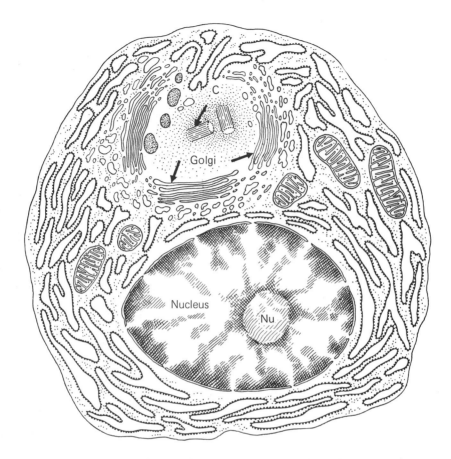

Figure 5–15. Ultrastructure of a plasma cell. The cell contains a well-developed granular endoplasmic reticulum, with dilated cisternae containing gamma globulins (antibodies). In plasma cells, the secreted proteins do not aggregate into secretory granules. Nu, nucleolus; C, centriole. (Redrawn and reproduced, with permission, from Ham AW: *Histology,* 6th ed. Lippincott, 1969.)

come specialized for storage of neutral fats. They are discussed in Chapter 6.

Leukocytes

Leukocytes or white blood corpuscles are frequently found in connective tissue. In general, they migrate across the capillary and venule walls from the blood. There is a continuous exchange of leukocytes between blood and connective tissue, and this process increases greatly during inflammation. Eosinophils and lymphocytes are the leukocytes most frequently encountered in normal connective tissue.

A. Eosinophils: The main morphologic characteristics of eosinophils are the granules in their cytoplasm (lysosomes). Electron microscopic examination shows that they have a membrane and, in their interior, a flat crystal embedded in a granular substance. The nucleus of these cells usually has 2 lobes (Fig 5–18).

The number of eosinophils increases during the course of allergic and parasitic diseases as well as other types of disease. It is believed that these cells contain histamine, though in much lower quantity than is found in mast cells.

The injection of a protein causes an increase in

the number of eosinophils in the injected area, and it is known that this attraction is due to the complex formed by the reaction of the injected protein and its antibody. It has also been demonstrated that, although the antigen-antibody complex is promptly phagocytosed by these cells, they are not active in the phagocytosis of bacteria and foreign particles.

The principal experiments that led to this concept were performed by injecting—separately—an antigen (bovine albumin) or its antibody into the peritoneal cavities of guinea pigs. The antigen was coupled with a red fluorescent dye; the antibody was coupled with a green fluorescent dye. It was observed that neither the antigens nor the antibodies were phagocytosed by the eosinophils. However, when the fluorescent antigen and antibody were administered together, the eosinophils manifested a yellow fluorescence, which suggests that the function of these cells is to engulf the antigen-antibody complex.

B. Lymphocytes: Connective tissue lymphocytes have a diameter of 6–8 μm (small lymphocytes). They have a small amount of slightly basophilic cytoplasm and a large, dark nucleus with condensed chromatin that sometimes shows an indentation. The nucleolus is

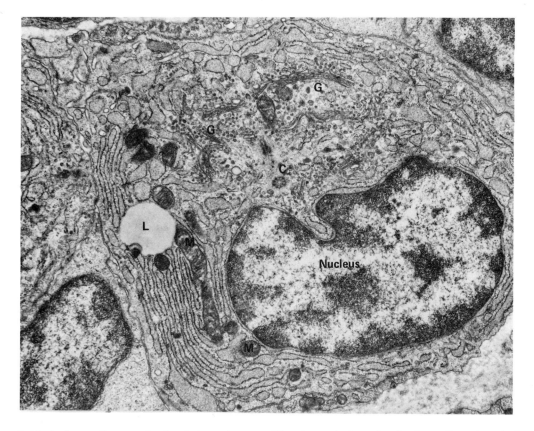

Figure 5–16. A plasma cell seen under the electron microscope. The micrograph shows the abundance of granular endoplasmic reticulum. Observe that many cisternae are dilated. M, mitochondria; G, Golgi apparatus; C, centriole; L, lipid droplet. × 18,000.

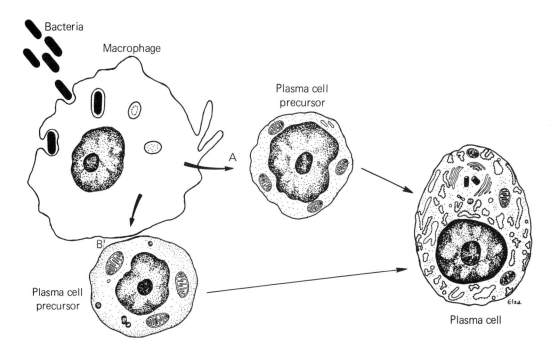

Figure 5–17. Possible relationships between macrophages and plasma cells. It has been shown that some kind of information passes from macrophages to plasma cell precursors. Bridges have been seen by some authors under the electron microscope between these 2 cell types (*B*).

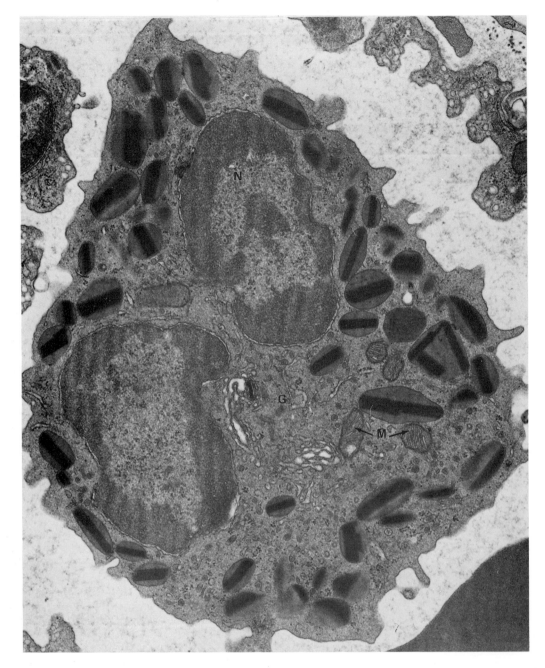

Figure 5—18. Electron micrograph of an eosinophil from rat connective tissue. Typical eosinophilic granules are clearly seen. Each granule has a disk-shaped crystal which is electron-dense and appears surrounded by a matrix which is enveloped by a unit membrane. N, nucleus; G, Golgi apparatus; M, mitochondria. ✕ 20,000. (Courtesy of KR Porter.)

not visible under the light microscope.

The lymphocytes of the connective tissue form a heterogeneous population. Some of them have a long life span (many months to several years), whereas others live for only a short time (a few days or weeks). At least 2 functional types have been recognized: (1) the *T lymphocytes,* which are responsible for initiating cell-mediated immune responses and have a long life; and (2) the *B lymphocytes,* which, when stimulated by

an antigen, divide several times and generate plasma cells which in turn secrete antibodies specific to the antigen. Their function is related to the humoral immune responses, and their life span is short.

The lymphocytes of the lamina propria of the intestinal epithelium migrate across it and are destroyed when they enter the lumen of the alimentary canal. This phenomenon also takes place in the tonsils, which accumulate large numbers of lymphocytes beneath the epithelium.

The relationships between cells found in different types of connective tissue are shown in Fig 5–19. For further discussions of lymphocytes, see Chapters 13, 14, and 15.

AMORPHOUS INTERCELLULAR SUBSTANCE

Amorphous intercellular substance is colorless, transparent, and homogeneous. It is difficult to study it in the fresh state. It fills the space between cells and fibers of connective tissue; it is viscous and acts as a barrier to the penetration of foreign particles into the tissues.

Intercellular substance is poorly preserved by histologic fixatives. In common preparations, it appears as a granular material among the cells and fibers of connective tissue. Histologic preservation of this substance is possible with the freeze-drying technic, which consists of freezing tissue rapidly to the temperature of liquid nitrogen (-200 °C) and removing water by means of sublimation performed at high vacuum at a temperature of -30 °C. The water, instantaneously solidified during freezing, is removed without passing through the liquid phase during drying. This method does not really fix the tissues, but it dehydrates them so that their morphologic and chemical characteristics are maintained almost unaltered. The tissues can then be fixed by nonpolar substances, and the intercellular substance can be stained by several methods including the PAS technic. It appears as a homogeneous component among the structural elements of connective tissue.

The exact chemical nature of amorphous intercellular substance of connective tissue is not completely clear, but it is composed mainly of acid mucopolysaccharides and complexes of protein with carbohydrates referred to as glycoproteins.

The term *acid mucopolysaccharides* was used originally to designate extracted polysaccharides of connective tissue rich in hexosamine or materials stained by histochemical reactions with basic dyes. In the last few years, other terms have been introduced to further classify these substances: *glycosaminoglycans* (polysaccharides that contain amino sugars), *galactosaminoglycans* (polysaccharides that contain galactosamine), *glucosaminoglycuronates* (polysaccharides that contain amino sugars and uronic acids), *glucosaminoglycans* (polysaccharides that contain glucosamine), *deoxylglucosaminoglycans,* etc. The terms proteoglycans, glycoproteins, mucoproteins, etc are often used synonymously with the term acid mucopolysaccharides. In this book, the following terms will be used: (1) *acid mucopolysaccharides* or *proteoglycans* or *glycosaminoglycans* and (2) *structural glycoproteins.* The acid mucopolysaccharides are protein-polysaccharide complexes having a large polysaccharide moiety including characteristic repeating disaccharide units.

The most common form of uronic acid is glucuronic acid, and the most common hexosamines are glycosamine and galactosamine. The acid mucopolysaccharides of connective tissue form very large molecules which become even larger by their association with other proteins. Polymerization of these acid mucopolysaccharides is variable and is in direct proportion to the viscosity of the amorphous substance.

The structural glycoproteins are conjugated proteins containing as prosthetic groups one or more saccharides with relatively few sugar residues, in the great majority of cases without repeating units in their carbohydrate fraction. These are glycoproteins extracted from connective tissue by a specific procedure and are different from serum glycoproteins. They are synthesized by fibroblasts in the connective tissue–cartilage cells in cartilage and smooth muscle cells in the walls of vessels.

The general type of synthesis for both groups of substances (collectively called glycoconjugates) consists of the formation of a protein core and the subsequent addition of repeating, usually similar acid mucopolysaccharide units or structural glycoproteins. It is generally accepted that the polypeptide units of the glycoproteins assembled within the liver cell occur on membrane-bound ribosomes. Initial sugar molecules are added while this core material traverses the lumen of granular or smooth endoplasmic reticulum. Other sugar components on the external surface of the molecule are added at the Golgi apparatus level. Polymerizing and transfer enzymes have been isolated, the first mainly from smooth and the second from granular endoplasmic reticulum. In different tissues (aorta, cartilage, cornea, heart valves, skin, synovial membranes, and tendons) they yield similar but not identical structural glycoproteins, and they are unrelated to collagen or elastin.

Table 5–1 illustrates the chemical composition of the most common acid mucopolysaccharides in connective tissue, some of which are sulfated. Hyaluronic acid is the most common nonsulfated acid mucopolysaccharide in connective tissue. It is not known whether the peptide core is present to start with or whether the linkage develops later in the ground substance itself. Chondroitin sulfate is the most abundant of the sulfated acid mucopolysaccharides but not so abundant as hyaluronic acid. Sulfated acid mucopolysaccharides give a solid appearance to tissues where they are present, whereas tissues containing hyaluronic acid are soft.

These acid mucopolysaccharides are covalently bound to proteins. Because they have numerous negative radicals in their molecules, the acid mucopolysaccharides are polyanions and are able to combine with a great number of cations by electrovalency. In connective tissue, sodium is the most frequent cation bound to acid mucopolysaccharides.

Acid mucopolysaccharides play an important role in regulating the amount of water in connective tissue.

Each molecule of acid mucopolysaccharide is extremely hydrophilic and combines with a great number

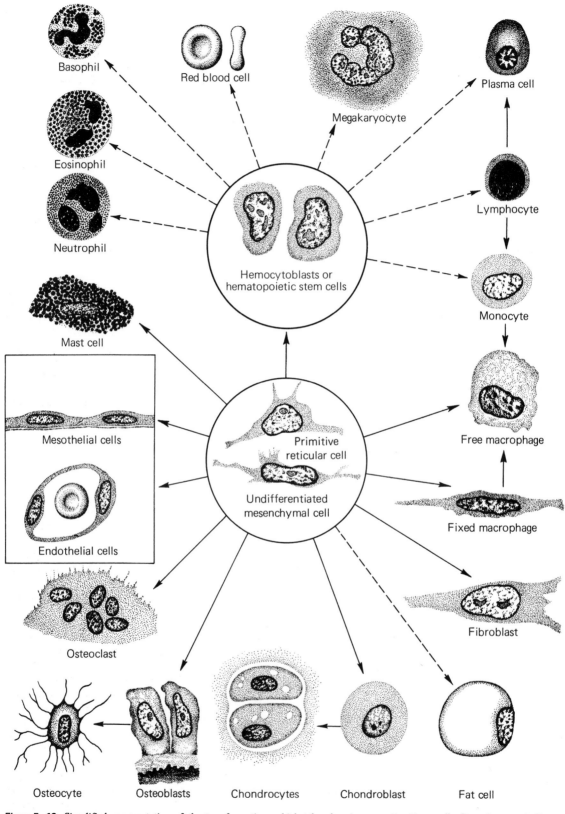

Figure 5—19. Simplified representation of the transformations which take place in connective tissue cells. Dotted arrows indicate that intermediate cell types exist between the pointed ones. The 2 cell types enclosed in the rectangle at left are epithelial morphologically, but they originate from the mesenchyme and retain several mesenchymal properties.

Table 5—1. Main components of connective tissue acid mucopolysaccharides or proteoglycans.

Acid Mucopolysaccharides	Disaccharide Unit	Location
Hyaluronic acid*	D-Glucuronic acid + N-acetyl-D-glucosamine	Skin, umbilical cord, vitreous, synovial fluid, heart valves, cornea; produced also by bacteria
Chondroitin*	D-Glucuronic acid + N-acetyl-D-galactosamine; some sulfate esters	Cornea, embryonic cartilage
Chondroitin-4-sulfate* (sulfate of chondroitin A)	D-Glucuronic acid + N-acetyl-D-galactosamine-4-sulfate	Cartilage, bone, cornea, skin
Chondroitin-6-sulfate* (sulfate of chondroitin C)	D-Glucuronic acid + N-acetyl-D-galactosamine-6-sulfate	Cartilage, tendon, umbilical cord, intervertebral disk, embryonic cartilage
Dermatan sulfate (chondroitin sulfate B)	L-Iduronic acid + N-acetyl-D-galactosamine-6-sulfate	Skin, tendon, ligaments, heart valves
Keratan sulfate	D-Galactose + N-acetyl-glucosamine-6-sulfate	Cartilage, intervertebral disk, bone, cornea

*Hydrolyzed by testicular hyaluronidase.

of molecules of water. Almost all water present in the amorphous intercellular substance of connective tissue is in the form of solvation water of acid mucopolysaccharide molecules. Even so, this water permits the diffusion of numerous water-soluble substances throughout connective tissue without fluid movement. The solvation water forms several layers around the acid mucopolysaccharide molecules, which become more irregular and unstable as they become more distant from these macromolecules. It is impossible to aspirate liquid from connective tissue with a hypodermic syringe because most of the water in amorphous intercellular substance is conjugated to acid mucopolysaccharide.

One interesting aspect of the distribution of the different acid mucopolysaccharides in vertebrate tissue is the variation of their relative proportions with age. Induction of calcification, control of metabolites, ions, and water, and healing of wounds are important roles of these compounds. They are genetically controlled, and disturbances in their metabolism results in pathologic conditions—the so-called lysosomal diseases. In some of these disorders, the degradation of dermatan sulfate or heparan sulfate is blocked at the lysosomal level by biochemically defective fibroblasts. Lack of hydrolase in the lysosomes has been found as the cause

of these disorders in humans. Examples are Hurler's syndrome, Hunter's syndrome, Sanfilippo syndrome, and Morquio's syndrome.

Glycoprotein molecules sometimes show significant variations in their side chains in response to changes in environmental conditions. They may influence the processes of development and adaptation, thus functioning as secondary informational macromolecules.

In connective tissue, in addition to the amorphous substance, there is a very small quantity of fluid—called *tissue fluid*—that is similar to blood plasma in its content of ions and diffusible substances. Tissue fluid contains a small percentage of plasma proteins of low molecular weight which pass through the capillary walls as a consequence of the hydrostatic pressure of the blood. Under normal conditions, the quantity of tissue fluid is insignificant.

Edema

The water in the intercellular substance of connective tissue comes from the blood, passing through the capillary walls into the intercellular regions of the tissue. The capillary wall is impermeable to macromolecules but permits the passage of water and small molecules, including low molecular weight proteins.

Blood brings to connective tissue the different nutrients required by the cells and carries metabolic waste products away to the detoxifying and excretory organs (liver, kidney, etc).

There are 2 forces acting on the water contained in the capillaries: (1) the hydrostatic pressure of the blood, a consequence of the pumping action of the heart, which forces water to pass through the capillary walls; and (2) the osmotic pressure of the blood plasma, which draws water back into the capillaries. Osmotic pressure is due mainly to plasma proteins because the ions and crystalloids that pass easily through the capillary walls have approximately the same concentration inside and outside these blood vessels. Therefore, osmotic pressure exerted by these ions and crystalloids is approximately equal on either side of the capillaries and cancel each other. However, the osmotic pressure exerted by the blood protein macromolecules (colloid osmotic pressure)—which are unable to pass through the capillary walls—is not counterbalanced by outside pressure and therefore tends to bring water into the blood vessel.

Normally, water passes through capillary walls to the surrounding tissues at the arterial end of a capillary. This occurs because the hydrostatic pressure at this level is greater than the colloid osmotic pressure. However, hydrostatic pressure decreases along the length of the capillary toward the venous end. As hydrostatic pressure falls, osmotic pressure rises because of the progressive increase in the concentration of proteins, which is determined by the passage of water from the capillaries. As a result of the increase in protein concentration and the fall in hydrostatic pressure, osmotic pressure becomes greater than hydrostatic pressure at the venous end of the capillary, and

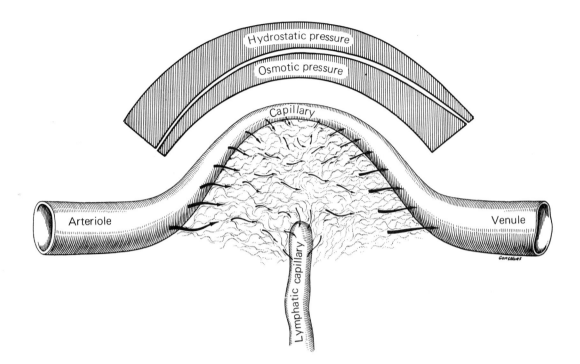

Figure 5–20. Movement of water through connective tissue. From the arterial to the venous parts of the blood capillaries there is a decrease in hydrostatic pressure and an increase in osmotic pressure (upper part of drawing). Water leaves the capillary through its arterial end and penetrates back into the blood at the venous end of the capillaries. Some water is drained by the lymphatic capillaries.

water is thus drawn back into the capillary (Fig 5–20).

It has been demonstrated that the quantity of water drawn back is less than that which passes out through the capillaries. Thus, the portion of water that remains in the connective tissue is brought back to the blood by the lymphatic vessels. The smallest lymphatic vessels are the lymphatic capillaries, which originate in connective tissue with blind ends. Terminal lymphatic vessels drain into veins at the base of the neck.

There is, therefore, little free water in the tissue because of the equilibrium that exists between the water entering and the water leaving the intercellular substance of connective tissue.

In several pathologic conditions, the quantity of tissue fluid may increase considerably, causing edema. Histologically, this condition is characterized by enlarged spaces between the components of the connective tissue caused by the increase in liquid. Macroscopically, edema can appear as an increase in volume that yields easily to localized pressure, creating a depression which slowly disappears ("pitting edema").

Edema may result from venous obstruction or decrease in venous blood flow (eg, congestive heart failure). It may also be caused by starvation because the consequent protein deficiency results in lack of plasma proteins and, in turn, a fall in colloid osmotic pressure. Water therefore accumulates in the connective tissue.

Another possible cause of edema is increased

permeability of the blood capillary endothelium due to mechanical injury or to some substance produced in the body (eg, histamine).

Edema may be caused also by the obstruction of lymphatic vessels, eg, by plugs of parasites or tumor cells.

TYPES OF CONNECTIVE TISSUE

There are several types of connective tissue that consist of the basic components already described— fibers, cells, and amorphous intercellular substance. The names given to the different types denote either the component that predominates in the tissue or a structural characteristic of the tissue.

The classification shown in Fig 5–21 does not include all possible types of connective tissue.

Connective Tissue Proper

In connective tissue proper, no single component predominates. There are 2 types: loose and dense.

A. Loose Connective Tissue: This tissue—also called areolar tissue—is the more abundant of the 2 types. It fills spaces between fibers and muscle sheaths, supports epithelial tissue, and forms a layer which encircles the lymphatic and blood vessels. Loose connec-

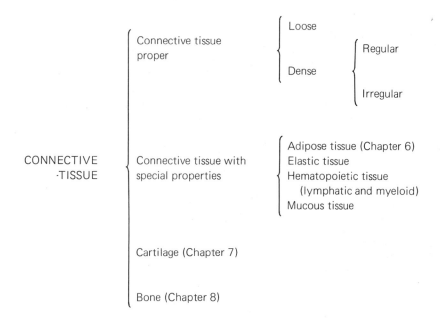

CONNECTIVE
-TISSUE

Connective tissue proper
- Loose
- Dense
  - Regular
  - Irregular

Connective tissue with special properties
- Adipose tissue (Chapter 6)
- Elastic tissue
- Hematopoietic tissue (lymphatic and myeloid)
- Mucous tissue

Cartilage (Chapter 7)

Bone (Chapter 8)

Figure 5–21. Simplified scheme of the interrelationships of the principal types of connective tissue.

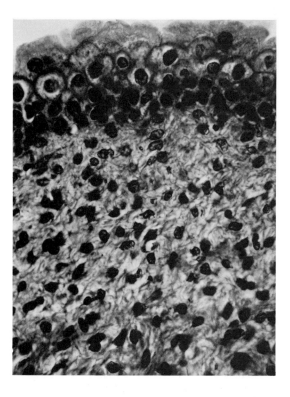

Figure 5–22. Photomicrograph of a section through the wall of the urinary bladder. Under the transitional epithelium there is a layer of loose connective tissue containing numerous cells. H&E stain, X 400.

tive tissue is found mainly in the papillary layer of the dermis, in the hypodermis, in the serosal linings of peritoneal and pleural cavities, and in glands and mucous membranes (wet membranes that line the hollow organs) supporting the epithelial cells.

Loose connective tissue is composed of all the main components of connective tissue proper (Fig 5–22). The most numerous cells are the fibroblasts and macrophages, but all of the other types of connective tissue cells are present also. Collagenous, elastic, and reticular fibers also appear in this tissue, though the proportion of reticular fibers is small. They tend to accumulate only where connective tissue comes into contact with other structures.

Loose connective tissue has a delicate consistency; it is flexible and not very resistant to stress.

B. Dense Connective Tissue: This type of tissue is composed of the same components found in loose connective tissue, but there is a clear predominance of collagenous fibers. Histologic preparations reveal that this tissue has fewer cells than loose connective tissue. The fibroblasts are most common. Dense connective tissue is less flexible and far more resistant to stress. It is known as irregular dense connective tissue when the collagenous fibers are arranged in bundles without a definite orientation. The collagenous fibers form a 3-dimensional network in this tissue and provide adequate resistance to stress from all directions (Fig 5–23). This type of tissue is encountered in the dermis of the skin and in the submucosa of the digestive tract.

The collagenous bundles of regular dense connective tissue are arranged according to a definite pattern. The collagenous fibers of this tissue are formed in response to prolonged stresses exerted in the same direc-

Figure 5—23. Irregular dense connective tissue. This tissue contains many randomly placed collagen fibers. H&E stain, × 320.

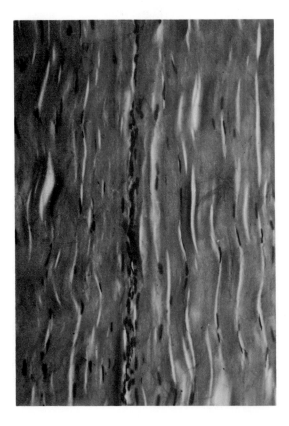

Figure 5—24. Regular dense connective tissue (longitudinal section through a tendon). There are numerous collagen bundles in parallel array. H&E stain, × 320.

tion. The fibers are arranged in a plane and offer great resistance to traction forces.

Tendons are the most common example of regular dense connective tissue. They are elongated, cylindric structures that function to attach striated muscle to bone; they are white and inextensible by virtue of their richness in collagenous fibers. They have parallel, closely packed bundles of collagenous fibers separated by a small quantity of amorphous intercellular substance. Their fibroblasts contain elongated nuclei parallel to the fibers and a sparse cytoplasm which tends to envelop the collagenous bundles. Their cytoplasm is rarely revealed in hematoxylin and eosin stains—not only because it is sparse but also because it has the same pink color as the fibers (Fig 5—24).

The collagenous bundles of the tendons (primary bundles) aggregate into larger bundles (secondary bundles) that are enveloped by loose connective tissue containing blood vessels and nerves. Externally, the tendon is surrounded by a sheath of dense connective tissue. In some tendons, this sheath is made up of 2 layers, both lined by squamous cells of mesenchymal origin. One layer is fixed to the tendon and the other is attached to the neighboring structures. Thus, a cavity containing a viscous fluid (similar to synovial fluid) is formed between the 2 layers. This fluid, which contains water, proteins, acid mucopolysaccharides, and ions, permits an easy sliding movement of the tendon.

Elastic Tissue

Elastic tissue is composed of bundles of thick, parallel elastic fibers. Around each bundle there is a small amount of loose connective tissue, and flattened fibroblasts, similar to those of tendons, are found between the elastic fibers. The abundance of elastic fibers

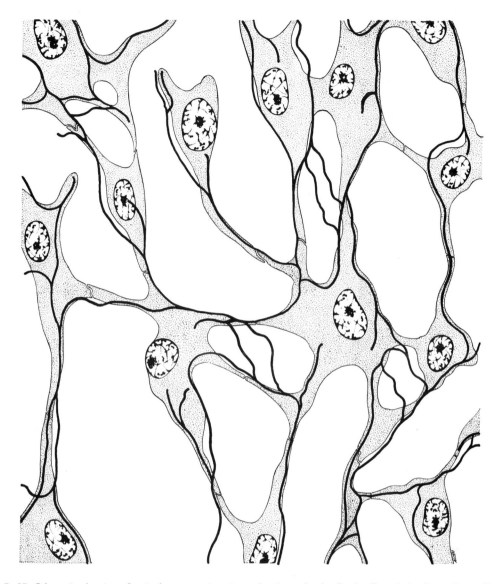

Figure 5–25. Schematic drawing of reticular connective tissue showing only the fixed cells and the fibers. Free cells are not represented. Reticular fibers are enveloped in the cytoplasm of reticular cells; however, the fibers are extracellular, being separated from the cytoplasm by the cell membrane.

in this tissue confers on it a typical yellow color and great elasticity. Elastic tissue occurs infrequently. It is present in the yellow ligaments of the vertebral column and in the suspensory ligament of the penis.

Reticular Tissue

Reticular tissue is composed of reticular fibers closely associated with primitive reticular cells which, according to some investigators, have the same potentiality as undifferentiated mesenchymal cells. Reticular tissue is encountered in the organs that produce blood cells (hematopoietic organs) and comprises the framework which supports the free cells found in these organs (Fig 5–25). Primitive reticular cells have long extensions which are in contact with those of neigh-

boring cells. Their nuclei are large, with fine chromatin and one or more visible nucleoli.

Mucous Tissue

Mucous tissue has an abundance of amorphous intercellular substance. It is a jellylike tissue containing collagenous fibers and a few elastic or reticular fibers. The cells in this tissue are chiefly fibroblasts. Mucous tissue is the chief component of the umbilical cord and is called Wharton's jelly. It is also found in the pulp of young teeth (see Chapter 16).

HISTOPHYSIOLOGY

Connective tissues have the functions of support, packing, storage, transport, defense, and repair. The functions of support and packing are obvious—epithelial, muscular, and nerve tissues are associated with connective tissue which supports and fills the tissue spaces between their cells. The support function is carried out mainly by connective tissue fibers.

Collagenous fibers constitute tendons, aponeuroses, capsules of organs, and membranes which envelop the central nervous system (meninges). They also make up the trabeculae and walls inside several organs, forming the most resistant component of the stroma (support tissue) of these organs.

Storage

Lipids, which are important nutritional reserves, are stored in adipose tissue, which is a type of connective tissue (see Chapter 6). In addition, because of its richness in acid mucopolysaccharides, loose connective tissue stores water and electrolytes. The most abundant electrolyte is sodium. Although only a small percentage of connective tissue consists of plasma proteins, because of its large size it is estimated that one-third of the plasma proteins of the body are stored in the intercellular connective tissue compartment.

Defense

Several defense mechanisms depend upon the cells and intercellular components of connective tissue. This tissue contains phagocytic cells (macrophages) and plasma cells, which synthesize antibodies. In addition, because of its viscosity, the intercellular substance acts as a barrier to the penetration of bacteria and inert particles. Bacteria that produce *hyaluronidase* have great invasive power, for this enzyme hydrolyzes hyaluronic acid and other acid mucopolysaccharides of the connective tissue, thus reducing the viscosity of the intercellular substance and facilitating their invasion.

The diverse mechanisms that constitute the reaction known as *inflammation* take place principally in connective tissue. Inflammation is a vascular and cellular defensive reaction against foreign bodies. In most cases, it is a reaction against pathogenic bacteria or irritating chemical substances. Blood flow and capillary permeability are increased, partly as a result of the liberation of histamine by the mast cells. Edema is formed in this way, and an increase of volume of the inflamed area can be observed.

Through their active ameboid movement, leukocytes cross the walls of venules and capillaries, invading the inflamed area. This migration is called *diapedesis.*

During the initial or acute phase of inflammation, the neutrophils predominate; when the inflammation persists and enters the *chronic phase,* the cell population changes. The main types of cells then found are lymphocytes, plasma cells, and monocytes, which may originate locally or come from the blood. Macrophages also appear, developing from monocytes or connective tissue cells.

The cells present in the inflamed area engulf the remains of cells and fibers altered by this process and produce antibodies against the invading microorganisms. If the bacteria are not destroyed, the surrounding connective tissue forms a fibrous wall around the inflammation.

Repair

Connective tissue has great regenerative capacity, and the areas destroyed by inflammation or traumatic injury are easily repaired. The spaces left by injuries to tissues whose cells do not divide (eg, cardiac muscle) are filled by connective tissue, which forms a scar. The healing of surgical incisions depends on the reparative capacity of connective tissue.

Transport

There is a close association between blood capillaries, lymphatic capillaries, and connective tissue. These vessels, except in nerve tissue, are always ensheathed by connective tissue. Consequently, the connective tissue carries nutrients from the blood to various tissues in the body and moves metabolic wastes from the cells to the blood.

Hormonal Effects

Different hormones influence the metabolism of connective tissue. An example is the hormone *cortisol (hydrocortisone),* produced by the cortical layer of the adrenal gland, which inhibits the synthesis of fibers by connective tissue cells. *Adrenocorticotropic hormone (ACTH),* elaborated by the pituitary, which stimulates the production of cortisol, has the same effect. Injection of either cortisol or ACTH has a detrimental effect on wound healing. These hormones also suppress or attenuate the inflammatory process. Their action is also directed against the cells of the connective tissue (lymphocytes, plasma cells, etc).

Both hormones, in addition to *cortisone* (which is similar to cortisol), have a beneficial effect on collagen diseases. The connective tissue fibers and the amorphous intercellular substance undergo alterations in these diseases (eg, rheumatic fever, rheumatic arthritis, systemic lupus erythematosus, polyarteritis nodosa).

Hypothyroidism causes an accumulation of acid mucopolysaccharides in connective tissues. Adult hypothyroidism is called *myxedema (mucous edema)* and is associated with an excess of acid mucopolysaccharides in the connective tissue.

Nutritional Factors

Vitamin C (ascorbic acid) deficiency leads to *scurvy,* a disease characterized by generalized degeneration of connective tissue. In the absence of this vitamin, the fibroblast stops synthesizing collagen and the destroyed fibers are not replaced. Ascorbic acid is a cofactor for the enzyme protocollagen proline hydroxylase, which is essential for the synthesis of collagen. Recent evidence suggests that hydroxylation of prolyl and lysyl residues is necessary for the normal extrusion of collagen from the cell. In this step of hydroxylation, iron, molecular oxygen, and a-ketoglutarate are also necessary. Changes in the concentration of these substances within the cell will influence the rate of collagen biosynthesis. The roles of vitamins A, C, and D in connective tissue are also discussed in Chapters 7 and 8.

Renewal of Collagen

Collagen is a stable protein, and its renewal is very slow. Its *turnover rate* is different in different anatomic structures. The collagen of tendons is renewed very slowly or not at all, whereas the collagen of loose connective tissue is renewed more rapidly.

In vitamin C deficiency, once collagenous fibers are removed they cannot be replaced. This leads to a generalized degeneration of connective tissue which becomes more pronounced in areas where collagen renewal takes place at a faster rate. The periodontal membrane that holds teeth in their sockets exhibits a relatively high collagen turnover; consequently, this membrane is markedly affected by scurvy.

The physiologic destruction of collagen is performed by collagenase, an enzyme produced by the connective tissue cells. This enzyme digests only collagen and not other proteins. It is active at the normal pH of the connective tissue (about 7.0). The existence of collagenase in mammals has recently been confirmed, although the fact of collagen removal has been known for some time. Some bacteria of the genus Clostridium that cause gas gangrene produce collagenase, which greatly increases the invasive power of these microorganisms.

● ● ●

References

Allison AC, Davies P, de Petris S: Role of contractile microfilaments in macrophage movement and endocytosis. Nature 232:153, 1971.

Bellamy G, Bornstein P: Evidence for procollagen, a biosynthetic precursor of collagen. Proc Nat Acad Sc USA 68:1138, 1971.

Bouteille M, Pease DC: The tridimensional structure of mature collagenous fibers: Their protein filaments. J Ultrastruct Res 35:314, 1971.

Carmichael GG, Fullmer HM: The fine structure of the oxytalan fiber. J Cell Biol 28:33, 1966.

Carneiro J, Leblond CP: Suitability of collagenase treatment for the radioautographic identification of newly formed collagen labeled with ^{3}H-glycine or ^{3}H-proline. J Histochem Cytochem 14:334, 1966.

Carneiro J, de Moraes FF: Radioautographic visualization of collagen metabolism in periodontal tissues of the mouse. Arch Oral Biol 10:833, 1965.

Chvapil M: *Physiology of Connective Tissue.* Butterworth, 1967.

Cohn ZA, Fedorko ME, Hirsch JG: The in vitro differentiation of mononuclear phagocytes. 4. The ultrastructure of macrophage differentiation in the peritoneal cavity and in culture. 5. The formation of macrophage lysosomes. J Exper Med 123:747, 757, 1966.

Combs JW: An electron microscope study of mouse mast cells arising in vivo and in vitro. J Cell Biol 48:676, 1971.

Cox JP, Karnovsky ML: The depression of phagocytosis by exogenous cyclic nucleotides, prostaglandins, and theophyllin. J Cell Biol 59:480, 1973.

Dehm P, & others: A transport form of collagen from embryonic tendon. Electron microscopic demonstration of an NH$_2$-terminal extension and evidence suggesting the presence of cystine in the molecule. Proc Nat Acad Sc USA 69:60, 1972.

De Petris S, Karlsbad G, Pernis B: Localization of antibodies in plasma cells by electron microscopy. J Exper Med 117:849, 1963.

Dische Z: Some biological aspects of structural characteristics of glycoproteins. Page 161 in: *The 4th International Confer-* *ence on Cystic Fibrosis of the Pancreas.* Karger (Basel), 1968.

Dougherty TF, Berliner DL: The effects of hormone on connective tissue cells. In: *Treatise on Collagen.* Vol 2, part A. Gould B (editor). Academic Press, 1968.

Eastoe JE: Composition of collagen and allied proteins. In: *Treatise on Collagen.* Vol 1. Ramachandran GN (editor). Academic Press, 1967.

Franzblau C: Elastin. In: *Comprehensive Biochemistry.* Vol 26, Part C. Florkin M, Stoltz, EH (editors). Elsevier, 1971.

Fullmer HM: The histochemistry of the connective tissues. Int Rev Connect Tissue Res 3:1, 1965.

Gould BS: Collagen biosynthesis. In: *Treatise on Collagen.* Vol 2, part A. Gould BS (editor). Academic Press, 1968.

Grant ME, Prockop DJ: The biosynthesis of collagen. (3 parts.) New England J Med 286:194, 242, 291, 1972.

Green H, Goldberg B, Todaro GJ: Differentiated cell types and the regulation of collagen synthesis. Nature 212:631, 1966.

Greenlee TK Jr, Ross R: The development of the rat flexor digital tendon: A fine structure study. J Ultrastruct Res 18:354, 1967.

Greenlee TK Jr, Ross R, Hartman JL: The fine structure of elastic fibers. J Cell Biol 30:59, 1966.

Harkness RD: Mechanical properties of collagenous tissues. In: *Treatise on Collagen.* Vol 2, part A. Gould BS (editor). Academic Press, 1968.

Hunter JAA, Finlay B: Scanning electron microscopy of connective tissues in health and disease. In: *International Review of Connective Tissue Research.* Vol 6. Hall DA, Jackson DS (editors). Academic Press, 1973.

Jackson SF: The morphogenesis of collagen. In: *Treatise on Collagen.* Vol 2, part B. Gould BS (editor). Academic Press, 1968.

Kefalides NA, Winzler RJ: The chemistry of glomerular basement membrane and its relation to collagen. Biochemistry 5:702, 1966.

Kivirikko KI: Biosynthesis of collagen. In: *Connective Tissues, Biochemistry and Pathophysiology.* Fricke R, Hartmann F (editors). Springer-Verlag, 1974.

Kornfeld Poullain N, Robert L: Effets de différents solvants organiques sur la dégradation alcaline de l'elastine. Bull Soc Chim Biol 50:759, 1968.

Lagunoff D: Membrane fusion during mast cell secretion. J Cell Biol 57:252, 1973.

Pease DC, Bouteille M: The tridimensional ultrastructure of mature collagenous fibrils: Cytochemical evidence for a carbohydrate matrix. J Ultrastruct Res 35:339, 1971.

Petruska JA, Hodge AJ: A subunit model for the tropocollagen macromolecule. Proc Nat Acad Sc USA 51:871, 1964.

Robert L, Parlebas J: Rapport entre la nature de la trame fibreuse et le taux d'incorporation d'aminoacides marqués dans différentes types de tissue conjonctif. Comptes Rendus Acad Sci (Paris) 261:842, 1965.

Robert L, Robert B: Structural glycoproteins, their metabolism in normal and pathological connective tissue. In: *Nutritional Aspects of the Development of Bone and Connective Tissue. Symposium, Cambridge, 1968.* Karger (Basel), 1969.

Robert AM, Robert B, Robert L: Chemical and physical properties of structural glycoproteins. Page 237 in: *Chemistry and Molecular Biology of the Intercellular Matrix.* Vol 1. Balars EA (editor). Academic Press, 1970.

Robert B & others: Studies on the nature of the "microfibrillar" component of elastic fibers. Europ J Biochem 21:507, 1971.

Robertson WV: Metabolism of collagen in mammalian tissues. In: *Connective Tissue: Intercellular Macromolecules.* New York Heart Assoc (editor). Little, Brown, 1964.

Ross R: The connective tissue fiber forming cell. In: *Treatise on Collagen.* Vol 2, part A. Gould BS (editor). Academic Press, 1968.

Ross R: The elastic fiber: A review. J Histochem Cytochem 21:199, 1973.

Ross R, Bornstein P: Elastic fibers in the body. Sc Am 224:44, June 1971.

Ross R, Klebanoff SJ: The smooth muscle cell. 1. In vivo synthesis of connective tissue proteins. J Cell Biol 50:159, 1971.

Schoenberg MD & others: Cytoplasmic interaction between macrophages and lymphocytic cells in antibody synthesis. Science 143:064, 1964.

Schubert M, Hamerman D: *A Primer on Connective Tissue Biochemistry.* Lea & Febiger, 1968.

Simkin JL: Biosynthesis of plasma glycoproteins. Exposés annuels de biochimie médicales 30:19, 1970.

Sutton JS, Weiss LV: Transformation of monocytes in tissue cultures into macrophages, epithelioid cells and multinucleated giant cells: An electron microscope study. J Cell Biol 28:303, 1966.

Szigetti M & others: Distribution of ingested ^{14}C-cholesterol in the macromolecular fractions of rat connective tissue. Connect Tissue Res 1:145, 1972.

Trelstad RL, Coulombre AJ: Morphogenesis of collagen in the chick cornea. J Cell Biol 50:840, 1971.

Velican C: Macromolecular changes in atherosclerosis. In: *Handbuch der Histochimie.* Vol 8, part 2 (suppl). Gustav Fischer, 1974.

6...
Adipose Tissue

Adipose tissue is a special type of connective tissue in which adipose cells (adipocytes) predominate. These cells may be found either isolated or in small groups within connective tissue itself, but most are found in the adipose tissue spread throughout the body. Adipose tissue is, in a sense, one of the largest organs in the body. In men of normal weight, adipose tissue represents 15–20% of the body weight; in women of normal weight, 20–25% of body weight.

Adipose tissue is important as a reservoir of energy for mammals because they use up energy continuously although they eat intermittently. Adipose tissue helps to shape the surface of the body; forms pads that act as shock absorbers, chiefly in the soles and palms; and, since fat is a poor heat conductor, contributes to the thermal insulation of the body. It also fills up spaces between other tissues and helps to keep some organs in position. Animals that hibernate have a special variety of adipose tissue that supplies the heat necessary to permit them to return to activity after hibernation.

The 2 types of adipose tissue are characterized by the structure of their cells, localization, color, vascularization, and functions: *common, yellow,* or *unilocular adipose tissue,* whose cells, when completely developed, contain only one droplet of fat in their cyto-

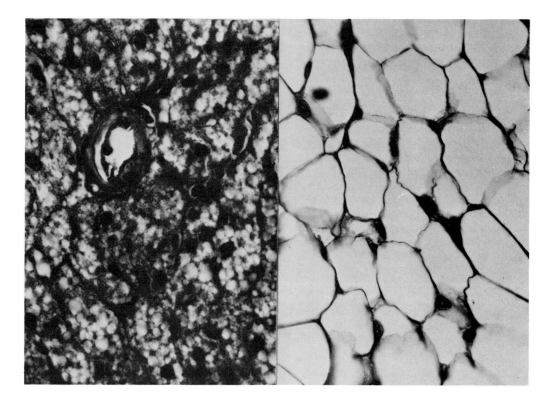

Figure 6–1. Photomicrographs of unilocular adipose tissue. **Left:** Tissue in formative stage. **Right:** Fully formed (mature) tissue. H&E stain, × 320.

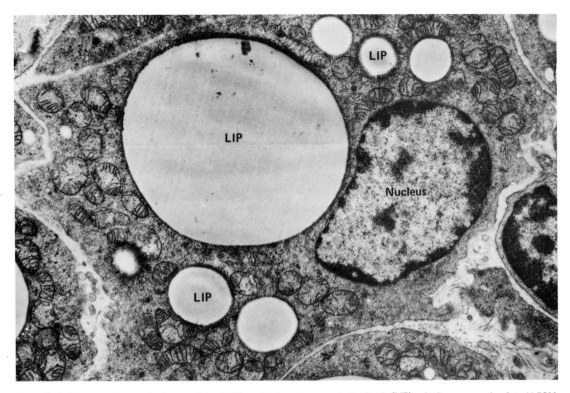

Figure 6—2. Electron micrograph of young fat cells. The cytoplasm is accumulating lipids (LIP), which appear as droplets. X 7500.

plasm; and *brown* or *multilocular adipose tissue,* composed of cells containing several lipid droplets and mitochondria and with a rich capillary supply.

UNILOCULAR ADIPOSE TISSUE

The color of unilocular adipose tissue varies from white to dark yellow, depending on the diet, and is mainly due to the presence of carotenoids dissolved in fat droplets of the cells. All adipose tissue in adults is probably of this type. It is found throughout the human body except for the eyelids, the penis and scrotum, and the lobule of the auricle, and its accumulation in some parts is determined by age and sex.

In the newborn, unilocular adipose tissue has a uniform thickness throughout the body; with age, it tends to disappear from some parts of the body and increase in others since its arrangement is partly regulated by sex hormones and adrenocortical hormones, which determine the accumulation of fat and are largely responsible for the male or female contour of the body.

Histologic Structure of Unilocular Tissue

Unilocular adipose cells are spherical when isolated but become polyhedral in adipose tissue, where they are closely packed. Lipid droplets are removed by the alcohol and xylol used in routine histo-logic technics. In standard microscope preparations, each cell shows a thin layer of cytoplasm as a ring around the vacuole left by the removed lipid droplet, the so-called signet ring cell (Fig 6—1). The rim of cytoplasm that remains after removal of the triglycerides (neutral fats) frequently ruptures and collapses, distorting the tissue structure.

Adipose cells are coated by a glycoprotein layer—glycocalyx—and their plasma membranes form numerous pinocytotic vesicles.

The cytoplasm surrounding the nucleus of these cells contains a Golgi apparatus, mitochondria of the filamentous and ovoid variety, a paucity of granular endoplasmic reticulum, and free ribosomes. The cytoplasm surrounding the lipid droplet contains vesicles of smooth endoplasmic reticulum and occasional microtubules (Fig 6—2).

Upon examination with the electron microscope, each adipose cell usually shows other lipid droplets than the large one seen with the light microscope. There is some question about whether or not the lipid droplet of the fat cell is membrane-bound. According to some authorities, the large lipid droplet is surrounded by a fenestrated envelope. Others have described in isolated fat cells an electron-dense line surrounding the lipid droplet outside of which lies a flattened double membrane envelope of endoplasmic reticulum, or have observed that the droplet is surrounded in an orderly fashion by fine filaments, or have noted the presence of an electron-dense layer which binds the lipid droplet. Similar structures surround the smaller lipid droplets, which occur individually or as aggregates of very small droplets. Groups of smaller individual droplets without any envelopes also occur.

Unilocular adipose tissue is subdivided into incomplete lobules by a partition of connective tissue containing blood vessels and nerves. Reticular fibers branch from these partitions and support individual fat cells.

Although blood vessels are not always apparent, adipose tissue is richly vascularized. Considering the amount of cytoplasm that exists in fat cells, the ratio of blood volume to volume of cytoplasm is greater in adipose tissue than in striated muscle.

Histophysiology of Unilocular Tissue

The lipids stored in adipose cells are chiefly neutral fats or triglycerides—ie, esters of fatty acids and glycerol. The fatty acids stored by these cells originate (1) in digested food, brought to the adipose cells in the form of chylomicrons; (2) in triglycerides synthesized

in the liver and transported to the adipose tissue in the form of very low density lipoproteins; and (3) by synthesis from glucose in the adipose cells. The deposition of unchanged fatty acids explains why a mammal fed lipids of another species may have in its adipose tissue neutral fats typical of the species utilized as food.

Chylomicrons are particles up to 3 μm in diameter present in blood plasma. They are composed of a central core of neutral fats and cholesterol esters absorbed by the small intestine and are surrounded by a stabilizing monolayer consisting of protein-free cholesterol and phospholipids. Chylomicrons and very low density lipoproteins are hydrolyzed in the blood capillaries of the adipose tissue by a lipase known as lipoprotein lipase, an enzyme synthesized in adipocytes and transmitted to the walls of adjacent capillaries. The hydrolyzed fatty acids pass within pinocytotic vesicles through the capillary walls into the intercellular space. Free fatty acids (presumably bound to albumin)

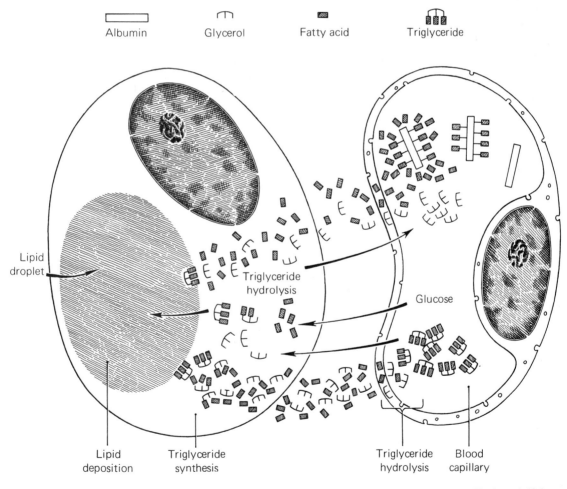

Figure 6–3. Probable pathways of lipid transport from the capillary lumen to the adipocytes and vice versa. The lower half shows the process of lipid deposition, utilizing glucose and triglycerides as precursors; the upper half shows lipid mobilization and its passage to the bloodstream. Triglycerides are hydrolyzed, and the molecules of fatty acid thus formed are carried in vesicles which fuse at the cell membrane. Thus, fatty acids are released into the extracellular space and from there are taken up by endothelial pinocytosis and liberated into the capillary lumen, from which site they are carried away by blood proteins.

are transported to the adipocytes, induce vesicle formation, and enter the cell where they combine with an intermediate product of glucose metabolism, α-glycerol phosphate, to form neutral fat molecules. These are then deposited in the fat droplets. Mitochondria, endoplasmic reticulum, and probably microtubules are organelles that are very active in the process of uptake and storage of lipids. Thus, the fatty acids cross the following layers in passing from the endothelium into the adipose cell: (1) capillary endothelium, (2) basement membrane, (3) connective tissue ground substance, (4) basement membrane of adipose cells, and (5) adipose cell membrane. The movement of fatty

acids across the cell cytoplasm into the lipid droplet is not so easily defined.

Adipose cells are also able to synthesize fatty acids from glucose, a process accelerated by insulin. Insulin also accelerates the intake of glucose into the adipose cells and increases the activity of lipoprotein lipase.

Stored lipids are mobilized by humoral and neurogenic mechanisms, resulting in the liberation of fatty acids and glycerol into the blood. An enzyme known as *hormone-sensitive lipase* (triglyceride lipase) is activated by adenylate cyclase, which is stimulated by epinephrine. Norepinephrine is liberated at the endings

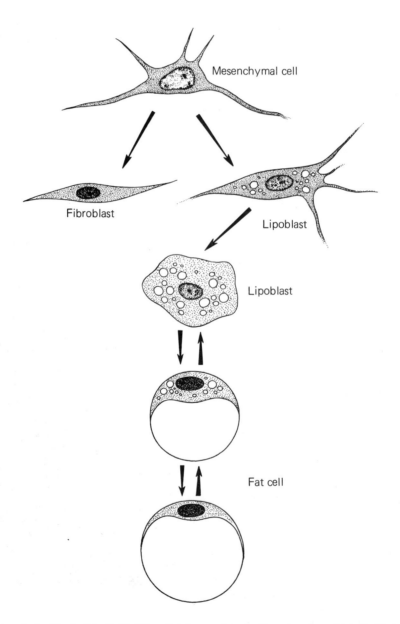

Mesenchymal cell

Fibroblast

Lipoblast

Lipoblast

Fat cell

Figure 6–4. Development of unilocular fat cells. Undifferentiated mesenchymal cells are transformed into lipoblasts that accumulate fat and thus give rise to mature fat cells. When a large amount of lipids is mobilized by the body, mature fat cells return to the lipoblast stage. Undifferentiated mesenchymal cells also give rise to other cell types, including fibroblasts.

of the postganglionic sympathetic nerves present in adipose tissue. The activated enzyme breaks down triglyceride molecules located mainly at the surface of the lipid droplets. The relatively insoluble fatty acids are transported by albumin to the other tissues of the body, while the more soluble glycerol remains free and is taken up by the liver (Fig 6–3).

Growth hormone, glucocorticoids, prolactin, corticotropin, and thyroid hormone also have roles in different steps in the metabolism of adipose tissue.

Under circumstances of bodily need, mobilization of lipids does not occur in uniform proportion in all parts of the body. Subcutaneous, mesenteric, and retroperitoneal deposits are the first to be mobilized, while adipose tissue in the pads of the hands and feet resists long periods of starvation. After such periods, unilocular adipose tissue loses nearly all of its fat and becomes a tissue containing polyhedral or spindle-shaped cells with very few lipid droplets. These cells remain as such and are not transformed into typical fibroblasts or other types of connective tissue cells.

Both types of adipose tissue are richly innervated by the autonomic nervous system. This innervation plays an important role in the mobilization of fats when the body is subjected to long periods of fasting or severe cold.

Histogenesis of Unilocular Tissue

Most histologists believe that the adipose cells develop from lipoblasts. These cells are similar to fibroblasts but are able to accumulate fat in their cytoplasm. The lipid droplets appear initially at one pole of the cell and then at the opposite pole. They are at first isolated from one another but soon fuse to form the single larger droplet that is characteristic of unilocular tissue cells (Fig 6–4). When fibroblasts or adipose cells contain more than one lipid droplet, they are said to be in the multilocular stage.

Adipose cells were at one time believed not to undergo division. The new lipoblasts develop from undifferentiated mesenchymal cells. Man is one of the few mammals who is born with fat stores; they begin to accumulate at the 30th week of gestation. After birth, the development of new adipose cells is common mainly around small blood vessels, where undifferentiated mesenchymal cells are usually found.

Recently, technics have become available for estimating the size and number of the adipose cells in the body. These involve lipid analysis of a sample of adipose tissue obtained by needle biopsy, in which a count of adipocytes has also been made. When these data are combined with a measure of total body fat, it is possible to estimate the total number of fat cells in the body as well as to determine the average lipid content per cell, which is a measure of its size.

With these technics, it has been determined that cells of adults of normal weight contain an average of 0.6 μg of lipid and that the average number of cells is 25×10^9. It is believed that, during a finite postnatal period, nutritional and other influences can cause an increase in the number of adipocytes, but after that period the cells do not increase in number but only accumulate more lipid under conditions of excess caloric intake. It has been postulated that this early increase in the number of adipocytes may predispose to increased adiposity in later life.

MULTILOCULAR ADIPOSE TISSUE

Multilocular adipose tissue is also called *brown adipose tissue* because of its characteristic color, which is due in part to the high content of cytochromes in the mitochondria of its cells. Unlike unilocular tissue, which is present throughout the body, brown adipose tissue has a more limited distribution. It is common in hibernating animals and is improperly called the hibernating gland.

In rats and several other mammals, this tissue is found mainly about the shoulder girdle. In the human embryo and the newborn, a small quantity of multilocular adipose tissue is encountered in the same area, remains restricted to this localization after birth, and probably does not persist into adulthood. The function of this tissue in man appears to be restricted to the first months of postnatal life, when it produces heat and thus protects the newborn against cold.

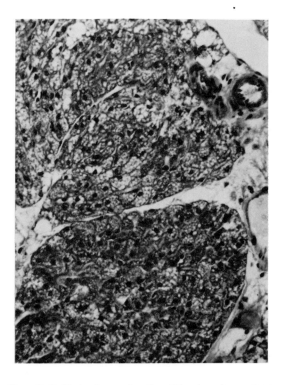

Figure 6–5. Photomicrograph of multilocular adipose tissue (brown fat). The cells exhibit a glandlike arrangement, and their cytoplasm contains numerous small lipid droplets. H&E stain, × 320.

Histologic Structure of Multilocular Tissue

Multilocular tissue cells are polygonal in shape and are smaller than those of unilocular adipose tissue. Their cytoplasm contains a great number of lipid droplets of different sizes (Fig 6–5) and numerous spherical mitochondria with long cristae occupying their whole width. Granular and smooth endoplasmic reticulum is not abundant.

Brown adipose tissue resembles an endocrine gland, for its cells assume an almost epithelial arrangement of closely packed masses associated with blood capillaries. This tissue is subdivided by partitions of connective tissue into lobules which are better delineated than in unilocular adipose tissue lobules.

Histophysiology of Multilocular Tissue

The physiology of multilocular tissue is understood best in the study of hibernating species.

In animals ending their hibernation period and in human newborns under conditions of low temperature, nerve impulses liberate norepinephrine into the tissue. This substance activates the hormone-sensitive lipase present in adipose cells, promoting hydrolysis of triglycerides into fatty acids and glycerol. Oxygen consumption and liberation of heat are increased, elevating the temperature of the tissue and warming the blood passing through it. Warmed blood circulates throughout, heating the body and carrying fatty acids not metabolized in the adipose tissue, which will be utilized by other organs.

It has recently been demonstrated that the mitochondria of multilocular adipose tissue can uncouple and recouple the process of oxidative phosphorylation. The mitochondria can therefore shift, according to the needs of the body, from the production of heat to the accumulation of ATP or vice versa.

Histogenesis of Multilocular Tissue

Multilocular tissue develops differently from unilocular tissue. The mesenchymal cells that constitute the brown tissue resemble epithelium, suggesting an endocrine gland, before they accumulate fat. Apparently there is no formation of brown adipose tissue after birth, nor is one type of adipose tissue transformed into another.

●   ●   ●

References

Christiansen EN, Pederson JI, Grav HJ: Uncoupling and recoupling of oxidative phosphorylation in brown adipose tissue mitochondria. Nature 222:857, 1969.

Cushman SW: Structure-function relationship in the adipose cell. 1. Ultrastructure of the isolated adipose cell. J Cell Biol 46:326, 1970.

Hales CN & others: Localization of calcium in the smooth endoplasmic reticulum of rat isolated fat cells. J Cell Sci 15:1, 1974.

Imaizumi M: On the time structure of the surface of lipid droplets in adipose cells. Arch Histol Jap 30:353, 1969.

Lindberg O & others: Studies of the mitochondrial energy transfer system of brown adipose tissue. J Cell Biol 34:293, 1967.

Napolitano L: The differentiation of white adipose cells: An electron microscope study. J Cell Biol 18:663, 1963.

Renold AE, Cahill GF Jr (editors): *Handbook of Physiology.* Section 5: *Adipose Tissue.* American Physiological Society, 1965.

Sheldon H: The fine structure of the fat cell. In: *Fat as a Tissue.* Rodahl K, Issekutz B Jr (editors). McGraw-Hill, 1964.

Slavin BG: The cytophysiology of mammalian adipose cells. Internat Rev Cytol 33:297, 1972.

Smith RE, Hock RJ: Brown fat: Thermogenic effector of arousal in hibernators. Science 140:199, 1963.

Wassermann F, McDonald TF: Electron microscopic study of adipose tissue (fat organs), with special reference to the transport of lipids between blood and fat cells. Z Zellforsch Mikrosk Anat 59:326, 1963.

Williamson JR: Adipose tissue: Morphological changes associated with lipid mobilization. J Cell Biol 20:57, 1964.

7...
Cartilage

Cartilage is a type of connective tissue in which the intercellular material has a rigid consistency, although the tissue is less resistant to pressure than bone. Its surface is usually resilient and smooth. The main functions of cartilage are to support soft tissues and, by virtue of its smooth surface, to provide a sliding area for joints, thus facilitating bone movements. Cartilage is essential for the growth of long bones both before and after birth. As with other differentiated types of connective tissue in general, cartilage contains much intercellular material, known as cartilage matrix, with cavities (lacunae) containing cartilage cells (chondrocytes).

The weight-bearing capacity of cartilage is exceeded only by that of bone, a tissue highly perfected for support and protection.

The physiologic properties of cartilage depend mainly on the physicochemical characteristics of its matrix, which contains either collagen or collagen plus elastin, associated with acid mucopolysaccharides. Chondrocytes synthesize and maintain the matrix.

Since collagen and elastin are pliable, the hard consistency of most cartilage tissue depends on the proteoglycans, whose molecules appear to combine, by means of weak chemical bonds, with the collagenous fibrils and the soluble collagen present in the matrix. Variations in the content and type of connective tissue fibers give special properties to cartilage.

In areas subjected to heavy weight-bearing or to strong pulling forces, the content of collagenous fibers is great, and the cartilage in such areas is almost inextensible. Areas of the body where the demands of weight-bearing and stress are less great contain cartilage with elastic fibers and fewer collagenous fibers, resulting in a more flexible and elastic type of cartilage.

Cartilage is devoid of blood vessels. It is nourished by diffusion from capillaries in adjacent connective tissue or by means of synovial fluid from joint cavities. In some instances, blood vessels pass through cartilage to nourish other tissues. Cartilage has no lymphatic vessels or nerves and has a low metabolic rate.

The 3 types of cartilage are *hyaline* (the most common form), the matrix of which contains a moderate number of collagenous fibers; *elastic,* the matrix of

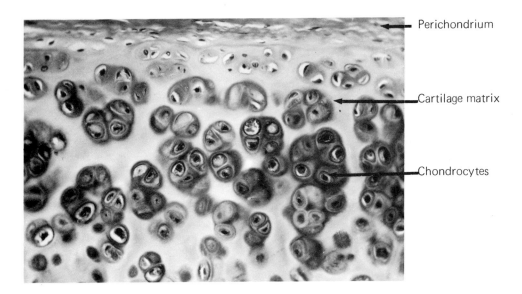
Perichondrium

Cartilage matrix

Chondrocytes

Figure 7–1. Photomicrograph of hyaline cartilage. Most chondrocytes are organized in isogenic groups. A condensation of the matrix—the capsule—forms around chondrocytes. The upper part of the figure shows the perichondrium, with cells being transformed into chondrocytes. H&E stain, × 300.

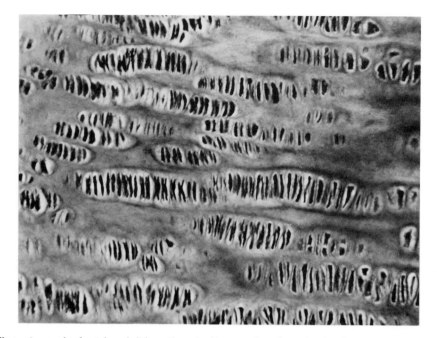

Figure 7—2. Photomicrograph of epiphyseal disk cartilage. In this type of cartilage, the chondrocytes are arranged side by side in parallel columns. H&E stain, X 320.

which contains collagenous fibers plus a large number of elastic fibers; and *fibrous (fibrocartilage),* which contains a matrix formed mostly by collagenous fibers.

Perichondrium (Fig 7—1), which merges gradually with cartilage on one side and with adjacent connective tissue on the other, is a special layer of connective tissue covering cartilage in most places (see p 111).

HYALINE CARTILAGE

Hyaline cartilage (Fig 7—1) is the most common and best studied of the 3 types. Most of the experimental data on cartilage have been obtained from studies of hyaline cartilage, but the findings are probably applicable to other types as well.

Fresh hyaline cartilage is bluish-white and translucent. In the embryo, it serves as a temporary skeleton until it is replaced gradually by bone. Between the diaphysis and the epiphysis of growing long bones the epiphyseal disk, composed of hyaline cartilage, is responsible for the longitudinal growth of bone (Fig 7—2).

In adults, hyaline cartilage is present mainly in the walls of the respiratory passages (trachea and bronchi), on the ventral ends of the ribs, and on bone surfaces within joints (articular cartilages).

Matrix

Forty percent of the dry weight of hyaline cartilage consists of collagenous fibers and fibrils embedded in an amorphous intercellular substance. In routine histologic preparations, collagenous fibers do not stand out from the amorphous substance for 2 reasons: (1) the collagen is mainly in the form of fibrils, the majority of which have submicroscopic dimensions; and (2) the fibers and fibrils have a refractive index very near to that of the amorphous intercellular substance which surrounds them.

Electron micrographs, however, show that isolated collagenous fibrils, finer than those of the connective tissue itself, are the dominant component of the matrix. These are similar in periodicity. There are also, however, a great number of very fine collagenous fibrils with nearly invisible periodicity and others, even finer, with no periodicity at all. This probably indicates that the collagen of hyaline cartilage remains in a different state of maturity (polymerization) than that of connective tissue proper. Collagenous bundles only appear in certain instances, eg, articular cartilage.

Information about the composition of the amorphous intercellular substance is incomplete. The most abundant component of this substance has in the past been referred to as chondromucoprotein or proteoglycan, a designation used to describe the mucopolysaccharide-protein complexes isolated from cartilage. In this book the terms proteoglycans, acid mucopolysaccharides, and glycosaminoglycan-protein complexes are understood to be equivalent. Cartilage proteoglycan, in addition to protein, contains principally chondroitin-4-sulfate, chrondroitin-6-sulfate, and keratan sulfate, covalently linked. The relative proportions of protein and of these 3 constituents in the cartilage varies with the anatomic site and with the age of the animal. The effect of aging probably has relevance to the function of cartilage.

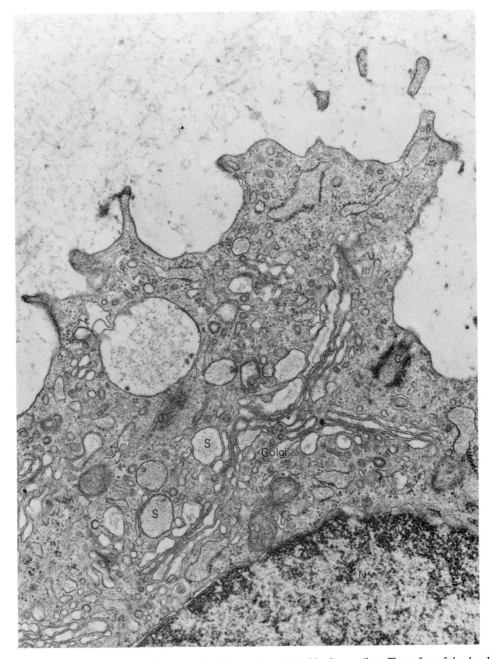

Figure 7–3. Electron micrograph of part of a young chondrocyte from tracheal hyaline cartilage. The surface of the chondrocyte is increased by projections and foldings which facilitate metabolic exchange. There are secretory vacuoles (S) next to the Golgi complex. Observe also a centriole (C) and part of the nucleus (N). Reduced from X 37,000. (Courtesy of M Weinstock.)

A correlation has been shown between the hardness of cartilage and a higher content of keratan sulfate than chondroitin sulfate.

Certain disease processes may exert their ill effects by interfering with the biosynthesis or favoring the degradation of proteoglycans in such a way as to interfere with its normal function.

Narrow bands of matrix with few or no collagenous fibrils surround the chrondocytes. They are rich in amorphous intercellular substance and show more intense basophilia, metachromasia, and PAS positivity than the rest of the matrix. The bands represent what the early histologists called capsules.

Chondrocytes

At the periphery of hyaline cartilage, the chondrocytes have an elliptic shape, with the long axis parallel to the surface. Farther in, they are round and

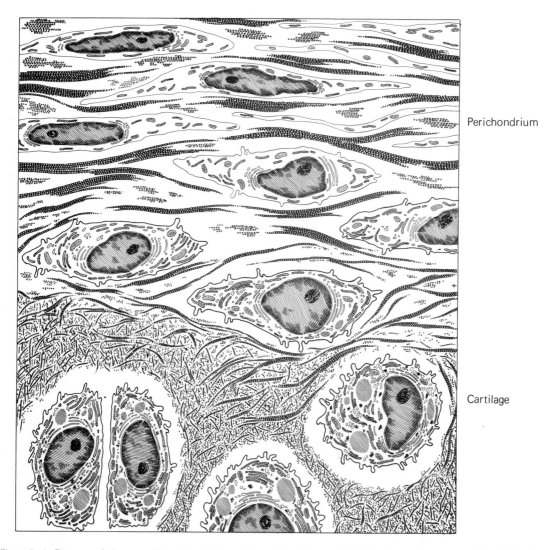

Perichondrium

Cartilage

Figure 7—4. Diagram of the area of transition between the perichondrium and the hyaline cartilage. As perichondrial cells are transformed into chondrocytes, they become round, with an irregular surface. Cartilage matrix contains numerous fine collagen fibrils.

usually appear in groups (Fig 7—1) of up to 8 cells originating from mitotic divisions of a single cell called a chondroblast. These groups are designated isogenous groups. In cartilage found in epiphyseal plates, the chondrocytes are accumulated in rows (Fig 7—2).

The cells and the matrix of cartilage shrink during histologic preparation, which accounts both for the irregular shape of the chondrocytes and for their separation from the capsule. In vivo, however, the chondrocytes or groups of chondrocytes occupy the lacunae completely. Upon examination with the light microscope, their surface appears smooth, but the electron microscope reveals indentations and protrusions, larger and more frequent in young chondrocytes (Fig 7—3). This structural characteristic increases their surface area, permitting easier exchange with the extracellular medium; this has an important function in maintaining nutrition of these cells since they are located at a dis-

tance from the bloodstream. They have a round nucleus with one or more nucleoli. Young chondrocytes are flat, whereas older ones are round and hypertrophied. Until recently, chondrocytes were described according to their morphology and metachromatic staining. Recent evidence suggests that the chondrocyte is a cell which synthesizes large amounts of chrondroitin sulfate proteoglycan and collagen of the composition $(a1[II])_3$. Chondrocytes produce this type of collagen, which is composed only of $a1$ collagen chains found in the skin, bones, and cornea. The biosynthesis of proteoglycan appears to be initiated on the granular endoplasmic reticulum where the protein core is formed. Enzymes present on the endoplasmic reticulum add the xylose, galactose, sulfate, and other residues that make up the complete molecule of chondroitin sulfate proteoglycan.

Perichondrium

Except in the articular cartilage of joints, all hyaline cartilage is covered by a layer of connective tissue, the "perichondrium," that is essential for the growth and maintenance of cartilage (Figs 7—1 and 7—4). It is made up of connective tissue that is very rich in collagenous fibers in which are cells resembling fibroblasts. These extend from the periphery of the perichondrium but are more numerous closer to the cartilage. Morphologically, the cells of the inner layer of the perichondrium (chondrogenic cells) are similar to the fibroblasts and are considered to be so by some authors. Others, however, postulate that they are undifferentiated mesenchymal cells which can be differentiated directly into chondroblasts.

Histophysiology

Since cartilage is devoid of blood capillaries, chondrocytes respire under low oxygen tension. There is evidence that hyaline cartilage cells metabolize glucose mainly by anaerobic glycolysis to produce lactic acid as the end product. Nutrients from the blood diffuse from the perichondrium to the more deeply placed chondrocytes. Because of this, the maximum width of the cartilage is limited. The nutrients diffuse through the solvation water of the matrix. There is almost no free water in cartilage matrix.

By means of radioautography, it has been demonstrated that chondrocytes synthesize the matrix of cartilage. In the growing cartilage of young animals, these cells have a well-developed granular endoplasmic reticulum and Golgi complex. Studies using injection of ^{35}S in the form of sulfate, which is incorporated into the acid sulfated mucopolysaccharides, revealed that radioactivity appeared first in the cytoplasm of the chondrocytes and afterward in the intercellular substance. Similar results were obtained after administration of the amino acid proline (a unique constituent of collagen) which had been tritiated. Radioautographic studies with the electron microscope after ^{3}H-proline administration demonstrated that radioactivity appeared first in the granular endoplasmic reticulum, then in the Golgi apparatus, and finally in the intercellular substance. There is also evidence that synthesis and sulfation of the mucopolysaccharides take place in the Golgi apparatus. Additionally, the core protein synthesized in the granular endoplasmic reticulum combines here with the repeated units of polysaccharides to form the proteoglycans.

Chondrocyte function depends on a proper hormonal balance. Although knowledge in this field is incomplete, it is known that the synthesis of acid sulfated mucopolysaccharides is accelerated by growth hormone, thyroxine, and testosterone. It is retarded by cortisone, hydrocortisone, and estradiol. Cortisone decreases the synthesis of adenosine triphosphate (ATP) in cartilage, resulting in partial inhibition of the penetration of sulfate ions into the chondrocytes as well as preventing the utilization of the intracellular sulfate required for sulfation of acid mucopolysaccharides.

Histogenesis

Cartilage derives from the mesenchyme (Fig 7—5). The first modification observed is the rounding

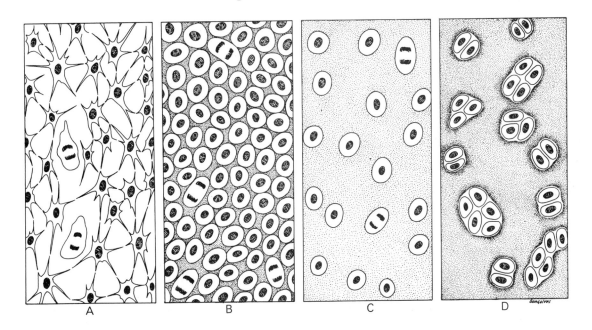

Figure 7—5. Histogenesis of hyaline cartilage. *A:* The mesenchyme, which is the precursor tissue of all types of cartilage. *B:* Mitotic proliferation of the mesenchymal cell gives rise to a very cellular tissue. *C:* Rounded cells are separated from each other by the formation of a great amount of matrix. *D:* Multiplication of cartilage cells gives rise to isogenic groups which are surrounded by a condensation of the matrix (capsule).

off of the mesenchymal cells, which retract their protoplasmic extensions and multiply rapidly, forming
condensed agglomerations. The cells formed by this
direct differentiation of the mesenchymal cells, now
called *chondroblasts,* have basophilic cytoplasm. Differentiation of mesenchymal cells into chondrocytes
may involve selective replication of regions of DNA
concerned with the control of genes responsible for
specialized macromolecule synthesis. Synthesis of the
matrix then begins to separate the chondroblasts from
each other. The differentiation of cartilage takes place
from the center outward; therefore, the more central
cells have characteristics of chondrocytes while the
peripheral cells are typical chondroblasts. The superficial mesenchyme develops into perichondrium.

Growth

The growth of cartilage is attributable to 2 processes: *interstitial growth,* due to mitotic division of
the preexisting chondrocytes; and *appositional growth.*
Both are ascribed to the cells of the perichondrium,
and in both cases newly formed chondrocytes synthesize collagenous fibrils and amorphous intercellular
substance. Real growth is thus much greater than that
due to the simple increase in the number of cells. Interstitial growth is the less important of the 2 processes
and occurs only during the early phases of cartilage
formation; it helps to expand cartilage from within. As
the matrix becomes increasingly more rigid and thick,
interstitial growth becomes less pronounced. Cartilage
then grows only by apposition. Cells of the perichondrium adjacent to the cartilage multiply and differentiate into chondrocytes, which are then incorporated
into the existing cartilage. During growth, superficial
areas of cartilage show transitions between chondrocytes and cells resembling the fibroblasts of the perichondrium (Figs 7–1 and 7–4).

Regressive Changes

In contrast to other tissues, hyaline cartilage is
frequently subjected to degenerative processes. The
most common is calcification of the matrix, and this is
preceded by an increase in the size and volume of the
cells followed by their death. Although calcification is
a regressive alteration, it occurs normally in certain
cartilages, providing a model for bone development.
(See Endochondral Ossification, Chapter 8.)

Regeneration

Except in young children, damaged cartilage regenerates with difficulty and often incompletely. In
adults, regeneration occurs because of the activity of
the perichondrium. When cartilage fractures, cells from
the perichondrium invade the fractured area and generate new cartilage. In extensively damaged areas (or
occasionally in small areas), the perichondrium, instead
of forming new cartilage, generates a scar of dense connective tissue.

ELASTIC CARTILAGE

Elastic cartilage is found in the auricle of the ear,
in the walls of the external auditory canals, in the
Eustachian tubes and epiglottis, and in some of the
cartilage in the larynx.

Basically, elastic cartilage is similar to hyaline cartilage; however, in addition to collagenous fibers, it
contains an abundant network of fine elastic fibers
which merge with the perichondrium. Fresh elastic cartilage has a yellowish color caused by the presence of
elastin in the elastic fibers, which may be demonstrated by standard stains (eg, orcein) (Fig 7–6).

Elastic cartilage may be present by itself or in
combination with hyaline cartilage. Because the chondrocytes of elastic and hyaline cartilage tissues are very
similar, elastic cartilage is frequently found to be gradually continuous with hyaline cartilage. As with hyaline cartilage, elastic cartilage possesses perichondrium
and grows mainly by apposition. It is less susceptible
to degenerative processes than hyaline cartilage.

FIBROCARTILAGE

Fibrocartilage is a tissue with characteristics intermediate between those of dense connective tissue and

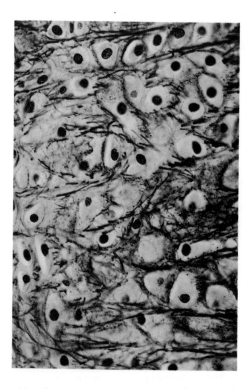

Figure 7–6. Photomicrograph of elastic cartilage. Weigert staining method for elastic fibers. × 350.

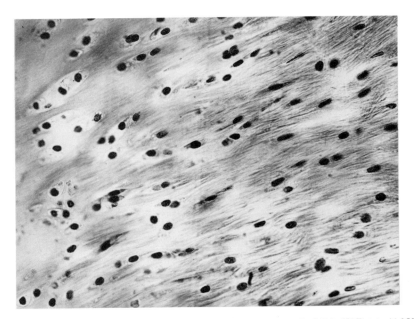

Figure 7—7. Photomicrograph of fibrocartilage from a human intervertebral disk. H&E stain, × 350.

hyaline cartilage. It is found in intervertebral disks, in attachments of certain ligaments to bones, and in the symphysis pubica. Fibrocartilage is always associated with dense connective tissue, and the border areas between these 2 tissues are not clear-cut but show a gradual transition.

Fibrocartilage contains chondrocytes similar to those of hyaline cartilage, either singly or in small groups. Very often, the chondrocytes are arranged in long columns. Fibrocartilage matrix is acidophilic because it contains a great number of collagenous fibers, which are easily seen under the light microscope (Fig 7–7). The amorphous intercellular substance is extremely rare; it is limited to the outer edges of the lacunae which contain the chondrocytes, constituting basophilic, metachromatic, and PAS-positive capsules.

In fibrocartilage, the numerous collagenous fibers form irregular bundles between the bulky groups of chondrocytes or a parallel arrangement along the columns of chondrocytes. This orientation depends upon the stresses acting on fibrocartilage since the collagenous bundles take up a direction parallel to those stresses. There is no perichondrium in fibrocartilage.

Fibrocartilage develops from dense connective tissue by means of differentiation of fibroblasts into chondrocytes.

INTERVERTEBRAL DISKS

Each intervertebral disk is situated between the vertebrae and held to them by means of ligaments. The disks have 2 components: the annulus fibrosus and the nucleus pulposus.

The *annulus fibrosus* has an external layer of dense connective tissue, but it is mainly composed of fibrocartilage in which collagenous bundles are concentrically arranged.

The *nucleus pulposus* is situated in the center of the annulus fibrosus. It is a tissue with unique characteristics, derived from the notochord, and is composed of a few round cells embedded in an amorphous semifluid substance. It is very rich in water and is under pressure. In children, the nucleus pulposus is large, but with age it is gradually reduced in size and is partially replaced by fibrocartilage.

Herniation of the Intervertebral Disk

Rupture of the annulus fibrosus (more frequent in the posterior region, where there are fewer collagenous bundles) causes dislocation of the semifluid nucleus pulposus from the intervertebral disk. It can thus enter the vertebral canal, compressing the spinal cord and nerve roots and causing neurologic disturbances. This condition is known as herniation of the intervertebral disk and is generally accompanied by severe pain in the areas innervated by the compressed nerve fibers. It is most frequent in the lower lumbar region. The collagen fibrils are thicker in the annulus fibrosus than in the nucleus pulposus, but they decrease in diameter with age. This probably is related to the fact that the annulus fibrosus gradually becomes weaker in the maturing tissue. A specific hydroxylysine-linked hexose is associated with this physical change.

•   •   •

References

Anderson DR: The ultrastructure of elastic and hyaline cartilage in the rat. Am J Anat 114:403, 1964.

Campo RD, Dziewiatkowski DD: Turnover of the organic matrix of cartilage and bone as visualized by autoradiography. J Cell Biol 18:19, 1963.

Cooper GW, Prockop DJ: Intracellular accumulation of protocollagen and extrusion of collagen by embryonic cartilage cells. J Cell Biol 38:523, 1968.

Fewer D, Threadgold J, Sheldon H: Studies on cartilage. 5. Electron microscopic observations on the autoradiographic localization of S^{35} in cells and matrix. J Ultrastruct Res 11:166, 1964.

Godman G, Porter KR: Chondrogenesis, studied with the electron microscope. J Biophys Biochem Cytol 8:719, 1960.

Godman GC, Lane N: On the site of sulfation in the chondrocyte. J Cell Biol 21:353, 1964.

Happey F & others: Variations in the diameter of collagen fibrils, bound hexose and associated glycoproteins in the intervertebral disc. In: *Connective Tissues*. Fricke R, Hartmann F (editors). Springer, 1974.

Levitt D, Ho PL, Dorfman A: Differentiation of cartilage. In: *The Cell Surface in Development*. Moscona AA (editor). Wiley, 1974.

Palmoski MJ, Goetinek PF: Synthesis of proteochondroitin sulfate by normal, nanomelic, and 5-bromodeoxyuridine-treated chondrocytes in cell culture. Proc Nat Acad Sc 67:3385, 1972.

Revel JP: Role of the Golgi apparatus of cartilage cells in the elaboration of matrix glycosaminoglycans. In: *Chemistry and Molecular Biology of the Intercellular Matrix*. Vol 3. Balasz EA (editor). Academic Press, 1970.

Revel JP, Hay ED: An autoradiographic and electron microscopic study of collagen synthesis in differentiating cartilage. Z Zellforsch Mikrosk Anat 61:110, 1963.

Rosenberg L, Hellmann W, Kleinshmidt AK: Macromolecular models of protein-polysaccharides from bovine nasal cartilage based on electron microscopic studies. J Biol Chem 245:4123, 1970.

Roy S, Meachim G: Chondrocyte ultrastructure in adult human articular cartilage. Ann Rheumat Dis 27:544, 1968.

Salpeter MM: ^{3}H-proline incorporation into cartilage: Electron microscope autoradiographic observations. J Morphol 124:387, 1968.

Sheldon H, Kimball FB: Studies on cartilage. 3. The occurrence of collagen within vacuoles of the Golgi apparatus. J Cell Biol 12:599, 1962.

Trelstad RL & others: Isolation of two distinct collagens from chick cartilage. Biochemistry 9:4993, 1970.

Tsiganos CP, Muir H: The natural heterogeneity of proteoglycans of vaccine and human cartilage. In: *Chemical and Molecular Biology of the Intercellular Matrix*. Balazs EA (editor). Academic Press, 1970.

8...
Bone

During the process of evolution, a basic structural protein emerged which was modified to varying degrees of rigidity, elasticity, and strength depending upon environmental influences and the functional requirements of the animal organism. This protein is the *collagen,* and the chief examples among its various modifications are skin, basement membrane, cartilage, and bone.

Bone is one of the hardest tissues of the human body and second only to cartilage in its ability to withstand stress. As the main constituent of the skeleton, it supports fleshy structures, protects vital organs such as those contained in the cranial and thoracic cavities, and also contains the bone marrow, where blood cells are formed.

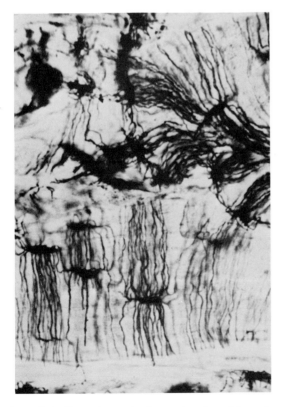

Figure 8—1. Photomicrograph of ground section of bone. Lacunae and canaliculi appear black. X 490.

Besides these functions, bones form a system of levers which multiply the forces generated during skeletal muscle contraction, transforming them into bodily movements.

Bone is composed of intercellular calcified material, the *bone matrix,* and different cell types: *osteocytes,* which are found in cavities (lacunas) within the matrix; *osteoblasts,* which synthesize the organic components of the matrix; and *osteoclasts,* which are multinucleated giant cells involved in the resorption of bone tissue, thus participating in the bone remodeling process.

Since diffusion does not take place through the calcified matrix of bone, the exchanges between osteocytes and blood capillaries depend on the canaliculi, which perforate the matrix. These canaliculi permit the osteocytes to communicate with their neighbors, with the internal and external surfaces of the bone, and with the blood vessels within the matrix.

Because of its hardness, bone is difficult to cut in the microtome; therefore, special technics must be used for its study. One of these consists of grinding thin slices of bone with abrasives until they become transparent. The preparation thus obtained is referred to as a ground section. This technic does not preserve the cells but it does permit detailed study of the matrix, its lacunas, and its canaliculi. Owing to differences in refractive index between lacunas and canaliculi (which are both filled with air) and the medium used in mounting, light rays striking the lacunas and canaliculi are deflected and do not penetrate the objective lens of the microscope. Lacunas and canaliculi consequently appear black in ground sections (Fig 8—1).

Another technic which is frequently used because it permits the observation of cells is based on the decalcification of bone already prepared in a standard fixative. The mineral is removed by immersion in a dilute acid solution (eg, 5% nitric acid) or in a solution containing a chelating substance (eg, ethylenediaminetetraacetic acid, EDTA). The decalcified tissue is then sectioned and stained by routine technics.

All bones are protected at both internal and external surfaces by layers of connective tissue called *endosteum* and *periosteum,* respectively.

BONE CELLS

Osteocytes

Osteocytes are found within the bone matrix in lacunas from which canaliculi radiate (Figs 8–1 and 8–3). They are flat, almond-shaped cells, with cytoplasmic processes which, at least in newly formed bone tissue, fully occupy the canaliculi (Fig 8–3). These processes gradually retract, leaving an amorphous, PAS-positive ground substance in the distal portions of the canaliculi.

Destruction of osteocytes is followed by matrix resorption—a fact which suggests a possible role of these cells in maintaining the matrix. Histochemical studies show that osteocytes and osteoblasts contain calcium phosphate bound to protein or glycoprotein. Consequently, bone cells are able to concentrate calcium phosphate in their cytoplasm. However, the significance of this observation is not known.

Osteoblasts

Osteoblasts are responsible for the synthesis of the organic components of bone matrix (collagen and glycoproteins). They are exclusively located at the surfaces of bone tissue, side by side, in a way resembling simple epithelium (Fig 8–2). When they are intensely engaged in matrix synthesis, osteoblasts have a cuboid shape and a basophilic cytoplasm. When their synthe-

sizing activity declines, they become flat, and cytoplasmic basophilia decreases.

Osteoblasts also present cytoplasmic processes which bring them into contact with neighboring osteoblasts. These expansions are more evident when the cell begins to be surrounded by matrix. Once it is trapped by the newly synthesized matrix, the osteoblast becomes an osteocyte. Lacunas and canaliculi appear because the matrix is formed around a cell with its cytoplasmic processes.

During synthesis, osteoblasts have the ultrastructure of cells synthesizing proteins for export, with well-developed granular endoplasmic reticulum and Golgi apparatus. They are polarized cells; extrusion of the synthesized molecules takes place by the cell surface in contact with bone matrix. The large, round nucleus has a finely dispersed chromatin and is found at the side of the cell away from the matrix.

The newly synthesized, not yet calcified matrix adjacent to osteoblasts is termed *osteoid*. In active osteoblasts, PAS-positive cytoplasmic granules have been found. These granules are probably precursors of the neutral mucopolysaccharides of the matrix.

The role of osteoblasts in secreting bone collagen has been studied by radioautography in animals injected with ^{3}H-glycine (since glycine constitutes one-third of the amino acid residues in collagen). Thirty minutes after ^{3}H-glycine administration, the label was found mainly in osteoblasts; 4 hours later, it was

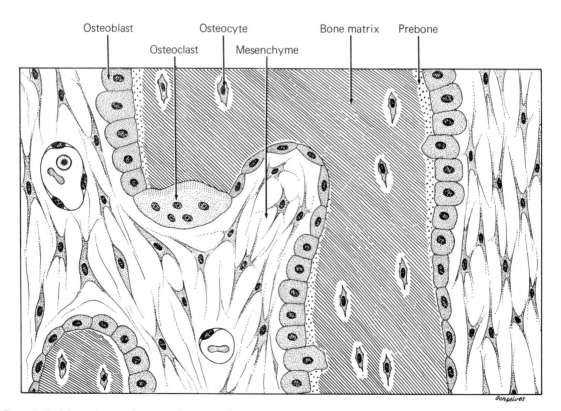

Figure 8–2. Advanced stage of intramembranous ossification. The lower part of the drawing shows an osteoblast being entrapped in the newly formed bone matrix.

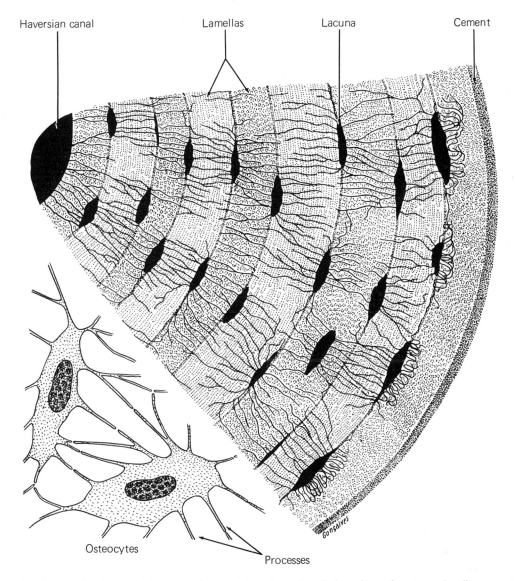

Figure 8–3. Schematic drawings of 2 osteocytes and part of a Haversian system. Collagen fibers of contiguous lamellas are sectioned at different angles. Observe the numerous canaliculi which form intercommunications of the lacunas with each other and with the Haversian canals. (Redrawn and reproduced, with permission, from Leeson TS, Leeson CR: *Histology,* 2nd ed. Saunders, 1970.)

located in osteoid; and after 35 hours, a radioactive band was observed in the calcified matrix (Fig 8–4A). The extracellular label appeared as a radioactive band which was displaced from the proximity of the osteoblasts by the nonradioactive matrix formed after utilization of the labeled, injected glycine. On the seventh (Fig 8–4B) and especially on the 45th day (Fig 8–4C) after the labeling injection, radioactivity was found deep in the matrix. Thus, the distance between the radioactive matrix and the osteoblast layer indicates the amount of bone formed in the interval between the injection of ^{3}H-glycine and the death of the animal.

Osteoclasts

Osteoclasts are very large motile cells with 6–50 or more nuclei; they appear on bone surfaces wherever bone resorption occurs (Fig 8–2). In histologic sections, areas of bone resorption may be identified by the presence of osteoclasts. They are often found in shallow pits of the bone matrix, which are called the *lacunas of Howship.* Their cytoplasm is foamy, slightly basophilic in younger cells and acidophilic in older cells. Osteoclasts contain numerous lysosomes and consequently give a positive histochemical reaction for acid phosphatase.

Electron micrographs show that the osteoclast surface facing bone matrix is folded into irregular, often subdivided projections. Besides establishing a device whereby small particles may be easily trapped and subjected to enzymatic activity, this arrangement

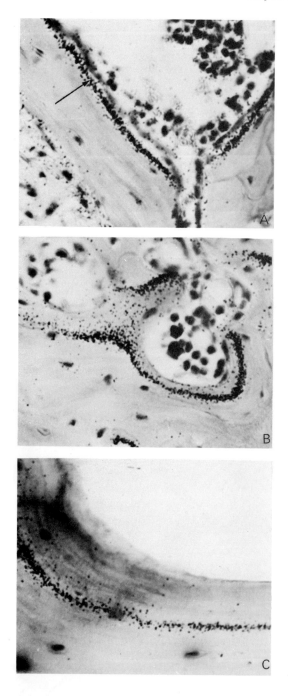

increases the active surface considerably.

Crystals containing calcium have been observed in the spaces between the folds as well as in cytoplasmic vacuoles, probably derived from the surface membrane of the osteoclasts. Disintegrating collagenous fibers have also been reported in the extracellular space close to the folds of the osteoclast, but they never occur within the cytoplasm.

The precise role of osteoclasts in bone resorption is not yet clear. There is evidence that they secrete collagenolytic enzymes which attack the bone matrix. They are also engaged in the elimination of debris formed during bone resorption.

BONE MATRIX

Inorganic matter represents about 50% of the dry weight of bone matrix. Calcium and phosphorus are especially abundant, but bicarbonate, citrate, magnesium, potassium, and sodium are also found. X-ray diffraction studies have shown that calcium and phosphorus form hydroxyapatite crystals with the composition $Ca_{10}(PO_4)_6(OH)_2$. In electron micrographs, hydroxyapatite crystals of bone appear as needles or elongated crystals measuring $40 \times 25 \times 3$ nm. They lie alongside the collagenous fibrils but are always surrounded by an amorphous ground substance. The surface ions of hydroxyapatite are hydrated, and a layer of water and ions forms around the crystal. This layer, the *hydration shell,* facilitates the exchange of ions between the crystal and the body fluids.

The organic matter is composed of collagenous fibers (95%) and the amphorous ground substance, which contains neutral and acid mucopolysaccharides associated with proteins. One of these proteins, osteomucoid, differs from collagen in the absence of hydroxyproline, the small content of proline and glycine, and the abundance of tyrosine and leucine. Among the acid mucopolysaccharides of bone are chrondroitin-4-sulfate, chondroitin-6-sulfate, and keratan sulfate.

Because of its high collagen content, decalcified bone matrix takes selective stains for collagenous fibers. It is also stained by the PAS technic, in which case the color intensity is proportionate to the quantity of galactose, fucose, and other carbohydrates present in neutral glycoproteins.

The association of hydroxyapatite with collagenous fibers is responsible for the hardness and resistance that are characteristic of bone. After a bone is decalcified, its shape is preserved but it becomes as flexible as a tendon. Removal by incineration of the organic part of the matrix—which is mainly collagenous in nature—also leaves the bone with its original shape; however, it becomes fragile and breaks easily when handled.

Figure 8—4. Radioautographs of bone tissue from mice injected with ^{3}H-glycine and killed at different intervals after the injection. *A:* From a mouse killed 4 hours after injection. At this time, osteoid is strongly radioactive (arrow). It contains labeled collagen synthesized by the osteoblasts using ^{3}H-glycine. There is some radioactivity remaining in the osteoblasts. Bone marrow cells (upper right) are also radioactive. *B:* From a mouse killed 7 days after injection. The radioactive band was pushed into the calcified matrix by the nonradioactive collagen formed after utilization of all labeled glycine. *C:* From a mouse killed 45 days after injection. The radioactive band is deeply placed by comparison with the sections from previous intervals. H&E stain.

PERIOSTEUM & ENDOSTEUM

Internal and external surfaces of bones are covered by layers of connective tissue named *endosteum* and *periosteum*. Bone surfaces not covered by connective tissue or by osteoblasts are subjected to resorption through the activity of osteoclasts which immediately appear in the area. For this reason, special attention is given to the periosteum and the endosteum in bone surgery.

The *periosteum* is a layer of dense connective tissue that is very fibrous externally but more cellular and vascular near the bone tissue (Fig 8–5).

Periosteal collagenous fibers are called *Sharpey's fibers.* They bind the periosteum to the underlying bone tissue.

Periosteal cells with morphologic characteristics

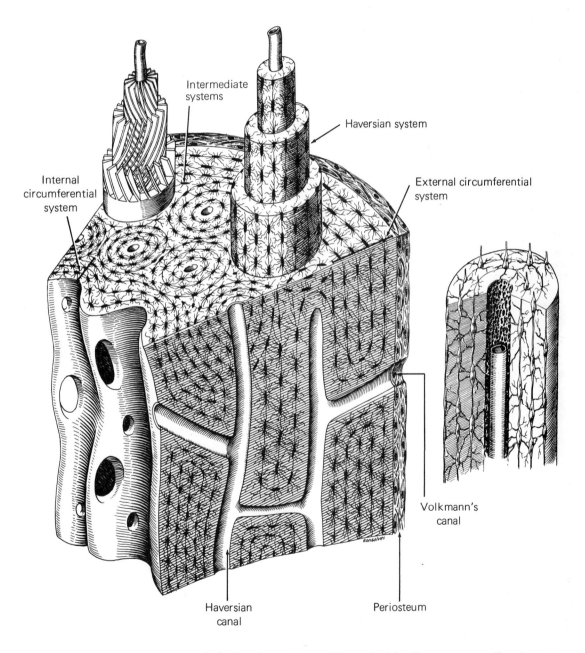

Figure 8–5. Schematic drawing of the wall of a long bone diaphysis. Observe the 4 lamellar arrangements: Haversian system, external and internal circumferential systems, and intermediate system. The Haversian system shows the orientation of collagen fibers in each lamella. At right is a Haversian system showing lamellas, a central blood capillary, and many osteocytes with their processes.

of fibroblasts are easily transformed into osteoblasts and then, through mitosis, into other osteoblasts. Periosteal cells play a prominent role in bone growth and repair.

The *endosteum* has the same components as the periosteum, and nearly the same structure, but it is considerably thinner and does not have 2 layers, as the periosteum does.

Within the connective tissue of the periosteum and endosteum, blood vessels are found which penetrate within the bone itself through canals called Volkmann's canals. The principal functions of the periosteum and endosteum are nutrition of osseous tissue and provision of a continuous supply of new osteoblastic cells for repair or growth of bone.

TYPES OF BONE TISSUE

Gross observation of bone in cross section shows dense areas without cavities—corresponding to *compact bone*—and areas with numerous interconnecting cavities—corresponding to *spongy bone*. Under the microscope, however, both compact bone and the walls separating the cavities of spongy bone have the same basic histologic structure.

In long bones, the extremities—called epiphyses—are composed of spongy bone covered by a thin layer of compact bone. The cylindric part—*diaphysis*—is almost totally composed of compact bone, with a small component of spongy bone in its inner position around the bone marrow cavity.

Short bones usually have a core of spongy bone completely surrounded by compact bone.

The flat bones which form the calvarium have 2 layers of compact bone called *plates*, separated by a layer of spongy bone called the *diploë*.

The cavities of spongy bone and the marrow cavity in the diaphyses of long bones contain *bone marrow*, of which there are 2 kinds: *red bone marrow*, in which blood cells are forming; and *yellow bone marrow*, composed mainly of fat cells.

Histologically, there are 2 varieties of bone tissue: *immature, primary,* or *woven bone;* and *mature, secondary,* or *lamellar bone.* Both varieties contain the same structural components, but in immature bone collagenous bundles are randomly placed while in mature bone these bundles are organized into *bone lamellas.*

Primary Bone Tissue

In the formation of each bone, as well as in the repair process, the first bone tissue to appear is immature. It is temporary and is replaced in adults by secondary bone tissue except in a very few places, eg, near the sutures of the flat bones of the skull, in tooth sockets, and in the insertions of some tendons.

Besides the irregular array of collagenous fibers, other characteristics of primary bone tissue are a smaller content of minerals (it is more easily penetrated by x-rays) and a higher percentage of osteocytes than in the secondary bone tissue.

Secondary Bone Tissue

Secondary bone is the variety usually found in adults. Characteristically, it shows collagenous fibers arranged in lamellas of $3-7$ μm, which are parallel to each other or concentrically organized around a vascular canal. The whole complex of concentric lamellas surrounding a canal containing blood vessels, nerves, and loose connective tissue is called the *Haversian system* (Fig 8–3). Lacunas with osteocytes are found between and occasionally within the lamellas. In each lamella, collagenous fibers are parallel to each other. Surrounding adjacent lamellas or Haversian systems there is often a deposit of glycoproteins called the *cementing substance.*

In the diaphysis, the lamellas exhibit a typical organization consisting of Haversian systems, an outer circumferential system, an inner circumferential system, and an intermediate system. The 4 systems are easily identified in cross section (Fig 8–5). Secondary bone tissue that contains Haversian systems is sometimes called *Haversian bone tissue.* It is usually found only in diaphyses, though small Haversian systems may be found in other places.

Each Haversian system is a long, often bifurcated cylinder parallel to the diaphyses. It consists of a central canal (of Havers) surrounded by $4-20$ concentric lamellas. Each canal contains blood vessels, nerves, and loose connective tissues. The Haversian canals communicate with the marrow cavity, with the periosteum, and with each other through transverse or oblique canals called Volkmann's canals (Fig 8–5). Volkmann's canals do not have concentric lamellas. Instead, they seem to perforate the lamellas (Fig 8–5). Actually, all vascular canals found in bone tissue come into existance when matrix is laid down around preexisting blood vessels.

Examination of Haversian systems with polarized light shows bright anisotropic layers alternating with dark isotropic layers. When observed under polarized light at right angles to their length, collagenous fibers are birefringent (anisotropic). The alternating aspect is due to the distribution of collagenous fibers in the lamellas. In each lamella, fibers are parallel to each other and follow a helical course. The pitch of the helix is, however, different for different lamellas, so that at any given point fibers from adjacent lamellas intersect at approximately right angles (Fig 8–5). Therefore, a cross-section of a Haversian system shows transverse sections of collagenous fibers from one lamella and oblique, almost longitudinal, sections of collagenous fibers from the following lamella. The structure of Haversian systems as shown in the light microscope is compatible with this interpretation. In one lamella, the collagenous fibers are sectioned transversely and appear granular; in the next, the fibers are sectioned obliquely and have an elongated appearance (Fig 8–3).

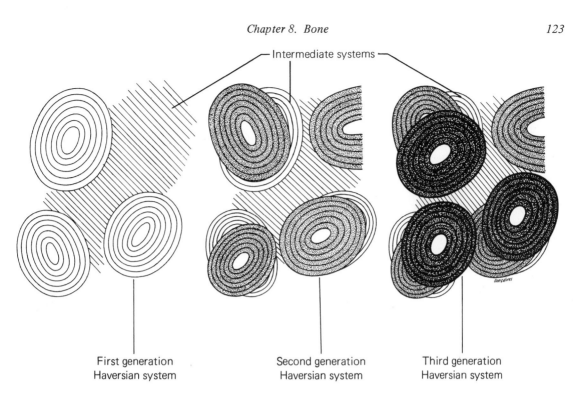

Intermediate systems

First generation
Haversian system

Second generation
Haversian system

Third generation
Haversian system

Figure 8—6. Schematic view of diaphyseal bone remodeling. Three generations of Haversian system are shown. At right, the contribution of first and second generation Haversian systems to the formation of intermediate systems can be seen.

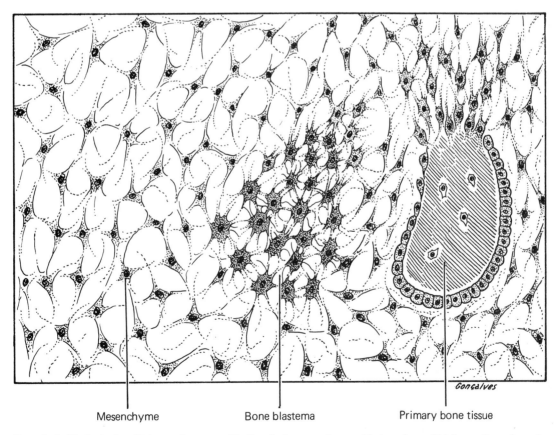

Mesenchyme

Bone blastema

Primary bone tissue

Figure 8—7. The beginning of intramembranous ossification. In the mesenchyme, a blastema from which bone cells are formed.

There is great variability in the diameter of Haversian canals. Each system is formed by successive deposition of lamellas, starting from the periphery, so that younger systems have larger canals.

During growth—and even in adult bone—there is continuous destruction and rebuilding of Haversian systems, so that one often sees systems with only a few lamellas and a large central canal.

Internal and external circumferential systems are, as their names indicate, located around the marrow cavity and immediately beneath the periosteum. Their lamellas have a circular distribution, with the medullary canal as the center. The external circumferential system has more lamellas than the internal system (Fig 8–5).

Between 2 circumferential systems there are numerous Haversian systems, and among them are triangular or irregularly shaped groups of parallel lamellas called intermediate systems. The intermediate systems are composed mainly of lamellas left by Haversian systems destroyed during growth and remodeling of bone (Fig 8–6).

HISTOGENESIS

Bone tissue arises either by intramembranous ossification, which occurs within a layer (membrane) of connective tissue, or by endochondral ossification, which takes place within a cartilaginous model. The model is gradually destroyed and replaced by bone formed by incoming cells from adjacent periosteal connective tissues.

In both processes, the bone tissue which appears first is primary or immature. It is a temporary tissue and is soon replaced by the definitive, lamellar variety of bone. During bone growth, areas of primary bone, areas of resorption, and areas of lamellar bone appear side by side. This combination of bone synthesis and removal occurs not only in growing bones but also throughout adult life, though its rate of change then is considerably slower.

Intramembranous Ossification

Intramembranous ossification is so called because it takes place within membranes of connective tissue. The frontal and parietal bones of the skull—as well as parts of the occipital and temporal bones and the mandible and maxilla—are formed by intramembranous ossification. Intramembranous ossification also contributes to the growth of short bones and the thickening of long bones.

In the connective tissue layer, the starting point for ossification is called the *primary ossification center*. The process begins by differentiation into osteoblasts of groups of cells resembling young fibroblasts. Osteoid synthesis and calcification follow, surrounding some osteoblasts which then become osteocytes (Fig 8–7). Several such groups arise almost simultaneously

at the ossification center, so that the fusion of matrix spicules gives the bone a spongy structure (Fig 8–8). The connective tissue that remains among the bone spicules is penetrated by growing blood vessels and undifferentiated mesenchymal cells, which give rise to the bone marrow cells.

Cells of the connective tissue membrane divide, giving rise to more osteoblasts, which are responsible for the growth of the ossification center. The several ossification centers of a bone grow radially and finally fuse together, replacing the original connective tissue. In newborn infants, the fontanels are soft areas in the skull which correspond to parts of the connective tissue not yet ossified.

In cranial flat bones, especially after birth, there is a marked predominance of bone formation over bone resorption at both the internal and the external surfaces. Thus, 2 layers of compact bone (internal and external plates) arise, whereas the central portion (diploë) maintains its spongy nature.

That portion of the connective tissue layer which does not undergo ossification gives rise to the endosteum and the periosteum of the intramembranous ossification.

Endochondral Ossification

Endochondral ossification takes place over a piece of hyaline cartilage whose shape resembles a small version of the model of the bone to be formed. This

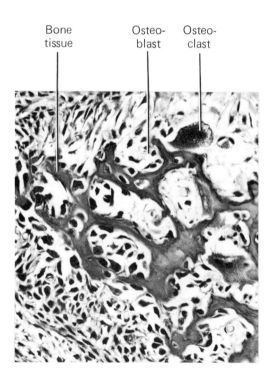

Bone tissue   Osteo-blast   Osteo-clast

Figure 8–8. Photomicrograph of intramembranous ossification from the head of a young rat. Bone tissue shows osteocytes in lacunas. Around the newly formed bone tissue there are numerous osteoblasts and an osteoclast. Mallory azan stain, X 350.

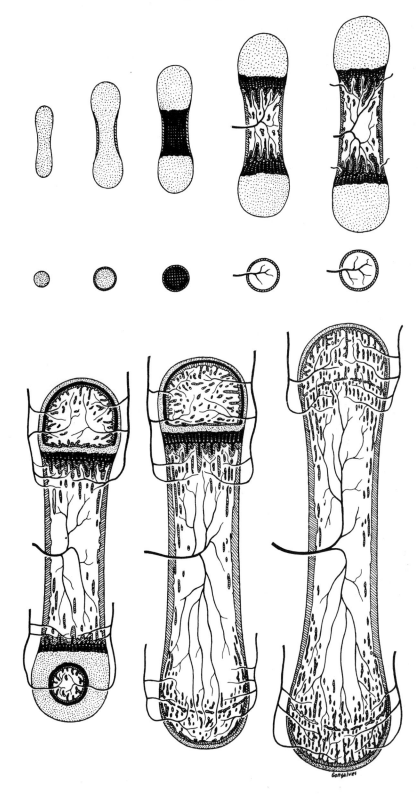

Figure 8–9. Formation of a long bone on a model made of cartilage. The hyaline cartilage is stippled, the calcified cartilage is black, and bone tissue is indicated by oblique lines. The 5 small drawings in the middle row represent cross-sections through the mid regions of the figures shown in the upper row. (For details, see text.) (Redrawn and reproduced, with permission, from Bloom W, Fawcett DW: *A Textbook of Histology,* 9th ed. Saunders, 1968.)

type of ossification is principally responsible for the formation of short and long bones (Fig 8–9).

Basically, endochondral ossification consists of 2 processes. The first process is hypertrophy and destruction of the chondrocytes of the model of the bone, leaving cavities separated by the septa of a calcified cartilage matrix. In the second process, undifferentiated mesenchymal cells and blood capillaries penetrate into the spaces left by destroyed chondrocytes. The undifferentiated cells give rise to osteoblasts, which form an osseous matrix on the remnants of the calcified cartilage matrix. In this way, bone tissue appears at the site where there was cartilage, but there is no transformation of the cartilage into bone tissue. The septa of calcified cartilage tissue serve as supports for the beginning of ossification (Fig 8–9).

Long bones are formed from cartilaginous models with dilated extremities (epiphyses) and a cylindric segment (diaphysis). The first bone tissue to be formed appears by means of intramembranous ossification at the perichondrium surrounding the diaphysis (Fig 8–9). Thus, a hollow bone cylinder (bone collar) is produced in the deep portions of the perichondrium surrounding the cartilage. (The perichondrium is then called periosteum because it covers the newly developed bone.) While the bone collar is being formed, those cartilage cells within the cartilage model at the same level increase their size and degenerate, leaving large cavities. Cartilage matrix becomes reduced to slender calcified partitions.

Blood vessels, coming from the periosteum through holes made by osteoclasts in the bone collar, penetrate the calcified cartilage matrix. Along with the blood vessels, undifferentiated mesenchymal cells also invade the area; they proliferate and give rise to osteoblasts and bone marrow stem cells. These form a continuous layer over the calcified cartilaginous matrix and start to synthesize bone matrix. Thus, primary bone synthesis takes place over the remnants of calcified cartilage (Fig 8–10).

In histologic sections, calcified cartilage can be distinguished as basophilic whereas the bone tissue deposited over it is acidophilic.

The ossification center described above, which appears in the diaphysis, is called the *primary ossification center*. Its rapid longitudinal growth ends by occupying the whole diaphysis, which then becomes composed completely of bone tissue. This expansion of the primary ossification center is accompanied by expansion of the periosteal bone cylinder (bone collar), which also grows in the direction of the epiphyses. From the beginning of the formation of the ossification center, osteoclasts are active, and resorption of the bone occurs at the center, which results in formation of a marrow cavity which grows toward the epiphyses as ossification continues toward the ends of the finally complete bone model.

At later stages in embryonic development, a secondary ossification center arises at each epiphysis though, even within one bone, all centers do not develop simultaneously. The function of these centers is

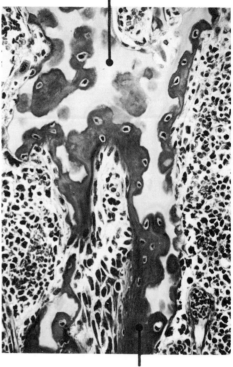

Remnants of cartilage matrix

Bone tissue

Figure 8–10. Photomicrograph of endochondral ossification from the finger of a human fetus. Remnants of calcified cartilage matrix appear covered by primary bone tissue. Calcified cartilage matrix has no cells, while bone matrix contains many osteocytes. Mallory trichrome stain, × 238.

similar to that of the primary center, but their growth is radial instead of longitudinal. Furthermore, since the articular cartilage has no perichondrium, the equivalent of a bone collar is not formed here (Fig 8–9).

When bone tissue that originated at the secondary centers occupies the epiphysis, cartilage remains restricted to 2 places: articular cartilage, which persists throughout adult life and does not contribute to bone formation; and epiphyseal cartilage or the epiphyseal plate (Figs 8–11 and 8–12). The epiphyseal plate is a cartilaginous disk that is replaced continuously by expanding bone mainly from the diaphyseal center. It connects the epiphysis to the diaphysis. No further longitudinal growth of the bone takes place after epiphyseal cartilage is replaced by bone tissue.

Epiphyseal cartilage is divided into 5 zones (Fig 8–12), starting from the epiphyseal side of cartilage: (1) The *resting zone* consists of hyaline cartilage without morphologic changes in the cells. (2) In the *proliferative zone*, chondrocytes divide rapidly and form parallel rows of stacked cells along the long axis of the bone. (3) The *hypertrophic cartilage zone* is characterized by large chondrocytes whose cytoplasm has accumulated glycogen. The matrix is reduced to thin septa between the chondrocytes. (4) Simultaneously

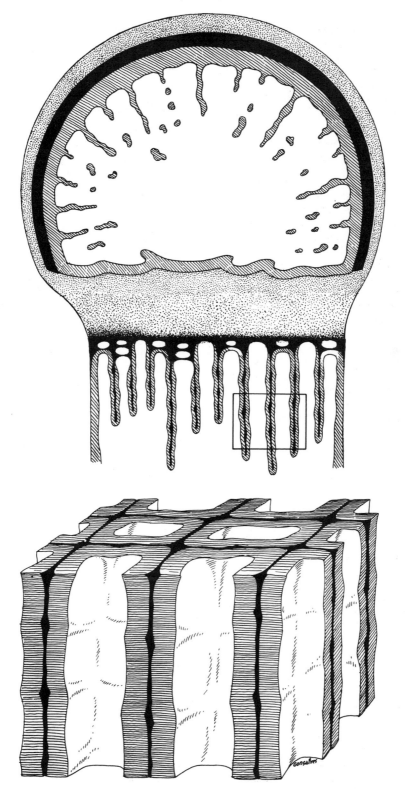

Figure 8–11. Schematic drawings showing the 3-dimensional shape of bone spicules in the epiphyseal disk area. Hyaline cartilage is stippled, calcified cartilage is black, and bone tissue is indicated by parallel lines. The upper drawing shows the region represented 3-dimensionally in the lower drawing. (Redrawn and reproduced, with permission, from Ham AW: *Histology,* 6th ed. Lippincott, 1969.)

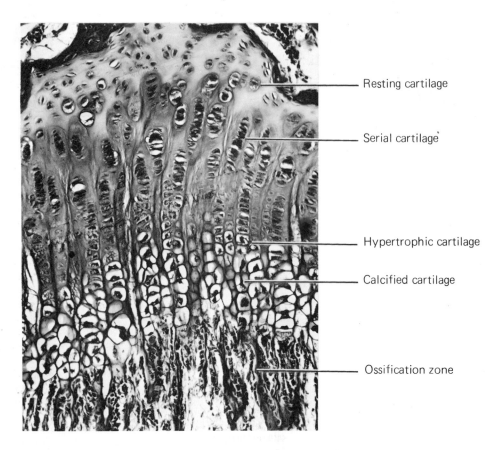

Resting cartilage

Serial cartilage

Hypertrophic cartilage

Calcified cartilage

Ossification zone

Figure 8–12. Photomicrograph of the epiphyseal plate, showing the changes which take place in the cartilage and the bone spicules formed. H&E stain, × 110.

with the death of chondrocytes occurring in the *calcified cartilage zone,* the thin septa of cartilage matrix become calcified by the deposition of hydroxyapatite (Figs 8–11 and 8–12). (5) In the *ossification zone,* bone tissue appears. Blood capillaries and undifferentiated cells formed by mitosis of cells originating from the periosteum invade the cavities left by the chondrocytes. The undifferentiated cells form osteoblasts, which in turn form a discontinuous layer over the septa of calcified cartilage matrix. Over these septa, the osteoblasts lay down bone matrix (Fig 8–10).

The bone matrix calcifies, and some osteoblasts are transformed into osteocytes. In this way, *bone spicules* are formed with a central area of calcified cartilage and a superficial layer of primary bone tissue. The spicules are so called because of their appearance in histologic sections; in fact, they are sections of walls which delineate elongated cavities containing capillaries, bone marrow cells, and undifferentiated cells (Fig 8–11).

GROWTH & REMODELING OF BONE

Bone growth is generally associated with partial resorption of preformed tissue and the simultaneous laying down of new bone. This permits the shape of the bone to be maintained while it grows.

Cranial bones grow mainly by formation of bone tissue by the periosteum located between the sutures and on the external bone surface. At the same time, resorption takes place on the internal surface. Since bone is an extremely plastic tissue, it responds to the growth of the brain and forms a skull of adequate size. Consequently, the skull will be small if the brain does not develop completely and larger than normal in a person suffering from hydrocephalus, a disorder characterized by abnormal accumulation of spinal fluid and dilatation of the cerebral ventricles.

The growth of long bones is a more complex process. The epiphyses increase in size owing to the radial growth of the cartilage, followed by endochondral ossification. In this way, the spongy part of the epiphysis increases.

The diaphysis (the bone formed between the 2 epiphyseal plates) consists initially of a bone cylinder. Because of the faster growth of the epiphyses, the

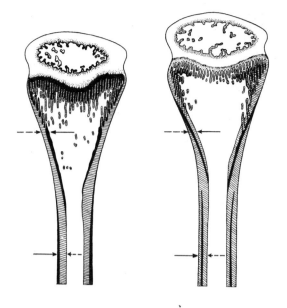

extremities of the diaphysis soon become larger, forming 2 *diaphyseal funnels* separated by the *diaphyseal shaft.*

The diaphyseal shaft increases in length mainly as a result of the osteogenic activity of the epiphyseal plate; it increases in width as a result of the formation of bone by the periosteum on the external surface of the bone. At the same time, bone is removed from the internal surface, and in this way the bone marrow cavity increases in diameter.

In both diaphyseal funnels, owing to the osteogenic activity of the endosteum, deposition of bone occurs on its internal surface (Fig 8–13). At the same time, bone is resorbed in certain areas from the external surface. The narrow parts of the diaphyseal funnels therefore become gradually cylindric, and this is due mainly to the osteogenic activity of the epiphyseal plate (Fig 8–14). As a result of this process, the cylindric diaphyseal shaft increases in length, and the 2 diaphyseal funnels grow farther apart as the bone lengthens. Gradually, osteogenic activity in the endosteum of the cylindric portion of the diaphyseal funnel ceases, permitting the bone marrow cavity to maintain or to increase its diameter slowly by resorption. As the central bone spicules become eroded to make room for the bone marrow cavity, the epiphyseal cartilage remains firmly attached to the diaphyseal funnel by means of the peripheral spicules (Figs 8–13 and 8–14).

In brief, it can be said that long bones become longer as a result of the activity of the epiphyseal plates and wider as a result of the apposition of bone

Figure 8–13. Drawings based on radioautographs of animals injected with radioactive phosphate at several time intervals before being killed. Black areas indicate radioactive matrix, solid arrows indicate zones of bone deposition, and broken arrows indicate zones of bone resorption. In diaphyseal funnels, bone deposition occurs mainly at the internal surface. In the diaphysis, bone is laid down mainly on the center surface. (Based on the work of CP Leblond & others. Redrawn and reproduced, with permission, from Greep RO, Weiss L: *Histology,* 3rd ed. McGraw-Hill, 1973.)

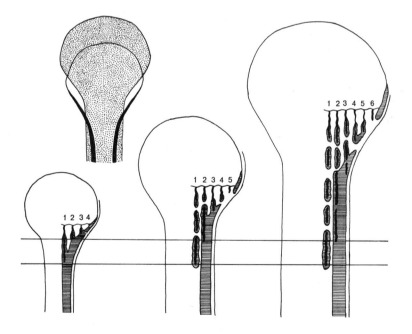

Figure 8–14. *Upper left:* The importance of bone resorption in the external surface of the funnel for bone growth. *Lower drawings:* Bone growth taking place by diaphyseal displacement. (Use the 2 parallel lines as reference). Observe also how epiphyseal bone spicules contribute to the diaphyseal development, eg, spicule 2 is being incorporated into the diaphysis. (Based on the work of CP Leblond & others.)

formed by the periosteum. After the disappearance of
the epiphyseal plates—normally at about age 20—the
longitudinal growth of bones becomes impossible, although widening may still occur.

FRACTURE REPAIR

When a bone is fractured, the damage suffered by
the blood vessels produces a localized hemorrhage with
the formation of a blood clot. Destruction of bone
matrix and death of bone cells adjoining the fracture
also occur.

During repair, the blood clot, the remaining cells,
and the damaged bone matrix are removed. The periosteum and the endosteum around the fracture respond
with intense proliferation of their fibroblasts and other
undifferentiated cells which form a cellular tissue surrounding the fracture and penetrate between the extremities of the fractured bone (Fig 8—15A and B).
Some of these cells differentiate into macrophages
which engulf the remains of the damaged tissue and
the bloot clot.

Immature bone is then formed by endochondral
ossification of small fragments of cartilage appearing in
the connective tissue that develops first in the fracture.
It is also formed by means of intramembranous ossification. Therefore, areas of cartilage, areas of intramembranous ossification, and areas of endochondral ossification are encountered simultaneously when repair is
taking place. Repair progresses in such a way that,
after a period of time, irregularly formed trabeculae of
immature bone temporarily unite the extremities of
the fractured bone, forming a *bone callus* (Figs 8—15C
and 8—16).

Normal stress imposed on the bone during repair
and during the patient's gradual return to activity serves
to remodel the bone callus. Since these strains are identical to those that occurred during the growth of the
bone, thus conditioning its structure, remodeling of
the callus reconstitutes the bone as it was prior to
fracture. The primary bone tissue of the callus is therefore gradually reabsorbed and replaced by lamellar
bone, resulting in restoration of the original bone
structure (Fig 8—15D).

HISTOPHYSIOLOGY

Support & Protection

Bones form the skeleton, the function of which is
to bear the weight of the body. Voluntary (skeletal)
muscles are inserted on the bones. Long bones constitute a system of levers that increase the forces produced by muscular contractions. Bones protect the
central nervous system, which is enclosed in the skull
and the spinal canal, and also the bone marrow.

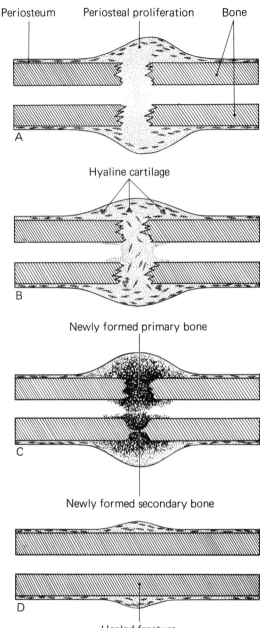

Figure 8–15. Repair of a fractured bone by formation of new
bone tissue through proliferation of periosteal and endosteal
cells.

Plasticity

In spite of its hardness, bone is capable of remodeling its internal structure according to the different stresses to which it is subjected. Thus, for example,
the positions of the teeth in the jawbone may be modified by lateral pressures produced by orthodontic ap-
pliances. Bone formation takes place on the side where
traction is applied and is reabsorbed where pressure is
exerted (on the opposite side). In this way, teeth move
within the jawbone while the alveolar bone is being

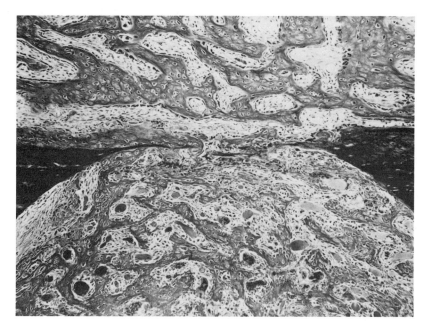

Figure 8–16. Photomicrograph of a mouse bone callus 7 days after fracture. The early callus contains mainly primary bone tissue made by cells originating in the periosteum. Mallory stain, ✕ 118.

remodeled. This capacity for reconstruction is a characteristic of all bones.

Calcium Reserve

The skeleton contains 99% of the total calcium of the body and acts as a calcium reservoir. The concentration of calcium in the blood and in tissues is quite stable. Calcium is important for the activity of several enzymatic systems, including those responsible for muscular contraction and transmission of nerve impulses. Calcium in the extracellular compartment is essential to several functions such as coagulation of the blood and cell adhesion.

There is a continuous interchange between blood calcium and bone calcium. The calcium absorbed from a meal, which would otherwise increase the blood calcium level, is rapidly deposited in bones or excreted in the feces or urine. Calcium in bones is mobilized when the concentration in blood decreases.

Bone calcium is mobilized by 2 mechanisms, one rapid and the other slow. The first is the simple transference of ions from hydroxyapatite crystals to interstitial fluid—from which, in turn, calcium passes into the blood. This purely physical mechanism is aided by the large surface area of the hydroxyapatite crystals. The younger, slightly calcified lamellas that exist even in adult bone because of continuous remodeling receive and lose calcium more easily. These lamellas are more important for the maintenance of calcium concentration in the blood than the older, greatly calcified lamellas, whose role is mainly that of support and protection.

The second mechanism for mobilizing calcium depends on the action of parathyroid hormone on bone.

Parathyroid hormone activates and increases the number of cells promoting resorption (osteoclasts) of the bone matrix, with the consequent liberation of calcium.

Another hormone, *calcitonin,* which is synthesized by the clear (C) cells of the thyroid gland, inhibits matrix resorption and calcium mobilization. Its effect on bone, therefore, is opposite to that of parathyroid hormone.

Since the concentration of calcium in tissues and blood must be kept constant, nutritional deficiency of calcium results in decalcification of bones; they then are more liable to fracture and are more permeable to x-rays. Decalcification of bone may also be caused by excessive production of parathyroid hormone (hyperparathyroidism), which results in intense resorption of bone, elevation of blood calcium, and abnormal deposits of calcium in several organs, mainly the kidneys and arterial walls.

Nutrition

Especially during growth, bone is sensitive to several nutritional factors. Insufficient dietary protein causes a deficiency of amino acids necessary for the synthesis of collagen by osteoblasts. Deficiency of calcium leads to incomplete calcification of the organic bone matrix; it may be due either to the lack of calcium in the diet or to the lack of vitamin D, which is important for the absorption of calcium by the small intestine.

Calcium deficiency in children causes rickets, a disease in which the bone matrix does not calcify normally and the bone spicules formed by the epiphyseal plate become distorted when subjected to the normal strains of body weight and muscular activity. Consequently, ossification processes at this level are hindered and the bones not only grow more slowly but also become deformed.

Calcium deficiency in adults gives rise to *osteomalacia,* characterized by deficient calcification of recently formed bone and by partial decalcification of already calcified matrix. However, since adults have no epiphyseal cartilage, the deformation of long bones and some retardation of growth that is characteristic of rickets in children does not occur, and of course growth is not affected. Osteomalacia may be aggravated during pregnancy since the developing fetus requires a great deal of calcium.

Besides the aforementioned effect on intestinal absorption, vitamin D has a direct effect on ossification, as has been demonstrated with in vitro experiments. Bone tissue cultivated in a medium rich in calcium but deficient in vitamin D does not calcify properly. Excessive amounts of vitamin D are toxic, however, and give rise to bone resorption.

Vitamin A is also related to the distribution and activity of the osteoblasts and osteoclasts; it therefore affects the balance between production and resorption of bone. This vitamin is essential to normal growth in response to mechanical factors acting on bones, an effect that becomes evident when, as a result of vitamin A deficiency, the bones of the skull do not develop fast enough to respond to the pressure exerted by the growing brain, resulting in damage to the central

nervous system. This development does not occur in laboratory control animals receiving adequate doses of vitamin A, for the skull then grows to the exact size necessary to contain the brain.

In vitamin A deficiency, the osteoblasts do not synthesize the bone matrix normally and the individual therefore does not reach his normal stature. Vitamin A excess accelerates ossification of the epiphyseal plates but has no important effect on the growth of cartilage in these plates. Consequently, epiphyseal cartilage is rapidly replaced by bone and body growth ceases. For these reasons, either vitamin A deficiency or administration of toxic doses of vitamin A may cause small stature.

Another vitamin which acts directly on bone is vitamin C (ascorbic acid), which is essential for collagen synthesis by the cells which produce this substance, including osteoblasts. Vitamin C deficiency interferes with bone growth and hinders repair of fractures.

Hormonal Factors

In addition to parathyroid hormone and calcitonin, several other hormones act on bone.

The anterior lobe of the pituitary synthesizes growth hormone, which, in stimulating overall growth, has a marked effect on epiphyseal cartilage. Consequently, lack of growth hormone during the growing years causes pituitary dwarfism, and growth hormone excess causes gigantism because of excessive growth of

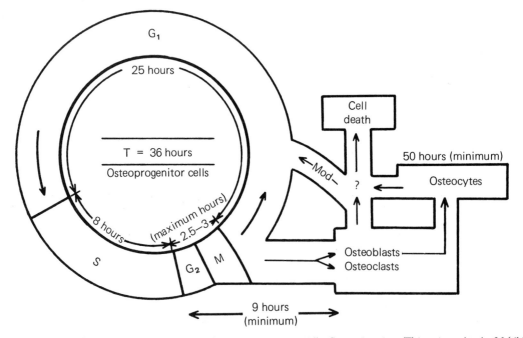

Figure 8–17. Osteoblasts and osteoclasts originating from osteoprogenitor cells. Generation time (T) is estimated to be 36 (tibia of young rats). The period of DNA synthesis (S) is 8 hours; G_1 consumes 25 hours of the cycle, whereas G_2 and mitosis (M) take 2.5–3 hours. The minimum time for an osteoprogenitor cell to be transformed into an osteoblast or osteoclast is 9 hours. Once formed, osteocytes remain as such for at least 50 hours or, very often, longer. Osteoblasts and osteoclasts can modulate (Mod) back to an osteoprogenitor cell; it is not certain whether osteocytes can do so. (Slightly modified and reproduced, with permission, from Young RW: J Cell Biol 14:357, 1962.)

long bones. Adult bones cannot increase in length when stimulated by an excess of growth hormone because of the lack of epiphyseal cartilage, but they do increase in width by periosteal growth. This causes *acromegaly,* a disease in which the bones—mainly the long ones—become very thick.

The sex hormones, both male (androgens) and female (estrogens), have a complex effect on bones and are, in a general way, stimulators of bone formation. They influence the time of appearance and the development of ossification centers. Thus, precocious sexual maturity due to sex hormone–producing tumors or to the administration of sex hormones retards bodily growth, for in these instances epiphyseal cartilage is quickly replaced by bone. In hormone deficiencies due to abnormal development of the gonads or castration, epiphyseal cartilage remains functional for a longer period of time, resulting in tall stature.

Interrelationships Between the Cells of Bone

Radioautographic studies performed after the administration of ^{3}H-thymidine to young animals—whose bone cells proliferate rapidly—reveal that these cells represent different aspects of an osteoprogenitor showing modulations between the 3 types of bone cells (Fig 8–17). The osteoblasts, osteocytes, and osteoclasts do not divide after having been formed from the osteoprogenitor cell, which is a slightly differentiated mesenchymal cell. In the epiphyseal disk, the osteoprogenitor cell has a "generation time" of about 36 hours; this means that during this interval its number doubles. Some of the new cells thus formed are modified, giving rise to osteoblasts, or form osteoclasts by fusion.

A. Fate of the Osteoblasts: Most of the osteoblasts give rise to osteocytes; others remain as osteoblasts for long periods of time; and some return to the state of the osteoprogenitor cell.

B. Fate of the Osteocytes: When destruction of the matrix occurs during the process of remodeling, it appears that some of the osteocytes die, but most probably return to the state of the osteoprogenitor cell. As a result of the intensive remodeling of bone that takes place in the epiphyseal disk, many of the osteocytes remain as osteocytes for a short period (minimum of 50 hours). In other sites (eg, in the systems of Havers), the cells may persist as osteocytes for a long time.

C. Fate of Osteoclasts: The osteoclasts are formed by the fusion of osteoprogenitor cells. These young osteoclasts, which have few nuclei, are joined by other progenitor cells. At the same time, some of the nuclei leave the osteoclasts, taking with them a portion of cytoplasm and returning to the osteoprogenitor cell state. At the end of the remodeling process, at a specific place, the osteoclasts become fragmented, thus forming mononucleated elements and returning to the state of the osteoprogenitor cells.

JOINTS

Bones are joined to one another to form the skeleton by means of connective tissue structures called joints. Joints may be classified as *diarthroses,* which permit free bone movement, and *synarthroses,* in which very limited or no movement occurs. There are 3 types of synarthrosis: synostosis, synchondrosis, and syndesmosis.

Synostosis

In joints of this type, bones are united by bone tissue. No movement takes place. In elderly people, this type of synarthrosis unites the skull bones. In children and young adults, these bones are united by dense connective tissue.

Synchondrosis

Synchondroses are articulations in which the bones are joined by hyaline cartilage. Limited movement may take place. The ribs are attached to the sternum in this way.

Syndesmosis

As is the case with synchondroses also, a syndesmosis permits a certain amount of movement. The bones are joined by connective tissue (eg, the inferior tibiofibular articulation).

Diarthrosis

Diarthroses are joints that generally unite long bones and have great mobility. In a diarthrosis, a capsule joins the extremities of the bones and encloses a

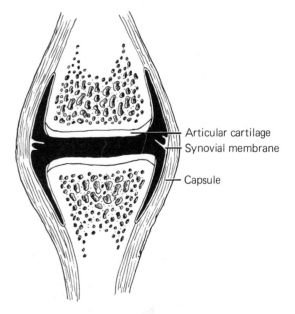

Articular cartilage
Synovial membrane

Capsule

Figure 8–18. Schematic drawing of a diarthrosis. Processes of the synovial membrane are shown in white; the joint cavity is shown in black.

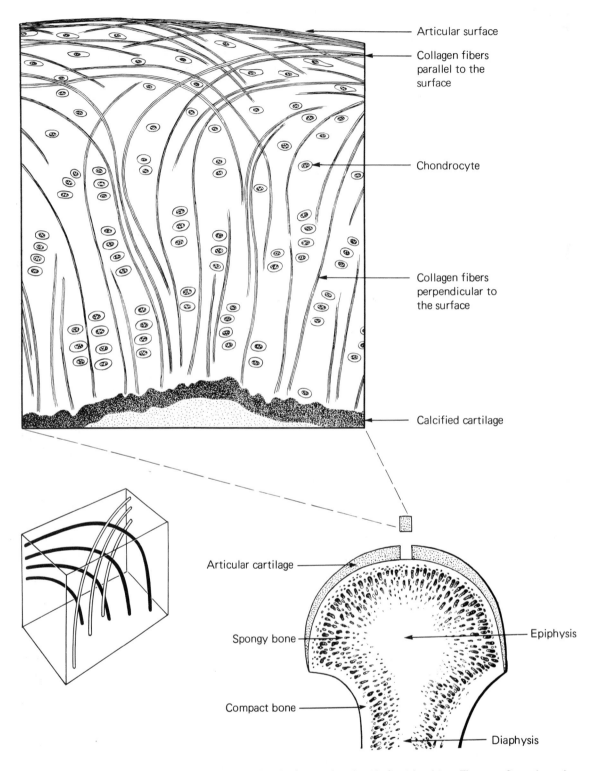

Figure 8—19. Articular surfaces of diarthroses are covered by hyaline cartilage devoid of perichondrium. The upper figure shows that in this cartilage collagen fibers are first perpendicular and then parallel to the cartilage surface. Deeply located chondrocytes are globular and are arranged in elongated rows. Superficially placed chondrocytes are slender and are not organized in groups. The lower left drawing shows the organization of collagen fibers in articular cartilage in 3 dimensions.

sealed cavity—the *articular cavity*—which contains a colorless, transparent, viscous fluid, rich in hyaluronic acid, called *synovial fluid.* The sliding of articular surfaces covered by hyaline cartilage and having no perichondrium is facilitated by the synovial fluid (Figs 8–18 and 8–19).

The capsules of diarthroses (Fig 8–18) vary in structure according to the joint. Generally, however, this capsule is composed of 2 layers, one external *(fibrous layer)* and one internal *(synovial layer).*

The fluid encountered in the articular cavity is formed by the synovial layer, which is arranged in folds that occasionally penetrate deep into the interior of the articular cavity. The internal surface of the synovial membrane is lined by a layer of squamous or cuboid cells. Underneath these cells is a layer of loose or dense connective tissue with areas of adipose tissue. The lining cells of the synovial membrane originate in the mesenchyme. They are separated from each other by a small amount of connective tissue ground substance (Figs 8–20 and 8–21).

Observations made with the electron microscope have shown 2 cell types lining the synovial membrane (Fig 8–21). Some of these cells resemble macrophages and are called M cells. They have a large Golgi apparatus and many lysosomes but only a small amount of granular endoplasmic reticulum. The other cell type has structural features of a fibroblast and is called an F cell. Cells of this type have a well-developed granular endoplasmic reticulum and are more electron-dense than M cells. M cells and F cells may represent only different functional stages of the same cell type.

Radioautographs analyzed under the light microscope show that the cells covering synovial membrane synthesize hyaluronic acid and proteins, which are secreted into the synovial fluid. Both M cells and F cells are phagocytic, but M cells are much more active in this respect.

The fibrous layer is made of dense connective tissue and is more developed in parts subject to great strain. This layer envelops the ligaments of the joint and some of the tendons inserted into the bone near the joint.

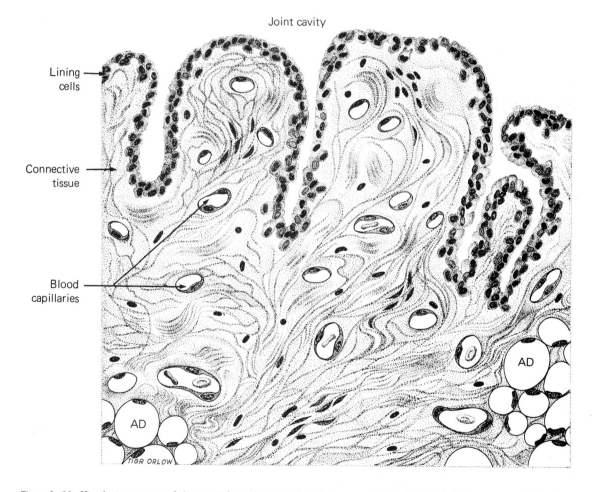

Figure 8–20. Histologic structure of the synovial membrane, with its lining connective cells in epitheloid arrangement. There is no basal lamina between the lining cells and the underlying connective tissue. This tissue is rich in blood capillaries and contains a variable amount of adipose cells (AD). (Reproduced, with permission, from Cossermelli W: *Reumatologia Básica.* Sarvier, 1972.)

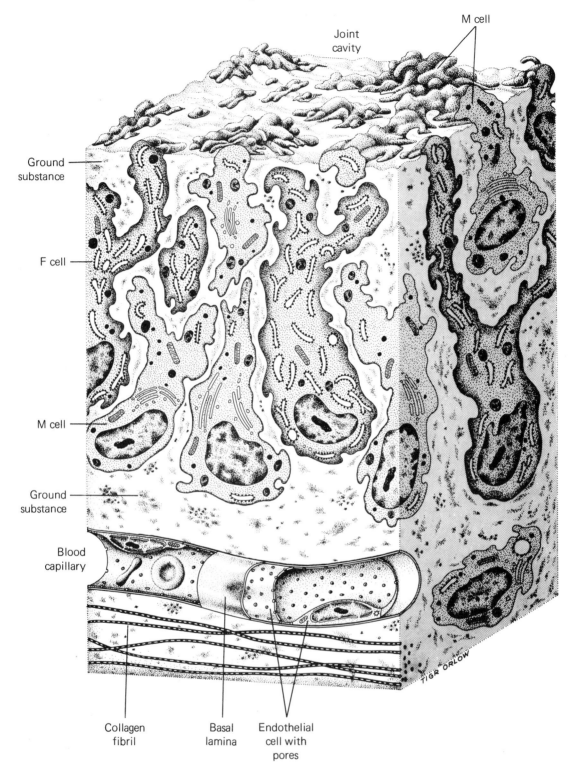

Figure 8–21. Schematic representation of the ultrastructure of a synovial membrane. F and M cell types are separated by a small amount of connective tissue amorphous ground substance. No basal lamina is seen separating the lining cells from the connective tissue. Blood capillaries are of the fenestrated type, which facilitates exchange of substances between the blood and the synovial fluid. (Redrawn and reproduced, with permission, from Cossermelli W: *Reumatologia Básica.* Sarvier, 1972. Based on a drawing in Barland PA & others: J Cell Biol 14:207, 1962.)

• • •

References

Barland P, Novikoff AB, Hamerman D: Electron microscopy of the human synovial membrane. J Cell Biol 14:207, 1962.

Barland P, Smith C, Hamerman D: Localization of hyaluronic acid in synovial cells by radioautography. J Cell Biol 37:13, 1968.

Blau S & others: Cellular origin of hyaluronate protein in the human synovial membrane. Science 150:353, 1965.

Bourne GH (editor): *The Biochemistry of Physiology of Bone.* Vol 1. *Structure.* Academic Press, 1972.

Cameron DA: The fine structure of osteoblasts in the metaphysis of the tibia of the young rat. J Biophys Biochem Cytol 9:583, 1961.

Carneiro J, Leblond CP: Role of osteoblasts and odontoblasts in secreting the collagen of bone and dentin, as shown by radioautography in mice given tritium-labelled glycine. Exp Cell Res 18:291, 1959.

Carneiro J, Leblond CP: Suitability of collagenase treatment for the radioautographic identification of newly-formed collagen labeled with ^{3}H-glycine or ^{3}H-proline. J Histochem Cytochem 14:334, 1966.

Cherubino P, Kataoka K: Scanning electron microscope observations of the synovial membrane of rabbit knee joints after experimentally induced hemarthrosis. Arch Histol Jap 35:417, 1973.

Gaillard PJ: The cellular basis of hormone response. Pathol Biol 9:619, 1961.

Glimcher MJ, Krane SM: The organization and structure of bone, and the mechanism of calcification. In: *Treatise on Collagen.* Vol 2, part B. Gould BS (editor). Academic Press, 1968.

Ham AW, Harris WR: Repair and transplantation of bone. In:

The Biochemistry and Physiology of Bone. Bourne GH (editor). Academic Press, 1956.

Jowsey J: Studies of Haversian systems in man and some animals. J Anat 100:857, 1966.

Kashiwa HA: Localization of phosphate in bone cells of fresh calvaria by means of a dilute silver acetate solution. Anat Record 162:177, 1968.

Kaufman EJ & others: Collagenolytic activity during active bone resorption in tissue culture. Proc Soc Exper Biol Med 120:632, 1965.

Lacroix P: Bone and cartilage. In: *The Cell.* Vol 5. Brachet J, Mirsky AE (editors). Academic Press, 1961.

Lacroix P, Bundy A (editors): *Radioisotopes and Bone: A Symposium.* Blackwell, 1962.

Nichol G Jr (editor): *Workshop Conference on Cell Mechanisms for Calcium Transfer and Homeostasis.* Academic Press, 1971.

Owen M: Cell population kinetics of an osteogenic tissue. (Part 1.) J Cell Biol 19:19, 1963.

Owen M: The origin of bone cells. Int Rev Cytol 28:213, 1970.

Owen M, MacPherson S: Cell population kinetics of an osteogenic tissue. (Part 2.) J Cell Biol 19:33, 1963.

Roberts ED & others: Electron microscopy of porcine synovial cell layer. J Comp Pathol 79:41, 1969.

Taylor AN, Wasserman RH: Immunofluorescent localization of vitamin D-dependent calcium-binding protein. J Histochem Cytochem 18:107, 1970.

Vaughan JM: *The Physiology of Bone.* Clarendon Press, 1970.

Wright V, Dowson D, Kerr J: The structure of joints. In: *International Review of Connective Tissue Research.* Vol 6. Hall DA, Jackson DS (editors). Academic Press, 1973.

9 . . .
Nerve Tissue

During the evolution of the metazoa, 2 intergrative systems were developed—the nervous and endocrine systems—that serve to coordinate the functions of specialized organs and tissues. Both developed from epithelia, and the nervous system probably appeared first. Of all types of cells, nerve cells undergo the greatest increase in volume and surface area during the processes of development and maturation.

Nerve tissue is found all over the body as a communications network. Anatomically, the nervous system is divided into the *central nervous system,* consisting of the brain and the spinal cord; and the *peripheral nervous system,* which is composed of nerves and small aggregates of nerve cells called *nerve ganglia.*

Structurally, nerve tissue is made up of 2 main components: *nerve cells* or *neurons,* which usually show numerous long processes; and several types of *glial cells* or *neuroglia,* which support the neurons and participate also in neural activity, neural nutrition, and the defense processes of the central nervous system.

In the central nervous system, the nerve cell bodies are concentrated in groups located at different areas from their processes. The brain and spinal cord are composed of *gray matter* and *white matter.* The former (gray when fresh) contains mainly nerve cell bodies and neuroglia but also a complicated network of processes of nerve cells. White matter does not contain nerve cell bodies; it consists of neuronal processes and neuroglia. It takes its name from the presence of a whitish material called *myelin* that envelops most of the neuronal processes. In the brain stem, there are regions that contain both nerve cells and myelinated fibers and where gray matter is mixed with white matter.

Neurons respond to environmental changes (stimuli) by modifications in the differences of electrical potential that exist between the inner and the outer surfaces of their membranes. Cells with this property (eg, neurons, muscle cells, some gland cells) are called "excitable." Neurons react promptly to stimuli, and modification of electrical potential may either be restricted to the place that received the stimulus or may be spread throughout the neuron by the membrane. This propagation is called the *nerve impulse,* which transmits information to other neurons, muscles, and glands.

The 2 fundamental functions of the nervous system are (1) to detect, analyze, utilize, and transmit all information generated by sensory stimuli such as heat and light and by mechanical and chemical changes that take place in the internal and external milieu; and (2) to organize and coordinate, directly or indirectly, most functions of the body, especially the motor, visceral, endocrine, and mental activities.

NEURONS

The nerve cells or neurons are independent anatomic and functional units with complex morphologic characteristics. Most neurons consist of 3 parts: the *dendrites,* which are multiple elongated processes specialized in receiving stimuli from the environment, from sensory epithelial cells, or from other neurons; the *cell body* or *perikaryon,* which represents the trophic center for the whole nerve cell and is also receptive to stimuli; and the *axon,* which is a single process specialized in generating or conducting nerve impulses to other cells (nerve, muscle, and gland cells). The final portion of the axon is usually branched and is called the *telodendron.* Each branch of the telodendron terminates in the next cell by dilatations, the *end bulbs,* which are important in the transmission of information to the next cell in the chain (Fig 9–1).

Neurons usually receive information through dendrites and cell bodies and transmit them via the telodendrons. This sequence, called *dynamic polarization* by Cajal, is the general rule, but some exceptions have been observed.

Neurons and their processes are extremely variable in size and shape (Fig 9–2). Perikaryons can be spherical, ovoid, or angular in contour; some are very large, measuring up to 150 μm in diameter. (When isolated, a corpuscle of this size is visible to the naked eye.) However, other nerve cells are among the smallest cells in the body, and the perikaryons of granular cells of the cerebellum measure 4–5 μm in diameter.

According to the size and shape of their processes, most neurons can be placed in one of the following categories: *multipolar neurons,* which have more than 2 cell processes, one being the axon and the rest dendrites; *bipolar neurons,* with one dendrite and

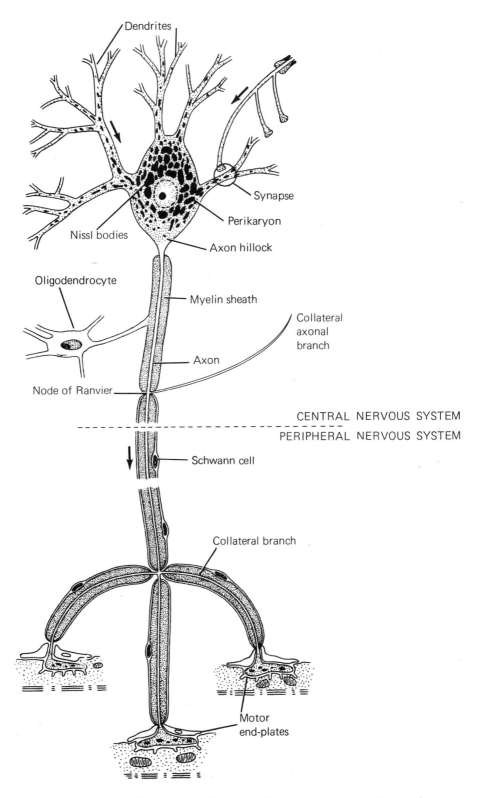

Figure 9–1. Schematic drawing of a motor neuron. The myelin sheath is produced by oligodendrocytes in the central nervous system and by Schwann cells in the peripheral nervous system. The neuronal cell body has a large nucleus with a well-developed nucleolus. The perikaryon contains Nissl bodies, which are also found in large dendrites. An axon from another neuron is shown at upper right. It has 3 end bulbs, one of which synapses with the neuron. Note also 3 motor end-plates, which transmit the nerve impulse to striated skeletal muscle fibers. Arrows show the direction of the nerve impulse.

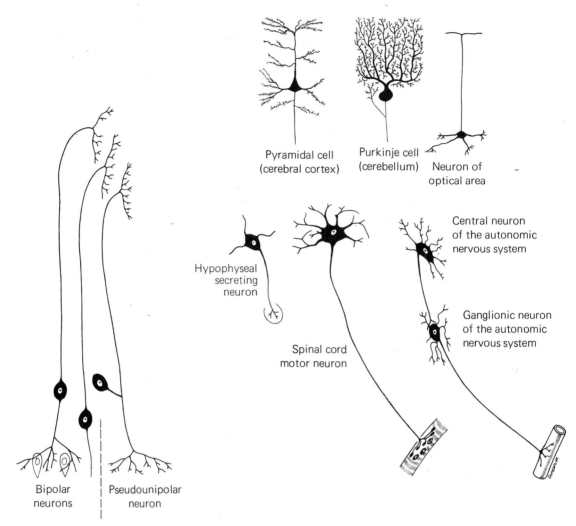

Figure 9–2. Diagrams of several types of neurons Neurons have a very complex morphology. Except for the bipolar and pseudo-unipolar neurons, which are not very numerous in nerve tissue, all others shown here are of the common multipolar variety.

one axon; and *pseudounipolar neurons,* which show a single process close to the perikaryon but which divides into 2 branches, forming a T shape, one branch extending to a peripheral ending and the other toward the central nervous system (Fig 9–2).

In the embryo, a pseudounipolar neuron starts as a bipolar cell with a dendrite and an axon, each arising from opposite ends of the perikaryon. During later development, the 2 processes come together on one side of the cell and fuse for a certain distance close to the perikaryon. Certain cells, like the amacrine cells of the retina, do not have axons in the ordinary sense and their processes appear to be both axonic and dendritic.

Most neurons of the body are multipolar. Bipolar neurons are found in the cochlear and vestibular ganglia as well as in the retina and the olfactory mucosa. Pseudounipolar neurons are found in the spinal ganglia; they are also found in most cranial ganglia, which are sensory ganglia located at the dorsal roots of the spinal nerves.

Neurons can also be classified according to their functional roles. *Motor neurons* control effector organs (eg, exocrine and endocrine glands) and muscle fibers. *Sensory neurons* are involved in the reception of sensory stimuli from the environment and from within the body. *Interneurons* establish interrelationships among other neurons, forming complex functional chains or circuits.

During mammalian evolution there was a great increase in the number and complexity of interneurons. The most highly developed functions of the nervous system cannot be ascribed to simple neuron circuits; rather, they depend on complex interactions established by the processes of many neurons.

In the central nervous system, nerve cell bodies are present only in the gray matter. White matter contains neuronal processes but no perikaryons. In the peripheral nervous system, perikaryons are found in ganglia and in some sensory regions (eg, retina, olfactory mucosa).

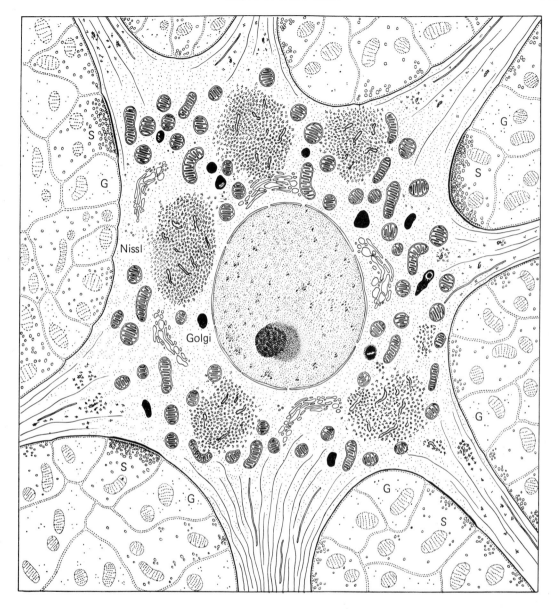

Figure 9–3. Ultrastructure of a neuron. The neuronal surface is completely covered either by synaptic end processes of other neurons (S) or by processes of glial cells (G). At synapses, the neuronal membrane is thicker and is called the postsynaptic membrane. The neuronal process devoid of ribosomes (lower part of figure) is the axon.

Perikaryon or Soma

The perikaryon is the part of the neuron that contains the nucleus and surrounding cytoplasm exclusive of the cell processes. It is primarily a trophic center, but it also has a receptive function. The perikaryon of most neurons receives a great number of nerve endings that convey excitatory or inhibitory stimuli generated in other nerve cells (Fig 9–3). The nerve cell body varies in diameter from 0.1–13.5 nm.

Nucleus

Most nerve cells show a spherical, usually large, palely staining nucleus with a prominent nucleolus.

The nucleus is most often located in the center of the cell body except in the nerve cells of Clarke's column of the spinal column, where the nucleus is situated eccentrically, as it is also in some sympathetic ganglia. Binuclear nerve cells are seen in sympathetic and sensory ganglia. The chromatin is usually finely dispersed, which means that the chromosomes are uncoiled and have transcriptional activity. In females, between the large nucleolus and the nuclear membrane, a special chromatin clump is found in neurons. This is the sex chromatin, first discovered in nerve cells from female cats and later located in many other cells of the body of females. This chromatin represents one of the X chromosomes which remains condensed during the interphase of the cell cycle.

Granular (Rough) Endoplasmic Reticulum

Perikaryons contain a highly developed granular endoplasmic reticulum organized into collections of parallel cisternae. In the cytoplasm between the cisternae, there are also a great number of free ribosomes which usually form rosettes; these cells synthesize both structural proteins and proteins for transport. When appropriate stains are used, granular endoplasmic reticulum and free ribosomes appear under the light microscope as basophilic granular areas called *Nissl bodies* (Figs 9—1 and 9—4).

The number of Nissl bodies varies according to neuronal type and functional state. They are particularly abundant in large neurons—especially motor neurons (Fig 9—4).

Injury to axons or neuron exhaustion by strong or prolonged stimuli causes a reduction in the number of Nissl bodies. This alteration is called *chromatolysis* and occurs simultaneously with nuclear migration to the periphery of the perikaryon. Moderate stimuli may increase the amount of RNA in the perikaryon.

Golgi Apparatus

The Golgi apparatus is located only in the perikaryon, around the nucleus. The neuronal Golgi apparatus

usually consists of multiple arrays of smooth cisternae parallel to each other and to the nuclear membrane and surrounding flat vesicles. There are also a number of smaller, spherical vesicles (Fig 9—3). With the use of osmic acid or silver impregnation technics, the Golgi apparatus takes on the appearance of a network of irregular filaments. Some profiles of smooth endoplasmic reticulum are seen near the Golgi area.

Mitochondria

Mitochondria are found in neurons and are especially abundant in the axon terminals (telodendrons). In the perikaryon, they are small and scattered in the cytoplasm. Mitochondria are usually present also in dendrites.

Neurofilaments & Microtubules

Hollow fibrils with a diameter of 10 nm and a wall thickness of 3 nm, called neurofilaments, are abundant in perikaryons and cell processes. There is evidence that neurofilaments can agglutinate as a result of the action of fixatives. When impregnated with silver, they form neurofibrils which are visible with the light microscope. Thus, neurofibrils are probably stained artifacts produced by reagents which cause neurofilaments to clump together. In tissue cultures under certain conditions, it is possible to see neurofibrils in living neurons. The neurofilaments can probably be seen because they are often parallel and very close to each other, though they are actually beyond the limit of resolution of the light microscope. The perikaryon also contains microtubules with a diameter of 24 nm similar to those found in many other cells (Fig 9—5).

Inclusions

In certain areas of the central nervous system, the perikaryons contain dark brown or black granules. Areas where this pigmentation is seen are the dorsal motor nucleus of the vagus nerve, the spinal and sympathetic ganglia, the substantia nigra of the midbrain, and the locus ceruleus in the floor of the fourth ventricle. The functional role of this melanin pigment in nerve cells is obscure. Another pigment sometimes found in nerve cell bodies is *lipofuscin.* This is a light brown lipid-containing pigment which accumulates in increasing amounts with age. It probably represents a residue of material undigested by lysosomes. Lipid droplets occur quite frequently in nerve cell bodies.

Dendrites

Most nerve cells show numerous dendrites, which increase considerably the receptive area of the cell. This makes it possible for one neuron to receive a great number of telodendrons from other nerve cells. It has been estimated that up to 200,000 axonal terminations establish functional contact with the dendrites of one type of nerve cell found in the cerebellum and called the Purkinje cell. In other nerve cells, that number may be even higher. Neurons with only one dendrite (bipolar neurons) are uncommon and are found only in

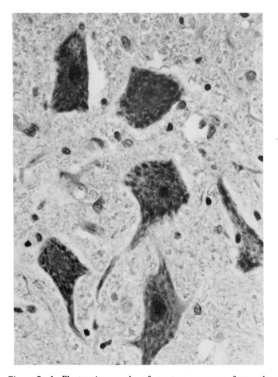

Figure 9—4. Photomicrograph of motor neurons from the human spinal cord. The cytoplasm contains a great number of Nissl bodies, making it difficult to see the cell nucleus. The large nucleoli are easily seen. H&E stain, X 360.

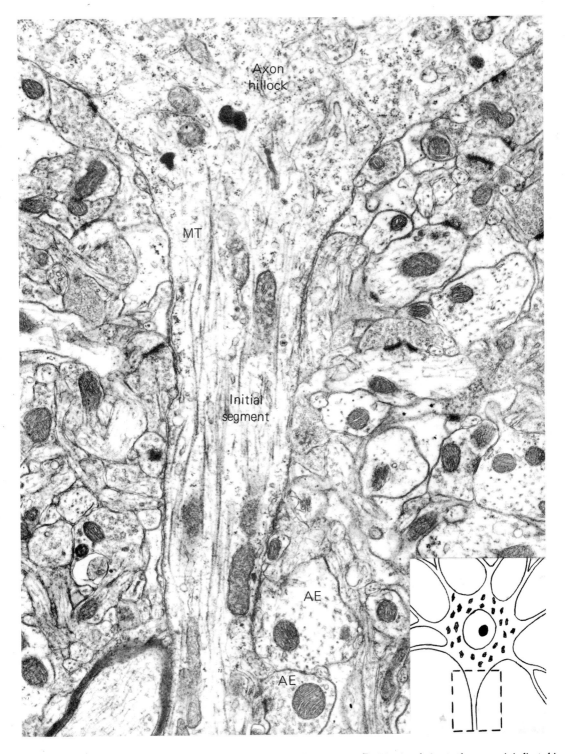

Figure 9–5. Electron micrograph of the axon hillock and the axon's first segment. (Position in relation to the neuron is indicated in the inset.) The axon hillock is poor in ribosomes and endoplasmic reticulum. The arrangement of the microtubules (MT) in bundles is already seen in the axon hillock and becomes more pronounced in the initial segment of the axon. Two axon endings (AE) synapse with the initial segment. Note that there is very little intercellular material in the nerve tissue. (See also Fig 9–3.) ×26,000. (Courtesy of A Peters.)

special sites. In contrast to axons (nerve fibers), which have a constant diameter from one end to the other, dendrites become thinner while they divide into branches.

Structurally, dendrites are very similar to perikaryons; however, they are devoid of Golgi apparatus. Nissl bodies and mitochondria are present except in very thin dendrites. Neurofilaments (10 nm) and microtubules (about 24 nm) are found in dendrites but are more numerous in axons. Dendrites are usually short and divide like the branches of a tree. In some instances, however, they assume a characteristic form; thus, the dendrites of Purkinje cells of the cerebellum branch in one plane only, assuming the shape of a fan (Fig 9–2) and increasing the surface area of each Purkinje cell from 250 sq μm in early development to 27,000 sq μm in the mature cell. Dendrites are usually observed enveloped in a large number of small thorny spines or gemmules. These represent sites of synaptic contact.

Axons

Each neuron has only one axon; it is a cylindric process which varies in length and diameter according to the type of neuron. Some neurons have a short axon, but the axons are usually very long processes. For example, axons of the motor cells of the spinal cord which innervate the foot muscles may have a length of up to 100 cm (about 40 inches). However, since dendrites of a nerve cell are more numerous, their total volume is usually greater than that of the axons.

All axons start from the perikaryon or, in a few cases, from the stem of a major dendrite with a short pyramidal *initial segment* called the *axon hillock* (Fig 9–5) that can be differentiated from dendrites by distinctive histologic features: (1) The granular endoplasmic reticulum and ribosomes found in perikaryons and dendrites do not extend into this initial axonal segment. (2) The initial segment of the axon is often constricted to form the *axon neck*. (3) In the initial segment, the microtubules are arranged in fascicles or bundles, which is a feature not seen in other neuronal components. The plasma membrane of the axon is called the *axolemma* and its contents *axoplasm*. In some cases, the axon arises directly from a principal dendrite and the cell body is used only for trophic purposes and not for conduction.

In contrast to dendrites, axons have a constant diameter and do not branch profusely. Occasionally, the axon, shortly after its departure from the cell body, gives rise to a branch which returns to the area of the nerve cell body. In the central nervous system, the axons give rise to branches at right angles to their main direction. These branches are known as *collaterals* (Fig 9–1).

Axonal cytoplasm (axoplasm) is poor in organelles and possesses few mitochondria and microtubules, though neurofilaments are more frequent. New cytoplasm and other constituents are formed in the cell body and flow out into the axon.

SYNAPSES

When axons are artificially stimulated, they conduct the nerve impulse in both directions from the stimulation point. The impulse directed to the cell body, however, does not excite other neurons, and only the impulse reaching the final arborization of the axon, the telodendron, can excite the next neuron in the chain.

This dynamic polarization and the transmission of the nerve impulse depends on highly specialized structures called synapses, which are classically defined as the contact of one axon with the dendrites or perikaryon and, very rarely, with the axon of another neuron. The recent trend is to consider the nerve endings on effector cells, such as gland or muscle cells, as synapses also.

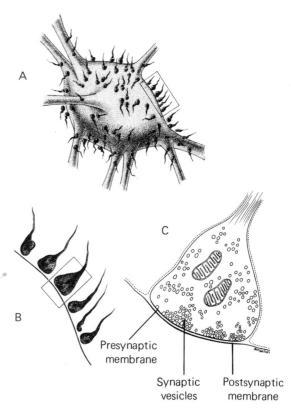

Figure 9–6. *A:* External morphology of a neuron and some of its processes. Axon endings from other neurons are shown in black. The area outlined by a rectangle appears enlarged at *B*. *B:* At synaptic junctions, the 2 cell membranes are separated by a slender space—the synaptic gap. *C:* Ultrastructure of the synapse outlined in *B*. Presynaptic and postsynaptic membranes are thicker than the neuronal cell membrane elsewhere. The axon ending shows 2 mitochondria as well as numerous synaptic vesicles that contain a chemical mediator. Liberation of the mediator substance transmits the nerve impulse from the presynaptic to the postsynaptic membrane. (Redrawn and reproduced, with permission, from De Robertis, Novinsky, & Saez: *Biologia Celular,* 8th ed. El Ateneo [Buenos Aires], 1970.)

Morphologically, several types of synapses can be identified. The telodendron may form bulbous expansions, basketlike structures, or club-shaped terminations (Fig 9–6). These synaptic end bulbs are often called *boutons terminaux* or *boutons en passage* if they make contact in other places also. The analysis of a synapse under the electron microscope shows that it is actually a specialized, localized region of contact between 2 cells (Fig 9–6). It is composed of a telodendron membrane (presynaptic membrane), a region of extracellular space (the synaptic gap), and a postsynaptic membrane belonging to a dendrite, perikaryon, or axon of another cell. At a synapse, the plasma membranes of the 2 neurons are usually separated by a distance of 20 nm (the synaptic gap). These membranes are firmly bound together at the synaptic region, and in some instances dense filaments form bridges between them. The plasma membranes of the 2 neurons are thicker at the presynaptic and postsynaptic areas of the synapse than elsewhere and show a condensation of the cytoplasm near the synaptic membranes. Cytoplasmic filaments resembling desmosomes are anchored to the inside of each of these membranes.

The cytoplasm in the endings of the telodendron typically contains numerous small vesicles with a diameter of 20–65 nm. They are the *synaptic vesicles*. Neurofilaments are absent, but mitochondria are numerous. The synaptic vesicles contain substances called *chemical mediators* or *neurotransmitters* that are responsible for the transmission of the nerve impulse across the synapse. These mediators are liberated at the presynaptic membrane and act on the postsynaptic membrane to promote the conduction of nerve impulses across the synaptic cleft.

NEUROGLIA

Several cell types found in the central nervous system in association with the neurons are classified as *neuroglia* or *glial cells*. The several types of neuroglia show morphologic, embryologic, and functional differences.

Routine hematoxylin and eosin preparations are not adequate to study neuroglia, since with this staining technic only their nuclei can be seen among the larger nuclei of nerve cells. The cytoplasm and processes of the neuroglia are not visible, for it is impossible to distinguish them from the processes of the neurons. The neuroglia play an important role in the normal function of the nervous system. For the study of the morphology of neuroglia, therefore, special technics of silver or gold impregnation are used.

It has been estimated that in the central nervous system there are 10 neuroglia for each neuron. However, since neuroglia are much smaller, they occupy only about half of the total volume of the nerve tissue.

Neuroglia include several varieties: astrocytes, oligodendrocytes, microglia, and ependymal cells. Astrocytes and oligodendrocytes are referred to as the *macroglia*.

Neuroglial cells are thought not to generate action potentials, and they do not form synapses with other cells. They form the myelin sheaths of the axons and are necessary for tissue culturing of neurons, which do not grow unless neuroglia are present in the culture.

1. ASTROCYTES

Astrocytes are the largest neuroglia, possessing numerous long processes. They have spherical, centrally located nuclei which stain lightly (Fig 9–7). Many of their processes have expanded pedicles at their ends which attach to the walls of blood capillaries. These pedicles are called the "vascular feet" of the neuroglia. Processes of the astrocytes are also present at the periphery of the brain and spinal cord, forming a layer under the pia mater. This layer, which also contains processes of other neuroglia, separates the connective tissue of the pia mater from nerve cells. There are usually 2 types of astrocytes: protoplasmic, found in the gray matter of the brain and spinal cord; and fibrous, found chiefly in the white matter. In tissue culture, astrocytes show constant movement.

Protoplasmic Astrocytes

Protoplasmic astrocytes have abundant granular cytoplasm. Their processes have many branches, are shorter than those of fibrous astrocytes, and are relatively thick (Fig 9–7). Their processes cover the surface of nerve cells, the synaptic areas, and blood vessels.

Some small protoplasmic astrocytes are located close to nerve cell bodies and represent one type of neuronal *satellite cell*, a term applied to all neuroglia. Most satellite cells are oligodendrocytes, but some are protoplasmic astrocytes.

Fibrous Astrocytes

Fibrous astrocytes have long, slender, smooth processes that branch infrequently. In special silver-stained preparations, their cytoplasm shows fibrillar material that is probably formed by the precipitation of very thin filaments abundant in the cell bodies and processes of fibrous astrocytes (Fig 9–8).

2. OLIGODENDROCYTES

Oligodendrocytes are much smaller than astrocytes, and their processes are less numerous and shorter than those present in other neuroglia (Fig 9–7). Oligodendrocytes are found both in gray and in white matter. In gray matter, they are mainly localized close to the perikaryons and are known as satellite cells. Satellite cells of the nerve ganglia in the peripheral

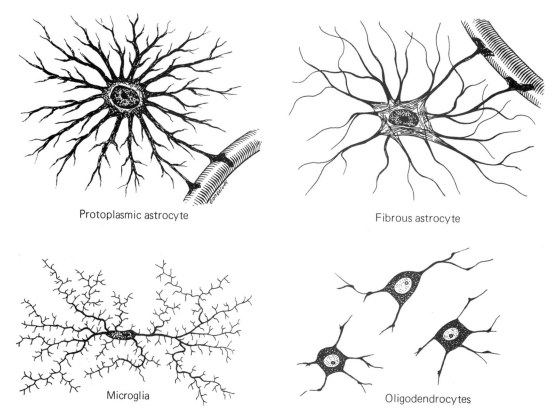

Protoplasmic astrocyte

Fibrous astrocyte

Microglia

Oligodendrocytes

Figure 9—7. Drawings of neuroglial cells as seen in slides specially stained by metallic impregnation. Observe that only astrocytes exhibit vascular end-feet. These processes terminate on the walls of blood capillaries.

nervous system have different morphologic characteristics and are not considered neuroglia.

The number of oligodendrocytes increases with increasing complexity of the nervous system in different species. Human nerve tissue has the highest number of oligodendrocytes per nerve cell.

In white matter, oligodenodrocytes appear in rows among the myelinated nerve fibers. Under the electron microscope, observation of fetal nerve tissue shows that the myelin sheath of central nervous system tissue is produced by the processes of oligodendrocytes. In this aspect of their function they are analogous to the Schwann cells of peripheral nerves.

The cytoplasm of oligodendrocytes is electron-dense and consists mainly of mitochondria, ribosomes, and microtubules, and these characteristics permit their identification in electron micrographs. Their nuclei are round, small, and dense.

In tissue culture, oligodendrocytes show intense movements characterized by rhythmic pulsations.

3. MICROGLIA

The cell bodies of microglia are small, dense, and elongated. Their nuclei show condensed chromatin and

an elongated shape along the axis of the cell body. The shape of the nuclei of microglia permits their identification in hematoxylin and eosin preparations, for other neuroglia have spherical nuclei. Microglia have short processes covered by numerous small expansions, giving them a thorny appearance (Fig 9—7). Microglia are not numerous, but they are found in both white and gray matter.

In contrast to all other neuroglia, which originate from the ectoderm of the neural tube, microglia are believed to originate from the mesenchyme which forms the pia mater. Microglia are sometimes phagocytic and are functionally similar to connective tissue macrophages. They are therefore part of the macrophage (reticuloendothelial) system, although this idea is controversial at present.

4. EPENDYMAL CELLS

Ependymal cells derive from the internal covering of the neural tube and retain their epithelial arrangement, whereas the other cells from the neural tube develop processes and give rise to neurons or to other neuroglia. They form the epithelial layer of the choroid plexus.

Ependymal cells line the cavities of the brain and spinal cord and are bathed by the cerebrospinal fluid, which fills these cavities. They are columnar cells with wide bases; they sometimes divide, developing long, threadlike processes that penetrate deeply into nerve tissue. Their nuclei are long, and in embryonic life they have cilia, which sometimes are observed also in adult organisms in some parts of the lining of the ventricles. In certain parts of the central nervous system, ependymal cells are continuous with and homologous to the cuboid cells of choroid plexuses.

HISTOPHYSIOLOGY OF NEUROGLIA

In the central nervous system, connective tissue layers form the protective and vascular coats (meninges) of the tissue. A very small amount of connective tissue penetrates into the nerve tissue, forming sheaths around the larger blood vessels.

In spite of its size, the central nervous system is poor in connective tissue content, and its nerve cells and their processes are supported by neuroglia. Because of their number and their long processes, astrocytes seem to be the most important supporting elements.

The vascular feet and the presence of pinocytotic vesicles in astrocytes suggest that they play a role in the transport of substances from blood capillaries to neurons and vice versa. There is evidence that astrocytes transport ions through an energy-dependent mechanism (ion pump) and are responsible for the equilibrium of electrolytes within the central nervous system. It is known that the "scars" formed in the central nervous system after lesions of these tissues result from hyperplasia and hypertrophy of astrocytes.

Satellite cells or *perineural oligodendrocytes* seem to live symbiotically with the neurons. Cytochemical studies performed in neurons and satellite cells isolated by microsurgery have shown a metabolic dependency between them. Any stimulus which alters the chemical composition of the nerve cell also is reflected in the

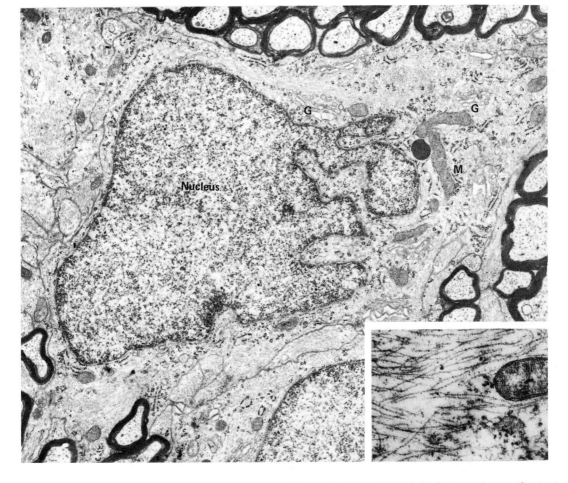

Figure 9–8. Electron of a fibrous astrocyte. G, Golgi apparatus; M, mitochondrion X 12,000. In the inset, the magnification is X 42,000 and shows the abundant filaments in the cytoplasm. (Courtesy of A Peters.)

satellite cell. In tissue cultures, neurons do not survive unless they are kept with their satellite cells.

NERVE FIBERS

Nerve fibers consist of axons enveloped by special sheaths. Groups of nerve fibers constitute the tracts of the brain, spinal cord, and peripheral nerves. According to their location either in the central or the peripheral nervous system, nerve fibers exhibit differences in their enveloping sheaths.

All axons in adult nerve tissue are ensheathed by single or multiple folds of a sheath cell. In peripheral nerve fibers, the sheath cell is the Schwann cell, or neurolemma sheath, and in central nerve fibers it is the oligodendrocyte. Axons of small diameter are surrounded by a single fold of the sheath cell and are called *unmyelinated nerve fibers* because in the light microscope myelin was not seen (Fig 9–9). Progressively thicker axons are ensheathed by increasingly numerous concentric wrappings of the enveloping cell,

called *myelin sheaths,* and are known as myelinated nerve fibers (Fig 9–10). Axonal conduction of the impulse is progressively faster in axons with larger diameters and thicker myelin sheaths.

Myelinated Fibers

In these fibers, the cytoplasm of the covering Schwann cell winds around the axon. In this process, the membranes of the sheath cell unite and form a lipoprotein complex called *myelin* which can be partly removed (the lipid component) by standard histologic procedures. Its presence can be demonstrated by osmium tetroxide, which preserves myelin and stains it black (Fig 9–12).

The myelin sheath shows gaps along its path called the *nodes of Ranvier.* The distance between 2 nodes is called an *internode* of myelin and consists of one Schwann cell (Figs 9–1 and 9–13). The thickness of the myelin sheath varies according to the axonal diameter, but it is constant along the extent of a particular axon. The length of the internodes varies from 0.08–1 mm. Under the light microscope, the myelin sheath shows cone-shaped clefts called *clefts* or *incisures of Schmidt-Lanterman.* Their apexes do not always point in the same direction (Fig 9–13).

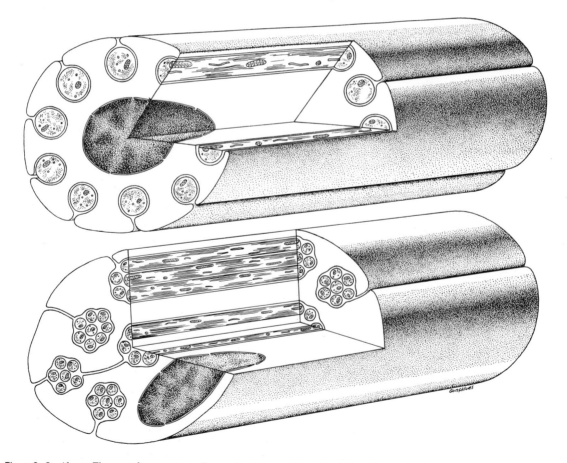

Figure 9–9. *Above:* The most frequent type of unmyelinated nerve fiber, in which each axon has its own mesaxon. *Below:* Many very thin axons are sometimes found together surrounded by the Schwann cell. In such cases there is one mesaxon for several axons.

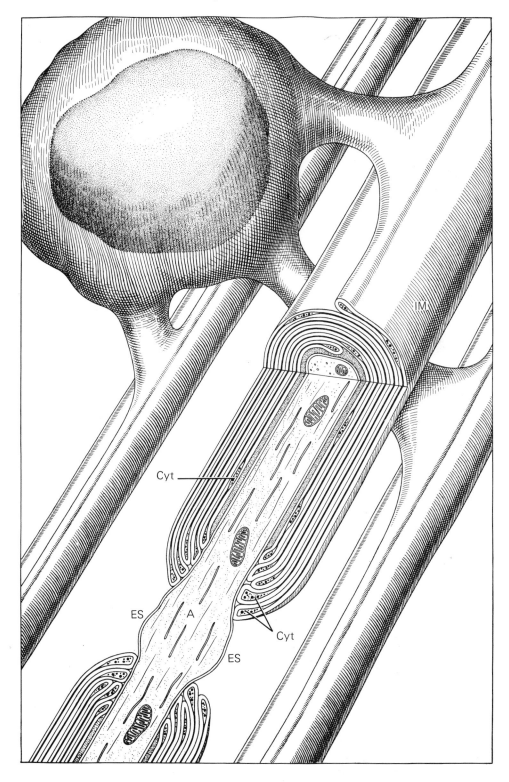

Figure 9–10. Myelin sheath of the central nervous system. The same oligodendrocyte forms myelin sheaths for several nerve fibers (3–50). In the central nervous system, the nodes of Ranvier are covered sometimes by processes of other cells or there is at that point considerable extracellular space (ES). The axolemma shows a thickening where the cell membrane of the oligodendrocyte comes into contact with it, thus limiting the periaxonal space as in the peripheral nervous system (not represented in this drawing). At upper left is a surface view of the cell body of an oligodendrocyte. (Redrawn and reproduced, with permission, from Bunge & others: J Biophys Biochem Cytol 10:67, 1961.) IM, inner mesaxon; Cyt, cytoplasm of glial cell; A, axon.

Diffraction studies with x-rays and microscopy under polarized light show that myelin is composed of bimolecular lipid layers alternating with layers of elongated protein molecules parallel to the axon. Thus, myelin actually consists of several layers of modified cell membranes. Embryo studies have shown that the first step in myelin formation is axon penetration into an existing groove of the Schwann cell cytoplasm. The edges of the groove come together to form a mesaxon, so that the plasma membranes of the 2 edges fuse together on their outer surface. Next, through a process not yet fully understood, the mesaxon wraps itself around the axon several times, the number of turns determining the thickness of the myelin layer. After this process, an internal and an external mesaxon can be seen (Figs 9–11 and 9–12). The clefts of Schmidt-Lanterman represent areas in which the cytoplasm of the Schwann cells is present within the myelin layer. These cytoplasmic areas were left behind during the winding process of the cytoplasm around the axon.

Schwann cells have elongated nuclei which lie parallel to the axon. With the myelin sheath, they assume a cylindric form. The nodes of Ranvier, which are indentations in the myelin sheath, are covered by interdigitating processes of adjacent Schwann cells (Fig 9–13).

There are no Schwann cells in the central nervous system; the myelin sheath is formed by the processes of the oligodendrocytes, so that different branches of one cell can envelop several axons (Fig 9–9). The nodes of Ranvier are not always covered in the central nervous system, and Schmidt-Lanterman clefts are not present.

Unmyelinated Fibers

Unmyelinated nerve fibers do not show Ranvier nodes, for their Schwann cells are laterally united to form a continuous sheath.

The gray matter of the central nervous system is rich in unmyelinated nerve fibers. These fibers are enveloped by the terminal expansion of the processes of neuroglia, for, again, Schwann cells are not present in the central nervous system.

NERVES

In the peripheral nervous system, the nerve fibers are grouped in bundles to form the nerves. Except for a few very thin nerves made up of unmyelinated fibers,

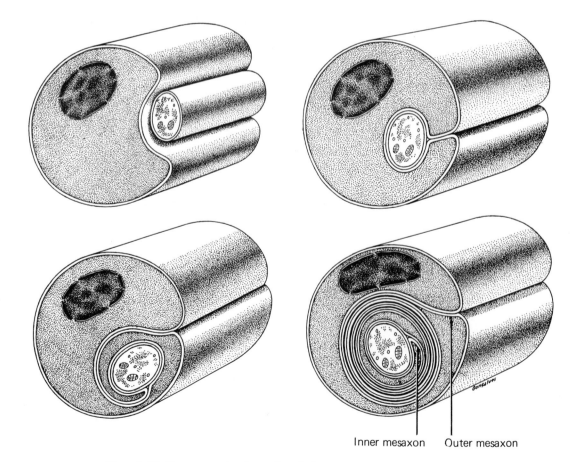

Inner mesaxon   Outer mesaxon

Figure 9–11. Four consecutive phases of myelin formation in peripheral nerve fibers.

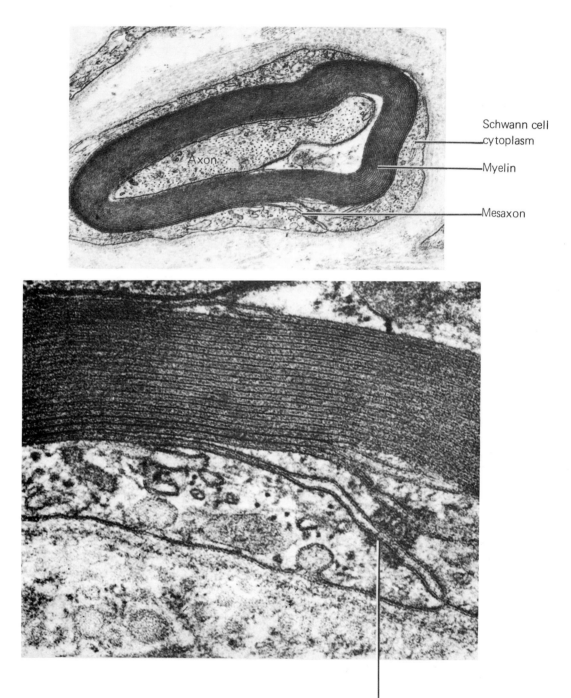

Schwann cell
cytoplasm

Myelin

Mesaxon

Axon

Outer mesaxon

Figure 9–12. Electron micrographs of a myelinated nerve fiber. X 20,000; X 80,000.

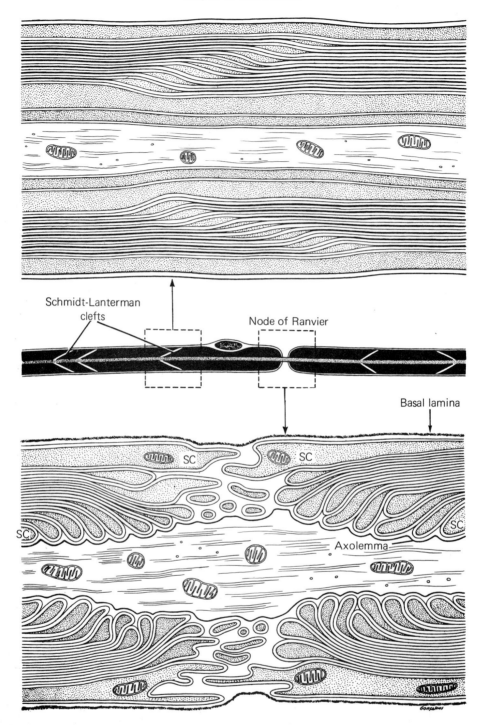

Figure 9–13. In the center drawing is shown a myelinated peripheral nerve fiber as seen under the light microscope. The stippled process is the axon enveloped by the myelin sheath (in black) and by the cytoplasm of Schwann cells or neurolemma. A Schwann cell nucleus is seen, as well as the Schmidt-Lanterman clefts and a node of Ranvier. The upper drawing shows the ultrastructure of the Schmidt-Lanterman cleft. This cleft is formed by portions of the Schwann cell cytoplasm, separated by the myelin layers during its formation. The lower drawing shows the ultrastructure of a node of Ranvier. Note the appearance of loose interdigitating processes of the outer leaf of the cytoplasm of the Schwann cells (SC) and that a close contact of the inner leaf of the cytoplasm with the axolemma exists, thus acting as a sort of barrier to the movement of materials in and out of the space between the axolemma and the membrane of the Schwann cell. This space is called periaxonal space. The basal lamina around the Schwann cell is continuous. Covering the nerve fiber is a connective tissue layer—mainly reticular fiber—which forms the outer sheath of the peripheral nerve fibers and is known as the sheath of Key and Retzius.

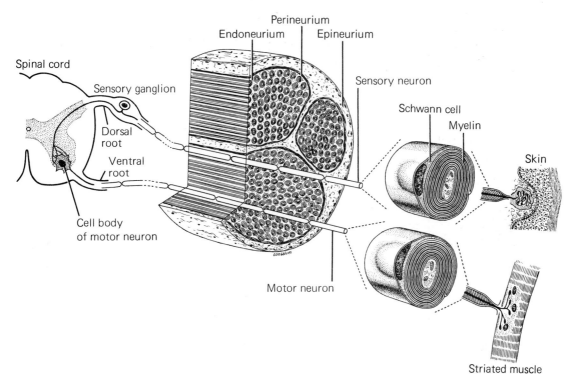

Figure 9—14. Schematic representation of a nerve and also of the simplest reflex arc. In this example, the sensory stimulus starts in the skin and the motor fiber innervates a striated skeletal muscle.

nerves are whitish because of their myelin content.

The stroma of the nerves consists of an external fibrous coat of dense connective tissue called *epineurium*. From it, dense septa penetrate into the nerve to form the *perineurium,* which surrounds bundles of nerve fibers. The *endoneurium,* which consists of a very thin layer of loose connective tissue, is in close contact with the individual nerve fibers (Fig 9–14). Because of their proximity to nerve fibers, the nuclei of fibroblasts of the endoneurium are difficult to distinguish from the nuclei of Schwann cells. Very delicate reticular fibers of the endoneurium form an incomplete envelope—called the connective tissue sheath of Key and Retzius—around each nerve fiber. While the other axonal sheaths (Schwann cells, myelin) originate from the neural ectoderm, the sheath of Key and Retzius derives from the mesenchyme.

The nerves establish communication between the nerve centers and the sense organs and effectors (muscles, glands, etc). They possess afferent and efferent fibers in relation to the central nervous system. The afferent fibers carry the information obtained from the interior of the body and the environment to the nerve centers. The efferent fibers carry impulses from the central nervous system to the effector organs commanded by these centers. Nerves possessing only sensory fibers (afferent) are called *sensory nerves;* those composed only of fibers carrying impulses to the effectors are called *motor nerves.* Most nerves have both sensory and motor types of fibers and are called *mixed*

nerves (Fig 9–14); these nerves have both myelinated and unmyelinated fibers (Fig 9–15).

AUTONOMIC NERVOUS SYSTEM

The autonomic nervous system is related to the control of smooth muscle, the secretion of some glands, and the modulation of cardiac rhythm. Its function is to make adjustments in certain activities of the body in order to maintain a constant internal environment (homeostasis). Although the autonomic nervous system is by definition a motor system, fibers which receive sensation originating in the interior of the organism accompany the motor fibers of the autonomic system.

Although the term autonomic might imply that this part of the nervous system functions independently, this is not the case; its functions are constantly subject to the influences of conscious activity.

The concept of the autonomic nervous system is mainly functional. Anatomically, it is composed of collections of nerve cells located in the central nervous system; of fibers which leave the central nervous system through cranial or spinal nerves; and of nerve ganglia situated in the paths of these fibers. The term "autonomic" covers all the neural elements concerned with visceral function.

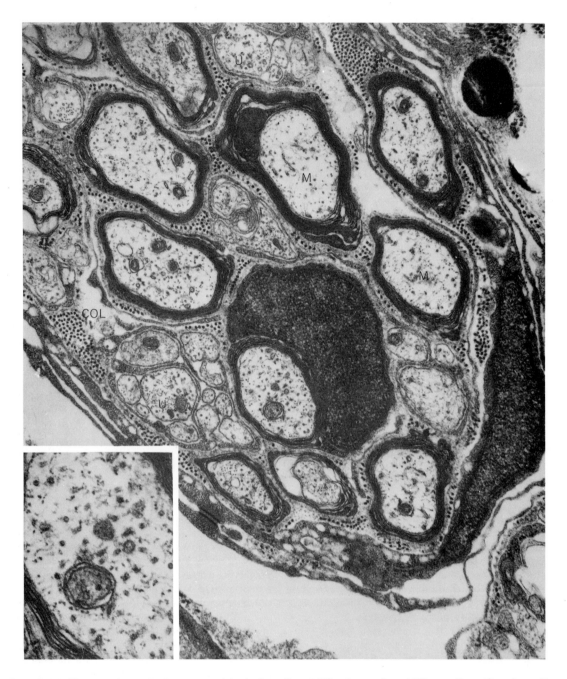

Figure 9–15. Electron micrograph of a nerve containing both myelinated (M) and unmyelinated (U) nerve fibers. The collagen fibers (COL) seen in cross section belong to the endoneurium. Near the center of the figure there is a Schwann cell nucleus. × 30,000. The inset shows part of an axon, where numerous neurofilaments and microtubules are seen. × 60,000.

The first neuron of the autonomic chain is located in the central nervous system. Its axon forms a synapse with the second multipolar neuron in the chain, located in a ganglion of the peripheral autonomic system. The nerve fibers (axons) of the first neuron to the second are called preganglionic fibers; the axons of the second neuron to the effectors—muscle or epithelium—are called postganglionic fibers. The chemical mediator present in the synaptic vesicles of all preganglionic endings and at anatomically parasympathetic postganglionic endings is acetylcholine. It is released from the terminals by nerve impulses.

The adrenal medulla is the only organ that receives preganglionic fibers because the majority of the cells, after migration into the gland, do not differentiate into ganglion cells but into secretory cells. Thus, its innervation is still preganglionic.

The autonomic nervous system is composed of 2 parts which differ both anatomically and functionally: the sympathetic system and the parasympathetic system (Fig 9—16).

Sympathetic System

The nuclei of the sympathetic system, which represent accumulations of nerve cell bodies, are located in the thoracic and lumbar segments of the spinal cord. The axons of these neurons—preganglionic fibers—leave the central nervous system by the ventral roots and white communicating rami of the thoracic and lumbar nerves. For this reason, the sympathetic system is also called the thoracolumbar division of the autonomic nervous system. The ganglia of the sympathetic system form the vertebral chain and plexuses situated near the viscera. The chemical mediator of the postganglionic fibers of the sympathetic system is norepinephrine. This substance is also produced by the medulla of the adrenal. Its secretion has an effect similar to that of stimulation of the sympathetic nervous system.

Parasympathetic System

The parasympathetic system has its nuclei in the medulla and midbrain and in the sacral portion of the spinal cord. The preganglionic fibers of these neurons leave through 4 of the cranial nerves (III, VII, IX, and X) and also through the second, third, and fourth sacral spinal nerves. The parasympathetic system is therefore also called the craniosacral division of the autonomic system.

The second neuron of the parasympathetic chain is found in ganglia smaller than those of the sympathetic system; it is always located near or within the effector organs. These neurons are frequently located in the walls of organs (eg, stomach, intestines), in which case the preganglionic fibers penetrate into the organs and synapse there with the second neuron in the chain.

The chemical mediator released by the pre- and postganglionic nerve endings of the parasympathetic system is acetylcholine. Acetylcholine is readily inactivated by acetylcholinesterase, and this is one of the

reasons why parasympathetic stimulation has both a more discrete and a more localized action than sympathetic stimulation.

Distribution

Most of the organs innervated by the autonomic nervous system receive both sympathetic and parasympathetic fibers (Fig 9—16). Generally, in organs where the sympathetic system is the stimulator, the parasympathetic system has an inhibitory action, and vice versa. For example, stimulation of the sympathetic system accelerates cardiac rhythm, whereas stimulation of parasympathetic fibers slows it down. In some instances, the activity of these 2 components is complementary and not antagonistic. This is true in the case of some salivary glands, whose secretion is greater when stimulated by both systems than when stimulated by either one separately.

HISTOPHYSIOLOGY OF NERVE TISSUE

The integrative function of nerve tissue depends basically on the generation and spreading of nerve impulses and on the production of neurohormones by special nerve cells. (The neurohormones are discussed in Chapter 21.)

Axonal conduction of nerve impulses is one of the basic and better understood functions of nerve tissue. Several cell components were thought to be implicated in the process of impulse conduction, but it is now well established that the key role is played by the cell membrane.

Passage of the impulse is characterized by changes in membrane permeability, resulting in an inward movement of sodium and an outward movement of potassium. Since the increase in permeability is greater for sodium than for potassium, positive ions accumulate on the undersurface of the cell membrane. During the passage of the impulse, therefore, the outer surface of the axon membrane becomes negatively charged relative to the internal surface (Fig 9—17).

In unmyelinated fibers, the impulse is conducted as a spreading wave of modification in membrane permeability. As this wave moves along the fiber, the membrane behind the wave returns to its resting stage (Fig 9—17). This is possible because of the presence of an active ion-transporting mechanism that redistributes the sodium and potassium ions on both sides of the axon membrane in concentrations equal to those present before stimulation. The wave progresses along the axon up to the endings of the telodendron, where it promotes the liberation of the chemical mediator into the synaptic gap.

In myelinated nerve fibers, local changes occur only at the nodes of Ranvier. At the internodes, the insulating effect of myelin prevents the continuous propagation of the impulse. Therefore, the impulse jumps from one node to the other. This type of con-

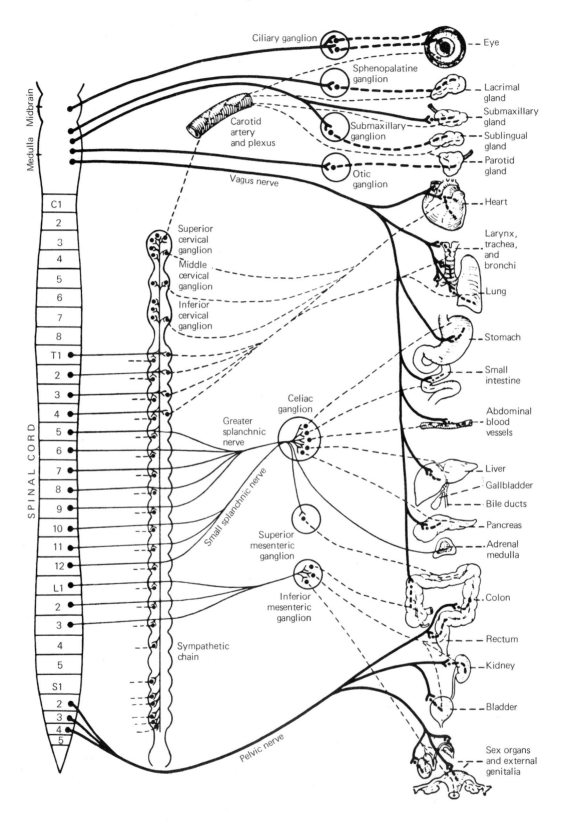

Figure 9–16. Diagram of the efferent autonomic pathways. Preganglionic neurons are shown as solid lines, postganglionic neurons as dotted lines. The heavy lines are parasympathetic fibers; the light lines are sympathetic. (Reproduced, with permission, from Youmans: *Fundamentals of Human Physiology,* 2nd ed. Year Book, 1962.)

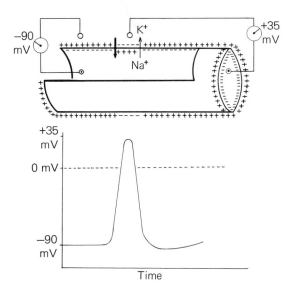

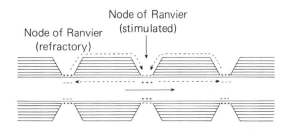

Figure 9–18. Conduction of the nerve impulse through a myelinated nerve fiber. In this fiber, the movements of Na⁺ and K⁺ described in unmyelinated fibers (Fig 9–17) take place only at the nodes of Ranvier. The presence of a myelin sheath covering each internode makes a continuous transmission of the impulse impossible, for myelin is a good electrical insulating material. The electrical field generated at each node jumps the internode and excites the next node. This type of conduction is called saltatory and is very fast. After its stimulation, the node of Ranvier remains refractory for a short time. For this reason, even if the electrical field produced at each node spreads in both directions (dotted arrows), physiologic nerve impulses move in one direction only (solid arrow in the center of the fiber).

Figure 9–17. Conduction of the nerve impulse through an unmyelinated nerve fiber. In the resting axon there is a difference of −90 mV between the interior of the axon and the outer surface of its membrane (resting potential). During the impulse passage, Na⁺ (thick arrow) passes into the axon interior, while K⁺ (thin arrow) migrates in the opposite direction. The amount of Na⁺ that enters the axon is larger than the amount of K⁺ that leaves it. In consequence, there is a change in membrane polarity. It becomes relatively positive on its inner surface. The resting potential is thus replaced by an action potential, which in the example given above is equal to +35 mV. In unmyelinated fibers, the nerve impulse is a wave of change in membrane permeability that moves along the axon and promotes the liberation of a chemical mediator when it reaches the axon terminal (telodendron). The above graph shows schematically what is registered by a cathode ray oscilloscope during passage of the nerve impulse through a small segment of the nerve fiber. (Conduction in a myelinated nerve fiber is illustrated in Fig 9–18.) The electrodes were placed as shown in the upper drawing, one inside the axon and the other on the external surface of the axonal membrane.

duction is called *saltatory conduction* and is faster than continuous conduction (Fig 9–18). Because membrane permeability is changed only at the nodes of Ranvier and not at the internodes, the transport of ions is less in saltatory conduction than in continuous conduction; consequently, less energy is expended in the process.

The energy used in the conduction of the impulse is restored by an increase in the axonal metabolism, with enhanced oxygen consumption and heat production.

Nerve impulse conduction can be blocked by cold, heat, or pressure on the nerve fiber. More complete blocking is obtained by application of local anesthetics.

According to their conductive properties, nerve fibers may be divided into 3 classes: A, B, and C. Type A fibers are myelinated, have large diameters and long

internodes, and conduct impulses with high velocity (15–100 m/second). Type B fibers have smaller diameters, shorter internodes, and medium velocity of conduction (3–14 m/second). Type C fibers are thin and unmyelinated, with slow conduction velocity (0.5–2 m/second).

Nerve impulses are transmitted from one neuron to another or to an effector cell by the chemical mediators liberated at synapses (Figs 9–19 and 9–20). The transmission substance is stored in synaptic vesicles and liberated by the nerve impulse. It crosses the presynaptic membrane and attaches to specific receptors in the postsynaptic membrane, where it causes a localized increase in the permeability to ions. This change in membrane permeability spreads along the nerve cell and is responsible for the propagation of the impulse.

After performing its function, the transmission substance is removed by enzymatic mechanisms which are specific for the particular transmitter. The entire process is very rapid and can occur, for brief periods of time, over 100 times a second.

The main chemical mediator is acetylcholine, but in postganglionic endings of the sympathetic system it is norepinephrine. Synaptic vesicles containing norepinephrine are larger than those containing acetylcholine, and they usually have an electron-dense core separated from its limiting membrane by a light zone (Fig 9–20).

Besides acetylcholine and norepinephrine, whose roles as transmitters are well established, there are probably other chemical mediators also. This function has been suggested for gamma-aminobutyric acid (GABA) and glutamic acid.

In mammals, gamma-aminobutyric acid is localized exclusively in the central nervous system. There is suggestive evidence but no definitive proof that it may function as an inhibitory chemical transmitter. In the nervous system of crustaceans, the role of gamma-aminobutyric acid as an inhibitory transmitter seems well established. The present concepts of the production, liberation, and inactivation of the best-known chemical mediators are summarized in Fig 9–21.

The abundance of RNA in the perikaryon suggests intense protein synthesis, which has been confirmed by radioautographic studies using ^{3}H-leucine and other labeled amino acids. The actively synthesized and labeled protein molecules migrate through the axons at a speed of 0.8 mm/day. In nongrowing animals, these protein molecules are probably used to replace similar molecules broken down in the axon. It has been shown that smaller molecules can also be transported along the axon—a process that occurs at a speed greater than that specified above. Experimental evidence has also been presented to show that transport can also occur in a centripetal direction from the axon to the perikaryon.

Almost no ribosomes are present in the axon, and these cellular processes depend on their perikaryons for the synthesis of proteins. The observations recently reported of substances which inhibit protein synthesis

acting on the memory of animals call attention to the importance of Nissl bodies and protein metabolism in the function of the nervous system.

A trophic function has been ascribed to the nervous system of mammals for the structures it innervates. It is known that denervation of organs such as glands and muscles can lead to their atrophy, with functional and morphologic recuperation after reinnervation. Whether this atrophy is solely a consequence of disuse is still an open question. In the lower vertebrates, it has been shown beyond doubt that the peripheral nerves have a trophic function which does not depend on the nerve impulse.

DEGENERATION & REGENERATION

Central or peripheral neurons do not divide; their destruction therefore represents a permanent loss. Neuronal processes in the central nervous system are, within very narrow limits, replaceable by growth

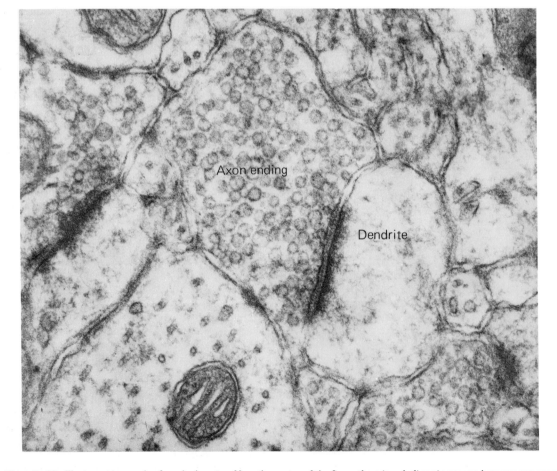

Figure 9–19. Electron micrograph of cerebral cortex. Near the center of the figure there is a cholinergic synapse between one axon ending and a dendrite. At the synapse, both the axonal (presynaptic) membrane and the dendritic (postsynaptic) membrane are thicker. The axon ending contains numerous synaptic vesicles. × 90,000. (Courtesy of A Peters.)

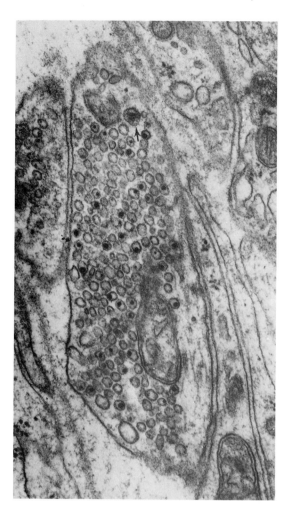

Figure 9—20. Norepinephrine nerve ending of pineal gland. There are many vesicles of 50 nm with a dark, electron-dense core. There are also a few large, pale vesicles, whose function is not known. (Courtesy of A Machado.)

through the synthetic activity of their perikaryons. Peripheral nerve fibers, however, can regenerate if their perikaryons are not destroyed.

Death of a nerve cell is limited to its perikaryon and processes. The neurons functionally connected to the dead neuron do not die, except for those neurons with only one link. In this instance, the isolated neuron undergoes *transneuronal degeneration.*

In contrast to nerve cells, neuroglia of the central nervous system and Schwann cells and ganglionic satellite cells of the peripheral nervous system are able to divide by mitosis. Consequently, spaces left in the central nervous system by nerve cells lost by disease or injury are occupied by neuroglia.

Since nerves are widely distributed throughout the body, they are often subjected to injury. When a nerve is transected, degenerative changes take place and are followed by a reparative phase.

In a wounded nerve fiber, it is important to dis-

tinguish the changes occurring in the proximal segment from those in the distal segment. The proximal segment maintains its continuity with the trophic center (perikaryon) and very often regenerates. The distal segment, separated from the nerve cell body, degenerates totally and is absorbed by the tissue macrophages (Fig 9—22).

Axonal injury causes the following changes in the perikaryon: (1) chromatolysis, ie, dissolution of Nissl substances with a consequent decrease in cytoplasmic basophilia; (2) increase in the volume of the perikaryon; and (3) migration of the nucleus to a peripheral position in the perikaryon. The proximal segment of the axon degenerates close to the wound for a short distance, but growth starts as soon as debris is removed by macrophages.

In the nerve stub distal to the injury, both the axon (now separated from its trophic center) and the myelin sheath degenerate completely, and their remnants are removed by macrophages (Fig 9—22B). While these regressive changes take place, the Schwann cells proliferate actively, giving origin to solid cellular columns. These rows of Schwann cells serve as guides to the sprouting axons which are formed during the reparative phase.

After these regressive changes, the proximal segment of the axon which is connected to the trophic center grows and branches, forming several filaments that progress in the direction of the columns of Schwann cells (Fig 9—22C). Only those fibers that penetrate these Schwann cell columns will continue to grow and therefore be able to reach an effector organ (Fig 9—22D). When there is an extensive gap between the distal and proximal segments, or when the distal segment disappears altogether (as in the case of amputation of a limb), the newly grown nerve fibers may form a painful bulbous mass, improperly called an *amputation neuroma* (Fig 9—22E).

Regeneration is functionally efficient only when the fibers find the columns of Schwann cells directed to the correct place. This possibility is increased for the reason that each regenerating fiber gives origin to several filaments and each column of Schwann cells receives filaments from several regenerating fibers. In an injured mixed nerve, however, if the regenerated sensory fibers grow into columns connected to motor end-plates that were occupied by motor fibers, the function of the muscle will not be reestablished.

GANGLIA

An aggregation of nerve cell bodies outside the central nervous system is called a *nerve ganglion.* Ganglia are usually ovoid structures encapsulated by dense connective tissue and associated with nerves.

Intramural ganglia are very small, consisting of only a few nerve cells, and are located within viscera, especially the walls of the digestive tract. All intra-

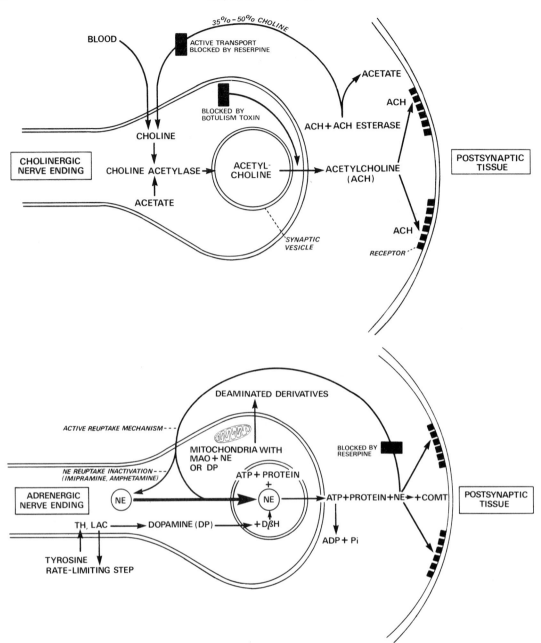

Figure 9–21. Schematic view of the production, liberation, and utilization of acetylcholine and norepinephrine. ***Top:*** *Acetylcholine* (ACH) is synthesized at the nerve ending from choline and acetate with the participation of the enzyme choline acetylase. The acetylcholine thus produced is stored in synaptic vesicles. When the nerve impulse reaches the axonal terminal, quanta of acetylcholine are liberated; they activate specific receptors located in the outer part of the cell membrane of perikaryons, dendrites, or effector cells (muscles, glands). Immediately after this activation, acetylcholine is hydrolyzed to acetate and choline by the enzyme acetylcholinesterase. By active transport, choline molecules reenter the axon ending, where they are utilized again. Reserpine inhibits the active transport of choline, thus preventing its reutilization. ***Bottom:*** *Norepinephrine* (NE) is synthesized in the nerve ending and probably also in the perikaryon, migrating through the axon to its terminal. It is synthesized from tyrosine through a dopamine step by the action of 3 enzymes: tyrosine hydrolase (TH), aromatic L-amino acid decarboxylase (LAC), and dopamine β-hydroxylase (DβH). Norepinephrine is stored in vesicles which also contain protein and ATP. Norepinephrine is released in quanta, and the ATP and protein are liberated at the same time. Cells sensitive to norepinephrine contain specific receptors in their membranes to which the mediator is attached, thus producing its effects. A portion of norepinephrine is degraded by the enzyme catechol-O-methyltransferase (COMT); however, some norepinephrine is transported back into the nerve endings and is used again. The ATP serves as energy source for this reuptake of norepinephrine. Reentry is blocked by reserpine. Exogenous norepinephrine injected into an animal is also stored in synaptic vesicles. Note that monoamine oxidase (MAO) is intracellular, so that some norepinephrine is being constantly deaminated in adrenergic endings.

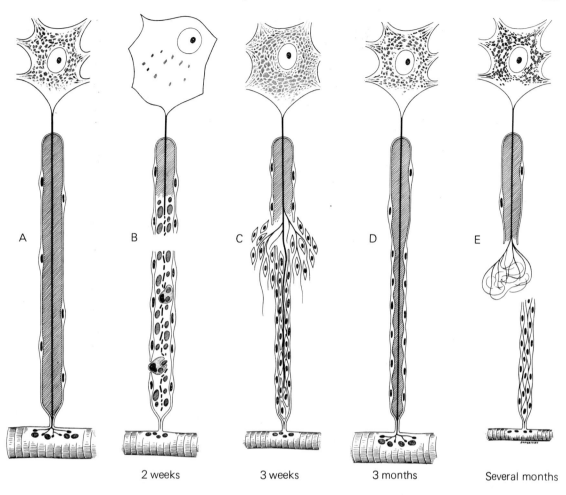

A B C D E

2 weeks   3 weeks   3 months   Several months

Figure 9–22. Main changes which take place in an injured nerve fiber. *A:* Normal nerve fiber, with its perikaryon and the effector cell (striated skeletal muscle). Note the position of the neuron nucleus and the amount and distribution of Nissl bodies. *B:* When the fiber is injured, the neuronal nucleus moves to the cell periphery and Nissl bodies become greatly reduced in number. The nerve fiber distal to the injury degenerates along with its myelin sheath. The debris is phagocytosed by macrophages. *C:* The muscle fiber shows a pronounced disuse atrophy. Schwann cells proliferate, forming a compact cord which is penetrated by the growing axon. The axon grows at the rate of 0.5–3 mm/day. *D:* In this example, the nerve fiber regeneration was successful. Observe that the muscle fiber was also regenerated after receiving nerve stimuli. *E:* When the axon does not penetrate the cord of Schwann cells, its growth is not organized. Then the axons may form an "amputation neuroma." (Redrawn and reproduced, with permission, from Willis RA, Willis AT: *The Principles of Pathology and Bacteriology,* 3rd ed. Butterworth, 1972.)

mural ganglia belong to the parasympathetic system.

Two types of nerve ganglia can be distinguished on the basis of differing morphology and function: *craniospinal ganglia* (sensory), which occur at the dorsal (posterior) root of the spinal nerves and also in the path of some cranial nerves; and *autonomic ganglia,* which are associated with the nerves of the autonomic system.

A capsule of connective tissue surrounding each ganglion is continuous with the connective tissue within it and with the perineurium and epineurium of the pre- and postganglionic nerves.

In ganglia, the body of each ganglion cell is enveloped by a layer of small cuboid cells called *satellite capsule cells.* A thin fibrous layer of connective tissue envelops each perikaryon with its satellite cells.

Craniospinal Ganglia

Craniospinal ganglia are located in the dorsal roots of the spinal nerves and in the paths of some cranial nerves. Their function is to carry to the central nervous system impulses generated by various sensory receptors.

Craniospinal ganglia have pseudounipolar neurons whose T-shaped process sends one branch to the periphery and the other to the central nervous system. The 2 branches of the single T-shaped process constitute one axon, and the peripheral branch has a dendritic arborization. In this instance, the dendrites are not expansions of the cell body but of an axon. The nerve impulse goes directly from the periphery to the central nervous system, bypassing the perikaryon. The perikaryons of pseudounipolar neurons therefore do

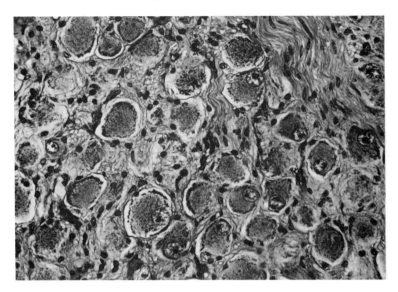

Figure 9—23. Photomicrograph of a spinal ganglion section, showing neurons, satellite cells, and nerve fiber. H&E stain, X 300.

not receive nerve impulses, and their function is exclusively trophic. The single process of this cell makes several irregular turns around the cell body before its bifurcation, which occurs outside the capsule of satellite cells.

The ganglia from the acoustic nerve are the only cranial ganglia whose cells are bipolar. During the expansion of the craniospinal ganglia, the neurons, which are initially bipolar, fuse the initial segments of their prolongations, giving rise to the T-shaped process.

Craniospinal ganglia contain, side-by-side, small nerve cell bodies 15—30 μm in diameter and large ones about 120 μm in diameter. The cell bodies predominate in the periphery of the ganglion, where they form the cortical zone, which is poor in nerve fibers. The central part of the ganglion shows a great predominance of nerve fibers, forming an axial or medullary zone where only a few perikaryons occur in isolated groups.

In histologic sections, perikaryons of pseudounipolar neurons appear as globular bodies. The site of emergence of the single process is rarely seen. These

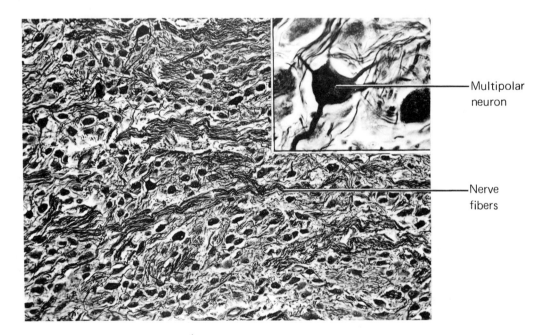

Multipolar
neuron

Nerve
fibers

Figure 9—24. Photomicrographs of silver-stained section from an autonomic nerve ganglion. Neurons and nerve fibers appear black. X 80. The inset shows a multipolar ganglion neuron. X 250.

neurons usually show fine Nissl bodies and droplets with lipofuscin (Fig 9–23).

Autonomic Ganglia

Autonomic ganglia usually appear as bulbous dilatations in autonomic nerves. Some, however, are located within certain organs, especially in the walls of the digestive tract, where they constitute the intramural ganglia. Intramural ganglia are devoid of connective tissue capsules, and their cells are supported by the stroma of the organ in which they are found.

In autonomic ganglia, the cell bodies do not show the peripheral localization seen in craniospinal ganglia; consequently, a cortical layer is not observed. Autonomic ganglia usually have multipolar neurons, which may appear star-shaped in histologic sections (Fig 9–24). As with craniospinal ganglia, autonomic ganglia show neurons with fine Nissl bodies.

The neurons of the autonomic ganglia are frequently enveloped by a layer of satellite cells, which is usually incomplete. In the intramural ganglia, only a few satellite cells are seen around each neuron.

GRAY MATTER & WHITE MATTER

The central nervous system is composed of white matter and gray matter. White matter contains myelinated fibers, oligodendrocytes, fibrous astrocytes, and microglial cells. Gray matter contains perikaryons, unmyelinated and myelinated fibers (mostly the former), protoplasmic astrocytes, oligodendrocytes, and microglial cells. The characteristic color of the white matter is a clue to the large number of myelinated nerve fibers.

Localization of gray matter and white matter varies according to the area and the organization of the nerve tissue considered. In cross-sections of the spinal cord, white matter appears externally and gray matter appears internally, assuming the shape of an H (Fig 9–25). In the horizontal bar of this H is an opening, the central canal, which is a remnant of the embryonic neural tube lumen and is lined by ependymal cells. The gray matter of the ventral bars of the H forms the anterior horns, which contain motor neurons that make up the ventral roots of the spinal nerves. It also forms the posterior horns, which receive sensory fibers from the neurons located in the spinal ganglia (dorsal roots).

Spinal cord neurons are large and multipolar, especially in the anterior horns, where very large motor neurons are found (Fig 9–25).

The cerebellum has 2 hemispheres separated by the *vermis*. The surface of the cerebellum has many furrows perpendicular to the vermis. These furrows divide the organ into lobules, each of which has a superficial layer of gray matter (cortex) and a core of white matter (Fig 9–26). In the interior of the white matter, isolated regions of gray matter also appear.

The cerebellar cortex has 3 layers: an inner molecular layer, a central layer of Purkinje cells, and an outer granular layer (Fig 9–27). The neurons of the granular layer are the smallest in the human body (5 μm in diameter) and have a typical structure. Each granular cell (cerebellar granule) has 3–6 dendrites and, as usual, one axon. The Purkinje cells are quite large. The dendrites of Purkinje cells divide repeatedly in one plane, forming a sort of fan (Fig 9–2). The most superficial layer of the cerebellum (the molecular layer) has few perikaryons and many unmyelinated nerve fibers.

Like the cerebellum, the cerebrum also has a cortex of gray matter and a central area of white matter in which are found the nuclei of gray matter. The surface of the cerebrum is increased by many gyri, which are elevations separated by depressions named sulci. The cytology of the cerebral cortex varies according to the area. The majority of the cells of the cortex have peri-

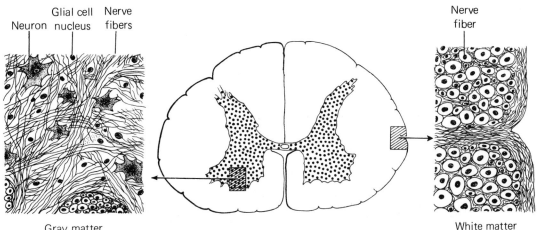

Figure 9–25. *Center:* Cross section through the spinal cord. *Left:* Gray matter. *Right:* White matter.

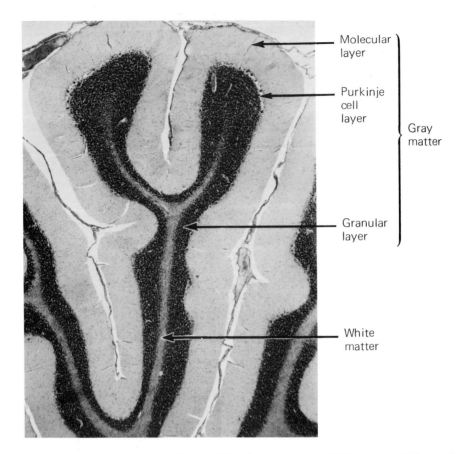

Figure 9–26. Photomicrograph of a portion of cerebellum. Each lobule contains a core of white matter and 3 layers of gray matter: granular, Purkinje, and molecular layers. H&E stain, × 28.

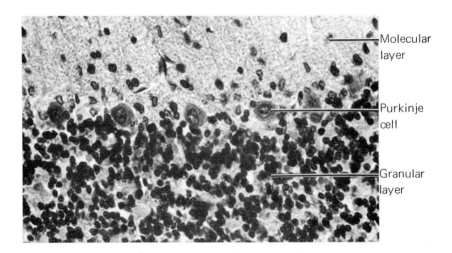

Figure 9–27. Photomicrograph of cerebellar cortex. H&E stain, × 250.

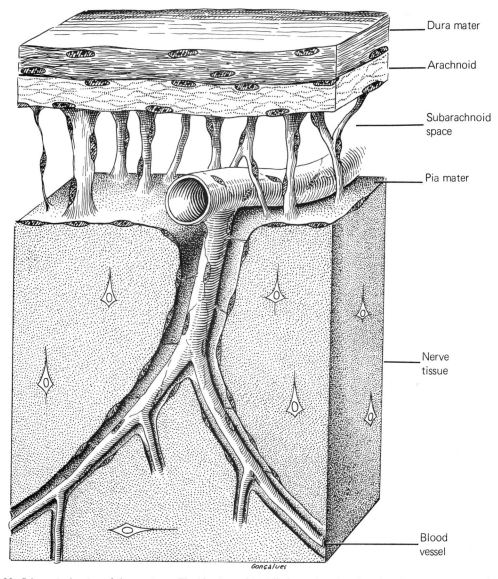

Dura mater

Arachnoid

Subarachnoid space

Pia mater

Nerve tissue

Blood vessel

Gonçalves

Figure 9—28. Schematic drawing of the meninges. The blood vessel initially located in the subarachnoid space penetrates the nerve tissue and is partly enveloped by the pia mater.

karyons which are pyramidal, stellate, or spindle-shaped.

MENINGES

The central nervous system is protected by the skull and the vertebral column. It is also encased in membranes of connective tissue called the meninges.

Starting with the outermost layer, the meninges are named *dura mater, arachnoid,* and *pia mater.* Dura mater is also called *pachymeninx.* The arachnoid and the pia mater are linked together and are often con-sidered as a single membrane called the *pia-arachnoid* or *leptomeninx* (Fig 9—28).

Dura Mater

The dura mater or pachymeninx is the external meninx, made of dense connective tissue continuous with the periosteum of the skull bones. The dura mater which envelops the spinal cord is separated from the periosteum of the vertebrae by the epidural space, which contains thin-walled veins, loose connective tissue, and fat.

The dura mater is always separated from the arachnoid by a thin space, the subdural space. The internal surface of all dura mater, as well as its external surface in the spinal cord, is covered by simple squamous epithelium of mesenchymal origin (Fig 9—28).

Arachnoid

The arachnoid has 2 components: a layer in contact with the dura mater and a system of trabeculae connecting that layer with the pia mater. The cavities between the trabeculae form the *subarachnoid space,* which is filled with cerebrospinal fluid. The subarachnoid space is completely separated from the subdural space.

The arachnoid is composed of connective tissue devoid of blood vessels. Its surfaces are covered by the same type of simple squamous epithelium that covers the dura mater. Since, in the spinal cord, the arachnoid has fewer trabeculae, it can be more clearly distinguished from pia mater.

In some areas, the arachnoid perforates the dura mater, forming protrusions which terminate in venous sinuses in the dura mater. These protrusions, which contain centrally located trabeculae, are called *arachnoid villi.* Their function is to absorb cerebrospinal fluid.

Pia Mater

The pia mater contains many blood vessels and is located quite close to the nerve tissue, but it is not in contact with nerve cells or fibers. Between the pia mater and the neural elements is a thin layer of neuroglial processes, firmly adherent to the pia mater.

The pia mater follows all the irregularities of the surface of the central nervous system and penetrates into it to some extent along with the blood vessels. Its external surface is covered by squamous cells of mesenchymal origin.

Blood vessels penetrate the central nervous system through tunnels covered by pia mater and called the *perivascular spaces* (Fig 9–28). The pia mater disappears before the blood vessels are transformed into capillaries. In the central nervous system, the blood capillaries are completely covered by expansions of the neuroglial cell processes.

Blood-Brain Barrier

There is a barrier which makes difficult the passage of certain substances from the blood to nerve tissue. This functional barrier is termed the *blood-brain barrier.* For example, intravenously injected trypan blue appears in the intercellular spaces of all tissues except the central nervous system.

The blood-brain barrier is a consequence of the reduced permeability which is a property of blood capillaries of nerve tissue. There is sufficient evidence to show that the continuous endothelial cells of these capillaries represent the main structural component of the barrier. The cytoplasm of these endothelial cells does not have the pores found in many other locations. It is also possible, as many authors believe, that the expansions of neuroglial cell processes which envelop the capillaries are partly responsible for their low permeability. These capillaries, in contrast to those in all other locations, are not sheathed by connective tissue.

THE CHOROID PLEXUS & THE CEREBROSPINAL FLUID

Choroid Plexus

The choroid plexuses (telae choroideae) are invag-

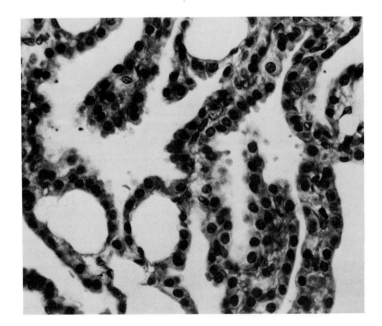

Figure 9–29. Photomicrograph of the choroid plexus. The numerous folds are covered by simple cuboid epithelium. H&E stain, × 400.

inated folds of pia mater that penetrate into the interior of the ventricles. They are found in the roofs of the third and fourth ventricles and in part in the walls of the lateral ventricles.

The choroid plexuses are composed of loose connective tissue of the pia mater, covered by a simple cuboid or low columnar epithelium of neural tube origin (Fig 9—29). The epithelial cells possess numerous irregular microvilli whose free ends are dilated. Their cytoplasm is rich in mitochondria, and there are junctional complexes near their free ends.

The connective tissue of the choroid plexuses is quite cellular, containing many macrophages. These cells avidly engulf intravenously injected supravital dyes such as trypan blue. The blood-brain barrier does not exist in the choroid plexuses. The endothelium of their fenestrated capillaries exhibits pores closed by thin diaphragms. The endothelial cells are held together by tight junctions. These cells are the site of the "blood–cerebrospinal fluid barrier."

The main function of the choroid plexuses is to secrete cerebrospinal fluid, a thin watery fluid which is actively secreted by the epithelial cells covering the plexuses. Among the plexuses are also a few absorbing cells.

Cerebrospinal Fluid

This liquid is elaborated by the choroid plexuses. It contains only a small percentage of solids and completely fills the ventricles, the central canal of the spinal cord, the subarachnoid space, and the perivascular space. It is important for the metabolism of the central nervous system and represents a protective device, forming a liquid layer in the subarachnoid space. This layer cushions the nerve tissue against trauma.

Adult males have about 100 ml of cerebrospinal fluid. The fluid is clear, has a low density (1.004—1.008), and is very low in protein content. It contains relatively high concentrations of sodium, potassium, and chloride, a few desquamated cells, and 2—5 lymphocytes per microliter.

Cerebrospinal fluid is continuously produced, which explains its outflow (up to 200 ml/day) in cranial lesions that penetrate the arachnoid. Substances entering the cerebrospinal fluid must pass through the cells of the choroid plexus.

Cerebrospinal fluid circulates through the central nervous system and is absorbed by the veins and lymphatic vessels around nerve tissue. Nerve tissue is completely devoid of lymphatic vessels.

• • •

References

Blunt MJ, Wendell-Smith CP, Baldwin F: Glia-nerve fibre relationships in mammalian optic nerve. J Anat 99:1, 1965.

Bourne GH (editor): *The Structure and Function of Nervous Tissue.* Vol 1. Academic Press, 1968.

Brightman MW, Palay SL: The fine structure of ependyma in the brain of the rat. J Cell Biol 19:415, 1963.

Bunge RP: Glial cells and the central myelin sheath. Physiol Rev 48:197, 1968.

Cajal S: *Histologie du Système Nerveux de l'Homme et des Vertébrés.* Vol 2. Paris: Librairie Maloine, 1911.

Davis R, Koelle GB: Electron microscopic localization of acetylcholinesterase at the neuromuscular junction by the gold-thiocholine and gold-thiolacetic acid methods. J Cell Biol 34:157, 1967.

De Robertis EDP: *Histophysiology of Synapses and Neurosecretion.* Macmillan, 1963.

De Robertis EDP: Ultrastructure and cytochemistry of the synaptic region. Science 156:907, 1967.

Droz B: Protein metabolism in nerve cells. Int Rev Cytol 25:363, 1969.

Eccles J: The synapse. Sc Am 212:56, Jan 1965.

Friede RL: Enzyme histochemistry of neuroglia. In: *Biology of Neuroglia.* De Robertis EDP, Correa R (editors). Elsevier, 1965.

Friede RL, Samorajski T: The clefts of Schmidt-Lanterman: A quantitative electron microscopic study of their structure in developing and adult sciatic nerves of the rat. Anat Record 165:89, 1969.

Friede RL, Samorajski T: Myelin formation in the sciatic nerve

of the rat: A quantitative electron microscopic, histochemical, and radioautographic study. J Neuropath Exper Neurol 27:546, 1968.

Hamberger A, Hansson HA, Sjöstrand J: Surface structure of isolated neurons: Detachment of nerve terminals during axon regeneration. J Cell Biol 47:319, 1970.

Hydén H: *The Neuron.* Elsevier, 1967.

Jacobson M, Hunt RK: The origins of nerve-cell specificity. Sc Am 228:26, Feb 1973.

Kirkpatrick JB & others: Purification of intact microtubules from the brain. J Cell Biol 47:384, 1970.

Kreutzberg GW: Neuronal dynamics and axonal flow. 4. Blockage of intra-axonal enzyme transport by colchicine. Proc Nat Acad Sc USA 62:722, 1969.

Nathaniel EJH, Pease DC: Collagen and basement membrane formation by Schwann cells during nerve regeneration. J Ultrastruct Res 9:550, 1963.

Peters A, Palay SL, Webster HF: *The Fine Structure of the Nervous System: The Cells and Their Processes.* Hoeber, 1970.

Schmitt FO, Samson FE: Neuronal fibrous proteins. Neurosci Res Prog Bull 6:117, 1968.

Sotelo C, Palay SL: The fine structure of the lateral vestibular nucleus in the rat. 1. Neurons and neuroglia cells. J Cell Biol 36:151, 1968.

Webster HD: The geometry of peripheral myelin sheaths during their formation and growth in rat sciatic nerves. J Cell Biol 48:348, 1971.

Weiss P: Neuronal dynamics. Neurosci Res Prog Bull 5:371, 1967.

10 . . .
The Sense Organs

The sensory organs have the function of receiving information from the environment and from within the body and transmitting it to the central nervous system. In the distal portions of these organs we find special structures, the *receptors,* which have the ability to convert various forms of energy into changes of *membrane potential;* this is called the *generating potential.* This initial generating potential is transformed in the nerve fibers into *action potentials* which are transmitted along these fibers to the central nervous system. The receptors act, therefore, as transducers which transform one type of energy into another. Receptors are usually nerve endings or cells specialized for this function. Various kinds of physical or chemical stimuli create an action potential in these nerve endings, eg, mechanical stimuli (pressure, tactile sensitivity, etc), thermal stimuli (heat and cold), electromagnetic energy (light), and chemical stimuli and concentration (taste, olfaction, blood CO_2 and O_2 concentration).

Most of these generating potentials are probably produced by changes in permeability of the membrane of the receptors, but the exact mechanism is not well understood.

Classification of Receptors

It is difficult to classify the receptors rationally. The principal receptors can be provisionally classified as follows:

(1) A system of receptors related to *somatic* and *visceral sensitivity.* These receptors are sensitive to pressure, vibration, temperature, and pain. In this group we include the mechanoreceptors responsible for giving information on the degree of distention of hollow viscera, the digestive tract, the carotid sinus, etc.

(2) A *proprioceptor system,* which provides information on the position in space of the different parts of the body. This system comprises the receptors of the vestibular part of the ear and receptors from the muscles, tendons, and joints.

(3) A *chemoreceptor system* which participates in the gustatory and olfactory senses. This group also includes the receptors sensitive to CO_2 and O_2 present in the walls of blood vessels and those sensitive to food found in the digestive tract.

(4) An *audioreceptor system* responsible for hearing.

(5) A *photoreceptor system* responsible for vision.

RECEPTORS RELATED TO SUPERFICIAL & DEEP SENSATION

These receptors can be divided on morphologic grounds into free and encapsulated according to the absence or presence of a special connective tissue capsule. They are composed of nerve endings and are responsible for the following senses:

Touch

The sense of touch depends upon Meissner's corpuscles and free endings surrounding the hair follicles. Meissner's corpuscles are most numerous in the dermis of the palms, the soles, the tips of the fingers and toes, the nipples, and the lips. They are elongated structures composed of a thick connective tissue capsule which surrounds nerve endings and is continuous with the endoneurium of the nerve fiber. They are usually located in the papillae of the outer layer of the dermis near the epidermis (Fig 10–1).

Pressure

The main receptor for perception of pressure is the Vater-Pacini corpuscle, which takes the form of a nonmyelinated nerve ending surrounded by thin concentric layers of connective tissue. In transverse section, this corpuscle resembles a sliced onion. It is found mainly in the deep layer of the dermis, in the loose connective tissue in general, in mesentery and visceral ligaments, and in the external genitalia of males and females (Figs 10–1 and 10–2).

Cold & Heat

The receptors thought in the past to be responsible for perception of cold and heat were the encapsulated corpuscles of Krause and Ruffini, respectively (Fig 10–1). This view has been challenged recently and most probably is not tenable any more. Temperature receptors presently are considered to be unencapsulated nerve endings similar to those that transmit pain impulses. The corpuscles of Krause are numerous in

Vater-Pacini

Meissner

Free endings

Ruffini

Krause

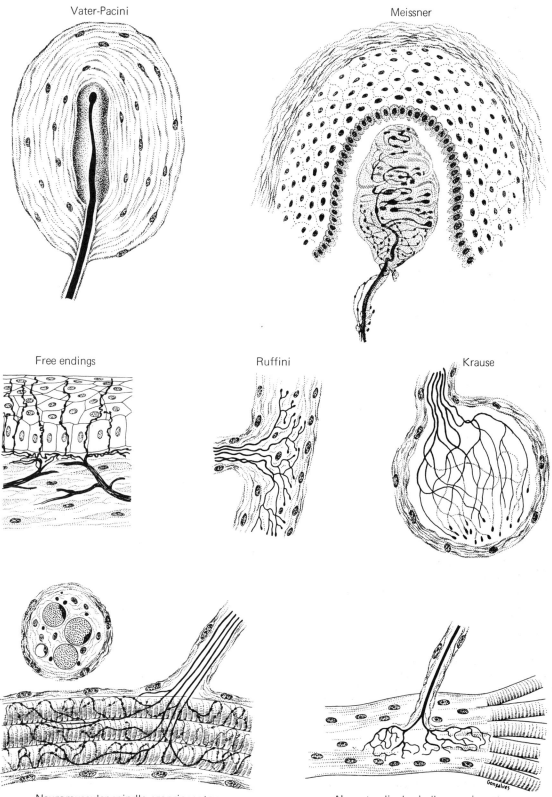

Neuromuscular spindle proprioceptor

Neurotendinal spindle proprioceptor

Figure 10–1. Various types of sensory endings of nerves. (Based partially on a drawing in Ham AW: *Histology*, 6th ed. Lippincott, 1969.)

the skin, the conjunctiva, the mucous membranes of the mouth, and the genital organs. They appear as terminations of nerve fibers in the form of solitary slight thickenings or as free enlarged herniations. Ruffini's corpuscles—particularly abundant in the subcutaneous connective tissue of the plantar surface of the foot— have a more flattened form than Krause's corpuscles, with an abundance of fibroblasts, connective tissue bundles, granular material, and nuclei.

THE PROPRIOCEPTOR SYSTEM

The proprioceptor system comprises the vestibular receptors from the ear and nerve endings of muscles, tendons, and joints. The vestibular receptors will be discussed in the section on the ear. In the *neuromuscular spindles,* sensory nerve endings envelop one or more muscle fibers in an irregular circular and spiral arrangement. They end by branching and forming nodular swellings (Fig 10–1). Each spindle is enveloped by an elongated connective tissue capsule. In tendons, aponeuroses, and joint ligaments, the so-called *neurotendinal spindles* have been observed. These are encapsulated structures that resemble the Ruffini corpuscles. In contrast to the neuromuscular spindles, they are not interspersed between the tendon fibers (Fig 10–1).

The structures mentioned above are sensitive to increases in tension and permit a blindfolded person to

know the exact position of his limbs and also to regulate the amount of effort required to perform certain movements which call for variable amounts of muscular force.

THE CHEMORECEPTOR SYSTEM

Taste

Taste is made possible by the *taste buds* —structures present in practically all of the oral cavity mucosa but particularly numerous in the fungiform and circumvallate papillae of the tongue. They are ovoid, lightly staining, small bodies which contrast with the darkly staining epithelium in which they are embedded (Fig 10–3). They are composed of spindle-shaped cells disposed perpendicularly to the epithelial surface. These cells converge on the apex of the taste bud, forming a small pit which is filled with thin processes of the cell apex, the *taste hairs,* that project into its lumen. The receptor cells receive sensory fibers from the facial and glossopharyngeal nerves that end in the taste bud in a net of irregular varicose terminal branches.

Four fundamental taste sensations have been described in man: acid, bitter, sweet, and salty. Putting small drops of solutions with different tastes on the fungiform papillae shows that some papillae are insensitive to some tastes whereas others are able to

Figure 10–2. Photomicrograph of a transverse section of a human Vater-Pacini corpuscle. Observe the concentric layers of connective tissue. H&E stain, × 320.

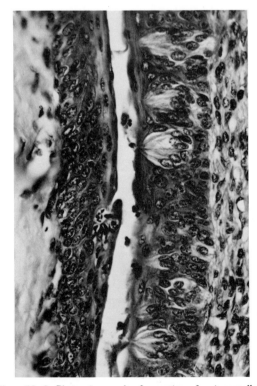

Figure 10–3. Photomicrograph of a section of a circumvallate papilla of the tongue, showing the taste buds immersed in the epithelial layer. H&E stain, × 400.

transmit more than one taste sensation. No structural differences have been described that might explain the differences in sensitivity of the taste buds to various substances.

These 4 fundamental taste receptors are not evenly distributed in the tongue, and for this reason certain regions of this organ are more sensitive to certain tastes than to others.

Olfaction

The olfactory chemoreceptors are located in a specialized area of the mucous membrane in the roof of the nasal cavity, the *olfactory epithelium.* This is a columnar pseudostratified epithelium, 0.06 mm thick, composed of 3 types of cells:

The *supporting cells* have broad, cylindric apexes and narrower bases. On their free surface they have microvilli which are submerged in the layer of mucus that covers the entire epithelial layer. They have a terminal web which is attached to zonula adherens of a well-developed junctional complex which binds the supporting cells to the adjacent olfactory cells. The cells have a reddish-brown pigment which is responsible for the dark gray color of the olfactory mucosa (Fig 10–4).

The *basal cells* are small, spherical or cone-shaped, and form a single layer in the basal region of the epithelium. They have branching processes.

Between the basal cells and the supporting cells are the *olfactory cells,* bipolar neurons that can be distinguished from the supporting cells by the unusual position of their nuclei found between the connective tissue and the nuclei of the supporting cells. Their apexes show dilated areas from which arise 6–8 small cilia, each inserted in its respective basal body. These cilia are long and nonmotile and are considered to be receptors, ie, they represent cellular projections which elicit a response when in contact with an odoriferous substance (Fig 10–5). Their proximal segment shows the usual 9 plus 2 organization of longitudinal cilial microtubules. In the outer part of the cilium (70% of its length), all tubular filaments are single instead of the 9 double microtubules found in the periphery of other cilia. The cilia are sensitive to chemical stimuli, and their mass enlarges considerably the receptor's surface. In some species (but not in humans), the surface of the cilia of the olfactory mucosa is equal in area to the body surface (Fig 10–6). The efferent axons of these neurons reunite in small bundles which are directed toward the central nervous system. It has been calculated that man has 10^7 receptors distributed in an area of 5 sq cm. In the lamina propria of this mucosa, in addition to the abundant vessels and nerves, glands of the tubulo-alveolar type are observed in conjunction with PAS-positive seromucous cells. The excretory ducts of these glands open onto the epithelial surface, and it is the continuous flow of their secretion that cleans the apical portion of the olfactory cells. In this manner, compounds which stimulate the sense of olfaction not only are constantly being removed, thus keeping the receptors in a state of readiness to respond to new stimuli, but the mucus secreted is used to dissolve the substance to which the olfactory receptors respond by generating a receptor potential.

THE EYES

The eye is a complex and highly developed photosensitive organ which permits a fairly accurate analysis of the form, light intensity, and color reflected from objects. The eyes are located in protective bony structures of the skull—the *orbits*—and are basically made up of a dark globe, a lens system to focus the image, a layer of photosensitive cells, and a system of cells and nerves whose function it is to transmit the information collected to the central nervous system. Each eye is composed of 3 concentric layers: (1) an external layer that consists of the *sclera* and the *cornea;* (2) a middle layer—also called the *vascular layer* or *uveal tract* —consisting of the *choroid, ciliary body,* and *iris;* and (3) an inner layer of nerve tissue, the *retina,* which communicates with the central nervous system through the *optic nerve* (Figs 10–7 and 10–8) and extends forward at the *ora serrata.* Beyond this point it forms a continuous layer of unpigmented epithelium over the ciliary body and a layer of pigment epithelium over the posterior iris.

The *lens* of the eye is a biconvex transparent structure kept in position by a circular ligament, the *zonule* or *ligament of Zinn,* which extends from the lens into a thickening of the middle layer called the *ciliary body,* and by close apposition to the vitreous on its posterior side (Figs 10–7 and 10–8). Partially covering the anterior surface of the lens is an opaque

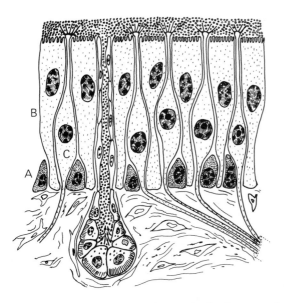

Figure 10–4. Olfactory mucosa showing the 3 cell types and the gland. A: basal cells, B: supporting cells, C: olfactory cells.

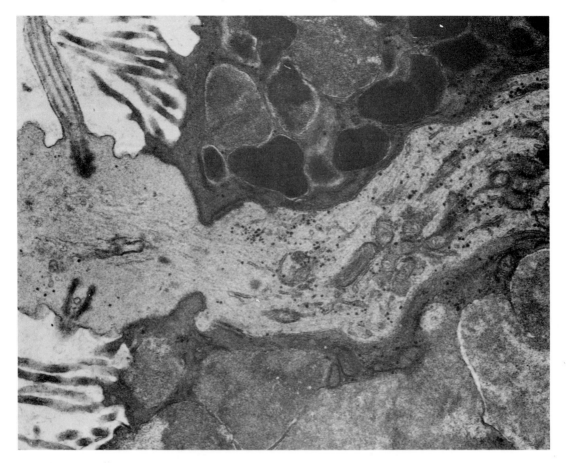

Figure 10–5. Electron micrograph of a section of olfactory mucosa from a frog. In the center is a pale olfactory cell with its terminal dilatation, with 2 basal corpuscles from which cilia emerge. × 28,000. (Courtesy of KR Porter.)

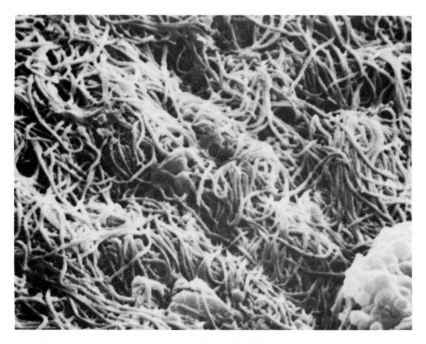

Figure 10–6. Scanning electron micrograph of the surface of the olfactory mucosa of a turtle. Observe the dense net of cilia covering its surface. × 6600. (Courtesy of PP Graziadei.)

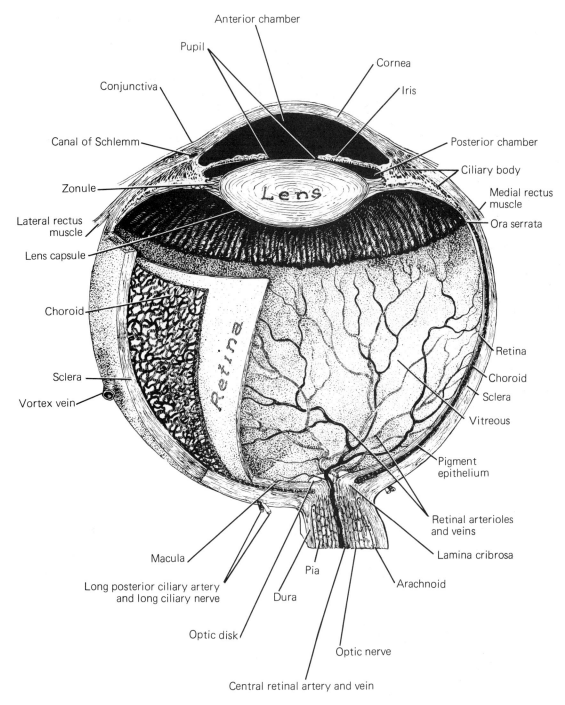

Figure 10–7. Internal structures of the human eye. (Redrawn from an original drawing by Paul Peck and reproduced, with permission, from *The Anatomy of the Eye*. Courtesy of Lederle Laboratories.)

pigmented expansion of the middle layer called the *iris.* The round hole in the middle of the iris is the *pupil.*

The eye is composed of 3 compartments: *the anterior chamber,* which occupies the space between the cornea, the iris, and the lens; the *posterior chamber,* between the posterior iris, the ciliary process, the zonular attachments, and the lens; and the *vitreous space* behind the lens and zonular attachments and surrounded by the retina (Figs 10–7 and 10–8). Both the anterior and the posterior chambers contain a protein-rich fluid called *aqueous humor.* The vitreous space is filled by a viscous, gelatinous substance called *vitreous.*

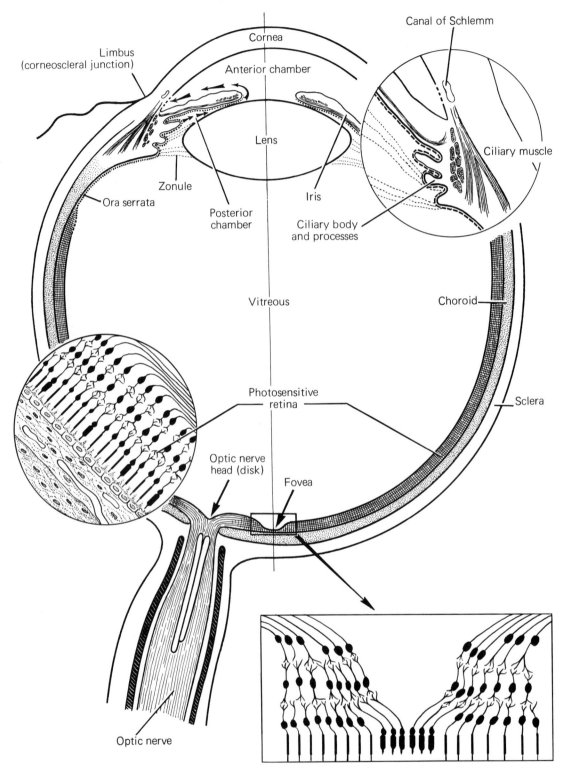

Figure 10–8. Diagram showing the structure of the eye, retina, fovea, and ciliary body. Arrows in the anterior chamber show the direction of flow of aqueous. (Modified and reproduced, with permission, from Ham AW: *Histology,* 6th ed. Lippincott, 1969.)

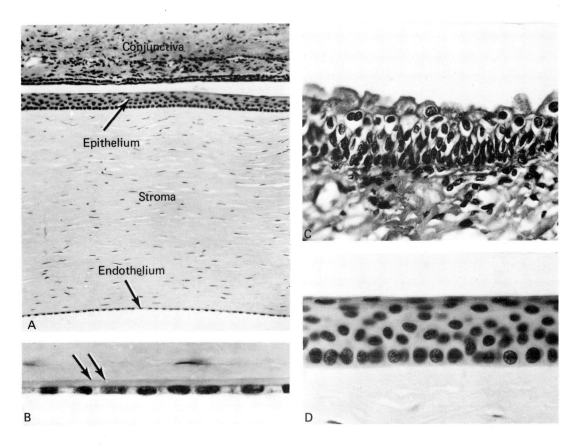

Figure 10–9. Photomicrographs of a transverse section of cornea. *A:* The cornea and conjunctiva seen in small enlargement. × 80. *B:* The posterior corneal epithelium (arrows indicate Descemet's membrane). × 400. *C:* Conjunctival epithelium. × 300. *D:* Anterior corneal epithelium. × 400.

External Layer or Tunica Fibrosa

The opaque white posterior five-sixths of the external layer of the eye is the *sclera,* forming in the human a segment of a sphere approximately 22 mm in diameter (Figs 10–7 and 10–8). The sclera consists of tough, dense connective tissue made up mainly of flat collagenous bundles which intersect in various directions—maintaining, however, a parallel position in relation to the surface of the organ—a moderate amount of ground substance, and a few fibroblasts. The external surface of the sclera—the *episclera*—is connected by a loose system of thin collagenous fibers to a dense layer of connective tissue called *Tenon's capsule* and comes into contact with the loose conjunctival stroma at the limbus. Between Tenon's capsule and the sclera is *Tenon's space.* It is because of this loose space that the eyeball can make rotating movements in all directions. Between the sclera and the choroid is a thin layer of loose connective tissue rich in melanocytes, fibroblasts, and elastic fibers called the *suprachoroidal lamina.* The sclera is relatively avascular.

In contrast to the posterior five-sixths of the eye, the anterior one-sixth—the cornea—is colorless and transparent (Fig 10–7). A transverse section of the cornea shows that it consists of 5 regions: epithelium, Bowman's membrane, stroma, Descemet's membrane, and endothelium (Fig 10–9). The corneal epithelium is stratified, squamous, and nonkeratinized and consists of 5 or 6 layers of cells. In the basal regions of these cells there are numerous mitotic figures which are responsible for the remarkable regenerating capacity of the cornea. The turnover time for these cells is approximately 7 days. The surface corneal cells show microvilli protruding into the space filled by the precorneal tear film. The cornea has one of the richest sensory nerve supplies of any eye tissue.

Beneath the corneal epithelium lies a thick homogeneous layer 7–12 μm in diameter. Study with the electron microscope shows that it consists of collagenous fibers crossing at random and a condensation of the intercellular substance, but no cells are found. This is *Bowman's membrane,* which contributes greatly to the stability and strength of the cornea. Below the *stroma* are several lamellas of parallel collagenous bundles which cross at an angle to each other. The collagen fibrils within each lamella are parallel to each other and run the full length of the cornea. Between the several layers, the cytoplasmic extensions of the fibroblasts are flattened like the wings of a butterfly. Both cells and fibers of the stroma are immersed in an amorphous metachromatic glycoprotein substance rich in chondroitin sulfate. Migrating lymphoid cells are also normally present in the cornea. The stroma normally is avascular.

Descemet's membrane can be seen with the light microscope to be a thick (5–10 μm in diameter) homogeneous structure. Electron microscopic and x-ray studies, however, suggest that Descemet's membrane is really composed of fine collagenous filaments which have a uniform distribution.

The *endothelium* of the cornea is typical simple squamous epithelium. These cells possess organelles characteristic of cells engaged in active transport and protein synthesis for secretion.

The *corneoscleral junction* or *limbus* is an area of transition from the collagenous bundles of the transparent cornea to the white opaque fibers of the sclera. It is highly vascularized, and its blood vessels assume an important role in corneal inflammatory processes. The cornea—an avascular structure—receives its metabolites by diffusion from the vessels and from the fluid of the anterior chamber of the eye. In the region of the limbus in the stromal layer, an irregular endothelium-lined channel and other collecting channels come together to form the *canal of Schlemm* (Figs 10–7 and 10–8), which drains the fluid from the anterior chamber of the eye. The aqueous passes through the trabecular meshwork into the canal of Schlemm, and the canal communicates externally with the venous system.

Middle or Vascular Layer

The middle (vascular) layer of the eye consists of 3 parts: choroid, ciliary body, and iris (Fig 10–7).

A. Choroid: The choroid is a highly vascularized coat. Between its blood vessels are found loose connective tissue rich in fibroblasts, macrophages, lymphocytes, mast cells, plasma cells, collagenous fibers, and elastic fibers. Melanocytes are abundant in this layer and give it its characteristic black color. The inner layer of the choroid is richer in small vessels than the outer layer and is therefore called the *choriocapillary layer.* It has an important function in nutrition of the retina, and damage of this tissue causes serious damage to the retina. A thin (3–4 μm), amorphous hyaline membrane separates the choriocapillary layer from the retina. This is known as *Bruch's membrane* and extends from the optic disk to the ora serrata. It is PAS-positive. The membrane is composed of a basement membrane of pigment epithelium (see p 179), a collagen layer, and an elastic layer close to the choriocapillaris. The suprachoroidea (connective tissue) layer lies between the choroid and the sclera.

B. Ciliary Body: The ciliary body is an anterior dilatation of the choroid at the level of the lens (Figs 10–7 and 10–8). It constitutes a continuous thickened ring which lines the inner surface of the anterior portion of the sclera. In transverse section, it forms a triangle. One of its faces is in contact with the vitreous, one with the sclera, and the third with the lens and the posterior chamber of the eye. This last face has an

irregular surface and presents outgrowths called *ciliary processes* (Figs 10–7 and 10–8). The histologic structure of the ciliary body is basically loose connective tissue (rich in elastic fibers, vessels, and melanocytes) surrounding the *ciliary muscle* (Fig 10–8). This structure is composed of 3 bundles of smooth muscle fibers which insert on the sclera on one side and on different regions of the ciliary body on the other. One of these bundles has the function of stretching the choroid, whereas another bundle, when contracted, relaxes the tension on the lens. These muscular movements are important in visual accommodation, as will be seen later in discussing the lens. The 2 surfaces of the ciliary body which face the vitreous, posterior chamber, and lens are covered by the anterior extension of the retina (Fig 10–8). In this region, the retina consists of only 2 cell layers. The layer directly adherent to the ciliary

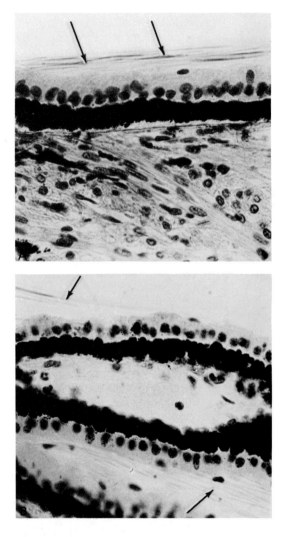

Figure 10–10. Photomicrographs of a ciliary body. *A:* Note the double layer, of which one consists of pigmented cells. *B:* The ciliary process is covered by epithelium on both sides. Arrows indicate zonular fibers. H&E stain, × 400.

body consists of simple columnar cells rich in melanin. It corresponds to the forward projection of the pigment layer of the retina. The second layer, which covers the first, is derived from the sensory layer of the retina and consists of simple colorless columnar epithelium (Fig 10–10A).

C. Ciliary Processes: The ciliary processes are ridgelike extensions of the ciliary body which have a loose connective tissue core and are covered by the 2 simple epithelial layers described above (Fig 10–10B). The outer colorless layer in the ciliary processes is called the *ciliary epithelium,* and its cells, when observed in the electron microscope, have the infoldings of the membrane at the cell basis that is characteristic of ion- and water-transporting cells (see Chapter 4). These cells secrete *aqueous humor.* This fluid, produced at the ciliary processes, flows toward the lens and passes between it and the iris, reaching the anterior chamber of the eye (see arrows in Fig 10–8). Once in the anterior chamber, it reverses its direction and proceeds to the angle formed by the cornea with the basal part of the iris. It then penetrates into the tissue of the limbus in a series of labyrinthine spaces (trabecular meshwork) and finally reaches an irregular canal (canal of Schlemm) lined by endothelial cells (Figs 10–7 and 10–8). This structure communicates with small veins of the sclera through which the aqueous humor escapes. Any impediment to the drainage of aqueous humor caused by an obstruction in the outflow channels results in an increase in the intraocular pressure, leading to *glaucoma.*

D. Iris: The iris is a membranous extension of the choroid which partially covers the lens, leaving a round opening in the center called the *pupil* (Fig 10–7). The anterior surface of the iris is irregular and rough, with grooves and ridges; the posterior surface is smooth. The anterior surface is covered by simple squamous epithelium—a continuation of the corneal endothelium. Beneath this layer is loose, poorly vascularized

connective tissue with few fibers and many fibroblasts and melanocytes. The next layer is rich in blood vessels embedded in loose connective tissue. The posterior surface of the iris is covered by 2 layers of epithelium (described above) which also cover the ciliary body and its processes. The heavy pigmentation in this layer prevents the passage of light into the interior of the eye except through the pupil.

The function of the abundant melanocytes or melanin-containing pigment cells in several regions of the eye is to keep stray light rays from interfering with image formation. The melanocytes of the stroma of the iris are responsible for the so-called color of the eyes, ie, the color of the iris. Thus, if the layer of pigment in the interior region of the iris consists of only a few cells, the light reflected from the black pigment epithelium present in the posterior surface of the iris will be blue. As the amount of pigment increases, the iris assumes various shades of greenish-blue, gray, and finally brown. Albinos have almost no pigment, and the pink color of their irides is due to the reflection of light incident from the blood vessels of the iris.

The interior of the iris contains smooth muscle bundles radially disposed from the periphery to the inner border. Just before they reach the border, they divide to assume the form of a Y with a long stalk. The branches of the Y interlace and form a special muscle whose fibers run in a circular direction. This is the *sphincter of the pupil,* responsible for contraction of the pupil. The long stalks of the Y form the *dilator of the pupil,* which has an action opposite to that of the sphincter. These 2 muscles have parasympathetic and sympathetic innervation, respectively.

Lens

This biconvex structure is characterized by great elasticity, a feature that it loses with age as the lens hardens. The lens has 3 principal components:

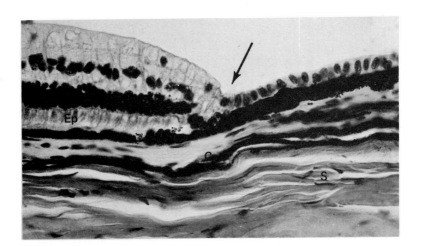

Figure 10–11. Photomicrograph of a section of retina in the transition (arrow) between the photosensitive *(left)* and blind *(right)* parts. Note the pigment epithelium (Ep), the choroid (C), and the sclera (S). H&E stain, × 200.

Ganglionic

Bipolar

Nuclei of the
rods and cones

Pigment

Choroid

Sclera

Figure 10–12. Photomicrograph of a section of the photosensitive part of a retina, showing its layers. H&E stain, × 200.

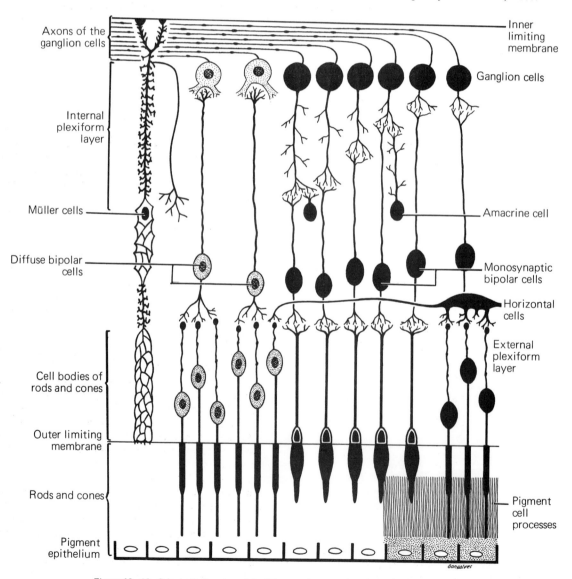

Axons of the
ganglion cells

Inner
limiting
membrane

Ganglion cells

Internal
plexiform
layer

Müller cells

Amacrine cell

Diffuse bipolar
cells

Monosynaptic
bipolar cells

Horizontal
cells

External
plexiform
layer

Cell bodies of
rods and cones

Outer limiting
membrane

Rods and cones

Pigment
cell
processes

Pigment
epithelium

Figure 10–13. Schematic drawing of the 3 layers of retinal neurons. (Modified from Cajal.)

A. Lens Fibers: The lens fibers are elongated and appear as thin hexagonal prismatic elements. They are highly differentiated cells derived from cells of the embryonic lens. They eventually lose their nuclei and become greatly elongated, attaining dimensions of 7–10 mm in length, 8–10 μm in width, and 2 μm in thickness. The cells of the epithelium and the fibers show many interdigitations on their surfaces. Their cytoplasm has few organelles and stains lightly. They are bound together occasionally by gap junctions. The lens fibers usually follow the direction of the lens surface.

B. Lens Capsule: The lens is enveloped by a thin (10–20 μm) homogeneous, refractile, carbohydrate-rich capsule coating the outer surface of the epithelial cells. It is elastic and consists mainly of thin lamellas of collagenous fibers and amorphous glycoprotein.

C. Subcapsular Epithelium: This consists of a single layer of cuboid epithelial cells. It is present only on the anterior surface of the lens. From these cells originate the lens fibers, which are added to the lens during its growing process.

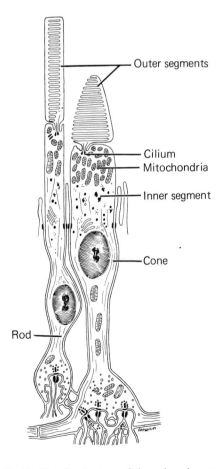

Outer segments

Cilium
Mitochondria

Inner segment

Cone

Rod

Figure 10–14. The ultrastructure of the rods and cones. (Redrawn and reproduced, with permission, from Chevremont M: *Notions de Cytologie et Histologie.* S.A. Desoer Editions [Liège], 1966.)

The lens is held in position by a radially oriented layer of fibers, the *zonule,* which inserts on one side on the lens capsule and on the other on the ciliary body. This system is important in the process known as *accommodation,* which permits focussing on near and far objects by changing the curvature of the lens. Thus, when the eye is at rest or gazing at distant objects, the lens is kept stretched by the zonule in a plane vertical to the optical axis. When we wish to focus on a near object, part of the ciliary muscle contracts, resulting in forward displacement of the choroid and ciliary body. Consequently, the tension exerted by the zonule is relieved and the lens becomes thicker, thus keeping the object in focus.

Vitreous

The vitreous occupies the region of the eye behind the lens. It is a transparent gel which consists of water (about 99%), highly hydrophilic polysaccharides whose principal component is hyaluronic acid, and collagenlike fibers.

Retina

The retina, the inner layer of the eyeball, consists of 2 portions. The posterior portion is photosensitive; the anterior part is not photosensitive and constitutes the inner lining of the ciliary body and the posterior part of the iris (Figs 10–8 and 10–11). The retina derives from an evagination of the anterior cephalic vesicle or prosencephalon. This so-called *optic vesicle,* upon coming into contact with the ectoderm, gradually invaginates in its central region, forming a double-walled calyx or cup. In the adult, the outer wall gives rise to a thin membrane called the *pigment epithelium;* from the inner layer is derived the optical or functioning part of the retina. The pigment epithelium consists of simple columnar epithelium made up of melanin-rich cells. This layer adheres strongly to Bruch's membrane of the inner choroid and weakly to the functional retina. *Detachment of the retina* (a relatively common and serious disorder) occurs at this region of weak adhesion. The optical part of the retina—the posterior or photosensitive part—is a more complex structure and consists of the following layers: (1) an outer layer of photosensitive cells, the *rods* and *cones* (Figs 10–8, 10–12, and 10–13); (2) a layer of *bipolar neurons,* which bind the rods and cones to the ganglion cells; and (3) a layer of *ganglion cells,* which establishes contact with the bipolar cells through its dendrites and sends axons to the central nervous system. These axons come together in one bundle, forming the *optic nerve.*

Between the layer of rods and cones and that of the bipolar cells, a region has been described where the synapses between these 2 types of cells occur. This is the *external plexiform* or *synaptic layer.* The region where the synapses between the bipolar and ganglion cells are established is called the *internal plexiform layer* (Fig 10–13). The retina has an inverted structure, for the light will first cross the ganglion layer and then the bipolar layer to reach the rods and cones.

If a needle were inserted through the posterior

part of the eyeball, it would pass through the sclera, the choroid, the pigment epithelium of the retina, the rods and cones, the bipolar layer, and the ganglion layer to enter the vitreous.

The structure of the retina will now be examined in greater detail. The rods and cones are cells with 2 poles whose only dendrite is photosensitive, whereas the other pole establishes synapses with the cells of the bipolar layer (Figs 10–12 and 10–13). These photosensitive dendrites assume the form of a rod or cone, giving these cells their names. Both rod cells and cone cells penetrate a thin layer called the *external limiting membrane.* Note in Fig 10–13 that whereas the nuclei of the cones are disposed near the limiting membrane, this does not occur with the nuclei of the rods. The external limiting membrane is not a membrane in the customary sense but consists of zonulae adherentes which usually join the inner segments of rods and cones to Müller cells; infrequently, Müller cells to Müller cells; and rarely, photoreceptors to photoreceptors.

The *rod cells* are thin, elongated cells (50 X 3 μm) composed of 2 portions as shown in Figs 10–13 and 10–14. The external photosensitive rod-shaped dendrite is composed mainly of numerous flattened disks piled up like a stack of coins. This *outer segment* is separated from the rest of the cell—the *inner segment*— by a constriction. Just below this constriction there is a basal corpuscle from which a cilium arises and passes to the outer segment. The inner segment is rich in glycogen and has a remarkable aggregation of mitochondria, most of them near the constriction (Figs 10–14 and 10–15). This local accumulation of mitochondria probably is related to the production of energy necessary for the visual process.

The flattened vesicles of the rod cells contain the pigment called *visual purple* or *rhodopsin,* which is bleached by light and thus initiates the visual stimulus. It has been estimated that the human retina has approximately 120 million rods. They are extremely sensitive to light and are considered to be the receptors used when low levels of light are present, such as during the period of dusk or at night.

Radioautographic studies show that the proteins of the disks of the rods are synthesized in the inner segment of these cells. From there, they migrate to the outer segment and aggregate at its basal region, where they are assembled into disks (Fig 10–14). These structures gradually migrate to the cell apex, where they peel off and are phagocytosed and digested by the cells of the pigment epithelium. This phenomenon is notable for the large amount of new protein synthesized by these photoreceptors; it has been observed in various species, and is widespread. It has been calculated that in the monkey approximately 90 disks per cell are produced daily. Each pigment cell is thought to phagocytose 2000–4000 disks daily. The whole process of migration, from assembly at the basal cell region to its apical peeling off, takes 9–13 days. In the cones the process is somewhat different, for the synthesized protein is not concentrated in recently assembled disks but is distributed uniformly throughout

the external segment. It has been shown that, in the disease called *hereditary retinal dystrophy* in the rat, the disks peeled off from the rods are not phagocytosed and are deposited at the surface of the pigment layer.

The *cone cells* are also elongated (60 X 1.5 μm). They have a structure similar to that of the rods, with internal and external segments, basal body with cilium, and an accumulation of mitochondria (Fig 10–14). The cones differ from the rods in their conical form and the structure of their external segments. This region is also composed of stacked flattened vesicles, but they are not independent of the outer enveloping membrane, arising as invaginations of this structure (Fig 10–14). The cones contain the visual pigment *iodopsin,* which is most sensitive to red light; and the human retina has approximately 6 million cones. While the cones are only sensitive to light of a higher intensity than the rods, they are believed to permit better visual acuity than the rods.

The layer of bipolar cells consists of 2 types of cells (Fig 10–12): (1) *diffuse bipolar cells,* which have synapses with 2 or more photoreceptors; and (2) *monosynaptic bipolar cells,* which establish contact with the axon of only one cone photoreceptor and only one ganglion cell. There are, therefore, a certain number of cones which transmit their impulses directly to the central nervous system (Fig 10–13).

The cells of the ganglion layer, besides establishing contact with the bipolar cells, project their axons to a specific region of the retina where they come together to form the *optic nerve.* This region is deprived of receptors and is therefore called the *blind spot* of the retina, the *papilla of the optic nerve,* or the *optic nerve head* (Figs 10–8 and 10–13). The ganglion cells are typical nerve cells with a large clear nucleus, basophilic substance, etc. These cells, like the bipolar cells, are also classified as diffuse or monosynaptic types in their connections with other cells.

Besides these 3 main types of cells (photoreceptors, bipolar cells, and ganglion cells), other types of cells are distributed more diffusely in the layers of the retina:

(1) The *horizontal cells* (Fig 10–13) establish contact between different photoreceptors. Their exact function is not known, but it is possible that they act to integrate stimuli.

(2) The *amacrine cells* are various types of neurons which establish contact between the ganglion cells. Their function is obscure.

(3) The *supporting cells* are neuroglia which present, besides the astrocyte and microglial cell types, some large, extensively ramified cells called *Müller cells.* They are believed to perform in the retina the functions performed by the neuroglia in the nervous system.

Retinal Histophysiology

Light passes through the layers of the retina to the rods and cones, where it is absorbed, thus initiating a series of reactions that result in what we call vision.

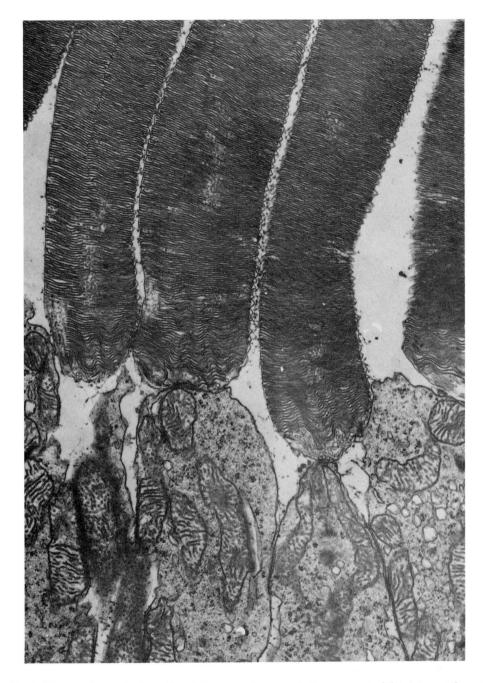

Figure 10—15. Electron micrograph of a section of the retina of a mouse. In the upper part of the picture are the outer segments. The photosensitive region consists of parallel membranous disks. Mitochondrial accumulation occurs in the inner portion. X 10,000. (Courtesy of KR Porter.)

This is an extraordinarily sensitive process, for there is experimental evidence to suggest that one photon is enough to trigger the production of potentials in a rod. Light acts to bleach the visual pigments, and this photochemical process is enormously amplified by some mechanism that causes the local production of potentials which will be transmitted to the central nervous system. Although the changes promoted by light in the visual pigments have been fairly well studied, the molecular processes related to energy transduction and amplification leading to the production of potentials in the photoreceptors are as yet completely unidentified. In a second step, the bleached visual pigment is restored and the process begins all over again. It is known that the stacked, flattened vesicles are the sites where these processes occur and that the visual pig-

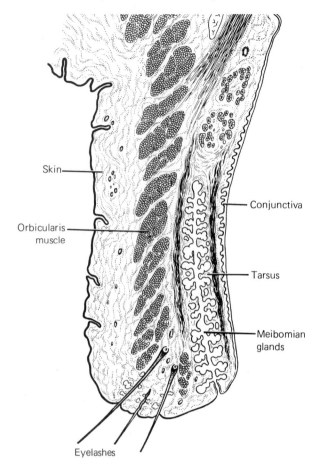

Skin

Orbicularis
muscle

Conjunctiva

Tarsus

Meibomian
glands

Eyelashes

Figure 10—16. Diagram illustrating the lid structure.

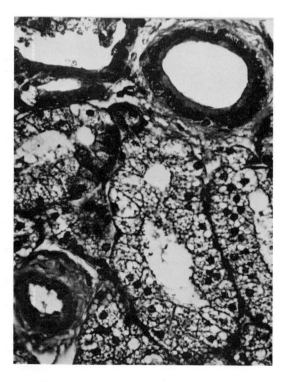

Figure 10—17 (at left). Photomicrograph of a section of a human lacrimal gland. A duct is shown in the upper right region. In the center is the secretory portion. H&E stain, × 350.

ments are situated on the membranes of these vesicles. The visual pigments are composed of an aldehyde of vitamin A_1 (called retinene$_1$) bound to specific proteins. There is evidence that the cones may contain 2 or 3 different pigments in man, thus providing a possible chemical basis for the classical tricolor theory of color vision. The presence of a localized accumulation of mitochondria near the photosensitive site of the rods and cones suggests that this process is highly energy-consuming. This seems to be one more example of mitochondrial aggregation near sites of energy consumption.

The retina is a poorly vascularized structure presenting few capillaries practically restricted to the ganglion and bipolar cell layers. In the photosensitive cell layer, capillaries are almost nonexistent. This poor vascularization probably explains the high glycolytic activity of this tissue. The clinical observation that the retina is damaged when it becomes detached suggests that the photosensitive cells derive at least part of their metabolites from the choriocapillary layer.

At the posterior pole of the optical axis lies the *fovea* (Fig 10–8), a shallow depression in whose center the retina is very thin. This is because the bipolar and ganglion cells accumulate in the periphery of this depression, so that its center consists only of cone cells (Fig 10–8). In this area, blood vessels do not cross over the photosensitive cells. Therefore, light falls directly on the cones in the central part of the fovea—a peculiarity that is probably related to the extremely precise visual acuity of this region.

Light not absorbed by the photoreceptors is absorbed by the pigment cells of the retinal pigment layer and the choroid.

The structure of the retina varies according to the region studied. The fovea has only cones, and the blind spot has no receptors. Other structural variations of physiologic significance are also observed in the retina. The number of ganglion cells per unit area is such an example. Thus, it has been shown that in the periphery of the retina these cells are relatively few in number— hundreds of cells per square millimeter—which is in sharp contrast to the periphery of the fovea, where the cells are counted in hundreds of thousands per square millimeter. This explains why vision at the peripheral part of the retina is much less sharp than at or near the fovea.

Although the retina has approximately 126 million receptors, not all the information gathered by the receptors is relayed to the central nervous system. This is because the optic nerve does not have more than 1 million axons. It is evident, therefore, that much of the information collected by the photoreceptors is selected and grouped (or processed) during its flow through the bipolar and ganglion cells. These cells probably integrate and code the information obtained, sending to the central nervous system only a summary of the data. The retina in humans is therefore mainly a *receptor-integrating structure.*

The retina is an extremely complex organ, as emphasized by the observation that in the primate retina at least 15 different types of neurons are present and that these cells form at least 38 distinct kinds of synapses with one another.

ACCESSORY STRUCTURES OF THE EYE

Conjunctiva

The conjunctiva is a thin, transparent mucous membrane which covers the anterior portion of the eye up to the cornea and the internal surface of the eyelids. It has a stratified columnar epithelium, and its lamina propria is composed of loose connective tissue.

Eyelids (Fig 10–16)

The eyelids are movable folds of tissue which serve to protect the eye. The skin of the lids is loose and elastic, permitting extreme swelling and subsequent return to normal shape and size. The *tarsal plates* consist of dense fibrous tissue with some elastic tissue. They are lined posteriorly by conjunctiva and fuse medially and laterally to form the *medial* and *lateral palpebral tendons (ligaments),* which attach to the orbital bones. The *orbital septum* is the fascia lying posterior to the orbicularis oculi muscle and is the barrier between the lid and the orbit.

The *orbicularis oculi* muscle, which is supplied by the seventh cranial nerve, is roughly circular. Its function is to close the lids. The *levator palpebrae* muscle, supplied by the third nerve, inserts into the tarsal plate and the skin and serves to elevate the lid. The superior tarsal muscle (of Müller), supplied by sympathetic nerves, originates in the levator muscle and inserts at the superior edge of the tarsus, coursing deep to the levator aponeurosis.

The 3 types of glands in the lid are the Meibomian glands and the glands of Moll and Zeis. The Meibomian glands are long sebaceous glands in the tarsal plate. They do not communicate with the hair follicles. There are about 25 in the upper lid and 20 in the lower lid, appearing as yellow vertical streaks deep to the conjunctiva. The Meibomian glands produce a sebaceous substance which creates an oily layer on the surface of the tear film. This helps to prevent rapid evaporation of the normal tear layer. The glands of Zeis are smaller, modified sebaceous glands which are connected with the follicles of the eyelashes. The sweat glands of Moll are unbranched sinuous tubules which begin in a simple spiral and not in a glomerulus as do ordinary sweat glands.

There is a *gray line* (mucocutaneous border) on the margins of both the upper and the lower eyelids. If an incision is made along this line, the lid can be cleanly split into a posterior portion, containing the tarsal plate and conjunctiva, and an anterior portion, containing the orbicularis oculi muscle, skin, and hair follicles.

The blood supply to the lids is derived mainly from the ophthalmic and lacrimal arteries. The

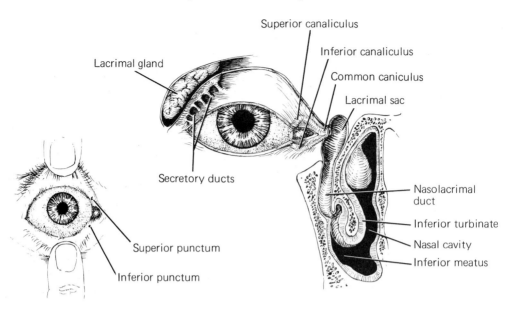

Figure 10–18. The lacrimal drainage system. (Redrawn with modifications and reproduced, with permission, from Thompson: Radiography of the nasolacrimal passageways. Medical Radiography and Photography 25:66, 1949.)

lymphatics drain into the preauricular, parotid, and submaxillary lymph glands.

Lacrimal Apparatus

The lacrimal apparatus (Figs 10–17 and 10–18) consists of the lacrimal gland, accessory glands, canaliculi, tear sac, and nasolacrimal duct. The lacrimal gland is a tear-secreting gland located in the anterior superior temporal portion of the orbit. Several secretory ducts connect the gland to the superior conjunctival fornix. The tears pass down over the cornea and bulbar and palpebral conjunctiva, moistening the surfaces of these structures. They drain into the lacrimal canaliculi through the lacrimal puncta, round apertures about 0.5 mm in diameter on the medial aspect of both the upper and lower lid margins. The canaliculi are about 1 mm in diameter and 8 mm long, and join to form a common canaliculus just before opening into the lacrimal sac. Diverticuli may be a part of the normal structure and are susceptible to fungal infection.

The lacrimal sac is the dilated portion of the lacrimal drainage system which lies in the bony lacrimal fossa.

The nasolacrimal duct is the downward continuation of the lacrimal sac. It opens into the inferior meatus lateral to the inferior turbinate.

All of the passages of the lacrimal drainage system are lined with epithelium. The tears pass into the puncta by capillary attraction. The combined forces of the capillary attraction in the canaliculi, gravity, and the pumping action of the orbicularis oculi muscle on the lacrimal sac tend to continue the flow of tears down the nasolacrimal duct into the nose and nasopharynx.

THE EAR OR VESTIBULOCOCHLEAR APPARATUS

The functions of the vestibulocochlear apparatus (Fig 10–19) are related to equilibrium and hearing (stato-acoustic). It consists of 3 parts: (1) the *external ear,* which receives the sound waves; (2) the *middle ear,* where these waves are transmitted from air to bone and by bone to the internal ear; and (3) the *internal ear,* where these vibrations are transduced to specific nerve impulses which pass via the acoustic nerve to the central nervous system. The internal ear also contains the vestibular organ, which functions to maintain equilibrium.

External Ear

The external ear has an irregular form and consists mainly of a plate of elastic cartilage covered by a layer of skin on both sides. Sebaceous glands and a few sweat glands are present in its dermis.

The *external auditory meatus* extends from the external ear to the tympanic membrane. It has the form of a somewhat flattened canal with rigid walls. The external third of the meatus is supported by an elastic cartilage continued from the external ear. The remainder is formed by the temporal bone. The meatus is lined by skin with numerous hairs, sebaceous glands, and a type of modified sweat gland—the *ceruminous glands*—coiled tubular apocrine glands which produce a brownish, semisolid fatty substance called *cerumen* (earwax). The hairs and cerumen probably have a protective function.

Across the deep end of the external auditory meatus lies an oval membrane, the *tympanic membrane.* It

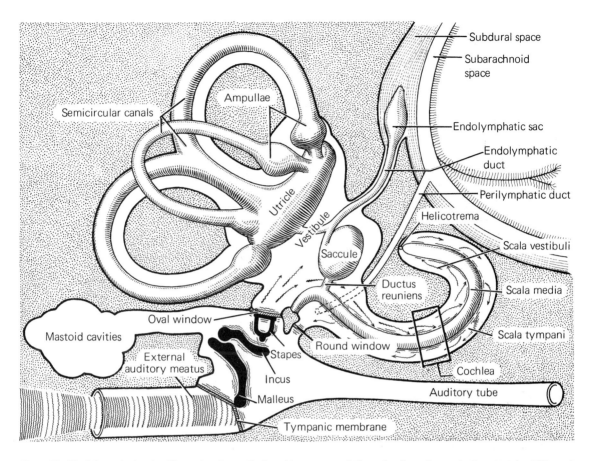

Figure 10–19. Schematic drawing illustrating the vestibulocochlear organ and the path of sound waves in the external, middle, and internal ear. (Redrawn and reproduced, with permission, from Best CH, Taylor NB: *The Physiological Basis of Medical Practice.* Williams & Wilkins, 1971.)

is covered by a thin outer layer of epidermis and, on its inner surface, by simple cuboid epithelium. Between these 2 epithelial coverings is a tough connective tissue layer composed of collagenous and elastic fibers and fibroblasts. In the anterior upper quadrant of the tympanic membrane, it is flaccid and devoid of fibers, forming *Shrapnell's membrane.* The tympanic membrane is the structure that transforms sound waves into mechanical vibrations (Fig 10–19).

Middle Ear

The middle ear, in the interior of the temporal bone, is an irregular cavity that separates the tympanic membrane (and external ear) from the bony surface of the internal ear. It communicates anteriorly with the pharynx by the *auditory tube (Eustachian tube)* and posteriorly with the air-filled cavities of the mastoid process of the temporal bone. The middle ear is lined by simple squamous epithelium that rests on the thin lamina propria which is strongly adherent to the subjacent periosteum. Near the auditory tube and in its interior, the simple epithelium that lines the middle ear is gradually transformed into pseudostratified columnar ciliated epithelium. The walls of the tube are usual-

ly collapsed, but they separate during the process of swallowing, thus balancing the pressure of the air in the middle ear with the atmospheric pressure. In the medial bony wall of the middle ear are 2 oblong regions devoid of bone and covered by a membrane; these are the *oval* and *round windows,* which will be described later (Fig 10–19).

The tympanic membrane is connected to the oval window by 3 small bones—the *auditory ossicles: malleus, incus,* and *stapes* (Fig 10–19)—which transmit the mechanical vibration generated in the tympanic membrane to the inner ear. The malleus inserts itself in the tympanic membrane and the stapes in the membrane of the oval window. These bones are articulated by synovial joints, and like all structures of this cavity they are also covered by simple squamous epithelium. In the middle ear, 2 small muscles are present which insert themselves in the malleus and stapes. They have a function in sound conduction, as will be seen later.

Internal Ear

The internal ear—also called the *labyrinth*—is a complex structure that consists of a series of fluid-filled membranous sacs and canals lodged in cavities of corresponding form in the petrous part of the temporal bone. The membranous sacs and canals form the so-called *membranous labyrinth,* whereas the corresponding osseous portion is the *osseous labyrinth* (Fig 10–19). The membranous structures sometimes impinge upon and adhere to the osseous labyrinth. Usually, however, there is a fluid-filled space between both labyrinths. This *perilymphatic fluid* contrasts with the *endolymphatic fluid* in the interior of the membranous labyrinth. The space filled with perilymph–also called the *perilymphatic space*–is a continuation of the arachnoid space of the meninges, contains stellate cells, and has, therefore, the same composition as cerebrospinal fluid (Fig 10–19). The membranous labyrinth is bound to the periosteum of its osseous counterpart by thin vascularized strands of connective tissue. The membranous labyrinth consists mainly of a lining of simple squamous epithelium surrounded by a thin connective tissue layer. This epithelium–despite being deeply situated in the temporal bone–is of ectodermal origin. It derives from the *auditory vesicle* developed from the ectoderm of the lateral part of the embryo's head. During embryologic development, this vesicle invaginates into the subjacent connective tissue, loses contact with the cephalic ectoderm, and moves deeply into the rudiments of the future temporal bone. During this process it undergoes a complex series of changes in form, giving rise to the various compartments of the membranous labyrinth. In certain regions its epithelial lining becomes differentiated to form special receptor organs known as the *maculae,* the *cristae,* and the *organ of Corti.*

Because the middle ear is derived from endoderm–ie, the first pharyngeal pouch–it presents a unique situation in that it is a structure of endodermal origin (the middle ear) sandwiched between 2 structures of ectodermal origin.

The osseous labyrinth consists of a central irregular cavity, the *vestibule,* with the *semicircular canals* on one side and the *cochlea* on the other (Fig 10–19). The arrangement of the membranous labyrinth in the osseous labyrinth is illustrated in Fig 10–19. Note that the vestibule houses 2 distinct elongated structures: the *saccule* and the *utricle.* The semicircular canals open into the utricle. Each of these canals has a dilatation–the *ampulla*–in one of its extremities. The saccule–also in the vestibule–communicates with the utricle and cochlea by short ducts. The duct which connects the utricle to the saccule assumes the form of a Y whose stalk ends as a blind sac in a special structure, the *endolymphatic sac* (Fig 10–19).

Histology of the Membranous Labyrinth

A. Saccule and Utricle: These structures are composed of a thin sheath of connective tissue lined by simple squamous epithelium. The membranous labyrinth is bound to the periosteum of the osseous labyrinth by thin strands of connective tissue. In the wall of the saccule and utricle, one can observe small regions, called *maculae,* of differentiated neuroepithelial cells to which come branches of the vestibular nerve.

The maculae of the saccule and of the utricle are disposed perpendicularly to one another, and both have a similar histologic structure (Fig 10–20). They consist basically of 2 cell types: *receptors* and *supporting cells.* In the *receptor cells* one can distinguish 2 forms. Both, however, are characterized by the presence of long extensions, resembling stereocilia, of its surface membrane and of one typical cilium with its accompanying basal body (Figs 10–20 and 10–21). It is easy to understand why these cells are classically referred to as *hair cells.* The abundance of mitochondria present in these cells is probably related to their sensory activity. One of these cells has the form of a goblet and is surrounded by a net of afferent nerve endings; the other is columnar and presents afferent and efferent nerve endings (Fig 10–20).

The *supporting cells* disposed between the receptors are columnar and prismatic, with their nuclei at the base of the cell and microvilli in its surface membrane (Fig 10–20). Covering this neuroepithelium is a thick, gelatinous glycoprotein layer, probably secreted by the supporting cells, with surface deposits of crystal bodies composed mainly of calcium carbonate and called *otoliths (otoconia)* (Figs 10–20 and 10–22).

B. Semicircular Canals: These structures have the same general form as the osseous labyrinth. Their receptor areas, however, are present in their ampullae, have an elongated ridgelike form, and are called *cristae ampullares.* They have a structure similar to that of the maculae, but their glycoprotein layer is thicker, has a conical form called a *cupula,* and is not covered by otoliths. The cupula extends across the ampullae, establishing contact with its opposite wall (Fig 10–23).

C. Endolymphatic Duct and Sac: The endolymphatic duct initially has a simple squamous epithelial lining. As it nears the endolymphatic sac, it gradually changes into tall columnar epithelium composed of 2 cell types, one of which has microvilli on its surface and abundant pinocytotic vesicles and vacuoles. It has been suggested that these cells are responsible for the absorption of endolymph and the digestion of foreign material and cellular remnants.

Cochlea

This structure–a diverticulum of the saccule–is highly specialized as a sound receptor. It is a spiral osseous canal 35 mm long. The membranous inner portion is triangular in shape when cut transversely and occupies only a small portion of the osseous cavity (Fig 10–24). One side of this triangle is attached to the bony encasement. The spiral cochlea is coiled around a cone-shaped structure composed of spongiform bone, the *modiolus,* in which there are channels for nerve fibers and vessels. This structure contains also the *spiral ganglion* (Fig 10–25). Lateral to the modiolus is a thin osseous ridge called the *osseous spiral lamina* (Figs 10–24 and 10–25). The modiolus and spiral lamina form a cone-shaped screw with the spiral lamina functioning as the thread.

Transverse section of the coils of the cochlea shows that its membranous portion is triangular in

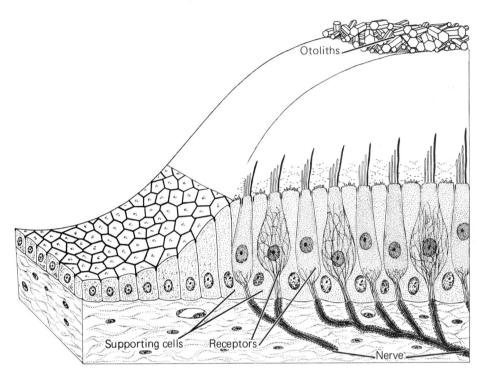

Figure 10–20. The structure of maculae.

shape with its apex pointed to the modiolus and resting on the osseous spiral lamina (Fig 10–24). The base of this triangle forming the membranous spiral lamina is in contact with the lateral bony walls of the osseous labyrinth which shows a region with differentiated cells of stratified epithelium called the *stria vascularis* (Fig 10–24). Another side of the triangle forms the *vestibular* (or *Reissner's*) *membrane,* (Fig 10–24).

The vestibular membrane presents a complex structure, the so-called *organ of Corti,* which contains receptor cells responsible for hearing. The membranous triangle divides the space limited by the osseous cochlea into 3 different portions: an upper portion, the *scala vestibuli;* a middle portion, the *scala media;* and a lower portion, the *scala tympani.* The scala vestibuli opens into the vestibule (Fig 10–19), whereas the scala tympani communicates through the round window with the tympanic cavity or middle ear (Fig 10–19). The vestibular and tympanic cavities are filled with perilymph and communicate in their extremities through a small hole (the *helicotrema*). At its point of origin, the scala media communicates through a duct with the saccule and ends as a blind sac (Fig 10–19).

The cochlea has the following histologic structure:

Figure 10–21 (at right). Scanning electron micrograph of the surface of the macula of a guinea pig's saccule. Observe the stereocilia grouped in bundles, in which a motile cilium—usually with a wavy aspect—can often be observed. X 7000. (Courtesy of Lim DJ, Lane WC: Arch Otolaryng 90:283, 1969.)

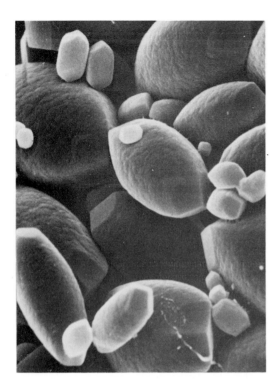

Figure 10—22. Scanning electron micrograph of the surface of a pigeon's macula showing the statoconia or otoliths. (Courtesy of DJ Lim.)

The *vestibular membrane* consists of a very thin layer of connective tissue covered by simple squamous epithelium (Fig 10—24). The *stria vascularis* is lined by stratified epithelium containing 2 main cell types. One is rich in mitochondria and has deep and abundant infoldings of the membrane in its basal portion. These are the characteristics of an ion- and water-transporting cell. The epithelium of the stria vascularis is one of the few examples of an epithelium that contains blood vessels. These characteristics suggest that this region may be involved in the secretion and maintenance of the unusual ionic composition of the endolymph. This fluid is rich in potassium and contains little sodium—a composition usually characteristic of the intracellular medium. This contrasts with the extracellular fluids, including the perilymph, which have just the opposite ionic composition, ie, are rich in sodium and poor in potassium.

Spiral Organ of Corti

This organ rests on the osseous and membranous spiral lamina. It consists of a series of complex structures which are sensitive to the vibrations induced by sound waves. The membranous lamina presents a thickened region composed of a layer of organized collagen-like fibers—the *basilar membrane*—which supports the organ of Corti. The membranous lamina begins medially in the osseous spiral lamina and ends laterally on an eminence of the periosteum called the *spiral crest* (Fig

10—24). Examining Fig 10—24 from right to left, one observes, first, a region composed of loose connective tissue and covered by epithelium—called *spiral limbus* —from which derives a glycoprotein-rich amorphous structure, the *tectorial membrane.* This is oriented in a lateral and horizontal direction, establishing contact with the sensory cells of Corti's organ. In doing so it creates a channel known as the *internal spiral tunnel* (Fig 10—24). The lateral wall of this tunnel is composed of a layer of so-called *inner sensory* or *hair cells;* supporting cells which form the so-called *pillar cells* on the side of the inner tunnel (Fig 10—24); and 3 rows of *outer sensory hair cells.* The cochlear sensory cells, when examined under the electron microscope, show 2 types of cells similar to those described in the macula.

The *inner sensory (or hair) cells* are gobletlike, have modified stereocilia at their free surface, and an accumulation of mitochondria in the base of the cell. Afferent and efferent nerve endings can be seen in these cells. The *outer hair cells* are elongated and also have local accumulations of mitochondria and modified stereocilia. Neither type has cilia, as does the macula. This cell type is innervated by the cochlear nerve.

Histophysiology of the Vestibule & Cochlea

A. Vestibular Function: Increase or decrease in the velocity of circular movement—also called angular acceleration and deceleration—stimulates a flow of liquid in the semicircular canals as a consequence of the inertia of the endolymph. This flow induces lateral movement of the conic cap (cupula) that covers the crista ampullaris. This movement exerts bending and tensile forces on the sensory cells of the crest. Measurement of electrical impulses along the vestibular nerve fibers indicates that movement of the cupula in one direction provokes excitation of the receptors, with production of potentials in the vestibular nerves, whereas movement in the opposite direction inhibits neuronal reactivity. When uniform movement returns, acceleration ceases, the cupula returns to its normal position, and excitation or inhibition of the receptors no longer occurs.

The mechanism of transformation of mechanical into electrical energy is still unknown. The semicircular canals serve to facilitate the reception of information about fluid displacement and therefore body position following circular acceleration; in lower mammals the macula of the saccule and of the utricle also responds to linear acceleration. By virtue of their greater density, the otoliths are displaced when there is an increase or decrease of linear velocity, causing tension in the gelatin layer and thus deforming the sensory cells. Consequently, excitation of the receptors occurs, with production of action potentials that are transmitted to the central nervous system by way of the vestibular nerves. The macula is also sensitive to the action of gravity on the otoliths. Their stimulation is important for the conscious perception of movement and orientation in space.

In summary, then, the vestibular apparatus is composed of many sensitive areas intimately con-

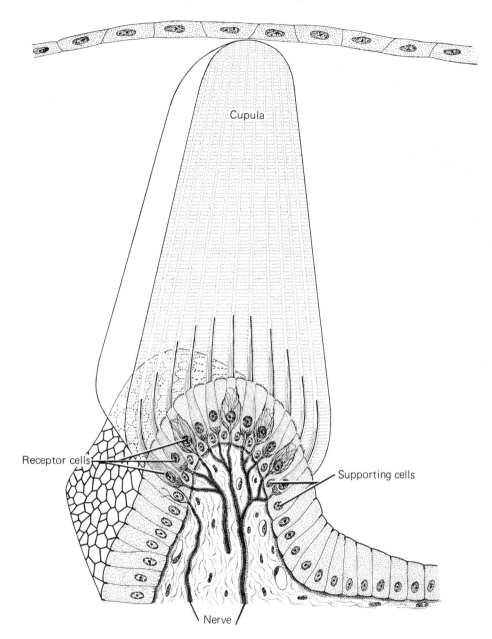

Figure 10−23. Schematic drawing of the structure of the crista ampullaris.

cerned with maintenance of equilibrium.

B. Cochlear Function: In the cochlea, mechanical stimuli (vibrations) induced by sound waves stimulate the production of a generating potential which is conveyed to the central nervous system by way of the cochlear nerve. The sound is transformed into vibrations by the tympanic membrane and transmitted across chains of small bones to the oval window. The eardrum vibrates when exposed to sound waves but ceases to vibrate when the stimulus is withdrawn. The result is that it functions like a resonator softener. The small bones of the ear function as a series of levers that convert the vibrations of the tympanic membrane into mechanical displacement that is conveyed to the oval window and then to the perilymph of the vestibular scala (Fig 10−19). Contraction of the tensor muscles of the malleus and incus results in consecutive traction on the small bones with a decrease in the transmission of sound. In general, an excessively loud sound produces contraction of these muscles, and this has a protective effect on the neurons of the spiral ganglia, which are very sensitive and can be damaged irreversibly by prolonged or repetitive exposure to very loud sounds. Vibrations that reach the perilymph of the vestibular scala are then transmitted to the tympanic scala and dissipate in the round window (Fig 10−19).

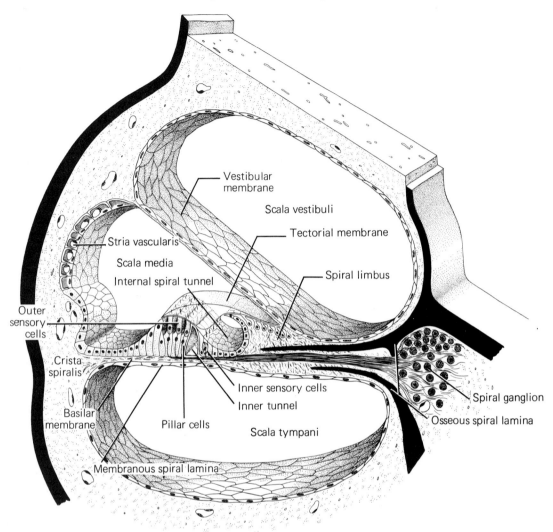

Figure 10–24. The structure of the cochlea. (Redrawn and reproduced, with permission, from Bloom W, Fawcett DW: *A Textbook of Histology,* 9th ed. Saunders, 1968.)

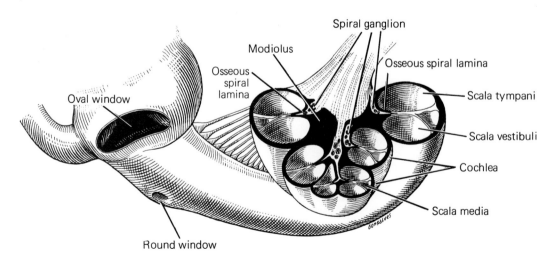

Figure 10–25. Schematic drawing of the disposition of the spiral ganglion and scalas of the cochlea.

Contrary to what was believed until recently, the membranous spiral lamina situated under the organ of Corti is not a dense structure, so that the whole membranous cochlea vibrates when a sound passes from the vestibular scala to the tympanic. Even though this is a controversial point, some authors believe that vibration of the organ of Corti results in displacement of the tectorial membrane, resulting in pressure on the sensory cells and causing deformation of the stereocilia. This process could generate the action potential in the auditory nerve by an unknown mechanism. It is known that in the cochlea sensitivity to sound varies in accordance with the region. Thus, high sounds generate waves that reach maximal vibration in the base of the cochlea, whereas low sounds vibrate maximally in the apex of the cochlea.

•   •   •

References

Cutaneous & Deep Sensory Mechanisms

Cordier R: Sensory cells. In: *The Cell.* Vol 6. Brachet J, Mirsky AE (editors). Academic Press, 1964.

Loewenstein WR: Biological transducers. Sc Am 203:99, July 1960.

Moulton DG, Beidler LM: Structure and function in the peripheral olfactory system. Physiol Rev 47:1, 1967.

Nishi K, Oura C, Pallie W: Fine structure of Pacinian corpuscles in the mesentery of the cat. J Cell Biol 43:539, 1969.

Okano M, Weber AF, Frommes SP: Electron microscopic studies of the distal border of canine olfactory epithelium. J Ultrastruct Res 17:487, 1967.

Ottoson D: Generation and transmission of signals in the olfactory system. Page 35 in: *Olfaction and Taste.* Zotterman Y (editor). Macmillan, 1963.

The Eye

Bok D, Hall MO: The role of the retinal pigment epithelium in the etiology of inherited retinal dystrophy in the rat. J Cell Biol 49:664, 1971.

Botelho SY: Tears and the lacrimal gland. Sc Am 211:78, Oct 1964.

Davson H (editor): *The Eye.* Academic Press, 1962.

Duke-Elder S, Wybar KC: *System of Ophthalmology: The Anatomy of the Visual System.* Mosby, 1961.

Hogan MJ & others: *Histology of the Eye.* Saunders, 1971.

Jakus MA: *Ocular Fine Structure.* Churchill, 1964.

Miller WH: Visual photoreceptor structures. In: *The Cell.* Vol 4, Brachet J, Mirsky AE (editors). Academic Press, 1960.

Orzalesi N, Riva A, Testa F: Fine structure of the human lacrimal gland. J Submicroscop Cytol 3:283, 1971.

Polyak S: *The Vertebrate Visual System.* Univ of Chicago Press, 1957.

Rodieck RW: *The Vertebrate Retina.* Freeman, 1974.

Smelser GK (editor): *The Structure of the Eye: A Symposium.* Academic Press, 1961.

Stell WK: The morphological organization of the vertebrate retina. In: *Physiology of Photoreceptor Organs.* Vol 7. Fuortes MGF (editor). Springer, 1972.

Tormey JM: Fine structure of the ciliary epithelium of the rabbit, with particular reference to "infolded membranes," "vesicles," and the effects of Diamox. J Cell Biol 17:641, 1963.

Villegas GM: Ultrastructure of the human retina. J Anat 98:501, 1964.

Young RW: The renewal of rod and cone outer segments in the rhesus monkey. J Cell Biol 49:303, 1971.

The Ear

Anson BJ, Donaldson JA: *Surgical Anatomy of the Temporal Bone and Ear.* Saunders, 1973.

Duval AJ, Flock A, Wersäll J: The ultrastructure of the sensory hairs and associated organelles of the cochlear inner hair cell, with reference to directional sensitivity. J Cell Biol 29:497, 1966.

Hinojosa R, Rodriguez-Echandia EL: The fine structure of the stria vascularis of the cat inner ear. Am J Anat 118:631, 1966.

Kimura RS, Schuknecht HF, Sundo I: Fine morphology of the sensory cells in the organ of Corti in man. Acta oto-laryng 58:390, 1965.

Wersäll J, Flock A, Lundquist P-G: Structural basis for directional sensitivity in cochlear and vestibular sensory receptors. In: *Sensory Receptors.* Vol 30. Cold Spring Harbor Symposium on Quantitative Biology, 1965.

11...
Muscle Tissue

Muscle tissue is responsible for body movements. It consists of elongated cells—the muscle fibers—that are characterized by the presence of great numbers of contractile cytoplasmic filaments. The muscle cells are of mesodermal origin, and their differentiation occurs mainly by a gradual process of lengthening with simultaneous synthesis of the protein of the filaments.

Three types of muscle tissue may be distinguished in mammals on the basis of morphologic and functional characteristics: *Smooth muscle* consists of collections of fusiform cells which, in the light microscope, do not show striations. Their contraction process is slow and not subject to voluntary control. *Striated skeletal muscle* is composed of bundles of very long cylindric multinucleated cells which present cross-striations. Their contraction is quick, forceful, and under voluntary control. *Striated cardiac muscle* also presents cross-striations and is composed of irregularly shaped or branched individual cells which are parallel to and in contact with their neighbors, forming the intercalated disks, structures that are found only in cardiac muscle. Their contraction is involuntary, vigorous, and rhythmic (Fig 11—1).

We will see in this chapter that each type of muscle tissue has a structure adapted to its physiologic role.

Muscle cells are highly differentiated and are named according to their structural characteristics. Thus, the cytoplasm of muscle cells (excluding the myofibrils) is called *sarcoplasm;* the endoplasmic retic-

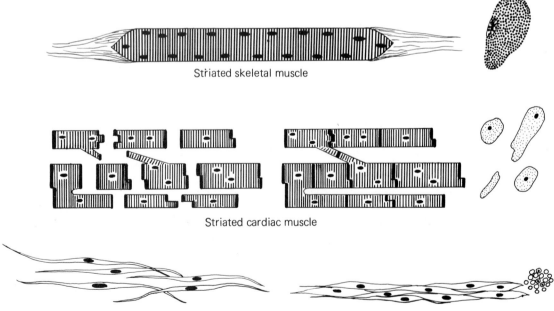

Striated skeletal muscle

Striated cardiac muscle

Dissociated smooth muscle

Smooth muscle

Figure 11—1. Diagram of the structure of the 3 muscle types. *Above:* Striated skeletal muscle. *Center:* Cardiac muscle. *Below:* Smooth muscle. The drawings at right show these muscles in cross section. Skeletal muscle is composed of large, elongated, multinucleated units (fibers). Cardiac muscle is composed of irregular branched cells bound longitudinally. Smooth muscle is an agglomerate of fusiform cells. (Redrawn and reproduced, with permission, from Passmore R, Robson JS [editors]: *A Companion to Medical Studies.* Vol 1. Blackwell, 1968.)

ulum is called *sarcoplasmic reticulum;* and their mitochondria are called *sarcosomes.* The *sarcolemma* is the cell membrane with the basement membrane and the few attached connective tissue fibrils. In current usage, the sarcolemma is often called simply the *cell membrane* or *plasmalemma.*

STRIATED SKELETAL MUSCLE

Striated skeletal muscle consists of bundles of very long (up to 30 cm) cylindric multinucleated cells with a diameter of 10–100 μm called *muscle fibers.* The nuclei are ovoid and are usually found at the periphery of the cell under the cell membrane. This characteristic nuclear location is helpful in distinguishing skeletal muscle from cardiac muscle, which has centrally located nuclei.

Organization of Striated Skeletal Muscle

The masses of fibers that make up the different types of muscle are not grouped in random fashion but are arranged in regular bundles surrounded by an external membrane of connective tissue called the *epimysium* (Fig 11–2). From the epimysium, thin septa of connective tissue extend inward, dividing the muscle bundles into fascicles. These septa are called *perimysia.* Each muscle fiber is surrounded by a very delicate layer of connective tissue composed of reticular fibers, the *endomysium* (Fig 11–2).

This disposition of connective tissue not only binds the muscle fibers together and permits some freedom of movement among them but also binds the muscle tissue to the structures (tendon, periosteum, skin, aponeurosis, etc) with which it comes in contact. The blood vessels penetrate into the muscle inside the connective tissue septa and form a rich capillary network which runs between and parallel to the muscle fibers.

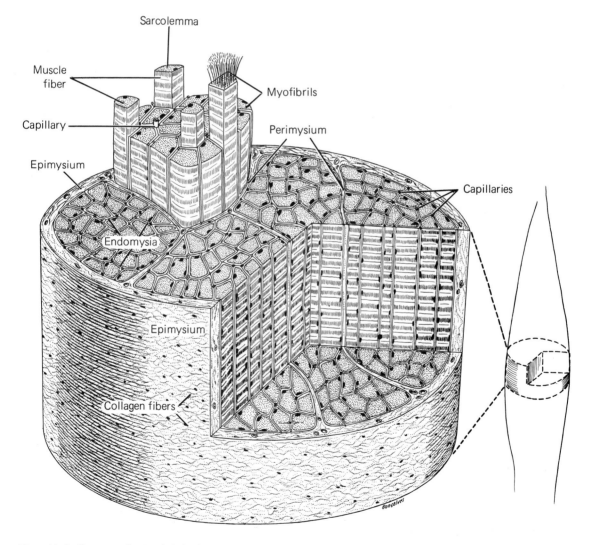

Figure 11–2. Structure of striated skeletal muscle. To the right is a drawing showing where the enlarged segment was taken from a muscle.

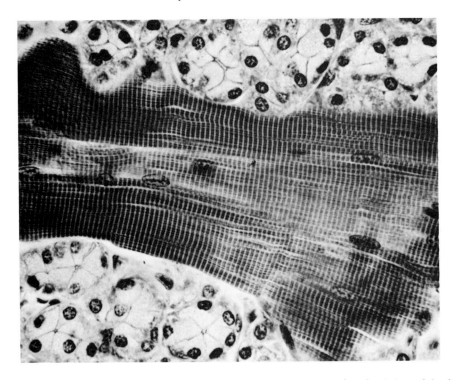

Figure 11–3. Photomicrograph of a section of the tongue of a rat, showing the transverse (cross) striations of the skeletal muscle fibers cut longitudinally. ✕ 700.

The capillaries are of the continuous type. Lymphatics are found in the connective tissue area. The muscles taper off at their extremities, and a transition from muscle into tendon occurs. Analysis of this transitional region with the aid of the electron microscope reveals that collagen fibers of the tendon insert themselves in complex infoldings of the plasmalemma of the muscle fibers present at this zone. Except in a few instances, each individual muscle fiber has near its center a motor nerve ending, the so-called *motor end-plate,* whose structure is shown in Fig 11–10 and will be described in greater detail below.

As observed with the light microscope, longitudinally sectioned muscle cells or muscle fibers, when stained with hematoxylin and eosin, show cross-striations composed of alternating light and dark bands (Fig 11–3). The darker bands are called *A bands* (anisotropic, ie, birefringent in polarized light); the lighter bands are called *I bands* (isotropic). Each I band is bisected by a dark transverse line, the *Z band.* Upon closer examination, we see that each muscle fiber shows also many longitudinal fibrils called *myofibrils* separated by the sarcoplasm in which large numbers of mitochondria are present. The myofibrils are cylindric, with a diameter of 1–2 μm.

Further analysis of this banding pattern reveals that the striation of the myofibril is due to the repetition of similar units called *sarcomeres.* Each of these units is the portion of the myofibrils found between 2 successive Z bands and contains one A band separating 2 semi-I bands (Figs 11–3 and 11–4). Closer observa-

tion of the A band shows the presence of a lighter zone in its center—the H band—which is centered on the M line. The disposition of these sarcomeres is almost parallel in the several myofibrils of a muscle fiber. Consequently, in the light microscope, they form a system of parallel cross-striations which is characteristic of the so-called striated muscle cells.

Study of the sarcomere with the electron microscope reveals that the pattern described above is due mainly to the presence of 2 types of filaments—thick and thin filaments—disposed parallel to the long axis of the myofibrils in a symmetric pattern. The thick filaments are composed predominantly of myosin and the thin filaments mainly of actin.

Inserted in the Z band is a platelike formation of thin filaments which run in the I zone and between the thick filaments as far as the outer border of the H band. The other type of filament is thicker and occupies the central dark portion of the sarcomere (Figs 11–4 and 11–5). As a result of this arrangement, the I bands consist of the portions of the thin filaments which are not invaded by the thick filaments. The A bands are composed mainly of thick filaments and the portion of the thin filaments between them; the H bands consist only of thick ones.

Thus, the thin and thick filaments overlap for some distance at the A band. As a consequence of this symmetric arrangement, a cross section at this point shows each thick filament surrounded by 6 thin filaments in the form of a hexagon (Fig 11–5).

The striated muscle filaments contain at least 4

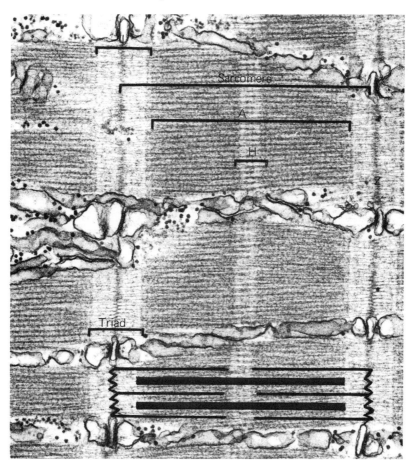

Figure 11—4. Electron micrograph of skeletal muscle of a tadpole. Observe the sarcomere, with its A, I, Z, and H bands. The position of the thick and thin filaments in the sarcomere is shown in the lower part. Reduced from X 42,000. (Courtesy of KR Porter.)

main proteins: tropomyosin, troponin, actin, and myosin; myosin and actin together represent 55% of the total protein of striated muscle. Other proteins such as actinin, β-actinin, and myoglobin are present, but their functions are not well understood.

Tropomyosin is composed of long, very thin molecules about 40 nm in length containing 2 polypeptide chains in an *a*-helical form and running on the surface alongside each groove of the double helix of G-actin (see below).

Troponin is another globular protein that appears at regular intervals of about 40 nm along the tropomyosin molecule. In the thin filament, one tropomyosin molecule covers 7 actins, with one troponin molecule on each tropomyosin.

Actin presents as long fibrous (F-actin) structures comprising 2 strands of spherical or globular (G-actin) monomers 5.6 nm in diameter twisted around each other in a double helical formation (Fig 11—5). A notable characteristic of all actin molecules is their asymmetry, which makes it possible to distinguish a front and a back. Therefore, each actin filament has a polarity which is very important for muscular contraction.

Each globular monomer of G-actin contains a binding site for myosin. The thin filaments are composed of actin, which has a molecular weight of 47,000. The thin actin filaments anchor perpendicularly on the Z line, having opposite polarity on each side of the Z line.

Myosin is a much larger and more complex molecule, with a molecular weight of about 500,000. It is a thin rodlike molecule, 200 nm long and 2–3 nm in diameter, made up of 2 helices twisted together and running from one end of the rod to the other, and has a small globular lateral projection at one end. This projection carries an ATPase site which is responsible for the biologic activity of the myosin, ie, to hydrolyze ATP and to combine with actin. When submitted to brief proteolysis, it can be cleaved into 2 fragments, *light* and *heavy meromyosin* (Fig 11—5). The light portion of the molecule constitutes the greater part of the rod portion of the molecule; heavy meromyosin constitutes its globular projection and can be split by proteolysis into 2 fragments: HMMS-1 and HMMS-2. The rod-shaped molecules are arranged within the thick filaments with their globular heads toward the 2 ends,

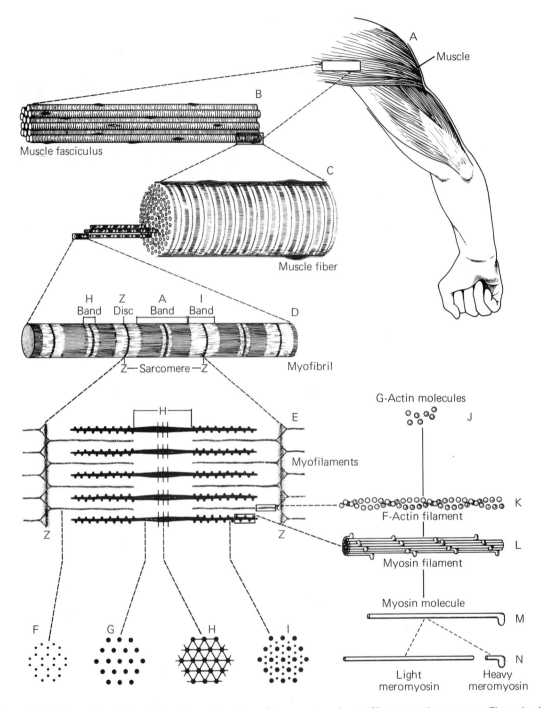

Figure 11–5. Diagram illustrating the structure and position of the myosin and actin filaments in the sarcomere. The molecular structure of these components is shown at right. (Drawing by Sylvia Colard Keene. Reproduced, with permission, from Bloom W, Fawcett DW: *A Textbook of Histology,* 9th ed. Saunders, 1968.)

thus leaving the bare M zone in the middle (Figs 11–4 and 11–5). The heavy meromyosin portion has ATPase activity, and this is also where a binding site to actin is located.

Hydrolysis of ATP takes place in the myosin head regions. ATP is attached to a particular site on the surface and is converted into a "charged" intermediate form which has a great tendency to attach to an actin molecule in the thin filament. This new structure is immediately altered by splitting of ATP into ADP and free phosphate ions by the action of myosin ATPase, liberating energy.

Careful electron microscopic analysis of thin sections of striated muscle shows the presence of cross-bridges between the thin (actin) and thick (myosin) filaments. These structures are considered important in the process of muscle contraction (Fig 11–7).

The chemical study of myosin shows that the ability to combine with actin and the ATPase activity are localized in the heavy meromyosin. As counterpart, each G-actin unit on the F-actin molecule has an active site capable of combining with heavy meromyosin.

Contraction Mechanism

Sufficient evidence has been presented to support the so-called *sliding interdigitating filament hypothesis* of muscle contraction (proposed by Hanson and Huxley) according to which, when muscle contracts, the thin and thick filaments slide past each other. The result is that the thin filaments slide into the A band with the following consequences: (1) The H band becomes narrower and is gradually obliterated. (2) The I band decreases in size. (3) As the 2 lines are pulled closer together, the sarcomere (and the muscle itself) are shortened (Figs 11–6 and 11–10).

This sliding movement is possible because heavy meromyosin forms cross-bridges and binds the thick filaments to the thin ones during muscle contraction (Fig 11–6). Flexible regions have been found at the base of the globular head and at the junction of the heavy meromyosin with the rest of the myosin molecule.

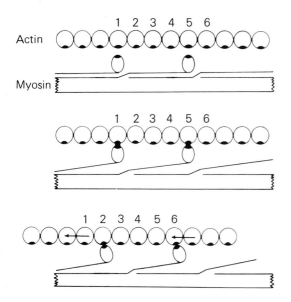

Figure 11–6. Diagram illustrating the hypothesis of the successive bindings, tiltings, and releases that would explain the sliding of the filaments. *Above:* There is no binding. *Center:* The heads of myosin bind to the sites in actin at a certain angle. Cross bridges on opposite sides of the clear H zone pivot in opposite directions, drawing in the filaments. *Below:* Tilting the myosin heads to a different angle promotes a partial sliding of the thin filaments. This process presumably repeats itself frequently, promoting an ample overall sliding movement.

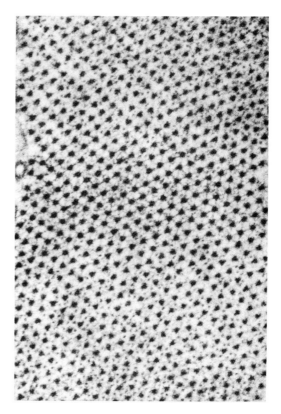

Figure 11–7. Transverse section of striated muscle showing the thin and thick myofibrils. In the center, the bridges connecting both structures are shown.

There is ample information on the exact movements that occur at this site during muscle contraction; successive bindings, tiltings, and releases of the cross-bridges, as illustrated in Fig 11–6, could promote sliding between the filaments.

Sarcolemma

The structure of the sarcolemma is similar to that of other cell membranes, including the presence on its surface of a glycocalyx. Periodically, it presents tubular fingerlike, radially oriented invaginations which penetrate deep into the muscle fibers (Fig 11–8). These tubules surround each of the many myofibrils present in the cell and form the T tubular system, so called because the position of the tubules is transverse to that of the myofibrils. In mammals, these tubules occur at the junctions of each A band with its adjacent I band (Fig 11–9).

The sarcolemma participates with the motor nerve endings of the nerve fiber in the formation of the so-called motor end-plate. This neuromuscular synapse can be easily demonstrated by gold or silver impregnation technics.

When the nerve fiber ends in the muscles, it branches into many terminal twigs, each presenting an irregular dilatation of its extremity which interlocks in a localized site with infoldings of the plasmalemma (Fig 11–10). The myelin sheath becomes gradually

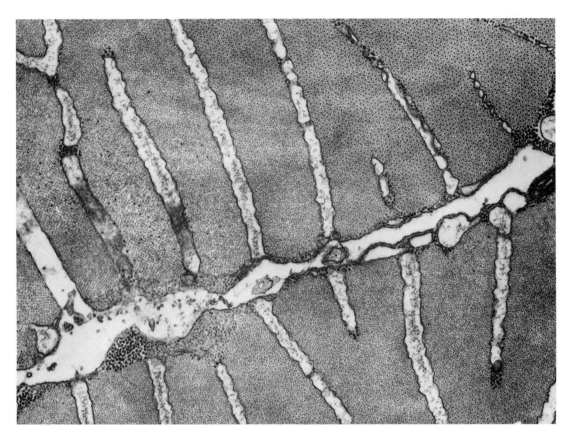

Figure 11—8. Electron micrograph of a transverse section of fish muscle, showing the surface of 2 cells limiting an intercellular space. Observe the invagination present in the sarcolemma, forming the tubules of the T system. The dark, coarse granules in the cytoplasm *(lower left)* are glycogen particles. X 60,000. (Courtesy of KR Porter.)

thinner and disappears. The axon near the nerve ending is covered with a thin cytoplasmic layer of Schwann cells and is packed with microvesicles and mitochondria. These vesicles are the synaptic vesicles described in Chapter 9 and contain acetylcholine. Between the membrane of the nerve endings and the plasmalemma of the muscle fibers, a deposit of amorphous substance—glycocalyx—has been described. This is thrown into numerous folds called junctional folds. The nerve membrane in this area is not covered by Schwann cells but by glycocalyx only. The space between the muscle cell membrane and the nerve ending is called the synaptic cleft.

The use of cytochemical methods at the electron microscopic level has shown that the site of acetylcholinesterase activity is at the region of the plasmalemma facing the motor end-plate. This enzyme hydrolyzes the acetylcholine liberated by exocytosis from the vesicles, thus avoiding prolonged contact of this substance with the receptors present in the muscle cell membrane. The acetylcholine makes the muscle cell membrane more permeable to sodium, which results in its depolarization, spreading throughout the muscle fiber via the tubules of the sarcoplasmic reticulum. As a result, the muscle fiber contracts.

Between the myofibrils and sarcolemma, numerous elongated nuclei are found. The sarcoplasm presents a typical but not very well developed Golgi apparatus and abundant elongated mitochondria (sarcosomes) located near the nuclei or distributed in rows between the myofibrils.

Sarcoplasmic Reticulum

This organelle is the smooth endoplasmic reticulum of the muscle cell and is present as a network of membrane-limited flattened cisternae disposed around each of the myofibrils (Fig 11–11). Each tubule of the T system lies between 2 cisternae of the sarcoplasmic reticulum, forming a typical structure called a *triad*. In cross section, the triad is seen to consist of 3 vesicles or channels: a small central one (T tubule) and 2 larger lateral ones (sarcoplasmic reticulum). Although these membranes are very close together, no communication exists between the content of the T tubules and the sarcoplasmic reticulum. This close proximity is important in transmission of the nerve impulse and will be referred to later on.

In mammalian muscle cells, there are 2 triads in each sarcomere and the tubules are present at the junctions between the A and I bands (Fig 11–9). In am-

Figure 11—9. Electron micrograph of a longitudinal section of the skeletal muscle of a monkey. Observe the mitochondria (**M**) between the myofibrils and the various bands of the sarcomere. The arrows show triads—2 for each sarcomere in this muscle. X 30,000.

phibia, as illustrated in Fig 11—11, only one triad is present which is at the level of the Z bands.

Differential centrifugation has made it possible to isolate the sarcoplasmic reticulum. In vitro experiments with this organelle have resulted in evidence for the existence of an active calcium transport mechanism in its membrane. This system can therefore concentrate calcium and, in this way, regulate the calcium concentration of the sarcoplasm bathing the myofilaments. When the nerve signal to start the contraction arrives at the muscle cell, calcium is released from the sacs of the sarcoplasmic reticulum that surround the myofibrils at the level of the H zone and diffuses into the sarcoplasm, whereupon contraction of the myofibrils begins. In this process, it has been proposed that the calcium ions unite with troponin and that this complex (calcium-troponin), through some unknown mechanism, suspends the blocking effect of tropomyosin on the active binding site of G-actin so that G-actin unites temporarily with the globular portion of the myosin molecule. As soon as calcium ions diffuse back into the endoplasmic reticulum, the active binding sites of G-actin are again blocked by tropomyosin, with the result that contraction ceases and relaxation occurs.

Other Components of the Sarcoplasm

Glycogen is found in abundance in the sarcoplasm in the form of coarse granules (Fig 11—8). It serves as a depot of energy which is mobilized during muscle contraction.

Another component of the sarcoplasm is *myoglobin,* a pigment similar to hemoglobin which is principally responsible for the dark red color of some muscles. Myoglobin acts as an oxygen depot and is present in great amounts in the muscle of animals that dive (eg, seals and whales). Muscles that have to maintain activity for prolonged periods usually are red and have a high content of myoglobin. This is the case, for example, with the pectoral muscles of flying birds.

Muscle cells have negligible amounts of granular endoplasmic reticulum and ribosomes, an observation that is consistent with the insignificant protein synthesis known to occur in this tissue.

Propagation of the Stimulus

The liberation of acetylcholine at the motor endplate promotes a transient local increase in the permeability of the plasmalemma. This change in permeability is transmitted along the surface of the membrane

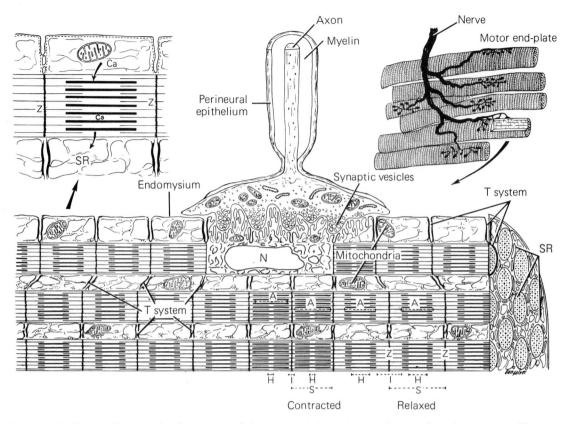

Figure 11–10. Diagram illustrating the ultrastructure of the motor end-plate and the mechanism of muscle contraction. The upper right drawing shows the branching of a small nerve with a motor end-plate for each muscle fiber. The aspect of one of the bulbs of an end-plate is seen highly enlarged in the central drawing. The axon loses its myelin sheath and dilates, establishing close, irregular contact with the muscle fiber. Muscle contraction begins with the release of acetylcholine from the synaptic vesicles of the end-plate. This substance promotes a local increase in the permeability of the sarcolemma. This process is propagated to the rest of the sarcolemma, including its invaginations, all of which constitutes the T system, and is transferred to the sarcoplasmic reticulum (SR). The increase of permeability in this organelle liberates calcium ions that will activate myosin ATPase activity, in turn triggering the sliding mechanism of muscle contraction. Consequently, the actin filaments slide between the myosin filaments and thus reduce the distance between the Z bands. This promotes a reduction in the size of all bands with the exception of the A and Z bands.

and deep into the muscle fibers through the tubules of the T system. This explains how the myofibrils of a muscle fiber are all stimulated simultaneously and almost immediately after delivery of the impulse at the surface of the fiber.

Experiments performed with microelectrodes at the surface of isolated muscle fibers have shown that very weak stimuli can promote localized muscle contractions only when applied at sites where the T system originates. These observations are compatible with the assumptions outlined above. The fact that mammalian muscle contains 2 tubules of the T system per sarcomere (as compared to only one in amphibia) suggests that transmission is better in mammalian muscle. This stimulus is probably transmitted to the sarcoplasmic reticulum as a result of its close attachment to the T tubules, promoting an increase of permeability in its membranes and a transfer of calcium to the sarcoplasm. This ion apparently is necessary for the ATPase activity of myosin, promoting the hydrolysis of ATP and the liberation of energy for muscle contraction.

After contraction, calcium is transported back to the sarcoplasmic reticulum with inhibition of myosin ATPase.

System of Energy Production

Striated skeletal muscle cells are highly adapted for discontinuous production of mechanical work through chemical energy. Therefore, they must have depots of energy to cope with bursts of activity. The most readily available energy is stored in the form of ATP and phosphocreatine, both of which are energy-rich compounds. Chemical energy is also available in glycogen depots, which can constitute about 0.5–1% of muscle weight. A small part of the energy from the glycogen is made available during glycolysis. The major portion of energy used by the muscle, however, is produced in the mitochondria through oxidative phosphorylation of blood glucose. This process uses oxygen from the bloodstream or from myoglobin.

In mammals, the main sources of energy for skeletal muscle are the circulating fatty acids and acetoace-

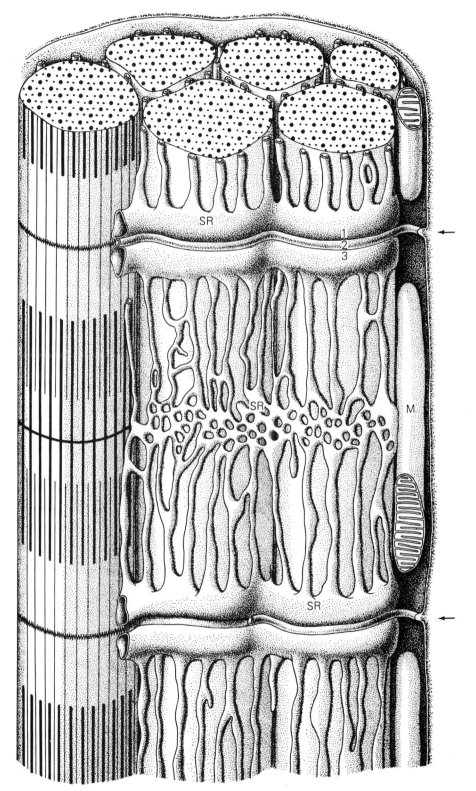

Figure 11—11. Diagram of a segment of amphibian skeletal muscle. To the right is the cut sarcolemma, with the invaginations of the T system (arrows). This system makes contact with the sarcoplasmic reticulum (SR), forming the triads (1, 2, and 3). At M, a mitochondrion is shown, and in the cut surface of the myofibrils are the actin and myosin filaments. Observe that the actin filaments are arranged as a hexagon around the myosin. (Redrawn and reproduced, with permission, from Bloom W, Fawcett DW: *A Textbook of Histology,* 9th ed. Saunders, 1968.)

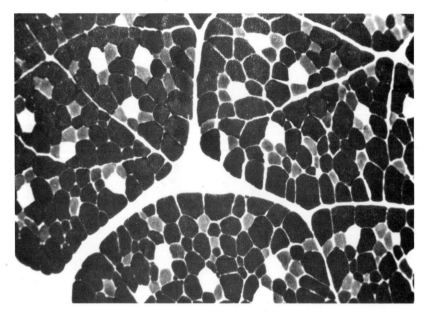

Figure 11–12. Transverse section of a striated muscle (rectus lateralis), stained by the histochemical technic for myosin **ATPase**, showing 3 types of fibers in the muscle. (Reproduced, with permission, from Khan MA & others. Stain Technol 47:277, 1971.)

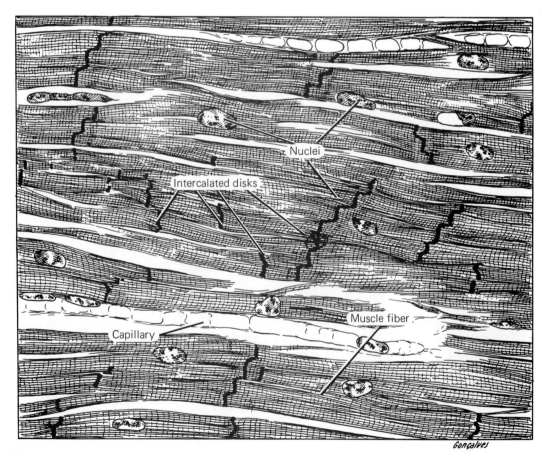

Figure 11–13. Diagram of a section of heart muscle. Observe the presence of central nuclei and intercalated disks.

tate. However, when these muscles are very active, they rapidly metabolize glucose, which then becomes the main source of energy.

From the morphologic, histochemical, and functional point of view, we may classify skeletal muscle fibers into 3 types: red, white, and intermediate. *Red fibers* have a high content of myoglobin and cytochrome, which are responsible for the dark red color (Fig 11–12). They contract at a slower rate than white fibers but are capable of continuous and vigorous activity. Their energy derives mainly from oxidative phosphorylation, and they consequently contain great numbers of mitochondria. These are the fibers in the breast muscle of migrating birds and mammalian limbs. *White fibers* have a low content of myoglobin and cytochrome and fewer mitochondria (Fig 11–12). The breast muscles of chickens and turkeys contain these fibers. They contract rapidly but do not support continuous heavy work. The energy for their activity is derived mainly from anaerobic glycolysis. *Intermediate fibers* have characteristics between the 2 extremes described above (Fig 11–12). In humans, the skeletal muscles are frequently composed of mixtures of these 3 types of fibers.

STRIATED CARDIAC MUSCLES

Striated cardiac muscle is composed of elongated cells grouped in irregular anastomosing columns. These cells present bands forming cross-striations but can easily be distinguished from the skeletal muscle fibers because they have one or 2 centrally located nuclei (Fig 11–13). The arrangement of the columns of cardiac cells is quite irregular, and they are often disposed in different positions in the same microscopic preparation. Surrounding these columns of cells is a delicate sheath of connective tissue equivalent to the endomysium of skeletal muscle. A rich network of capillaries winds among the cells.

Cardiac muscle cells are similar to skeletal muscle cells in many ways but differ from them in having more sarcoplasm, mitochondria, and glycogen. A unique characteristic of cardiac muscle is the presence of darkly stained transverse lines which cross the muscle fiber at the junction of 2 adjacent cells. These so-called *intercalated disks* (Figs 11–13 and 11–14) may extend uninterruptedly across the fiber but more often are disposed in an irregular stepwise pattern (Fig 11–13). Study of the intercalated disks under the electron microscope shows that they are the result of the presence of specialized areas for the maintenance of cell cohesion (Fig 11–15). Thus, in this region, structures similar to the zonula occludens, gap junctions,

Figure 11–14. Electron micrograph from a longitudinal section of the heart of a monkey, showing the typical steplike disposition of the intercalated disks and an abundance of mitochondria. X 7000.

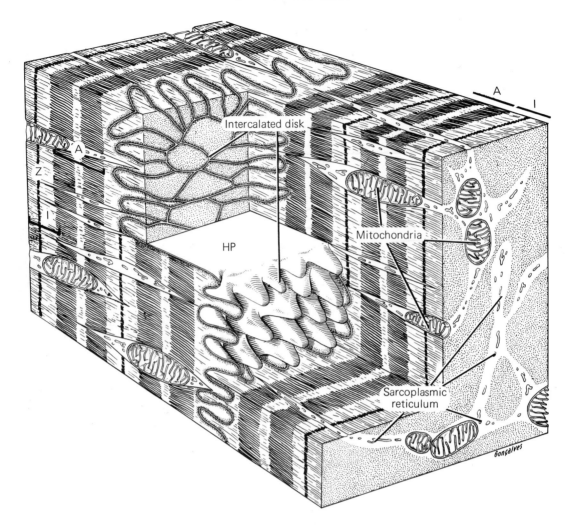

Figure 11–15. Ultrastructure of heart muscle in the region of an intercalated disk. Contact between cells is accomplished by interdigitation in the vertical region and is smooth in the horizontal plane (HP). Straight membrane contacts occur in the interdigitating region. (Redrawn and reproduced, with permission, from Marshall JM: The heart. *In:* Mountcastle VB [editor] : *Medical Physiology,* 13th ed. Mosby, 1974. Based on the results of Fawcett DW, McNutt NS: J Cell Biol 42:1, 1969; modified from Poche R, Lindner E: Z Zellforsch Mikrosk Anat 43:104, 1955.)

and desmosomes (described in Chapter 4 for epithelial cells) are observed. These specialized areas are responsible for binding the cardiac muscle cells together. This binding role is emphasized if cardiac tissue is perfused by calcium-free Ringer's solution. In these conditions, the cardiac cells frequently separate along the intercalated disks. It is known that calcium ions are important for the binding between cells and that their absence loosens these bonds.

Special emphasis is placed on the presence of the so-called gap junctions found along the sides of the intercalated disks of the cardiac muscle cells, for evidence has been presented to show that they are areas of low electrical resistance which permit the spread of excitation from cell to cell and consequently through the whole organ. This explains why (functionally) the heart behaves like a syncytium.

Cardiac muscle cells have the same A, I, Z, and H bands described for skeletal muscle. Their filaments, however, are not grouped in discrete packages as the myofibrils of the skeletal fiber but form a large cylindric mass of parallel filaments incompletely divided by portions of the sarcoplasm (Fig 11–16).

The system of tubular invaginations of the sarcolemma (T system) is larger in cardiac than in skeletal muscle. It is located at the level of the Z lines, establishing in this region contacts with the sarcoplasmic reticulum, which is extensively branched in this type of muscle. Consequently, the triad is not as conspicuous as that observed in skeletal muscle. As a result of this disposition, no region in the cardiac muscle cell is more than $1-3$ μm from the extracellular space—a convenient circumstance not only for transmission of impulses but also for the availability of metabolites.

Figure 11–16. Electron micrograph from a longitudinal section of heart muscle. Observe the alternation of microfilaments and dense mitochondria rich in cristae. Note the smooth endoplasmic reticulum (SER). × 30,000.

The transduction of chemical into mechanical energy is similar in this muscle to that observed in skeletal muscle.

This type of cell contains less sarcoplasmic reticulum than does the skeletal muscle cell.

Nerves & the Impulse-Generating & Conduction System of the Heart

A network of specialized modified cardiac muscle cells is found below the connective tissue layer which lines the heart and the inner wall of this organ. This system, called the impulse-generating and conduction system, makes it possible for the atria and ventricles to beat in succession, permitting the cardiac muscle to act efficiently as a pump. Further details about this system are presented in Chapter 12.

This network consists of groups of cardiac cells— *Purkinje fibers*—which also present transverse striations and intercalated disks and are irregularly disposed in columns. These cells are characterized by a great quantity of sarcoplasm, very rich in glycogen, which fills the center of the cell. The large amount of sarcoplasm displaces the myofilaments toward the periphery. There are no T tubules in the Purkinje fibers.

The heart receives innervation from both the sympathetic and the parasympathetic nervous systems, which form plexuses in the base of the organ. There are in the heart no nerve endings comparable to the motor end-plates of the musculoskeletal system. However, the nervous system exerts a regulatory action on the heart, adapting the cardiac rhythm to the necessities of the organism as a whole.

It is accepted that the cardiac muscle cells have the capacity for autostimulation independently of nerve impulses. Each of these cells maintains its own rhythm, but, since they are closely united, those that maintain a faster rhythm transmit their impulses to all of the others and thus the entire organ.

The fibers of the conduction system of the heart normally initiate and stimulate the propagation of the impulses at a more rapid rate than heart muscle, but the muscle cells of the heart are capable of making the organ function at a slower rate in case of failure of the conduction system.

SMOOTH MUSCLE

This type of muscle is composed of long spindle-like cells which can measure 5–10 μm in diameter and

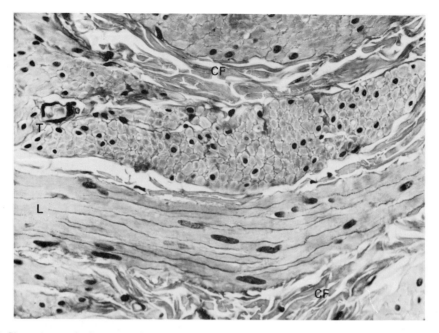

Figure 11–17. Photomicrograph of a section of urinary bladder. Smooth muscle cells are sectioned transversely (T) and longitudinally (L). Note the collagen fibers (CF). H&E stain, × 400.

30–200 μm in length (Fig 11–17). These cells are usually arranged in layers, mainly in the walls of hollow viscera (such as the digestive tract), blood vessels, etc. They are held in place by a fine network of reticular fibers (Fig 11–18). Smooth muscle cells can also be found dispersed in the connective tissue of certain organs such as the prostate and seminal vesicles and in the subcutaneous tissue of the scrotum and nipple. They may also become grouped, forming small muscles such as the arrector pili muscle, or may be the predominant tissue of an organ, as is the case with the uterus.

Blood vessels and nerves penetrate and ramify in the smooth muscle. In cross-section, smooth muscle appears as a collection of rounded or polygonal struc-

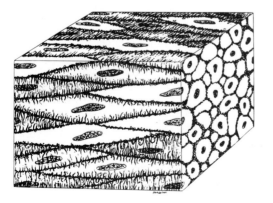

Figure 11–18. Diagram of a segment of smooth muscle. All cells are surrounded by a net of reticular fibers. In cross section, the cell exhibits variable diameters.

tures which occasionally have nuclei in their centers (Fig 11–18). If the section is longitudinal, a layer of parallel spindle-shaped cells will be seen (Figs 11–17 and 11–18).

Structure of Smooth Muscle Cells

Smooth muscle cells also have a distinctive surrounding layer of amorphous glycoprotein (glycocalyx). Their plasmalemma characteristically has an abundance of pinocytotic vesicles in different stages of development. The plasmalemmas of adjoining muscle cells are often very close together, forming tight junctions probably of the occludens and gap type. It is probable that these structures not only participate in the cell-to-cell transmission of impulses but also bind them together. The cell presents a centrally located oblong nucleus. In a clear juxtanuclear zone of sarcoplasm, a few mitochondria and elements of the granular endoplasmic reticulum and glycogen granules can be observed (Fig 11–19). A small Golgi apparatus is also present. In glutaraldehyde-fixed material, most of the cytoplasm consists of thin filaments arranged in parallel with the long axis of the cell. No cross-striations are found in these filaments. Scattered between these filaments are irregular electron-dense structures of as yet unknown nature.

Although it is known that smooth muscle contains myosin, no clear equivalent of the thick filaments present in other types of muscle has been consistently observed. Thin filaments are usually seen and probably correspond to actin. Some investigators believe that the myosin in this muscle is normally in a depolymerized state and that it would polymerize during muscle contraction, creating conditions for the

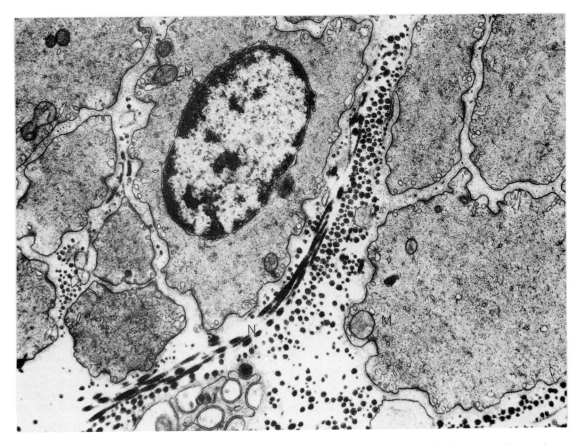

Figure 11—19. Electron micrograph of a transverse section of smooth muscle. The cells have variable diameters and many pinocytotic vesicles on their surface. There are few mitochondria (M). Between the cells are collagen fibers and a small amyelinated nerve (N). Reduced from × 7500.

occurrence of a possible sliding mechanism as described for striated muscle. Recently, however, it has become possible to observe thick filaments (presumably of myosin) regularly disposed between thin filaments in smooth muscle fixed by special technics.

Although nerve endings have been described in smooth muscle, their control by the nervous system is variable. In some cases, as in the smooth muscle of the ductus deferens, the nerve supply is abundant; in other cases, such as in the smooth muscle of the intestinal wall, this tissue (as in the heart) has an inherent rhythm which is only modulated by its motor nerve supply. In this case, the junctions are important in the transmission of the stimulus from cell to cell.

REGENERATION OF MUSCLE TISSUE

Muscle tissue has practically no regenerative capacity. Although mitoses have been observed in smooth muscle cells, they are not significant for wound healing. The fact is that muscle hyperplasia does not occur to any significant extent in muscle after birth. Large defects of muscle tissue are therefore repaired by the proliferation of connective tissue cells and scar formation.

Muscle tissue usually reacts to stimuli (such as overexertion) by a process of growth of its fibers (hypertrophy). In most mammals, skeletal muscle hypertrophy is stimulated by male sex hormones. Disuse of a muscle or loss of the motor nerve supply leads to a rapid and reversible atrophy of muscle tissue.

● ● ●

References

Ballard FB & others: Myocardial metabolism of fatty acids. J Clin Invest 39:717, 1960.

Bennett T, Cobb JL: Studies on the avian gizzard: Morphology and innervation of the smooth muscle. Z Zellforsch Mikrosk Anat 96:173, 1969.

Bintliff S, Walker BE: Radioautographic study of skeletal muscle regeneration. Am J Anat 106:233, 1960.

Bourne GH (editor): *The Structure and Function of Muscle.* Academic Press, 1972.

Burnstock G: Structure of smooth muscle and its innervation. Page 1 in: *Smooth Muscle.* Bülbring E & others (editors). Williams & Wilkins, 1970.

Challice CE, Viragh S (editors): *Ultrastructure of the Mammalian Heart.* Academic Press, 1973.

Cobb JL, Bennett T: A study of nexuses in visceral smooth muscle. J Cell Biol 41:287, 1969.

Constantin LL, Franzini-Armstrong C, Podolsky RJ: Localization of calcium accumulating structures in striated muscle. Science 147:158, 1965.

Endo M: Entry of a dye into the sarcotubular system of muscle. Nature 202:1115, 1964.

Fawcett DW: The sarcoplasmic reticulum of skeletal and cardiac muscle. Circulation 24:336, 1961.

Forssmann WG, Girardier L: A study of the T system in rat heart. J Cell Biol 44:1, 1970.

Franzini-Armstrong C, Porter KR: The Z disc of skeletal muscle. Z Zellforsch Mikrosk Anat 61:661, 1964.

Garamvölgyi N, Vizi ES, Knoll J: The regular occurrence of thick filaments in stretched mammalian smooth muscle. J Ultrastruct Res 34:135, 1971.

Gauthier GF, Padykula HA: Cytological studies of fiber types in skeletal muscle: A comparative study of the mammalian diaphragm. J Cell Biol 28:333, 1966.

Hanson J, Lowy L: Molecular basis of contractility in muscle. Brit M Bull 21:264, 1965.

Harman JW, O'Hegarty MT, Byrnes CK: The ultrastructure of human smooth muscle. 1. Studies of cell surface and connections in normal and achalasic esophageal smooth muscle. Exp Mol Pathol 1:204, 1962.

Huxley HE: Muscle cells. Page 365 in: *The Cell.* Vol 4. Brachet J, Mirsky AE (editors). Academic Press, 1960.

Huxley HE: The mechanism of muscular contraction. Science 164:1356, 1969.

Huxley HE, Haman T: Changes in the cross striations of muscle during contraction and stretch and their structural interpretation. Nature 173:973, 1954.

McNutt NS: Ultrastructure of intercellular junction in adult and developing cardiac muscle. Am J Cardiol 25:169, 1970.

McNutt NS, Fawcett DW: The ultrastructure of the cat myocardium. J Cell Biol 42:46, 1969.

Murray JM, Weber A: The cooperative action of muscle proteins. Sc Am 230:58, 1974.

Page S: Structure of the sarcoplasmic reticulum in vertebrate muscle. Brit M Bull 24:170, 1968.

Rice RV & others: Regular organization of thick filaments in mammalian smooth muscle. Nature 231:242, 1971.

Somlyo AP, Somlyo AV: Vascular smooth muscle. 1. Normal structure, pathology, biochemistry and biophysics. Pharmacol Rev 20:197, 1968.

Sommer JR, Johnson EA: A comparative study of Purkinje fibers and ventricular fibers. J Cell Biol 36:497, 1968.

Thaemert JC: Ultrastructure of cardiac muscle and nerve contiguities. J Cell Biol 29:156, 1966.

Uehara Y, Burnstock G: Demonstration of gap junctions between smooth muscle cells. J Cell Biol 44:215, 1970.

12...
Circulatory System

The circulatory system consists of the blood and lymphatic vascular systems. The blood vascular system comprises the following structures: (1) the heart, whose function is to pump the blood; (2) a series of efferent vessels, the arteries, which become smaller as they branch more and more abundantly and whose function it is to carry the blood and, with it, nutrients and oxygen to the tissues; (3) a diffuse network of thin tubules—the capillaries—which anastomose profusely and through whose walls the interchange between blood and tissues takes place; and (4) the veins, the afferent vessels of the heart, which represent the convergence of the capillaries into a system of larger channels and which convey into the vascular system products of metabolism, CO_2, etc.

The lymphatic vascular system begins in dead-end tubules, the lymphatic capillaries, which gradually anastomose in vessels of steadily increasing size and which terminate in the blood vascular system, emptying into the large veins near the heart. The function of the lymphatic system is to return to the blood the fluid of the tissue spaces, which, on penetrating the lymphatic capillaries, contributes to the formation of the liquid part of the lymph and, by passing through the lymph glands, contributes to the circulation of lymphocytes and other immunologic factors.

The entire circulatory system is internally lined by a simple squamous cellular lining, the endothelium discussed in Chapter 4. The composition of the circulatory system, beginning with the simplest structures and proceeding to the more complex ones, is discussed in the following pages.

Capillaries

The capillaries are composed of only a single layer of endothelial cells of mesenchymal origin, rolled up in the form of a tube, bounding a cylindric space. The average diameter of the capillaries is small, varying from 7–9 μm. When transversely cut, their walls are observed to consist, in general, of 2 or 3 cells (Fig 12–1). The external surfaces of these cells rest on a basal lamina which is a product mainly of epithelial origin, and their walls are held together by structures similar to the zonula occludens discussed in Chapter 3. The capillaries can be grouped into 3 types according to the structure of the endothelial cell walls. The type described above and illustrated in Fig 12–2 is called a

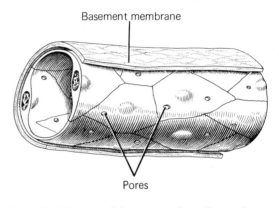

Figure 12–1. Diagram of the structure of a capillary with pores on its wall. It is composed of 2 endothelial cells. Not all capillaries have perforated walls. The basement membrane surrounds the capillary.

continuous capillary. A *fenestrated* or *perforated capillary* is the next type, characterized by the presence of pores *(fenestrae)* in the walls of the endothelial cells. These pores are often closed by a diaphragm of complex structure and unknown chemical composition which is thinner than the cell membrane (Figs 12–1, 12–3, and 12–4). Perforated capillaries are usually encountered in tissues in which rapid interchange of substances occurs between the tissues and the blood, as is the case with the kidney, intestine, and endocrine glands. Electron microscopic studies show that the diaphragm present in some pores of these capillaries has a sievelike structure, which suggests that in this region are located the capillary pores described by physiologists. It has been shown that macromolecules injected into the bloodstream can and do cross the capillary wall through these orifices to enter the tissue spaces (Fig 12–5). This seems to be a more important means of transcapillary transport than that which occurs as a result of pinocytosis as described in Chapter 3.

The third type of capillary, the *sinusoidal capillary* (Fig 15–20), has the following characteristics: (1) a tortuous path and a greatly enlarged diameter (30–40 μm), which slows the circulation of blood in them; (2) absence in the walls of a continuous lining of endothelial cells, thereby leaving open spaces between

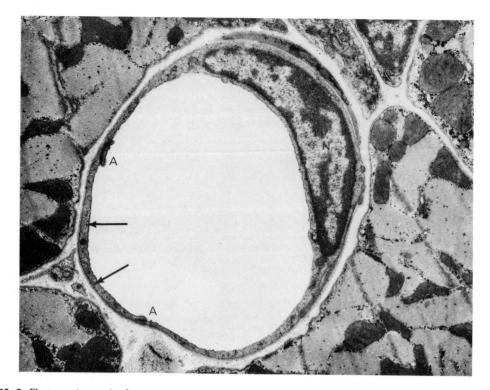

Figure 12–2. Electron micrograph of a transverse section of a capillary from the myocardium. This is a continuous capillary. Note the pinocytotic vesicles in the cytoplasm (arrows) and the nucleus (N). × 12,600. (Courtesy of J Rhodin.)

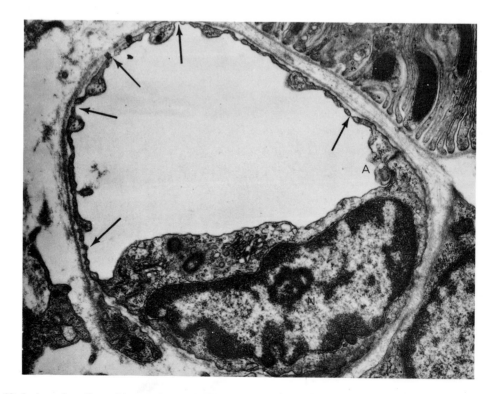

Figure 12–3. A renal capillary with pores in its endothelial cell (arrows). In this cell the Golgi apparatus (G), nucleus (N), and 2 centrioles (C) can be seen. × 20,000. (Courtesy of J Rhodin.)

Figure 12—4. Electron micrograph of the endothelium of a fenestrated capillary. The arrows show the pores. In the center is a large pinocytotic vesicle. Some blood vessels have many of these vesicles in different stages of evolution, causing a ruffled appearance (see also Fig 12—5).

cells through which the capillary communicates with the underlying tissue; (3) the presence in and around the wall—in addition to the usual endothelial cells—of cells with phagocytic activity; and (4) absence of a continuous basal lamina.

The sinusoidal capillaries are found mainly in the liver and in hematopoietic organs such as the bone marrow and spleen. These structural details suggest that in the sinusoidal capillaries the interchange between blood and tissues is greatly facilitated so that cells can easily pass back and forth between the 2 compartments.

In abnormal states such as inflammation, injection of snake or bee venom, etc, capillary permeability increases greatly. Electron microscopic examination shows that these conditions promote weakness and separation of the points of close contact between the endothelial cells. Under these circumstances, electron-dense colloidal substances were observed to pass from the lumens of the capillaries between the endothelial cells into the surrounding tissues. The leukocytes pass from the bloodstream between these cells to the tissue spaces by a process called *diapedesis.* Comparing the permeability of various organs illustrates well the differences in permeability of the different types of capillaries. It has been calculated that the permeability in the kidney glomerulus is 100 times greater than that in muscle.

In various locations on the outside of the walls of capillaries and metarterioles, there are mesenchymal cells which partially surround the endothelial cells through long cytoplasmic processes. These *adventitial cells* or *pericytes* are enclosed in their own basement

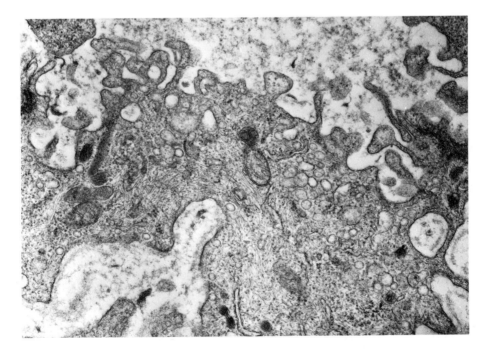

Figure 12—5. Electron micrograph of a section of a continuous capillary. Observe the ruffled appearance of its interior surface, the large and small pinocytotic vesicles, and numerous microfilaments in the cytoplasm. Reduced slightly from × 30,000.

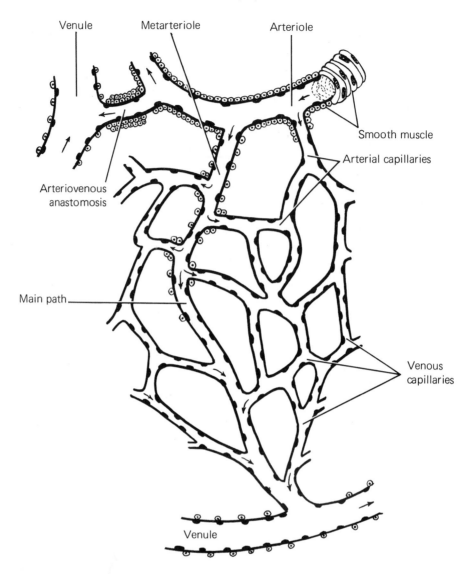

Figure 12–6. Branching of an arteriole to form a capillary network which terminates in a venule. The continuous layer of smooth muscle from the arteriole becomes discontinuous in the metarterioles. In arteriovenous anastomosis, blood passes directly from the arterial to the venous system. When blood pressure is lowered—as a result of the opening of the arteriovenous anastomosis or of contraction of the metarterioles—blood flow may be restricted to the main paths as indicated by arrows in the drawing. It is thus possible to regulate the extension of the capillary network utilized in a given territory. (Reproduced, with permission, from Copenhaver WM, Bunge RP, Bunge MB: *Bailey's Textbook of Histology,* 16th ed. Williams & Wilkins, 1972.)

membrane. These perivascular cells have great potentiality for transformation into other cells. Whether they are contractile or not has been the subject of much controversy, but recent evidence suggests the possibility of active contraction by these pericytes. The presence of abundant microfibrils in their cytoplasm is believed by some authors to be related to this type of movement.

As illustrated in Fig 12–6, the capillaries anastomose profusely, forming a rich network between the small arteries and veins. It can be seen that the arterioles branch into small vessels which present a discontinuous layer of smooth muscle, the *metarterioles.*

These in turn branch into capillaries which form an abundant network. The constriction of the metarterioles helps to regulate—but does not stop completely— the circulation in the capillaries, and maintains differences in pressure in the 2 systems. A simple ring of smooth muscle cells, called a sphincter, has been proposed as existing at the point of origin of capillaries from the metarteriole. This precapillary cell can completely stop the blood flow within the capillary. The entire network does not always function simultaneously, and the number of functioning and open capillaries depends not only on the state of contraction of the metarterioles but also on arteriovenous anastomoses which enable the metarterioles to empty directly into small veins as illustrated in Fig 12—6. These interconnections are abundant in skeletal muscle and the skin of the hands and feet. When the vessels of the arteriovenous anastomosis contract, all of the blood must pass through the capillary network. When it relaxes, some of the blood flows directly to a vein instead of circulating in the capillaries. Thus, capillary circulation is controlled by different mechanisms, including neural and chemical ones and the position of capillaries relative to the heart level.

The wealth of the capillary network is a function of the metabolism of the tissues and represents a transition zone between the high-pressure system (arterial) and low-pressure system (venous). Tissues with high metabolic rates such as the kidney, liver, and cardiac and skeletal muscle have an abundant capillary network; the opposite is true of tissues with low metabolic rates such as smooth muscle and tendons.

An idea of the importance of the capillaries in the economy of the organism can be gained by noting that in the human body the surface area of the capillary network is approximately 6000 sq m. Its total diameter is approximately 800 times larger than that of the aorta. A unit volume of fluid within a capillary is exposed to a larger surface area than the same volume in the other parts of the system. The flow of blood in the aorta is about 320 mm/second; in the capillaries, about 0.3 mm/second. The capillary system may thus be compared with a lake where a full-flowing river enters and leaves; because of their thin walls and slow blood flow, the capillaries are a favorable place for the interchange of water and solutes between blood and tissues. Large colloidal molecules cannot escape.

GENERAL STRUCTURE OF THE BLOOD VESSELS

All blood vessels with lumens above a certain diameter present a common general structure which will be discussed here in order to simplify the more detailed study of the various types of arteries and veins to be presented later on. However, it must be made clear that, within a definite framework, there are marked structural differences between different types of blood vessels and that there really exists a gradual transition from one structural type to another.

A blood vessel is usually composed of the following layers (Fig 12—7):

(1) An *internal tunic (tunica intima),* consisting of (a) a layer of endothelial cells lining the interior of the vessel; (b) a delicate subendothelial layer composed of loose connective tissue; and (c) an internal elastic limiting membrane formed by a tubular perforated membrane of elastic substance. Owing to the contraction of the vessel, this membrane is generally observed in sections in a scalloped form (Fig 12—8).

(2) A *middle tunic (tunica media),* consisting mainly of smooth muscle cells positioned circularly. Interposed among the muscle cells are variable amounts of elastic tissue arranged in the form of elastic laminas or fibers. Elastic laminas are usually fenestrated. Through these fenestrae (holes) substances can diffuse and nourish cells deep in the walls of the vessels.

Smooth muscle cells are the chief sites of metabolic activity, both in the internal and middle tunics.

(3) An *adventitial tunic (tunica adventitia),* consisting of connective tissue with elastic fibers, which gradually fuses with the connective tissue that envelops the neighboring organs, thus uniting the vessel to the

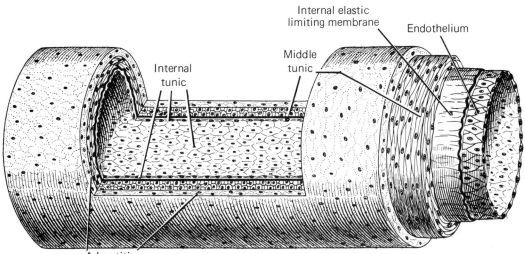

Figure 12—7. Drawing of a medium-sized artery (muscular artery) showing its layers. The usual appearance seen in histologic preparations is not shown because the layers appear thicker and the lumen larger. Experimental work suggests, however, that the drawing is more closely similar to the in vivo architecture of the vessel. After death, the vessel contracts, the layers become thicker, and the lumen becomes smaller and corrugated.

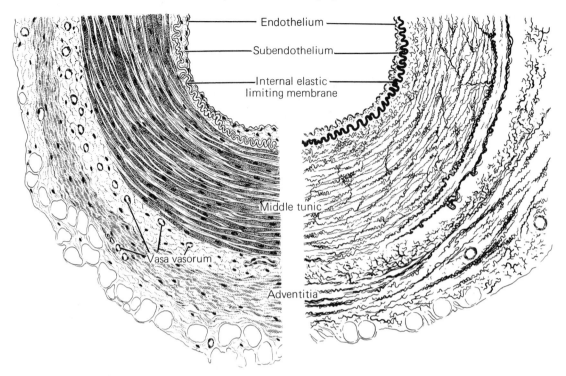

Endothelium

Subendothelium

Internal elastic
limiting membrane

Middle tunic

Vasa vasorum

Adventitia

Figure 12–8. Comparative diagrams of a medium-sized artery prepared by H&E staining *(left)* and by Weigert's staining method for elastic structures *(right).* Observe the layers. The middle tunic is composed of a mixture of smooth muscle cells and elastic membranes. The adventitia has many elastic and collagenous fibers.

organs. Deep within this tunic is often found an elastic tissue called the *external elastic limiting membrane.*

(4) *Vasa vasorum,* large nutrient vessels which usually have in their walls small arteries and veins that branch profusely. In these arteries, these vessels are less frequent and reach only the adventitial layer, whereas in the veins they are more numerous, reaching the middle layer. The greater abundance of vessels in the veins can be attributed to the relative lack of nutritional substances in venous blood. The vasa vasorum are present in the tunica adventitia and in the outer part of the tunica media. The external layers of the large arteries receive metabolites from the adventitial vessels. In the intima and the inner half of the media, changes in the macromolecular organization and composition of the ground substance, collagen, and elastic fibers might be of great significance in the nutrition of cells in these avascular areas. The muscular layer (tunica media), however, is nourished by arterioles that derive from the region where its collateral branches emerge. The intima and deeper part of the medial layer are nourished directly from the arterial lumen.

(5) *Nonmyelinated vasomotor nerves,* which form a network in the adventitial layer and end among the smooth muscle cells of the middle layer. Myelinated fibers reach the internal layer, forming the sensory fibers of the veins.

Arteries

The arteries may be classified according to their

increasing size into (1) arterioles; (2) arteries of medium size, or muscular arteries; and (3) large or elastic arteries, where elastic tissue predominates.

Arterioles are very fine, generally less than 0.5 mm in diameter. They exhibit a tunica intima with no subendothelial layer and with a thin internal elastic limiting membrane. The middle tunic is muscular, generally composed of 4–5 circularly arranged layers of smooth muscle cells. The adventitial tunic is narrow, poorly developed, and shows no external elastic limiting membrane (Fig 12–9). The arterioles have relatively narrow lumens.

Small and *medium-sized arteries* (muscular arteries) have the general structure of vessels illustrated in Figs 12–8 and 12–10. They are characterized by a thick muscular layer which can have as many as 40 layers of smooth muscle cells. These cells are intermixed with variable amounts of elastic material depending on the size of the vessel.

Large arteries include the aorta and its large branches. They have a yellowish color owing to the accumulation of elastic material in the middle tunic. This type of artery presents the following characteristics: (1) The internal tunic, thicker than that of a muscle artery, is lined by endothelial cells. In the electron microscope, the endothelial cell shows microvilli, pinocytotic vesicles, granular endoplasmic reticulum, microfibrils, intercellular junctions, and lysosomes. In large arteries, subendothelial basement membrane is sometimes not seen, but mainly fibrillar connections be-

Internal elastic limiting membrane

Middle tunic

Adventitia

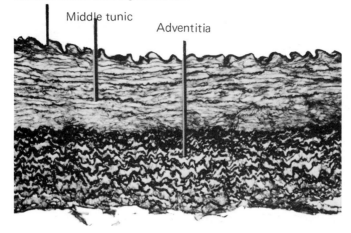

Figure 12—9. Photomicrograph of a section of a medium-sized arteriole stained by Weigert's method for elastic structures. × 110.

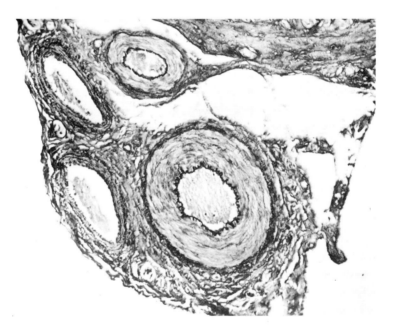

Figure 12—10. Photomicrograph of 2 small arteries *(right)* and venules *(left)*. The arteries have thicker walls than the venules. The elastic material is restricted to an internal limiting membrane. In the middle tunic, the elastic membranes are often replaced by smooth muscle. Weigert's stain, × 150.

tween the basal plasma membrane and various components of the internal tunic are always seen. Some of the endothelial cells are phagocytic. Endothelial cells develop from preexisting ones by mitosis. In medium- and large-sized arteries, a folded endothelium whose cells bulge into the lumen of this vessel is often observed. This sometimes occurs as a result of postmortem contraction of the muscle of the arteries. The subendothelial layer is thick. The fibers of the subendothelial layer exhibit mainly a longitudinal orientation and play an important role in the free play of the endothelial layer of cells during the rhythmic contrac-

tions and dilatations of the vessel. An internal elastic limiting membrane is not always evident since it is confused with the membranes of the next layer. (2) The middle tunic consists of a series of concentrically arranged perforated elastic membranes whose number increases with age (40 in the newborn; 70 in the adult); elastic structures, once formed, usually become metabolically inert as shown by radioautographic studies, especially in older animals. The laminas exhibit a progressive increase in thickness by deposition of elastic units composed of microfibrils, fibrils, and amorphous material. Between these membranes there are smooth

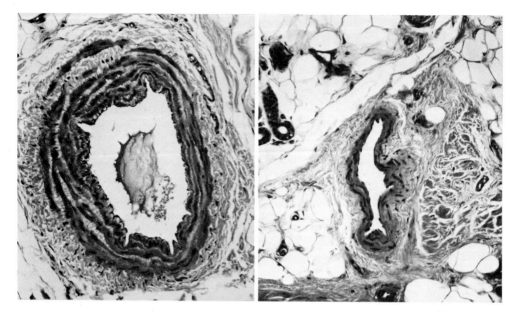

Figure 12–11. Photomicrographs of sections of a small artery *(left)* and a venule *(right)*. The elastic material disappeared in the small artery. H&E stain, X 100.

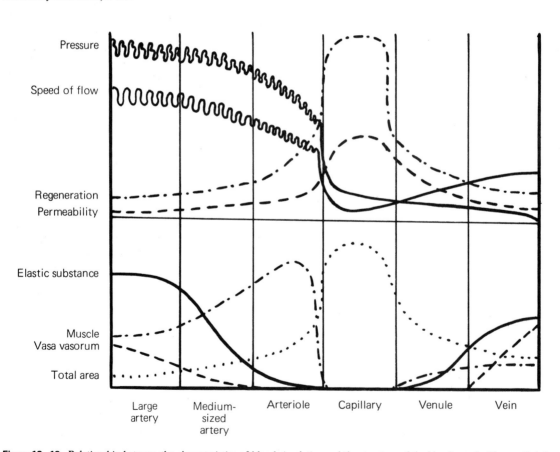

Figure 12–12. Relationship between the characteristics of blood circulation and the structure of the blood vessels. Observe that the arterial blood pressure and rapidity of flow decrease and become more constant as the distance from the heart gradually increases. This coincides with a reduction in number of elastic fibers and an increase in the number of smooth muscle cells in the arteries. The graphs illustrate the gradual changes in vessel structure and their biophysical properties. Observe that regenerative capacity and permeability are highly developed in the capillaries. (Reproduced, with permission, from Cowdry EV: *Textbook of Histology.* Lea & Febiger, 1944.)

muscle cells, fibroblasts, and an amorphous substance consisting of glycoprotein and acid mucopolysaccharide macromolecules with a composition similar to that of the amorphous components in the connective tissue. (3) The adventitial tunic does not show an external limiting membrane, is relatively underdeveloped, and contains elastic and collagen fibers.

The smooth muscle cells have a slender and elongated cytoplasm which shows many fine myofilaments, arranged parallel to the longitudinal axis of the cell. These cells have a PAS-positive basal lamina and a network of reticular fibers around them. The elongated nucleus reflects in its length and shape the degree of cell contraction. With the electron microscope, the myofilaments terminate in peripheral condensations under the plasma membrane. They do show pinocytotic vesicles. The histologic findings in these smooth muscle cells vary with their position within the walls and the vascular system, but all of them are regarded as components of the arterial smooth muscle cell compartment at different functional and structural stages. Structural differences are recognized between the smooth muscle cells and the fibroblasts. Embryologically, smooth muscle cells derive from the mesenchymal component of the visceral mesoderm, whereas fibroblasts originate from the somatic mesoderm. The smooth muscle cell appears to be a typical secretory cell during certain periods of life and in different experimental conditions or disease states. It synthesizes and releases components of the ground substance of the arterial wall collagen and reticular and elastic fibers. During these periods of secretion, an extensive endoplasmic reticulum can be seen in the cytoplasm accompanied by a developed Golgi apparatus. Dedifferentiation of smooth muscle cells toward more primitive cells can be observed in aortic explants. This transformation was indicated by a decrease in the myofilaments of the cell, with a concomitant increase in organelles appearing then like a fibroblast or even an undifferentiated cell.

Histophysiology of the Arteries

The large arteries are also called *carriers* since their major function is transporting blood. The function of the medium-sized arteries, also known as *distributing arteries,* is to furnish blood to the various organs. The accumulation of elastic material is characteristic of the structure of the large arteries. This layer has an important function in regulating blood flow. Thus, it is this elastic tissue that, by dilating periodically, absorbs the intermittent impact of the cardiac pulse. During *diastole,* the large arteries return to normal size, impelling the blood forward. The consequence of this action is that the arterial pressure and blood flow decrease and become less variable as the distance from the heart increases (Fig 12–12).

The muscular layer in the medium-sized or distributing arteries can, by contracting or not contracting, control the flow of blood to the various organs.

The blood vessels undergo progressive and gradual changes from birth to death, and it is difficult to say where the normal growth processes end and the processes of involution begin. Each artery exhibits its own aging pattern. The artery that changes most preco-

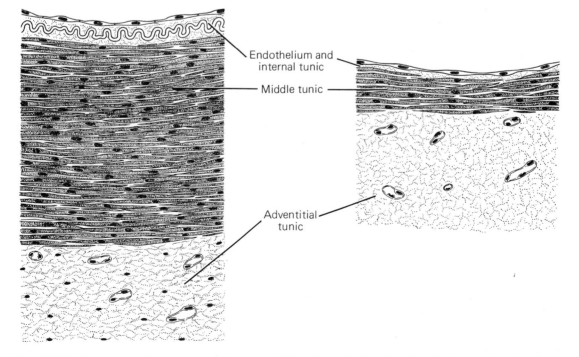

Figure 12–13. Diagram comparing the structure of an artery *(left)* and a venule. Note that the tunica intima and tunica media are highly developed in the artery but not in the venule.

ciously, beginning at 20 years of age, is the coronary. The other arteries begin to be modified only after age 40. When the middle layer of an artery is weakened by an embryologic defect or lesion, the wall of the artery gives way, dilating extensively. If this process progresses, it is called an aneurysm and might result in rupture of the wall.

The alterations in arteriosclerosis generally begin in the subendothelial layer, passing from there to the middle layer. The lesion of the middle layer, with the destruction of the elastic tissue and the consequent loss of elasticity observed in arteriosclerosis, results in serious circulatory disturbances; the mechanisms leading to elastic structural alterations are usually related to the existence of hemodynamic and mechanical stresses acting probably on inadequate cross-linked elastic micromolecules and deficiently developed elastic structures. Fig 12–12 illustrates the relationship between the structure and the biophysical characteristics of blood vessels.

Certain arteries irrigate only definite areas of specific organs, and obstruction results in necrosis (death of the tissues owing to lack of metabolites). These are the so-called infarcts which occur commonly in the heart, kidneys, cerebrum, and some other organs. In other regions, such as the skin, arteries anastomose frequently, and the obstruction of one artery does not lead to tissue necrosis because blood flow is maintained.

Experiments suggest that the polypeptide angiotensin promotes hypertension by binding itself initially to vascular endothelial cells. It is believed that this initial endothelial stimulus is later transmitted to arterial smooth muscle cells, promoting their contraction and consequent increase in blood pressure.

Carotid & Aortic Bodies

Small structures encountered in the bifurcation of the common carotid artery and the aorta are believed to perform the function of respiratory chemoreceptors. They are richly vascularized, exhibiting sinusoidal capillaries surrounded by clear cells, and have the function of detecting alterations in the pH and the CO_2 and oxygen tensions of the blood, transmitting this information to nearby nerve endings. Thus, they are specialized sense organs with the important homeostatic function of maintaining the partial pressures of CO_2 and oxygen in the blood at normal levels.

Arteriovenous Anastomosis

Direct communications between the arterial and venous circulation are often observed. These arteriovenous anastomoses are distributed throughout the body and generally occur in small vessels. The lumens of these anastomoses vary considerably depending on the physiologic condition of the organ, and changes in terminal diameter regulate the circulation in particular areas (Fig 12–6). In the ear of a rabbit, using the technic of injecting microspheres of a certain size which obliterate the capillaries, it is possible to calculate that about one-third of the blood flow can pass through the arteriovenous anastomoses. Besides these direct communications, more complex structures called *glomi* occur, mainly in the fingerpads, the fingernail beds, and the ears. In these structures, the arterioles which establish continuity with venules lose their internal elastic membranes and acquire a thick layer of smooth muscle cells arranged longitudinally. This muscle layer forms a continuous or discontinuous sheet that partially or completely surrounds the lumen of a vessel. Contraction of this layer can therefore promote

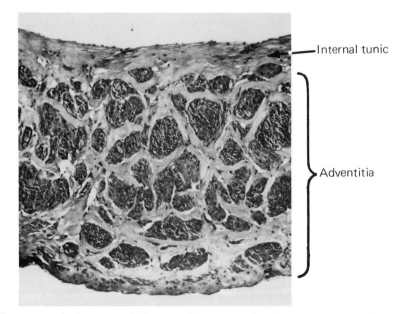

Figure 12–14. Photomicrograph of a section of a large vein. Observe the well-developed adventitia with longitudinal smooth muscle bundles. H&E stain, × 100.

the complete or partial transitory closure of blood vessels. The systems have an important role in control of the circulation in various organs and participate in several physiologic phenomena such as menstruation, protection against low temperatures, and erection. The arteriovenous anastomoses are richly innervated by the sympathetic and parasympathetic nervous systems. Control of this activity appears to be mainly neural. Besides controlling the blood flow in the various organs, these anastomoses have—mainly in the skin of the extremities—a thermoregulatory function.

Veins

As in the case of the arteries, it is customary to arbitrarily classify the veins into venules and veins of small, medium, and large size.

The *venules* are small, with a diameter of 0.2—1 mm. They are characterized by an internal layer composed of endothelium; a thin middle layer consisting of a few cell layers of smooth muscle; and an adventitial layer, which is the thickest layer and is composed of connective tissue rich in collagenous fibers. Venules thus have very thin walls (Figs 12—10, 12—11, and 12—13). Venules with luminal diameters up to 50 μm have the structure and other biologic features of capillaries and therefore also participate in inflammatory processes and in the interchange of metabolites between the blood and tissues.

Most veins are *small* or *medium-sized veins* with the exception of the main trunks, and have a diameter of 1—9 mm. The internal tunic usually has a thin subendothelial layer, but this layer may at times be absent. The middle layer consists mainly of small bundles of smooth muscles intermixed with collagen fibers and with a delicate network of elastic fibers. The collagenous adventitial layer is well developed.

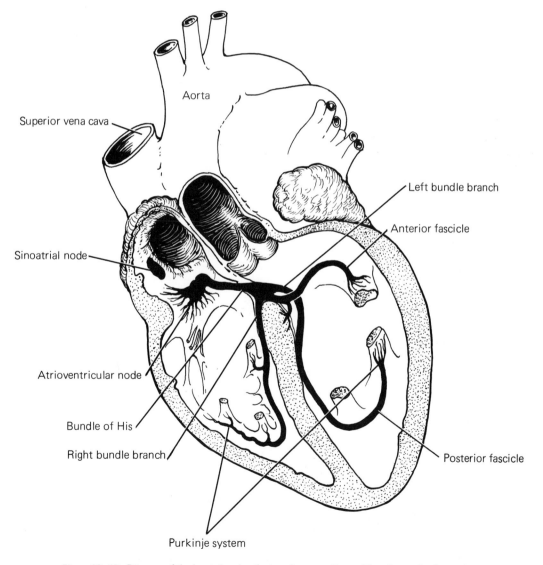

Figure 12—15. Diagram of the heart showing the impulse-generating and impulse-conducting system.

Connective tissue

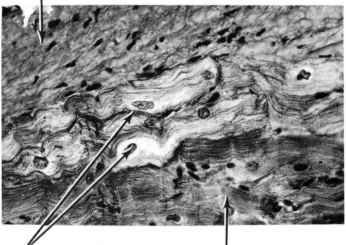

Conducting system   Heart muscle

Figure 12—16. The conducting system of the heart is characterized by a reduced number of myofibrils present mainly in the periphery of the muscle fiber. The light area around the nuclei of the conducting fibers in vivo consists of glycogen. H&E stain, X 400.

Large veins have a well-developed internal tunic. The middle tunic is much smaller, with a few smooth muscle cells and abundant connective tissue. The adventitia is the thickest layer, containing bundles of smooth muscle arranged longitudinally along the vein (Fig 12–14). Besides these different layers, small or medium-sized veins exhibit valves in their interior. These structures consist of 2 semilunar folds of the internal layer of the vessel which project into the lumen. They are composed of elastic connective tissue and lined on both sides by endothelium.

The valves are especially numerous in the veins of the limbs (arms and legs). It is known that they help to propel the venous blood in the direction of the heart— thanks to the contraction of the skeletal muscles which surround most of these veins.

Heart

The heart is a muscular organ which contracts rhythmically, pumping the blood in the circulatory system. Its walls consist of 3 tunics: the internal, or *endocardium;* the middle, or *myocardium;* and the external, or *pericardium.* The heart has a fibrous central region which serves as a support: the *fibrous skeleton.* The heart also contains the cardiac valves and an impulse-generating and conducting system.

The *endocardium* is homologous with the internal layer of the veins. It is lined with endothelium which rests on a thin subendothelial layer of loose connective tissue. Uniting the myocardium with the subendothelial layer is a subendocardial layer of connective tissue containing veins, nerves, and branches of the impulse-conducting system.

Myocardium consists of cardiac muscle fibers (see Chapter 10) arranged in layers which cover the heart chambers in a complex spiral manner. A large number of these layers insert themselves on the fibrous cardiac skeleton. The muscle cells of the heart can be grouped into 2 populations: the contractile cells for the contraction and the conductive cells for the rapid conduction of impulses. The arrangement of these muscle fibers is extremely varied—to the point that, in histologic preparations of a small area of the heart, we often encounter fibers oriented in many directions.

The intercalated disk, a specialized attachment of 2 plasma membranes across a thin interspace which is so characteristic of cardiac muscle, is composed of 3 types of junctional specialization: the fascia adherens, the desmosome, and the gap junction (nexus). In fascia adherens, the 2 plasma membranes are often deeply interdigitated but lie parallel to each other and separated by a 20–30 nm interspace. The cytoplasm adjacent to the membrane shows filaments. The fascia adherens covers a large area of the plasma membrane area as opposed to the desmosome (Chapter 4), which is a small round area. The gap junction (Chapter 4) is a very important part of the intercalated disk because it is used as the site of propagation of excitation from one cell to the other, thus coordinating the contraction of the organ acting as an electrical syncytium.

Epicardium is the serous membrane of the heart, forming the visceral lining of the pericardium. It is externally covered by simple squamous epithelium (mesothelium) supported by a thin layer of connective tissue. A subepicardial layer consisting of loose connective tissue contains veins, nerves, and nerve ganglia. It is in this layer that the adipose tissue which generally surrounds the heart accumulates.

The *fibrous skeleton of the heart* is composed of dense connective tissue. Its principal components are the *septum membranaceum,* the *trigona fibrosa,* and the *annuli fibrosi.*

These structures have the general appearance of an aponeurosis, with thick collagen fibers oriented in various directions. Certain regions contain nodules or areas of fibrous cartilage.

The *cardiac valves* consist of a central portion of dense fibrous aponeurosislike tissue lined on both sides by an endothelial layer.

Impulse-Generating & Conducting System of the Heart

This system consists of 2 nodes located in the atrium: the *sinoatrial node* and the *atrioventricular node.* There is also the *atrioventricular bundle,* or bundle of His, which originates in the node of the same name and is directed toward the ventricles, bifurcating and sending branches to both ventricles (Fig 12–15).

The initial stimulus of contraction originates in the form of depolarization in the cells of the sinoatrial node; in this way, it is spread by the atrial muscles to the atrioventricular node and from there to the ventricles.

The sinoatrial node is a mass of spindle-shaped, specialized cardiac muscle cells, rich in sarcoplasm and poor in myofibrils, surrounded by a dense fibroelastic capsule. The atrioventricular node has a similar structure, but its cells branch and their extensions intertwine, forming a net.

The atrioventricular bundle and its branches, which run inside the endocardium, resemble a group of modified cardiac fibers, rich in glycogen and poor in myofibrils. The glycogen accumulates in the center of these cells, displacing its myofibrils to the periphery and giving this tissue its characteristic appearance (Fig 12–16). *Purkinje fibers* are found in the subendothelial connective tissue of the endocardium. After traversing the subendocardial tract, the branches of the atrioventricular bundle subdivide and penetrate the ventricles, thus becoming intramyocardial. This sequence is important in that it carries the stimulus to the interior of the ventricular muscle. No nerve endings resembling motor plates exist in heart muscle cells.

When anomalies or lesions of the generating and conducting system occur, changes in the sequence of the heart's contractile processes can be observed. These changes can be analyzed and studied with the electrocardiograph, which records the electrical phenomena occurring during heart movements.

Lymphatic Vascular System

Besides the blood vessels, the human body has a system of thin channels lined with endothelium which collects the fluid from the tissues and returns it to the blood. The fluid thus collected and transported is called lymph; in contrast to the blood, it circulates in only one direction, ie, toward the heart.

The *lymphatic capillaries* originate in the various tissues as thin, blind vessels. They consist only of a single layer of endothelium. These thin vessels gradually converge until they end in 2 large trunks, the *thoracic duct* and the *right lymphatic duct,* which empty into the junction of the internal jugular vein with the left subclavian vein and into the confluence of the subclavian vein and the right internal jugular vein. Interposed in the path of the lymphatic vessels are lymph nodes, whose morphology and functions are discussed in Chapter 14. With rare exceptions such as the nervous system and the bone marrow, a lymphatic system is found in almost all organs.

The *lymphatic vessels* have a structure similar to that of veins except that they have thinner walls and are without a clear-cut separation between the 3 layers: internal, middle, and adventitial. Like the veins, they have numerous internal valves. These valves are, however, more numerous in lymphatic vessels. Between the valves the lymphatic vessels are dilated, thus assuming a nodular appearance.

As in the veins, lymph circulation in the lymphatic vessels is aided by the action of external forces (mainly muscular contraction) on its walls. These forces act discontinuously, and lymph flow occurs mainly as a result of the presence of many valves in these vessels and the rhythmic contraction of the smooth muscle present in their walls.

The *lymphatic ducts* of large size have a structure similar to that of a vein with a reinforcement of smooth muscle in the middle layer. In this layer the muscle bundles are longitudinally and circularly arranged, with longitudinal fibers predominating. The adventitia is relatively underdeveloped. As in the case of the arteries and veins, the lymphatics contain vasa vasorum and a rich neural network.

•   •   •

References

Abramson DL (editor): *Blood Vessels and Lymphatics.* Academic Press, 1962.

Bennett HS, Luft JH, Hampton JC: Morphological classification of vertebrate blood capillaries. Am J Physiol 196:381, 1959.

Clementi F, Palade GE: Intestinal capillaries. 1. Permeability to peroxidase and ferritin. J Cell Biol 41:33, 1969.

Cliff WJ: The aortic tunica media in growing rats studied with the electron microscope. Lab Invest 17:599, 1967.

Fernando NVP, Movat HZ: The smallest arterial vessels: Terminal arterioles and metarterioles. Exp Mol Pathol 3:1, 1964.

Forssman WG, Girardier L: A study of the T system in rat heart. J Cell Biol 44:1, 1970.

Fritz KE, Jarmolych J, Daoud AS: Association of DNA synthesis and apparent dedifferentiation of aortic smooth muscle cells in vitro. Exp Mol Pathol 12:354, 1970.

Fryer DG, Birnbaum G, Luttrell CN: Human endothelium in cell culture. J Atherosclerosis Res 6:151, 1966.

Giacomelli F, Wiener J, Spiro D: Cross-striated arrays of filaments in endothelium. J Cell Biol 45:188, 1970.

Hayes JR: Histological changes in constricted arteries and arterioles. J Anat 101:343, 1967.

Hofmann BF: Physiology of atrio-ventricular transmission. Circulation 24:506, 1961.

Hüttner I, Boutet M, More RH: Gap junctions in arterial endothelium. J Cell Biol 57:247, 1973.

Karnovsky MJ: The ultrastructural basis of capillary permeability studied with peroxidase as a tracer. J Cell Biol 35:213, 1967.

Matter A: A morphometric study on the nexus of rat cardiac muscle. J Cell Biol 56:690, 1973.

Maul GG: Structure and formation of pores in fenestrated capillaries. J Ultrastruct Res 36:768, 1971.

Papp M & others: An electron microscopic study of the central lacteal in the intestinal villus of the cat. Z Zellforsch Mikrosk Anat 57:475, 1962.

Reynolds SRM, Zweifach BW: *The Microcirculation: A Symposium on Factors Influencing Exchange of Substances Across the Capillary Wall.* Univ of Illinois Press, 1959.

Rhodin JAG: Ultrastructure of mammalian venous capillaries, venules and small collecting veins. J Ultrastruct Res 25:452, 1968.

Rhodin JAG, Del Missier P, Reid LC: The structure of the specialized impulse-conducting system of the steer. Circulation 24:349, 1961.

Richardson JB, Beaulines A: The cellular site of action of angiotensin. J Cell Biol 51:419, 1971.

Scott MN, Fawcett DW: Myocardial ultrastructure. In: *The Mammalian Myocardium.* Langer GA, Brady TW (editors). Wiley, 1974.

Todd TW: The specialized systems of the heart. In: *Special Cytology.* Vol 2. Cowdry EV (editor). Hoeber, 1932.

Walford RL, Carter PK, Schneider RB: Stability of labeled aortic elastic tissue with age and pregnancy in the rat. Arch Path 78:43, 1964.

Willms-Kretschner K, Magno G: Ischemia of skin: Electron microscopic study of vascular injury. Am J Path 54:327, 1969.

Wissler RW: The arterial medial cell, smooth muscle or multifunctional mesenchyme? J Atherosclerosis Res 8:201, 1968.

13...
Blood Cells

Blood is the fluid, contained in a closed compartment, the circulatory system, that flows in a regular unidirectional movement, propelled mainly by the rhythmic contractions of the heart.

Microscopic observation of capillaries in vivo (in the conjunctiva of the eye in man; in the mesentery in animals) shows that the homogeneity of blood is only apparent. The blood is actually made up of 2 parts: *formed elements,* or blood cells, and *plasma,* the liquid phase in which the former are suspended. The formed elements of the blood are the *erythrocytes,* or red blood cells; the *platelets;* and the *leukocytes,* or white blood cells.

If blood is removed from the circulatory system, a clot develops. This clot contains formed elements and a clear yellow liquid called *serum* which is separated from the coagulum during the phenomenon of coagulation. Blood serum is equivalent in composition to plasma except that it lacks *fibrinogen*—a protein present in plasma—and some other clotting factors necessary for formation of the clot and contains *serotonin* in increased amounts.

Blood collected and kept from coagulating by the addition of anticoagulants (heparin, citrate, etc) separates, when centrifuged, into layers which reflect its heterogeneity (Fig 13–1). The result obtained by this sedimentation, carried out in glass tubes of standard size, is called the *hematocrit.*

The hematocrit permits estimation of the volume of packed erythrocytes per unit volume of blood. The normal value is 40–50% in the adult male, 35–45% in the adult female, approximately 35% in a child up to age 10 years, and 45–60% in the newborn. In pregnancy, this value is diminished by physiologic hemodilution. The hematocrit is normally higher in venous blood than in arterial blood because of the hydration of red cells and their increase in size. This value is usually different also in different compartments of the blood vascular system.

The translucent, yellowish, and somewhat viscous supernatant obtained when the hematocrit is measured corresponds to the plasma of the blood. The formed elements of the blood separate into 2 easily distinguishable layers. The lower layer represents 42–47% of the entire volume of blood present in the hematocrit

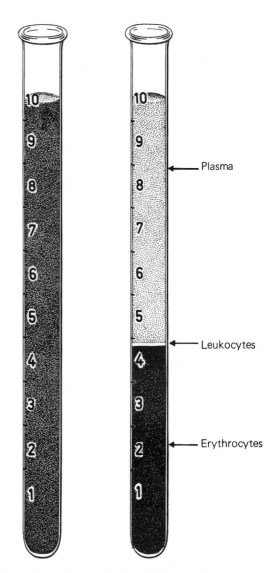

Figure 13–1. Hematocrit tubes with blood. *Left:* Before centrifugation. *Right:* After centrifugation. In the centrifuged tube, the red blood cells represent 43% of the blood volume. Between the sedimented red blood cells and the supernatant light-colored plasma is a thin layer of leukocytes called the buffy coat.

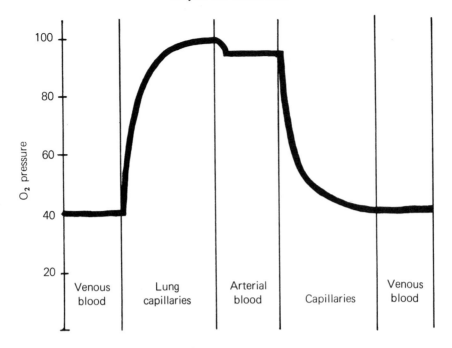

Figure 13–2. Blood oxygen content in each type of blood vessel. The amount of oxygen (O_2 pressure) is highest in lung capillaries and in arteries and decreases in tissue capillaries, where exchange takes place between blood and tissues.

tube. It is red and is made up of erythrocytes. The layer immediately above (1% of the blood volume), which is white or grayish in color, is called the *buffy coat* and consists of leukocytes. This separation occurs because the leukocytes are less dense than the erythrocytes. Covering the leukocytes is a fine layer of platelets not distinguishable by the naked eye.

The leukocytes, some of which are phagocytic and constitute one of the chief defenses against infection, circulate through the body via the blood vascular system. By crossing the capillary wall, these cells can become concentrated rapidly in the tissues and thus participate in the process of inflammation. The blood vascular system is also the vehicle of transport of oxygen (O_2) (Fig 13–2) and carbon dioxide (CO_2); the former is mainly bound to the hemoglobin of the erythrocytes, whereas the latter, in addition to being bound to the proteins of the erythrocytes (mainly hemoglobin), is also carried in solution in the plasma as CO_2 or in the form of HCO_3^-.

The plasma transports metabolites from their site of absorption or synthesis, distributing them to different areas of the organism. It also transports the residues of metabolism, which are removed from the blood by the excretory organs. The blood, being the distributing vehicle for the hormones, permits the exchange of chemical messages between distant organs for normal cellular function. It further participates in the regulation of heat distribution and in acid-base and osmotic balance.

Composition of Plasma

The plasma is an aqueous solution containing sub-

stances of small or large molecular weight which correspond to 10% of its volume. The plasma proteins account for 7% and the inorganic salts for 0.9%; the remainder of the 10% consists of several organic compounds of different origin—amino acids, vitamins, hormones, lipids, etc.

Through the capillary walls, the plasma is in equilibrium with the interstitial fluid of the tissues; consequently, the composition of plasma is usually an indicator of the mean composition of the extracellular fluids in general.

Plasma proteins can be separated in the ultracentrifuge or by electrophoresis into *albumin; alpha, beta, and gamma globulins;* and *fibrinogen.* Albumin is the main component and has a fundamental role in maintaining the osmotic pressure of the blood. The gamma globulins are antibodies and are usually called *immunoglobulins.* Fibrinogen is necessary for the formation of fibrin in the final step of coagulation. This change occurs in the presence of thrombin.

Several substances which are insoluble or only slightly soluble in water can be transported by the plasma because they combine with albumin or with the alpha and beta globulins, which act, therefore, as carriers. For example, lipids are insoluble in the plasma but combine with the hydrophobic portions of protein molecules. Since these molecules also have hydrophilic parts, the whole lipid-protein complex becomes soluble in water.

Staining of Blood Cells

Blood cells are generally studied in smears or films prepared by spreading a drop of blood thinly

Figure 13–3. Preparation of a blood smear. *A:* A drop of blood is placed on a microscope slide. A second slide is moved over the first at an angle of 45 degrees. *B:* When the slide edge touches the blood drop, the blood spreads along the edge. *C:* With a uniform movement of the oblique slide, a thin film of blood is spread on the horizontal fixed slide. *D:* The final result of this process. The table (shown in C) serves as a support throughout: The slide with the blood was on the table and fixed by the left hand of the operator from the beginning of the process.

over a microscope slide (Fig 13–3). The blood should be evenly distributed over the slide and allowed to dry rapidly in air. In such films the cells are clearly visible and distinct from one another. Their cytoplasm is spread out, thus facilitating observation of their fine structure.

Blood smears are routinely stained with special dye mixtures first discovered by Dimitri Romanovsky and later modified by other investigators. In 1891, Romanovsky observed that a mixture of solutions of methylene blue and eosin in certain proportions stained purple the nuclei of leukocytes and malaria parasites. Today it is known that this staining is due to the oxidation of the methylene blue and the formation in the mixture of new compounds called azures.

Stains currently used to study blood cells differ slightly in the proportion of their components and in the way in which the methylene blue is oxidized. They are named for the investigator who first introduced the modification. Leishman's, Wright's, and Giemsa's stains are examples of modified stains which are collectively known as Romanovsky-type mixtures.

After application of a Romanovsky-type mixture, there are essentially 4 types of staining characteristics which are expressions of the affinity of their cellular structures for the respective dyes of the mixture: (1) affinity for methylene blue (a basic dye) is known as

basophilia (blue); (2) affinity for the azures is known as *azurophilia* (purple); (3) affinity for the eosin (an acid stain) is known as *acidophilia* or *eosinophilia* (yellowish-pink); and (4) affinity for a complex dye present in the mixture—incorrectly thought to be neutral—is known as *neutrophilia* (salmon-pink to lilac).

FORMED ELEMENTS OF BLOOD

Erythrocytes

The erythrocytes of mammals have no nuclei and in man they are shaped like biconcave disks 7.2 μm in diameter (Fig 13–4). The biconcave shape provides the erythrocytes with a large surface, thus facilitating gas exchange, which occurs at a point no more than 0.85 μm from the surface of the cell.

Erythrocytes with diameters greater than 9 μm are called *macrocytes,* and those with diameters less than 6 μm are called *microcytes.* The presence of a high percentage of erythrocytes of abnormal variation in size is called *anisocytosis.*

The erythrocyte is quite flexible, and this property permits it to adapt to the sometimes irregular shape and small diameter of the capillaries. Observations in vivo show that when traversing the angles of

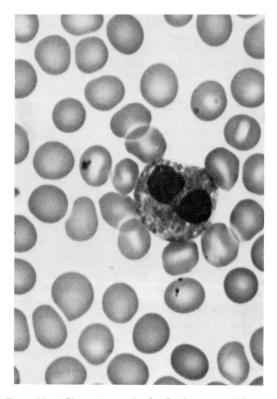

Figure 13–4. Photomicrograph of a Leishman-stained human blood smear. There are numerous erythrocytes and one granulocyte (eosinophil).

Neutrophilic granulocyte

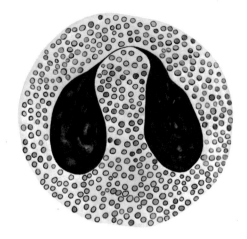

Eosinophilic granulocyte

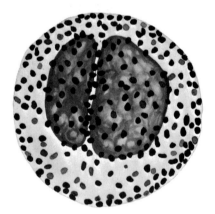

Basophilic granulocyte

Lymphocyte

Monocyte

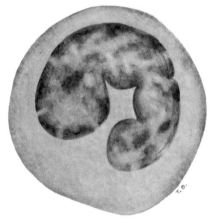

Monocyte

Figure 13–5. The 5 types of human leukocytes. *A:* Neutrophilic granulocyte. *B:* Eosinophilic granulocyte. *C:* Basophilic granulocyte. *D:* Lymphocyte. *E* and *F:* Monocytes. The drawings were made from blood smears stained by the Romanovsky technic. (This illustration is reproduced in color on p xiv.)

capillary bifurcation the erythrocyte changes its shape easily.

The normal concentration of erythrocytes in blood is approximately 4.5–5 million/μl in women and 5 million/μl in men.

Owing to their richness in hemoglobin, a basic protein, erythrocytes are acidophilic, staining with eosin. Besides hemoglobin, the erythrocytes contain a lipoprotein stroma. If placed in a hypotonic solution, they undergo tumefaction and become spherical, and the hemoglobin escapes and is dissolved in the surrounding liquid. This phenomenon is called *hemolysis.* The membranous material or empty shell that remains after this treatment is called the *ghost* and corresponds to the stroma. It consists of 50–60% protein and 35–40% lipid by weight. Since the ghost can assume again the biconcave disk shape, it is deduced that the stroma is responsible for the shape of the erythrocyte; it is known that this phenomenon requires the extrusion of Na^+ and water. Thus, the shape of the erythrocyte is maintained at the expense of energy; this process requires ATP, which is generated through glycolysis.

The red cell membrane, composed of proteins, carbohydrates, and lipids, gives to the cell its discoid appearance, and its flexibility allows great changes in the shape of the cell when it passes through capillaries. The cell membrane also acts as a semipermeable barrier, maintaining differences in the concentrations of sodium and potassium between the plasma and the interior of the cell and maintaining active transport systems for cation transfers against concentration gradients. Because red cells are not rigid particles, the viscosity of the blood remains low.

Erythrocytes recently released by the bone marrow into the bloodstream contain ribosomal RNA (rRNA), which, in the presence of supravital dyes (eg, brilliant cresyl blue), can be precipitated and stained. Under these conditions, the young erythrocytes, which are called *reticulocytes,* appear to have in their interior a stained netlike structure or just a few stained dots. The reticulocytes normally constitute about 1% of the total number of circulating red blood cells since that is the rate at which erythrocytes are replaced daily by the bone marrow. The process by which the reticulocytes are released from the bone marrow into the circulation is not completely understood.

Sometimes—mainly in disease states—nuclear fragments (containing DNA) remain in the erythrocyte after extrusion of its nucleus, which occurs at the orthochromatic normoblast stage of development. These nuclear remainders are Feulgen-positive and stain with basic dyes. Often they take the form of one or 2 small granules (1 μm in size) and are called *Howell-Jolly bodies.* When they appear as circular filaments, they are called *Cabot rings.*

The hemoglobin molecule (a conjugated protein) consists of 4 subunits, each containing a heme group linked to a polypeptide. The heme group is a porphyrin derivative containing iron (Fe^{2+}).

Owing to variations in each polypeptide chain attached to the heme, various types of hemoglobin can be distinguished, several of which are considered normal: hemoglobins A_1 (HbA_1), A_2 (HbA_2), and F (HbF) are found normally in postnatal life.

HbA_1 represents 97% of the normal hemoglobin in adults; HbA_2 represents 2%. The third type (1%), fetal hemoglobin (HbF), represents the predominant hemoglobin of the fetus—around 80% of the hemoglobin in newborns—and decreases progressively to lower levels until the eighth postnatal month, when it represents a small percentage similar to that found in adults.

Combined with oxygen or CO_2, the hemoglobin forms *oxyhemoglobin* and *carbaminohemoglobin,* respectively. These combinations are unstable. On the other hand, the combination of hemoglobin with carbon monoxide forms *carboxyhemoglobin,* which is very stable.

The erythrocytes of man survive in the circulation for about 120 days. This is measured by labeling young erythrocytes with ^{14}C-glycine or ^{15}N-glycine and determining their survival. Worn-out erythrocytes are removed from the circulation by cells of the macrophage system of the body.

Erythrocytes lose their mitochondria and ribosomes during maturation to adult cells from reticulocytes, a process which takes 24–48 hours. They depend continually on the system of anaerobic glycolysis and the pentose phosphate pathway for energy. They do not synthesize hemoglobin because they do not have a nucleus and have lost their ribosomes in prior stages of differentiation.

Leukocytes

On the basis of specific granules in their cytoplasm as viewed in the light microscope, the white blood cells were classified in 2 groups: *granulocytes* and *agranulocytes.* On the basis of the appearance of their nuclei, the leukocytes can also be separated into *polymorphonuclear* and *mononuclear* cells. In addition, they can be classified as myeloid or lymphoid cells depending on the site of production of the cells.

The granulocytes have irregularly shaped nuclei and, in their cytoplasm, the so-called *specific granules—neutrophils, eosinophils,* and *basophils.* These cytoplasmic granules confer the specific staining affinity which characterizes the 3 types. A granule is specific when it has its own characteristics (dimensions, form, staining affinity, and ultrastructure) and is consistently present in a certain type of leukocyte and in most of its precursors.

Agranulocytes have nuclei with a regular shape; the cytoplasm does not possess specific granules but can have nonspecific granules characterized as azurophilic which are also present in the other leukocytes. Depending upon the appearance of their nuclei and the cytoplasmic coloration, the agranulocytes can be classified as *lymphocytes* or *monocytes.*

The leukocytes are involved in the cellular and humoral defense of the organism against foreign material, alive or dead. They are spherical cells when in suspension in the circulating blood but are capable of becoming amebiform on encountering a solid substrate. As a consequence of the process of *diapedesis,* leukocytes leave the capillaries constantly, passing between the endothelial cells of their walls and penetrating into the connective tissue, where they appear so frequently that they are considered normal cellular components of this tissue.

The number of leukocytes per microliter of blood in the normal adult is 4–11 thousand; at birth, it varies between 15 and 25 thousand, and by the fourth day it falls to 12 thousand. At 4 years, the average is around 8 thousand with a maximum normal limit of 12 thousand. The white count reaches normal adult values at about 12 years of age. There is a qualitative variation depending on age; thus, at birth there is a preponderance of neutrophils, but by the second week the lymphocytes constitute around 60% of the leukocytes and predominate during infancy until age 4, when the granulocytes and lymphocytes are equal in number. There follows a progressive increase in the percentage of granulocytes, and at age 14–15 years the percentages typical of the adult (50–70%) are reached. Not only the percentage but also the absolute number of each cell type per unit of blood volume must be taken into consideration when studying physiologic and pathologic variations in the number of blood cells.

Neutrophils

These cells, which develop in the bone marrow and are released into the circulation, are about 12 μm in diameter, with a nucleus consisting of 2–5 lobes (usually 3 lobes) linked to each other by fine threads of chromatin (Fig 13–5). The very young neutrophil has a nonsegmented nucleus in the shape of a horseshoe.

The nuclei of all granulocytes follow a similar chromatin pattern in which dense masses of chromatin

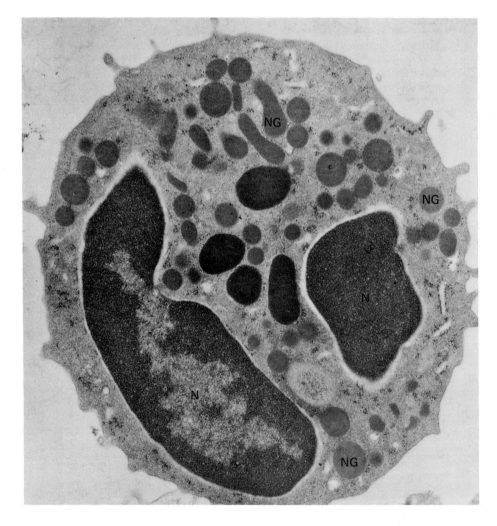

Figure 13—6. Electron micrograph of a rabbit neutrophil. Note the nucleus (N) and specific neutrophilic granules (NG). The chromatin bridge linking the 2 nuclear lobes does not appear in this section. × 23,000. (Courtesy of DF Bainton and MG Farquhar.)

are distributed mainly at the periphery close to the nuclear membrane (Fig 13–6). The zones of loosely arranged chromatin are located mainly in the center of the nucleus.

Neutrophils with more than 5 lobes are called *hypersegmented* and represent old cells. Although under normal conditions the maturation of the neutrophil is parallel to the increase in the number of nuclear lobes, this relationship is not absolute. In some pathologic conditions, young cells can appear with 5 or more lobes.

In the living neutrophil, the shape of the nucleus is variable. The chromatin bridges which unite the nuclear lobes frequently change their position and vary in number. Therefore, for the same cell the number of lobes is variable from time to time depending on the moment when it is observed.

The abundant cytoplasm of the neutrophil is filled with specific granules whose dimensions (0.3–0.8 μm) lie close to the limit of resolution of the optical microscope. These granules are stained a salmon-pink color by the Romanovsky-type mixtures (Fig 13–5). There are great differences in size and staining properties of the neutrophilic granules among mammals. For this reason, these granulocytes are also called heterophils. In the rabbit and guinea pig, heterophils have large acidophilic granules. It is obvious that experimental results obtained with heterophils from other mammals cannot be assumed to be valid for humans.

The granules present in the neutrophils (50–200 in each cell) are surrounded by a membrane and can be separated into 2 types: azurophilic and specific (Fig 13–6). The distinction between the 2 types is made clear by the different chronologic appearance of each type of granule during the development of the granulocytes in the bone marrow; by the histologic appearance of the 2 types of granules in the electron microscope; and by the enzymic content of each type, which

accounts for the differences in function. The azurophilic granules appear first in the promyelocyte stage of maturation and decrease in number with each successive division of the cell; they are present in mature cells, but most of them lose their staining characteristics; they are large and appear electron-dense under the electron microscope. They contain lysosomal enzymes and peroxidase. The specific granules appear at the myelocyte stage; they are smaller and contain alkaline phosphatase and bactericidal substances (cationic proteins). With Romanovsky-type stains, the azurophilic granules are stained reddish-purple, whereas the specific granules are salmon-pink. Both types of granules are formed in the Golgi apparatus but at different sites. Granules undergo Brownian movement or a rapid movement involving one or more granules showing small or great displacement. Neutrophils contain a significant amount of glycogen in their cytoplasm.

After the segmentation of its nucleus, the neutrophil is in the final stage of differentiation, having a very limited protein synthesis. The mature neutrophil contains rare profiles of the granular endoplasmic reticulum, rare free ribosomes, few mitochondria, a rudimentary Golgi apparatus, and a few granules of glycogen. It is a terminal cell in the sense that once it has performed its phagocytic function it is unable to replace the used proteins and eventually dies.

Neutrophils constitute the first line of cellular defense against the invasion of microorganisms. They are active phagocytes of small particles, and this might be due to the specialization of their membrane for this process. These cells are inactive and spherical while circulating but change shape as soon as they touch a solid substrate, over which they start sending out pseudopodia at a speed of 19–36 μm/minute. Once over a supporting surface, these granulocytes undergo a process called "expansion" or spreading, characterized by the emission of cytoplasmic processes in various direc-

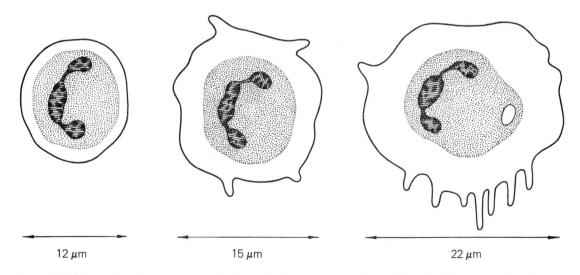

12 μm   15 μm   22 μm

Figure 13–7. Neutrophils undergo a process called "expansion" when in contact with a solid surface. Processes spread out from the hyaloplasm; at the same time, the cell increases its diameter.

tions which are transformed into fringes of hyaloplasm (cytoplasm without granules), attaining a diameter of 20 μm. It is interesting to note that the granules keep a distance of 3–5 μm from the cell boundary where an undulatory movement is taking place (Fig 13–7). In this process, the cells do not adhere to the substrate but maintain themselves at a higher level, touching it by filamentous projections of the hyaloplasm.

The particle to be phagocytosed by the neutrophil is surrounded by pseudopodia which fuse around it (Fig 13–8); thus, the particle eventually occupies a vacuole (phagosome) delimited by a membrane derived from the cell surface and containing extracellular fluid and its contents. Immediately afterward, azurophilic and specific granules fuse their membrane to that of

the phagosome and empty their contents into its interior, thus saving the cytoplasm from exposure to enzymes present in the granules. In this process there is an expenditure of granules and consequent decrease in their number in the interior of the cell. The presence in the azurophilic granules of D-amino acid oxidase is important in the digestion of bacterial cell walls containing D-amino acids. Lysozyme present in these granules is also important for the destruction of bacterial cell walls.

A third enzyme is also instrumental in the bactericidal effect of polymorphonuclear neutrophils. During the process of phagocytosis, peroxide is formed. Myeloperoxidase, which is present in the neutrophils, combines with the peroxide and halide to act on the tyro-

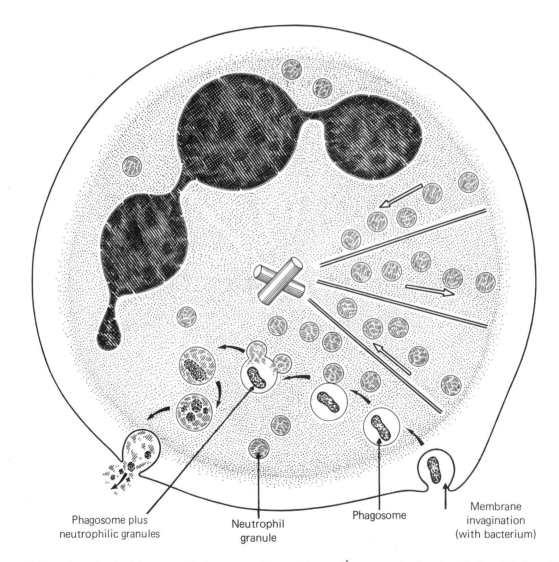

Phagosome plus
neutrophilic granules

Neutrophil
granule

Phagosome

Membrane
invagination
(with bacterium)

Figure 13–8. Some details of the neutrophil ultrastructure. Neutrophilic granules move constantly; microtubules radiate from the centrioles. The direction of this movement is indicated by white arrows. The lower part of the figure shows the process of intracellular digestion of a phagocytosed bacterium (black arrows). Neutrophilic granules fuse together with phagosomes. The bacterium may be digested in the secondary phagosomes thus formed. Later, the digestion products usually are expelled from the neutrophil.

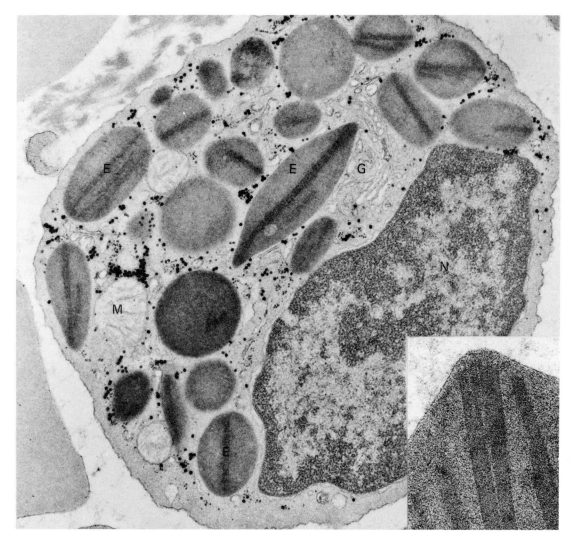

Figure 13–9. Electron micrographs of rabbit eosinophils. Observe the nuclear lobe (N), the Golgi complex (G), the mitochondrion (M), and the eosinophilic granules (E). × 21,500. The inset shows a higher magnification of an eosinophilic granule; the internum with its crystalloid organization is visible. × 132,000. (Courtesy of DF Bainton and MG Farquhar.)

sine molecule of the bacterial cell wall, thus destroying it.

Under the action of certain toxic substances such as streptolysin (streptococcus toxin), the neutrophils undergo rupture of the membranes of the granules, resulting in a tumefaction process followed by agglutination of the organelles and final destruction of the neutrophils themselves.

The neutrophils are quite metabolically active and are capable of both aerobic and anaerobic glycolysis. They apparently depend mainly on the latter process for their energy supply. The Krebs cycle is less important, as might be expected in view of the paucity of mitochondria in these cells. Phagocytosis by the neutrophil stimulates hexose monophosphate shunt activity and increases glycogenolysis.

Eosinophils

The eosinophil has a diameter of about 9 μm (slightly smaller than the neutrophil). In general, its nucleus is bilobate. The endoplasmic reticulum, mitochondria, and Golgi apparatus are poorly developed in eosinophils. The main identifying characteristic of the eosinophil is the presence of ovoid granulations which are stained by eosin (acidophilic granules). These granules are larger than those of the neutrophils, measuring 0.5–1.5 μm along their main axis (Fig 13–9). The granules are lysosomes containing acid phosphatase, cathepsin, and ribonuclease but not lysozyme.

The electron microscope shows that the eosinophilic granules are surrounded by unit membrane. Parallel to the granule's longer axis, an electron-dense, elongated crystalloid or *internum* is found which is relatively resistant to mechanical trauma and osmotic lysis (Fig 13–9). The internum consists of phospholipids and unsaturated fatty acids. In man, granules with more than one internum are rare, this being a common characteristic in other species. The layer surrounding the internum, which is less dense to the electrons, is called the *externum* or *matrix* and is rich in acid phosphatase.

The eosinophils are endowed with ameboid movement and are capable of phagocytosing. The eosinophils phagocytose in a slower but more selective way than the neutrophils.

It has been observed that an increase in the absolute number of eosinophils in the blood *(eosinophilia)* is associated with allergic reactions in the organism.

It was experimentally observed that the eosinophil does not phagocytose isolated bovine serum albumin (antigen) or its antibody (specific gamma globulin). However, the eosinophil phagocytoses the complex of this antigen with its antibody (see Chapter 5). It appears to be a function of the eosinophil to perform this type of selective phagocytosis.

In the same way as the neutrophil, the eosinophil also exhibits the phenomenon of granule coalescence with the phagosomes, at which time the respective membranes fuse. In the eosinophil after fusion, it can be observed that only the network or *externum* of the granule appears to fulfill the function of destroying the engulfed material since the internum remains intact within the vacuole for a long time. This fact is compatible with the hypothesis that hydrolytic enzymes are localized in the externum of the granule.

Eosinophils contain profibrinolysin, which suggests that they may play a role in keeping the blood liquid, especially when its fluidity is altered by pathologic processes.

Corticosteroids (hormones from the adrenal complex) produce a rapid fall in the number of blood eosinophils; however, this hormone has no effect on bone marrow eosinophils.

Basophils

Basophils measure about 12 μm in diameter and have a large nucleus with an irregular twisted shape, generally in the form of an S (Fig 13–5). The cytoplasm of the basophil is filled with granules that are larger than those seen in other granulocytes. Often the granules partially obscure the nucleus. These granules are irregular in size and shape and stain metachromatically. In smears stained by Romanovsky-type mixtures,

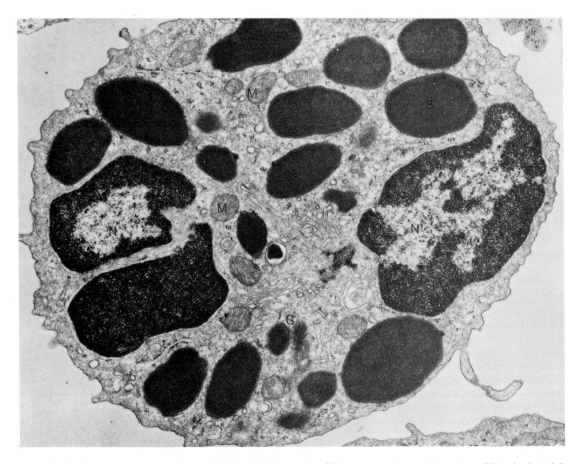

Figure 13–10. Electron micrograph of a rabbit basophil. The nucleus (N) appears in 3 separated sections. Note the basophilic granules (B), the mitochondria (M), and the Golgi apparatus (G). (Reproduced, with permission, from Terry RW, Bainton DF, Farquhar MG: Lab Invest 21:65, 1969.)

they appear violet (Fig 13–5).

Under the electron microscope, the granules of the basophils appear delimited by unit membrane and contain particles of uniform size in each granule (Fig 13–10). The size of these particles varies from one granule to another. Some investigators interpret this variation in size as a reflection of different phases of a secretory cycle. The substances secreted—histamine and heparin—can be demonstrated in the granules of the basophils.

There is some similarity between the granules of the basophils and those of the mast cells (see Chapter 5). Both are metachromatic and contain heparin and histamine. Although the participation of the mast cells in anaphylaxis and in other processes related to allergic reactions is well documented, the role of the basophil in these processes is still controversial.

Like the other granulocytes, the basophils are capable of ameboid movement and phagocytosis, although they are not very active in this respect.

It is possible that in response to the action of certain antigens the basophils can liberate their granules, as happens with the mast cell, but this has not been definitely proved. Despite the similarities they present, mast cells and basophils are not the same cell, for in the same species they present different ultrastructures.

Lymphocytes

These are spherical cells with diameters of 6–8 μm. Lymphocytes with these dimensions are known as *small lymphocytes* (Fig 13–5). In the circulating blood there occurs a small percentage of *medium-sized lymphocytes* and *large lymphocytes.* This is a meaningless morphologic distinction which is a holdover from the long period during which the role of the lymphocytes was poorly understood.

The small lymphocyte, which is the type that is predominant in the blood, has a spherical nucleus, sometimes with an indentation. Its chromatin is distributed in coarse clumps, so that the nucleus appears dark in the usual preparations, a characteristic which facilitates the identification of the lymphocyte (Figs 13–5 and 13–11). In these preparations, the nucleolus of the lymphocyte is not visible, but it can be demonstrated by special staining technics and with the electron microscope.

The cytoplasm of the small lymphocyte is scanty, and in blood smears it appears as a slender ring around the nucleus. It is slightly basophilic, taking a light blue color in stained smears (Fig 13–5). Sometimes the cytoplasm is not visible. It may contain granules which stain purple by the azures of the Romanovsky-type mixtures. These are called *azurophilic granules* (Fig 13–11) and are not exclusive to lymphocytes; they also appear in monocytes and in immature precursors and mature granulocytes. Under the electron microscope, the cytoplasm of the lymphocyte appears poor in organelles but contains many free ribosomes and polyribosomes (Fig 13–12).

The cytologic criteria that separate the large from the small lymphocytes are the following: (1) abundance of cytoplasm with an increased number of polyribosomes; (2) decrease in the nucleus of coarse clumps of chromatin; (3) appearance of nucleoli in the lighter-stained nuclei; and (4) increase in the number of mitochondria and in the size of the Golgi apparatus. Both large and small lymphocytes show motility and mobility both in vitro and in vivo.

Although they are morphologically similar, lymphocytes of blood constitute a heterogeneous cell population. They vary in size and in density. Experimental evidence, based on studies of electrophoretic mobility, surface topography, histologic localization, buoyant density, and responsiveness to mitogens, suggests the existence of at least 4 fractions (subgroups) of lymphocytes with different and characteristic immunologic functions. They vary also in life span, for some lymphocytes live only a few days whereas others survive in the circulating blood for many years.

A further separation of lymphocytes can be done by the recognition of special molecular arrangements on the surface membrane of these cells. It has been shown that some carry specific antigen-binding structures—receptors—on their membrane which are absent from others, and also that they show differences in the position and class of immunoglobulins they contain. Cells binding more than 2 antigens appear to bind them at independent sites.

The simple appearance of the small lymphocytes gives little indication of the capacity of this cell to be

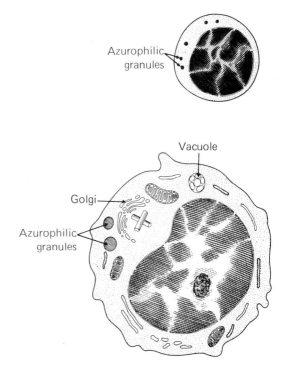

Figure 13–11. The lymphocyte as seen with the light microscope *(above)* and the electron microscope *(below).* Cytoplasmic organelles are scanty.

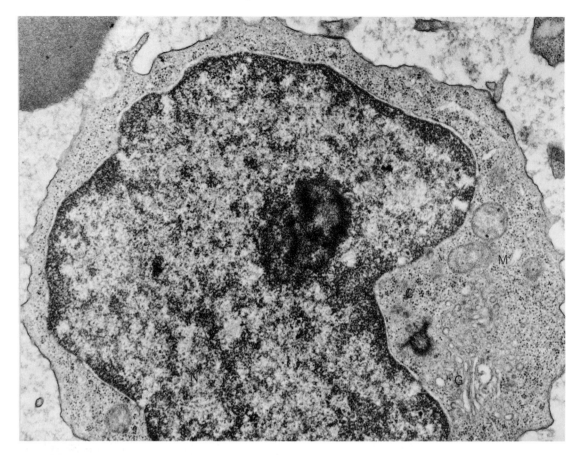

Figure 13—12. Electron micrograph of a human blood lymphocyte. This cell is poor in endoplasmic reticulum, containing a moderate quantity of free ribosomes. Observe the nucleus (N), the nucleolus (Nu), the centriole (C), the mitochondria (M), and the Golgi complex (G). Reduced from X 22,000. (Courtesy of DF Bainton and MG Farquhar.)

transformed into other types of cells. This transformation can be induced by many substances to which lymphocytes might be exposed in vitro. These nonspecific agents complement the specific agents which apparently stimulate specific receptors on the membrane of the cell. In this latter case, only a part of the lymphocyte population responds to the agent, whereas the rest of the lymphocytes do not. The specific or nonspecific agents probably activate different metabolic pathways or points on the pathways. The activated cells divide mitotically and give rise to large or small cells. This information has been obtained by following labeled blast cells and by observing the radioactivity in developing small cells. Small lymphocytes very seldom divide, although this is common in large lymphocytes or blast forms.

There is also a separation of functions among lymphocytes. It appears from recent experimental data that precursor cells originate in the bone marrow in late fetal and postnatal life and are capable of differentiating and becoming immunocompetent cells in areas outside the bone marrow. In birds, this differentiation occurs in 2 distinct areas: the *bursa of Fabricius* and the *thymus*. In the bursa of Fabricius, which is a mass of lymphoid tissue in the cloaca of birds, the undifferentiated cells of bone marrow origin are induced to become progenitor cells of lymphocytes necessary for the production of plasma cells, which produce antibodies—immunoglobulins—to specific antigens. They are involved in the humoral immunity of the body. These lymphocytes are called *B (bursa-dependent) lymphocytes* (Fig 13–13).

In the thymus, undifferentiated cells of bone marrow origin are induced to become progenitor cells of lymphocytes which are involved in the cellular immunity of the organism. These lymphocytes are called *T (thymus-dependent) lymphocytes* (Fig 13–13).

In mammals, the bursa of Fabricius does not

Figure 13—13 (on facing page). Scanning electron micrograph of lymphocytes from normal peripheral blood. *Above:* A B lymphocyte, with its typical villous surface. *Below:* A typical T lymphocyte, which has a smooth surface and only a few microvilli. (Reproduced, with permission, from Polliack A & others: J Exper Med 138:607, 1973.)

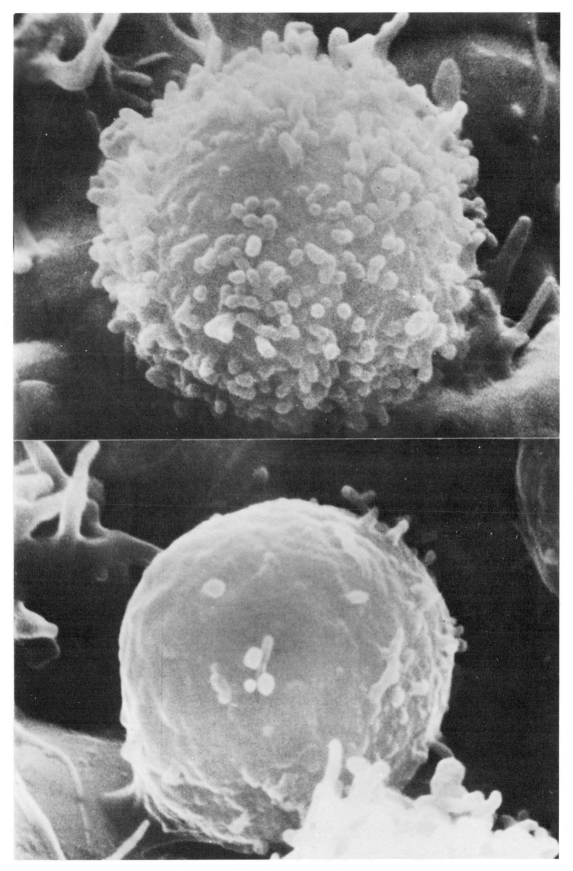

[Legend on facing page.]

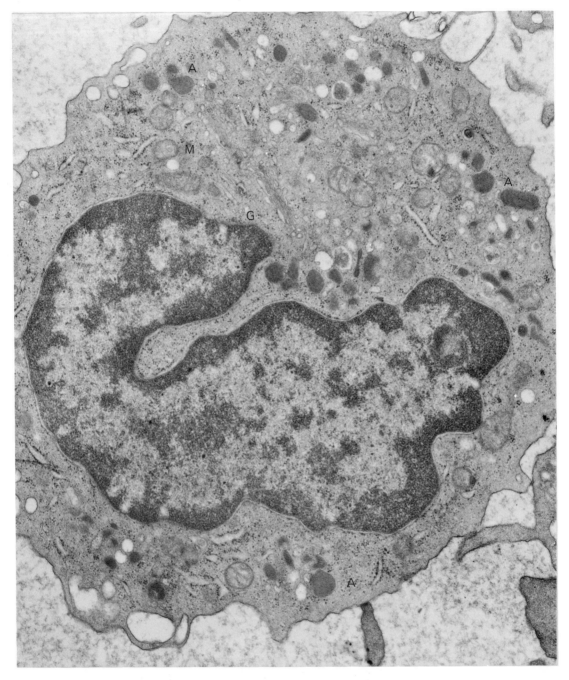

Figure 13–14. Electron micrograph of a human monocyte. Note the Golgi complex (G), the mitochondria (M), and the azurophilic granules (A). Endoplasmic reticulum is poorly developed. There are some free ribosomes. × 22,000. (Courtesy of DF Bainton and MG Farquhar.)

exist, but the progenitor marrow cells differentiate into B cells in the so-called bursa-equivalent area which is not well defined but appears to be associated with areas of the gastrointestinal tract of mammals. These 2 organs are called central lymphoid organs, and cells differentiated in these organs colonize other areas of the body where lymphoid tissue is found in encapsulated, diffuse, or organ form.

When in contact with an antigen, B lymphocytes differentiate into plasma cells which synthesize antibodies which are secreted into the blood, intercellular fluid, and lymph.

However, in the blood, most lymphocytes belong to type T and are responsible for the cell-mediated immune reactions which do not depend on free circulating antibodies. Graft rejection is an example of a cell-mediated immune reaction. In this type of immune response, T lymphocytes produce factors which remain attached to the cell surface. For this reason, cell-mediated reactions take place only when the lymphocyte itself is present to elaborate these factors in the environment. T lymphocytes also play a vital role in determining the type and amount of antibodies produced by the B lymphocytes.

Lymphocytes function also as *memory cells.* These are lymphocytes which have been in the presence of an antigen but have not become differentiated into plasma cells. When they later come into contact with the same antigen again, they rapidly divide several times by mitosis and give rise to plasma cells which synthesize antibody against the antigen. Memory cells explain why the second injection of an antigen is followed by a higher and faster production of antibody than the first injection.

Monocytes

These agranulocytes have diameters varying from 9–12 μm (Fig 13–5). The nucleus is oval, horseshoe-shaped, or kidney-shaped and is generally eccentrically placed. The chromatin appears in a looser and more delicate arrangement than in the lymphocytes, this being the most constant characteristic of the monocyte (Fig 13–14). Owing to the delicate distribution of their chromatin, the nuclei of the monocytes are more lightly stained than those of the lymphocytes, which are the blood cells with which they may most easily be confused although the monocytes are generally larger (Fig 13–5). The nucleus of the monocyte contains 2 or 3 nucleoli which can sometimes be seen in blood smears stained by Romanovsky-type mixtures.

The cytoplasm of the monocyte is basophilic and frequently contains very fine azurophilic granules, some of which are at the limits of optical microscopic resolution. These granules may fill all of the cytoplasm, giving it a bluish-gray color. Evidence obtained by examining the enzymic contents suggests that the azurophilic granules of the monocytes are lysosomes. Fig 13–14 shows the ultrastructure of the monocyte. In the electron microscope, one or 2 nucleoli are seen in the nucleus and a small quantity of granular endoplasmic reticulum, ribosomes, polyribosomes, and many small elongated mitochondria are observed. A well-developed Golgi apparatus involved in the packaging of the lysosomelike granules is also present in the

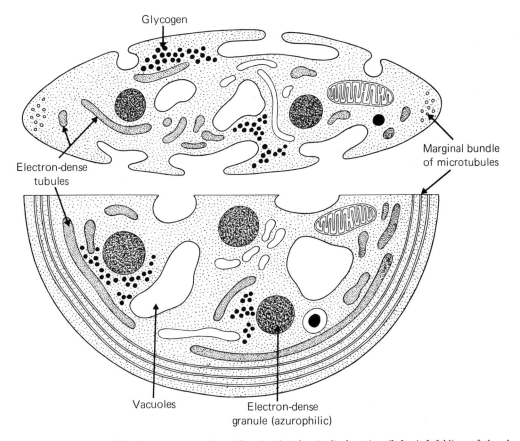

Glycogen

Marginal bundle of microtubules

Electron-dense tubules

Vacuoles

Electron-dense granule (azurophilic)

Figure 13–15. Ultrastructure of platelets in cross section *(above)* and in longitudinal section *(below).* Infoldings of the plasma membrane give rise to numerous vacuoles. The large electron-dense granules are the azurophilic granules of light microscopy. Near the edge of the platelet, there is a marginal bundle of microtubules. Glycogen granules, mitochondria, and electron-dense tubules are present in the hyalomere.

cytoplasm. Microfibrils and microtubules are usually observed in areas near the indentation of the nucleus. Many microvilli and pinocytotic vesicles are found on the cell surface.

Monocytes are found in the blood, connective tissue, and other tissues and in body cavities. They belong to the *mononuclear phagocytic system (reticuloendothelial system)* and have receptor sites on their surface membrane for immunoglobulins and complement. They have their origin in the bone marrow and are transported in the body via the bloodstream.

The monocytes move through the bloodstream unidirectionally; after crossing the capillary wall and penetrating the connective tissues, they are transformed into phagocytic cells of the macrophage system. The half-life of the monocyte in the blood is a few days, and there is no strong evidence of recirculation after they enter the tissues. In the tissues they interact with the lymphoid cell component of the immune defense system of the organism, and they are important in the recognition and interaction of the immunocompetent cellular system with the antigen.

PLATELETS

The platelets have no nuclei. They are fragments of cytoplasm 2–5 μm in diameter covered with cell membrane and derived from giant cells of the bone marrow called *megakaryocytes.* They are found exclusively in mammals. The concentration of these corpuscles in human blood varies within a wide range. Platelet counts are difficult to make with precision because the cells have a tendency to agglutinate into clumps. The normal count ranges from 150–300 thousand/μl of blood. Platelets have a life span of 8 days.

In common stained blood smears, the platelets often appear in clumps. Each platelet has a peripheral light blue-stained transparent part, the *hyalomere,* and a central portion containing granules stained purple, the *chromomere* or *granulomere.* The hyalomere sends out fine processes, conferring an irregular outline on the corpuscle.

The ultrastructure of platelets is represented in a semischematic way in Fig 13–15. The hyalomere is homogeneous and shows microfilaments and microtubules, the latter being concentrated in the platelet periphery under the unit membrane and called the *marginal bundle of microtubules* (Fig 13–16). The mi-

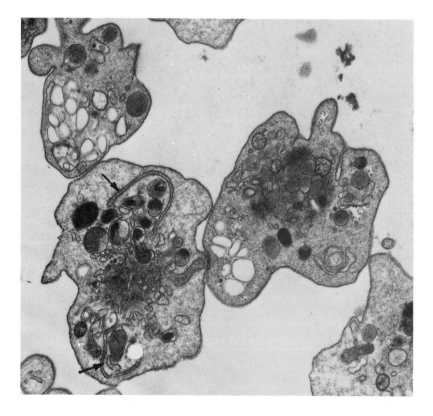

Figure 13–16. Electron micrograph of human platelets. Arrows indicate electron-dense tubules. The system of vacuoles and the electron-dense (azurophilic) granules are also seen. × 17,000.

crofilaments are made of contractile protein. Microtubules and microfilaments probably play an important role in maintaining the discoid shape of the platelets and participate in the formation of pseudopodia and surface projections during movement and adhesion of platelets. An exterior coat outside the unit membrane, 15–20 nm in width, consists of acid mucopolysaccharides and glycoproteins. This coat represents the adhesive layer of the platelet. The granulomere contains mitochondria, vacuoles, electron-dense granules, glycogen granules, a system of tubules and vesicles, and other granules, often called a granules, measuring 0.15–0.2 μm in diameter. The content of the latter is granular and corresponds to the chromomere. The a granules enclosed by unit membrane contain substances involved in the function of the platelets such as lysosomal-type enzymes (acid phosphatase, β-glucuronidase, etc) and acid mucopolysaccharides. The mitochondria, acting also as a calcium depot, show changes in appearance during platelet coagulation. The system of tubules and vesicles, in which the Golgi apparatus must also be included, forms an extensive network communicating with the cell surface such as that which participates in the formation of granules from Golgi saccules. A more clearly delineated section called the *dense tubular system,* which is associated with the circumferential band of microtubules, may serve as a template for the organization of the microtubules.

Platelets are related to the function of hemostasis. When rupture of a vessel occurs, the platelets agglutinate, forming a plug which can, up to a certain point, close the gap. They also participate in the formation of *thromboplastin,* a factor essential to the transformation of fibrinogen into fibrin, which forms the blood clot.

Several important physiologic substances are accumulated and transported in the platelets, eg, epinephrine and serotonin (5-hydroxytryptamine), although these compounds are not synthesized by platelets. Epinephrine and serotonin are vasoconstrictors and aid in occlusion of ruptured blood vessels by promoting contraction of vascular smooth muscle. They are liberated from the platelets through the action of *thrombin,* an enzyme synthesized in the plasma during blood coagulation.

Viruses, bacteria, and other small particles are phagocytosed by platelets. Although the role of platelets in the defense against infection is not an important one, it is interesting to note that in viral diseases there is often a decrease in the platelet count (thrombocytopenia).

● ● ●

References

Archer GT, Hirsch JG: Isolation of granules from eosinophil leucocytes and study of their enzyme content. J Exper Med 118:227, 1963.

Baggiolini M, Hirsch JG, de Duve C: Resolution of granules from rabbit heterophil leukocytes into distinct populations by zonal sedimentation. J Cell Biol 40:529, 1969.

Bainton DF, Farquhar MG: Origin of granules in polymorphonuclear leukocytes: Two types derived from opposite faces of the Golgi complex in developing granulocytes. J Cell Biol 28:277, 1966.

Bainton DF, Farquhar MG: Segregation and packaging of granule enzymes in eosinophilic leukocytes. J Cell Biol 45:54, 1970.

Behnke O: Electron microscopic observations on the membrane systems of the rat blood platelet. Anat Record 158:121, 1967.

Bessis M: *Living Blood Cells and Their Ultrastructure.* Springer, 1973.

Campbell FR: Nuclear elimination from the normoblast of fetal guinea pig liver as studied with electron microscopy and serial sectioning techniques. Anat Record 160:539, 1968.

Campbell FR: Ultrastructural studies of transmural migration of blood cells in the bone marrow of rats, mice and guinea pigs. Am J Anat 135:521, 1972.

Gowans JL, Knight EJ: The route of recirculation of lymphocytes in the rat. Proc Roy Soc London s.B 159:745, 1965.

Hanifin JM, Cline MJ: Human monocytes and macrophages: Interaction with antigen and lymphocytes. J Cell Biol 46:97, 1970.

McFarland W, Schecter GP: The lymphocyte in immunological reactions in vitro: Ultrastructural studies. Blood 35:683, 1970.

Miller F, de Harven E, Palade GE: The structure of eosinophil leukocyte granules in rodents and in man. J Cell Biol 31:349, 1966.

Nichols BA: Differentiation of monocytes: Origin, nature, and fate of their azurophil granules. J Cell Biol 50:498, 1971.

Nossal GJV: Genetic control of lymphopoiesis, plasma cell formation and antibody production. Internat Rev Exper Path 1:1, 1962.

Polliack A & others: Identification of human B and T lymphocytes by scanning electron microscopy. J Exper Med 138:607, 1973.

Polliack A & others: Scanning electron microscopy of human lymphocyte–sheep erythrocyte rosettes. J Exper Med 140:146, 1974.

Roelants GE & others: Active synthesis of immunoglobulin receptors for antigen by T lymphocytes. Nature 247:106, 1974.

Simpson CF, Kling JM: The mechanism of denucleation in circulating erythroblasts. J Cell Biol 35:237, 1967.

Tanaka Y, Goodman JR: *Electron Microscopy of Human Blood Cells.* Harper, 1972.

Ullyot JL, Bainton DF, Farquhar MG: Cytochemical studies of human neutrophilic leukocyte granules. J Histochem Cytochem 18:681, 1970.

Watanabe L, Donahue S, Hoggott N: Method for electron microscopic studies of circulating human leukocytes: An observation of their fine structure. J Ultrastruct Res 20:366, 1967.

Wintrobe M & others: *Clinical Hematology,* 7th ed. Lea & Febiger, 1974.

14...
The Life Cycle of Blood Cells

The blood cells usually do not multiply in the bloodstream, and, because of their short life span, are continuously being replaced by new cells produced in the *hematopoietic organs*. Erythrocytes, granulocytes, monocytes, and platelets are formed in the bone marrow, whereas lymphocytes are formed mainly in the lymph nodes, spleen, thymus, and lymphatic nodules of the mucosa of the gastrointestinal tract. Recent information indicates that lymphocytes might be produced in the marrow.

Before attaining complete maturity and being released into the circulation, the blood cells go through various stages of differentiation and maturation. Because these processes are continuous, cells with characteristics that are intermediate between 2 typical stages are frequently encountered in smears of blood or bone marrow.

It is probable that all of the formed elements of the blood originate from a single type of precursor cell *(unitarian* or *monophyletic theory)*. In the past, some investigators favored the concept that there is more than one type of precursor cell *(polyphyletic theory)*. The simplest polyphyletic theory assumes the existence of 2 stem cells, one for the cells that derive from myeloid tissue and the other for cells that derive from lymphatic tissue. The other extreme is the complete polyphyletic theory, which maintains that there is a primitive stem cell for each type of blood cell.

These theories represent an effort to resolve the difficulties of following the various stages of cell differentiation in bone marrow and lymphoid tissue. When cells at different stages of differentiation are arranged in a definite sequence—eg, in the stratified squamous epithelium (skin, esophagus) or in the seminiferous tubules (testis)—it is easy to follow each cell through its various stages of differentiation. In the hematopoietic organs, however, although the cells develop in clusters (groups of cells of the same origin), this definite sequence does not exist and the various stages of differentiation can be followed only by observing criteria for their morphologic characterization. Since the less clearly differentiated cells have more similarities among themselves than do cells that have reached a more highly developed stage, the main difficulties and controversies arise in relation to these less mature cells.

According to the unitarian theory, all of the blood cells derive from the *hemocytoblast,* a free cell which arises directly from the embryonic mesenchymal cell and has a strictly hematopoietic potential. The mitotic multiplication of the cells that derive from the hemocytoblast, which are at the observed intermediate stages of differentiation, is almost sufficient to maintain the number of peripheral blood cells at a constant level. For this reason, the number of hemocytoblasts encountered in the hematopoietic organs is small and mitosis of these cells is very rare.

Hemocytoblast

Although research workers acknowledge the difficulty of characterizing a stem cell which shows no signs of differentiation, it is customary to designate as hemocytoblasts those cells whose direction of differentiation cannot be predicted with any assurance. The ultimate fate of the hemocytoblast presumably is influenced by the microenvironment: In the bone marrow it usually becomes a granulocyte, megakaryocyte, or erythrocyte; in the lymphoid environment it becomes a lymphocyte. Cells capable of incorporating radioactive thymidine are sometimes found in the peripheral blood and have been shown to act like stem cells (see also Chapter 15).

On a Giemsa-stained smear, the hemocytoblast generally appears as a large cell, although some question about its size has recently been raised, limiting it to 8—12 μm rather than 30 μm as formerly thought. When stained with Giemsa's stain, it shows a basophilic sky-blue cytoplasm without granules and a large nucleus with a delicate pale network of fine chromatin. It also presents 2 or 3 large nucleoli which are clearly visible in smears. The cell has very little cytoplasm and sharp and even borders (Figs 14—1 and 14—2). Hemocytoblasts constitute only 0.5—1% of the cells found in the hematogenic bone marrow, and this is one of the main difficulties in identifying these cells.

ERYTHROCYTIC SERIES

According to their state of further differentiation and maturation, the erythrocytic cells are classified as *proerythroblasts, basophilic erythroblasts, polychromatophilic erythroblasts, normoblasts* (orthochromatic

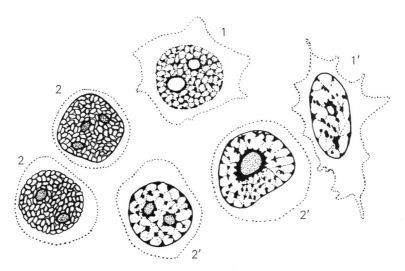

Figure 14—1. Hemocytoblasts. *1, 2:* Hemocytoblasts in bone marrow smears. *1', 2':* Hemocytoblast structure in paraffin sections. The delicate chromatin pattern of hemocytoblast nuclei is best preserved in bone marrow smears.

erythroblasts), *reticulocytes,* and *erythrocytes.* A mature cell has achieved all of its specific functions.

The basic process in the maturation of the erythrocyte or red cell series is the synthesis of hemoglobin and the formation of a small corpuscle, the erythrocyte, which has the greatest possible area for the diffusion of oxygen (Fig 14—3). In this maturation process,

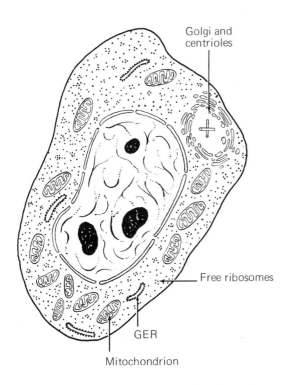

Figure 14—2. Ultrastructure of hemocytoblast. Organelles are poorly developed. The chromatin pattern is fine, pale, and regular in appearance. GER, granular endoplasmic reticulum.

the unit of erythropoiesis is the *erythrocytic island* (Fig 15—1). This island consists of one or 2 centrally located primitive cells called *reticulum cells,* surrounded by erythroblasts and normoblasts which remain in contact with the body of the reticulum cell during the entire process of maturation and development. The reticulum cells have many pseudopods which sometimes encircle the erythroblast. Through these contacts, by a process similar to pinocytosis, iron is transferred from the reticulum cell to the maturing erythroblasts in the form of ferritin. The relationship of the reticulum cell to the stem cell and the proerythroblast has not been determined.

This reticulum cell also has a role in phagocytosis of expelled nuclei of normoblasts and of aged or damaged erythrocytes. The hemoglobin-containing material ingested by this cell is changed by lysosomal enzymes into ferritin and deposited within the cytoplasm or in membrane-bound residue as hemosiderin. This is the material that gives the Prussian blue reaction that is characteristic of the presence of iron in cells or tissues. In humans, hemosiderin is the main storage form of iron. It has also been found that transferrin, an iron-binding plasma globulin, provides iron for the formation of heme by the maturing erythroblasts.

During maturation of the cells of the erythrocytic series, the following major morphologic and histologic changes occur, corresponding to the biochemical events of the developing erythroid cell: (1) the cell volume decreases; (2) the nucleoli diminish in size until they become invisible under the light microscope; (3) the nuclear chromatin becomes increasingly more dense until the nucleus presents a pyknotic appearance and is finally extruded from the cell; (4) there is a decrease in the number of polyribosomes (basophilia) and an increase in the amount of hemoglobin (acidophilia) within the cytoplasm; and (5) the quantity of mitochondria diminishes (Fig 14—3).

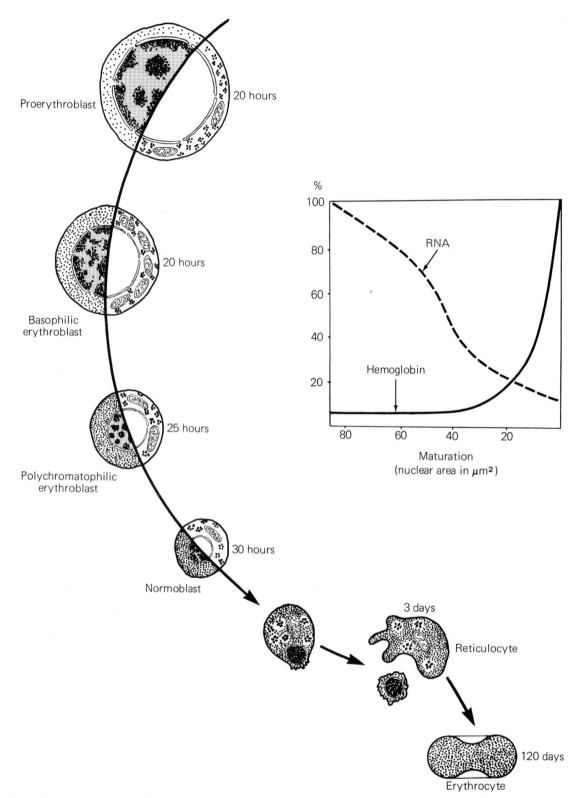

Proerythroblast

20 hours

Basophilic
erythroblast

20 hours

%
100

80

RNA

60

40

Hemoglobin

20

80   60   40   20

Maturation
(nuclear area in μm²)

Polychromatophilic
erythroblast

25 hours

Normoblast

30 hours

3 days

Reticulocyte

120 days

Erythrocyte

Figure 14–3. Summary of erythrocyte maturation. The stippled part of the cytoplasm shows that hemoglobin concentration increases continously from the proerythroblast to the erythrocyte stage. There is also a decrease in nuclear volume and an increase in chromatin condensation, followed by extrusion of a pyknotic nucleus. In the graph, the higher concentrations of hemoglobin and RNA were considered to be 100%. The notations of times are average life spans.

Proerythroblast (Pronormoblast)

The proerythroblast is a large cell (22–28 μm in diameter) which contains all of the elements characteristic of a cell undergoing intense protein synthesis. The nucleus is spherical and centrally located, occupying 80% of the cell, with a delicately structured chromatin and 1 or 2 large nucleoli. The cytoplasm is characteristically intensely basophilic, with a pale region around the nucleus. Electron microscopic examination demonstrates that this pale perinuclear halo contains mitochondria, the Golgi apparatus, and a pair of centrioles. The remaining cytoplasm contains numerous polyribosomes, but the endoplasmic reticulum is not well developed.

The main function of the proteins synthesized by the proerythroblast is to increase the cell's mass of protoplasm, since this cell divides actively. Hemoglobin synthesis also begins to appear, and the presence of this protein can be detected by microspectrophotometry. Pinocytosis is present, and ferritin can be seen in the cytoplasm. At this stage, the amount of hemoglobin is too small to be detected by the usual staining technics.

Basophilic Erythroblast (Basophilic Normoblast)

The basophilic erythroblast is smaller (16–18 μm in diameter) than the proerythroblast and has a nucleus of the same shape as the proerythroblast that occupies three-fourths of the cell. The chromatin is condensed in coarser granules, and the heterochromatin and euchromatin are arranged in such a way as to give a clockface appearance. There are no visible nucleoli (Figs 14–4, 14–5, and 14–6). Polyribosomes are present in the cytoplasm, and their large number explains the basophilia of this cell. The Golgi apparatus is well developed, and there is an abundance of mitochondria. Microtubules and microfibrils are also present in the cytoplasm. The basophilic erythroblast undergoes one mitotic division. Hemoglobin continues to be formed.

Polychromatophilic Erythroblast (Polychromatophilic Normoblast)

The polychromatophilic erythroblast is even smaller (12–15 μm in diameter) than the basophilic erythroblast, with a nucleus that occupies half of the cell or less and contains even more condensed chroma-

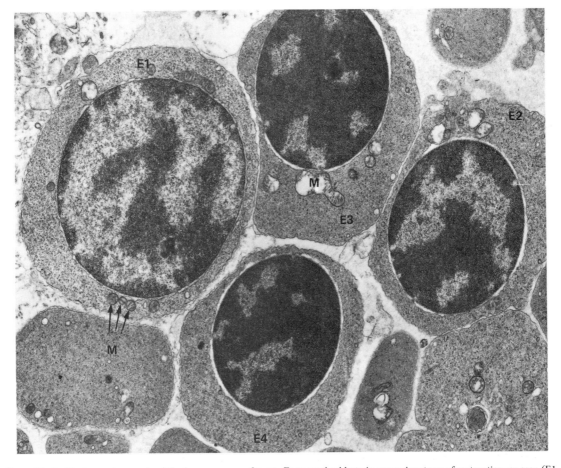

Figure 14–4. Electron micrograph of the bone marrow of a rat. Four erythroblasts in successive stages of maturation are seen (E1, E2, E3, and E4). As the cell matures, its chromatin becomes condensed and the accumulation of hemoglobin increases the electron density of the cytoplasm. Note the mitochondria (M). × 11,000.

Proerythroblast

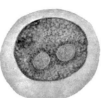

Hemocytoblast

Basophilic erythroblast

Neutrophilic promyelocyte

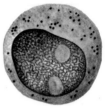

Myeloblast

Basophilic promyelocyte

Polychromatophilic erythroblast

Neutrophilic myelocyte

Eosinophilic promyelocyte

Normoblast

Neutrophilic metamyelocyte

Eosinophilic myelocyte

Basophilic myelocyte

Reticulocyte

Neutrophil with
band-shaped nucleus

Eosinophilic
metamyelocyte

Erythrocyte

Mature neutrophil

Mature eosinophil

Mature basophil

Figure 14–5. Maturation of the erythrocytic and granulocytic series. Romanovsky staining was used except for the reticuloycte, which was treated additionally by cresyl blue in order to precipitate and stain the RNA found in this cell. (This illustration is reproduced in color on p xv.)

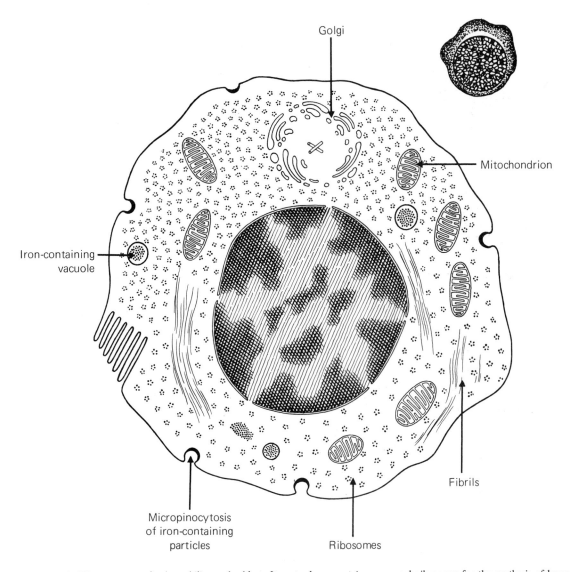

Figure 14–6. Ultrastructure of a basophilic erythroblast. Its cytoplasm contains many polyribosomes for the synthesis of hemoglobin. The upper right drawing shows the structure of the same cell as seen in bone marrow smears. The light area near the nucleus contains the Golgi complex and the centrioles.

tin in a checkerboard pattern. This polychromatophilic erythroblast contains hemoglobin in sufficient quantity to cause a cytoplasmic acidophilia (pink), which, added to the basophilia, gives a grayish-pink color to the cytoplasm (Figs 14–4 and 14–5). The rest of the organelles decrease in size, but pinocytosis in the plasma membrane is still present. After a number of cell divisions each of which increases the degree of differentiation, the final step in mitotic division of the erythrocytic series occurs at this stage.

Normoblast (Orthochromatic Erythroblast)

The normoblast has a diameter of 8–10 μm. The nucleus shows very condensed chromatin, has become smaller so that it occupies less than one-fourth of the cell area, and is found eccentrically. The cytoplasm of

this cell is usually acidophilic but may contain traces of basophilia (Fig 14–5). Many single ribosomes are still seen, but the mitochondria and the Golgi apparatus are becoming smaller and beginning to degenerate. After 3 mitotic divisions, the pyknotic nucleus becomes incapable of further replication and is then extruded.

Reticulocytes

Microcinematography has demonstrated that at any given moment the normoblast puts forth a series of cytoplasmic protrusions—one containing the nucleus, which is expelled encased in a thin layer of cytoplasm containing hemoglobin. The extruded nuclei, separated from the normoblasts, are engulfed by the macrophages of the bone marrow or the reticular cells.

Expulsion of nuclei may also occur at an earlier maturation stage than the normoblast, in which case the erythrocyte will be larger than normal and is called a *macrocyte*. The remaining part of the cell has no nucleus and is called a *reticulocyte*. Under the electron microscope, it still presents 2 centrioles, some mitochondria, remnants of the Golgi apparatus, and polyribosomes. These last organelles still synthesize the small quantity of hemoglobin (almost 20%) necessary to complete the total hemoglobin content of the mature erythrocyte. As polyribosomes cannot be renewed because of the absence of a nucleus, protein synthesis ceases within a short time.

The reticulocyte is capable of contracting itself, forming folds at certain points and projections at others. It appears that the reticulocyte enters the circulation by sending forth a pseudopodium which penetrates the wall of the sinusoidal capillary and becomes larger until it passes through into the lumen. The maturation period of the reticulocytes in the circulation is 24–28 hours, with a total life span of approximately 72 hours. During this period, autophagia and ejection of different organelles occur.

The reticulocyte differs from the erythrocyte in that it contains vestiges of RNA, thus showing a slight diffuse basophilia superimposed on the intense acidophilia of the hemoglobin. The reticulocytes are polychromatophilic red cells. In blood smears stained by the usual methods, the reticulocyte appears larger than the erythrocyte, measuring approximately 9 μm in diameter.

When treated with supravital dyes such as cresyl blue, the ribonucleoprotein of the reticulocytes precipitates, forming a reticulum of variable appearance and size which stains dark blue (Fig 14–5). During this period of maturation, all of the polyribosomes become monoribosomes.

The reticulocyte represents a young erythrocyte. An increase in the number of reticulocytes in the blood indicates increased production of erythrocytes as long as the number of reticulocytes in the bone marrow does not decrease. A high reticulocyte count in the blood accompanied by a decrease of their number in the bone marrow indicates more rapid liberation of these cells into the circulation without a corresponding increase in reticulocyte formation in the bone marrow.

Erythrons (Fig 14–7)

The erythron is the total cell population of erythrocytes and their precursor cells and can be thought of as a widely dispersed but functionally single organ. Its principal function is to supply the organism with the oxygen necessary for tissue metabolism. Moreover, it carries CO_2, a gas which is also transported dissolved in the plasma for elimination from the lungs.

The erythron can be divided into 2 functional compartments: (1) the *circulating* or *blood compartment*, represented by the erythrocytes in the blood; and (2) the *medullary compartment*, or *erythropoietic pool*, where formation of new elements takes place.

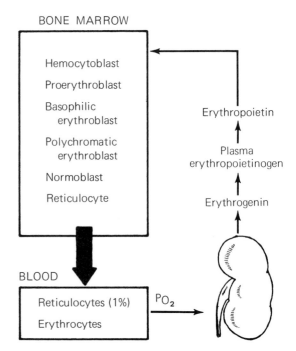

Figure 14–7. The erythron is composed of both the medullary and circulating blood compartments. Reticulocytes pass from the bone marrow to the blood, where they complete maturation into erythrocytes. A fall in blood oxygen tension (P_{O_2}) stimulates the kidney to produce erythrogenin, a renal factor interacting with a plasma globulin erythropoietinogen to produce an active hormone, erythropoietin, which accelerates the mitotic rate and the maturation of red cells in the medullary compartment. Thus, the number of liberated reticulocytes and erythrocytes in the blood increases.

As continuous synthesis and accumulation of hemoglobin-carrying cells occurs, continuous renewal of the cells released into the circulation is required since the mature erythrocyte in man has a half-life of approximately 120 days.* Continuing cell renewal depends upon the existence of another cellular compartment which, via homeostatic mechanisms, makes immature forms of cells available for maturation (Fig 14–8). This can be easily shown by injecting ^{59}Fe and observing the process of its incorporation into the hemoglobin molecule of maturing cells. Such experiments have demonstrated that the pool of proerythroblasts is increased not only by mitosis of existing proerythroblasts but also by the emergence of unlabeled erythroblasts from an early compartment. This precursor compartment is called the committed stem cell compartment and depends on a multipotential cell compartment for maintaining numbers of cells. The committed stem cell, according to some workers, is sensitive to erythropoietin, a hormone controlling the erythropoiesis. The same hormone also influences the differentiated compartment. A feedback mechanism

*In other animals the red cell has a longer or shorter life span, but the measurement is always in days.

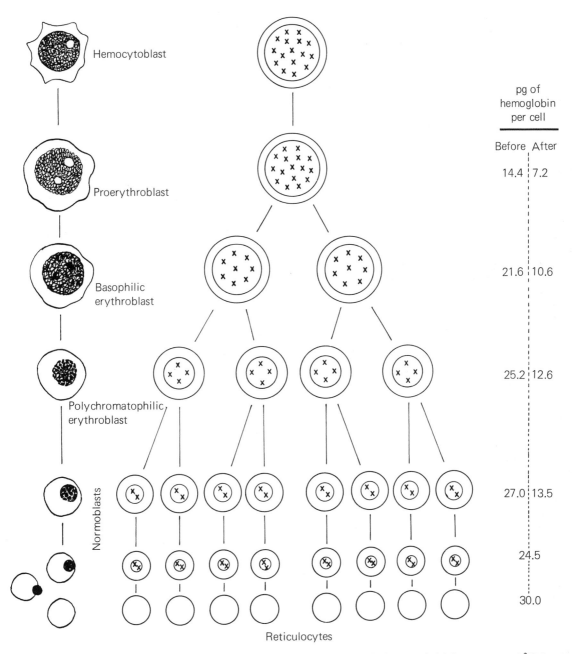

pg of
hemoglobin
per cell

Before After

Figure 14—8. Radioautographic data on the rate of erythrocyte maturation obtained after a single labeling injection of ^{3}H-thymidine. Silver granules in the radioautographs are represented by crosses. In each mitotic division, the number of silver granules per nucleus is reduced by half. In adult bone marrow, hemocytoblasts are few in number, and they rarely divide. The erythrocytes are normally produced by multiplication of proerythroblasts, basophilic erythroblasts, and polychromatophilic erythroblasts.

exists between the multipotential and the committed cell compartments. These *stem cells* (or *hemocytoblasts* of the early workers) appear to be small mononuclear cells similar to mature lymphocytes. The proponents of the *unitarian theory*—Maximow and, more recently, Yoffey—hold that these cells, which are similar to lymphocytes, act as precursors of proerythroblasts. There is speculation that erythropoietin might act as a derepressor of a repressor of genes in the cell

that are responsible for the formation of mRNA necessary for differentiation of the erythroid series, thus increasing their iron uptake, hemoglobin production, and stroma formation. Erythropoietin is essential for the maintenance of the precursor cells by enabling them to continue to proliferate into hemoglobin-synthesizing elements. It has been shown that erythropoietin might alter the hematopoietic internal microenvironment in order to obtain an optimal area for erythropoiesis. The cell cycle of these stem cells, or erythropoietin-responsive or sensitive cells, has a variable resting G_1 phase with an S phase of 6–12 hours and an M (mitotic) phase of 30–45 minutes. Erythropoietin acts on cells at the G_1 level and differentiates them into proerythroblasts. Experimentally, antibodies to erythropoietin can almost completely terminate erythrocyte production. It appears that, in man, after an erythropoietic stimulus (eg, hemorrhage, high altitude), new reticulocytes enter the circulation within approximately 5 days, and it has been calculated that the time required for maturation in each stage is approximately 1 day. The erythropoietic pool accounts for approximately one-thirtieth of the circulating red cell volume.

The blood compartment consists of erythrocytes and a small percentage of reticulocytes. The medullary compartment contains principally nucleated elements (proerythroblasts, normoblasts) and a relatively small number of erythrocytes and reticulocytes (Fig 14–7). The latter remain in the bone marrow for 36–44 hours before entering the circulation.

Since the erythron has no large reserve compartment of mature forms, the concentration of erythrocytes in the blood expresses the rate of medullary production. Therefore, an increase in the production of erythrocytes with no increase in their destruction results in a greater concentration of these cells in the blood.

Under conditions of hypoxia (deficient supply of oxygen to the tissues), the production of erythrocytes increases. This occurs, for example, in people who live at high altitudes where the atmospheric oxygen concentration is low. The same occurs after hemorrhage and in persons with chronic pulmonary dysfunction. Thus, hypoxia is a fundamental physiologic stimulus for erythropoiesis. Oxygen supply and demand regulate the red cell production.

Erythropoietin is a glycoprotein hormone with a molecular weight of 45,800 when obtained from anemic sheep plasma. It contains 30% carbohydrate with a large component, 10.5%, being sialic acid. It is found in the plasma and urines of anemic and hypoxic experimental animals and man and has a half-life of approximately 1–2 days in humans and a few hours in laboratory animals. However, other organs must also produce erythropoietin, for this substance still appears in the blood of animals which have undergone bilateral nephrectomy. Thus, the feedback mechanism of production and release of erythropoietin is related to the need for oxygen in the tissues and the number of circulating erythrocytes carrying oxygen.

Numerous substances are essential for the proper functioning of the erythron and for the production of erythrocytes. Among these are iron, vitamin B_{12}, and folic acid.

Several hormones (eg, thyroxine, testosterone, cortisol) stimulate erythropoiesis, but the mechanisms of action are unknown and probably indirect. Injection of estrogens lowers the red cell count, and growth hormone acts directly upon the erythron; this has been demonstrated by perfusion of the femur of the dog, which is followed by an increase in the number of erythrocytes in the blood and in the percentage of erythroblasts in the bone marrow.

GRANULOCYTIC SERIES

The myeloblast is the most immature recognizable cell in this series and gives rise to the 3 types of granulocytes. The presence of azurophilic granules in the cytoplasm identifies a cell as a promyelocyte. When the various specific cytoplasmic granules are fully developed, the cell is called a *neutrophilic, eosinophilic,* or *basophilic myelocyte* according to the staining characteristics of the granules. The subsequent stages of maturation are from the *myelocyte* to the *metamyelocyte,* then to the *granulocyte with a band-shaped nucleus,* and finally to the *mature granulocyte* (neutrophilic, eosinophilic, or basophilic). Only the last 2 forms are normally seen in the circulation.

Myeloblast

The myeloblast is 15–20 μm in diameter, with a large spherical nucleus which has a delicate chromatin and one or 2 nucleoli. Its cytoplasm is scanty and more basophilic than that of the hemocytoblast from which it is derived, and there is no clear zone around the nucleus (Fig 14–5). Examination with the electron microscope shows many mitochondria, ribosomes, and dispersed granular endoplasmic reticulum.

Promyelocyte

The promyelocyte is smaller than the myeloblast. The nucleus is spherical, at times with a small indentation. The chromatin is coarser than in the myeloblast, and nucleoli are prominent (Fig 14–5).

The cytoplasm of the promyelocyte is more basophilic than that of the myeloblast and contains azurophilic granules, usually at the periphery. These granules are different from the specific granules which appear in the next stage of maturation, the myelocyte. They show a homogeneous density, are surrounded by a membrane, and contain lysosomal enzymes. The granular endoplasmic reticulum is well developed.

Myelocyte

The myelocyte is 16–24 μm in diameter. The nucleus is ovoid and usually eccentric, with coarse chromatin. Different stages in the development of the myelocyte can be identified depending on the number of the specific granules, the appearance of the nucleus (from spherical to ovoid to kidney-shaped), and the relative size of its cytoplasm. A slight cytoplasmic basophilia and azurophilic granules are still encountered (Figs 14–5, 14–9, and 14–10).

What characterizes an immature cell of the granulocytic series as a myelocyte is the beginning of the appearance of the specific granules: *neutrophilic, eo-*

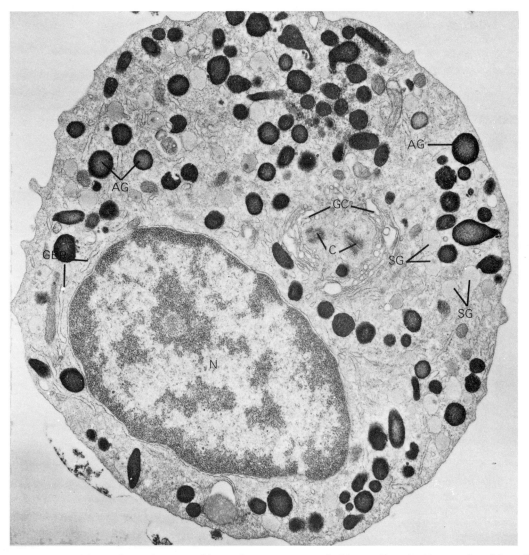

Figure 14—9. Neutrophilic myelocyte from normal human bone marrow treated with peroxidase. At this stage, the cell is smaller than the promyelocyte and the cytoplasm contains 2 different types of granules: (1) large, peroxidase-positive azurophilic granules (AG); and (2) the generally smaller specific granules (SG), which do not stain for peroxidase. Note that the peroxidase reaction product is present only in azurophilic granules and is not seen in the granular endoplasmic reticulum (GER) or Golgi cisternae (GC), which are located around the centriole (C). N, nucleus. × 15,000. (Courtesy of DF Bainton.)

sinophilic, and *basophilic.* The 3 different lines of granulocytes in the peripheral blood can be traced from this stage. The process of further maturation in each cell is characterized principally by changes in the size, shape, and appearance of the nucleus and by relative increases in the amount of cytoplasm. The granules appear first in the perinuclear region and later fill the cytoplasm. They are usually smaller than the azurophilic granules. Depending on the number of granules, the cytoplasm is bluish-pink in neutrophils to orange-salmon in eosinophils to dark purple and spotted in basophils. In this stage, the cell still divides.

Metamyelocyte

The metamyelocyte is characterized by a nucleus with a deep indentation, indicating the beginning of lobe formation. The cytoplasm is a deeper pink color. The nuclear pattern becomes denser, and azurophilic granules are still seen in the cytoplasm. The modifications which characterize the metamyelocytes are not easily identifiable in the basophilic cells, so that the basophilic metamyelocyte is not easily seen (Fig 14—5). The metamyelocyte does not divide.

Granulocyte With a Band-Shaped Nucleus

Before assuming the lobate form typical of a mature cell, the granulocyte goes through an intermediate stage in which the nucleus appears as a curved rod (Fig 14—5). This cell is found in the peripheral blood, and stimulation of granulocytopoiesis is asso-

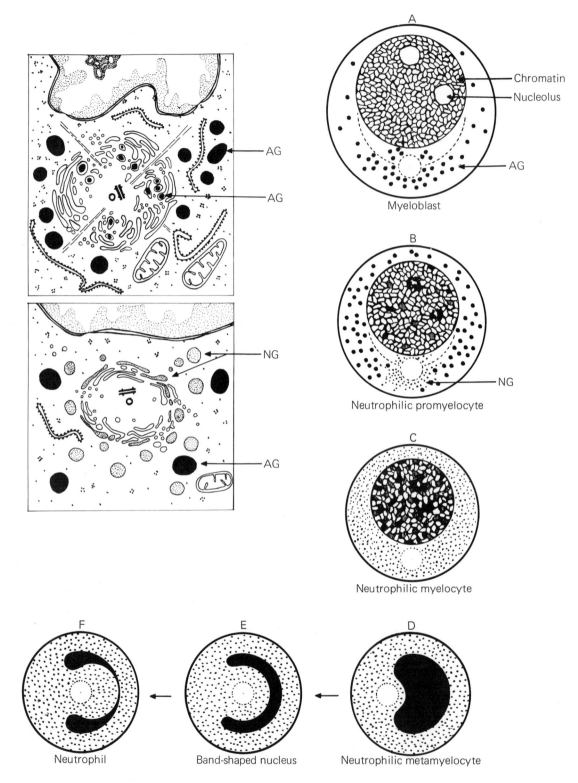

Figure 14–10. Several stages of neutrophil maturation. Note the changes in nuclear shape and structure. The light area close to the nucleus contains the Golgi complex and the 2 centrioles. This is the region where the neutrophilic granules (NG) and the azurophilic granules (AG) first appear. At upper left is shown the ultrastructure of the light juxtanuclear area. Both neutrophilic and azurophilic granules are formed in the cisternae of the Golgi complex. Observe that azurophilic granules are formed deep in the Golgi complex, close to the centrioles, whereas the neutrophilic granules are formed later in the maturation process in the outer cisternae of the Golgi complex.

ciated with the appearance of larger than normal numbers of these cells in the peripheral blood. The normal percentage in blood is 3–5%. The appearance of large numbers of immature cells in the blood is called a "shift to the left" and is of clinical significance.

KINETICS OF THE NEUTROPHILS

The kinetics of the neutrophils are better understood than is the case with other granulocytes, mainly because these cells are more numerous in the blood and thus easier to study.

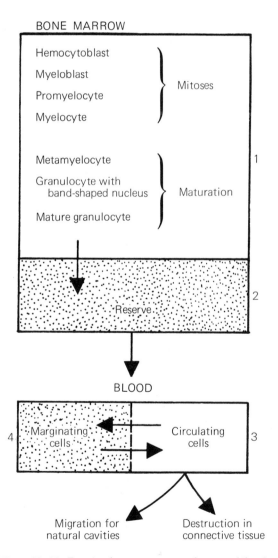

Figure 14–11. Functional compartments of neutrophils. *1:* Medullary formation compartment. *2:* Medullary reserve compartment. *3:* Circulating compartment. *4:* Marginating compartment. The size of each compartment is roughly proportionate to the number of cells.

As shown in Fig 14–11, the neutrophils and their precursor cells may be regarded as occupying 4 different functional compartments: (1) the medullary formation compartment, where new neutrophils are formed; (2) the medullary reserve compartment, in which mature neutrophils remain for a variable period before entering the blood; (3) the circulating compartment, consisting of the neutrophils suspended in the plasma and circulating in the blood vessels; and (4) the marginating compartment, in which neutrophils are present but do not circulate. These latter neutrophils are in the capillaries, temporarily excluded from the circulation by vasoconstriction, or—especially in the lungs—at the periphery of the vessels, adhering to the endothelium, and not in the main bloodstream.

Neutrophils originate in the medullary formation compartment and enter first the medullary reserve compartment and then the circulating compartment. There is a constant interchange of cells between the circulating and marginating compartments. The marginating compartment and the circulating compartment thus contain equal numbers of neutrophils and the medullary compartment contains more neutrophils than are present in the circulating blood. This is why neutrophilia does not necessarily imply an increase in neutrophil production. (*Neutrophilia* is an increase in the number of neutrophils in the circulation and *neutropenia* a decrease.) Intense muscular activity or administration of epinephrine, for example, causes the neutrophils in the marginating compartment to move into the circulating compartment, with an apparent neutrophilia even though neutrophil production has not increased.

Neutrophilia may also result from the liberation of greater numbers of neutrophils of the medullary reserve compartment. This type of neutrophilia is transitory and is followed by a "recovery" period during which no neutrophils are liberated.

Increased production of neutrophils without neutrophilia occurs when there is an increase in the number of cells in the marginating compartment. An increase in the functional marginating compartment absorbs the excess production of cells by the bone marrow and maintains a normal level of circulating neutrophils.

The neutrophilia that occurs during the course of bacterial infections is due to an increase in neutrophil production and a shorter stay of these cells in the medullary reserve compartment. In such cases, immature forms such as neutrophils with band-shaped nuclei, neutrophilic metamyelocytes, and even myelocytes may appear in the bloodstream. The neutrophilia that occurs during infection is of longer duration than that which occurs as a result of intense muscular activity.

Control of Neutrophilogenesis

There seems to be some mechanism that stimulates the production of neutrophils by the bone marrow which is set in motion by a decrease in the number of these cells. This conclusion arises from the observa-

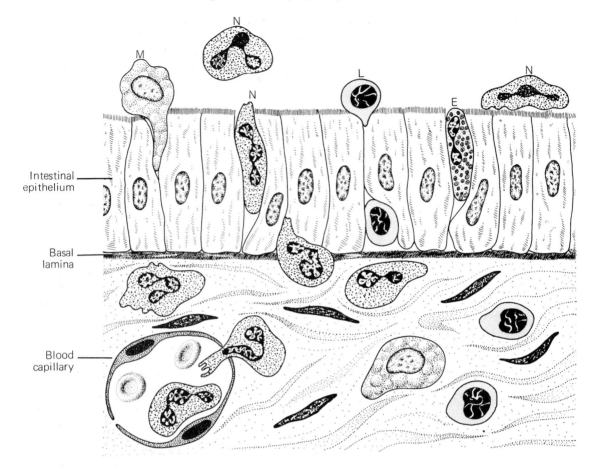

Intestinal epithelium

Basal lamina

Blood capillary

Figure 14—12. Migration of leukocytes through the simple columnar epithelium of the intestinal mucosa. By ameboid movement, leukocytes cross the basal lamina, pass between the epithelial cells, and enter the intestinal lumen. In this way, many leukocytes are destroyed and are replaced by new ones. Note the monocyte (M), the lymphocyte (L), the neutrophilic granulocytes (N), and the eosinophilic granuloycyte (E).

tion that destruction of neutrophils (eg, by the injection of an antineutrophil antibody) immediately stimulates the production of these cells. Leukapheresis, which consists of withdrawing blood and reinfusing it after removal of most of the leukocytes, also causes neutrophilia, and this observation rules out the possibility that a substance liberated by dead neutrophils (present in experiments with antineutrophil antibody) stimulates the production of these cells by the bone marrow. These and similar experiments suggest that the production of neutrophils is controlled by a humoral mechanism which has not yet been identified.

Destruction of Granulocytes

By various technics, including radioautography performed after the injection of labeled thymidine, it has been shown that the bone marrow of a man weighing 70 kg generates 150×10^9 granulocytes per day.

Because the number of these cells in the blood remains constant, an equivalent destruction of granulocytes must occur in the same period of time. The process by which this destruction is effected is not com-

pletely clear, though some of the means by which granulocytes are destroyed are known.

It is known that the granulocytes pass through the blood capillary wall and appear in the connective tissues. This phenomenon is widespread throughout the body. The granulocytes leave the vessels at random, regardless of their age, and once they have reached the connective tissue it seems that they rarely return to the blood. There occurs, therefore, a constant and unidirectional flow of granulocytes into the connective tissues of all organs, where many of these cells die.

Destruction of a large number of granulocytes occurs also in the alimentary tract and in the lungs. These cells pass through the mucosa, principally where the epithelium is simple (stomach, intestines), to the lumen of the alimentary tract, where they die (Fig 14—12). They also die in the lung alveoli after passing through the lining of simple squamous epithelium. The half-life of circulating neutrophils is about 6—7 hours.

LYMPHOCYTIC & MONOCYTIC SERIES

Study of the precursor cells of lymphocytes and monocytes is particularly difficult because these cells do not contain specific cytoplasmic granules nor the nuclear lobulation that is present in the granulocytes, both of which facilitate the distinction between young and mature forms. Lymphocytes and monocytes are distinguished mainly on the basis of size, chromatin structure, and the presence of nucleoli in smear preparations. As the lymphocytic and monocytic cells mature, their chromatin becomes more compact, the nucleoli become less visible, and the cells decrease in size.

The circulating lymphocytes originate mainly in the lymphatic tissue of the central and peripheral lymphoid organs and, to a lesser extent, in the bone marrow. The precursor cell is the *lymphoblast,* which forms the mature *lymphocytes.* However, many lymphocytes of the blood and lymph have a great capacity for differentiation. It is not possible to distinguish the lymphocytes with this capacity by light microscopy, but electron and scanning microscopy have revealed differences between mature lymphocytes which appeared identical under the light microscope. It must be concluded, therefore, that there is a circulating cell which is morphologically indistinguishable from a mature lymphocyte which is a stem cell of the lymphocytic series and in this way functionally similar to the lymphoblast. Many researchers maintain that this cell is comparable to the hemocytoblast and can, after proper stimulation, give rise to any type of blood cell.

Lymphoblast

The lymphoblast is the largest cell of the lymphocytic series. It is spherical, with a basophilic cytoplasm and no azurophilic granules. The chromatin is relatively condensed and in blocks, foreshadowing the chromatin of a mature lymphocyte. The lymphoblast has 2 or 3 nucleoli.

Prolymphocyte

The prolymphocyte is smaller than the lymphoblast, has a basophilic cytoplasm, and may contain azurophilic granules. The chromatin of the prolymphocyte is condensed, but to a lesser degree than that of the medium-sized and small lymphocytes. The nucleoli are not easily visible because of the condensed chromatin.

The prolymphocyte gives rise directly to the circulating lymphocyte.

Monocyte

The monocyte derives from a stem cell in the bone marrow. It then is liberated into the peripheral blood and from there enters the tissues, where it is transformed into a macrophage or a reticulum cell. The precursor cell cannot be identified accurately. Some cells called monoblasts are considered the precursor cells and show a characteristic positive alpha-naphthol-

acetate esterase reaction. The average intravascular life span of monocytes is estimated to be between 30–72 hours, and they leave the bloodstream by diapedesis. Their life span in the tissues may be as long as 75 days, and these cells are seldom seen in division.

MEGAKARYOCYTIC SERIES

In adults, the platelets originate in the red bone marrow by fragmentation of the cytoplasm of the mature *granular megakaryocytes.* These in turn arise by differentiation of the *megakaryoblasts.*

Megakaryoblast

The megakaryoblast is 15–50 μm in diameter and has a large ovoid or kidney-shaped nucleus with numerous nucleoli. The cytoplasm of this cell is homogeneous and intensely basophilic (rich in free ribosomes) (Fig 14–13).

Megakaryocyte

This is a giant cell (35–150 μm in diameter) with an irregularly lobulated nucleus, coarse chromatin, and no visible nucleoli. It has abundant and slightly basophilic cytoplasm. The megakaryocyte contains numerous azurophilic granules which at times occupy most of the cytoplasm. These granules will form the chromomeres of the platelets (Fig 14–13).

Electron microscopy reveals that the cytoplasm of the megakaryoblast is rich in free ribosomes and contains very little smooth and granular endoplasmic reticulum. Membrane-surrounded granules corresponding to the azurophilic granules seen under the light microscope appear during the process of maturation of the granular megakaryocyte. These granules are formed in the Golgi apparatus and are later distributed throughout the cytoplasm. With maturation of the megakaryocyte there also occurs an increase in the quantity of smooth membranes which will then form *demarcation channels.* The membranes finally fuse and give rise to the membrane of the platelets.

In smear preparations of bone marrow, it is possible to observe platelets which are still bound to the cytoplasm of the megakaryocyte and in the various phases of separation. Furthermore, in cultures of megakaryocytes, the liberation of platelets can be observed under the microscope, which proves their megakaryocytic origin. In certain forms of *thrombocytopenic purpura,* a disease in which the number of blood platelets is reduced, several platelets appear bound to the cytoplasm of the megakaryocytes, indicating a defect in the liberation mechanism of these corpuscles.

In observations carried out using platelets marked in vitro with radioactive isotopes (^{32}P-labeled diisopropylfluorophosphate, ^{32}P, ^{35}S) and afterwards reinjected, the life span of these corpuscles was found to be approximately 10 days.

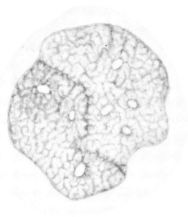

Megakaryoblast

Megakaryocyte

Platelets

Figure 14–13. Cells of the megakaryocytic series. They are shown in bone marrow smear with Romanovsky staining.

INTRAUTERINE HEMATOPOIESIS

There are 3 ill-defined stages of intrauterine hematopoiesis: a *primordial* or *prehepatic phase,* a *hepatosplenothymic phase,* and a *medullolymphatic* or *definitive phase.*

When one of these stages is initiated, the predominant processes of the previous phase persist for some time, though gradually decreasing in importance (Fig 14–14).

All formed elements of the blood are of mesenchymal origin. In organs of double embryonic origin such as the liver and thymus (endoderm and mesoderm), the cells originating in the mesoderm are responsible for hematopoiesis.

Primordial or Prehepatic Phase

In humans, the first blood cells appear in the mesoderm of the yolk sac during the third week of intrauterine life. The *blood islands* consist of elongated clusters of mesenchymal cells. The endothelium of the first vessels originates in the most superficial cells of these islands; the innermost cells become spherical and differentiate into hemocytoblasts.

By fusion of the endothelial cells of contiguous islands, the first blood vessels are formed. These vessels soon establish communication with those that appear in the body of the embryo. This permits the cells formed in the yolk sac to penetrate and circulate in the body of the embryo.

The hemocytoblasts of the yolk sac divide within the vessels to form the *primitive erythroblasts* (megaloblastic period erythropoiesis), which are larger than the *definitive erythroblasts.* The majority of the erythroblasts formed in the yolk sac do not lose their nuclei, so that at this stage the red cells are predominantly nucleated. Only at the end of the primordial phase do some erythrocytes appear as a result of extrusion of the nucleus from the erythroblasts.

The cells that arise by primitive red cell erythropoiesis are larger than those that develop as a result of definitive erythropoiesis, and this process is known as megaloblastic erythropoiesis.

During the primordial phase, the blood contains only the above-mentioned red cell series plus chains of Gower hemoglobin. No leukocytes or platelets are present.

Hepatosplenothymic Phase

This period begins in the second month, with hematopoiesis taking place in the liver and spleen. Subsequently, the thymus also starts producing blood cells, almost exclusively lymphocytes. In the mesenchyme which invades the endodermal primordium of the liver appear precursor cells of the granulocytes, megakaryocytes, and definitive erythroblasts. Of the latter, a large number reach the blood without losing their nuclei. Although hepatic hematopoiesis begins to decline in the fifth month, it persists until some weeks

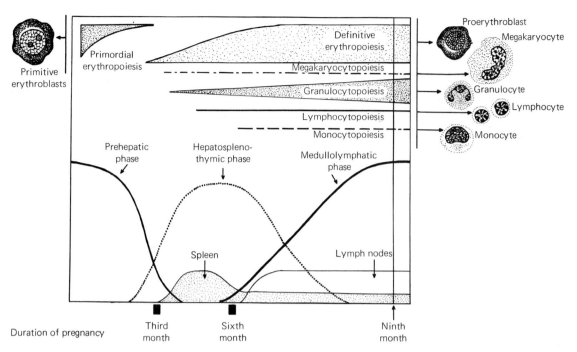

Figure 14—14. The main events in intrauterine hemocytopoiesis.

after birth. In the adult, the liver is not considered a hematopoietic organ.

The spleen produces mainly cells of the red cell series and, in smaller quantity, granulocytes and platelets. The production of lymphocytes in the spleen becomes important as birth becomes imminent.

The thymus begins to form lymphocytes in the second month of intrauterine life and produces almost no other type of blood cell. The number of erythroblasts and granulocytes produced in the thymus is insignificant.

Medullolymphatic Phase

The clavicle is the first bone to show hematopoietic activity. Its bone marrow begins to function between the second and third month of intrauterine life. The marrow of other bones soon begins to function, and in the fourth month bone marrow hematopoiesis is significant.

The bone marrow shows great erythrocytic, granulocytic, and megakaryocytic activity. Lymphocytes and monocytes are also produced.

During this period—and close to birth—the lymph nodes (which since the beginning of their existence have been lymphocyte-producing organs) become very active. Before birth, the lymph nodes may show discrete erythropoietic activity.

It is during this medullolymphatic period that a more functional separation is established between myeloid tissue (forming erythrocytes, platelets, and granulocytes) and lymphatic tissue (forming the lymphocytes).

RETICULOENDOTHELIAL SYSTEM (RES)

Aschoff in 1924 introduced the concept of the existence of a group of mesynchymal cells distributed throughout the body with different morphologic characteristics and different names but sharing the important properties of phagocytosis and storage of vital dyes. In this so-called *reticuloendothelial system (RES)* were incorporated all of the macrophages described by Metchnikoff in 1893 and the phagocytic endothelia of sinusoids seen in the liver, adrenal, spleen, pituitary, and bone marrow. Many of these cells were associated with reticular fibers.

Recently, this concept has been modified by following the further development and movement within the body of radioactively labeled cells. It was found that the so-called phagocytic cells of the sinusoids are not more phagocytic than endothelia of other capillaries and that what was observed as phagocytosis in the light microscope was actually a function of the perivascular macrophages of sinusoids. Since it has been shown that the Kupffer cells of the liver arise from the monocytes of blood or their precursors, which can also be transformed into macrophages, it has been suggested that the concept of a reticuloendothelial system be abandoned in favor of a *mononuclear phagocyte system* originating in the monocyte and its precursors and including all of its derivatives in the tissues—fixed or free macrophages in connective tissue and lymph tissue, Kupffer cells, alveolar macrophages, microglia cells, and perivascular macrophages of sinusoids. The cells of the mononuclear phagocyte system have receptor sites for immunoglobulins on their plasma membranes, attach themselves firmly to glass, and originate in the bone marrow in the form of promonocytes and monocytes.

• • •

References

Bainton DF, Farquhar MG: Segregation and packaging of granule enzymes in eosinophilic leukocytes. J Cell Biol 45:54, 1970.

Behnke O: An electron microscope study of the rat megacaryocyte. 2. Some aspects of platelet release and microtubules. J Ultrastruct Res 26:111, 1969.

Berman I: The ultrastructure of erythroblastic islands and reticular cells in mouse bone marrow. J Ultrastruct Res 17:291, 1967.

Bessis MC, Breton-Gorius J: Iron metabolism in the bone marrow as seen by electron microscopy: A critical review. Blood 19:635, 1962.

Bierman HR (editor): Leukopoiesis in health and disease. Ann New York Acad Sc 113:511, 1964.

Boyum A & others: Kinetics of cell proliferation of murine bone marrow cells cultured in diffusion chambers: Effect of hypoxia, bleeding, erythropoietin injections, polycythemia, and irradiations of the host. Blood 40:174, 1972.

Caffrey RW, Everett NB, Rieke WO: Radioautographic studies of reticular and blast cells in the hemopoietic tissues of the rat. Anat Record 155:41, 1966.

Fedorko ME: Formation of cytoplasmic granules in human eosinophilic myelocytes: An electron microscope autoradiographic study. Blood 31:188, 1968.

Fedorko ME, Hirsch JG: Cytoplasmic granule formation in myelocytes: An electron microscope radioautographic study on the mechanism of formation of cytoplasmic granules in rabbit heterophilic myelocytes. J Cell Biol 29:307, 1966.

Gowans JL: Life-span, recirculation and transformation of lymphocytes. Int Rev Exp Pathol 5:1, 1966.

Leblond CP, Sainte-Marie G: Models for lymphocyte and plasmocyte formation. In: *Haemopoiesis: Cell Production and Its Regulation.* Wolstenholme GE, O'Connor M (editors). Little, Brown, 1960.

Marchesi VT, Florey HW: Electron microscopy on the emigration of leukocytes. Quart J Exp Physiol 45:343, 1960.

Moore MAS, Metcalf D: Ontogeny of the haemopoietic system: Yolk sac origin of in vivo and in vitro colony forming cells in the developing mouse embryo. Brit J Haemat 18:279, 1970.

Spinak JL, Marmor J, Dickerman HW: Studies on splenic erythropoiesis in the mouse. 1. Ribosomal ribonucleic acid metabolism. J Lab Clin Med 79:526, 1972.

Thomas DB, Yoffey JM: Human fetal haemopoiesis. 1. The cellular composition of fetal blood. Brit J Haemat 8:280, 1962.

Yoffey JM, Courtice FC: *Lymphatics, Lymph and Lymphoid Tissue.* Harvard Univ Press, 1960.

15 . . .
Blood- & Lymph-Forming Organs

The cells of blood and lymph, some of which have a relatively short life span, are constantly being replaced by new cells formed in the bone marrow and lymphoid organs. The parenchyma of these organs consists of *hematopoietic* or *reticular* tissue, a variety of connective tissue already discussed in Chapter 5. Hematopoietic tissue is a 3-dimensional network of reticular fibers, blood vessels, sinusoids, and *reticular cells* whose meshes contain a variety of free cells.

Reticular cells—in the older literature sometimes called primitive reticular cells—are thought by some investigators to be derived from the mesenchyme and retain all of the potentialities of embryonic mesenchymal cells. They have a large ovoid, pale nucleus with finely dispersed chromatin. The nuclear envelope is visible under the microscope because there is a slight condensation of chromatin attached to its inner surface. One or 2 large nucleoli are usually found. Around the nucleus there is a small amount of cytoplasm from which arise long branching processes which are usually associated with reticular fibers. These processes are difficult to observe with the light microscope.

In man there are 2 types of hematopoietic tissue: *myeloid tissue,* found in the bone marrow, which forms erythrocytes, granular leukocytes, platelets, and monocytes; and *lymphoid tissue,* responsible for the formation of lymphocytes and cells that derive from them. Lymphoid tissue is found in several parts of the body but especially in the mucosa of the digestive or respiratory tract and in isolated organs such as the lymph nodes, spleen, and thymus.

Besides making cells for the blood and lymph, the hematopoietic tissue is also responsible for the synthesis of antibodies.

BONE MARROW

Bone marrow is found in the medullary canals of long bones and in the cavities of spongy bones. Two types have been described according to their appearance on gross examination: *red, hematogenous,* or *active bone marrow,* whose color is due to the presence of numerous erythrocytes and their precursors in several phases of maturation; and *yellow bone marrow,* rich

in adipose cells, which does not produce blood cells except upon conversion or transformation into red bone marrow induced by severe bleeding or hypoxia. In newborns, all of the bone marrow is red and is therefore active in the production of blood cells. As the child grows, most of the bone marrow changes into the yellow variety; in adults, red bone marrow is found only in the sternum, the vertebrae, the ribs, the clavicles, the bones of the pelvis, and the diploë of the skull bones; in young adults, red marrow is found also in the proximal epiphyses of the femur and humerus.

In both red and yellow bone marrow, small amounts of lymphoid tissue may form lymphatic nodules, the sites of proliferation of small lymphocytes. The bone marrow has no lymph vessels.

Active (Red) Bone Marrow

Like hematopoietic tissue in general, red bone marrow consists of reticular cells (some with a phagocytic tendency becoming macrophages) associated with reticular fibers and cells of the erythroid series in different stages of maturation. These elements (cells and fibers) form a sponge traversed by numerous sinusoid capillaries whose lining contains endothelial cells. Among the above-mentioned cells there is a variable number of adipose cells; in many cases, the boundary between red and yellow marrow is not clear.

The reticular cells, macrophages, and adipose cells are usually attached to the supporting stromal connective tissue. In the meshes of the myeloid tissue, there is a profusion of free cells consisting of blood elements (erythrocytes, granulocytes, monocytes, and platelets) and their precursors as described in Chapter 14. The bone marrow may present still other connective cells—especially plasma cells—in different phases of maturation.

When they reach maturation, the blood cells formed in myeloid tissue are carried by the circulating blood across the walls and into the lumens of the sinusoids. The incomplete walls of the sinusoids and their basement membranes facilitate penetration of the newly formed cells.

The free cells of the myeloid tissue have a tendency to remain in groups. In each group, one kind of cell predominates in different phases of maturation.

The blood that comes from the arterioles penetrates into the sinusoids and is there enriched by the elements formed in the meshes of the myeloid tissue. From the sinusoids, the blood passes to veins which leave the bone marrow.

The main functions of the red bone marrow are in the production of blood cells, the destruction of erythrocytes and the subsequent storage of iron, and the production of undifferentiated cells which are carried by the blood to the central lymphoid organs. These cells are precursors of B and T lymphocytes.

By inoculating different bone marrow cells into animals whose lymphoid organs have been destroyed by irradiation, it is possible to show that lymphocyte precursors come from bone marrow. Only bone marrow cells are able to repopulate the destroyed central organs of the lymphoid tissue. All others—even cells from peripheral lymphoid tissue—lack the capacity to promote this regeneration.

Iron is stored in bone marrow as *ferritin* and *hemosiderin* in the cytoplasm of reticular cells and other macrophagic cells (Fig 15–1). However, large amounts of ferritin and hemosiderin are also stored outside the bone marrow in hepatocytes, skeletal muscle fibers, and spleen macrophages.

Ferritin contains iron and a protein with a molecular weight of 480,000 called *apoferritin*. This protein makes an envelope around a central core of colloid iron. The whole particle has a diameter of 12 nm, and the iron core has a diameter of 5.5 nm. Under the electron microscope, each ferritin particle shows 4–6 electron-dense subunits, which permits the identification of ferritin in electron micrographs.

Hemosiderin is a heterogeneous complex containing apoferritin, other proteins, carbohydrates, lipids, and other molecules. The iron content is higher in hemosiderin than in ferritin. Hemosiderin exists in storage cells as granules 1–2 μm in diameter demonstrable by cytochemical reactions for iron.

Yellow Bone Marrow

In the yellow bone marrow there is a great predominance of adipose cells with an admixture of macrophages, undifferentiated mesenchymal cells, and reticular cells. Under stimulation, the reticular cells may proliferate, giving rise to myeloid cells and transforming the yellow marrow into red marrow again.

The yellow bone marrow has 2 main functions: It is a storage organ, by virtue of its richness in fat; and it represents a reserve of hematopoietic tissue, becoming the site of production of cells in clinical situations marked by frequent hemorrhages or excessive destruction of erythrocytes.

LYMPHOID TISSUE

The basic histologic organization of lymphoid tissue is similar to that of myeloid tissue. It contains reticular fibers and different types of fixed cells identical or similar to those found in bone marrow. Adipose cells, however, are not present. An important difference between myeloid and lymphoid tissue is the population of free cells, which in the latter is represented mainly by mature and precursor lymphocytic cells and their derivatives. The free cells are found in

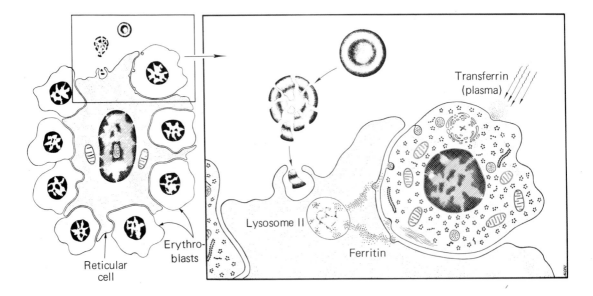

Figure 15–1. Phagocytosis of broken erythrocytes by bone marrow macrophages and transference of iron to erythroblasts. Engulfed erythrocytes are digested in secondary lysosomes and the iron is released as ferritin by a process which can be compared to reverse pinocytosis. The ferritin is taken up by the erythroblasts by means of true pinocytosis. Very often, erythroblasts in several stages of maturation are located in infoldings of the phagocytic cell cytoplasm. Erythroblasts receive iron also from transferrin, an iron-carrying β-globulin in blood plasma.

the meshes of a 3-dimensional network composed of reticular cells, macrophages, and reticular fibers.

There are 3 types of lymphoid tissue: *loose lymphoid tissue,* in which the meshwork of fixed cells predominates; *dense lymphoid tissue,* where free cells (mainly lymphocytes) predominate; and *nodular lymphoid tissue,* which also contains a predominance of free cells but appears as typical spherical structures called *lymphatic nodules.* These nodules are found in all of the lymphoid organs except the thymus.

Lymphatic nodules—also called lymphatic follicles—can also be found isolated in the loose connective tissue of several organs, mainly in the lamina propria of the digestive tract, the upper respiratory tract, and the urinary passages. These nodules do not have a connective tissue capsule and may occur in groups forming accumulations such as *Peyer's patches* in the ileum. Nodules are temporary structures and may disappear and reappear in the same place.

Each lymphatic nodule is a round structure which may attain a diameter of 0.2—1 mm (Figs 15—2 and 15—3). In histologic sections, the nodules are strongly stained by hematoxylin as a consequence of their richness in lymphocytes. The interior of the nodule often shows a less densely stained region called the *germinal center* (Fig 15—2). This is because the central region of many nodules is rich in immature lymphocytes with lightly staining nuclei; for this reason, it contrasts with smaller lymphocytes, which have darker nuclei and predominate in the periphery of the nodule, which is not well defined. At times they exhibit many mitotic figures. The presence of a germinal center may appear and disappear in one nodule according to its functional state.

In nodules in different phases of maturation, there is a predominance of free cells, principally *lymphoblasts;* small, medium, and large *lymphocytes; plasmablasts;* and *plasma cells.*

The activity of lymphatic nodules depends upon several factors including the effects of the bacterial flora. In animals kept in sterile conditions, nodules with germinal centers are rare. The opposite situation occurs in some infections, where the production of lymphocytes increases and germinal centers become frequent.

In newborns as well as in animals grown in aseptic environments, lymphatic nodules are very rare, which indicates that their formation depends on antigenic stimuli. In localized inflammations, there is an increase in the number of lymphatic nodules close to the inflamed site, and most nodules have a germinal center.

LYMPH NODES

The lymph nodes (sometimes called lymph glands) are encapsulated round or kidney-shaped organs composed of lymphoid tissue. They are distributed throughout the body, always along the course of the lymphatic vessels, which carry lymph into the thoracic and the right lymphatic ducts. They are found in the axillas and in the groin, along the great vessels of the neck, and in large numbers in the thorax, the abdomen, and especially in the mesentery. Kidney-shaped lymph nodes present a convex side and a depression, the hilus, through which the arteries and nerves penetrate and the veins leave the organ. The shape and internal structure of lymph nodes vary greatly, but all have the basic pattern of organization described below and illustrated in Figs 15—2 and 15—3.

The lymph which crosses the lymph node penetrates through the *afferent lymphatic vessels,* which enter at the convex edge of the organ, and exits through the *efferent lymphatic vessels* of the hilus (Fig 15—2).

The capsule of dense connective tissue which covers the lymph nodes sends trabeculae to their interior, dividing the parenchyma into incomplete compartments. The reticular fibers unite with this connective tissue and extend to the parenchyma, thus providing a network in which the cells are freely suspended.

Each lymph node has a *cortical region,* situated below the capsule (except at the hilus), and a *medullary region* which occupies the center of the organ and its hilus. The cortex of the lymph node differs from that of the thymus because it contains lymphatic nodules (Figs 15—2 and 15—3).

Besides the cortical and medullary regions, which are the 2 regions classically described, there is a *paracortical zone,* poorly defined morphologically but functionally distinct. The lymphocytes of the paracortical zone—the T lymphocytes—have special properties which make them different from the other lymphocytes of the lymph node.

The cortical region is composed of loose lymphoid tissue that forms the *subcapsular* and *peritrabecular sinuses* and of lymphatic nodules (Figs 15—2 and 15—3) which may present germinal centers. The lymphatic sinuses are spaces lined intermittently by endothelial cells, with some reticular fibers, forming part of the loose wall and containing, in the lumen, many lymphocytes and free macrophages. They receive the lymph brought by afferent vessels and carry it toward the medullary region.

The medullary region consists of the *medullary cords,* composed of dense lymphoid tissue—where, usually, many plasma cells are encountered—and the *medullary sinuses* (loose lymphoid tissue), which receive and circulate the lymph from the sinuses of the cortical region (Fig 15—2). Medullary sinuses communicate with the efferent lymphatic vessels through which the lymph leaves the lymph node.

The paracortical or diffuse cortical zone consists of dense lymphoid tissue localized among the tissue of the deep cortical region—mainly between the cortical and the medullary regions.

Lymphocytes found in the paracortical region disappear when an animal has its thymus removed, especially if this is done at birth. This shows that they are *thymus-dependent,* belonging to· the population of *T*

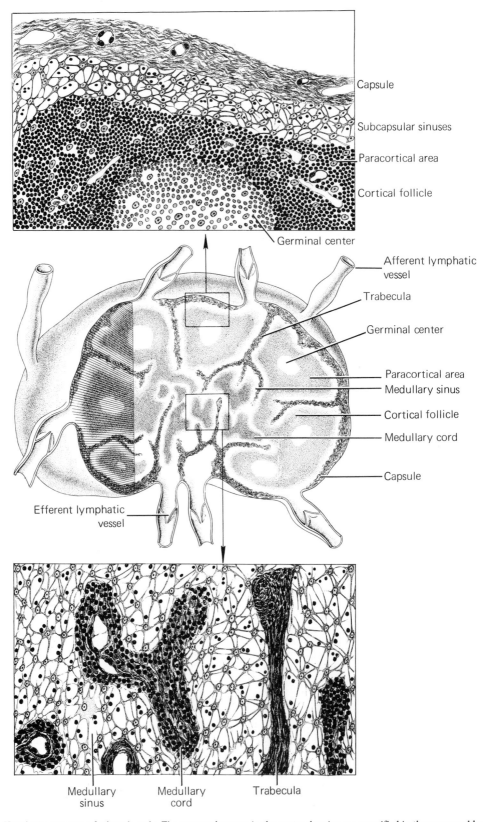

Figure 15–2. Histologic structure of a lymph node. The rectangular areas in the center drawing are magnified in the upper and lower drawings. The cortical layer is composed mainly of lymphatic nodules, whose germinal centers (lightly stained core of each nodule) are clearly seen in the center drawing.

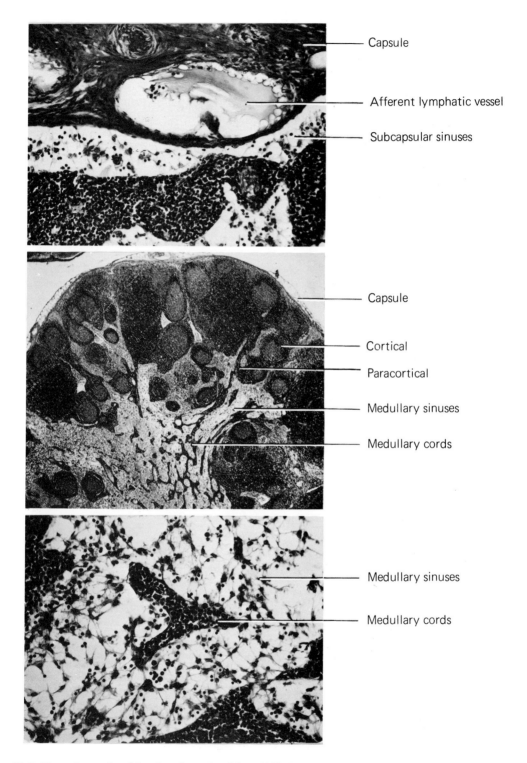

Capsule

Afferent lymphatic vessel

Subcapsular sinuses

Capsule

Cortical

Paracortical

Medullary sinuses

Medullary cords

Medullary sinuses

Medullary cords

Figure 15—3. Photomicrographs of lymph nodes, reduced from X 30 *(center)* and X 200 *(lower* and **upper)** magnification. H&E stain.

lymphocytes. They derive from precursor cells that migrate from the bone marrow to the thymus, where they divide by mitosis. T lymphocytes are most numerous in blood and lymph and are found also in the periarterial sheaths of the spleen and other lymphoid organs. They are responsible for cell-mediated immune responses such as delayed immune reactions and graft rejections. As explained in Chapter 14, these cells colonize the thymus-dependent zones in the peripheral lymphoid organs with long-lived lymphocytes which recirculate and are capable of further replication under proper stimulation.

Histophysiology

The lymph nodes are compared to filters through which the lymph flows and is cleared of foreign particles before proceeding to other parts of the body. Because the lymph nodes are spread throughout the body, the lymph formed in the tissues must cross at least one lymph node before entering the bloodstream.

Each node receives lymph from a limited region of the body of which it is said to be a *satellite node.* Malignant tumors often metastasize via satellite lymph nodes.

The afferent lymph penetrates through the convex side of the nodes, is collected by the subcapsular sinuses, passes to the peritrabecular and medullary sinuses, and leaves the lymph nodes by the efferent lymphatic vessels. The lymph crosses the nodes through passageways created by the loose lymphoid tissue that constitutes the sinuses, which are much more permeable to lymph than is the dense lymphoid tissue of the nodules. While the lymph is passing slowly through the sinuses, there is a close contact between the macrophages and the constituents of the lymph, facilitating the phagocytosis of foreign or other particles contained in the lymph.

Most antigens, when they are phagocytosed, start an immunologic response. In most of these situations, there is a great increase in the number of plasma cells and a consequent enlargement of the affected lymph node. In resting lymph nodes, only a few plasma cells are found (usually 1–3% of the total cell population).

The antibody-synthesizing plasma cells originate, in lymph nodes as well as in other lymphoid organs, from stimulated or sensitized small lymphocytes which are modified to form a larger cell called an *immunoblast* or *pyroninophil cell.* This cell divides several times in developing from its immature (immunoblast) stage into the plasma cell, which then is capable of synthesizing antibodies specific to the antigen.

The lymphocytes which are carried by the lymph to the bloodstream return to the lymphoid tissue and are again carried by the lymph to the blood. Blood lymphocytes return to lymphoid tissue by crossing the walls of postcapillary venules located in the paracortical zone of the lymph nodes. These venules are lined by tall cuboid endothelial cells, and their walls are very

Epithelium with some infiltration   Heavily infiltrated epithelium

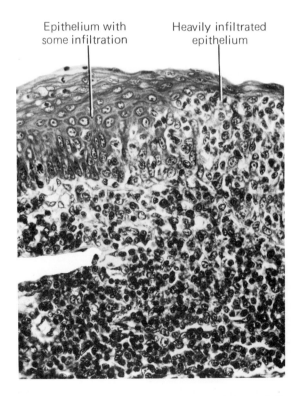

Figure 15–4. Photomicrograph of a palatine tonsil. The stratified squamous epithelium is infiltrated by lymphocytes. H&E stain, X 400.

thick in comparison with venules with lumens of the same size. They become thin-walled after thymectomy at birth. It may be speculated that lymphocytes possess membrane polysaccharides (glycocalyx) which have receptor molecules in the endothelial cells of those venules. This would permit the 2 cells to recognize each other. Lymphocytes which cross between the endothelial cells of the venules penetrate the paracortical zone and medullary sinuses and leave the node by the efferent vessels together with newly formed lymphocytes. In this way, most T lymphocytes recirculate many times.

Recirculation of lymphocytes also occurs through venules found in the spleen and in Peyer's patches of the ileum. However, the participation of other lymphoid organs in lymphocyte recirculation is negligible.

TONSILS

Tonsils are organs composed of agglomerations of lymphoid tissue under the epithelium of the mouth and pharynx. According to their location, they are called the *palatine tonsils,* the *pharyngeal tonsil,* and the *lingual tonsils.* In contrast to lymph nodes, the tonsils are not situated along the course of lymphatic vessels. Tonsils produce lymphocytes, many of which cross the epithelium and are deposited in the mouth and pharynx.

Palatine Tonsils

The 2 palatine tonsils are located in the oral part of the pharynx. The dense lymphoid tissue present in these tonsils forms, under the squamous stratified epithelium, a band which contains lymphatic nodules, generally with germinal centers. Each tonsil has 10–20 epithelial invaginations which penetrate deeply into the parenchyma, forming the *crypts,* which contain in their lumens desquamated epithelial cells, live and dead lymphocytes, and bacteria. They may appear like purulent spots during episodes of tonsillitis (Figs 15–4 and 15–5).

Separating the lymphoid tissue from subjacent organs is a band of dense connective tissue called the *capsule* of the tonsil. This capsule acts usually as a barrier against spreading tonsillar infections.

Pharyngeal Tonsil

This is a single tonsil situated in the superoposterior portion of the pharynx. It is covered by ciliated, cylindric, pseudostratified epithelium which is typical of the respiratory tract. Areas of stratified epithelium may also be observed.

The pharyngeal tonsil is composed of pleats of mucosa and shows diffuse lymphoid tissue and lymphatic nodules. It has no crypts.

The capsule of the pharyngeal tonsil is thinner than the capsules of the palatine tonsils.

Lingual Tonsils

The lingual tonsils are smaller and more numerous than the others. They are situated at the base of the tongue and are lined by squamous stratified epithelium. Each has a single crypt (Fig 15–5).

THYMUS

The thymus is a primary or central lymphoid organ situated in the mediastinum at about the level of the great vessels of the heart. It consists of lobules measuring about 0.5–2 mm in diameter and partially separated by septa of connective tissue of mesenchymal origin which envelops the organ (Fig 15–6).

In contrast to lymph nodes, the thymus has no afferent lymphatics or lymphatic nodules. Each lobule has a peripheral zone of dense *cortical* lymphoid tissue—resulting from the higher concentration of thymocytes or T lymphocytes—which surrounds a lightly staining central zone of loose lymphoid tissue, the *medullary zone* (Fig 15–6). The cortical and medullary zones of a lobule are continuous with those of adjacent lobules, and serial sections show that the parenchyma of the thymus is continuous. In the medulla are found *Hassall's corpuscles,* each consisting of flattened epithelial cells concentrically arranged, which are characteristic of the thymus (Fig 15–9).

Other lymphoid organs originate exclusively from mesenchyme, whereas the thymus has a double embryologic origin. Its lymphocytes arise from mesenchymal cells which invade an epithelial primordium that has its origin in the third and sometimes also the fourth pharyngeal pouch.

During intrauterine life, the thymus is colonized by lymphocyte-forming cells which come from the blood islands of the yolk sac and probably also from the hematopoietic tissue of the liver. After birth, it is believed that these colonizing cells originate only in the bone marrow.

The intense lymphocytic proliferation which takes place during embryologic development pulls apart the epithelial cells, but, since these cells have desmosomes, they remain attached to each other at the end of their processes, thus forming the epithelial blood-thymus barrier of the cortex of the thymus.

Thymus Cells

Both the cortical and the medullary zones have the same cellular types, although in different proportions. The most abundant are T lymphocytes and their precursor cells in various stages of differentiation and maturation and the *epithelial reticular cells* (Fig 15–7). Besides these cells, the thymus has a few mesenchymal reticular cells some of which are phagocytic.

The *epithelial reticular cells* are morphologically very similar to the reticular cells of mesenchymal origin which occur in other lymphoid organs and also, though in smaller numbers, in the thymus. Unlike the

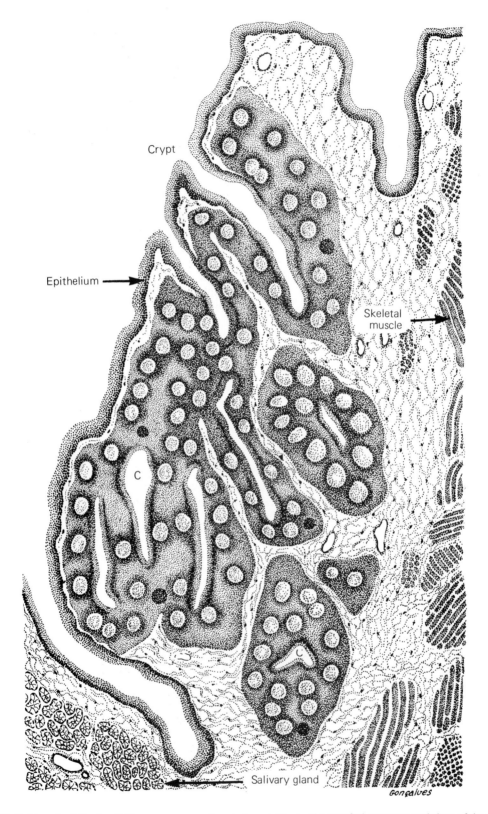

Crypt

Epithelium ➤

Skeletal
muscle ➤

C

Salivary gland ◄

Gonçalves

Figure 15–5. Lingual palatine tonsil. There are numerous lymphatic nodules near the stratified squamous epithelium of the oropharynx. The light areas in the lymphoid tissue are germinal centers. Note the cross sections of epithelial crypts (C).

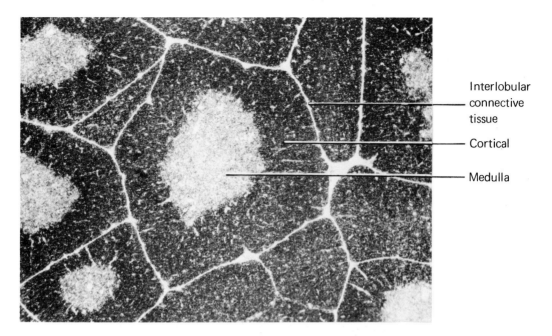

Interlobular connective tissue

Cortical

Medulla

Figure 15—6. Photomicrograph of the thymus. H&E stain, X 32.

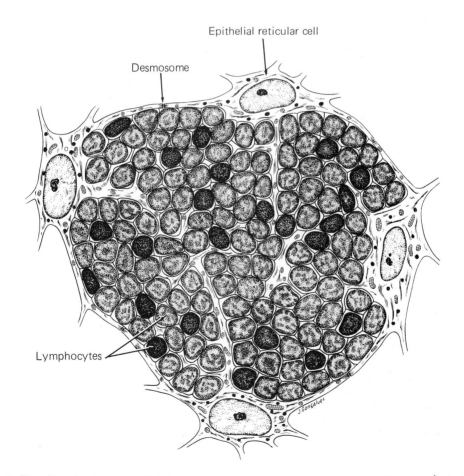

Figure 15—7. The relationship between epithelial reticular cells and thymus lymphocytes. Observe the long processes of epithelial reticular cells extending among the lymphocytes.

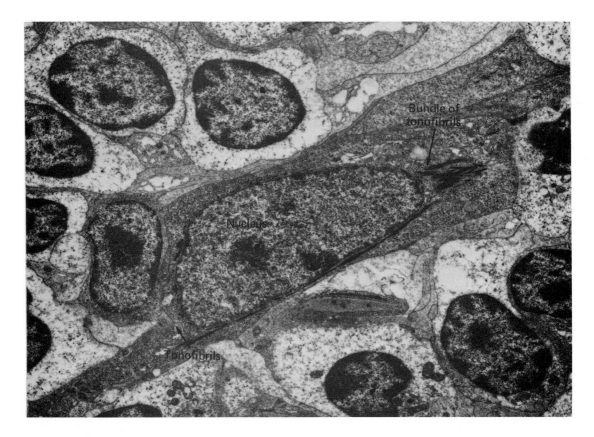

Figure 15—8. Thymic medulla seen under the electron microscope. An epithelial reticular cell appears obliquely across the figure. It has fine chromatin and exhibits tonofibrils in the cytoplasm. × 7100.

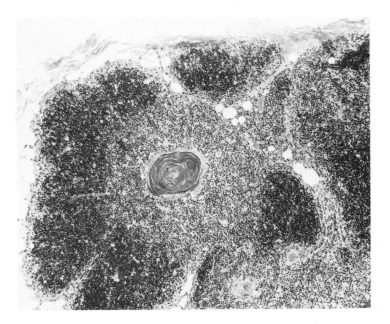

Figure 15—9. Photomicrograph of a human thymus, showing the cortical and medullary zones. Near the center, one Hassall corpuscle appears in the medulla. H&E stain, × 118.

mesenchymal cells, epithelial reticular cells have no reticular fibers, so that the reticulum which exists in the thymus and in whose meshes the lymphocytes proliferate is composed almost exclusively of cell processes.

The epithelial reticular cells have large nuclei with fine chromatin and cytoplasm and numerous processes which are linked by desmosomes to the desmosomes of adjacent cells of the same type (Fig 15—7). Besides the desmosomes, these cells have tonofibrils which are reminiscent of their epithelial origin (Fig 15—8). The electron microscope shows also, in their cytoplasm, dense granules which could be a kind of secretion (Fig 15—7).

The epithelial reticular cells envelop groups of lymphocytes which multiply in isolation from circulating antigens. Furthermore, they seem to form a complete network in the periphery of the lobules and around the blood and lymphatic vessels. This network of epithelial cells joined by desmosomes forms a continuous layer which separates the thymic parenchyma from the other histologic components of the organ, especially the vessels. Thus, between the epithelial cells and the capillaries, a space is encountered in which a basement membrane is seen and which also has macrophages. Through this blood-thymus barrier antigenic

material has difficulty in passing and coming into contact with the developing and programmed T lymphocytes although some antigens eventually do pass through. It has also been suggested that the dynamics of flow in this space direct these antigens toward the medulla of the organ and away from the cortex.

Cortical Zone

In the cortical zone, lymphocytes predominate—mainly small ones. These cells do not form nodules, as in other lymphoid organs, but are disposed in a continuous layer constituting a zone which passes from one lobule to the other. This area is a very active site of lymphocyte production. Many of the cells die in this area before they are released. Plasma cells are not usually seen in the thymus. Epithelial reticular cells are less numerous at the cortical layer, and here their processes are generally very thin and long because of the distention that results from the storage of lymphocytes.

Medullary Zone

Lymphoblasts, young lymphocytes, and epithelial reticular cells predominate in the medulla. Normally, small lymphocytes are rare. The medulla also contains

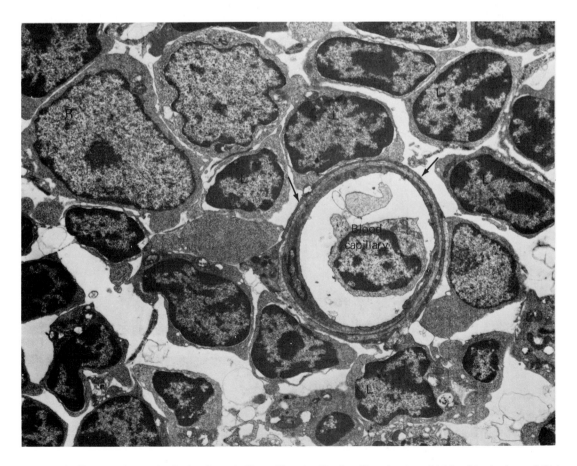

Figure 15—10. Electron micrograph of a thymic cortical layer. There is a blood capillary showing a thick basal lamina (arrows). Note the lymphocytes (L) and the reticular cell (R). X 28,500.

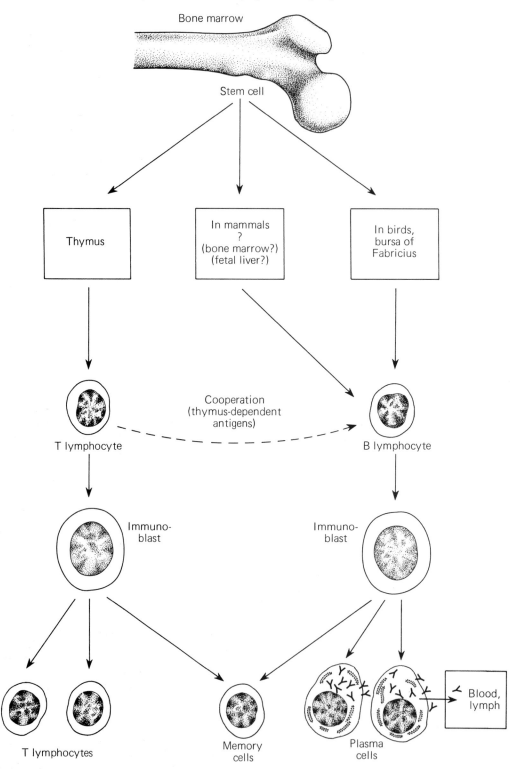

Figure 15–11. All lymphocytes originate from a stem cell, whose morphology is not clear. This cell migrates through the blood and invades the thymus, dividing many times to form T lymphocytes. (In birds, the stem cells are "conditioned" to become B lymphocytes in the bursa of Fabricius, a lymphatic organ located in the cloaca. The mammalian equivalent of the bursa of Fabricius is unknown. It may be the bone marrow itself or the fetal liver.) After encountering an antigen, the lymphocyte modulates into a larger cell—the immunoblast—which then proliferates and produces more T lymphocytes or plasma cells as the case may be. The so-called thymus-dependent antigens promote the transformation of B lymphocytes into plasma cells only when T lymphocytes are also present. This phenomenon is called cooperation between T cells and B cells in antibody production.

the Hassall corpuscles which are characteristic of the thymus (Fig 15–9).

Hassall bodies are 30–150 μm in diameter and consist of concentric layers of epithelial reticular cells. Some of these cells, mainly the innermost ones, can degenerate and die. It is not rare to find Hassall bodies with cores that consist only of cell remnants, sometimes calcified.

Evolution & Involution of the Thymus

In relation to body weight, the thymus shows its maximum development immediately after birth and undergoes accelerated involution after puberty. In the newborn, it weighs 12–15 g; at puberty, 30–40 g; and in old age, 10–15 g.

The thymus is very sensitive to radiation, infection, and disease. Thymuses observed at autopsies of children and adults who die after protracted illnesses are much smaller than normal.

Despite the processes of involution that accompany the passage of the years, the thymus remains capable of producing great numbers of lymphocytes when stimulated. The involutionary process of aging begins in the cortical zone, which gradually becomes thinner. The medulla begins its process of involution at puberty. Reticular cells of epithelial origin and Hassall corpuscles are more resistant to involution than lymphocytes. The thymus never disappears completely; it is still present even in very old people, represented by reticular cells, Hassall corpuscles, some lymphocytes, and a great amount of connective tissue.

Vascularization

Arteries which penetrate the thymus through the capsule distribute blood first to the cortical area; the smaller branches then reach the medulla.

Thymic capillaries have an endothelium without pores and a very thick basement membrane (Fig 15–10). The endothelial cells have thin processes which perforate the basement membrane and may come in contact with epithelial reticular cells.

As mentioned earlier, epithelial reticular cells surround all vessels of the thymus and constitute a layer which, although incomplete, separates the blood from the lymphocytes.

The medullary and cortical veins penetrate into the connective tissue septa and leave the thymus through its capsule.

The thymus does not have afferent lymphatic vessels and does not constitute a filter for the lymph as do lymph nodes. The few lymphatic vessels encountered in the thymus are all efferent and localized in the walls of blood vessels found in the septa and in the capsule.

Histophysiology

It was observed as long ago as 1961 that thymectomy in newborn rats caused atrophy of other lymphoid organs and a decrease in the number of circulating lymphocytes. We now know that undifferentiated cells whose morphology is little understood migrate through the blood from the bone marrow to the *thymus,* where they proliferate, giving rise to *T lymphocytes.* As explained in Chapter 13, these lymphocytes are responsible for cell-mediated immune reactions such as delayed hypersensitivity and graft rejection, whereas the *B lymphocytes* differentiate in plasma cells, which produce the humoral antibodies (Fig 15–11).

Leaving the thymus through the blood vessels in the medulla, T lymphocytes penetrate certain areas of other lymphoid organs called secondary or peripheral lymphoid organs. Those areas are called *thymus-dependent.* In mammals, thymus-dependent zones are the paracortical zone of lymph nodes, the periarterial sheaths in the white pulp of the spleen, and the loose lymphoid tissue found in Peyer's patches in the small intestine. The remaining lymphoid tissue of the body contains B lymphocytes.

In the light microscope, B and T lymphocytes are morphologically similar. Most T lymphocytes have the *theta antigen* on their cell membrane, which permits their identification. This antigen is probably produced by T lymphocytes during their maturation in the thymus. For each type of lymphocyte (B or T), there is a difference in the type of marker present on the surface membrane. These differences in markers are used to identify the 2 types of lymphocytes. These are shown in Table 15–1.

T lymphocytes are long-lived cells and constitute a population of cells comprising a portion of the lymphocytes of the thymus, most lymph and blood lymphocytes, and the lymphocytes found in all thymus-dependent zones.

Mitotic proliferation of lymphocytes is much higher in the cortical than in the medullary zone, being 5–10 times higher than in other lymphoid organs. One milligram of mouse thymus produces 1 million lymphocytes per day. The thymic mitotic rate is at its maximum at birth and decreases with age. However, only a small number of the lymphocytes produced daily in the thymus leave this organ. Most are destroyed inside the thymus, a process whose significance is not yet fully understood.

Thymectomy at Birth

When newborn animals are thymectomized—or in cases where the thymus does not develop during embryonic life—the following effects are observed: (1) There is no formation of T lymphocytes, with a consequent decrease in the number of lymphocytes in blood

Table 15–1. Differences in surface markers in T and B lymphocytes of the mouse.

Markers	T Lymphocytes	B Lymphocytes
Alloantigen	Present	Absent
Plasma cell alloantigen	Absent	Present on plasma cells only
Immunoglobulin determinants	Few	Numerous
Heterospecific antigen	Absent	Present

and lymph as well as a depletion of all thymus-dependent zones of the lymphoid tissue. (2) There is no delayed hypersensitivity reaction, and graft rejection does not occur. (3) There is atrophy of all lymphoid organs. (4) Finally, after 3–4 months of age, the thymectomized animal becomes weak, loses weight, and dies. In humans, many diseases with symptoms that are related to these events have been described, and in such cases death usually occurs shortly after birth.

The pool of T lymphocytes does not exist in thymectomized animals. Consequently, they do not show cell-mediated immune responses since T lymphocytes probably synthesize specific factors and keep them attached to their membranes.

On the other hand, the pool of B lymphocytes in thymectomized animals is nearly normal. They react to most antigens, producing plasma cells which synthesize antibodies. However, there are some antigens which require both T and B lymphocytes for antibody formation. For these antigens, T lymphocytes are important for the differentiation of B lymphocytes in plasma cells. When injected into animals thymectomized immediately after birth, these antigens do not elicit the formation of antibodies and are thus called *thymus-dependent antigens* (Fig 15–11).

The generalized atrophy of lymphoid organs observed in animals thymectomized immediately after birth is believed to be due to lack of a hypothetic humoral factor produced by the thymus which stimulates the development of lymphoid tissue in general. This hypothesis is based on strong experimental evidence. For example, implantation of thymus fragments in a small box whose walls are permeable to fluids and small molecules but not to cells prevents the lymphoid atrophy of thymectomized newborn animals. It has been observed also that implantation of fragments of thymus whose lymphocytes have been destroyed by irradiation has the same protective effect. It is believed that epithelial reticular cells secrete a hormone which has a trophic action on the lymphoid system. The electron microscope shows, in the cytoplasm of these cells, small granules which are very similar to secretory granules of some endocrine glands. However, the thymus hormone has not yet been clearly identified.

Animals thymectomized just after birth develop in a few weeks a progressive, fatal wasting disease characterized by weakness, weight loss, lethargy, and diarrhea. Since it is believed that this disease is due to widespread infections which may take place simultaneously in several organs, this outcome can be prevented by continuous injection of antibiotics or by keeping the thymectomized animals in a sterile environment.

Thymectomy in Adults

In adult animals, the effects of thymectomy are not as pronounced as in younger animals. There is usually a slight decrease of blood lymphocytes as well as in the weight of the lymphoid organs. Since they are long-lived, the T lymphocytes which exist at the time

of thymectomy maintain the pool of these circulating cells at a nearly normal level. On the other hand, since the trophic activity of the thymus is important only for the development of the lymphoid system, the lymphoid organs, once formed, become able to maintain themselves.

Thymus Grafting

In animals of any age, thymus grafting avoids the adverse effects of thymectomy. Studies of graft recipients whose cells have been labeled by chromosome markers show that there is an initial proliferation of lymphocytes from the graft. However, after the third week, lymphocytes divide for a few days but soon disappear entirely.

Hormones Which Act on the Thymus

The thymus is subject to the effects of several hormones. Injections of some adrenocorticosteroids cause a reduction in lymphocyte number and mitotic rate. There is atrophy of the cortical layer of the thymus. Adrenocorticotropic hormone (ACTH) produced by the anterior pituitary achieves the same effect by stimulating the activity of the adrenal cortex.

Male and female sex hormones also accelerate thymic involution; castration has the reverse effect.

Pituitary growth hormone (somatotropin, STH) stimulates thymic development in a nonspecific way, having a general effect on body growth.

ORGAN TRANSPLANTATION

Transplants are classified as *autografts* when the transplanted tissue or organ is taken from a different site on the same individual; *isografts* when the tissue or organ is taken from an identical twin; *homografts* or *allografts* when it is taken from an unrelated individual of the same species; and *heterografts* or *xenografts* when it is taken from an animal of a different species.

Autologous and isologous transplants take easily as long as an efficient blood supply is established. In such cases there is no rejection because the transplanted cells are genetically similar to those of the host and are composed of molecules that the organism recognizes as its own. For this reason, no antibodies are produced.

Homologous and heterologous transplants, on the other hand, contain cells whose constituents are foreign to the host and are therefore recognized and treated as such. Transplant rejection is due mainly to the activity of *graft rejection cells* (Fig 15–12). These cells are T lymphocytes which penetrate the transplant and act locally, destroying the transplanted cells. It seems that the graft rejection cells synthesize antibodies which remain attached to their surface.

We have said that homologous transplants are rejected. However, when this type of transplant is carried out between fraternal twins who shared the same pla-

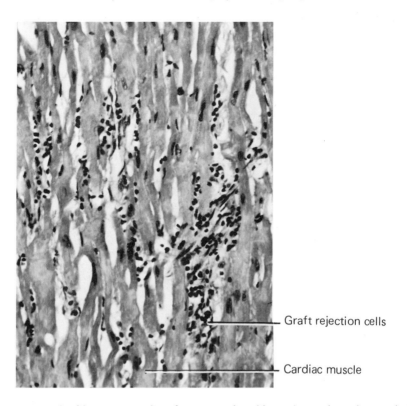

Graft rejection cells

Cardiac muscle

Figure 15—12. Photomicrograph of human myocardium from a transplanted heart. Among the cardiac muscle fibers which show degenerative changes there are many graft-rejecting cells. H&E stain, × 250.

centa, the graft is not rejected. This was verified after observing that fraternal twin calves that had shared a single placenta, although having different blood groups, had erythrocytes from each other and did not develop an immunologic reaction.

What occurs in these cases is that during embryonic life there is an exchange of blood between the animals. It is now known that an organism will never form antibodies against an antigen which was present in it before its antibody formation system started functioning. Only the molecules that enter the body after the organism has begun to synthesize antibodies are recognized as foreign and treated as antigens. In humans, the synthesis of antibodies begins a few days after birth. The infant is protected during the first few days of life mainly by antibodies received from the mother through the placenta. This is, therefore, a passive immunity which protects the child until his own cells begin to produce antibodies.

THE SPLEEN

The spleen is the largest accumulation of lymphatic tissue in the organism, and in humans it is the largest lymphatic organ in the circulatory system. Owing to its abundance of phagocytic cells and the close contact between the circulating blood and these cells, the spleen represents an important defense against microorganisms which penetrate the circulation and is also the site of destruction of many red cells. As is true of all other lymphatic organs, the spleen is the site of formation of lymphocytes, which pass into the blood. The spleen reacts promptly to antigens carried in the blood and is an important antibody-forming organ.

General Structure

The spleen is surrounded by a capsule of dense connective tissue which sends out trabeculae that divide the parenchyma or *splenic pulp* into incomplete compartments (Fig 15—13). The medial surface of the spleen presents a hilus at the level of which the capsule presents a number of trabeculae through which the nerves and arteries penetrate. Through the hilus leave also the veins proceeding from the parenchyma and the lymphatic vessels that originate in the trabeculae. The splenic pulp has no lymphatic vessels.

The connective tissue of the capsule and of the trabeculae contains some smooth muscle cells. In man, these cells are not numerous. In certain other mammals (cat, dog, horse) they are quite abundant, and their contraction causes the expulsion of accumulated blood in the spleen, which has a spongy structure and stores blood.

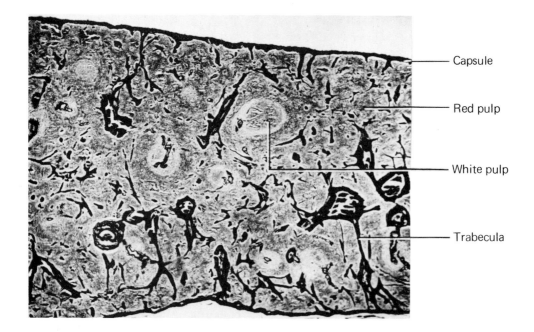

Capsule

Red pulp

White pulp

Trabecula

Figure 15—13. Photomicrograph of a silver-stained spleen section to show the general architecture of the organ. X 30.

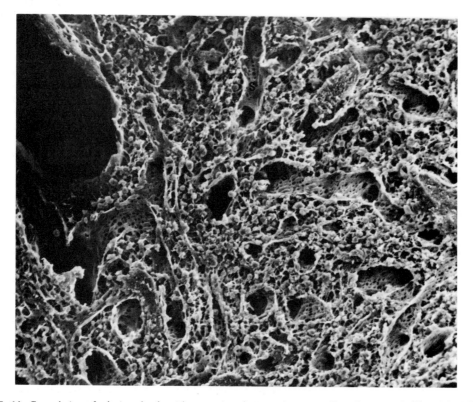

Figure 15—14. General view of splenic red pulp with a scanning electron microscope. Note the sinusoids (S) and the Billroth cords (C). X 360. (Reproduced, with permission, from Miyoshi M, Fujita T: Arch Histol Jap 33:225, 1971.)

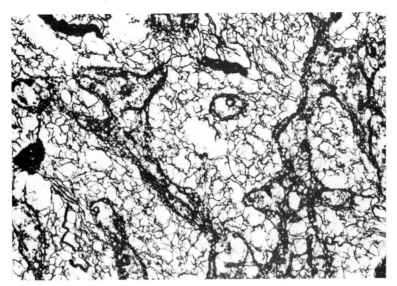

Figure 15–15. Photomicrograph of a network of splenic reticular fibers. Silver-stained section, X 200.

Splenic Pulp

On the surface of a fresh or fixed slice cut through the spleen one can observe white spots in the parenchyma with the naked eye. These are lymphatic nodules and are part of the so-called *white pulp,* which is not continuous. Among these nodules there appears a dark red tissue, rich in blood, called the *red pulp* (Figs 15–13, 15–14, 15–16, and 15–17).

Examination under a low-power microscope reveals that the red pulp is composed of elongated structures, the *splenic cords* or *Billroth cords,* between which are found the *sinusoids* (Fig 15–14).

All of the splenic pulp consists of connective tissue containing reticular fibers. Fixed cellular elements of this tissue are the reticular cells and macrophages, and the function of the reticular fibers is that of support (Fig 15–15).

The relationship between the reticular cells and the reticular fibers has not been fully explained. Electron microscopy has demonstrated that, in most cases, the reticular fibers are encased in extensions of primitive reticular cells. These fibers—as is generally true of all reticular fibers—are composed of a collagen fibril covered with an amorphous PAS-positive material.

Blood Circulation

The splenic artery divides as it penetrates the hilus, branching out into vessels of various sizes which follow the course of the connective tissue trabeculae and are called *trabecular arteries.* When they leave the trabeculae to enter the parenchyma, the arteries are immediately enveloped in a sheath of lymphocytes, becoming the *central arteries* or *white pulp arteries* or *follicular arteries.* Following a variable course, the lymphocytic sheath (white pulp) may thicken to form a lymphatic nodule, in which the vessel, now an arteriole, occupies an eccentric position. Even so, it is still called the central artery. During its course through the white pulp, the arteriole divides into numerous intercommunicating branches which will supply the lymphatic tissue surrounding it.

Before leaving the lymphatic tissue, the arteriole forms several more branches which reach into the red pulp and subdivide to form *penicilli,* arterioles with a diameter of approximately 25 μm. These penicilli possess smooth muscle in the first portion of these straight vessels, which is called the artery of the pulp. They are composed of an endothelium supported by a thick basal lamina. Near their terminations, some of these branches present a typical thickening, the *ellipsoid* or *sheathed artery.* This ellipsoid—cylindric, elliptic, or spherical in shape—consists of a sheath of phagocytic cells that surrounds the endothelium. Although the endothelial layer of the ellipsoid may be continuous, its basement membrane is not and in some specimens is nonexistent.

Beyond the ellipsoids, the vessels continue as simple arterial capillaries which transport blood to the sinusoids or red pulp sinuses. These sinusoids occupy the area between the Billroth cords (Fig 15–14). From the sinusoids the blood proceeds to the red pulp veins which join and penetrate the trabeculae, forming the *trabecular veins.* Thus originates the splenic vein, which emerges from the hilus of the spleen. The trabecular veins do not have individual muscle walls, ie, their walls are composed of trabecular tissue. They can be regarded as channels hollowed out in the connective trabecular tissue and lined by endothelium.

The exact manner in which blood flows from the capillary arteries of the red pulp to the interior of the sinusoids has not yet been completely explained. Some investigators consider that the capillaries open directly into the sinusoids; others maintain that the blood passes through the spaces between the reticular cells and then moves on to be collected by the sinusoids (Figs 15–16 and 15–19). In the first instance, this

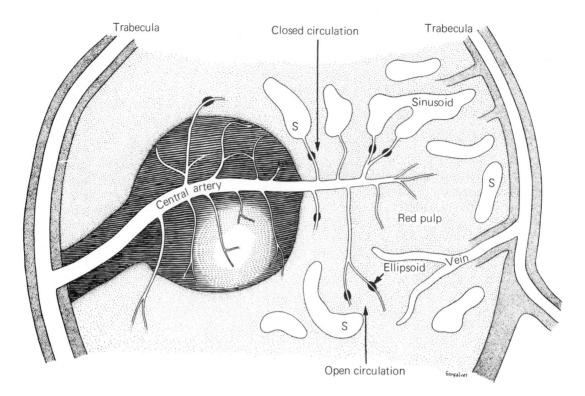

Figure 15–16. Schematic view of the blood circulation of the spleen. Theories of open and closed circulation are represented in this drawing. Splenic sinuses (S) are indicated. (Redrawn and reproduced, with permission, from Greep RO, Weiss L: *Histology,* 3rd ed. McGraw-Hill, 1973.)

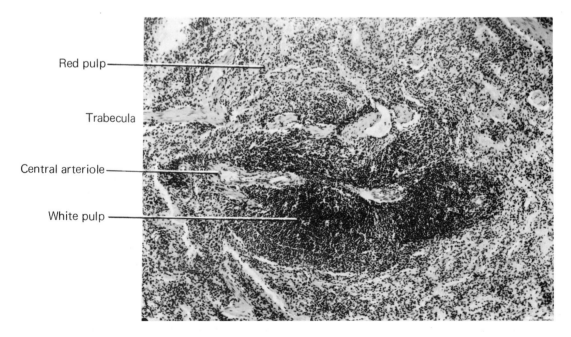

Figure 15–17. Photomicrograph of splenic white and red pulp. H&E stain, × 100.

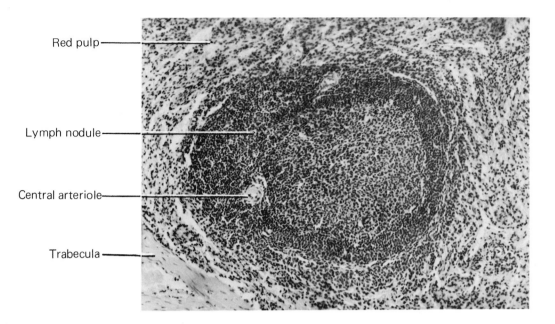

Red pulp

Lymph nodule

Central arteriole

Trabecula

Figure 15–18. Photomicrograph of the spleen, showing a lymphatic nodule (white pulp) surrounded by red pulp. H&E stain, X 100.

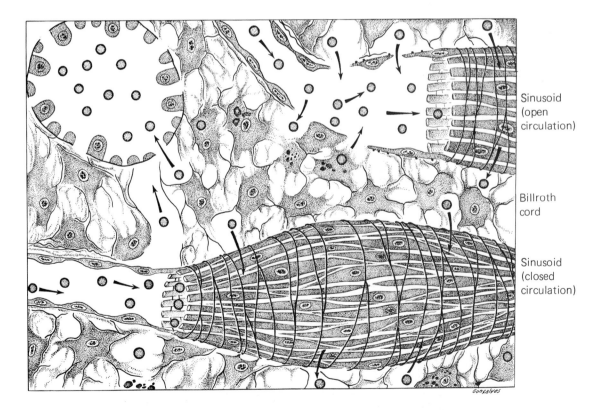

Sinusoid
(open
circulation)

Billroth
cord

Sinusoid
(closed
circulation)

Figure 15–19. Structure of the red pulp of the spleen, showing splenic sinusoids and Billroth cords with phagocytic cells (some with phagocytosed material). The relationship between reticular fibers and sinusoid lining cells is also shown. A sinusoid in cross section is shown at upper left. Both the open and closed theories of spleen blood circulation are illustrated.

would mean a *closed* circulation as proposed by the supporters of the "closed theory," who maintain that the blood always remains inside the vessels. In the second case, the circulation would *open* ("open theory") into the parenchyma of the organ between its cells and the blood would pass through the area between the cells in order to reach the sinusoids. Others maintain that in a distended spleen, full of blood, the circulation would be open, whereas in a spleen with little blood the arterial capillaries would connect directly with the sinusoids, establishing a closed circulation.

White Pulp

The white pulp consists of the lymphatic tissue arranged in cords or nodules around the arteries, called Malpighian corpuscles (Figs 15–16 and 15–17). As in lymphatic tissue in general, reticular cells and reticular fibers are both encountered and form a 3-dimensional mesh. The spaces in this mesh are occupied mainly by macrophages and by lymphocytes at various stages of maturation. The white pulp forms a sheath around the vessels and contains lymphatic nodules (Figs 15–16 and 15–17). These nodules are easily distinguished from other nodules encountered in the various lymphatic organs because of the presence of the central artery (Figs 15–16 and 15–18).

Between the lymphatic nodules and the red pulp lies a poorly delimited *marginal zone* of loose lymphoid tissue with few lymphocytes but with many macrophages having branching processes and showing active phagocytosis. The marginal zone retains great amounts of blood antigens and thus plays a major role in the immunologic activity of the spleen. The lymphocytes of the periarterial sheath are *thymus-dependent*, whereas the marginal zones are populated by B lymphocytes. Thus, the splenic white pulp has B and T lymphocytes segregated in 2 different sites.

Red Pulp

The red pulp is a reticular tissue with a special characteristic, ie, the presence of *splenic* or *Billroth cords*. The cords appear only in histologic preparations since the red pulp actually is a sponge the cavities of which are the sinusoids.

The cords are continuous and of varying thickness according to the local distention of the sinusoids. Besides the reticular cells, the splenic cords contain fixed and wandering macrophages, monocytes, lymphocytes, plasma cells, and many blood elements (erythrocytes, platelets, and granulocytes).

The *sinusoids* of the spleen differ from the common capillaries in 4 ways: (1) they have a dilated, irregular lumen; (2) their lining contains phagocytic cells; (3) among their lining cells are spaces which facilitate exchange between the sinusoids and adjacent tissues; and (4) the basement membrane–like material is not continuous everywhere along its wall.

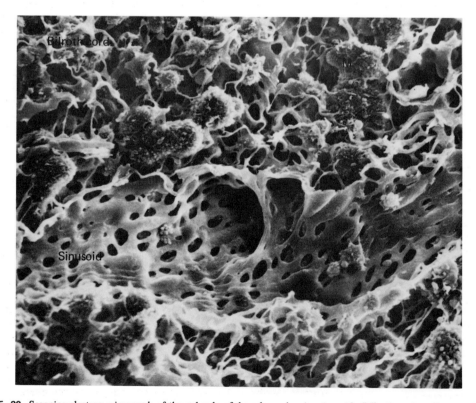

Figure 15–20. Scanning electron micrograph of the red pulp of the spleen, showing sinusoids, Billroth cords, and macrophages (M). × 1600. (Reproduced, with permission, from Miyoshi M, Fujita T: Arch Histol Jap 33:225, 1971.)

The cells which line the splenic sinusoids are elongated, with their long axis parallel to the sinusoids. These cells are enveloped in reticular fibers set mainly in a transverse direction, similar to the hoops of a barrel. The transverse fibers and those oriented in various directions join to form a network enveloping the sinusoid cells (Fig 15–19).

The spaces between the cells of the splenic sinusoids can be 2–3 μm in diameter or even larger, so that the erythrocytes are able to pass easily from the lumen of the sinusoids to the Billroth cords (Fig 15–20).

Histophysiology

The spleen is a lymphatic organ with special characteristics. Its best-known functions are (1) the formation of lymphocytes and monocytes, (2) the destruction of erythrocytes, (3) defense of the organism against foreign particles that enter the bloodstream, and (4) the storage of blood.

A. Production of Blood Cells: The white pulp of the spleen produces lymphocytes that migrate to the red pulp and reach the lumens of the sinusoids, where they are incorporated into the blood that is present there. A constant flow of lymphocytes is observed from the splenic parenchyma to the bloodstream as well as in the opposite direction. Radioautography after intravenous injection of radioactive lymphocytes has demonstrated that many of these labeled lymphocytes appear in the white pulp of the spleen.

In the fetus, the spleen also produces granulocytes (neutrophils, basophils, and eosinophils) and erythrocytes, but this activity ceases at the end of the fetal phase. In certain pathologic conditions (eg, leukemia), the spleen may recommence the production of granulocytes and erythrocytes, thus undergoing a process known as *myeloid metaplasia* (pathologic transformation of one kind of cell into another).

The spleen is an important source of monocytes, probably from the lining of the splenic sinusoids or from the reticular cells of the white and red pulps.

B. Destruction of Erythrocytes: The red blood cells have an average life span of 120 days, and at that time they are destroyed, mainly in the spleen. This phenomenon of the removal of degenerating erythrocytes (hemocatheresis) also occurs in other organs.

The macrophages of the red pulp—mainly those of the Billroth cords but also of the sinusoid lining—engulf entire pieces of the erythrocytes that frequently fragment themselves in the extracellular spaces.

The engulfed erythrocytes are altered and digested by the lysosomes of the phagocytes. The hemoglobin they contain is broken down, forming a pigment, *bilirubin,* which contains no iron, and a protein, *ferritin,* which does contain iron. These compounds are then returned to the blood.

Bilirubin is excreted by the hepatic cells together with the bile. Ferritin, which represents a form of mobile iron, will be used by the erythrocytes of the bone marrow, which will draw iron from it for the synthesis of new hemoglobin.

C. Defense: Since it contains both B and T lymphocytes and macrophages, the spleen is important in body defense. In the same way that lymph nodes "filter" the lymph, the spleen is considered as a "filter" for the blood.

The T lymphocytes found in the periarterial sheaths of the white pulp proliferate and enter the bloodstream. They participate in cell-mediated immune mechanisms.

Radioautographic studies with labeled antigens injected into the blood show that the antigens are preferentially retained by the surface of the macrophages and some by reticular cells found in the marginal zone. These cells have many long processes which branch profusely, thus increasing the cell surface.

Under the stimulus of antigens, splenic B lymphocytes proliferate and give rise to antibody-producing plasma cells.

Of all the macrophagic cells of the organism, those of the spleen are most active in the phagocytosis of living particles (bacteria and viruses) and inert particles that find their way into the bloodstream. After the injection of trypan blue, the macrophages of the spleen are among the first to accumulate this dye.

When there is an excess of lipids in the blood plasma (hyperlipidemia), the macrophages of the spleen accumulate considerable quantities of these substances. In diabetes, hyperlipidemia is frequent, and for this reason large macrophages, their cytoplasm containing numerous lipid droplets, are common in the spleens of diabetics.

D. Blood Storage: Owing to the spongy structure of the red pulp, the spleen stores blood, which can be returned to the circulation to increase the volume of circulating blood. In animals with spleens composed of a capsule and trabeculae rich in smooth muscle, the organ is emptied by muscular contraction. Because the human spleen is poor in smooth muscle fibers, the storage and expulsion of blood depends on changes in the diameter of the blood vessels. It has been demonstrated that in man the blood storage capacity of the spleen is very small.

Splenectomy

Although it has important functions, the spleen can be removed without serious damage to the individual. Other organs with cells similar to those found in the spleen will compensate for its loss.

After splenectomy, a temporary increase in the number of lymphocytes and platelets is observed in the blood. This is due to excessive compensatory lymphocyte production by other lymphatic organs (lymph nodes, isolated nodules, etc).

Splenectomy is beneficial in diseases where there is a deficiency in bone marrow function. In these cases, splenectomy is followed by bone marrow activation. This permits the conclusion that the spleen inhibits bone marrow function in such cases. This inhibiting effect has not been proved under normal conditions, but many investigators argue that the spleen has a regulating effect on bone marrow. This effect would be more pronounced in certain pathologic states.

•   •   •

References

Avrameas S, Leduc EH: Detection of simultaneous antibody synthesis in plasma cells and specialized lymphocytes in rabbit lymph nodes. J Exper Med 131:1137, 1970.

Bessis M, Thiery J: Electron microscopy of human white blood cells and their stem cells. Int Rev Cytol 12:199, 1961.

Binet JL, Mathe G: Optical and electron microscope studies of "immunologically competent cells" in graft reactions. Nature 193:992, 1962.

Clark SL Jr: Cytological evidence of secretion in the thymus. In: *The Thymus: Experimental and Clinical Studies.* Wolstenholme GE, Porter R (editors). Little, Brown, 1966.

Everett NB, Caffrey RW: Lymphopoiesis in the thymus and other tissues: Functional implications. Int Rev Cytol 22:205, 1967.

Gowans JL, Knight EJ: The route of recirculation of lymphocytes in the rat. Proc Roy Soc London s.B 159:257, 1964.

Hirasawa Y, Tokuhiro H: Electron microscopic studies on the normal human spleen, especially on the red pulp and the reticuloendothelial cells. Blood 35:201, 1970.

Ito T, Hoshino T: Fine structure of the epithelial reticular cells of the medulla of the thymus in the golden hamster. Z Zellforsch Mikrosk Anat 69:311, 1966.

Joel DD, Hess MW, Cottier H: Thymic origin of lymphocytes in developing Peyer's patches of newborn mice. Nature 231:24, 1971.

Leblond CP, Sainte-Marie G: Models for lymphocyte and plasmocyte formation. In: *Haemopoiesis: Cell Production and Its Regulation.* Wolstenholme GE, O'Connor M (editors). Little, Brown, 1960.

Martin CR: T and B lymphocytes and immune responses. Nature 242:19, 1973.

Mellors RC, Korngold L: The cellular origin of human immunoglobulins. J Exper Med 118:387, 1963.

Metcalf D, Brumby M: The role of the thymus in the ontogeny of the immune system. J Cell Physiol 67 (Part 2):149, 1966.

Miller JFAP: Immunity and the thymus. Lancet 1:43, 1963.

Miller JFAP: Origins of immunological competence. Brit M Bull 19:214, 1963.

Mishell RL, Dutton RW: Immunization of dissociated spleen cell cultures from normal mice. J Exper Med 126:423, 1967.

Miyoshi M, Fujita T: Stereo-fine structure of the splenic red pulp: A combined scanning and transmission electron microscope study on dog and rat spleen. Arch Histol Jap 33:225, 1971.

Osoba D, Miller JFAP: The lymphoid tissues and immune responses of neonatally thymectomized mice bearing thymus tissue in millipore diffusion chambers. J Exper Med 119:177, 1964.

Ouchi E, Selvaraj RJ, Sbarra AJ: The biochemical activities of rabbit alveolar macrophages during phagocytosis. Exp Cell Res 40:456, 1965.

Raviola E, Karnovsky MJ: Evidence for a blood-thymus barrier using electron opaque tracers. J Exper Med 136:466, 1972.

Sainte-Marie G: Cytokinetics of antibody formation. J Cell Physiol 67 (Part 2):109, 1966.

Thomas CE: An electron and light microscope study of sinus structure in perfused rabbit and dog spleens. Am J Anat 120:527, 1967.

Wagner H & others: Cell mediated immune response in vitro. J Exper Med 136:331, 1972.

Weiss L: Electron microscopic observations on the vascular barrier in the cortex of the thymus of the mouse. Anat Rec 145:413, 1963.

Weiss L: *The Cells and Tissues of the Immune System.* Prentice-Hall, 1972.

Yoffey JM: A note on the thick-walled and thin-walled arteries of bone marrow. J Anat 96:666, 1962.

Zamboni L, Pease DC: The vascular bed of red bone marrow. J Ultrastruct Res 5:65, 1961.

16 . . .
Digestive Tract

The digestive system consists of the digestive tract and its associated glands. Its function is to obtain from ingested food the metabolites necessary for the growth and energy needs of the body. Before it can be stored or used as energy, food must be digested and transformed into small molecules that can be easily absorbed through the lining of the digestive tract—all the while maintaining, however, a barrier between the environment and the internal milieu of the body. The first step in the complex process known as digestion occurs in the mouth, where food is ground up into smaller pieces by mastication and moistened by saliva. Digestion continues in the stomach and small intestine. In the small intestine, the food—transformed into its basic components (amino acids, monosaccharides, glycerides, etc)—is absorbed. Water absorption occurs in the large intestine, and as a result the contents become semisolid.

THE ORAL CAVITY

The oral cavity is lined with stratified nonkeratinized squamous epithelium. Its superficial cells are nucleated and have scanty granules of keratin in their interior. In the lips, a transition from squamous to keratinized epithelium can be observed. The lamina propria presents papillae similar to those in the skin and is continuous with a submucosa containing diffuse small salivary glands.

The roof of the mouth is composed of the hard and soft palates, both covered with the same type of stratified squamous epithelium. In the hard palate, the mucous membrane rests on bony tissue. The soft palate has a center of striated skeletal muscle and numerous mucous glands in its submucosa.

The palatine *uvula* is a small conical process that extends downward from the center of the lower border of the soft palate. It has as its core the musculus uvulus and areolar connective tissue and is covered by typical oral mucosa.

THE TONGUE

The tongue is a mass of striated muscle covered by a mucous membrane whose structure varies according to the region studied. The muscle fibers cross each other in 3 planes. They are grouped in bundles, usually separated by connective tissue. The mucous membrane is strongly adherent to the muscle because the connective tissue of the lamina propria penetrates into the spaces between the muscular bundles. On the lower surface of the tongue, the mucous membrane is smooth. The dorsal surface, however, is very irregular, covered anteriorly by a great number of small excrescences called papillae. The posterior region of the dorsal surface of the tongue is separated from the anterior portion by a V-shaped boundary. Behind this boundary, the surface of the tongue presents eminences composed mainly of small lymphatic aggregations of 2 types: (1) lymph follicles, which are small collections of lymph nodules; and (2) the lingual tonsils, where lymph nodules aggregate around invaginations of the mucous membrane (Fig 16–1).

The Papillae
The papillae are elevations or excrescences of the oral epithelium and of the lamina propria which assume different forms and functions. There are 3 types:

A. Filiform Papillae: Filiform papillae have an elongated conical shape. They are quite numerous and are present on the surface of the entire tongue. They do not contain taste buds (Fig 16–1).

B. Fungiform Papillae: The fungiform papillae have a narrow stalk and a dilated upper part with a smooth surface in the shape of a mushroom (Fig 16–1). They are less numerous than the filiform papillae and interspersed among them. They frequently contain taste buds and appear red in vivo.

C. Circumvallate Papillae: These are flattened structures surrounded by a deep groove. There are 7–12 of them in the V region of the tongue, and they have many taste buds on their lateral surface. Numerous excretory ducts of serous glands maintain a continuous flow of fluid over the taste buds, and this is important in removing food particles from the buds so

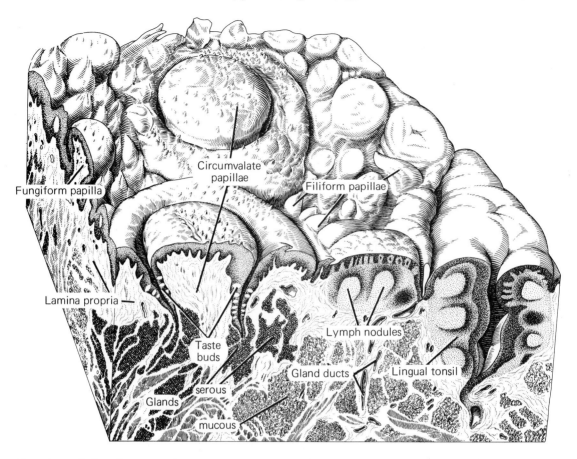

Figure 16—1. Surface of tongue on the region close to its V-shaped boundary between the anterior and posterior portions. Observe the lymph nodules, lingual tonsils, glands, and papillae. (After Braus.)

that they can receive and process new gustatory stimuli. In addition, to the serous glands associated with this type of papilla, other small mucous and serous glands dispersed throughout the lining of the oral cavity act in the same way to prepare the taste buds in other parts of the oral cavity—epiglottis, pharynx, palate, etc—to respond to taste stimuli.

THE PHARYNX

The pharynx represents a transition space between the oral cavity and the respiratory and digestive systems. It forms a communication between the nasal region and the larynx. A transition from stratified squamous nonkeratinizing epithelium to pseudostratified columnar ciliated epithelium can be observed, according to the different functions of the various parts of the pharynx (transport of food or air, respectively). Stratified columnar epithelium is also seen at transition areas.

The pharynx contains the tonsils (described in Chapter 15). The mucosa of the pharynx also has many small mucous glands in its dense connective tissue layer. Outside this layer, the constrictor and longitudinal muscle of the pharynx are located.

THE TEETH & ASSOCIATED STRUCTURES

The teeth are disposed in 2 curved arches inserted in the maxillary and mandibular bones. Each tooth is composed of a portion that projects above the *gingiva* (or *gum*)—the *crown*—and a *root* below the gingiva which holds the tooth in a bony socket called the *alveolus,* one for the root of each tooth (Fig 16—2).

The point of transition from crown to root is the *neck.* The first *deciduous* teeth are gradually replaced by *permanent teeth*. Both are similar in structure and are composed of a nonmineralized portion—the *pulp*—and 3 mineralized portions—the *enamel, dentin,* and *cementum* (Fig 16—2).

Each tooth has a central cavity—the *pulp cavity*—which has roughly the same shape as the tooth. In the region of the roots, this cavity extends to the apex of the root and forms an orifice through which pass the

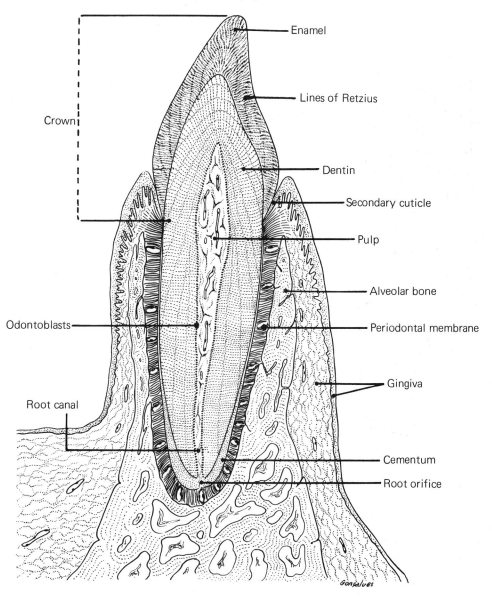

Crown

Odontoblasts

Root canal

Enamel

Lines of Retzius

Dentin

Secondary cuticle

Pulp

Alveolar bone

Periodontal membrane

Gingiva

Cementum

Root orifice

Gonçalves

Figure 16–2. Diagram of a sagittal section from an incisor tooth in position in the mandibular bone. (Redrawn and reproduced, with permission, from Leeson TS, Leeson CR: *Histology,* 2nd ed. Saunders, 1970.)

blood vessels and nerves of the tooth. The *periodontal membrane* or *ligament* is a collagenous fibrous structure surrounding the cementum of the root, helping to fix the tooth firmly in its bony socket.

The dentin is covered by enamel in the crown of the tooth and by cementum in its roots (Fig 16–2).

Dentin

Dentin is a calcified tissue similar to bone but harder because of its higher content of calcium salts. It is composed mainly of collagenous fibers, acid mucopolysaccharides, and calcium salts (80% of dry weight) in the form of crystals of hydroxyapatite. Its organic matrix is synthesized by the *odontoblasts,* cells which line the internal surface of the tooth, separating it

from the pulp cavity (Fig 16–3). Like the osteoblast, however, the odontoblast is a polarized slender cell, producing organic matrix only at the dentinal surface. The cytoplasm of each of these cells contains a nucleus at its base, a large Golgi apparatus, and many ribosomes, both free and attached to granular endoplasmic reticulum, and has a slender extension which penetrates perpendicularly through the entire width of the dentin, forming the *Tomes fibers.* These fibers gradually become longer as the dentin becomes thicker, running in small canals called the *dentinal tubules.* The Tomes fibers initially have a diameter of 3–4 μm, gradually become thinner, and end by branching near the junction between the dentin and the enamel (Fig 16–4). The periodontoblastic space between the process of

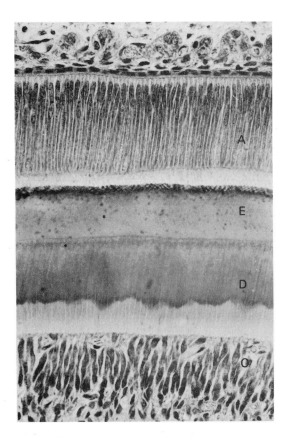

Figure 16–3 (at left). Photomicrograph of a section of an immature tooth, showing dentin (D) and enamel (E). The ameloblasts (A) and the odontoblasts (O) are both disposed as palisades. Masson's stain, × 350.

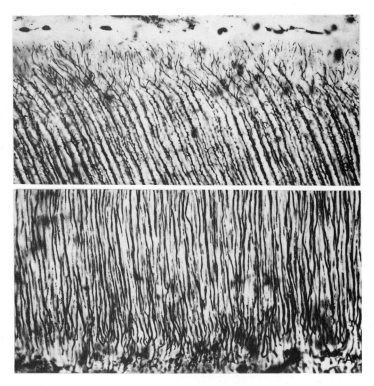

Figure 16–4. Photomicrograph of a section of a tooth, showing the Tomes fibers of the dentin. *A:* Initial portion. *B:* Terminal portion. These fibers gradually get thinner and terminate by branching into delicate extensions. × 400.

the cell and the tubule is full of tissue fluid.

The mineralization of the developing dentin begins by deposition of calcium salts in globules which gradually fuse together. However, this process is not complete, and noncalcified or partially calcified regions frequently remain between the globules as *interglobular spaces*. Dentin is sensitive to many stimuli such as heat, cold, acids, and trauma, and responds to all painful stimuli. However, nerve fibers are very scarce in the dentin, and it may be that the Tomes fibers act as receptors and transmit the impulses to the pulp tissue, which is richly innervated. In contrast to bone, dentin persists as a mineral for a long time after destruction of the odontoblasts. It is thus possible to maintain teeth whose pulp and odontoblasts have been destroyed by infection. In adult teeth, destruction of the covering enamel due to erosion by wearing usually triggers a reaction in the dentin which causes it to resume the synthesis of its components. Thus, production of newly formed, usually irregular dentin can be observed on the wall of the pulp cavity.

Enamel

Enamel is the hardest structure of the body and the richest in calcium. It contains about 97% calcium salts and 3% organic material. It is of epithelial ectodermal origin, whereas the other structures of the teeth derive from mesoderm. The organic matrix is not composed of collagenous fibers, and x-ray diffraction studies have demonstrated that its main component is a protein in the cross β configuration, rich in proline. Mature enamel can only be studied in preparations obtained by grinding because the organic matrix collapses when decalcified so that it cannot be embedded and sectioned. However, it can be studied in growing teeth, where enamel is incompletely calcified.

Enamel matrix is secreted by cells called *ameloblasts*. The cells of the inner dental epithelium of the developing dental organ differentiate into ameloblasts (Fig 16–3), which have all of the organelles necessary for the secretion of the organic matrix and which later become mineralized just as happens in other hard tissues of the body. The dentin appears first between the ameloblasts and odontoblasts and extends down the dental papilla. This first soft fibrillar dentin is called *predentin*. A broad apical process of the cell (Tomes process) is embedded in the enamel matrix. When the enamel is fully calcified, the ameloblasts become small cuboid cells and atrophy and disappear after forming the enamel cuticle which covers the external surface of the enamel.

Enamel is composed of elongated hexagonal rods or columns of structures in the shape of prisms—the *enamel prisms*—bound together by an interprismatic substance. Each rod runs through the entire thickness of the enamel layer. Both the enamel and the cementing substance are heavily calcified. Starting from the dentin, they run perpendicular to the surface of the tooth. In the mid region, they briefly take a spiral course and then become perpendicular again. In the lateral crown, the prisms are disposed in horizontal planes.

Pulp

The tooth pulp consists mainly of a loose type of connective tissue. Its main components are thin collagenous fibers arranged in no particular pattern plus a ground substance containing acid mucopolysaccharides. In very young teeth, these fibers are nonexistent or scarce. Reticular fibers are also present (Fig 16–5).

The pulp is a highly innervated and vascularized tissue. Numerous fibroblasts are present. Blood vessels and myelinated nerves extend through an orifice in the apex of the root and divide into numerous branches. Some nerve fibers lose their myelin sheath and are believed to extend for a short distance into the dentinal tubules. Surrounding the pulp and separating it from the dentin, large columnar cells are arranged in palisade formation. These are the odontoblasts (Fig 16–5), shown under the electron microscope to be highly polarized cells with characteristics of cells that synthesize proteins for export. Thus, their basal cytoplasm has an abundant granular endoplasmic reticulum. A well-developed Golgi apparatus and secretory granules are observed in the supranuclear area.

Associated Structures

The structures responsible for maintaining the teeth in maxillary or mandibular bone consist of the *cementum, periodontal membrane, alveolar bone,* and *gingiva.*

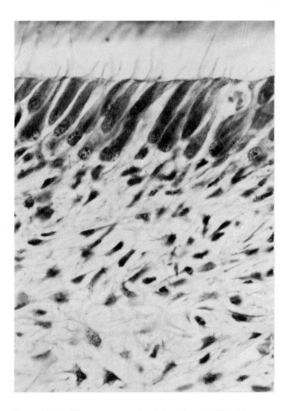

Figure 16–5. Photomicrograph of dental pulp. Fibroblasts are abundant. In the upper region are the odontoblasts, from which the Tomes fibers derive. H&E stain, X 400.

A. Cementum: This tissue covers the dentin of the root and is similar in structure to bone, although Haversian systems and blood vessels are absent. It is thicker in the apical region of the roots, and in this area there are cells with appearance of osteocytes, the *cementocytes.* Like the osteocytes, they are encased in lacunae which communicate through canaliculi. Like bony tissue, cementum is labile and reacts by resorption or production of new tissue according to the stresses to which it is submitted. When periodontal membrane is destroyed, the cementum undergoes necrosis and may be resorbed. Continuous production of cementum compensates for the normal growth which teeth undergo. This process maintains a close contact between the tooth's roots and their sockets.

B. Periodontal Membrane: Periodontal membrane is composed of a special type of dense connective tissue whose fibers penetrate the cementum of the tooth and bind it to the bony walls of its socket—permitting, however, limited movements of the tooth. It serves as periosteum to the alveolar bone. Its fibers are so disposed that the pressures exerted during mastication are supported by them. This disposition avoids the transmission of pressure directly to the bone—a process that would cause localized resorption of this structure.

The collagen of the periodontal membrane has characteristics that resemble those of immature tissue. Thus, it has a high protein turnover rate (as demonstrated by radioautography) and a large content of soluble collagen. The space between its fibers is filled with acid mucopolysaccharides. It is this high rate of collagen renewal in the periodontal membrane that allows processes affecting protein or collagen synthesis—eg, protein or vitamin C deficiency—to cause atrophy of this membrane. Consequently, the teeth become loose in their sockets and in extreme cases may even fall out.

C. Alveolar Bone: This portion of bone is in immediate contact with the periodontal membrane. It is an immature bone in which the collagen fibers are not arranged in the typical lamellar pattern present in adult bone. Many of the collagenous fibers of the periodontal membrane are arranged in bundles which penetrate into this bone and the cementum, forming a connecting bridge between these structures. The bone closest to the roots of the teeth forms the socket. The vessels and nerves run through this alveolar bone and the foramens of the root to enter the pulp.

D. Gingiva: The gingiva is mucous membrane firmly bound to the periosteum of the maxillary or mandibular bone. It is composed of stratified squamous epithelium and numerous connective tissue papillae. The epithelium binds itself to the tooth's surface by way of the epithelial attachment of Gottlieb. Between the enamel and the epithelium there is a small deepening surrounding the crown called the gingival crevice. These epithelial cells are fixed to the basement membrane by hemidesmosomes.

GENERAL STRUCTURE OF THE DIGESTIVE TRACT

The entire gastrointestinal canal presents certain common structural characteristics. The digestive tract is composed of 4 principal layers: the *mucous layer (mucosa),* the *submucosa,* the *muscle layer,* and the *serous layer.* The structure of these layers is summarized below and illustrated in Fig 16-6.

The *mucous layer* is composed of (1) an epithelial lining; (2) a lamina propria of loose connective tissue rich in blood and lymph vessels and smooth muscle cells, sometimes containing also glands and lymphoid tissue; and (3) *muscularis mucosae,* a continuous thin layer of smooth muscle separating the mucosa from the submucosa.

Submucosa is composed of loose connective tissue with many blood and lymph vessels and a *submucosal* (also called *Meissner's*) *nerve plexus.* It may also contain glands and lymphoid tissue.

The *muscle layer* contains the following elements: (1) Smooth muscle cells, spirally oriented, divided into 2 sublayers according to the main direction the muscle cells follow. In the internal layer (close to the lumen), the orientation is generally circular; in the external sublayer, mostly longitudinal. (2) The myenteric (or Auerbach's) nerve plexus, disposed between the 2 muscle sublayers. (3) Blood and lymph vessels in the connective tissue between the muscle sublayers.

The *serosal layer* is composed of (1) loose connective tissue, rich in blood and lymph vessels and adipose tissue; and (2) simple squamous covering epithelium (mesothelium).

The main functions of the mucosal epithelial lining of the digestive tract are to provide a selectively permeable barrier between the contents of the tract and the tissues of the body and to facilitate the transport and digestion of food. The cells in this layer produce mucus and numerous digestive enzymes.

The abundant lymphoid nodules present in the lamina propria and in the submucosal layer protect the organism (in association with the epithelium) from bacterial invasion. The importance of this function can be further emphasized if one considers that—with the exception of the oral cavity, esophagus, and anal canal—the entire digestive tract is lined by a simple and therefore a thin and vulnerable epithelium. Careful study of the lamina propria has demonstrated that there is a continuous small layer of macrophages and lymphoid cells just below the epithelium. Some of these lymphoid cells have been shown by immunofluorescent methods to actively produce gamma globulins, ie, antibodies.

The muscularis mucosae promotes the movement of the mucous layer independently of other movements of the digestive tract, increasing its contact with the food. The contractions of the muscle layer propel and mix the food in the digestive tract. The nerve plexuses of Meissner coordinate this muscular contraction.

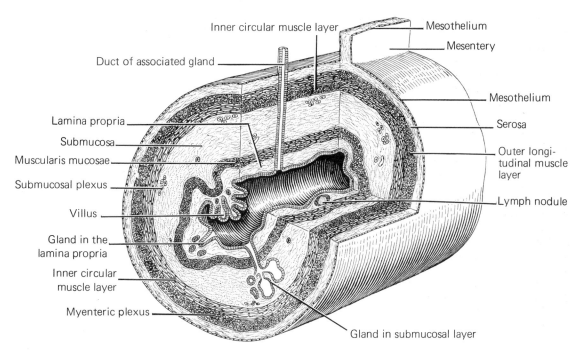

Figure 16—6. Schematic structure of a portion of the digestive tract with various possible components. (Redrawn and reproduced, with permission, from Bevelander G: *Outline of Histology,* 7th ed. Mosby, 1971.)

They are composed mainly of nerve cell aggregates (multipolar visceral neurons) which form small parasympathetic ganglia. A rich network of pre- and postganglionic fibers of the autonomic nervous system and some visceral sensory fibers in these ganglia permit communication between them. The number of these ganglia along the digestive tract is variable. They are more numerous in regions where motility is greatest.

In certain diseases such as Hirschsprung's disease or *Trypanosoma cruzi* infection (Chagas' disease), the digestive tract plexuses are severely injured and most of its neurons are absent or destroyed. This results in disturbances of digestive tract motility with frequent dilatations in some areas. The fact that the digestive tract receives abundant innervation from the autonomic nervous system provides an anatomic explanation of the widely observed action of emotional disturbances on the digestive tract—a phenomenon of importance in psychosomatic medicine.

ESOPHAGUS

This part of the gastrointestinal tract is a muscular tube whose function is to transport foodstuffs quickly from the mouth to the stomach. It is covered by nonkeratinized stratified squamous epithelium (Fig 16–7). In general, it has the same layers described for the rest of the digestive tract. In the submucosa are groups of small mucus-secreting glands, the *esophageal glands.* In the lamina propria of the region proximal to the stomach there are groups of glands called *esophageal cardiac glands.* At the distal end of the esophagus the muscular layer is composed only of smooth muscle cells; in the mid portion, a mixture of striated and smooth muscle cells; and at the proximal end, only striated muscle cells.

STOMACH

The stomach is a dilated segment of the digestive tract whose main function is to add fluid to the ingested food, transforming it into a viscous pulp and continuing the process of digestion. Three regions with different histologic structures can be observed in this organ: the *cardia,* the *body* and *fundus,* and the *pylorus* (Fig 16–8). The lining epithelium of all 3 regions consists of columnar mucus-secreting (PAS-positive) cells which can be distinguished from goblet cells by the fact that their nuclei are not flattened at the base of the cells but are round and in the center. The goblet cells are also single cells that do not form a continuous covering layer. The remainder of the surface of the stomach is characterized by the presence of invaginations of its lining epithelium into the lamina propria, forming microscopic furrows called *gastric pits* or *foveolae gastricae.* The entire mucous membrane of the stomach contains a great number of small glands which open into the bottom of these pits. Each of the 3

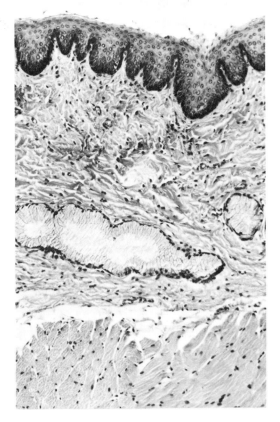

Figure 16—7. Photomicrograph of a section of the upper region of the esophagus. Mucous glands are in the submucosa; striated muscle is in the muscle layer. H&E stain, × 20.

regions of the stomach contains gastric glands of different structure, whereas the gastric pits have the same morphology in all parts of the stomach. The gastric glands are always in the lamina propria and never extend through the muscularis mucosae to the submucosa. The lamina propria of the stomach is composed of loose connective tissue interspersed with smooth muscle and lymphoid cells.

The various types of mucous membranes lining the different parts of the stomach are discussed in the following paragraphs.

Cardiac Region

The cardia is a narrow circular band at the transition between the esophagus and the stomach (Fig 16—8). Its lamina propria contains simple or branched tubular glands. The terminal portion of these glands is frequently coiled and often presents a large lumen. Their secretory cells produce mucus. These glands are similar in structure to the cardiac glands of the terminal portion of the esophagus.

Body & Fundus

The lamina propria of these areas is filled with characteristic branched tubular glands which open into

the bottom of the gastric pits. Different areas of these glands have a different cellular structure (Figs 16—8 and 16—9). It is customary to regard them as consisting of 3 regions from the end of the gastric pit to the base of the gland: the isthmus, the neck, and the base. Six different types of cells are present whose aspect, function, and location in the gland will be described: (1) isthmus mucous cells, (2) parietal or oxyntic cells, (3) neck mucous cells, (4) zymogenic cells, (5) argentaffin cells, and (6) cells producing glucagonlike substance.

(1) The *isthmus mucous cells* (Figs 16—8 and 16—9) are present in the upper region of the gland in the transitional region between the neck and the gastric pits. These cells are continuous with and quite similar to the covering epithelium of the stomach, but they are lower and have fewer mucous granules in their cytoplasm. They probably derive from mitotic activity of small undifferentiated cells in the neck region which are differentiating into covering epithelial cells (Figs 16—8 and 16—9).

(2) The *parietal* or *oxyntic cells* are present mainly in the isthmus region mixed with the undifferentiated cells described above and in the neck region between the neck mucous cells (Figs 16—8 and 16—9). They are scarcer in the gland's base. They are rounded or pyramidal cells with central round nuclei and intensely eosinophilic cytoplasm. They are disposed as if fitted between the basal regions of the other cells of the glands (Fig 16—8). When observed in the electron microscope, they present the following characteristics: (a) A deep circular cytoplasmic invagination is present, simulating different *intracellular canaliculi*. This invagination is lined with abundant microvilli (Fig 16—10). (b) No secretory granules are seen. (c) The rest of the cytoplasm consists mainly of spherical or elongated mitochondria densely packed with cristae and a Golgi apparatus near the base of the cell (Figs 16—10 and 16—11). These cells do not show any external coating of protein-polysaccharide on their plasma membranes.

The parietal cells produce the hydrochloric acid present in gastric juice. The intracellular canaliculi described above derive mainly from invaginations of the plasma membrane and are the probable site of secretion of hydrochloric acid. In human disease, the number of parietal cells is closely correlated with the acid-producing capacity of the stomach. In cases of atrophic gastritis, both parietal and zymogenic cells are much less numerous; consequently, the gastric juice has little or no acid and pepsin activity.

Parietal cells secrete 0.16 M hydrochloric acid, 0.07 M potassium chloride, traces of other electrolytes, and practically no organic matter. They deal mainly, therefore, with ions. There is evidence that the acid secreted originates from chlorides present in the blood plus a cation (H^+) resulting from the action of an enzyme—*carbonic anhydrase.* Carbonic anhydrase acts on CO_2 to produce carbonic acid, which dissociates into bicarbonate and one H^+. Both the cation and the chloride ion are actively transported across the cell membrane whereas water diffuses passively along the

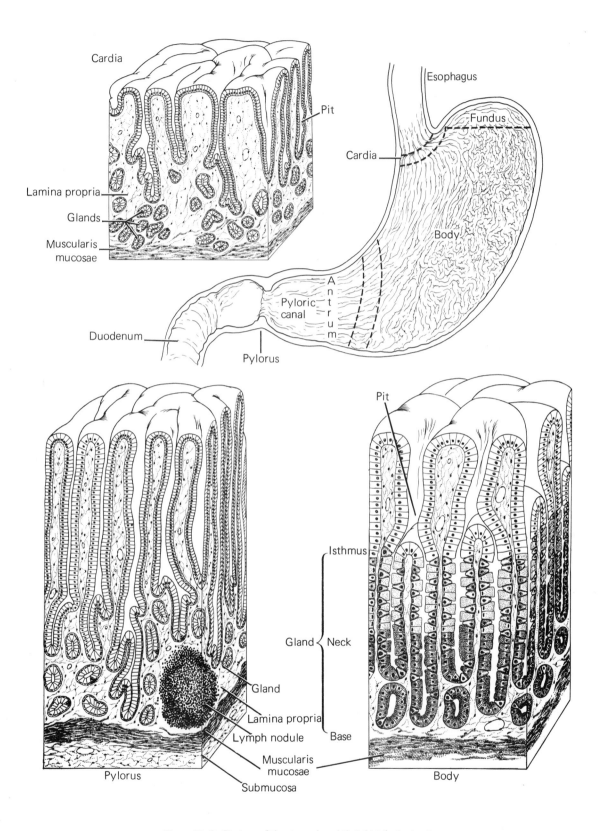

Figure 16—8. Regions of the stomach and their histologic structure.

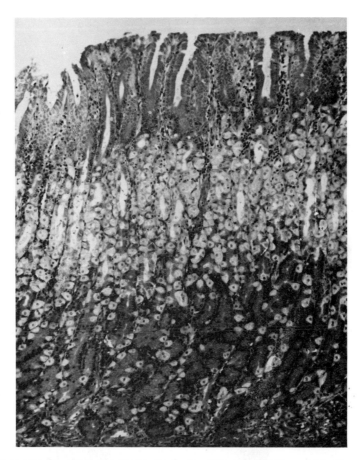

Figure 16–9. Photomicrograph of a section of a gland in the fundus of the stomach. The parietal cells predominate in the upper region of the gland, whereas the zymogenic cells predominate in the lower region. H&E stain, × 100.

osmotic gradient (Fig 16–13). The presence of abundant mitochondria in the parietal cells suggests that the metabolic processes in these cells are highly energy-consuming. As a matter of fact, this cell type presents histochemical peculiarities which characterize it as one of the cells with the highest observable energy metabolism.

Radioautographic studies performed with labeled vitamin B_{12} strongly suggest that the parietal cells are, in humans, the site of production of *intrinsic factor*. In other species, however, this substance may be present in other cells.

The presence of intrinsic factor is normally required for vitamin B_{12} absorption, and this vitamin binds strongly in the lumen of the stomach with intrinsic factor, a glycoprotein produced locally. This complex is absorbed by the cells in the ileum. This explains why lack of intrinsic factor can lead to vitamin B_{12} deficiency—a disease which results in a disorder of the red blood cell—forming mechanism known as *pernicious anemia* and usually caused by *atrophic gastritis.* In a high percentage of cases, pernicious anemia seems to be an autoimmune disease, since antibodies against parietal cell proteins are often detected in the blood of patients with the disease.

The secretion of the parietal cells is activated by different mechanisms. One is through cholinergic nerve endings. Histamine and a polypeptide called *gastrin,* both secreted in the gastric mucosa, act strongly to stimulate the production of hydrochloric acid.

(3) *Neck mucous cells* are sparse and located between the parietal cells in the necks of the glands. Despite being mucous cells, they have morphologic and histochemical characteristics that make their mucous secretions quite different from that of the surface-lining epithelial mucous cells. They are irregular in shape, having their nuclei at the base of the cell. In the electron microscope they show interdigitations of their lateral surfaces and desmosomes. Their ovoid or spherical granules are near the apical surface and are stained intensely with PAS or mucicarmine.

(4) Zymogenic cells (Fig 16–12) predominate in the lower region of the tubular glands and have all the characteristics of a protein-synthesizing cell. The granules present in their cytoplasm contain pepsinogen. Their basophilia is due to the large number of ribosomes present in the cytoplasm and in the granular endoplasmic reticulum (see Chapter 4). In humans, these cells produce the enzymes pepsin and lipase. Their lipolytic activity, however, is weak and of doubt-

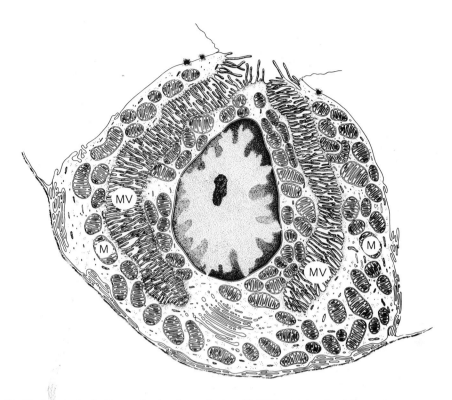

Figure 16—10. A parietal cell. Observe the abundance of microvilli (MV), mitochondria (M), and the intracellular canaliculi.

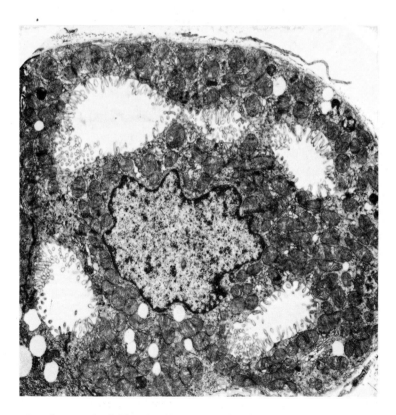

Figure 16—11. Cross-section of a parietal cell. Note the abundant mitochondria and the intracellular canaliculi lined by microvilli. X 300.

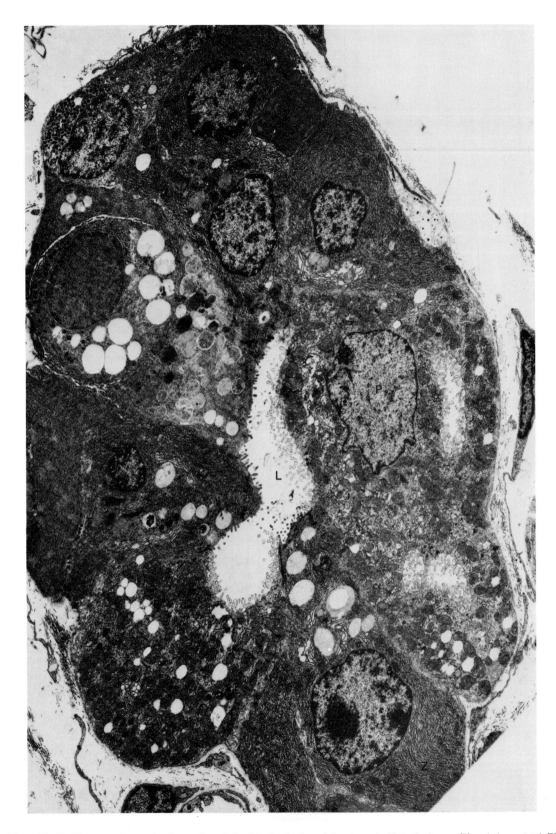

Figure 16—12. Electron micrograph of a section of gland in the fundus of the stomach. Note the lumen (L) and the parietal (P), zymogenic (Z), and argentaffin (A) cells. × 5300.

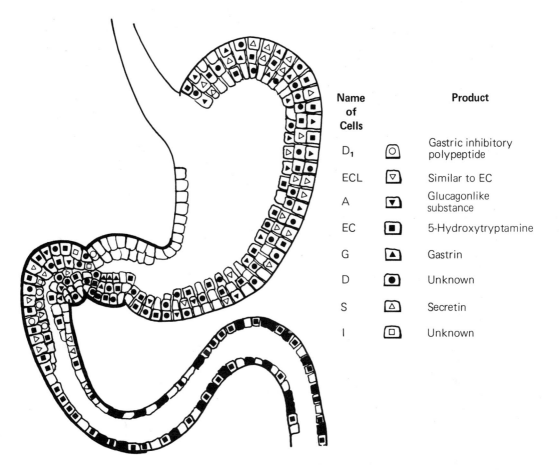

Name of Cells		Product
D₁	⟨◌⟩	Gastric inhibitory polypeptide
ECL	⟨▽⟩	Similar to EC
A	⟨▼⟩	Glucagonlike substance
EC	⟨■⟩	5-Hydroxytryptamine
G	⟨▲⟩	Gastrin
D	⟨◉⟩	Unknown
S	⟨△⟩	Secretin
I	⟨□⟩	Unknown

Figure 16–15. Distribution of endocrine cells in stomach and intestine. Some of them have an identifiable secretion or equivalent to that produced by certain cells of the pancreas. Others are only morphologically identified. (Slightly modified and reproduced, with permission, from Pearse AGE: Cell migration and the alimentary system: Endocrine contributions of the neural crest to the gut and its derivatives. Digestion 8:372, 1973. Copyright © 1973 by S Karger AG, Basel.)

product was originally a biogenic amine, during evolution most of these cells have been transformed into polypeptide hormone - secreting cells. Thus, a relationship exists between these APUD cells and the endocrine polypeptide cells of the pancreas and other organs. In regarding these cells as part of an entero-insular group, pathologists may be able to provide reasonable explanations of some obscure endocrine diseases. (See also Chapter 4.)

Pylorus

The pylorus presents deep gastric pits into which open tubular or ramified tubular glands, the *pyloric glands,* which are very similar to the glands of the cardiac region. In the pyloric region, however, are found long pits and short coiled glands—the reverse of the situation in the cardiac region. Recently, with the aid of the electron microscope and immunofluorescence, cells have been described in the pyloric glands which have the characteristics of APUD cells and are responsible for the production of the polypeptide gastrin (Figs 16–15 and 16–16).

Other Layers of the Stomach

The muscularis mucosae of the stomach is composed of 2 or 3 different layers. From this layer, perpendicular muscle fibers penetrate into the lamina propria; when they contract, folds are produced in the organ's internal surface. This contraction may also be important in compressing the glands of the stomach and eliminating their secretion.

The submucosa is composed of loose connective tissue and blood and lymph vessels and is infiltrated by lymphoid cells and mast cells. The muscularis externa is composed of spiral fibers oriented in 3 main directions: the external layer longitudinal, the middle layer circular, and the internal layer oblique. The serous layer is thin and covered by mesothelium.

Regeneration of Gastric Mucosa

The mucous membrane of the stomach regenerates when injured. Radioautographic studies using tritiated thymidine have established that the mitotic activity is confined mainly to cells of the necks of the glands. From this region arise 2 lines of cells. One is

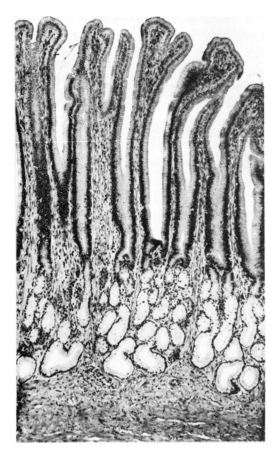

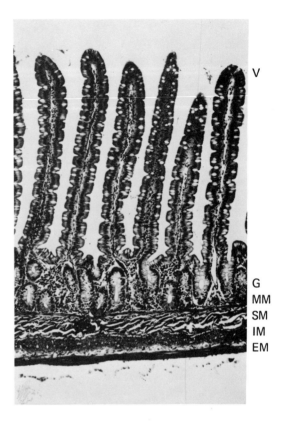

Figure 16—16. Photomicrograph of a section of the pyloric region of the stomach. Observe the deep gastric pits with short pyloric glands (lamina propria). H&E stain, × 40.

Figure 16—17. Photomicrograph of the small intestine. Observe the villi (V), the intestinal glands (G), muscularis mucosae (MM), submucosa (SM), and the external and internal muscle layers (EM and IM). H&E stain, × 40.

directed toward the surface of the mucous membrane and becomes differentiated into the mucous epithelial lining. This process is constant and relatively rapid. It is estimated that the rate of renewal of these epithelial cells is about 2—3 days. The epithelial lining of the stomach is therefore short-lived, and the cells are constantly shed into the lumen.

The other line of cells derived from mitosis of neck cells flows in an opposite direction. These cells slowly differentiate into parietal and zymogenic cells. This is a slow process, and regeneration of the secretory portion of the gastric glands is correspondingly slow.

THE SMALL INTESTINE

In small intestine, the processes of digestion are completed and the products of digestion are absorbed. The small intestine is relatively long—approximately 6 meters—and this permits prolonged contact between

food and digestive enzymes. The small intestine consists of 3 segments: *duodenum, jejunum,* and *ileum.* The 3 segments have many characteristics in common and will be discussed together.

Mucous Membrane of the Small Intestine

Grossly, the lining of the small intestine shows a series of permanent folds, *plicae circulares* or *valves of Kerckring,* consisting of mucosa and submucosa and having a semilunar, circular, or spiral form. Under magnification, the *intestinal villi* are easily seen. These structures, 0.5—1.5 mm long, are outgrowths of the mucous membranes (epithelium plus lamina propria) which project into the lumen of the small intestine. In the duodenum they are leaf-shaped, gradually assuming the form of a finger as the ileum is reached (Figs 16—17 and 16—19).

Between the areas where villi insert into the mucous membrane, one may observe small openings of simple tubular glands called *intestinal glands* (crypts or glands of *Lieberkühn*) (Figs 16—17 and 16—19). Analysis of transverse sections of the intestine shows that there exists a continuity between the epithelium

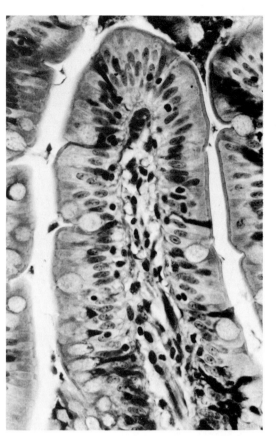

Figure 16–18 (at right). Photomicrograph of the tip of a villus of the human ileum. Observe the connective tissue core with blood and lymph vessels surrounded by the epithelial layer, in which goblet cells frequently occur. At right, the cuticle formed by microvilli present in the surface of the cell is clearly visible. H&E stain, × 450.

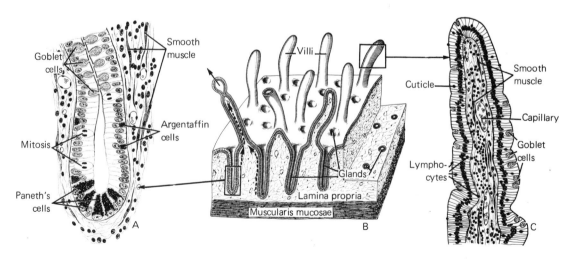

Figure 16–19. Schematic diagrams illustrating the structure of the small intestine. *A:* The intestinal glands present a lining of intestinal epithelium and goblet cells (upper portion). At a lower level, the immature epithelial cells are frequently seen in mitosis; note also the presence of Paneth and argentaffin cells. As the immature cells progress upward, they differentiate and develop microvilli seen as cuticle in the light microscope. Thus, in the blind end of these glands, cell proliferation and cell differentiation occur simultaneously. *B:* The small intestine under low magnification. In the villus to the left, observe the desquamation of a small group of epithelial cells. Because of constant mitotic activity of the cells from the blind end of the glands and the upward migration of these cells (dotted arrows), the intestinal epithelium is continuously renewed. Observe the glands of Lieberkühn. *C:* A villus tip seen with medium magnification, showing the columnar covering epithelium with its cuticle and a moderate number of goblet cells. In the connective tissue core of the villus, capillaries, smooth muscle cells, and leukocytes can be seen. Lymphocytes are constantly crossing the epithelial layer into the intestinal lumen in great numbers. Here they are digested and their amino acids and nucleotides are reabsorbed and reused by the organism. (Redrawn and reproduced, with permission, from Ham AW: *Histology,* 6th ed. Lippincott, 1969.)

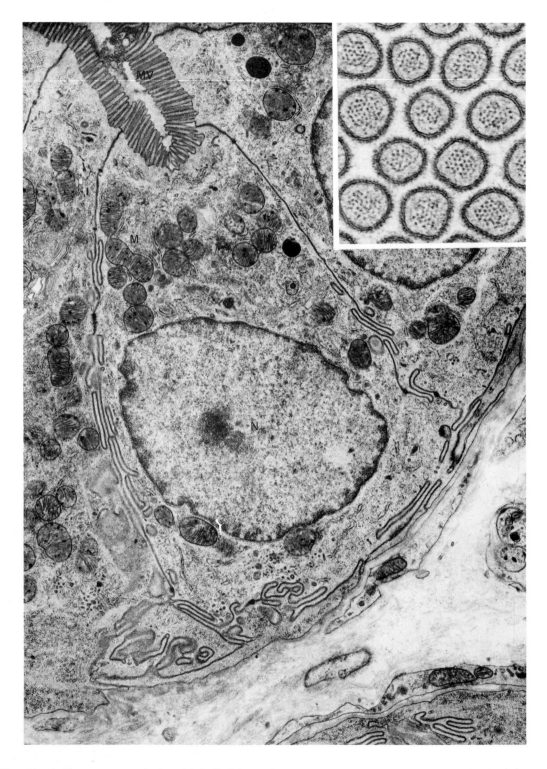

Figure 16–20. Electron micrograph of epithelial cell of the small intestine. Observe the accumulation of mitochondria (M) in their apexes. The luminal surface is covered with microvilli (MV) (shown in transverse section in the inset). N, nucleus. Reduced from × 8000. (Courtesy of KR Porter.)

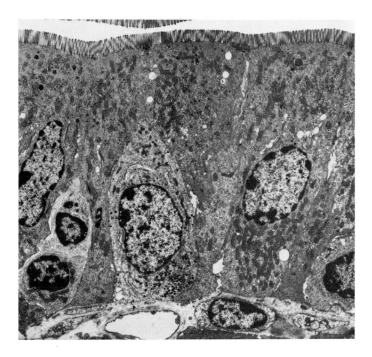

Figure 16—21. Section of epithelium of small intestine. With the light microscope, abundant microvilli at the cell apex can be seen to form the striated border or cuticle. At left are 2 lymphocytes crossing the epithelium. In the center is shown an argentaffin cell (**A**) with its basal secretory granules. Reduced from × 3000.

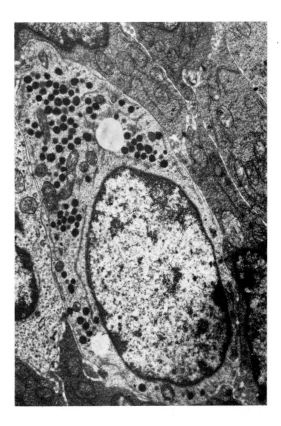

Figure 16—22 (at right). A secretin-producing cell from dog duodenum. × 10,250. (Courtesy of AGE Pearse.)

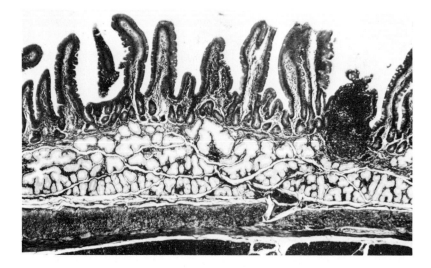

Figure 16—23. Photomicrograph of the duodenum, showing villi and duodenal glands in the submucosa. The dark structure at right is a lymph nodule; at the bottom are 2 smooth muscle layers. H&E stain, × 30.

of these glands and the epithelium which covers the villi. The rate of renewal of the epithelium of the villi is quite fast. The cells thus formed—owing to frequent mitosis—gradually slide upward in the direction of the tip of the villi where they are desquamated in small groups (Fig 16—19). About 250 g of mucous membrane are shed every day into the small intestine.

The epithelial cells of the entire gastrointestinal tract respond to certain stimuli (hormones, cholinergic neural activity) by production of new cells. Cells of the basal layer of the esophageal epithelium, of the isthmus between the gastric pits and the glands, of the lower half of the Lieberkühn glands, and of the lower third of the crypts of the large intestine are easily labeled with tritiated thymidine and consequently identified as proliferating cells. The rate of cell loss by migration or death is equal to the rate of production. The villus increases or decreases in size depending on the number of cells produced and desquamated in the lumen (Fig 16—19B). From this proliferative zone in each of the regions the cells move next to the maturation area where they undergo normal structural and enzymic maturation, thus providing the functional cell differentiation of each region.

In man, the renewal rate of the epithelium in the esophagus is approximately 2—3 days; in the epithelial lining of the remainder of the gastrointestinal tract, it is 1—2 days. The replacement time of the parietal and zymogenic cells extends from 1 year to many years.

The mucosa of the small intestine is lined with several types of cells. The most common are the *columnar (absorptive) intestinal* epithelial cells, followed by *goblet cells, argentaffin cells, Paneth cells, glucagonlike substance - producing cells, cholecystokinin-producing cells,* etc (Fig 16—15).

The *absorptive cells* are columnar cells characterized by the presence of a condensation of their apical surface, the *cuticle* (Fig 16—18). With the aid of the

electron microscope, the cuticle can be seen to be a layer of densely grouped microvilli (Figs 16—20 and 16—21). It is estimated that each of these cells has an average of about 3000 microvilli and that 1 sq mm of mucosa contains about 200 million of these structures. Thus, the microvilli have the important physiologic function of considerably increasing the area of surface contact of the intestines with food. Studies performed by isolating the cuticles of these cells by differential

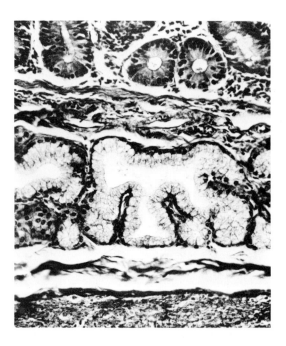

Figure 16—24. Details of the mucosal duodenal glands under higher magnification than that shown in Fig 16—23. H&E stain, reduced from × 200.

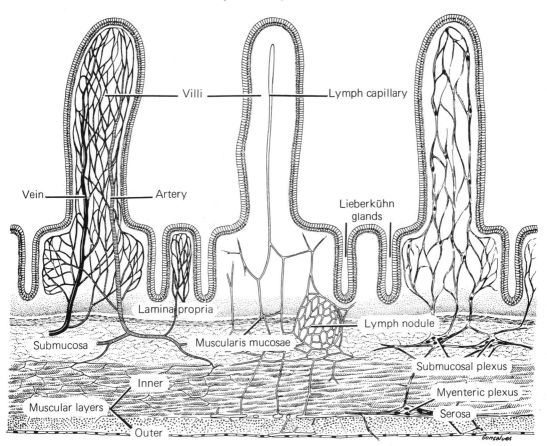

Figure 16–25. Diagram showing the blood circulation *(left)*, lymphatic circulation *(center)*, and innervation *(right)* of the small intestine.

centrifugation and then applying immunofluorescence technics suggest that the cuticle is the site of activity of the disaccharidases of the small intestine. These enzymes, bound to microvilli, hydrolyze the disaccharides into monosaccharides, which are easily absorbed. Deficiencies of these disaccharidases have been described in human diseases characterized by digestive disturbances. Some of these enzymatic deficiencies seem to be of genetic origin. An analogous localization has been postulated for dipeptidases which hydrolyze dipeptides into their component amino acids.

Another important function of the columnar intestinal cells, however, is to absorb the metabolites that result from the digestive process. This is discussed further below.

The *goblet cells* are interspersed between the absorptive cells. They are less abundant in the duodenum and increase in number as one approaches the ileum. The goblet cells produce acid glycoproteins whose main function is to lubricate the lining of the intestine.

The *argentaffin cells* have already been described in the section on the stomach. They are more numerous in the basal portion of the intestinal glands. It has been speculated that these cells may release 5-hydroxy-tryptamine, which actively stimulates the smooth muscle layer of the intestines and would therefore greatly increase the motility of this organ (Fig 16–21).

The *Paneth cells* in the basal portion of the intestinal glands are typical exocrine serous cells of the protein-synthesizing type described in Chapter 4. They have a well-developed granular endoplasmic reticulum and Golgi apparatus. Their wide distribution in many species and their high zinc content suggest that they may be of physiologic importance. They probably secrete the enzyme lysozyme. Radioautographic studies have shown that the renewal rate of the Paneth cells is about 30 days—much slower than the rate of 1 or 2 days noted in the case of the mucous and absorptive cells of the intestinal lining.

Cells that produce the hormones *secretin* and *glucagonlike substance* have recently been localized by means of immunohistochemical technics. They are cells of the APUD type (see above and Chapter 4) located between the absorptive cells in the villi. Fig 16–22 illustrates a secretin-producing cell. The cells that produce *cholecystokinin*—a polypeptide known to be present in the intestine and of physiologic importance in stimulating contraction of the gallbladder—have not yet been clearly identified.

The lamina propria of the small intestine is composed of loose connective tissue and blood and lymph vessels, nerve fibers, and smooth muscle cells. Just below the basement membrane, a continuous layer of antibody-producing lymphoid cells and macrophages has been described, forming an immunologic barrier at this region.

The lamina propria penetrates into the core of the intestinal villi, taking along blood and lymph vessels, nerves, and smooth muscle cells. These cells are probably responsible for the rhythmic movements of the villi, which are important for absorption.

The *muscularis mucosae* does not present any peculiarities in this organ. The submucosa contains, in the initial portion of the duodenum, clusters of ramified, coiled tubular glands which open into the intestinal glands. These are the *duodenal (or Brunner) glands* (Figs 16–23 and 16–24). Their cells are of the mucous type and produce in humans a neutral glycoprotein. The product of secretion of the glands is distinctly alkaline (pH 8.1–9.3), and it has been speculated that its function would be to protect the duodenal mucous membrane against the effects of the acid gastric juice.

Besides the duodenal glands, the intestinal submucosa also contains frequent isolated lymph nodules. Some of these nodules occasionally aggregate, forming *lymph follicles* that are also called *Peyer's patches*, occurring almost exclusively in the ileum.

Vessels & Nerves of the Small Intestine

The blood vessels which nourish the intestine penetrate the muscle layer and form a large plexus in the submucosa. From the submucosa, branches extend to the muscle layer, lamina propria, and villi. Each villus receives, according to its size, one or more branches which form a capillary network just below its epithelium. At the tips of the villi, one or more venules arise from these capillaries and run in the opposite direction, reaching the veins of the submucosal plexus (Fig 16–25). The lymph vessels of the intestine begin as blind tubes in the core of the villi. These structures, despite being larger than the blood capillaries, are difficult to observe because their walls are usually collapsed. These vessels run to the region of lamina propria above the muscularis mucosae, where they form a plexus. From there they are directed to the submucosa, where they surround lymph nodules. These vessels anastomose repeatedly and leave the intestine with the blood vessels.

The neural components of the intestine are composed mainly of submucosal plexuses of Meissner and myenteric plexuses of Auerbach, parasympathetic preganglionic fibers, and sympathetic postganglionic fibers from the celiac plexus. The cells of the ganglia can be identified as belonging to 2 types: one provides motor axons to the muscularis externa or to the muscularis mucosae and the smooth muscle cells of the villi; the other is found mainly in the myenteric plexus and is a connecting neuron with the cells of the first type. Other cells of microglial nature, called interstitial cells, are also seen in these nerve plexuses. Fibers of

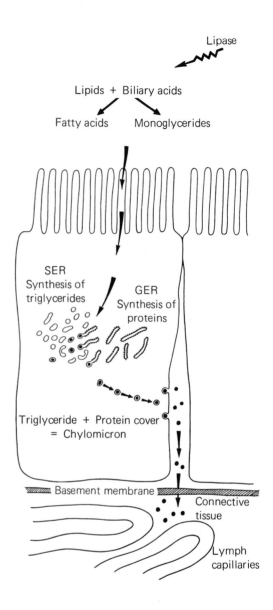

Figure 16–26. Drawing illustrating the sequence of processes that promote lipid absorption in the small intestine. Lipase promotes the hydrolysis of lipids to monoglycerides and fatty acids in the intestinal lumen. These compounds are stabilized in an emulsion by the action of biliary acids. The products of hydrolysis cross the microvilli membranes passively and are collected in the cisternae of the smooth endoplasmic reticulum, where they are synthesized back to triglycerides. These triglycerides are surrounded by a thin layer of proteins forming particles called chylomicrons (0.2–1 μm in diameter). The chylomicrons migrate to the lateral membrane, cross it by a process of membrane fusion (reverse pinocytosis), and flow in the extracellular space in the direction of the blood and lymph vessels. Most chylomicrons go to the lymph and a few to the blood vessels. The long chain lipids (more than C_{12}) go mainly to the lymph vessels. Fatty acids of less than 10–12 carbon atoms are not reesterified to triglycerides but leave the cell directly and enter the blood vessels. GER, granular endoplasmic reticulum; SER, smooth endoplasmic reticulum.

the parasympathetic system often come into contact with cells of the first type. The sympathetic fibers terminate on vessels and muscle cells. The plexuses form the intrinsic part of the intestinal innervation, and the pre- and postganglionic fibers form the extrinsic part.

HISTOPHYSIOLOGY

In the small intestine, the digestive process is completed and its products are absorbed. Lipid digestion occurs mainly as a result of the action of pan-

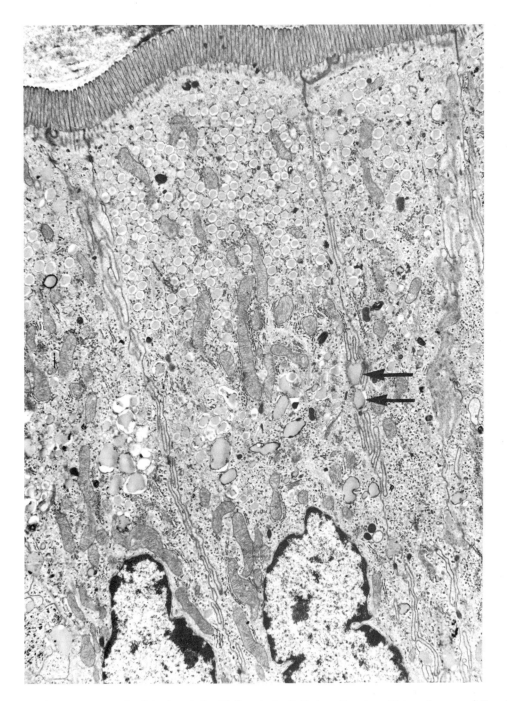

Figure 16—27. Electron micrograph of the intestinal epithelium in the lipid absorption phase. Observe the accumulation of lipid granules in vesicles of the smooth endoplasmic reticulum. (Compare with Fig 16—20.) These vesicles fuse near the nucleus, forming lipid droplets that migrate laterally and cross the cell membranes to the extracellular space (arrows). × 5000. (Courtesy of HI Friedman.)

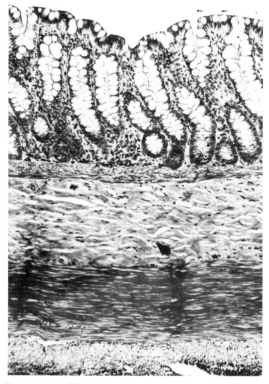

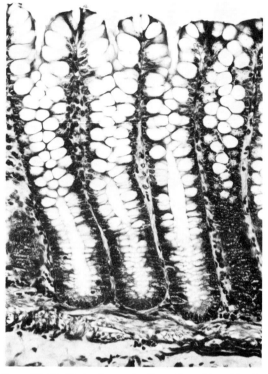

Figure 16–28. Photomicrograph of a section of large intestine with its various layers. Observe the absence of villi. H&E stain, X 30.

Figure 16–29. Photomicrograph of a section of large intestine. Observe the intestinal glands with abundant goblet cells. H&E stain, reduced from X 100.

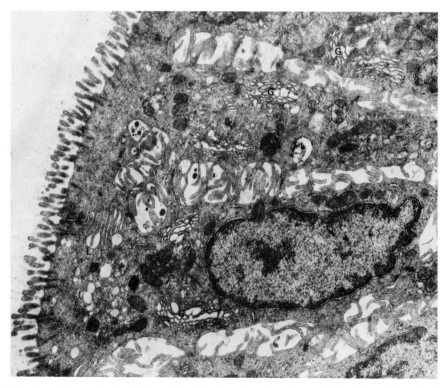

Figure 16–30. Electron micrograph of epithelial cells of the large intestine. Observe the luminal surface of the microvilli, the well-developed Golgi apparatus (G), lysosomes (L), and dilated intercellular spaces filled by microvilli. Reduced from X 5000.

creatic lipase and bile. In humans, most of the lipid absorption occurs in the duodenum and upper jejunum. Figs 16–26 and 16–27 illustrate present concepts of this process of absorption.

The amino acids and monosaccharides derived from digestion of the proteins and carbohydrates are absorbed by the epithelial cells by active transport without underlying visible morphologic change. In newborn animals, transfer of undigested proteins from colostrum occurs as a result of pinocytotic processes in the cell apex. In this way, antibodies secreted into the colostrum can be transferred to the young animal—an important aspect of the immune defense mechanism. This capacity to transfer proteins is almost completely lost after a few days and is minimal in adults. In diseases marked by severe damage to epithelial cells, the transfer of undigested proteins to the blood increases considerably. The presence of folds, villi, and microvilli greatly increases the surface of the intestinal lining—an important characteristic in an organ where absorption occurs so intensely. It has been calculated that the presence of villi increases the intestinal surface 8-fold whereas the microvilli increase it 20-fold. Both of these processes are therefore responsible for a 160-fold increase of the intestinal surface.

Another process that is probably of importance for intestinal function is the rhythmic movement of the villi. This occurs as a result of contraction of smooth muscle cells in the cores of the villi. These asynchronous movements occur at the rate of several strokes per minute. During digestion, their rate increases, and in fasting animals the rate is considerably lower.

For these reasons, in disorders marked by atrophy of the intestinal mucosa due to infections or nutritional deficiencies, the absorption of metabolites is greatly hindered, producing the so-called *malabsorption syndrome.*

THE LARGE INTESTINE

The large intestine consists of a smooth mucosal membrane with no folds except in its distal (rectal) portion. The epithelial lining is columnar and has—as in the small intestine—a thin cuticular region. No villi are present in this portion of the intestine. The *intestinal glands of Lieberkühn* are long and characterized by a great abundance of goblet cells and a small number of argentaffin cells (Figs 16–28, 16–29, and 16–30). The structure of this organ is well suited to its main functions: water absorption and formation of the fecal mass plus production of mucus and lubrication of the mucosal surface.

The lamina propria is rich in lymphoid cells and

nodules. The nodules frequently cross the muscularis mucosae and invade the submucosa. The muscle layer is composed of longitudinal and circular strands. This layer differs from the small intestine since the fibers of the outer longitudinal layer congregate in 3 thick longitudinal bands called *taeniae coli.* In the free portions of the colon, the serous layer is characterized by small pendulous protuberances composed of adipose tissue— the *appendices epiploicae.*

In the anal region, the mucous membrane presents a series of longitudinal folds, the *rectal columns of Morgagni.* About 2 cm above the anal opening, the intestinal mucosa is abruptly replaced by stratified squamous epithelium. In this region, the lamina propria contains a plexus of large veins that, when excessively dilated and varicose, produce hemorrhoids.

THE APPENDIX

The appendix is an evagination of the cecum characterized by a relatively small, narrow, and irregular lumen due to the presence of abundant lymphoid follicles in its wall. Its general structure is similar to that of the large intestine. However, it contains fewer and shorter intestinal glands and has no taeniae coli (Fig 16–31).

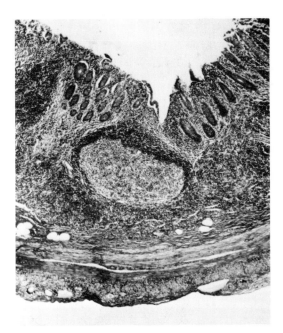

Figure 16–31. Photomicrograph of a section of appendix. There are few glands and abundant lymphoid follicles. H&E stain, × 20.

References

Berger EH: The distribution of parietal cells in the stomach: A histographic study. Am J Anat 54:87, 1934.

Cardell RR Jr, Bandenhausen S, Porter KR: Intestinal triglyceride absorption in the rat. J Cell Biol 34:123, 1967.

Creamer B: Variations in small-intestinal villous shape and mucosal dynamics. Brit MJ 2:1371, 1964.

Croft DN & others: DNA and cell loss from normal small-intestinal mucosa: A clinical method of assessing cell turnover. Lancet 2:70, 1968.

David H: The mechanism of desquamation of cells from the intestinal villi: An electron microscopic study. Virchows Arch Pathol Anat 342:19, 1967.

Deane HW: Some electron microscopic observations on the lamina propria of the gut, with comments on the close association of macrophages, plasma cells, and eosinophils. Anat Rec 149:453, 1964.

Doell RG, Rosen G, Kretchmer N: Immunochemical studies of intestinal disaccharidases during normal and precocious development. Proc Nat Acad Sc 54:1268, 1965.

Forssmann WG: Ultrastructure of hormone-producing cells of the upper gastrointestinal tract. Page 31 in: *Origin, Chemistry, Physiology and Pathophysiology of the Gastrointestinal Hormones.* Creutzfeldt W (editor). Schattauer, 1970.

Freeman JA: Goblet cell fine structure. Anat Rec 154:121, 1966.

Fresen O, Holzki J: Morphology, localization and behavior of the basal-granulated (enterochromaffin) cells in the human gastroduodenal mucosa. Z Zellforsch Mikrosk Anat 90:296, 1968.

Greco V & others: Histochemistry of the colonic epithelial mucins in normal subjects and in patients with ulcerative colitis. Gut 8:491, 1967.

Hakanson R, Owman C: Concomitant histochemical demonstration of histamine and catecholamines in enterochromaffin-like cells of gastric mucosa. Life Sc 6:759, 1967.

Hally AD: The fine structure of the Paneth cell. J Anat 92:268, 1958.

Hoedemseker PJ & others: Further investigations about the site of production of Castle's gastric intrinsic factor. Lab Invest 15:1163, 1966.

Hugon J, Borgers M: Fine structural localization of lysosomal enzymes in the absorbing cells of the duodenal mucosa of the mouse. J Cell Biol 33:212, 1967.

Ito S, Winchester RJ: The fine structure of the gastric mucosa in the rat. J Cell Biol 16:541, 1963.

Junqueira LCU, Tafuri WL, Tafuri CP: Quantitative and cytochemical studies on the intestinal plexuses of the guinea pig. Exp Cell Res (Suppl 5), 568, 1958.

Kotani M & others: Reutilization of DNA breakdown products from lymphocytes in lumen of intestine. Blood 29:616, 1967.

Leaming DB, Cauna N: A qualitative and quantitative study of the myenteric plexus of the small intestine of the cat. J Anat 95:160, 1961.

Leblond CP, Messier B: Renewal of chief cells and goblet cells in the small intestine as shown by radioautography after injection of thymidine H^3 into mice. Anat Record 132:247, 1958.

Leeson TS, Leeson CR: The fine structure of Brunner's glands in man. J Anat 103:263, 1968.

Lipkin M: Proliferation and differentiation of gastrointestinal cells. Physiol Rev 53:981, 1973.

Lorenzsonn V, Trier JS: The fine structure of human rectal mucosa: The epithelial lining of the base of the crypt. Gastroenterology 55:88, 1968.

McGuigan JE: Gastric mucosal intracellular localization of gastrin by immunofluorescence. Gastroenterology 55:315, 1968.

Mjör IA, Pindberg JJ: *Histology of the Human Tooth.* Munksgaard, 1973.

Pearse AGE: Cell migration and the alimentary system: Endocrine contributions of the neural crest to the gut and its derivatives. Digestion 8:372, 1973.

Pearse AGE, Polak YM: Endocrine tumours of neural crest origin: Neurolophomas, apudomas and the APUD concept. Med Biol 52:3, 1974.

Pearse AGE, Riechen ED: Histology and cytochemistry of cells of small intestine. Brit M Bull 23:217, 1967.

Penttilä A: Histochemical reactions of the enterochromaffin cells and the 5-hydroxytryptamine content of the mammal duodenum. Acta physiologica scandinav Suppl 281:7, 1966.

Pfeiffer CJ, Rowden G, Weibel J: *Gastrointestinal Ultrastructure.* Academic Press, 1974.

Pick J, De Lemos C, Cianella A: Fine structure of nerve terminals in the human gut. Anat Record 159:131, 1966.

Pittman FE, Pittman JC: An electron microscopic study of the epithelium of normal human sigmoid colonic mucosa. Gut 7:644, 1966.

Polak JM & others: Immunofluorescent localization of secretin and enteroglucagon in human intestinal mucosa. Scandinav J Gastroent 6:739, 1971.

Robertson RN: The separation of protons and electrons as a fundamental biological process. Endeavour 26:134, 1967.

Schade SG: Studies on antibody to intrinsic factor. J Clin Invest 46:615, 1967.

Sedar AW: Uptake of peroxidase into the smooth-surfaced tubular system of the gastric acid-secreting cell. J Cell Biol 43:179, 1969.

Troughton WD, Trier JS: Paneth cell and goblet cell renewal in mouse duodenal crypts. J Cell Biol 41:251, 1969.

Ugolev AM, Kooshuck KI: Hydrolysis of dipeptides in cells of the small intestine. Nature 212:859, 1966.

17 . . .
Glands Associated With the Digestive Tract

The subjects of this chapter are the salivary glands, pancreas, liver, and gallbladder. The function of the salivary glands is to wet and lubricate the oral cavity and its contents; to initiate the digestion of food; to promote the excretion of certain substances such as urea and thiocyanate; and to reabsorb sodium and excrete potassium.

The main functions of the pancreas are to produce digestive enzymes which act in the small intestine and to secrete the hormones insulin and glucagon into the bloodstream. The liver produces bile, an important fluid in the digestion of fats; plays a major role in lipid, carbohydrate, and protein metabolism; inactivates and metabolizes many toxic substances and drugs; and participates in iron metabolism and the synthesis of blood

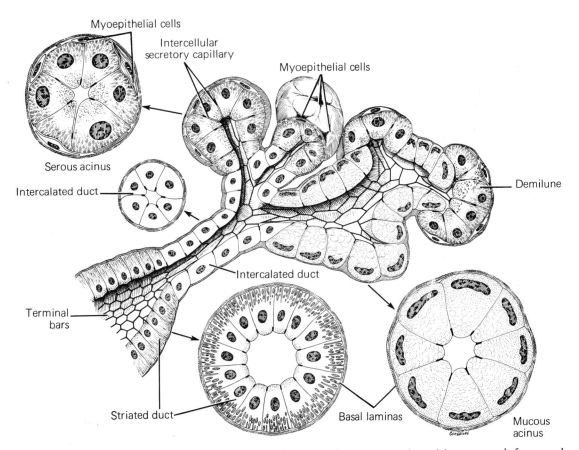

Figure 17–1. The structure of the submandibular (submaxillary) gland. In the secretory portion, acini are composed of serous and mucous cells and tubules of mucous cells. In serous cells, the nuclei are rounded, and in the basal third of the cell an accumulation of granular endoplasmic reticulum (ergastoplasm) is evident. The cellular apex is filled with secretory granules. The nuclei of mucous cells are flattened and located near the bases of the cells; they have no ergastoplasm and present distinct secretory granules. The ducts are short and are lined by cuboid epithelium. The striated ducts are composed of columnar cells with characteristics of ion-transporting cells (see Chapter 4), such as basal membrane invaginations and mitochondrial accumulation. (After Braus.)

proteins and factors necessary for blood coagulation. The gallbladder stores bile and reabsorbs water from it.

THE SALIVARY GLANDS

Besides the small glands scattered in the oral cavity described in the previous chapter, 3 large salivary glands are present: the *parotid, submandibular (submaxillary),* and *sublingual* glands.

Analysis of the structure of these glands shows that they are composed of morphologic and functional units called *adenomeres.* In Fig 17—1 is illustrated an adenomere of the submandibular gland. Note that it has a secretory portion composed of glandular cells and the conducting *intercalated striated* or *secretory* ducts. Near the bases of the cells of the secretory portion and of the intercalated ducts, myoepithelial cells are present (described in Chapter 4).

The large salivary glands are not mere collections of adenomeres but contain other components such as connective tissue, blood and lymph vessels, and nerves organized in a definite pattern.

Thus, these glands are surrounded by a capsule of connective tissue rich in collagen fibers. From this capsule, septa of connective tissue penetrate into the gland, dividing it into lobules. From these septa are derived fibers of connective tissue which individually involve the components of the adenomeres. Between these fibers and the cells, a distinct basal lamina can be observed under the electron microscope (Fig 17—1). The vessels and nerves enter the gland at the *hilus* and from there branch gradually to the lobules and adeno-

meres. A rich capillary network surrounds the components of the adenomeres. The striated ducts present in the lobules—also called *intralobular ducts*—converge and fuse into ducts in the septa separating the lobules, at which point they are called *extralobular ducts.* These are characterized by an abundant sheath of connective tissue and a lining of stratified columnar epithelium which is gradually transformed into stratified squamous epithelium.

The specific characteristics of each of the major salivary glands will now be considered individually.

Parotid Glands

The parotid gland is a branched acinous gland. Its secretory portion is composed almost exclusively of seromucous cells (Fig 17—2). In humans, these cells are PAS-positive, and a moderate amount of RNA as compared to the pancreas is present in their basal regions. Their secretory granules (Fig 17—3) are rich in proteins and have a high amylase activity. The other components of this gland are similar to the general description just given. In humans, the secretory cells represent about 90% of the cell volume; the striated ducts account for about 5%; and the remainder consists of extracellular ducts, connective tissue, vessels, nerves, etc.

Submandibular (Submaxillary) Glands

The submandibular gland is a branched tubuloacinar gland. Its secretory portion contains mucous cells and serous cells. The serous cells form acini or are eccentrically located in mucous acini, forming the *demilunes* (Fig 17—4). The serous cells are the main component and are easily distinguished from the mucous cells by their rounded nucleus and an acidophilic

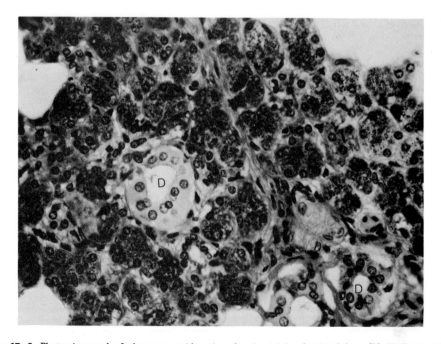

Figure 17—2. Photomicrograph of a human parotid section, showing acini and striated ducts (D). H&E stain, × 360.

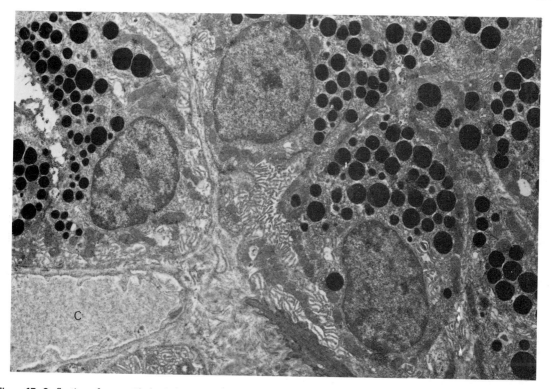

Figure 17–3. Section of a parotid gland showing 3 nuclei of secretory cells and their characteristic secretory granules. At lower left is a fenestrated capillary (C). (Courtesy of LL George.)

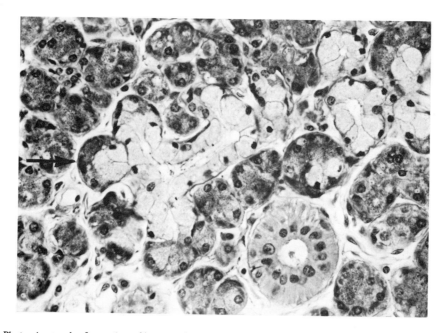

Figure 17–4. Photomicrograph of a section of human submandibular gland. Observe the presence of serous and mucous cells. In the lower right region is a striated duct. The arrow shows a demilune. H&E stain, × 360.

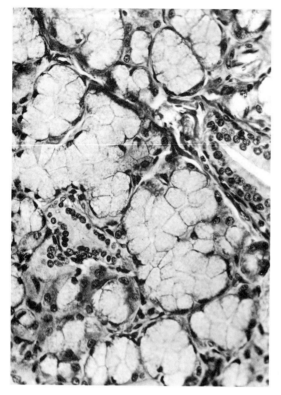

and PAS-positive cytoplasm. These cells are probably responsible for the weak amylolytic activity present in this gland and its saliva. In humans, this gland consists of 80% serous cells, 5% mucous cells, and 5% striated ducts; the remainder consists of vessels, nerves, and other ducts.

Sublingual Gland

The sublingual gland is also (like the submandibular gland) a branched tubulo-acinar gland. It presents, however, no acini formed exclusively by serous cells, and the mucous cells predominate in the sublingual gland. The serous cells also form demilunes in mucous acini. This gland consists of 60% mucous cells, 30% serous cells, and 3% striated ducts (Fig 17–5); the remainder consists of vessels, nerves, and other ducts. The bases of the cells of the striated ducts show the characteristics of ion-transporting cells (Fig 17–6).

Histophysiology of the Salivary Glands

As already mentioned, one of the main functions of the salivary glands is to wet and lubricate the oral cavity and the food. This function is performed by the water and the glycoproteins of saliva. The latter are synthesized mainly by the mucous cells and to a lesser degree by the serous cells of the glands. Human saliva is made up of secretions from the parotid glands (25%), the submandibular glands (70%), and the sublingual gland (5%).

Figure 17–5. Photomicrograph of a human sublingual gland showing the predominance of mucous cells. H&E stain, × 600.

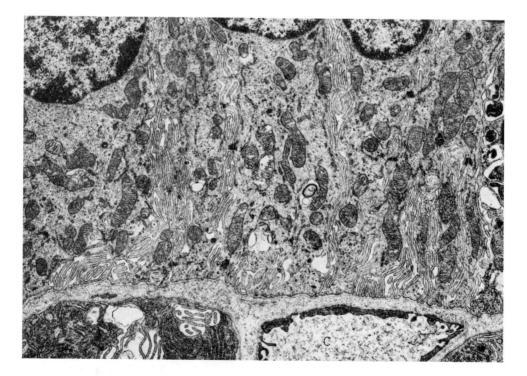

Figure 17–6. Electron micrograph of the basal portion of cells of a striated duct. Observe the membrane invaginations and mitochondria disposed in palisades, characteristics of ion-transporting cells. At the lower right is a fenestrated capillary (C). × 6000. (Courtesy of LL George.)

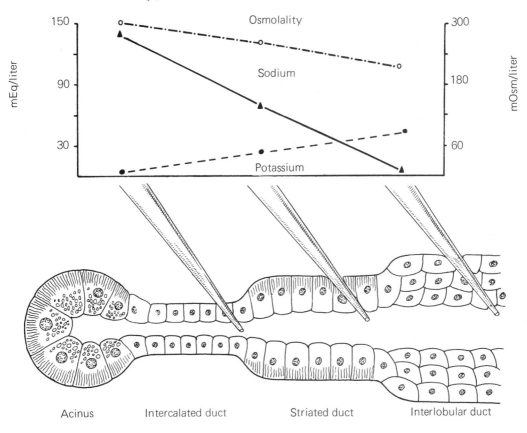

Acinus   Intercalated duct   Striated duct   Interlobular duct

Figure 17-7. Diagram illustrating the results obtained from micropuncture experiments in the salivary gland. When the puncture is close to the secretory portion in the intercalated duct, the sodium and potassium content and the osmolality of the saliva are equal to that observed in the blood. With gradual movement away from the intercalated ducts, the potassium content increases and sodium content and osmolality decrease. This strongly suggests that these changes occur in the epithelial lining of the ducts.

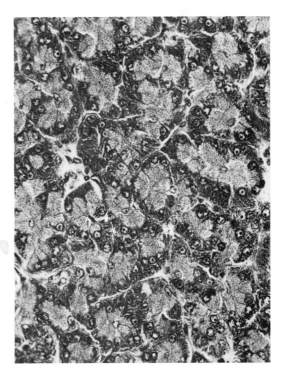

Another important function of these glands in humans is to begin the digestion of carbohydrates. The major part of the hydrolysis of ingested carbohydrates is due to salivary amylase activity. This digestion begins in the mouth but takes place also in the stomach before the gastric juice acidifies the food and therefore decreases considerably the amylase activity. Besides the amylase activity—present mainly in the parotid gland—weak ribonuclease and maltase activities have been described in human saliva.

The function of the intercalated ducts is unknown, although in some species their cells contain secretory granules.

Recent studies performed by inserting micropipettes into the striated and excretory ducts strongly suggest that the saliva produced by the secretory cells is isosmotic with blood and that these ducts actively reabsorb sodium and excrete potassium (Fig 17-7). This explains why saliva is hypotonic and has a higher concentration of potassium and a lower concentration

Figure 17-8 (at right). Photomicrograph showing the appearance of the acinar portion of the pancreas with its excretory cells. H&E stain, × 400.

of sodium than blood. The striated ducts bear morphologic and functional similarities to the renal tubules (Figs 17–6 and 20–9). Both have cells with characteristics of ion-transporting cells, and both are sensitive to aldosterone and vasopressin.

Human salivary glands, although sensitive to hormones, are controlled mainly by the sympathetic and parasympathetic nervous systems, both of which have nerve endings in these glands.

THE PANCREAS

The pancreas is a mixed exocrine and endocrine gland. The endocrine portion is composed of the *islets of Langerhans* (see Chapter 22). The exocrine portion is a compound acinar gland (Fig 17–8). It is quite similar in structure to the parotid. However, in histologic slides, the pancreas is characterized by the absence of striated ducts and the presence of the islets of Langerhans. Another characteristic detail is that the intercalated ducts penetrate into the lumen of the acini lining their initial portion (Fig 17–9). This intra-acinar portion of the intercalated duct is composed of rounded clear cells called *centro-acinar cells* (Fig 17–9). The intercalated ducts are tributary to larger interlobular ducts lined by columnar epithelium in which goblet cells can be observed.

The acinar cell in the human is PAS-positive and is therefore a serous cell. It has all the characteristics of a protein-secreting cell described in Chapter 4 and should be considered as such. In terms of RNA content it is one of the richest cells of the body—a character-

istic which coincides with its active protein-synthetic activity. It has been calculated that in the rat, under conditions of maximal stimulation, the pancreas can produce up to 1.5% of its total proteins in 1 hour. The number of zymogen granules in its cells is variable and depends on the digestive phase, attaining its maximum in fasted animals.

The pancreas is covered by a thin capsule of connective tissue which sends septa into it, separating the pancreatic lobules. The acini are surrounded by a basal lamina supported on a delicate sheath of reticular fibers. It has a rich capillary network.

The human exocrine pancreas secretes, besides water and ions, the following enzymes and proenzymes: trypsinogen, chymotrypsinogen, carboxypeptidase, ribonuclease, deoxyribonuclease, lipase, and amylase.

The control of pancreatic secretion is performed mainly through 2 hormones—*secretin* and *pancreozymin*—probably produced by the epithelial cells present at the apical portion of the intestinal villi.

Secretin promotes the secretion of an abundant fluid, poor in protein and enzyme activity and rich in bicarbonate. It functions mainly in water and ion transport. This action contrasts with that of pancreozymin, which promotes the secretion of a less abundant but protein- and enzyme-rich fluid. This hormone, therefore, acts mainly in the process of extrusion of the zymogen granules. In conditions of extreme malnutrition such as in the disease called kwashiorkor, the pancreatic cells undergo atrophy and lose much of their granular endoplasmic reticulum, and the production of digestive enzymes is hindered.

THE LIVER

With the exception of the skin, the liver is the largest organ of the body. It is situated in the abdominal cavity beneath the diaphragm. Most of its blood (about 70%) comes from the portal vein; a smaller percentage is supplied by the hepatic artery. Through the portal vein, all the material absorbed via the intestines reaches the liver except the lipids, which are transported mainly by the lymph vessels. The position of the liver is convenient for gathering, transforming, and accumulating metabolites and for neutralizing and eliminating toxic substances. This elimination occurs in the bile, an exocrine secretion of the liver which is of importance in the digestion of lipids.

In addition to these main functions, the liver has other important functions which will be studied later on.

The Liver Lobule

The main structural component of the liver is the liver cell or hepatocyte. These epithelial cells are grouped in plates which are interconnected in such a way as to show, in light microscope sections, structural

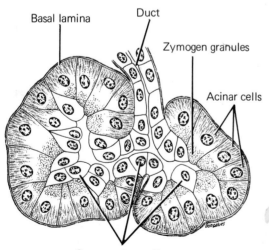

Basal lamina   Duct

Zymogen granules

Acinar cells

Centro-acinar cells

Figure 17–9. Schematic drawing of the structure of the pancreatic acini. The acinar cells are pyramidal, with granules at their apex and ergastoplasm at the cell base. The intercalated duct penetrates partially into the acini forming the centro-acinar cells.

units called by early investigators *liver lobules* (Fig 17–10). The liver lobule forms a prismatic polygonal mass of liver tissue about 0.7 × 2 mm in size (Figs 17–10 and 17–11). In certain animals (eg, the pig), these lobules are separated from each other and sharply delimited by a layer of connective tissue. This does not occur in humans, where the various lobules are in close contact along most of their extent, though in some regions the lobules are separated by connective tissue and blood vessels. These *portal spaces* at the corners of the polygons are occupied by the *portal canals* (also called *portal areas* or *portal tracts*). The human liver contains 3–6 portal canals per lobule, each containing a venule, a branch of the portal vein;

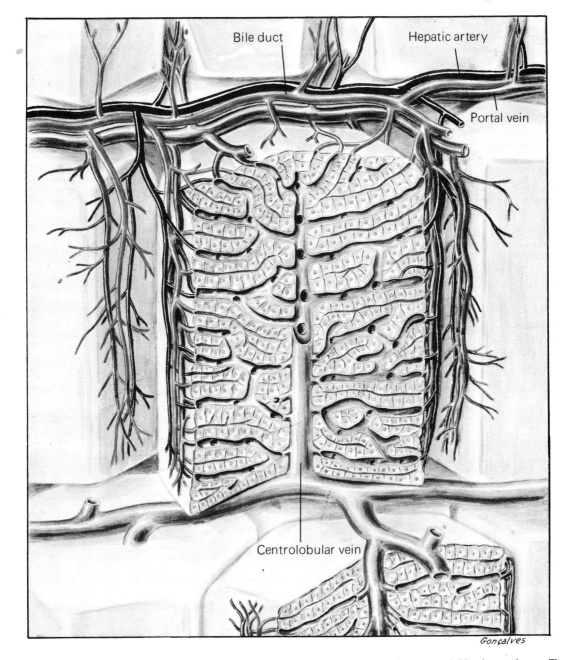

Figure 17–10. Schematic drawing of the structure of the liver. In the center, the liver lobule is surrounded by the portal space. The portal spaces are shown dilated here for the sake of clarity; in the human liver, these spaces are much smaller and in some places nonexistent. Arteries, veins, and bile ducts occupy the portal spaces. Lymph vessels and connective tissue are also present but are not shown in this illustration. Observe in the lobule the radial disposition of the plates formed by liver cells. The sinusoid capillaries separate cords of liver cells. The bile canaliculi can be seen between the liver cells. The intercalated (sublobular) veins derive from the lobules. (Redrawn and reproduced, with permission, from Bourne G: *An Introduction to Functional Histology.* Churchill, 1953.)

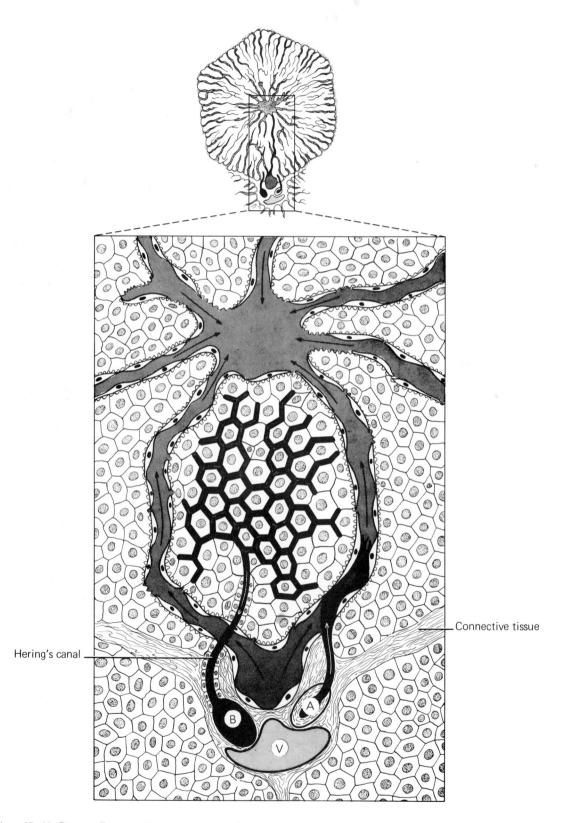

Hering's canal

Connective tissue

Figure 17–11. Diagram illustrating the direction of flow (arrows) of arterial blood (A), venous blood (V), and bile (B) in the liver lobule.

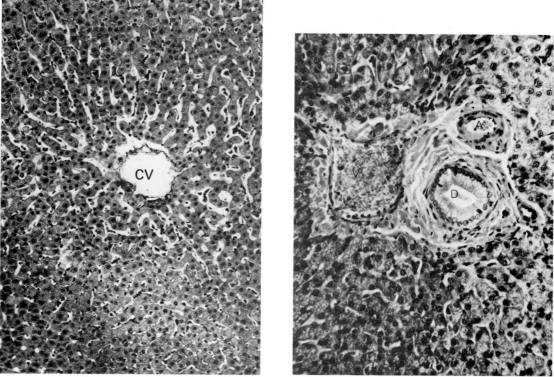

Figure 17–12. Photomicrograph of the liver. *Left:* A central vein (CV). Observe the liver plates that anastomose freely, limiting the space occupied by the sinusoids. H&E stain, X 200. *Right:* A portal space with its characteristic artery (A), vein (V), and bile duct (D) surrounded by connective tissue. Masson's stain, X 300.

an arteriole, a branch of the hepatic artery; a duct, part of the bile duct system; and lymphatic vessels. The venule is usually the largest of these tubular structures, containing blood coming from the superior and inferior mesenteric and splenic veins. The arteriole contains blood from the celiac trunk of the abdominal aorta. The duct, lined by cuboid epithelium, carries bile from the parenchymal cells and eventually empties into the bile duct. One or more lymphatics carries lymph into the blood circulation. All of these structures are embedded in a sheath of connective tissue (Figs 17–11 and 17–12).

The hepatocytes are radially disposed in the liver lobule. They are piled up, forming a layer one cell thick in a fashion similar to the bricks of a wall. These plates are directed from the periphery of the lobule to its center and anastomose freely, forming a complex labyrinthine and spongelike structure (Fig 17–10). The space left between these plates is filled by sinusoid capillaries, the so-called *liver sinusoids* (Figs 17–10, 17–11, and 17–12). As seen in Chapter 12, sinusoids are irregularly dilated capillaries composed of only one discontinuous layer of cells which can be of the typical endothelial or macrophagic type. These latter cells are fixed macrophages and have all the characteristics of this cell type. In the liver they are called *Kupffer cells.* The liver sinusoid capillaries have a lining with big gaps

in it, permitting an easy flow of macromolecules from the lumen to the liver cells. Between the liver cells and the wall of the sinusoid, a discrete space can be seen. It is usually filled by microvilli of the hepatocytes, reticular fibers, and extracellular fluid (Figs 17–13 and 17–15). This is the so-called *space of Disse* (Fig 17–13). The sinusoid is surrounded and supported by a delicate sheath of reticular fibers important in maintaining its form. The sinusoids arise in the periphery of the lobule where the ultimate branches of the portal veins and hepatic arteries are emptying and run in the direction of its center, where they abut in a vein called the *central vein* (Fig 17–12).

Liver Blood Supply

Blood circulation through the liver occurs in the following ways (Figs 17–10 and 17–11):

A. Portal Vein System:

1. The portal vein branches repeatedly and sends small venules, the *portal venules,* to the portal canals. These are the *interlobular branches.*

2. The interlobular venules penetrate into the lobules and empty their contents into the *liver sinusoids.*

3. These sinusoids run radially and converge in the center of the lobule to form the *central* or *centrolobular vein.* This vessel has very thin walls with few

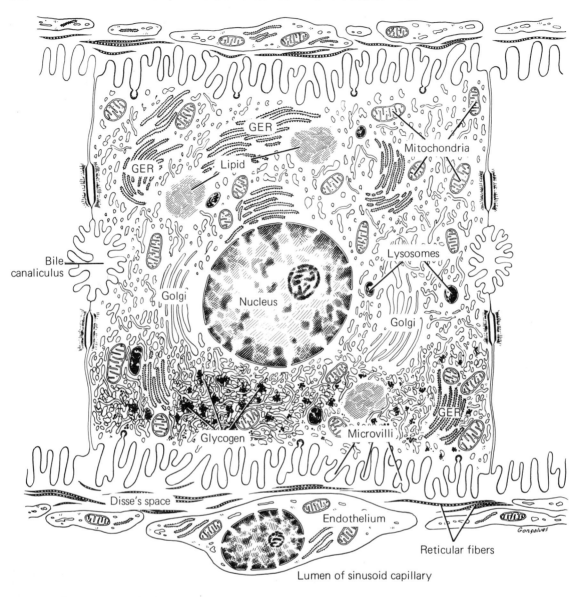

Figure 17–13. Diagram of the ultrastructure of a hepatocyte. GER, granular endoplasmic reticulum. × 10,000.

cells and little connective tissue and does not have the discrete layers described for veins of such size. The walls of this vein are penetrated by the emptying sinusoids.

4. As the central vein progresses along the lobule, it receives more and more sinusoids and gradually increases in diameter. At its end it leaves the lobule at its base, abutting into larger veins.

5. These veins form the so-called *sublobular veins,* which gradually converge and fuse, forming the 2 or more large hepatic veins that end in the inferior vena cava.

B. Arterial System: The hepatic artery branches repeatedly and forms the *interlobular arteries;* some irrigate the structures of the portal canals and others end directly in the sinusoids at varying distances from

the portal tracts, thus promoting a mixture of arterial and portal venous blood (Fig 17–11).

Blood therefore flows from the periphery to the center of the lobule. Consequently, the metabolites and all other toxic or nontoxic substances absorbed in the intestines reach first the peripheral cells and then the central cells of the lobule. This peculiarity partly explains why the cytologic and physiologic behavior of the perilobular cells is different from those of the centrolobular cells. This duality of behavior of the hepatocyte is particularly evident in pathologic specimens, where certain changes occur preferentially either in the central or in the peripheral cells of the lobule.

The description just given of the liver lobule with its blood supply corresponds to the classical concept of

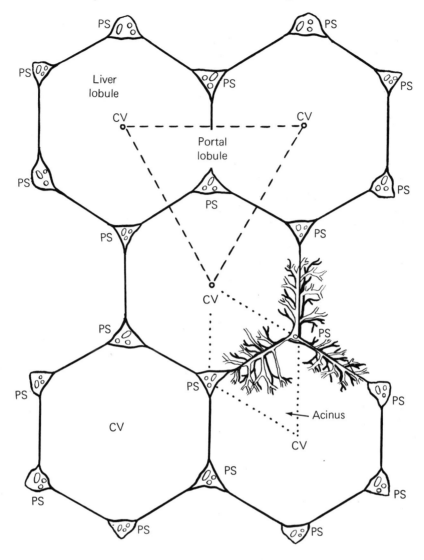

Figure 17–14. Schematic drawing illustrating the territories of the liver lobules, hepatic acini, and portal lobules. The classical lobule has a central vein (CV) and is outlined by lines that bind the portal spaces (PS) (solid lines). The portal lobules have their center in the portal space and are outlined by lines that bind the central veins (upper triangle). They comprise the portion of the liver from which bile flows to a portal space. Finally, the hepatic acinus comprises the region irrigated by one portal space (lower triangles). (Redrawn and reproduced, with permission, from Leeson TS, Leeson CR: *Histology,* 2nd ed. Saunders, 1970.)

this subject in which the centrolobular veins constitute the axis of these structures. (See the hexagons limited by portal spaces [PS] with the central vein [CV] in the center in Fig 17–14.)

Other points of reference may be used in analyzing possible functional units of the liver's structure. Thus, a new unit can be visualized, the so-called *portal lobule,* which has at its center the portal space and which is formed at its periphery by the regions of adjoining hepatic lobules, all of which drain bile into one portal canal. Thus, the portal lobule would be triangular, as opposed to the polygonal appearance of the classical liver lobule; would have a central vein in the tip of each of its angles; and would contain parts of 3

adjoining liver lobules. (See the dashed triangle in Fig 17–14 with the portal space [PS] at its center.)

Another way of looking at this problem is to regard as a unit of liver parenchyma that region which is irrigated by a terminal branch of the interlobular veins. This unit is called the *hepatic acinus.* These appear diamond-shaped in section (see dotted area CV, PS, CV, PS in Fig 17–14). In addition to the terminal branches of the portal vein, an arterial branch and a bile ductule are in the center of this mass of hepatic parenchyma, which is situated in adjacent areas of 2 different classical hepatic lobules (Fig 17–14). This proposal suggests that the liver is made up of acini, diamond-shaped in cross section, so that the cells

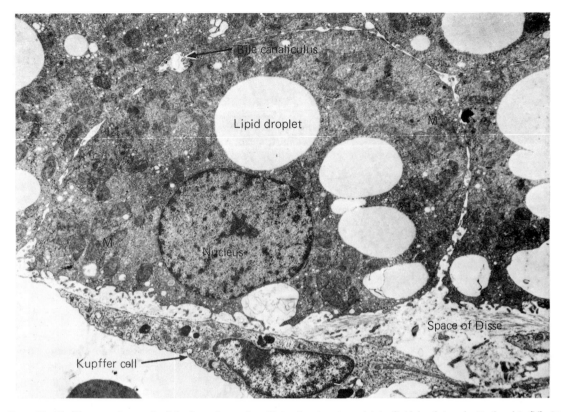

Figure 17—15. Electron micrograph of the liver of a monkey. Note a hepatocyte containing lipid droplets and mitochondria (M). At upper left is a bile canaliculus with microvilli. Below are a Kupffer cell and Disse's space. X 6300.

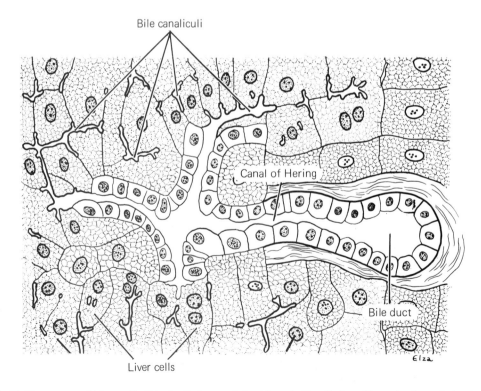

Figure 17—16. The passage of bile canaliculi to the Hering canals lined by cuboid epithelium. These structures abut onto the bile ducts of the portal spaces.

closer to the vessels would have the best supply. Outside of this zone 1, another zone 2 is visualized, and the rest of the liver parenchyma toward the central vein is called zone 3. This zonal arrangement probably explains some of the differences in the damage of liver parenchyma by various noxious agents or in different disease conditions.

The Hepatocyte

The liver cells are polyhedral, with 6 or more surfaces, and have a diameter of approximately 20–30 μm. In sections stained with hematoxylin and eosin, the cytoplasm of the hepatocyte is eosinophilic mainly because of the presence of large numbers of mitochondria and to some extent smooth endoplasmic reticulum. The cell surface is covered by glycocalyx. The hepatocytes located at different distances from the portal tracts show variations in structural, histochemical, and biochemical parameters. The surface of each liver cell is in contact with the following structures: the wall of the sinusoid capillaries through the space of Disse (Fig 17–13); the surface of another cell; and the wall of another cell but limiting a tubular space, the *bile canaliculus* (Fig 17–13).

These canaliculi are the first bile-transporting structures. They are tubular spaces limited only by the plasma membranes of 2 hepatocytes and have a small number of microvilli in their interior (Figs 17–13 and 17–15). The cell membranes near these canaliculi are firmly bound by the junctions as described in Chapter 4. The bile canaliculi form a complex anastomosing network which progresses along the plates of the liver lobule in the direction of the portal canals (Fig 17–11). The bile flow therefore progresses in a direction opposite to that of the blood, ie, from the center of the lobule to its periphery. At the periphery, the bile enters the *bile ductules* or *Hering's canals* (Fig 17–16). These are small ducts composed of cuboid cells with a clear cytoplasm and few organelles. After a short distance, these bile ductules cross the limiting plates of the portal tracts and end in the *bile ducts* in the portal canals (Figs 17–11, 17–12, and 17–16). These ducts are lined by a cuboid or columnar epithelium and have a distinct connective tissue sheath. They gradually enlarge and fuse, forming the right and left *hepatic ducts,* which leave the liver. The surface of the hepatocyte which faces the space of Disse presents many microvilli protruding in that space but always leaving a space between them and the cells of the sinusoidal wall (Figs 17–13 and 17–15). The liver cell presents one or 2 rounded nuclei with one or 2 typical nucleoli. It has an abundant endoplasmic reticulum both in its smooth and granular varieties (Fig 17–13). A network of interconnected cisternae, vesicles, and tubules forms a compartment of membrane-bound cavities, the so-called *GERL* (Golgi apparatus, G; endoplasmic reticulum, ER; and lysosomes, L). Materials synthesized at the ER level are transported to G and from there, in the form of secretory vesicles, are released; lysosomes are involved in different intercellular or extracellular functions. In these cells, the granular

endoplasmic reticulum forms aggregates dispersed in the cytoplasm which have been called *basophilic bodies* by classical microscopists. Several proteins—eg, blood albumin and fibrinogen—are synthesized in these structures. Various important processes occur in the smooth endoplasmic reticulum that is present diffusely throughout the cytoplasm. This organelle seems to be responsible for the process of conjugation, in which various substances are bound to sulfate or glucuronide, being inactivated or detoxified for excretion from the body. The smooth endoplasmic reticulum of the hepatocyte has been shown to be a labile system which reacts promptly to changes in the environment. Thus, the administration of certain drugs to laboratory animals promotes in a short time an increase in the smooth endoplasmic reticulum of the liver cell, with a parallel increase in the activity of enzymes responsible for the conjugation process which will inactivate these drugs.

Another typical component of the liver cell is glycogen (Fig 17–17). This polysaccharide appears in the electron microscope as coarse, electron-dense granules which frequently collect near areas of smooth endoplasmic reticulum, assuming the form of berries. The amount of glycogen present in the liver conforms to a diurnal rhythm and depends also upon the nutritional state of the animal. The liver glycogen pool is a depot of glucose and is mobilized every time the blood glucose level falls below normal. In this way the body maintains a steady level of blood glucose, the main metabolite used by the body. The liver cell has many mitochondria (1000–2000) with a spherical or ovoid form. Their cristae are not as numerous or as closely packed as in the mitochondria of the muscle cell, and this characteristic is consistent with the moderate oxygen consumption observed in this organ. Similar to what occurs in most cellular components, the proteins of the liver mitochondria are constantly being renewed. The average life span of the structural proteins of this organelle is calculated to be about 10 days. Other frequent cellular components are the lipid droplets, whose quantity varies greatly (Fig 17–15). Lysosomes are abundant in the hepatocytes, although their exact function in this cell is still a subject of speculation. It is known, however, that administration of the pancreatic hormone glucagon promotes the appearance of many autophagosomes in the liver cell. It has been speculated that they might be related to processes of turnover of the hepatocyte. The Golgi system consists of several aggregates, usually near the bile canaliculi. Its function in the hepatocyte is not clear, although there is evidence that it may participate in the formation of lysosomes. The presence of variable quantities of lipids, glycogen, and granular endoplasmic reticulum in the liver cell is responsible for its great morphologic variability.

HISTOPHYSIOLOGY & LIVER FUNCTION

The liver cell undoubtedly is the most versatile cell in the body. It is at the same time a cell with endocrine and exocrine functions, and it synthesizes and accumulates certain substances, detoxifies others, and transports others. This multiple functional activity is also related to the great morphologic variability of the hepatocyte. We shall now analyze the main activities of this cell.

Protein Synthesis

Besides synthesizing the proteins of its normal

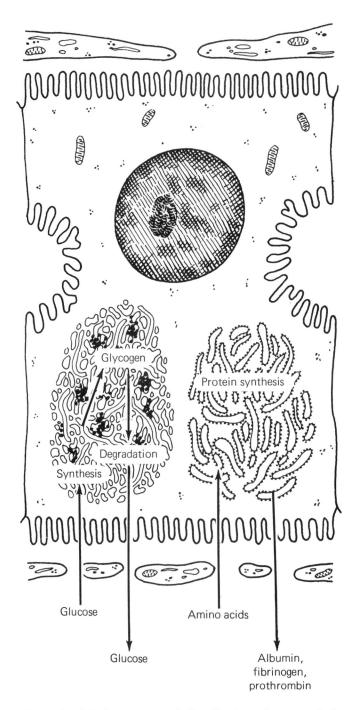

Figure 17—17. Protein synthesis and carbohydrate storage in the liver. Protein synthesis occurs in the granular endoplasmic reticulum, which explains why liver cell lesions lead to a decrease in the amounts of albumin, fibrinogen, and prothrombin in a patient's blood. In several diseases, glycogen degradation is depressed with abnormal intracellular accumulation of this compound.

turnover, the liver cell produces various proteins for export—among them the albumin, prothrombin, and fibrinogen of the blood plasma. These proteins are synthesized in the granular endoplasmic reticulum. Contrary to what is observed in other glandular cells, the hepatocyte does not store proteins in its cytoplasm as secretory granules but gradually releases the protein produced into the bloodstream. In a sense, therefore, it behaves during this activity as an endocrine gland (Fig 17–17).

Radioautographic studies using the electron mi-croscope show that protein is secreted in the granular endoplasmic reticulum of the hepatocyte. The protein migrates to the Golgi region and from there is extruded to the blood. About 5% of the protein exported by the liver is produced by the cells of the histiocyte system (Kupffer cells); the remainder is synthesized in the liver cells.

Bile Secretion

Bile production is a secretion in the sense that the hepatocytes transform and transport blood compo-

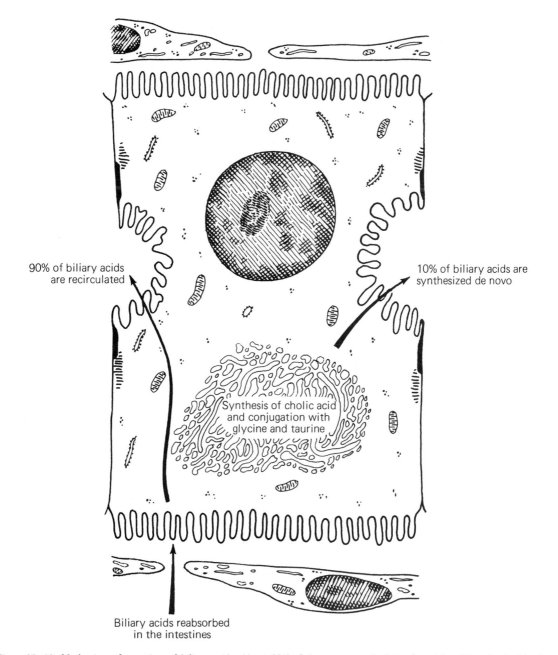

90% of biliary acids are recirculated

10% of biliary acids are synthesized de novo

Synthesis of cholic acid and conjugation with glycine and taurine

Biliary acids reabsorbed in the intestines

Figure 17–18. Mechanism of secretion of biliary acids. About 90% of these compounds derive from bile acids reabsorbed in the intestinal epithelium and recirculated to the liver. The remainder are synthesized in the liver by conjugating cholic acid with the amino acids glycine and taurine. This process occurs in the smooth endoplasmic reticulum.

nents into the bile canaliculi. Besides water, bile has 2 main components: bile acids and bilirubin. The secretion of bile acids is illustrated in Fig 17—18. About 90% of these substances are derived by absorption from the intestinal lumen through the intestinal epithe-

lium, being transported as such by the hepatocyte from the blood to the bile canaliculi. About 10% of these compounds, however, are synthesized in the hepatocyte by conjugation of cholic acid with the amino acids glycine and taurine at the level of the

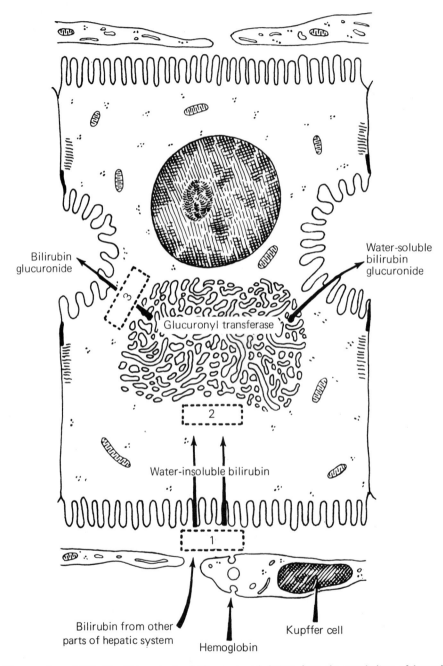

Figure 17—19. The secretion of bilirubin. This water-insoluble compound derives from the metabolism of hemoglobin in the macrophages of the macrophage system (or reticuloendothelial system), including the Kupffer cells of the liver sinusoids. In the hepatocytes, by means of glucuronyl transferase activity, bilirubin is conjugated in the smooth endoplasmic reticulum with glucuronide, forming a soluble compound. When bile secretion is blocked by one of several possible mechanisms, the yellow bilirubin glucuronide accumulates in the blood and jaundice appears. Several mechanisms can produce jaundice: (1) a defect in the capacity of the cell to trap and absorb bilirubin (rectangle 1); (2) inability of the cell to conjugate bilirubin because of deficiency in the enzyme glucuronyl transferase (rectangle 2); or (3) problems in the transfer and excretion of bilirubin into the biliary canaliculi (rectangle 3). One of the most frequent causes of jaundice, however, is obstruction of bile flow.

smooth endoplasmic reticulum. Thus, glycocholic and taurocholic acids are produced. Cholic acid is probably also synthesized at this level from cholesterol. The bile acids have an important function in emulsifying the lipids in the digestive tube and promoting their easier digestion by lipase and subsequent absorption.

Bilirubin is formed in the macrophage system (this includes the macrophages of the liver sinusoids) and from there is transported to the hepatocyte. This hydrophobic and therefore water-insoluble bilirubin is transported into the hepatocyte, where it is conjugated to glucuronic acid, forming a water-soluble *bilirubin glucuronide*. This process occurs at the smooth endoplasmic reticulum (Fig 17–19). In a further step, the bilirubin glucuronide is secreted into the bile canaliculi. The hepatocyte also has the ability to actively transport several dyes. This ability to eliminate dyes is used as a test of liver function. One of the dyes classically used for this purpose is sulfobromophthalein (Bromsulphalein, BSP).

Storage of Metabolites

Lipids and carbohydrates can be stored in the liver in the form of fat and glycogen (Figs 17–15 and 17–17). This capacity to store energetic metabolites is important because it supplies the body with energy between meals. Fig 17–17 shows how this is done for the carbohydrates. The liver also serves as the major storage compartment for vitamins.

Metabolic Function

The hepatocyte is also responsible for converting lipids and amino acids into glucose by means of a complex enzymatic process called *glyconeogenesis*. It is also the main site of amino acid deamination, with the production of urea. This compound is transported by the blood to the kidney and excreted by that organ.

Detoxification & Inactivation

Various drugs and substances can be inactivated by oxidation, methylation, and conjugation. The enzymes participating in these processes are considered to be located mainly in the smooth endoplasmic reticulum (Fig 17–18).

Liver Regeneration

Despite being an organ whose cells are renewed at a slow rate, the liver has an extraordinary capacity for regeneration. The loss of hepatic tissue due to the action of toxic substances or surgical removal triggers a mechanism by which the liver cells begin to divide actively, and this process goes on until restoration of the original mass of tissue has been achieved. In rats it has been shown that the liver can in 1 month regenerate a loss of 75% of its weight. Experimental evidence suggests that the process of regeneration is probably due to substances called *chalones* which act to inhibit the mitotic division of a certain cell type. This theory proposes that when a tissue is injured or partially removed the amount of chalones it produces decreases; consequently, a burst of mitotic activity occurs in this tissue. As regeneration proceeds, the amount of chalones produced is increased and the mitotic activity decreases. It is, therefore, a self-regulated process. There is evidence that this mechanism is present in different tissues and is probably a generalized phenomenon.

The regenerated liver tissue is usually similar to the removed tissue. However, in the case of continuous or repeated damage to this organ, an abundant production of connective tissue occurs simultaneously with liver cell regeneration. This exaggerated connective tissue production can disorganize the regeneration and produce a condition called *cirrhosis.*

THE BILIARY TRACT

The bile produced by the liver cell flows through the *biliary canaliculi, bile ductules,* and *bile ducts.* These structures gradually fuse, forming a rich network which gradually converges to form the *hepatic duct.* The hepatic duct, after receiving the *cystic duct* from the gallbladder, continues to the duodenum as the *common bile duct* (or ductus choledochus).

The hepatic, cystic, and common bile ducts are lined by a mucous membrane which presents a columnar epithelium composed of cells with abundant mitochondria. The lamina propria is thin and surrounded by an inconspicuous layer of smooth muscle. This muscle layer becomes thicker near the duodenum and finally forms, in the intramural portion, a sphincter which regulates bile flow.

THE GALLBLADDER

The gallbladder is a hollow, pear-shaped organ attached to the lower surface of the liver. It communicates with the common hepatic duct through the cystic duct. The wall of the gallbladder consists of the following layers (Fig 17–20): (1) a mucous layer composed of columnar epithelium and lamina propria, (2) a layer of smooth muscle, (3) a well-developed perimuscular connective tissue layer, and (4) a serous membrane.

The mucous layer is thrown into folds that are particularly evident in the empty bladder. The epithelial cells are rich in mitochondria and have their nuclei in their basal third (Fig 17–21). Microvilli are frequent in the apical region. Near the cystic duct, the epithelium invaginates into the lamina propria, forming tubulo-acinar glands with a wide lumen. The cells of these glands have characteristics of mucus-secreting cells and are probably responsible for the production of the mucus in bile.

The muscular layer is thin and irregular. A thick connective tissue layer binds the superior surface of the gallbladder to the liver. The opposite surface is covered by a typical serous layer, the peritoneum.

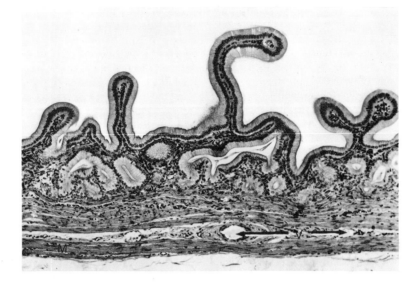

Figure 17–20. Photomicrograph of a section of gallbladder. Observe the lining columnar epithelium, the smooth muscle layer (M), and the blood vessels (V). H&E stain, × 30.

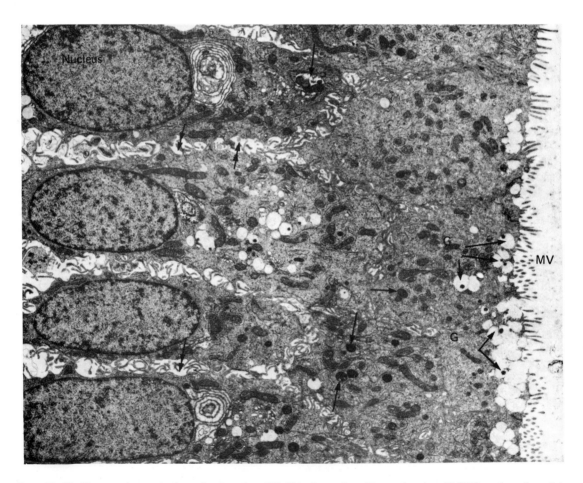

Figure 17–21. Electron micrograph of a section from the gallbladder of a monkey. Observe the microvilli (MV) on the surface of the cell and secretory granules (G) containing glycoprotein complexes. The single arrows indicate the lysosomes; the double arrows show the ample intercellular spaces. These are cells that transport sodium chloride from the lumen to the blood vessels, secrete mucous substances, and digest particles reabsorbed from the bile. × 6500.

The main function of the gallbladder is to store bile and reabsorb its water, concentrating it 5- to 10-fold. This process depends upon an active sodium chloride–transporting mechanism in its epithelium. The water reabsorption is considered as being an osmotic consequence of the sodium chloride pump. Because sodium and chloride ions are transported in equal amounts, no potential difference is evident between the 2 surfaces of this organ. Studies of its epithelial covering suggest that the sodium chloride and water cross the membrane of the cell apex and move laterally to the intercellular spaces and from there to the blood vessels of the lamina propria. Contraction of the smooth muscle of the gallbladder is induced by *cholecystokinin,* a hormone produced in the mucosa of the small intestine.

● ● ●

References

Pancreas & Salivary Glands

Amsterdam A & others: Concomitant synthesis of membrane protein and exportable protein of the secretory granule in rat parotid gland. J Cell Biol 40:187, 1971.

Junqueira LCU: Aspects of the biology of the animal cell secretion. In: *Funktionelle und morphologische Organization der Zelle: Sekretion und Exkretion.* Wohlfarth-Buttermann KE (editor). Springer, 1965.

Junqueira LCU: Control of cell secretion. In: *Secretory Mechanisms of Salivary Glands.* Schneyer LH, Schneyer CA (editors). Academic Press, 1967.

Junqueira LCU, de Moraes FF: Comparative aspects of the vertebrate major salivary glands' biology. In: *Functionelle und morphologische Organization der Zelle: Sekretion und Exkretion.* Wohlfarth-Buttermann KE (editor). Springer, 1965.

Junqueira LCU, de Moraes FF, Toledo AMS: Action of vasopressin on salivary secretion. Acta Physiol Lat Am 17:36, 1967.

Junqueira LCU, Hirsch GC: Cell secretion: A study of pancreas and salivary glands. Internat Rev Cytol 5:323, 1956.

Junqueira LCU, Hirsch GC, Rothschild HA: Glycine uptake by the proteins of the rabbit pancreatic juice. Biochem J 61:275, 1955.

Junqueira LCU, Rothschild HA, Fajer A: Protein production by the rat pancreas. Exper Cell Res 12:338, 1957.

Junqueira LCU, Rothschild HA, Vugman I: The action of atropine on pancreatic secretion. Brit J Pharmacol 13(1):71, 1958.

Munger BL: Histochemical studies on seromucous and mucous-secreting cells of human salivary glands. Am J Anat 115:411, 1964.

Opie EL: Cytology of the pancreas. In: *Special Cytology,* 2nd ed. Cowdry EV (editor). Hoeber, 1932.

Stormont DL: The salivary glands. In: *Special Cytology,* 2nd ed. Cowdry EV (editor). Hoeber, 1932.

Tandler B: Ultrastructure of the human submaxillary gland. 1. Architecture and histological relationship of the secretory cells. Am J Anat 111:287, 1962.

Young JA & others: A microperfusion investigation of sodium resorption and potassium secretion by the main excretory duct of the rat submaxillary gland. Pfleugers Arch 295:157, 1967.

Liver & Biliary Tract

Ashley CA, Peters T Jr: Electron microscopic radioauto-graphic detection of sites of protein synthesis and migration in liver. J Cell Biol 43:237, 1969.

Becker FF: The normal hepatocyte in division: Regeneration of the mammalian liver. In: *Progress in Liver Diseases.* Vol 3. Popper H, Schaffner F (editors). Grune & Stratton, 1970.

Bolender RP, Weibel ER: A morphometric study of the removal of phenobarbital-induced membranes from hepatocytes after cessation of treatment. J Cell Biol 56:746, 1973.

Bruni C, Porter KR: The fine structure of the parenchymal cell of the normal rat liver. 1. General considerations. Am J Path 46:691, 1965.

Diamond JM, Tormey JM: Studies on the structural basis of water transport across epithelial membranes. Fed Proc 25:1458, 1966.

Elias H: A re-examination of the structure of the mammalian liver. 2. The hepatic lobule and its relation to the vascular and biliary systems. Am J Anat 85:379, 1949.

Jones AL, Fawcett DW: Hypertrophy of the agranular endoplasmic reticulum in hamster liver induced by phenobarbital. J Histochem Cytochem 14:215, 1966.

Kaye GI & others: Fluid transport in the rabbit gallbladder: A combined physiological and electron microscopic study. J Cell Biol 30:237, 1966.

McMinn RMH, Kugler JH: The glands of the bile and pancreatic ducts: Autoradiographic and histochemical studies. J Anat 95:1, 1961.

Novikoff AB, Essner E: The liver cell: Some new approaches to its study. Am J Med 29:102, 1960.

Onstad GR, Schoenfield LJ, Higgins JA: Fluid transfer in the everted human gallbladder. J Clin Invest 46:608, 1967.

Orrenius S, Ericsson JLE, Ernster L: Phenobarbital-induced synthesis of the microsomal drug-metabolizing enzyme system and its relationship to the proliferation of endoplasmic membranes: A morphological and biochemical study. J Cell Biol 25:627, 1965.

Peters T Jr: The biosynthesis of rat serum albumin. 2. Intracellular phenomena in the secretion of newly formed albumin. J Biol Chem 237:1186, 1962.

Rouiller C (editor): *The Liver: Morphology, Biochemistry, Physiology.* 2 vols. Academic Press, 1963, 1964.

Simon FR, Arias IM: Alterations in liver plasma membranes and their possible role in cholestasis. Gastroenterology 62:341, 1972.

18 . . .
Respiratory System

The respiratory system includes the lungs and the system of tubes which link the pulmonary tissue with the external environment. It is customary to divide the respiratory system into 2 principal divisions (Fig 18−1): a *conducting portion,* which includes the nasal passages, nasopharynx, larynx, trachea, bronchi, and bronchioles; and a *respiratory portion,* which consists of the terminal part of the bronchial tree and the alveoli, the only part in which gases are exchanged. The 2 parts are connected by a *transitional portion,* which consists of the respiratory bronchioles.

NASAL CAVITY

The mucosal lining of the nasal cavity has a different histologic structure in different areas. Three regions can be distinguished: the vestibule, the respiratory area, and the olfactory area.

Vestibule
The vestibule, just behind the naris, is the most anterior and most dilated portion of the nasal cavity.

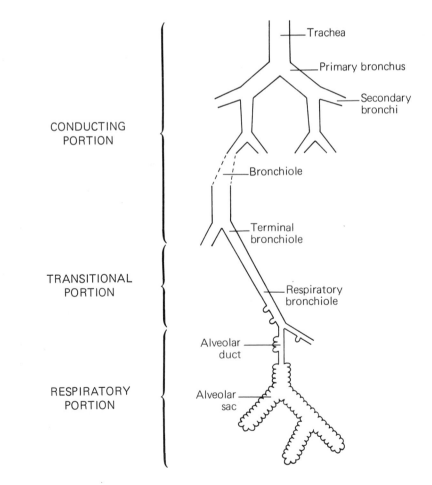

Figure 18−1. The main divisions of the respiratory tract.

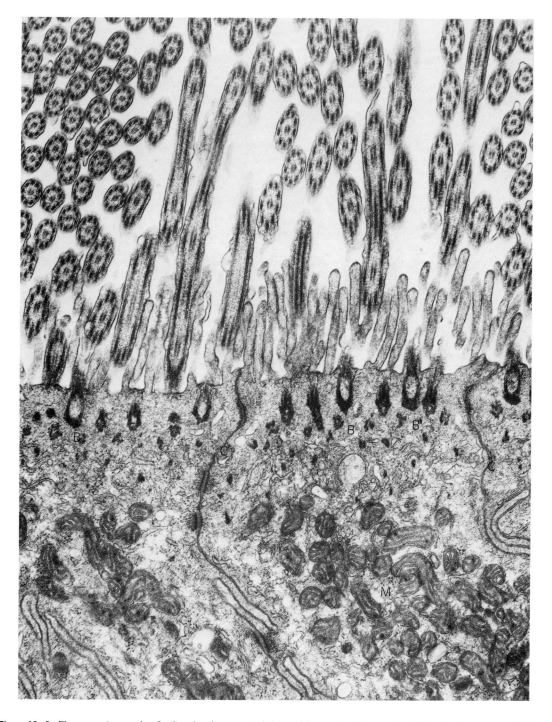

Figure 18–2. Electron micrograph of ciliated columnar epithelium. Observe the ciliary microtubules in transverse and oblique section. In the cell apex are the U-shaped basal bodies (B) where the cilia insert themselves. At (M), local accumulation of mitochondria is probably related to energy production for ciliary movement. At (C), observe junctional complexes. Note the emergence of microvilli between the ciliary roots. Reduced from × 10,000.

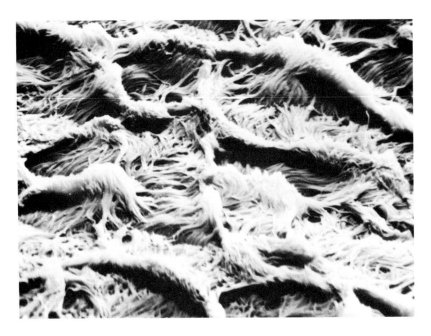

Figure 18–3. Scanning electron micrograph of the surface of a turtle's respiratory mucosa. Observe the wavelike ciliary formation. (Courtesy of PP Graziadei.)

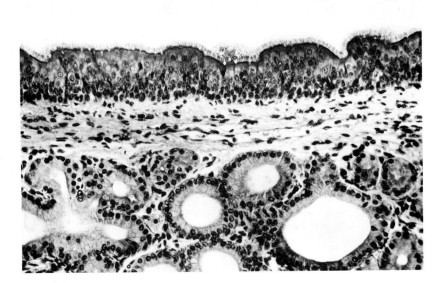

Figure 18–4. Photomicrograph of a section of tracheal mucosa. Observe the ciliated pseudostratified columnar epithelium and its lamina propria containing mucous glands. H&E stain, × 200.

Its epithelium consists of stratified nonkeratinized squamous epithelium and a lamina propria of dense connective tissue. The hairs and the cutaneous glands in this region constitute the first barrier to the entrance of coarse particles of dust and other substances into the upper respiratory passages.

Respiratory Area

The respiratory area constitutes a large part of the nasal cavity. The mucosa in this region consists of ciliated pseudostratified columnar epithelium with numerous goblet cells. This type of epithelium is found in the greater part of the upper respiratory tract. It lies on a basal lamina resting on a fibrous lamina propria which contains seromucous glands whose secretion helps maintain the surfaces of the nasal cavities in a humidified state. The lamina propria rests on the subjacent periosteum.

In the areas most exposed to air, the epithelium is higher and contains more goblet cells. The mucus produced by the glands and by the goblet cells is carried along the epithelial surface in the direction of the pharynx by the synchronized ciliary motion.

Along the lateral wall of each nasal cavity, the surface is irregular because of the presence of 3 bony expansions called *conchae*. At the level of the lower and middle conchae, the lamina propria contains an abundant venous plexus whose veins can become swollen in certain conditions such as influenza, allergic disorders, etc, hindering the free passage of air.

In passing through the nasal passages, the air is warmed, filtered, and humidified. This warming action is an important function of the venous plexus.

Olfactory Area

The olfactory region is located in the upper part of the nasal passages. It is discussed in Chapter 10.

PARANASAL SINUSES

The paranasal sinuses are cavities in the frontal, maxillary, ethmoid, and sphenoid bones that are lined with a thin respiratory type of epithelium that contains few goblet cells. The lamina propria contains only a few small glands and is continuous with the underlying periosteum. The mucus produced in these cavities drains into the nasal passages.

NASOPHARYNX

The nasopharynx is the first part of the pharynx, continuing caudally with the oral portion of this organ, *the oropharynx*. It is lined with respiratory-type epithelium which is replaced by stratified squamous epithelium in the portion that is in contact with the soft palate.

LARYNX

The larynx is an irregular tube that connects the pharynx to the trachea. Its walls contain a series of irregular cartilaginous pieces held together by fibroelastic connective tissue which holds the larynx open at all times. The larger cartilages (thyroid, cricoid, and a large part of the arytenoids) are of the hyaline type; the others are of the elastic type.

The mucous layer forms 2 pairs of folds that extend into the lumen of the larynx. The upper pair constitutes what is called the *false vocal cords* (or vestibular folds), and the lamina propria of this region is loose and contains numerous glands. The lower pair constitutes the *true vocal cords*. These structures consist of 2 cores of elastic tissue controlled by the *intrinsic muscles of the larynx*. Their contraction modifies the opening of the vocal cords, resulting in the production of sounds with different tones when air passes through the larynx.

The epithelial lining of the larynx is not the same in all portions. On the ventral side and on part of the dorsal side of the epiglottis—as well as in the vocal cords—the epithelium is subject to friction and wear and is of the stratified squamous, nonkeratinized type. In most other regions, however, it is of the respiratory type, with the cilia beating toward the mouth. The lamina propria is rich in elastic fibers and contains small glands of the mixed type which, however, are not present in the true vocal cords. A well-defined submucosa does not occur.

TRACHEA

The trachea is continuous with the larynx and terminates by branching in the 2 extrapulmonary bronchi (Fig 18–1). Its lining epithelium is of the respiratory type. In the trachea, the ciliated cells are most numerous and contain small mitochondria which are grouped mainly at the apical poles of the cells (Fig 18–2). Experimental evidence suggests that the beating of the cilia in waves (Fig 18–3) is accelerated by adenosine triphosphate (ATP), an observation that is consistent with the apical localization of the mitochondria in these cells. Each of these cells has about 270 cilia. Besides the cilia, their free surfaces contain scarce and short microvilli (Fig 18–2). Goblet cells and basal cells are also present in the epithelium. The basal cells do not reach the surface and have characteristics of immature epithelial cells. All cells of this pseudostratified ciliated columnar epithelium touch the basal layer, and the epithelium rests on a thick basement membrane.

The lamina propria is made up of loose connective tissue rich in elastic fibers. It contains glands mainly of the mucous type (Fig 18–4) whose ducts open into the tracheal lumen. The secretion of these glands, as well as of the goblet cells, forms a continuous mucous layer which is carried by the ciliary movement in the direction of the pharynx. This mucous substance constitutes an important barrier to dust particles which enter the conducting portion of the respiratory system with the inhaled air. In addition to the mucous barrier, the upper respiratory tract has another defense system against the external environment—the lymphoid barrier—which includes both accumulations of lymphocytes and lymphatic nodules along the conducting portion of the system (see discussion of tonsils in Chapter 15).

In the trachea, the submucosa is separated from the mucosa by an elastic membrane that consists of a dense band of elastic fibers.

The trachea characteristically has a variable (16–20) number of pieces of cartilage of the hyaline type (Fig 18–5). These pieces are incomplete C-shaped rings whose free extremities point to the dorsal region. In longitudinal section, they are ovoid. They are covered by perichondrium, which is a continuation of the fibrous connective tissue that binds the pieces of cartilage. This confers a certain extensibility on the tracheal tube. With age, these pieces of cartilage may become fibrous or may even calcify.

In the dorsal region, cartilage is replaced by smooth muscle bundles. These also occur between contiguous cartilaginous rings.

Externally, the trachea is covered by a layer of loose connective tissue which constitutes the adventitia that binds it to the neighboring tissues.

BRONCHIAL TREE

The trachea divides into 2 bronchi which enter the lungs at the hilus. These are called the *primary bronchi* (Fig 18–1). Also at each hilus, the arteries enter and the lymphatic vessels and veins leave the lungs. All of these structures are surrounded by dense connective tissue and form a unit called the *pulmonary root.*

After entering the lungs, the primary bronchi course downward and outward, giving rise to 3 bronchi in the right lung and 2 in the left, each of which supplies a pulmonary lobe. These bronchi, frequently called *lobar bronchi* (Fig 18–6), divide repeatedly, gradually giving rise to smaller bronchi the terminal branches of which are called *bronchioles* (Figs 18–1 and 18–7). Each bronchiole enters a pulmonary lobule, where it branches to form 5–7 *terminal bronchioles* (Figs 18–1 and 18–8). These are the last portions of the bronchial ramifications and are characterized by layers of smooth muscle and an absence of cartilage (Fig 18–8). They have the same structure as the bronchioles but have thinner walls lined exclusively by respiratory (ie, ciliated pseudostratified) epithelium.

The pulmonary lobules are pyramid-shaped, with the apex directed toward the hilus and the base directed toward the pulmonary surface. These lobules are delimited by thin connective septa which are easily seen in the fetus. In the adult, the septa are incomplete and the lobules are therefore poorly delineated. The region next to the pleura, where there is a large deposit

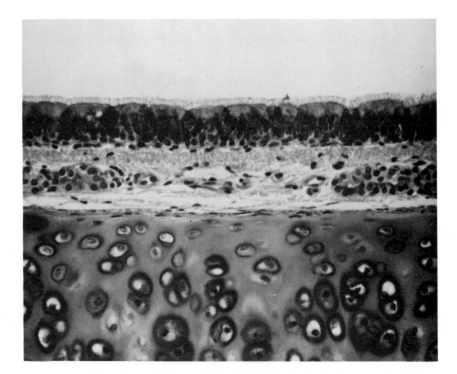

Figure 18–5. Photomicrograph of a section of dog trachea.

of carbon particles in the interlobular septa, is an exception. The terminal bronchiole supplies one or more *respiratory bronchioles* (Fig 18–8) which mark the beginning of the respiratory portion; this part also includes the *alveolar ducts, alveolar sacs,* and *alveoli* (Fig 18–9).

The primary bronchi in the extrapulmonary portion possess the same histologic picture as the trachea. As we proceed toward the respiratory portion, we can observe a simplification of the histologic structures with a decrease in the height of the epithelium. It must be stressed, however, that this simplification is slow and gradual, for no abrupt transition can be observed between the bronchi and the bronchioles. For this reason, the division of the bronchial tree into bronchi, bronchioles, etc is to some extent artificial despite the fact that it has a certain teaching and practical value.

Bronchi (Figs 18–6 and 18–7)

In the larger branches, the mucosa is identical to that in the trachea; in the smaller branches, the epithelium may be simple columnar with cilia. The lamina propria is rich in elastic fibers. Next to the mucosa is a smooth muscle layer consisting of 2 muscle bundles arranged spirally (Figs 18–6 and 18–7) which completely surround the bronchi. In histologic section, this muscular layer may appear discontinuous. The contraction of this muscle after death is responsible for the folded aspect of the bronchial mucosa observed in histologic section. External to this muscle layer are glands of the mucous or seromucous type whose ducts open into the bronchial lumen.

The cartilaginous pieces of the bronchi are surrounded by connective tissue rich in elastic fibers which is continuous with the connective fibers of the neighboring pulmonary tissue (Fig 18–6). Both in the adventitial and in the mucous layer, lymphatic nodules can be observed that become more abundant with age. These lymphatic nodules are particularly numerous at the branching points of the bronchial tree.

Bronchioles

These are intralobular segments with a diameter of 1 mm or less; they do not have cartilage, glands, or lymphatic nodules. The epithelium in the initial portions is ciliated columnar, becoming cuboid—with cilia or not—in the final portion (Fig 18–8). The goblet cells decrease in number and are often completely absent. The lamina propria is thin, consisting mainly of elastic fibers. Next to the mucous layer is the smooth muscle layer whose cells interlace with the elastic fibers; these fibers extend outward, continuing with the rest of the structure of the pulmonary parenchyma.

The musculature of the bronchi and bronchioles is under the control of the vagus nerve and the sympathetic nervous system. Stimulation of the vagus nerve decreases the diameter of these structures, whereas sympathetic stimulation produces the opposite effect. This explains why epinephrine and other sympathomimetic drugs are frequently employed to relax smooth muscle during asthmatic attacks. When the thicknesses of the bronchial and bronchiolar walls are compared, it can be seen that, proportionately, the bronchiolar muscle layer is better developed than the bronchial layer. Increased airway resistance in asthma is believed to be due mainly to the contraction of bronchiolar muscle.

Respiratory Bronchiole (Figs 18–8 and 18–9)

The respiratory bronchiole is a short tube coated with an epithelium which varies from low columnar to cuboid and occasionally has cilia, especially in the initial portion. The smooth muscle and elastic fibers are well developed, although they form a thinner layer than in the terminal bronchioles. The respiratory bronchiole can be considered as a terminal bronchiole in which a part of the wall has alveoli; consequently, its wall appears discontinuous in histologic sections (Figs 18–8 and 18–9). This is a region of transition between the conducting and respiratory portions of the respiratory system. These alveoli are saclike expansions in the walls of the bronchioles lined with an epithelium where gas exchange can occur efficiently, which justifies the term respiratory applied to this segment. The alveoli are more numerous at the distal ends of these bronchioles.

Alveolar Ducts (Fig 18–9)

The alveolar ducts are long, winding tubes formed by the branching of the respiratory bronchioles, which, in turn, may also branch. The term alveolar defines the principal characteristic of this segment, which presents numerous alveoli and alveolar sacs in its walls. On histologic section, the alveolar duct presents a very discontinuous wall; between the openings of 2 alveoli or alveolar sacs, an accumulation of collagen, elastic fibers, and smooth muscle cells usually is found. The epithelial coat is composed of low cuboid cells and is often difficult to see with the light microscope. The muscle bundles are distributed around the opening of an alveolus but do not extend to its walls. However, the collagen and elastic fibers are continuous with the alveolar walls, thus constituting their only supporting system (Fig 18–9). The alveolar ducts are the last segments which present smooth muscle cells.

Alveolar Sacs & Alveoli

The alveolar duct ends in simple alveoli or in alveolar sacs which contain 2 or more alveoli (Figs 18–9 and 18–10). Alveoli are small saclike evaginations of the respiratory bronchioles, alveolar ducts, and alveolar sacs (Figs 18–9 and 18–10). They represent the terminal portions of the bronchial tree, being responsible for the spongy structure of the pulmonary tissue. They are small pockets open on one side, similar to the honeycombs of a beehive. The wall of an alveolus consists mainly of a thin, double epithelial partition that contains capillaries. The wall is common to 2 neighboring alveoli and is thus termed an *interalveolar wall* or *septum* (Fig 18–10). The electron microscope has shown that the interalveolar wall has a very thin continuous epithelial lining that in several regions is below

Epithelium

Lamina
propria

Smooth
muscle

Cartilage

Perichondrium

Adventitia

Figure 18—6. Photomicrograph of a large bronchus. Observe the ciliated pseudostratified epithelium with many goblet cells, 2 cartilaginous plates, and smooth muscle. H&E stain, reduced from X 200.

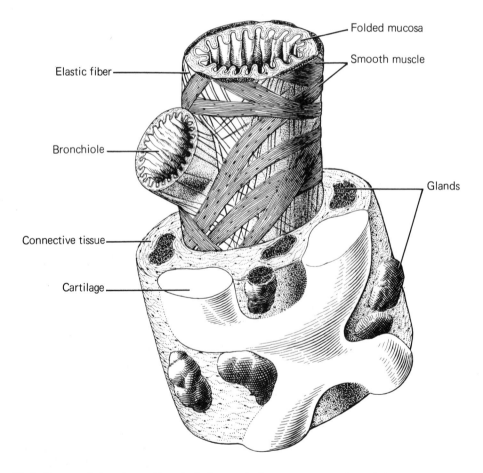

Folded mucosa

Smooth muscle

Elastic fiber

Bronchiole

Glands

Connective tissue

Cartilage

Figure 18—7. Diagram of a bronchus and bronchiole showing the discontinuous smooth muscle layer. The contraction of this muscle induces folding of the mucosa. The elastic fibers present in the bronchus continue into the bronchiole. In white is shown an irregular cartilaginous plate sectioned in 2 regions. The adventitia is not represented in this drawing.

Terminal bronchiole

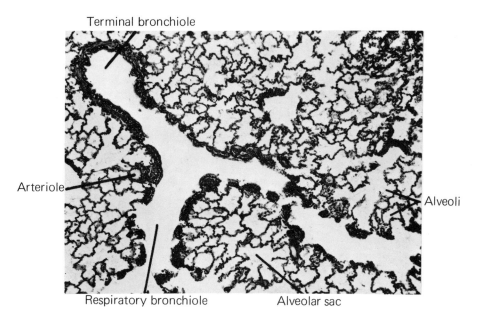

Arteriole

Alveoli

Respiratory bronchiole   Alveolar sac

Figure 18—8. Photomicrograph of a thick lung section showing a terminal bronchiole dividing into 2 respiratory bronchioles in which alveoli appear. The spongelike aspect of the lung is due to the abundance of alveoli and alveolar sacs. H&E stain, X 80.

the limits of resolution of the optical microscope (Figs 18—10 and 18—11). This explains why the classical histologists disagreed about whether the alveolar epithelium was continuous or discontinuous.

The air in the alveoli is thus separated from capillary blood by 4 layers of membranes and cells: the cytoplasm of the epithelial cell, the basement membrane of this cell, the basement membrane of the capillary, and the cytoplasm of the endothelial cell (Fig 18—11). Small tissue spaces are sometimes seen between the 2 basement membranes. The total thickness of these 4 layers varies from 0.3—0.7 μm. In certain places, fusion of the 2 basal laminas can occur, leaving no tissue space between (Figs 18—10 and 18—11). Between the epithelial and endothelial cells, leukocytes, macrophages, and occasional fibroblasts can be found, and some authors have also described rare smooth muscle fibers. The interalveolar wall is supported by reticular fibers and a network of elastic fibers which resist overexpansion (Fig 18—10).

The oxygen of the alveolar air passes into the capillary blood through the above-mentioned membranes (Fig 18—11); the CO_2 diffuses in the opposite direction. Liberation of the CO_2 from H_2CO_3 is catalyzed by the enzyme carbonic anhydrase present in red blood cells. It is not surprising, therefore, that the erythrocyte contains more of this enzyme than any other cell in the body. The lungs contain approximately 300 million alveoli, thus increasing considerably their internal exchange surface, which has been calculated to be approximately 70—80 sq m.

The interalveolar wall is composed of 3 main types of cells: endothelial cells, epithelial lining cells, and septal cells or great alveolar cells (Figs 18—10, 18—11, and 18—12).

Endothelial cells of the capillaries have a slightly smaller and more elongated nucleus than the epithelial lining cells, with which they are frequently confused. They can be recognized in sections because of their proximity to red blood cells. The endothelial lining of the capillaries is continuous and not fenestrated (Fig 18—11).

Epithelial lining or *squamous cells* have flattened nuclei which protrude slightly into the interior of the alveoli and are distinctly separated from each other. As the cytoplasm fans out from the perinuclear region, it becomes very thin (Figs 18—10 and 18—11). These cells completely cover the luminal surface of the alveoli. They have a poorly developed granular endoplasmic reticulum, present short microvilli in some surface regions, and are bound to neighboring cells by desmosomes. The endothelial and alveolar epithelial cells each form only about 1% of the volume of the lungs. It is only because of their extreme thinness that these cells can line such a large surface (Fig 18—13).

Septal cells or *great alveolar cells* are found side by side with the epithelial lining cells, with which they have tight junctions forming junctional complexes (Fig 18—12). They have a rounded cuboid shape, always remain over the basement membrane of the alveolar epithelium, and tend to appear in small groups at those points at which the alveolar walls unite and form angles. Their nuclei are larger and more "vesicular" than the nuclei of the neighboring cells (Figs 18—11 and 18—12). The cytoplasm is not thin like that of the epithelial lining and presents vacuoles when observed with the light microscope. According to several authors, these cells belong to the epithelium, for they have the same origin as the slender epithelial cells which coat most of the alveolar wall. They have abun-

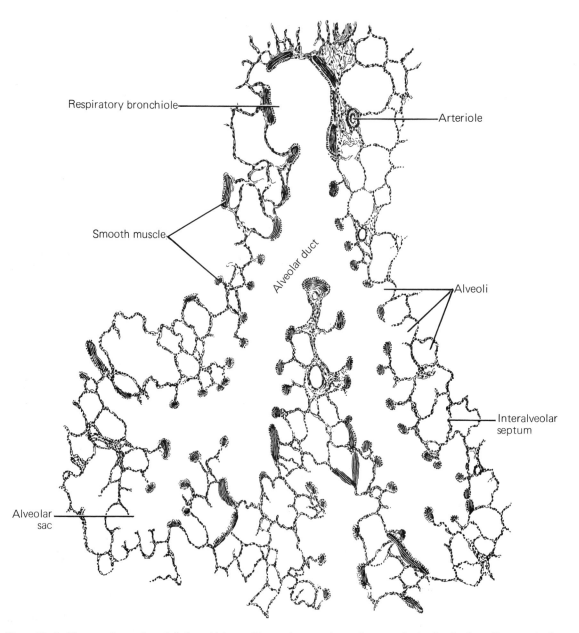

Figure 18—9. Diagram of a portion of the bronchial tree. Observe that smooth muscle present in the alveolar ducts disappears in the alveoli. (Redrawn from Baltisberger.)

dant microvilli on their free surfaces, mitochondria, Golgi apparatus, and a well-developed granular endoplasmic reticulum. The main characteristic of these cells is the presence in their cytoplasm of multilamellar bodies consisting of concentric or parallel lamellae limited by a membrane (Fig 18—12), with a diameter of 0.2 μm, which accounts for the vesicular appearance of their cytoplasm in the light microscope. Histochemical evidence suggests that these structures contain phospholipids.

It is known that the alveolar surface is covered by a lipoprotein layer in which the proteins and lipids are

distributed as a half unit membrane. This layer probably has the function of reducing the surface tension of the alveoli, thus maintaining a constant alveolar diameter. This lipoprotein film has recently been observed with the electron microscope and has been isolated in purified form from the lungs of humans and other species.

Various data suggest that the multilamellar bodies of the great alveolar cells and their products are eliminated into the alveolar lumen where they then form the lipoprotein covering of the alveolar wall. A substance called *surfactant,* produced by these cells and released at the surface, is composed of the phospholipid *dipalmitoyl lecithin.* They are therefore considered nowadays as secretory cells. In fetuses, this lipoprotein layer appears at the end of gestation and coincides with the appearance of multilamellar bodies in the septal cells. Surfactant plays an important role in lowering the surface tension at the fluid-air interface. Its presence reduces the effort required for inspiration. After covering the alveolar epithelium for some time, it is gradually transported by pinocytotic vesicles to the lymph vessels. This substance therefore undergoes a continuous cycle of secretion and reabsorption. The presence of surfactant is very important for the onset of breathing in the newborn.

Besides lipoproteins, neutral mucopolysaccharides also cover the alveolar cell surface. They probably represent the glycocalyx of these cells.

Alveolar Macrophages (Figs 18–10 and 18–13)

The alveolar macrophages, also called *dust cells,*

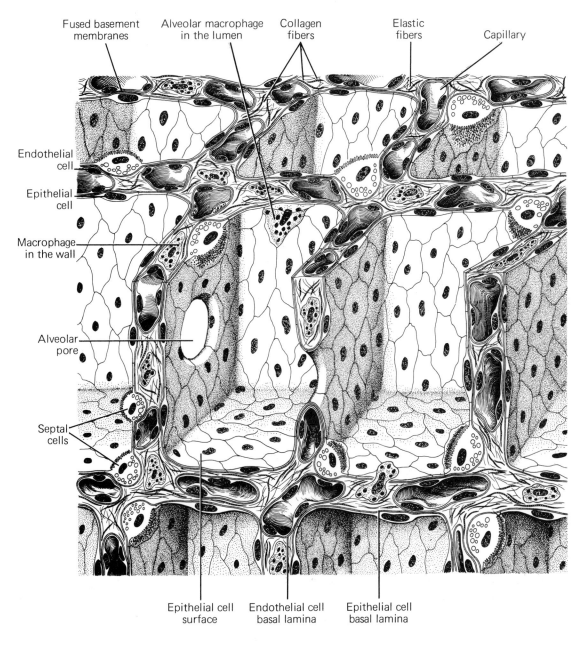

Figure 18–10. Three-dimensional diagram of pulmonary alveoli showing the interalveolar wall and its structure. Observe the capillaries, connective tissue, and macrophages. These cells can also be seen in the alveolar lumen or passing into them. Alveolar pores are numerous. The septal cells are identified by their abundant apical microvilli. The alveoli are lined by a continuous epithelial layer.

are probably derived from monocytes. They occur in the interior of the alveoli or are often seen protruding from the alveolar walls into the lumen. They frequently contain particles of phagocytosed carbon in their cytoplasm. In heart failure, the lungs become congested with blood and the red cells escape to the alveoli and are phagocytosed by these cells, which then can be identified by a positive histochemical reaction to iron (hemosiderin). In such cases they are commonly called *cardiac failure cells.*

Alveolar macrophages are scavenger cells on the surfaces of the alveoli. They have many lysosomes. Passing from the capillaries into the tissue spaces of the alveolar wall and then through the epithelium into the alveolar lumen, they are carried out of the alveolar area into the pharynx and are then swallowed or expelled in sputum.

Alveolar Pores (Figs 18–10 and 18–13)

The interalveolar septum may contain one or more pores, 10–15 μm in diameter, connecting neighboring alveoli. Their functional significance is not known. They might act to equalize pressure in the alveoli or might make possible collateral circulation of air when a bronchiole is obstructed.

PULMONARY BLOOD VESSELS

The circulation in the lungs includes nutrient and functional vessels.

The functional circulation is represented by pulmonary arteries and veins. The pulmonary artery is elastic in type and contains venous blood to be oxygenated in the pulmonary alveoli. Within the lung this artery branches, accompanying the bronchial tree (Fig 18–14). Its branches are always surrounded by the adventitia of the bronchi and bronchioles. At the level of the alveolar duct, the branches of this artery form a capillary network in close contact with the alveolar epithelium. The lung has the best-developed extremely fine capillary network in the body. The capillaries occur in all alveoli, including those present in the respiratory bronchioles.

Venules which originate in the capillary network occur singly in the parenchyma; they are supported by a thin covering of connective tissue and run into the interlobular septa (Fig 18–14). After the veins leave a lobule, they follow the bronchial tree in the direction of the hilus; until then, they are found singly in the pulmonary parenchyma.

The nutrient vessels include the bronchial arteries and veins, which are much smaller than the pulmonary artery and veins. The branches of the bronchial arteries

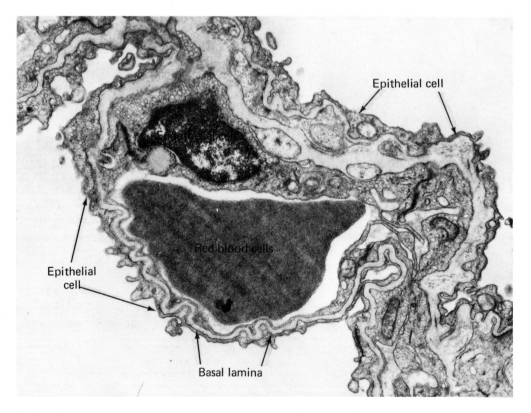

Figure 18–11. Electron micrograph of an alveolar wall from monkey lung. Observe a capillary containing a red blood cell covered by epithelial cells on both sides. The basal lamina is clearly seen. × 30,000.

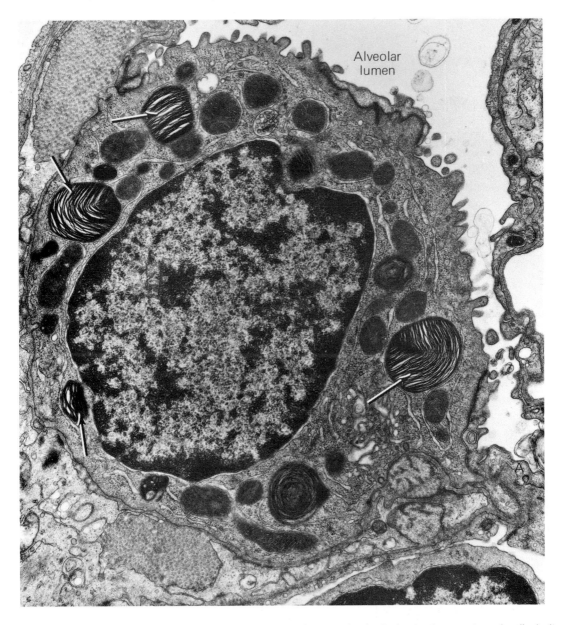

Alveolar
lumen

Figure 18–12. Type II alveolar epithelial cell from rat lung protruding into the alveolar lumen. Arrows point to lamellar bodies containing newly synthesized pulmonary surface-active material. At A, the cytoplasm of a type I epithelial lining cell. Note the microvilli of the type II cell and the junctional complexes with the type I cell. × 17,000. (Courtesy of M Williams.)

also accompany or follow the bronchial tree, but only as far as the respiratory bronchioles, at which point they anastomose with the pulmonary artery.

PULMONARY LYMPHATIC VESSELS

The lymphatic vessels (Fig 18–14) follow the bronchi and the pulmonary vessels; they also occur in the interlobular septa, and all of them drain into the lymph nodes in the region of the hilus. This lymphatic network is referred to as the deep network to distinguish it from the superficial network, which includes the lymphatic vessels present in the visceral pleura. The lymphatic vessels of this region also drain toward the hilus. They either follow the entire length of the pleura or penetrate the lung tissue via the interlobular septa.

In the terminal portions of the bronchial tree and beyond the alveolar ducts, lymphatic vessels do not occur.

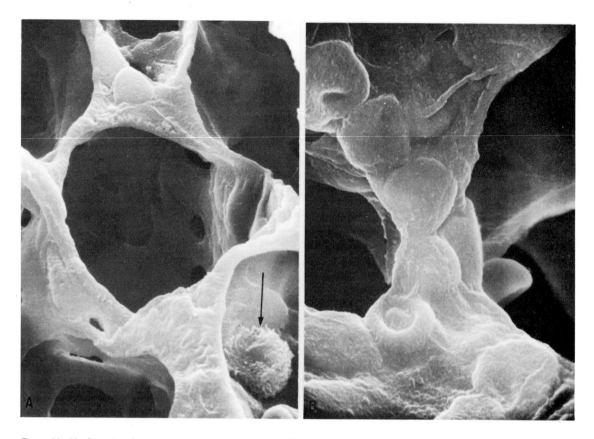

Figure 18–13. Scanning electron micrograph of mouse lung. Observe in *(A)* the thin septa and alveolar pores. At the arrow, a macrophage with its typical ruffled membrane. × 3200. In *(B)*, the alveolar wall is so thin that one can see the shape of the red blood cells in a capillary. × 6700. (Courtesy of Greenwood MF, Holland P: Lab Invest 27:296, 1972.)

PLEURA

The pleura (Fig 18–14) is the serous membrane that surrounds the lung. It consists of 2 layers, parietal and visceral, which are continuous in the region of the hilus. Both membranes are covered by mesothelial cells which rest on a fine connective tissue layer containing collagen and elastic fibers. The elastic fibers of the visceral pleura are continuous with those of the pulmonary parenchyma.

These 2 layers, therefore, delimit a cavity entirely lined by mesothelial squamous cells. Under normal conditions, this pleural cavity contains only a film of liquid which acts as a lubricating agent, permitting the smooth sliding of one surface over the other during respiratory movements. In certain pathologic states, the pleural cavity can become a real cavity, containing liquid or air in its interior. The walls of the pleural cavity, like all serosal cavities (peritoneal and pericardial), are quite permeable to water and other substances—which explains the high frequency of fluid accumulation in this cavity in pathologic conditions.

This fluid is derived from the blood plasma by exudation. Conversely, under certain conditions, liquids or gases present in the pleural cavity can be rapidly reabsorbed.

RESPIRATORY MOVEMENTS

During inhalation, contraction of the intercostal muscles elevates the ribs and contraction of the diaphragm lowers the bottom of the thoracic cavity, increasing its diameter and resulting in pulmonary expansion. The bronchi and bronchioles increase in diameter and length during inhalation. The respiratory portion also enlarges, mainly as a result of expansion of the alveolar ducts; the alveoli enlarge only slightly. The elastic fibers of the pulmonary parenchyma are stretched by this expansion, so that during exhalation caused by muscle relaxation the retraction of the lungs is passive, mainly because of the elastic fibers, which were under tension.

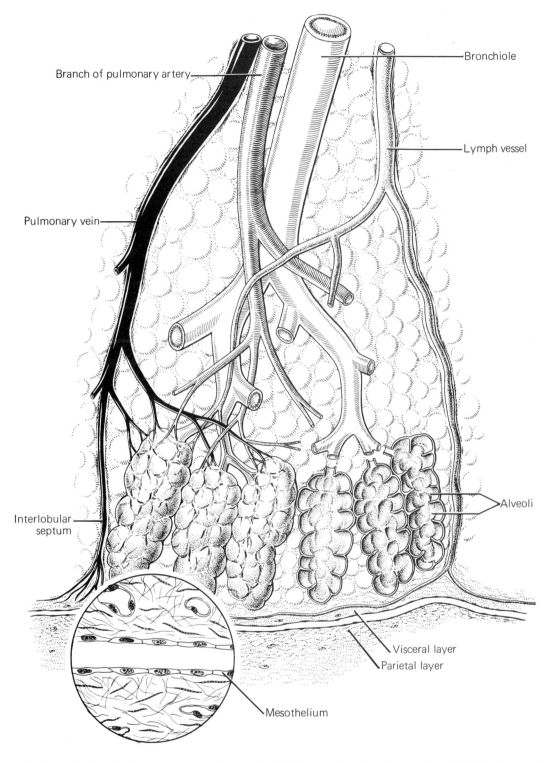

Branch of pulmonary artery

Bronchiole

Lymph vessel

Pulmonary vein

Interlobular septum

Alveoli

Mesothelium

Visceral layer

Parietal layer

Figure 18–14. Blood and lymph circulation in a pulmonary lobule. Both vessels and bronchi are enlarged out of proportion in this drawing. In the interlobular septa, only the vein (left) or lymph vessel (right) has been represented, although both actually coexist in this region. At lower left, an enlargement of the pleura showing its mesothelial lining. (Based partially on Ham AW: *Histology*, 6th ed. Lippincott, 1969.)

●   ●   ●

References

Ali MY: Histology of the human nasopharyngeal mucosa. J Anat 99:657, 1965.

Bertalanffy FD: Respiratory tissue: Structure, histophysiology, cytodynamics. 1. Review and basic cytomorphology. Internat Rev Cytol 16:233, 1964.

Buckingham S & others: Phospholipid synthesis in the large pulmonary alveolar cell. Am J Path 48:1027, 1966.

Clements JA: Surface tension in the lungs. Sc Am 207:120, Dec 1962.

Clements JA: The alveolar lining layer. In: *Ciba Foundation Symposium: The Development of the Lung.* Ciba, 1967.

Dermer GB: The pulmonary surfactant content of the inclusion bodies found within type II alveolar cells. J Ultrastruct Res 33:306, 1970.

Gil J, Weibel ER: Improvements in demonstration of lining layer of lung alveoli by electron microscopy. Resp Physiol 8:13, 1969.

Goldberg VE, Buckingham S, Sommers SC: Pilocarpine stimulation of granular pneumocyte secretion. Lab Invest 20:147, 1969.

Greenwood M, Holland P: The mammalian respiratory tract surface: A scanning electron microscope study. Lab Invest 27:296, 1972.

Hatasa K, Nakamura T: Electron microscopic observations of lung alveolar epithelial cells of normal young mice, with special reference to formation and secretion of osmio-philic lamellar bodies. Z Zellforsch Mikrosk Anat 68:266, 1965.

Heineman HO, Fishmann AP: Nonrespiratory functions of mammalian lungs. Physiol Rev 49:1, 1969.

Kalifat SR, Dupuy-Coin AM, Delarue J: Démonstration ultrastructurale de polysaccharides dont certains acides dans le film de surface de l'alvéole pulmonaire. J Ultrastruct Res 32:572, 1970.

Kuhn C III, Finke EH: The topography of the pulmonary alveolus: Scanning electron microscopy using different fixations. J Ultrastruct Res 38:161, 1972.

Miller WS: *The Lung,* 2nd ed. Thomas, 1947.

Nagaishi C: *Functional Anatomy and Histology of the Lung* University Park Press, 1972.

Sorokin SP: A morphologic and cytochemical study on the great alveolar cells. J Histochem Cytochem 14:884, 1966.

Tobin CE: Human pulmonic lymphatics. Anat Rec 127:611, 1957.

Weibel ER: Études morphométriques du poumon: Leur methodologie et leurs applications. Rev Tuberc Pneumol 32:185, 1968.

Weibel ER: The ultrastructure of the alveolar capillary membrane or barrier. In: *Pulmonary Circulation and Interstitial Space.* Fishman AP, Hecht HH (editors). Univ of Chicago Press, 1969.

19 . . .
Skin

The skin is the heaviest single organ of the body, accounting for about 16% of total body weight. It is composed of an epithelial layer of ectodermal origin, the *epidermis,* and a layer of connective tissue of mesodermal origin, the *dermis* or *corium.* Beneath the dermis, the *subcutaneous tissue* is also made up of connective tissue, often containing many adipose cells, the *panniculus adiposus,* which is not considered part of the skin. The subcutaneous tissue binds the skin loosely to the subjacent tissues. The epidermal appendages include the hairs, nails, and sebaceous and sweat glands.

The keratinized layer of the skin is relatively impermeable to water, thus avoiding extreme water loss by evaporation and making possible terrestrial life. The skin functions as a receptor organ in continuous communication with the environment (see Chapter 10) and protects the organism from impact and friction injuries. A pigment called *melanin,* produced and stored in the cells of the epidermis, provides further protective action against ultraviolet rays. The glands of the skin, the blood vessels, and the adipose tissue participate in the processes of thermoregulation and body

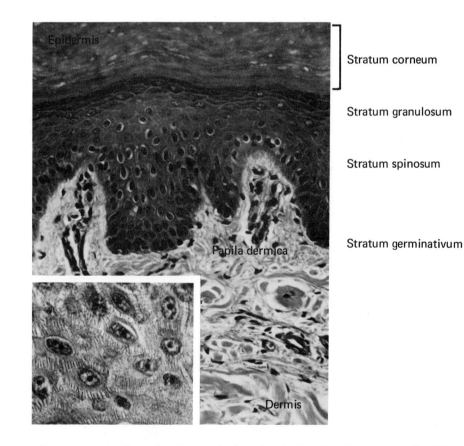

Figure 19—1. Photomicrographs of a section of human skin from the sole of the foot. Observe the papillae of the papillary layer and the thickness of the stratum corneum. The inset, at higher magnification, shows cells of the stratum spinosum with intercellular bridges and their tonofibrils. H&E stain, X 100 and X 600.

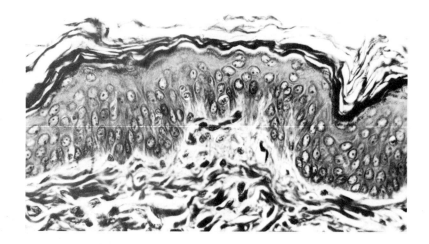

Figure 19—2. Photomicrograph of a section of human abdominal skin. Compare with Fig 19—1 and note the thinness of the epidermis and stratum corneum. The several layers are not as clearly seen as in Fig 19—1. H&E stain, × 310.

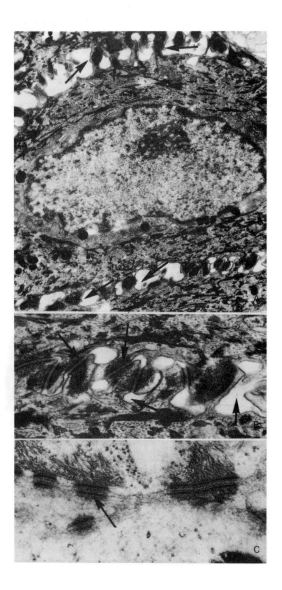

metabolism and in the excretion of various substances. Because skin is a mobile tissue, it has the ability to relax and extend over larger areas.

Upon close observation, human skin shows lines arranged in definite patterns which are unique to the area under examination and never exactly alike in any 2 individuals. These ridges appear first during intrauterine life at 13 weeks in the tips of the digits (fingerprints) and later in the volar surfaces of the hands and feet. The ridges and sulci and their configuration are known as *dermatoglyphics.* They are unique for each individual and so can be used for personal identification, appearing as loops, arches, whorls, or combinations of these forms. These configurations are probably determined by multiple genes, and dermatoglyphics is a field which has recently come to be of considerable medical and anthropologic interest.

EPIDERMIS

The epidermis consists essentially of stratified squamous keratinized epithelium, but it contains also 2 less abundant cell types: melanocytes and Langerhans cells. *Melanocytes* produce the pigment melanin and are derived from the embryonic neural crest and invade the epidermis between the 12th and 14th weeks of

Figure 19—3 (at left). Electron micrograph of the stratum spinosum of human skin. *A:* A cell of the stratum spinosum with its cytoplasm full of tonofibrils and with melanin granules. The arrows show the "intercellular bridges" with their desmosomes. Reduced from × 14,000. *B* and *C:* Desmosomes in greater detail. Observe that a dense substance appears between the cell membranes and that bundles of cytoplasmic filaments (tonofibrils) insert themselves on the desmosomes. Reduced from × 60,000 and × 75,000. (Courtesy of C Barros.)

human pregnancy. During the third to sixth months of intrauterine life, very few melanocytes remain in the dermis. The function of the Langerhans cells is not clear; they are probably of mesenchymal origin.

The thickness of the epidermis varies in different portions of the body. It is thicker on the palms of the hands and the soles of the feet, where it may be as thick as 1.5 mm (Figs 4–2, 19–1, and 19–2).

From the dermis outward, the epidermis consists of 5 layers as follows:

(1) The *stratum germinativum* consists of basophilic columnar or cuboid cells which rest on the dermal-epidermal junction that separates the dermis from the epidermis. Their long axes are perpendicular to the skin surface. Desmosomes are attached to the cells of this stratum, and hemidesmosomes are seen on the inner cell surface facing the basement membrane. The stratum germinativum is characterized by intense mitotic activity and is responsible, in conjunction with the initial portion of the next layer, for the constant renewal of the epidermal cells. The human epidermis is renewed about every 12–14 days. In vitro cultivation of living human epidermis, in contact with dermis which is killed repeatedly by freezing and thawing, demonstrates the emergence of a clear-cut basal lamina, and this strongly suggests an epidermal origin for this structure. All cells in the stratum germinativum have filaments about 10 nm in diameter. Analysis of isolated fibrillar protein shows that it contains proline, cystine, and methionine. As the cells progress upward, the number of filaments increases until they represent, in the stratum corneum, half of its total protein. Another amorphous protein around the filaments constitutes the rest of it.

(2) The *stratum spinosum* consists of cuboid, polygonal, or slightly flattened cells with a central nucleus and a cytoplasm with processes filled with bundles of fibrils. These bundles converge into many small cellular extensions, where they end on desmosomes located at the end of these expansions (Figs 19–1 and 19–3). The cells of this layer are firmly bound together by this system of fibril-filled cytoplasmic expansions and desmosomes which cover its whole surface, giving a prickle-studded appearance in the light microscope. These bundles of fibrils are visible under the light microscope and are called *tonofibrils*. They do not pass from one cell to another, although they were at one time believed to move across intercellular bridges which united cell to cell. They play an important role in maintaining cohesion among cells and helping them to resist the effects of abrasion, especially at the sites of the desmosomes. The epidermis of areas subject to continuous friction and pressure (such as the soles of the feet) has a thicker stratum spinosum with more abundant tonofibrils. The cells of epidermis receive their nutrients by diffusion from the underlying connective tissue.

The term *Malphigian layer* denotes the stratum germinativum and stratum spinosum considered together.

(3) The *stratum granulosum* is characterized by 3–5 layers of flattened polygonal cells containing centrally located nuclei and cytoplasm filled with coarse basophilic granules stained with hematoxylin. They are called *keratohyaline granules* and, because they are found immediately below the stratum lucidum and stratum corneum, they have been regarded as precursors of keratin. Biochemical studies have shown that keratohyaline granules contain a histidine-rich protein. These granules are not membrane-bound, and it is hypothesized that they become part of the interfilamentous matrix in the cell of the stratum corneum. PAS-positive nonglycogen substances are usually found in the intercellular spaces of this layer.

Another characteristic structure found with the electron microscope in the cells of the granular layer of epidermis is the *membrane-coating granule,* ovoid or rodlike in appearance. These granules, formed in association with the Golgi apparatus, move near the upper part of the cell near its plasma membrane. They eventually fuse with the membrane and discharge their contents into the intercellular spaces of the granular layer. Under high magnification in the electron microscope, these granules show a lamellar arrangement. Histochemical reactions show that they probably contain acid mucopolysaccharides and phospholipids. The function of this extruded material is not known, although a hypothesis has been advanced regarding its possible role as an intercellular cement substance which acts as a barrier to the penetration of foreign materials and provides, in the stratum corneum, the same attachment qualities as the tight junctions of other epithelia.

(4) The *stratum lucidum,* found usually in thick skin, is translucent and composed of a thin layer of flattened, eosinophilic, nonnucleated cells. These cells contain *eleidin,* which is probably a product of keratohyalin.

(5) The *stratum corneum* contains the flattened, nonnucleated, keratinized cells whose cytoplasm is filled with a birefringent scleroprotein called keratin (Figs 19–1 and 19–4). This protein consists of elongated protein chains rich in disulfide bonds. In this stage, the cell membrane becomes 15 nm thick and the unit membrane cannot be seen.

After the process of keratinization, which consists of the formation of fibrillar and amorphous proteins, keratohyalin, membrane-bound granules, and thickened plasma membranes, the cells of the stratum corneum have lost their nuclei and other organelles and are called horny cells. Lysosomal hydrolytic enzymes play a role in the disappearance of these structures, and they have been seen in the epidermal cells.

At the surface of the stratum corneum, the horny cells are continuously shed, and 2 types of layers of horny cells (hairy and nonhairy) have been described: that of the palms and soles, adapted for weight-bearing and friction; and that over the rest of the body, adapted for flexibility and impermeability. The formation of the keratinized cell layer was an important evolutionary event, permitting development of terrestrial life, and appeared first in reptiles.

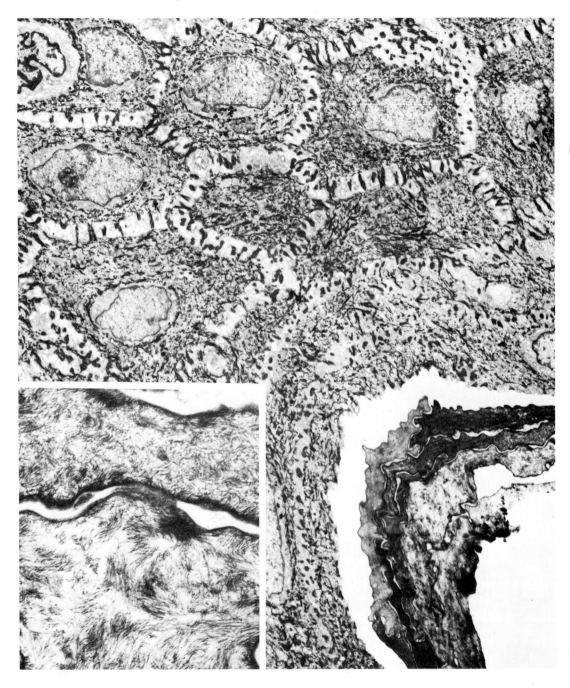

Figure 19—4. Electron micrograph of a section of human skin at the transition between the stratum spinosum and stratum corneum. Observe the cells with their typical cytoplasmic expansions, "intercellular bridges," and cytoplasmic tonofibrils. At lower right is the stratum corneum, seen in detail in the inset at left. Observe that these cells are packed with filaments. X 5500 and X 36,000. (Courtesy of C Barros.)

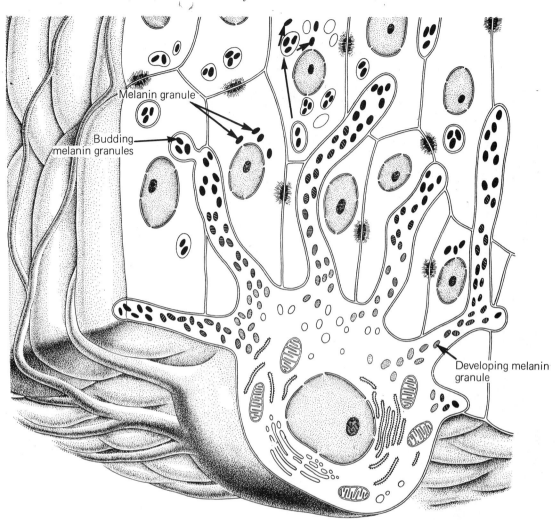

Melanin granule

Budding
melanin granules

Developing melanin
granule

Figure 19–5. Diagram of a melanocyte. Observe that its arms extend upward into the interstices between the epithelial cells. The melanin granules are synthesized in these cells, migrate to its arms, and are transferred by phagocytosis into the cytoplasm of the epithelial cells. This is observed in the upper left arm. Ribosomes, Golgi apparatus, granular endoplasmic reticulum, and mitochondria are also present. (Based on the work of Fitzpatrick & Szabó, 1959.)

The foregoing description of the epidermis corresponds to its most complex structure in areas where it is very thick, as on the soles of the feet. In other regions the epidermis is much thinner; the stratum granulosum and the stratum lucidum are often less well developed; and the stratum corneum may be quite delicate.

Renewal of the epidermis under normal conditions every 12–14 days is due to mitotic activity, observed mainly in the germinativum and spinosum layers. Mitosis is highest during periods of rest or sleep and is related to epinephrine, a potent mitotic inhibitor which is present in the bloodstream in greater amounts during periods of activity. During the process of keratinization, gradual cytoplasmic deposition of protein as fibrils and as an amorphous substance occurs in the cells as they migrate from the base to the surface

of the epidermis. Keratinization consists of the synthesis and deposition of a specific fibrous scleroprotein, called *keratin,* which fills the cytoplasm of the cells of this layer. During this process, the structure of keratin is reinforced by the formation of several disulfide bonds at the expense of preexistent sulfhydryl groups. Keratin, which shows great insolubility and resistance to enzymes, gives an a-diffraction pattern similar to that of myosin or fibrinogen. This a type of keratin is present in the epidermis of all vertebrates. Reptilian scales and bird feathers contain protein which gives a β-diffraction pattern. Lysosomes are known to increase considerably in keratinization, during which time their enzymes are thought to act in the cytoplasm, digesting the cellular organelles. This explains the loss of cell structure and the hyaline appearance of keratinized cells.

Melanocytes

The color of the skin results from several factors, but the most important are its content of melanin and carotene, the number of blood vessels, and the color of the blood flowing in them.

Melanin is a dark brown pigment produced by a specialized cell of the epidermis, the *melanocyte,* usually found beneath or between the cells of the basal layer and the upper layers of the epidermis. Melanocytes are also found in the hair matrix. They have rounded bodies from which long irregular extensions branch into the epidermis, running between the cells of the germinativum and spinosum layers. The tips of these extensions terminate in invaginations of the cells present in the 2 layers. The electron microscope shows a lack of desmosomal attachments and a paucity of tonofibrils in these cells (Figs 19–5, 19–6, and 19–7). The synthesis of melanin occurs in the interior of the melanocyte, and the enzyme tyrosinase plays an important role in this process. As a result of the activity of tyrosinase, tyrosine is transformed first into 3,4-dihydroxyphenylalanine (dopa) and then into dopaquinone, which is finally converted, after a series of transformations, into melanin (eumelanin). There is evidence that tyrosinase is synthesized in the ribosomes, transported in the lumen of the granular endoplasmic reticulum of melanocytes, and accumulated in vesicles formed at the Golgi zone (Fig 19–8). These tyrosinase-filled vesicles are called *stage II melanosomes* (formerly *premelanosomes*) and are the sites where the synthesis of melanin begins. Melanin gradually accumulates in these vesicles and forms the *stage III melanosome,* where tyrosinase coexists with melanin (Fig 19–8). In the last stage (stage IV), the synthesis of melanin ceases, the vesicle is filled with melanin, and no tyrosinase activity can be detected in it. It is then called a *melanin granule* (Figs 19–5, 19–6, 19–7, and 19–8). Thus, in the development of the mature melanin granule, we can distinguish 4 developmental stages:

Stage I: A vesicle surrounded by a membrane, showing the beginning of tyrosinase activity and the formation of fine granular material; at its periphery, electron-dense strands show an orderly arrangement of tyrosinase molecules on a protein matrix.

Stage II: The vesicle is ovoid now and shows, in its interior, parallel filaments with a definite periodicity of about 10 nm or cross-striations of about the same periodicity. Melanin is deposited on the protein matrix.

Stage III: As a result of increased melanin formation, the internal periodic fine structure is less visible.

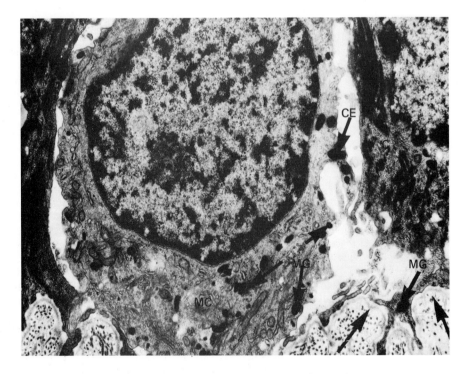

Figure 19–6. Electron micrograph of a melanocyte (MC) between 2 epidermal epithelial cells. Observe the presence of melanin granules (MG) in its cytoplasmic extensions (CE) and in the neighboring epithelial cells (C). No desmosomes bind the melanocytes to the epithelial cells. × 14,000. (Courtesy of C Barros.)

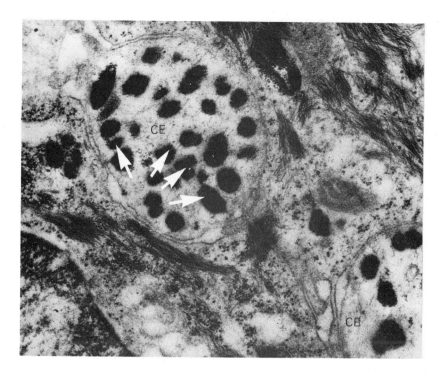

Figure 19-7. Electron micrograph showing 2 melanocyte extensions sectioned transversely and full of melanin granules. The cytoplasm of the surrounding cells contains tonofibrils. X 40,000. CE, cytoplasmic extensions. (Courtesy of C Barros.)

Stage IV: The mature melanin granule is visible in the light microscope.

Melanosomes found in blond and red hair contain a different pigment called *phaeomelanin,* and their shape is spherical, whereas melanosomes of black or brown hair follicles are ovoid.

When no tyrosinase activity exists in the melanocyte or when this activity is defective, no pigment is produced, resulting in the hereditary disorder known as *albinism.*

Once formed, the melanin granules migrate along the extensions of the melanocyte and are transferred to cells of the germinativum and spinosum layers of the epidermis. This transfer process has recently been shown, with the aid of cinemicrography in skin tissue culture, to occur mainly by active phagocytosis on the part of the keratinocytes and not by a "cytocrine" process as proposed by Masson. Whereas the melanocytes synthesize melanin, the epithelial cells act as a depot for this pigment and contain more of it than the melanocytes. Inside the keratinocytes, the melanin granules are linked with lysosomes and their enzymes. In this interaction between keratinocytes and melanocytes, which would result in pigmentation of the skin, the important factors are the rate of formation of melanin granules within the melanocyte, their transfer into the keratinocytes, and the ultimate disposition of the granules by the keratinocytes. It has been sug-

gested that a feedback mechanism may exist between melanocytes and keratinocytes.

The melanocytes can be easily visualized by incubating fragments of epidermis in dopa. This compound, under the action of tyrosinase, produces in the melanocyte an insoluble deposit of dark brown melanin. It is possible in this way to count the number of melanocytes of the epidermis per unit area. Such studies show that these cells are not distributed at random among keratinocytes; rather, there is a definite pattern in their disbribution called the epidermal-melanin unit. In man, the ratio of dopa-positive melanocytes to keratinocytes in the stratum germinativum is constant for each specific area of the body but varies from one region to another. Furthermore, the number of melanocytes per unit area is not influenced by sex or race, and skin color differences are due mainly to differences in the number and size of mature melanosomes in the keratinocytes and the way they are distributed in them. The morphology of the melanosome varies according to race.

Darkening of the skin after exposure to sun (tanning) is considered to be the result of a 2-step process. A physicochemical reaction occurs first, darkening the preexistent melanin and releasing it rapidly into the keratinocytes. In a second stage, the rate of melanin synthesis in the melanocytes accelerates, resulting in an increase in the amount of this pigment.

Melanocyte-stimulating hormone (a- and β-MSH),

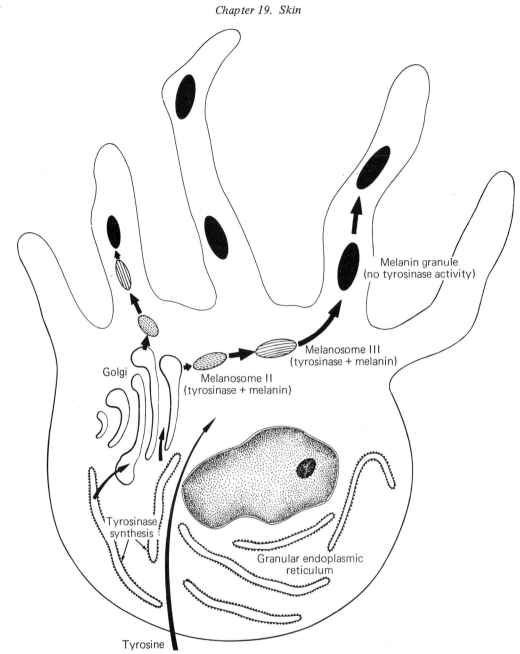

Melanin granule
(no tyrosinase activity)

Melanosome III
(tyrosinase + melanin)

Golgi

Melanosome II
(tyrosinase + melanin)

Tyrosinase
synthesis

Granular endoplasmic
reticulum

Tyrosine

Figure 19—8. Diagram of a melanocyte, illustrating the principal process occurring during melaninogenesis. Tyrosinase is synthesized in the granular endoplasmic reticulum and is accumulated in vesicles of the Golgi apparatus. The free vesicles are now called melanosomes. Melanin synthesis begins in the stage II melanosomes, where this compound is accumulated and forms stage III melanosomes. Later, this structure loses its tyrosinase activity and becomes a melanin granule. Melanin granules migrate to arm tips and are then transferred to the epithelial cells of the Malpighian layer.

produced in the intermediate lobe of the pituitary, has a marked influence on the melanophores of amphibia, promoting the centrifugal migration of their pigment in their long cytoplasmic processes and an increase in the number of melanosomes in the keratinocytes. Its action in man, however, is less dramatic. Lack of cortisol from the adrenal cortex causes overproduction of ACTH and probably MSH, both of which increase the pigmentation of the skin, as in Addison's disease (a disease due to dysfunction of the adrenal glands). The action of MSH is mediated through a-adrenergic receptors; the action of catecholamines is mediated through β-adrenergic receptors. Substances like ammoniated mercury may lighten the skin by exerting a mild peeling effect. Hydroquinone and its derivatives may inhibit the synthesis of melanin, with consequent depigmentation. Other substances such as dihydroxyacetone, when applied to the skin, react with the proteins of the keratin layer, darkening it promptly.

The Langerhans Cells

These star-shaped cells are found mainly in the stratum spinosum of the epidermis. After impregnation with gold chloride, they are delineated sharply against an unstained background. In the electron microscope they have an indented nucleus and a clear cytoplasm with no tonofilaments in their cytoplasm and no desmosomes in the plasma membrane. They have granules. Their functional significance is still obscure.

DERMIS

The dermis is composed of the connective tissue which supports the epidermis and binds it to the subjacent layer, the subcutaneous tissue. Its thickness varies according to the region of the body up to a maximum of 3 mm on the soles of the feet. The external surface of the dermis is very irregular and presents many outgrowths which follow similar infoldings of the epidermis (Fig 19–1). These structures are more numerous in skin subject to frequent pressure and are believed to increase and reinforce the dermo-epidermal junction. During embryonic development, dermis acts as the determinant of the developing pattern of the overlying epidermis. Dermis obtained from the sole always forms a heavily keratinized epidermis irrespective of its site of origin except when the cells are obtained from the corneal epithelium.

The distinctive dermo-epidermal junction is seen in histologic sections of the human skin, and this understructure of the epidermis is unique in each part of the body. Villouslike projections of the cytoplasm of basal cells interdigitate with brushlike projections of the connective tissue fibers, and the basal surface of the epidermis shows cones, ridges, and cords of different lengths extending into the dermal papillae. The epidermal growth seen between 2 dermal papillae is called an interpapillary peg. At the tip of the epidermal ridges, the ducts of the sweat glands enter. Flat dermoepidermal junctions occur in the eyelids and scrotum. At the tips of the digits, parallel ridges constitute an intricate system of valleys and tunnels. The sulci of the outer surface of the skin correspond to the valleys. A PAS-positive basement membrane always follows the surface of the basal cells of the stratum germinativum facing the dermis.

Two layers with rather indistinct boundaries have been described in the dermis. They are the outermost papillary layer and the deeper reticular layer. The *papillary layer* is thin and is composed of loose connective tissue. Many connective tissue cells are present, the most abundant being the mast cells. Extravasated leukocytes and macrophages are also seen. The papillary layer is so called because it penetrates into the papillae.

From this layer, collagenous fibrils insert into the basal lamina and extend perpendicularly into the dermis. They are thought to have a special function, binding the dermis to the epidermis, and are thus called anchoring fibrils. A layer of thin elastic fibers runs parallel to the basal cell layer of epidermis.

The *reticular layer* is thicker, composed of irregular dense connective tissue, and therefore has more fibers and fewer cells than the papillary layer. Both layers have many elastic fibers, which is in part responsible for the elasticity and firmness of the skin. The acid mucopolysaccharide content of the dermis is different in the various regions. The 3 principal glycosaminoglycans in the skin are hyaluronate, dermatan sulfate, and chondroitin sulfate A and C, and they are bound to protein, constituting proteoglycans. Fibroblasts obtained from skin grown in vitro produce both hyaluronate and various sulfated acid mucopolysaccharides.

Age changes in the dermis can be observed histologically and biochemically. Collagen fibers thicken with age, and collagen synthesis decreases because of the decline in growth rate; a decreased excretion of urinary hydroxyproline occurs in the aged. With age, elastic fibers steadily increase in number and thickness, so that the elastin content of human skin increases approximately 5-fold from fetal to adult life. The dermis has a rich network of blood and lymph vessels. In certain areas of the skin, blood can pass directly from arteries to veins through the arteriovenous anastomoses or shunts. They play a very important role in temperature and blood pressure regulation, since skin can accommodate about 4.5% of the blood volume. Blood flow is regulated by nerve impulses from the sympathetic vasoconstrictive nerves and by epinephrine and acetylcholine. Besides these components, the dermis also contains some epidermal derivatives, the hair follicles and the sweat and sebaceous glands. A rich supply of nerves is found in the dermis, and the effector nerves to the skin are postganglionic fibers of the ganglia of the paravertebral chain. The afferent nerve endings form a superficial dermal nerve network with free nerve endings, a hair follicle network, and the mucocutaneous end organs, Meissner and Vater-Pacini corpuscles.

SUBCUTANEOUS TISSUE

This layer consists of loose connective tissue that binds the skin loosely to the subjacent organs, making it possible for the skin to slide over them. The subcutaneous tissue often contains fat cells, varying in number according to the area of the body and in size according to the nutritional status of the individual.

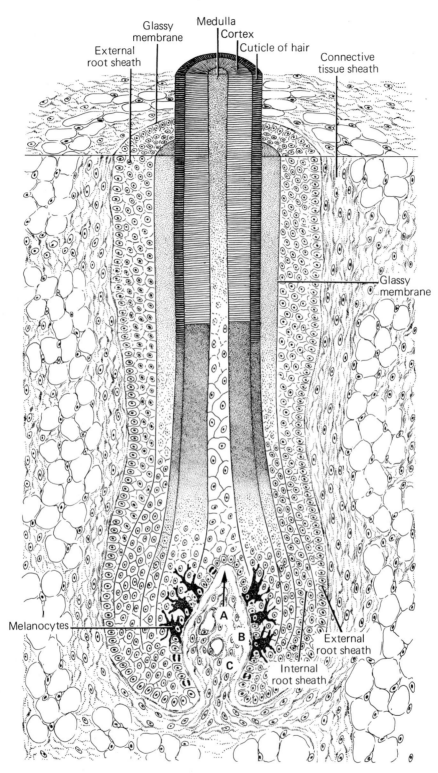

Figure 19–9. Drawing of a hair and its follicle. The follicle has a bulbous terminal expansion that contains a dermal papilla, which is covered by cells that form the hair root and develop into the hair shaft. The central cells *(A)* indicated by the arrow produce large, vacuolated, poorly cornified cells that form the medulla of the hair. The cells that produce the cortex of the hair are located laterally *(B)*. Cells forming the hair cuticle originate in the next layer *(C)*. The peripheral epithelial cells develop into the internal and external sheaths. The external sheath continues with the epidermis, while the cells of the internal sheath disappear at the level of the openings of the sebaceous gland ducts.

HAIRS

The hairs are thin keratinized structures derived partly from an epidermal invagination and partly from a dermal hair germinal center. Their color, size, and disposition are variable according to race, age, sex, and the region of the body. They are present almost everywhere on the surface of the body. Hairs grow discontinuously and have periods of growth followed by periods of rest. This growth does not occur synchronously in all regions of the body or even in the same area. This type of growth is known as *growth in mosaic*. The duration of the growth and rest periods also varies according to the region of the body. Thus, in the scalp, the growth periods may last for several years, whereas the rest periods average 3 months. Hair growth of certain regions of the body such as the scalp, face, and pubis is strongly influenced by sex hormones— especially androgen—but by adrenal and thyroid hormones also.

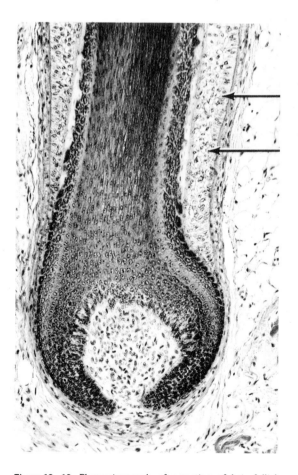

Figure 19–10. Photomicrograph of a section of hair follicle from a human lip. Observe the papilla and the outer root sheath (arrows), surrounded by a connective tissue sheath. H&E stain, × 118.

Each hair derives from an epidermal invagination, the *hair follicle,* which presents during its growth period a terminal dilatation called the hair bulb. At the base of the *hair bulb,* a dermal papilla can be observed (Figs 19–9 and 19–10). The cells covering this dermal papilla form the hair root that produces and is continuous with the hair shaft that protrudes beyond the skin surface.

During periods of growth, the cells of the hair bulb divide and differentiate into the following cell types:

(1) In certain types of thick hairs, the cells of the central region of the root at the apex of the dermal papilla produce large vacuolated and moderately keratinized cells which will form the *medulla* of the hair (Fig 19–9A).

(2) The cells located around the medulla multiply and differentiate into heavily keratinized, compactly grouped fusiform cells forming the *hair cortex* (Fig 19–9B).

(3) The next layer of bulb cells produces the hair cuticle, a layer composed of cells which, midway up the bulb, are cuboid, then become tall and columnar, and, higher up, change from horizontal to vertical, at which point they form a layer of flattened, heavily keratinized cells disposed as shingles covering the cortex (Fig 19–9C). The cuticle cells are the last cell line in the hair follicle to differentiate.

(4) Finally, the most peripheral cells give rise to the *internal root sheath,* which completely surrounds the initial part of the hair shaft. The sheath is composed of 3 layers: the cuticle, the middle (Huxley) layer, and Henle's outer layer. This sheath contains many granules similar to keratohyalin but called trichohyaline granules. The internal sheath is ultimately discharged inside the canal where the sebaceous glands abut in the hair follicle (Fig 19–11). The outer or external root sheath is the downgrowth of epidermal cells, and near the surface it shows all the layers of epidermis. Near the dermal papilla it is composed of cells corresponding to the stratum germinativum of the epidermis.

Separating the hair follicle from the dermis is a noncellular hyaline membrane, the *glassy membrane* (Fig 19–9), which probably represents a thickening of the basal lamina. The dermis which surrounds the follicle is denser, forming a special sheath of connective tissue. Bound to this sheath and connecting it to the papillary layer of the dermis are bundles of smooth muscle cells disposed in an oblique direction (Fig 19–11). Their contractions promote erection of the hair shaft into a more vertical position—commonly called "gooseflesh" in humans. These muscles are called the *arrector pili* muscles.

Hair color is due to the activity of melanocytes located between the papilla and the epithelial cells of the hair root and the amount of pigment present in the medullary and cortical cells of the hair shaft (Fig 19–9). These melanocytes probably produce and transfer melanin to the epithelial cells by a mechanism similar to that described for the epidermis.

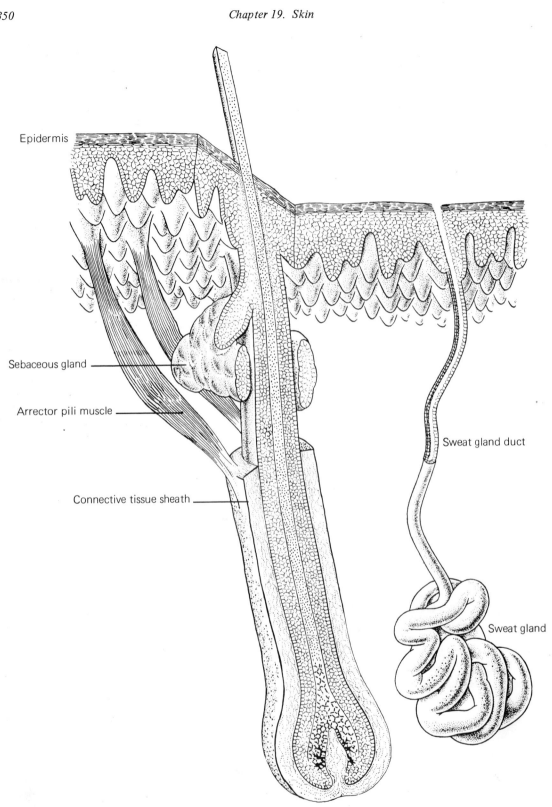

Epidermis

Sebaceous gland

Arrector pili muscle

Sweat gland duct

Connective tissue sheath

Sweat gland

Figure 19—11. Diagram of the relations between the skin, hair follicle, arrector pili muscle, and sebaceous and sweat glands.

Although the keratinization processes in the epidermis and hair appear to be similar, they differ in the following ways:

(1) The epidermis produces relatively soft, keratinized outer layers of dead cells which adhere slightly to the skin and desquamate continuously. In the hair and internal root sheath the opposite occurs, with the production of a hard and compact keratinized structure.

(2) Whereas in the epidermis keratinization occurs continuously and all over, in the hair it is intermittent and present only in the hair root. The hair papilla has an inductive action on the covering epithelial cells, promoting their proliferation and differentiation. This explains why processes which injure the dermal papillae promote the loss of hair.

(3) Contrary to what happens in the epidermis, where all cells differentiate in the same direction, giving rise to the final keratinized layer, in the hair root the cells differentiate into various cell types which are different in ultrastructure, histochemistry, and function. Mitotic activity in hair follicles and sebaceous glands is under the influence of androgens.

NAILS

The nails are cornified plates present on the dorsal surfaces of the terminal phalanges of the toes and fingers (Fig 19–12). The thickened epithelial surfaces of the phalanges on which the nail plate rests are called the *nail beds*. Seen from above, the nail body shows near the root a white, crescent-shaped area called the *lunula*. There is no generally accepted explanation for its presence. The proximal part of the nail, hidden in the nail groove, is the *nail root*. Processes of epithelial proliferation and differentiation which gradually produce the nail are localized in the nail root. The nail plate consists of a compact layer of highly adherent and keratinized epithelial cells. The nails grow in a distal direction, sliding over the skin of the nail bed,

which is called *hyponychium* and is continuous with the epidermis that covers the ventral surface of the digits. This underlying skin normally does not participate in the process of nail formation, and its main function is to act as a support. The horny epidermal extension of the tip of the proximal nail fold is called the *eponychium* or *cuticle*.

GLANDS OF THE SKIN

Sebaceous Glands

The sebaceous glands are found embedded in the dermis almost all over the body except in areas where hairs are not found. They are acinous glands which usually have various acini opening into a short duct. This duct usually ends in the upper portion of a hair follicle (Fig 19–11), but in certain regions, such as the glans penis, glans clitoridis, and lips, it opens directly onto the epidermal surface. The acini consist of an external layer of undifferentiated flattened epithelial cells which rests on the basement membrane. These cells proliferate and differentiate, filling the acini with rounded cells containing abundant fat droplets in their cytoplasm (Fig 19–13). Their nuclei gradually shrink, and the cells simultaneously become filled with fat

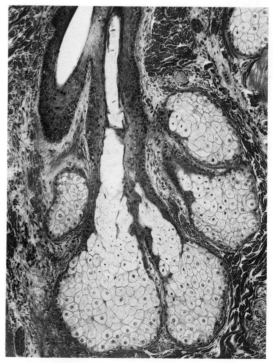

Figure 19–13. Photomicrograph of a sebaceous gland. It consists of various acini, which are limited externally by proliferating, flattened epithelial cells that give rise to the fat-filled round cells of the acinar center. H&E stain, × 100.

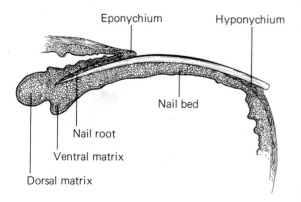

Eponychium   Hyponychium

Nail bed

Nail root

Ventral matrix

Dorsal matrix

Figure 19–12. The nail and its components.

droplets and burst. The product of this process is the secretion of the sebaceous gland, which is gradually moved to the surface of the skin. This is, therefore, a typical example of a holocrine gland, for its product of secretion, the sebum, is released with remnants of dead cells. This product is composed mainly of a complex mixture of lipids which contains triglycerides, free fatty acids, and cholesterol and its esters. The primary controlling factor of sebaceous glands in men is testicular testosterone; in women, it is a combination of ovarian and adrenal androgens, and the flow of sebaceous glands is continuous. A disturbance in the normal secretion and flow of sebum is one of the reasons for the development of acne. The preen glands of certain aquatic birds are modified sebaceous glands, and their product is spread by the bird on its feathers, rendering them impermeable to water.

Sweat Glands

The sweat glands are widely distributed in the skin. Certain regions such as the glans penis are exceptions.

The sweat glands are simple, coiled, tubular glands (Fig 19—14). Their ducts do not divide and are thinner in diameter than the secretory portion (Fig 19—11). This secretory part of the gland is embedded in the dermis, measures approximately 0.4 mm in diameter, and is surrounded by myoepithelial cells (described in Chapter 4). Contraction of these cells is believed to help to discharge the secretion. A fairly thick basement membrane lies on the outside of the secretory portion of the glands. Two cell types have been described in the secretory portion of these glands: (1) a *dark cell,* with characteristics of a serous cell having an abundant granular endoplasmic reticulum and

secretory granules containing glycoprotein; and (2) a *clear cell,* devoid of secretory granules, with a small amount of endoplasmic reticulum and presenting frequent invaginations of the plasma membrane in its basal portion. As explained in Chapter 4, this morphologic aspect is characteristic of cells which transport ions and water.

The ducts are composed of a double layer of cuboid cells (Fig 19—14). The cells of the inner layer have the characteristics of ion- and water-transporting cells.

The fluid secreted by these glands is not viscous and contains very little protein. Its main components are water, sodium chloride, urea, ammonia, and uric acid. Its sodium content of 85 mEq/liter is distinctly below that of blood (144 mEq/liter), and it has been suggested that the cells present in the inner layer of the sweat ducts are responsible for sodium reabsorption. The elimination of catabolites plus other considerations outlined above suggest that the sweat glands might have an excretory function.

Besides these *merocrine* sweat glands, another type of modified sweat gland—the *apocrine* gland—is present in the axillary, areolar, and anal regions. Apocrine glands are much larger (3—5 mm in diameter) than merocrine glands. They are found embedded in the subcutaneous tissue and open into hair follicles. They produce a viscous secretion and in females undergo histologic changes during the menstrual cycle. While the apocrine glands are innervated by adrenergic nerve endings, the merocrine glands receive cholinergic fibers.

The glands of Moll in the margins of the eyelids and the ceruminous glands of the ear are also considered to be modified sweat glands.

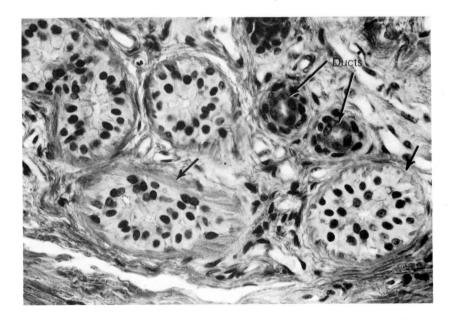

Figure 19—14. Photomicrograph of a human sweat gland. At upper right are 2 ducts transversely sectioned. Observe the myoepithelial cells, which form a sheath around the gland. H&E stain, × 360.

VESSELS & NERVES OF THE SKIN

The arterial vessels which nourish the skin form 2 plexuses, one located between the papillary and reticular layers and one between the dermis and the subcutaneous tissue. Thin branches leave these plexuses and vascularize the dermal papillae. Each papilla has only one arterial ascending and one venous descending branch. The veins are disposed in 3 plexuses, 2 of them in the position described for the arterial vessels and the third in the middle of the dermis. Arteriovenous anastomoses with glomi (see Chapter 12) are frequent in the skin. The lymphatic vessels begin as blind sacs in the papillae of the dermis and converge to 2 plexuses in the same way as the arterial vessels.

One of the most important functions of the skin is to receive stimuli from the environment, and it is therefore richly innervated. Besides the free nerve endings in the epidermis and the cutaneous glands, receptors are present in the dermis and subcutaneous tissue, being more frequently found in the dermal papillae (see Chapter 10). The hair follicles possess a rich network of nerve endings, and this has an important role in the processing of tactile impressions from the environment.

• • •

References

Briggaman RA, Dalldorf FG, Wheeler CE: Formation and origin of basal lamina and anchoring fibrils in adult human skin. J Cell Biol 51:384, 1971.

Bullough WS: Mitotic and functional homeostasis: A speculative review. Cancer Res 25:1683, 1965.

Cohen J, Szabó G: Study of pigment donation in vitro. Exper Cell Res 50:418, 1968.

Cummins H: Dermatoglyphics. In: *Dermatology in Medicine.* Fitzpatrick TB & others (editors). McGraw-Hill, 1971.

Epstein WL, Maibach HI: Cell renewal in human epidermis. Arch Dermat 92:462, 1965.

Fitzpatrick TB, Breathnach AS: Das epidermale Melanin-Einheit-System. Dermatol Wochenschr 147:481, 1963.

Fitzpatrick TB, Szabó G: The melanocyte: Cytology and cytochemistry. J Invest Dermat 32:197, 1959.

Fraser RDB, MacRae TP, Rogers CE: *Keratins: Their Composition, Structure, and Biosynthesis.* Thomas, 1972.

Frenk E, Schellhorn JP: Zur morphologie der epidermalen Melaninheit. Dermatologica 21:339, 1969.

Fukuyama K, Epstein WL: Protein synthesis studied by autoradiography in the epidermis of different species. Am J Anat 122:269, 1968.

Guevedo WC Jr: Epidermal melanin units: Melanocyte-keratinocyte interactions. Am Zool 12:35, 1972.

Halprin KM: Epidermal "turnover time": A reexamination. J Invest Dermat 86:14, 1972.

Hashimoto K: Cementosome: A new interpretation of the membrane-coating granule. Arch Dermat 240:349, 1971.

Kisstala U, Mustaballis KK: Electron microscopic evidence of synthetic activity of Langerhans cells of human epidermis. Z Zellforsch Mikrosk Anat 78:427, 1967.

Laidlaw GG: The dopa reaction in normal histology. Anat Record 53:399, 1932.

Lavker RM, Matoltsy AG: Formation of horny cells. J Cell Biol 44:501, 1970.

Masson P: Pigment cells in man. In: *The Biology of Melanosomes.* Miner RW, Gordon M (editors). Ann New York Acad Sc 4:15, 1948.

Matoltsy AG: Mechanism of keratinization. In: *Fundamentals of Keratinization.* Butcher EO, Sognnaes RF (editors). Publication No. 70. American Association for the Advancement of Science, 1962.

Menton DN, Eisen AZ: Structure and organization of mammalian stratum corneum. J Ultrastruct Res 35:247, 1971.

Montagna W: *The Structure and Function of Skin,* 3rd ed. Academic Press, 1974.

Munger BL: The cytology of apocrine sweat glands. 2. Human. Z Zellforsch Mikrosk Anat 68:837, 1965.

Snell RS: An electron microscopic study of keratinization in the epidermal cells of the guinea pig. Z Zellforsch Mikrosk Anat 65:829, 1965.

Snell RS: An electron microscopic study of the dendritic cells in the basal layer of guinea-pig epidermis. Z Zellforsch Mikrosk Anat 66:457, 1965.

Snell RS: The fate of epidermal desmosomes in mammalian skin. Z Zellforsch Mikrosk Anat 66:471, 1965.

Terzakis JA: The ultrastructure of monkey eccrine sweat glands. Z Zellforsch Mikrosk Anat 64:493, 1964.

Zelickson AS: *Ultrastructure of Normal and Abnormal Skin.* Lea & Febiger, 1967.

20...
Urinary Tract

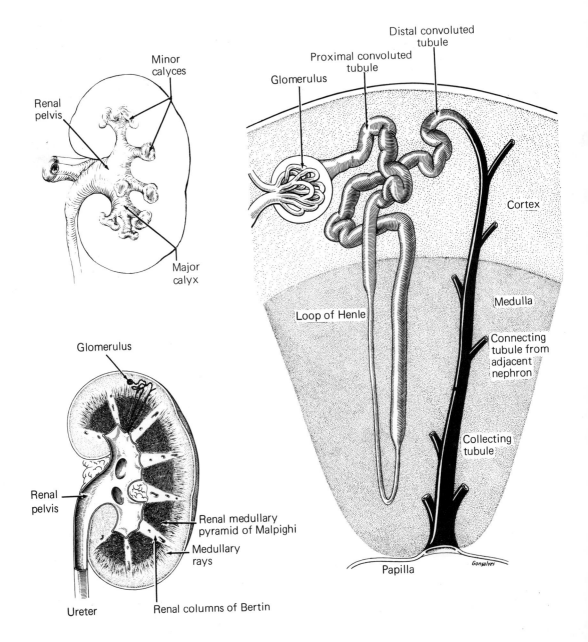

Figure 20–1. *Left:* The general organization of the kidney. *Right:* The cortical or medullary localization of nephron segments and collecting tubules (the latter shown in black).

The urinary system consists of the kidneys, the ureters, the bladder, and the urethra and contributes to the maintenance of homeostasis by producing the urine, in which various metabolic waste products are eliminated. The kidneys also regulate the fluid balance of the body and are the site of production of renin and erythropoietin. The urine produced in the kidneys passes through the ureters to the bladder and is released to the exterior through the urethra.

THE KIDNEYS

Each kidney is shaped like a red bean, with one concave border with a large indentation at the center in which the hilus—the area where the nerves and blood and lymph vessels enter and leave—is located and a convex surface on the opposite side (Fig 20–1). In the hilus also, the calyces unite to form the renal pelvis which is the superior, dilated part of the ureter. The kidney is covered by the *renal capsule,* composed of dense connective tissue, and has an outer *cortex* and an inner *medulla* (Figs 20–1 and 20–2).

In man, the renal medulla is composed of 10–18 conical or pyramid-shaped structures, the *Malpighian* or *medullary pyramids,* whose bases and sides are in contact with the cortical zone and whose vertices protrude into the renal calyces (Fig 20–1). These protrusions are the *renal papillae,* each of which is perforated by 10–25 orifices, the openings of the *collecting ducts,* forming the *area cribrosa.*

From the base of the medullary pyramid, 400–500 elongated formations of medullary substance called the *medullary rays* penetrate the cortex (Fig 20–1). Each medullary ray consists of a straight collecting tubule into which the distal convoluted tubules of many neighboring nephrons empty their contents through arched collecting tubules.

The cortex occupies the spaces between the Malpighian pyramids and between the bases of the pyramids and the renal capsule. The cortical tissue in the areas between the pyramids constitutes the *renal columns of Bertin.* In sections of fresh kidney, the cortex shows small red dots which correspond to special functional structures called the *renal corpuscles* or *corpuscles of Malpighi.*

The renal cortex consists mainly of nephrons; in the medulla, collecting tubules—structures which differ from the nephrons in morphology, physiology, and embryologic origin—are more conspicuous.

In some mammals, the kidney is composed only of one medullary pyramid and the cortex, which occupies the area between the base of the pyramid and the convex surface of the organ. The apex of the pyramid enters the ureter. This type of organization represents a lobe of kidney tissue, and such kidneys are called unilobar. In other mammals, including humans, the kidney is composed of many lobes (multilobar kidneys), each with a medullary pyramid and its corre-

sponding cortical tissue. The renal lobule consists of a medullary ray and the cortical tissue which surrounds it. Thus, each renal lobule contains the collecting tubules, the renal corpuscles, and the proximal and distal convoluted tubules of the cortical tissue, which surround the branched system of the collecting ducts. In the adult human, the renal lobes and lobules are not always clearly visible.

Many aspects of renal histology and physiology have been discovered using the technic of dissociation, which consists of macerating the organ in dilute acid and subsequently separating its components under a stereoscopic microscope with the aid of fine needles. The acid attacks the delicate connective tissue which supports and binds the renal tubules, permitting their isolation with relative ease.

Nephrons

Each kidney is composed of 1–4 million functional units called *nephrons.* Each nephron consists of (1) a dilated portion, the *renal corpuscle* or *Malpighian corpuscle;* (2) the *proximal convoluted tubule;* (3) the *thin* and *thick portions of the loop of Henle;* and (4) the *distal convoluted tubule* (Fig 20–1). The *collecting duct,* which is of different embryologic origin than the nephron, represents the excretory duct of the system, although in some areas it is involved in water transport across its cells.

The components of the nephron are invested by a basement membrane which is continuous with the limited amount of connective tissue of the organ.

The *renal corpuscle* consists of a tuft of capillaries, the glomerulus, surrounded by a double-walled epithelial capsule called *Bowman's capsule* (Figs 20–2 and 20–3). The internal leaflet of the capsule adheres to the capillaries of the glomerulus and is called the visceral layer, whereas the external leaflet forms the outer limit of the renal corpuscle and is called the parietal layer of Bowman's capsule (Figs 20–2 and 20–3). Between the 2 leaflets of Bowman's capsule is the *capsular space,* which receives the liquid filtered through the capillary wall and the internal leaflet. There is a relation between total glomerular volume and kidney weight expressed in a straight line on a logarithmic scale. In most mammals, development of renal corpuscles stops at birth.

Each renal corpuscle has a *vascular pole,* where the *afferent arteriole* enters and the *efferent arteriole* leaves, and a *urinary pole,* where the proximal convoluted tubule begins.

After entering the renal corpuscle, the afferent arteriole usually divides into 2–5 primary branches which divide again into narrow secondary branches; at regular intervals, these branches open into capillary loops. According to some investigators, the capillary loops originating from the same branch of the afferent arteriole anastomose only with each other and not with those of the other branches, whereas others have produced evidence that the capillary tuft is in fact an unrestricted network with numerous anastomoses. Direct connections between the afferent and the effer-

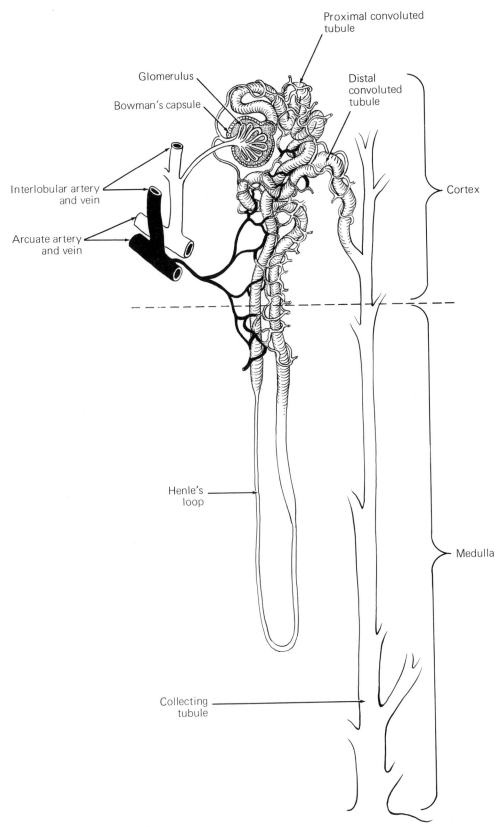

Figure 20—2. Vascular supply of the nephron in the outer zone of the cortex.

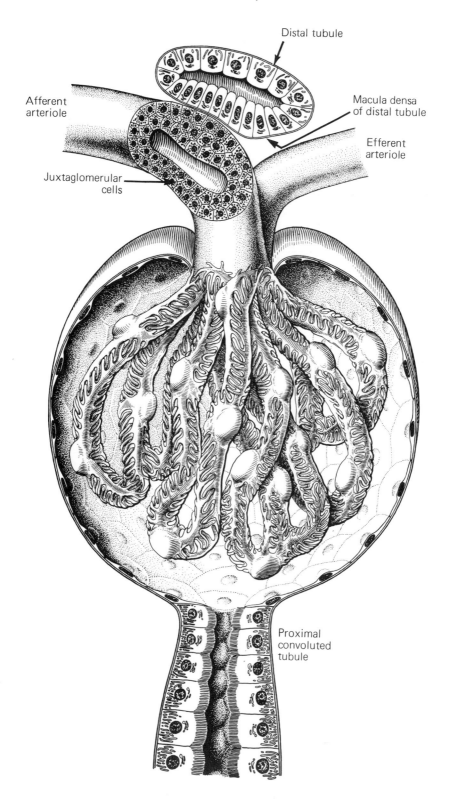

Distal tubule

Afferent
arteriole

Macula densa
of distal tubule

Efferent
arteriole

Juxtaglomerular
cells

Proximal
convoluted
tubule

Figure 20–3. The renal corpuscle. The upper part shows the vascular pole, with afferent and efferent arterioles and the macula densa. Note the juxtaglomerular cells in the wall of the afferent arteriole. Podocytes cover glomerular capillaries. Their nuclei protrude on the cell surface. Podocyte processes can be seen. Note the cells of the parietal layer of Bowman's capsule. The lower part of the drawing shows the urinary pole and the proximal convoluted tubule.

ent arterioles, by which the blood can circulate without passing through the glomerulus, have also been described.

The hydrostatic pressure of the arterial blood contained in the glomerular capillaries is regulated by the afferent arteriole. The wall of this arteriole contains a considerable amount of smooth muscle and is thus capable of changing luminal diameter; the lumens of the efferent arterioles remain constant in diameter.

The *parietal* layer of Bowman's capsule consists of simple squamous epithelium supported on a basement membrane and a thin layer of reticular fibers which anastomose with the reticular framework around the tubules of the organ. At the urinary pole, the epithelium changes into that of the proximal tubule.

Whereas the epithelium of the parietal layer remains unchanged, the internal or visceral layer is modified during embryonic development, acquiring a peculiar character. The cells of the internal layer, called *podocytes* (Figs 20–4 and 20–5), present a cell body from which arise several primary processes. From each primary process branch several secondary processes (Figs 20–3 and 20–4) which embrace the capillaries of the glomerulus. The secondary (foot) processes, at a regular distance of 25 nm from each other, are in direct contact with the basement membrane of the capillaries, but most of the cellular bodies of the podocytes and their primary processes do not reach the basement membrane (Figs 20–4 and 20–5). The foot processes from one epithelial cell embrace more than one capillary. The foot processes contain few or no organelles, but microfilaments are numerous.

The secondary processes of the podocytes interpenetrate, delimiting elongated spaces—the filtration slits—between them. Between these processes (and,

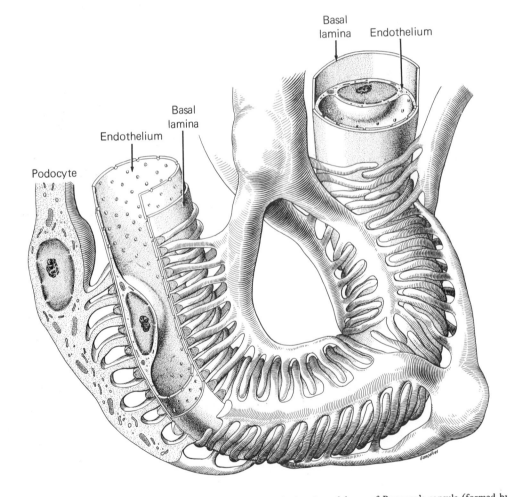

Figure 20–4. Schematic representation of a glomerular capillary, with the visceral layer of Bowman's capsule (formed by podocytes). In this capillary, endothelial cells are fenestrated; however, the basal lamina on which they rest is continuous. At left is a podocyte shown in partial section. As viewed from the outside, the nuclei of the podocytes are seen to protrude into Bowman's capsule. Each podocyte has many primary processes from which arise an even greater number of secondary processes. The secondary processes are in contact with the basal lamina of the capillary wall. (Redrawn and modified after Gordon. Reproduced, with permission, from Ham AW: *Histology,* 6th ed. Lippincott, 1969.)

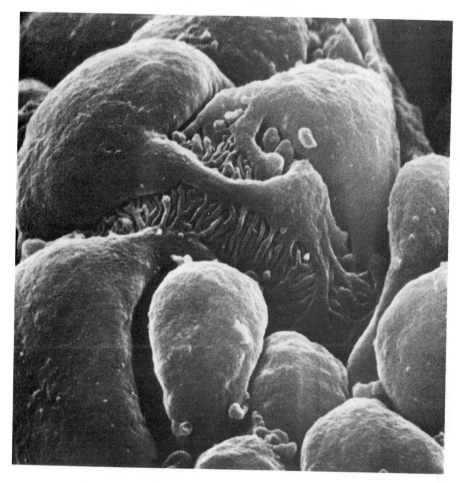

Figure 20—5. Scanning electron micrograph of a renal glomerulus from a newborn rat. The round structures are podocytes seen in surface views. Primary and secondary processes are apparent. X 12,000. (Reproduced, with permission, from Miyoshi M, Fujita T, Tokunaga J: Arch Histol Jap 33:161, 1971.)

therefore, over the filtration slits), a thin membrane has been described (Fig 20—6) which is about 6 nm thick and comparable to the diaphragm encountered in the pores of endothelial cells. The cytoplasm of the podocytes contains numerous free ribosomes, microtubules, and microfilaments (Fig 20—6). In spite of extensive study, the exact physiologic role of these cells is still not well understood. The glomerular capillaries are of the fenestrated type (Fig 20—6).

Between the fenestrated endothelial cells of the capillaries and the podocytes which cover their external surface is a typical basal lamina. This membrane is the only continuous structure which separates the blood contained in the capillary from the capsular space. With the aid of the electron microscope, one can distinguish a central electron-dense layer and on each side an electron-lucent layer. Histochemical methods are providing evidence that the 2 electron-lucent zones have different biochemical compositions.

The endothelial cells of the glomerular capillaries have a very thin cytoplasm which is thicker around the nucleus. The pores of these cells are more numerous than in the fenestrated capillaries of other organs, and according to most investigators they do not usually have the thin diaphragm commonly observed in the pores of endothelial cells of other fenestrated capillaries, whereas a few propose the existence of only a simple proteinaceous condensation in that area.

Besides the endothelial cells and the podocytes, the glomerular capillaries have *mesangial cells* adhering to their walls in places where the basement membrane does not completely surround a single capillary— constituting, in these places, a layer shared by 2 or more capillaries (Fig 20—7). The mesangial cells are sometimes placed under the endothelial cells, between these cells and the basement membrane of the capillary.

The mesangial cells possess many short extensions and are covered by a layer of amorphous material. Little is known about their cytophysiology, but it is possible that they are supporting elements for the capillaries. After the injection of ferritin (an electron-scattering, iron-containing protein easily identified with the electron microscope), the cytoplasm of the

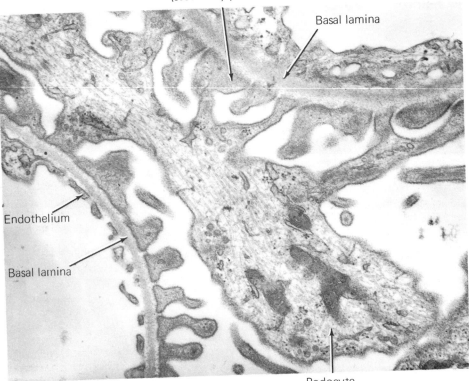

Figure 20—6. Electron micrograph of a glomerular capillary wall. Note the processes of the podocytes, the glomerular basal lamina, and the endothelium of the capillaries. X 36,000. (Courtesy of T de Brito.)

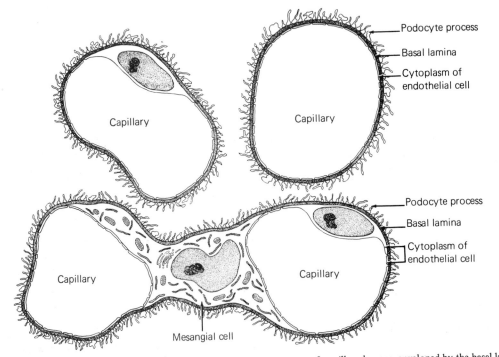

Figure 20—7. Mesangial cells of glomerular capillaries. They are located between 2 capillary lumens, enveloped by the basal lamina.

mesangial cells appears to be loaded with this protein. It is possible that these cells remove residues which are caught during filtration in the walls of the glomerular capillary.

Proximal Convoluted Tubule

This structure comprises an initial tortuous segment close to the renal corpuscle followed by a straight segment which penetrates the medulla for a short distance, continuous with that part of the nephron which is called *Henle's loop* (Figs 20–1 and 20–2). It is longer and larger than the distal convoluted tubule.

The proximal convoluted tubule, found in the cortex usually in cross sections, is lined by simple cuboid epithelium (Fig 20–8). The cells of this epithelium have a strongly acidophilic cytoplasm as a result of the presence of abundant elongated mitochondria. The cell apex in contact with the lumen of the tubule exhibits abundant microvilli about 1 μm in length which form the so-called *brush border* described long ago by the light microscopists (Fig 20–9). Because these cells are large, each transverse section of proximal tubule contains only 3 or 4 spherical nuclei which are usually located in the center of the cell (Fig 20–8). A well-developed, PAS-positive basement membrane is seen around the proximal tubule.

In the normal living animal, proximal convoluted tubules have wide lumens and flattened cells with a clear cytoplasm. The tubules are separated from each other by large interstitial spaces. Their lumens become wider as the medulla is approached. This has been shown through observation in living kidneys or in preparations carefully fixed by freezing in situ or by special

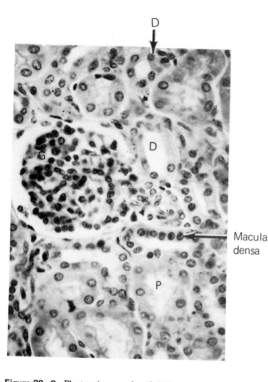

Figure 20—8. Photomicrograph of kidney cortical layer. Observe the glomerulus (G), the proximal convoluted tubule (P), and the distal convoluted tubule (D). H&E stain, × 250.

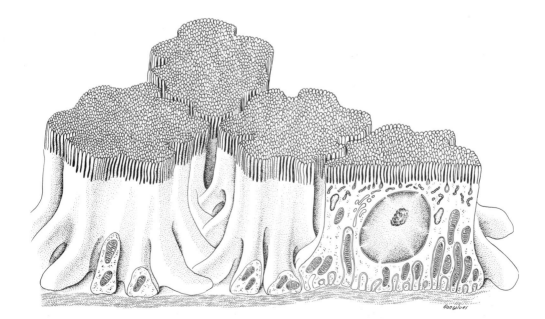

Figure 20—9. Schematic drawing of proximal convoluted tubule cells. These cuboid cells show abundant microvilli in their apical surfaces. They have 2 types of lateral processes: some along the whole side of the cell and others only in the basal half of the cell. The latter are longer than the former and penetrate deeply among the neighboring cells.

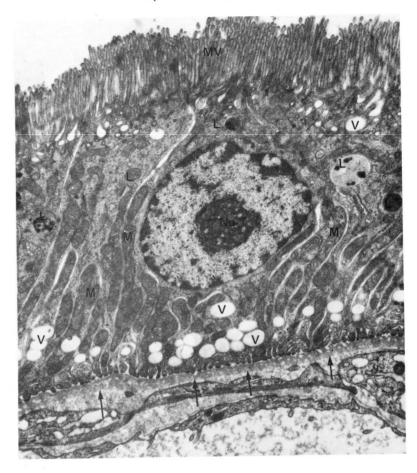

Figure 20–10. Electron micrograph of a proximal convoluted tubule wall. Observe the microvilli (MV), the lysosomes (L), the vacuole (V), the nucleolus (Nu), and the mitochondria (M). The arrows point to the basal lamina. × 10,500.

fixation for examination with the electron microscope. In the usual histologic preparations, however, the tubular lumens frequently appear greatly reduced or collapsed.

The apical cytoplasm of the cells has numerous canaliculi which arise from the base of the microvilli (Fig 20–10). The microvilli rest on a terminal web. Their membrane is continuous with the cytoplasmic membrane. Close to the canaliculi, small vesicles can be observed which might originate from them. These have been interpreted as being due to pinocytosis. The basal portion of these cells presents abundant lateral extensions that interdigitate profusely with analogous extensions of the neighboring cells (Fig 20–9). This process considerably increases the contact surface between neighboring cells and intercellular space. The mitochondria are concentrated at the base of the cell (Fig 20–10) and arranged parallel to the long axis of the cell. This mitochondrial location and the increase in the surface area of the cell membrane at the base of the cell through which the sodium pump operates are characteristics of cells engaged in ion transport (see Chapter 4).

Loop of Henle

The more numerous renal corpuscles located close to the medulla, the *juxtamedullary glomeruli,* have longer loops of Henle that penetrate more deeply into the medulla than those located next to the capsule which do not descend into the medulla for any great distance. Each loop of Henle is U-shaped and presents a thin segment followed by a thick one. In the long loops, the turn occurs always in the thin part; in the short loops, this happens in the thick part. Therefore, most of the thin portion is descending and most of the thick portion is ascending (Figs 20–1 and 20–2).

The thin part of the loop of Henle, which is a continuation of the proximal convoluted tubule, has an external diameter of about 12 μm, but the lumen is wide because its wall consists of flattened squamous cells whose nuclei protrude into the lumen (Fig 20–11). The thin part of Henle's loop resembles a blood capillary, with which it may be confused; differences in content, appearance of nuclei, and width of the lumen are the main criteria used for differentiation.

The transition between the proximal convoluted tubule and the loop of Henle may be abrupt or gradu-

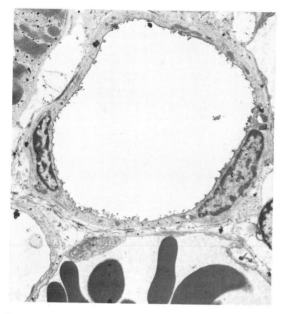

Figure 20—11. Electron micrograph of the thin part of Henle's loop composed entirely of squamous cells. Note fenestrated capillaries, the interstitium with bundles of collagen filaments, and the basal lamina. Reduced from X 4000. (Courtesy of J Rhodin.)

al. In the latter case, flat cells are interspersed between cuboid cells with brush borders.

The thick ascending part of the loop of Henle is similar in structure to that of the distal convoluted tubule.

Distal Convoluted Tubule

When the thick part of the loop of Henle penetrates the cortex, it preserves its histologic structure but becomes tortuous and is then called the distal convoluted tubule, which is the last segment of the nephron (Figs 20—1 and 20—8). This tubule is also lined by simple cuboid epithelium.

In histologic sections, the distinction between the proximal and distal convoluted tubules, both found in the cortex and having cuboid epithelium, is based on the following characteristics: The cells of the proximal tubules are larger, have brush borders, and are more acidophilic because of their abundance of mitochondria (Fig 20—12). The lumens of the distal tubules are larger; their walls have more cells with less acidophilia and nuclei; and they do not show brush borders or large numbers of microvilli. The cells of the distal convoluted tubule also have lateral extensions as described in the basal region of the proximal tubule cells, and the tubules show a basement membrane. The cells of the distal convoluted tubules show intercellular membranes.

Careful study of the distal convoluted tubule

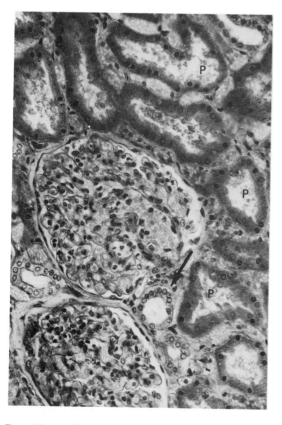

Figure 20—12. Photomicrograph of a kidney cortex showing a macula densa (arrow). P indicates proximal convoluted tubules. H&E stain, X 360.

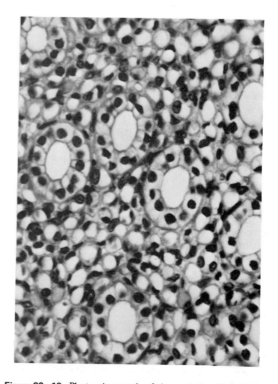

Figure 20—13. Photomicrograph of the medulla of the kidney, close to the papilla. There are several collecting tubules whose walls are composed of cuboid cells. H&E stain, X 250.

shows that along its path in the cortex it establishes contact with the vascular pole of the renal corpuscle of its own nephron, often close to the afferent and efferent arteriole. At this point of close contact, the distal tubule shows modifications along with the afferent arteriole. Its cells usually become cylindric, and their nuclei are closely packed together. Most of these cells have a Golgi apparatus in the basal region. This modified segment of the wall of the distal tubule, which appears darker in microscopic preparations (because of the close proximity of its nuclei), is called the *macula densa* (Figs 20–3 and 20–12). The exact functional significance of the macula densa is not clear. It may be related to the transmission to the glomerulus of information about the composition of the fluid in the distal tubule.

Collecting Tubules

The urine passes from the distal convoluted tubules to the collecting tubules, which join each other, forming larger straight tubules, the *papillary ducts of Bellini,* which widen gradually as they approach the papillae. Most of the collecting tubules are located in the medulla and follow a straight path (Fig 20–1).

The smaller collecting tubules are lined with cuboid epithelium and have a diameter of approximately 40 μm. As they penetrate deeper into the medulla and approach the papillae, their cells become higher until they are transformed into cylindric cells. The diameter of the collecting duct reaches 200 μm near the papillae.

Along their entire extent, the collecting tubules are composed of cells which stain weakly by the usual stains and whose intercellular limits are clearly visible under the light microscope (Figs 20–13 and 20–14). Each large collecting tubule is joined at right angles by several generations of smaller collecting tubules draining each medullary ray. Many nephrons are united with the straight collecting tubules through their arched collecting tubules.

Juxtaglomerular Apparatus

Next to the renal corpuscle the middle layer of the afferent arteriole is modified, consisting of cells having the appearance of epithelioid cells instead of smooth muscle fibers. These cells, called *juxtaglomerular (JG) cells* (Fig 20–3), have spherical nuclei and a cytoplasm full of granules which stains darkly by special technics (PAS-positive). The macula densa of the convoluted tubule is usually located next to the JG cells, forming, with them, the *juxtaglomerular apparatus.* In the area where the JG cells are present, the internal elastic membrane of the afferent arteriole disappears and the basement membrane, which is present

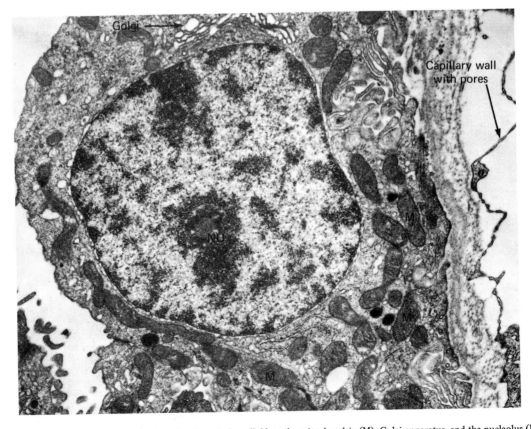

Figure 20–14. Electron micrograph of a collecting tubule wall. Note the mitochondria (M), Golgi apparatus, and the nucleolus (Nu). X 15,000.

around the convoluted tubule, is also absent at the macula densa.

When examined with the electron microscope, the JG cells present characteristics of secretory cells, including an abundant granular endoplasmic reticulum, a highly developed Golgi apparatus, and secretory granules. The recently formed secretory granules measure around 10–40 nm and join in clumps which appear to constitute the mature form of the secretory material (Fig 20–3).

The JG cells produce the enzyme *renin*, and the amount of renin present in a kidney is proportionate to the number of secretory granules in these cells; furthermore, fluorescent antibody (antirenin) has been shown to react specifically with the JG cells. Renin is known to act on a plasma protein called *angiotensinogen*, producing a decapeptide called *angiotensin I*. This substance, as a result of the action of converting enzyme present in the plasma, loses 2 amino acids, becoming an octapeptide called *angiotensin II*.

The main physiologic effect of angiotensin II is to increase the secretion of the hormone aldosterone by the adrenal cortex, thus influencing blood pressure. Aldosterone acts on the cells of the renal tubules (mostly the distal tubules), increasing the reabsorption of sodium and chloride. Sodium deficiency is known to be a stimulus for the liberation of renin, which indirectly accelerates the secretion of aldosterone, which in turn inhibits the excretion of sodium. Inversely, an excess of sodium in the blood depresses the secretion of renin with the consequent inhibition of the production of aldosterone and thus increases the concentration of urinary sodium. Thus, the juxtaglomerular apparatus has an important homeostatic role in the control of ionic balance.

Blood Circulation

Each kidney receives blood from its renal artery which, at the level of the hilus and before entering this organ, usually divides into 2 branches: one in the anterior part and the other in the posterior part of the kidney. While still in the hilus, these branches give rise to fine end arteries which further branch to form the *interlobar arteries* located between the renal pyramids of Malpighi (Fig 20–15). At the level of the base of the pyramids, the interlobar arteries form the *arcuate arteries*, which follow a path parallel to the capsule of the organ along the corticomedullary junction. Arcuate arteries originating from one interlobar artery do not communicate with vessels from other interlobar arteries. Thus, these arteries are terminal arteries. From the arcuate artery the *interlobular arteries* branch off at right angles and regular intervals and follow a course in the cortex perpendicular to the renal capsule. The interlobular arteries are situated between the medullary rays, which, with the adjacent cortex, form the lobules of the kidneys (Fig 20–15). From the interlobular arteries arise the *afferent arterioles of the glomeruli,* which supply the blood to the capillaries of the glomeruli. From there the blood passes into the *efferent arterioles* of the glomeruli, which at once branch

again to form a capillary network which will nourish the proximal and distal tubules of the renal cortex. The efferent arterioles derived from glomeruli located deeper in the juxtamedullary cortex and near the medullary region, in addition to providing capillaries to the tubules, form long and thin vessels which follow a deep straight path in the medulla; these vessels are the *arteriolae rectae,* or straight arterioles, and some arise directly from arcuate arteries.

In the medulla one can observe the *venulae rectae,* from which blood flows to the arcuate veins. These straight venules are situated very close and parallel to the straight arteries, with which they form a loop. These loops, formed by the straight arterioles and venules in the kidney medulla, are physiologically important and are called collectively the *vasa recta* of the kidney, containing mainly blood which has been filtered through the glomeruli.

The capillaries of the outer cortex and of the capsule of the kidney converge to form the *stellate veins,* so called because of their configuration when seen from the surface of the kidney and which empty into the interlobular veins.

The veins follow the same course as the arteries. Blood from the *interlobular veins* flows into the *arcuate* and from there to the *interlobar veins.* The interlobar veins form the *renal vein* through which the blood leaves the kidney.

HISTOPHYSIOLOGY OF THE KIDNEY

The kidney regulates the chemical composition of the internal environment by a complex process which involves *filtration, active absorption, passive absorption,* and *secretion.* Filtration takes place in the glomerulus, where an ultrafiltrate of blood plasma is formed. The tubules of the nephron reabsorb from this filtrate the substances that are useful for body metabolism, thus maintaining the homeostasis of the internal environment. They also transfer from the blood to the tubular lumen certain waste products which are eliminated with the urine. The collecting tubules absorb water, thus contributing to the concentration of the urine, which in general is hypertonic in relation to blood plasma. In this way the organism controls its water, intercellular fluid, and osmotic balance.

The 2 kidneys produce about 125 ml of filtrate per minute; of this amount, 124 ml are absorbed and only 1 ml is released into the calyces as urine. Every 24 hours, about 1500 ml of urine are formed.

Filtration

The blood flow in the 2 kidneys of an adult amounts to 1.2–1.3 liters of blood per minute, which means that all of the circulating blood in the body passes through the kidneys every 4–5 minutes. The glomeruli are composed of arterial capillaries whose hydrostatic pressure is higher than that in other capillaries. This pressure is about 75 mm Hg, representing

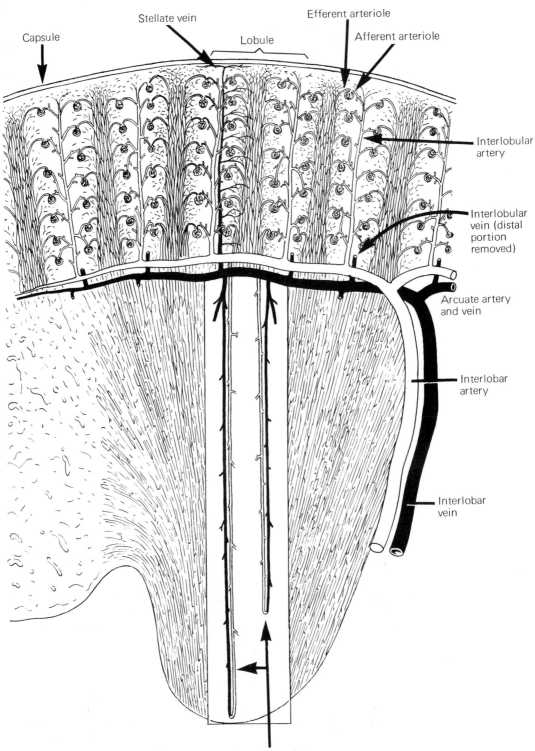

Figure 20–15. Circulation of blood in the kidney. Arcuate arteries are seen in the border between the cortical and medullary zones.

about 70% of the hydrostatic pressure in the aorta.

The glomerular filtrate is formed in response to the hydrostatic pressure of blood, to which the following forces are opposed: (1) osmotic pressure of plasma colloids (30 mm Hg): (2) pressure of the liquid contained in the tubular part of the nephron (10 mm Hg); and (3) interstitial pressure in the interior of the renal parenchyma (10 mm Hg), which acts on Bowman's capsule and is transmitted to the capsular liquid.

Since the hydrostatic pressure is 75 mm Hg and the forces which oppose it total 50 mm Hg, the resulting *force of filtration* is approximately 25 mm Hg.

The glomerular filtrate has a chemical composition similar to that of blood plasma but has almost no proteins because macromolecules do not cross the glomerular wall. The largest protein molecules which succeed in crossing the pores of the glomerular capillary walls have a molecular weight of about 70,000, and some plasma albumin fractions having the same molecular weight appear in very small amounts in the filtrate.

The endothelial cells of the glomerular capillaries are fenestrated and have numerous cytoplasmic pores mainly without diaphragms, so that the endothelium is easily permeated. According to most authors, filtration occurs at the basement membrane. Injections of larger molecules, such as ferritin (MW 460,000), show that they pass through the endothelial cells but are concentrated at the basement membrane. Much smaller proteins are able to pass through the filtration slits of the podocytes (foot processes).

Proximal Convoluted Tubule

The glomerular filtrate formed in the renal corpuscle passes into the proximal convoluted tubule, and the process of resorption and excretion then begins. The site of resorption of diverse substances can be precisely identified, and the points of resorption of various substances are different. Various amino acids are absorbed in different parts of the tubule. The proximal convoluted tubule absorbs all of the glucose and about 85% of the sodium chloride and water contained in the filtrate. The resorption of glucose is maximal near the renal corpuscle. The glucose and the sodium are absorbed by the tubular cells through an active process involving expenditure of energy. The water and the chloride ion probably diffuse passively, following the osmotic gradient. When the amount of glucose in the filtrate is excessive, it exceeds the absorbing capacity of the proximal tubule and the urine becomes more abundant and contains glucose.

The proximal convoluted tubule also absorbs, by an active process, all of the amino acids, ascorbic acid, and proteins present in the filtrate. The absorption of the proteins takes place by pinocytosis, which occurs at the base of the microvilli, and most of the products are eventually transferred from the filtrate into the interstitial tissue. The absorbed proteins appear first in the pinocytotic vesicles which are later joined by primary lysosomes, forming secondary lysosomes. In these, the proteins are digested and the resultant amino acids are probably reutilized by the tubular cells themselves or returned to the blood to be used by other cells.

Besides these activities, the proximal convoluted tubule transfers creatinine and excretes substances which are foreign to the organism such as para-aminohippuric acid, phenol red, and iodopyracet (an iodinated organic compound used as an x-ray contrast medium) from the interstitial plasma to the filtrate. This is an active process referred to in this organ as tubular excretion. Radioautographic experiments have shown that the cells of the convoluted tubule, although similar in histologic appearance, have varying absorption properties for different substances.

Loop of Henle

Although the filtrate which leaves the loop of Henle is hypotonic, this segment of the nephron is mainly responsible for the formation of a final hypertonic urine, and only animals with a loop of Henle in their kidneys are capable of producing hypertonic urine. The loop of Henle creates a gradient of hypertonicity in the medulla which influences the concentration of the urine as it flows in the collecting tubule.

The descending part of the loop of Henle is quite permeable, permitting the free passage of water and sodium. Since the interstitial fluid of the kidney medulla is hypertonic, sodium enters and water leaves the glomerular filtrate in the descending part of the loop of Henle.

The ascending part is impermeable to water and is highly active in transporting sodium to the interstitial fluid. Thus, it is directly responsible for the hypertonicity of the interstitial fluid of the medullary region. As a consequence of the loss of sodium, the filtrate which reaches the distal convoluted tubule is hypotonic.

Distal Convoluted Tubule

In the distal convoluted tubule, there is an ion exchange site at which, if aldosterone is acting, sodium is reabsorbed and potassium ions are excreted because of a decrease in the reabsorption of potassium—ie, it is the site of the mechanism for the control of total salt and water in the body mentioned above in the discussion of the JG apparatus. The distal tubule also secretes hydrogen ions and ammonium ion into tubular urine. This activity is very important for maintenance of the acid-base balance of the blood.

Collecting Tubules

Beginning in the distal tubule but becoming more important in the collecting tubules is the ADH-dependent mechanism for final dilution or concentration of urine. The walls of the distal tubules and the collecting tubules are freely permeable to water if large amounts of ADH are present.

Formation of Hypotonic or Hypertonic Urine

The loop of Henle forms a multiplying countercurrent system which concentrates the filtrate by repetitive transfer of relatively small amounts of sodium

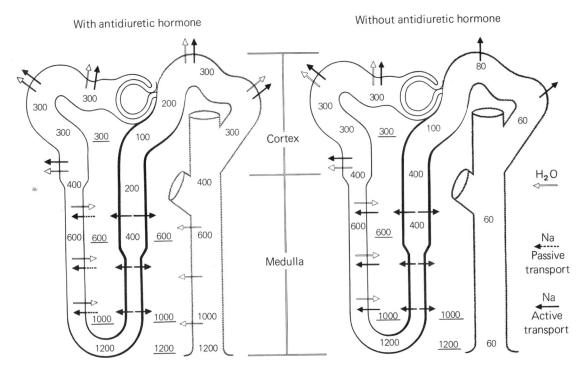

Figure 20–16. Multiplying countercurrent system formed by the loop of Henle. The segment of Henle's loop impermeable to water is represented by thick lines. The distal convoluted tubule and the collecting tubules, which are sensitive to antidiuretic hormone, are indicated by serrated lines. *Left:* Under the influence of ADH, the urine formed is hypertonic. *Right:* With very low levels of ADH or none at all, a great quantity of hypotonic urine is formed. The numbers in the tubules and interstitial spaces indicate the local concentration in mOsm/liter. (Redrawn and reproduced, with permission, from Pitts RF: *Physiology of the Kidney and Body Fluids,* 2nd ed. Year Book, 1968.)

along the length of the loop (Fig 20–16).

As already mentioned, the ascending part of the loop of Henle is impermeable to water; however, in this part sodium is transferred actively (sodium pump) to the intercellular space of the kidney medulla (Fig 20–16). Consequently, the interstitial fluid of the pyramid shows a gradient of hypertonicity increasing toward the papillae (Fig 20–16). Part of the sodium transferred to the intertubular environment by the ascending part of the loop is transferred passively to the filtrate by the descending part and passes again through the "sodium pump" present in the cells of the ascending part of the loop of Henle (Fig 20–16).

The hypotonic or isotonic urine which is present in the collecting tubules of the medulla (the interstitial fluid of the cortex is isotonic) will lose water into the interstitium if there is enough ADH to make the tubules permeable to water. Thus, a hypertonic urine is formed. When ADH is lacking, the walls of the collecting tubules are impermeable to water, so that concentration of the urine does not occur and the kidneys produce abundant hypotonic urine (Fig 20–16).

The permeability of the distal convoluted tubule to water also depends on ADH, but this tubule, being located in the cortex, where the interstitial fluid is isotonic, cannot contribute appreciably to urine concentration. The urine which leaves the distal convoluted tubule is at most isotonic (as a result of equilibration with the interstitial fluid of the region).

The vasa recta or straight vessels of the medullary region are situated so that the blood circulation does not disturb the osmotic gradient created by the sodium pump of the loop of Henle, and they form a countercurrent exchange system as shown in Fig 20–17.

The straight arterioles and veins are very thin vessels whose walls are similar to those of capillaries. Each straight vessel—an arterial and a venous part—forms a loop whose branches run side by side. While moving through the straight arterioles toward the inner medulla, the blood loses water and gains sodium, because in the medulla the interstitial fluid gradually becomes more and more hypertonic. When returning in the opposite direction, the blood is again exposed to the same gradient—now decreasing—and therefore loses sodium and gains water. The water lost by the descending vessel is gained by the ascending one, and the sodium which enters the descending vessel is recovered by the ascending one.

The function of the osmotic changes in the blood of the straight vessels is to keep constant the osmotic

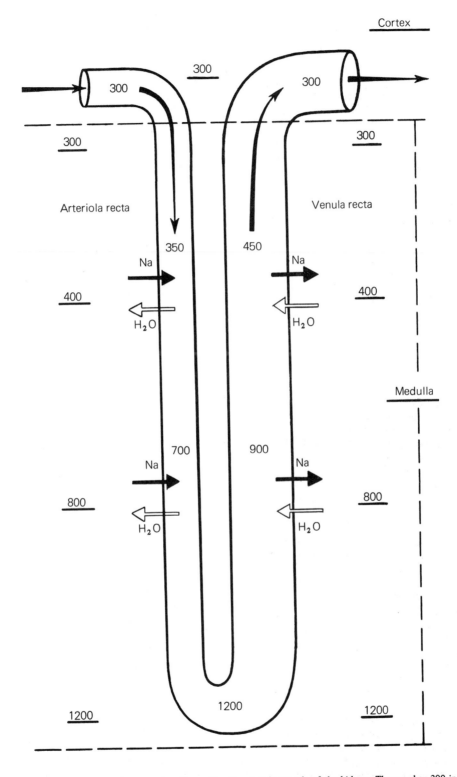

Figure 20–17. The countercurrent exchange system formed by the straight vessels of the kidney. The number 300 in the cortical segment of the arteriole and venule represents blood osmolarity (more precisely, 285–295 mOsm/liter). The sodium and water exchanges between these straight vessels and the interstitium are passive, depending on the osmotic gradient formed by the loop of Henle.

gradient which exists in the kidney medulla. It must be emphasized that these movements of water and sodium are passive, taking place without utilization of energy.

Hormonal Effects

As explained above, water balance is controlled in part by the posterior lobe of the pituitary, which produces ADH. When there is a high intake of water, production of ADH is inhibited, the walls of the distal tubules and collecting tubules become impermeable to water, and water therefore is not reabsorbed. The result is the formation of large amounts of hypotonic urine with excess water eliminated while the ions necessary for the osmotic balance are retained. When small amounts of water are ingested or when a great loss of water occurs (eg, by excessive sweating), the walls of the distal and collecting tubules become permeable to water, which is then absorbed, and the formed urine is hypertonic.

Steroid hormones of the adrenal cortex, mainly *aldosterone,* increase the tubular absorption of sodium from the glomerular filtrate and thus decrease sodium elimination by the urine. Aldosterone facilitates the elimination of potassium and hydrogen. This hormone is very important in maintaining ionic equilibrium in the body. Aldosterone deficiency in adrenalectomized animals and in humans with Addison's disease produces an excessive loss of sodium by the urine.

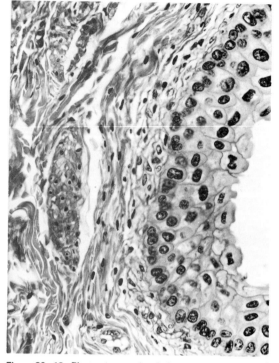

Figure 20–18. Photomicrograph of the urinary bladder wall. H&E stain, reduced from X 320.

BLADDER & URINARY PASSAGES

The bladder and the urinary passages store the urine formed in the kidneys and conduct it to the exterior. The calyces, pelvis, ureter, and bladder have the same basic histologic structure. The walls of the ureters become gradually thicker with increasing proximity to the bladder.

The mucosa of these organs consists of transitional epithelium and a lamina propria of loose or dense connective tissue. There is no submucosa (Fig 20–18).

Under the electron microscope, the superficial cells of the transitional epithelium show numerous cytoplasmic filaments beneath the plasma membrane covering their free surfaces. In this same region—but more deeply located—numerous vesicles with a membrane similar to the plasma membrane can be observed.

The muscular layers in the calyces, renal pelvis, and ureters have a helical arrangement. As the ureteral muscle fibers reach the bladder, they become longitudinal; therefore, the intravesical part of the ureter is composed of longitudinal fibers which then fan out distally to form the superficial trigone whose muscles continue dorsally to the verumontanum in the male and the external urethral meatus in the female.

Beginning 2–3 cm proximal to the bladder, Waldeyer's sheath or muscle is found on the outer surface of the ureter. It extends to the ureteral meatus,

below which it fans out to form the deep trigone, which ends at the bladder neck.

The muscle fibers of the bladder run in every direction (without distinct layers) until they approach the bladder neck, where 3 distinct layers can be identified: (1) The internal longitudinal layer, which, distal to the bladder neck, becomes circular around the prostatic urethra and the prostatic substance in the male. They extend to the external meatus in the female. These fibers form the true involuntary urethral sphincter. (2) The middle layer, which ends at the bladder neck. (3) The outer longitudinal layer, which continues to the end of the prostate and to the external urethral meatus in the female.

The ureters pass through the wall of the bladder obliquely, so that a valve is formed that prevents the backflow of urine. The intravesical ureter has only longitudinal muscle fibers.

The urinary passages are covered externally by an adventitial membrane—except for the upper part of the bladder, which is covered by (serous) peritoneum.

Urethra

The urethra is a tube which carries the urine from the bladder to the exterior. In the male, the sperms also pass through the urethra during ejaculation. In the female, the urethra is exclusively an organ of the urinary system.

A. Male Urethra: The male urethra consists of 4 parts: a *prostatic part,* a *membranous part,* a *bulbous part,* and a *pendulous part.*

The prostate (see Chapter 23) is situated very close to the bladder, and the initial part of the urethra passes through it. The ducts which transport the secretions of the prostate open into the prostatic urethra.

In the dorsal and distal part of the prostatic urethra there is an elevation, the *verumontanum,* which protrudes into its interior. In the tip of the verumontanum opens a blind tube called the prostatic utricle which has no known function. On the sides of the verumontanum open the ejaculatory ducts through which the seminal fluid enters the posterior urethra to be stored just prior to ejaculation. The prostatic urethra is lined by transitional epithelium.

The membranous urethra extends for only 1 cm and is lined with pseudostratified columnar epithelium. Surrounding this part of the urethra there is a sphincter of striated muscle, the *external sphincter* of the urethra.

The voluntary external striated sphincter adds further closing pressure to that exerted by the involuntary urethral sphincter formed by the continuation of the internal longitudinal muscle of the bladder.

The bulbous and pendulous parts of the urethra are located in the *corpus spongiosum* of the penis. Distally, the urethral lumen dilates, forming the *fossa navicularis.* The epithelium of this portion of the urethra is mostly pseudostratified and columnar, with areas that are squamous and stratified.

The glands of Littré are mucous glands found along the entire length of the urethra but mostly in the pendulous part. The secretory portions of some of these glands are directly linked to the epithelial lining of the urethra; others possess excretory ducts.

B. Female Urethra: The female urethra is a tube 4–5 cm long, lined with squamous stratified epithelium with areas of pseudostratified columnar epithelium. The mid part of the female urethra is surrounded by an external striated voluntary sphincter.

● ● ●

References

Barajas L, Latta H: A 3-dimensional study of the juxtaglomerular apparatus in the rat. Lab Invest 12:257, 1963.

Bing J, Karimierczac J: Renin content of different parts of the juxtaglomerular apparatus. Acta path microbiol scandinav 54:80, 1962.

Boudeau JE, Carone FA, Ganote CE: Serum albumin uptake in isolated perfused renal tubules. J Cell Biol 54:382, 1972.

Bulger RE & others: Human renal ultrastructure. 2. The thin limb of Henle's loop and the interstitium in healthy individuals. Lab Invest 16:124, 1967.

Caulfield JB, Trump BF: Correlation of ultrastructure with function in the rat kidney. Am J Path 40:199, 1962.

Dirks JH, Clapp JR, Berliner RW: The protein concentration in the proximal tubule of the dog. J Clin Invest 43:916, 1964.

Ericsson JLE, Trump BF: Electron microscopic studies of the epithelium of the proximal tubule of the rat kidney. 1. The intracellular localization of acid phosphatase. Lab Invest 13:1427, 1964.

Farquhar MG, Wissig SL, Palade GE: Glomerular permeability. 1. Ferritin transfer across the normal glomerular capillary wall. J Exper Med 113:47, 1961.

Ganote CE & others: Ultrastructural studies of vasopressin: Effect on isolated, perfused, renal collecting tubules of the rabbit. J Cell Biol 36:355, 1968.

Hartroft PM, Sutherland LE, Hartroft WS: Juxtaglomerular cells as the source of renin: Further studies with the fluorescent antibody technique and the effect of passive transfer of antirenin. Canad MAJ 90:163, 1964.

Hatt PI: The juxtaglomerular apparatus. In: *Ultrastructure of the Kidney.* Dalton AJ, Haguenau F (editors). Academic Press, 1967.

Latta H, Maunsbach AB: The juxtaglomerular apparatus as studied electron-microscopically. J Ultrastruct Res 6:547, 1962.

Latta H, Maunsbach AB, Osvaldo L: The fine structure of renal tubules in cortex and medulla. In: *Ultrastructure of the Kidney.* Dalton AJ, Haguenau F (editors). Academic Press, 1967.

Maul CG: Structure and formation of pores in fenestrated capillaries. J Ultrastruct Res 36:768, 1971.

Maunsbach AB: Observations on the ultrastructure and acid phosphatase activity of the cytoplasmic bodies in rat kidney proximal tubule cells, with a comment on their classification. J Ultrastruct Res 16:197, 1966.

Menefee MG, Mueller CB: Some morphological considerations of transport in the glomerulus. In: *Ultrastructure of the Kidney.* Haguenau F (editors). Academic Press, 1967.

Michielsen P, Creemers J: The structure and function of the glomerular mesangium. In: *Ultrastructure of the Kidney.* Dalton AJ, Haguenau F (editors). Academic Press, 1967.

Miller F, Palade GE: Lytic activities in renal protein absorption droplets: An electron microscopical cytochemical study. J Cell Biol 23:519, 1964.

Miyoshi M, Fujita T, Tokunaga J: The differentiation of renal podocytes: A combined scanning and transmission electron microscope study in rats. Arch Histol Jap 33:161, 1971.

Murakami T, Miyoshi M, Fujita T: Glomerular vessels of the rat kidney with special reference to double efferent arterioles: A scanning electron microscopic study of corrosion casts. Arch Histol Jap 33:179, 1971.

Oliver C, Essner E: Protein transport in mouse kidney utilizing tyrosinase as an ultrastructural tracer. J Exper Med 136:291, 1972.

Osvaldo L, Latta H: The thin limb of the loop of Henle. J Ultrastruct Res 15:144, 1966.

Post RS: The distribution of normal serum proteins within rat and human renal tubule cytoplasm as demonstrated by immunofluorescence. J Lab Clin Med 67:189, 1966.

Staehelin LA, Chlapowski FJ, Bonneville MA: Luminal plasma membrane of the urinary bladder. 1. Three-dimensional reconstruction from freeze-etch images. J Cell Biol 53:73, 1972.

Straus W: Occurrence of phagosomes and phagolysosomes in different segments of the nephron in relation to the reabsorption, transport, digestion and extrusion of intravenously injected horseradish peroxidase. J Cell Biol 21:295, 1964.

21...
Pituitary & Hypothalamus

As explained in Chapter 3, the process of cell specialization led to the evolutionary development of Metazoa, a group of organisms in which the efficient performance of several functions was undertaken by formations of cell aggregates: the tissues. As a consequence of this process, certain systems appeared which had the function of integrating and coordinating the work of the various tissues. The *endocrine system* coordinates the activity of the tissues by means of substances called *hormones.*

A hormone is an organic chemical liberated at a specific time in small but precisely appropriate amounts by endocrine cells into the tissue fluids or vascular system. In general, the hormones exert their effects at a distance from the site of secretion and have the function of coordination of parts of the organism. The tissues and organs the hormones act on are called *target organs.* Biologists believe that the endocrine and nervous systems, both of which have the function of integrating the activities of diverse parts of the organism, are not clearly separated in function. The hormones of many endocrine glands have an effect on the nervous system, and several endocrine organs are stimulated or inhibited by neural mechanisms. Thus, most biologic phenomena are under the overlapping authority of both systems. This interlocking mechanism is so remarkable that its nervous and endocrine elements are coming to be regarded as constituting a single system called the *neuroendocrine system.*

The structure, histophysiology, and cytophysiol-ogy of the endocrine glands comprise the subject matter of this and the following chapters.

PITUITARY
(Hypophysis)

The *pituitary gland* or *hypophysis* is a small organ weighing about 0.5 g whose normal dimensions in man are about 10 × 13 × 6 mm. It lies at the base of the brain below the hypothalamus, with which it has important anatomic and functional relations, in a bony cavity called the *sella turcica.*

The pituitary is formed early in embryonic life and has a double embryonic origin, developing partly from ectoderm and partly from oral nerve tissue. The part that arises from nerve tissue develops from an evagination of the floor of the diencephalon and grows caudally without detaching itself from the brain, thus forming a stalk. An outpocketing of the ectoderm of the roof of the primitive mouth of the embryo grows cranially, forming a cavity called *Rathke's pouch;* at a later stage, a constriction at the base of this pouch separates it from the buccal cavity. Its anterior wall develops at the same time, reducing the size of the lumen of Rathke's pouch, which becomes a small fissure (Fig 21–1).

The part of the pituitary that develops from nerve

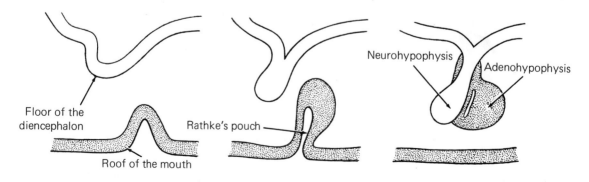

Figure 21–1. Diagram of the development of the adenohypophysis and neurohypophysis. The ectoderm of the roof of the mouth and its derivatives is stippled (lower portion). In the upper portion is the neural ectoderm from the floor of the diencephalon.

tissue is known as the *neurohypophysis*. It consists of a large portion, the *pars nervosa* or *infundibular process,* and the *infundibulum* or *neural stalk* (Fig 21—2). The infundibulum is composed of the stem, bulb, and median eminence of the tuber cinereum. The infundibulum merges with the hypothalamus, which serves to connect the pituitary with the central nervous system. Through the infundibulum pass important nerve tracts and substances which will act upon the anterior lobe of the pituitary.

The part of the pituitary that arises from oral ectoderm is known as the *adenohypophysis* and is subdivided into 3 portions: a large part, the *pars distalis* or *anterior lobe;* a cranial part, the *pars tuberalis,* which surrounds the infundibulum; and an intermediate part, the *pars intermedia,* between the neurohypophysis and the pars distalis, separated from the latter by the remaining fissure of the primitive cavity of Rathke's pouch, the residual cleft (Fig 21—2). The *posterior lobe* of the pituitary consists of the pars nervosa and the pars intermedia. The gland is usually covered by a connective tissue capsule and is situated in a depression of the sphenoid bone. Loose connective tissue with abundant venous drainage is found between the periosteum of the sphenoid bone and the capsule of the gland.

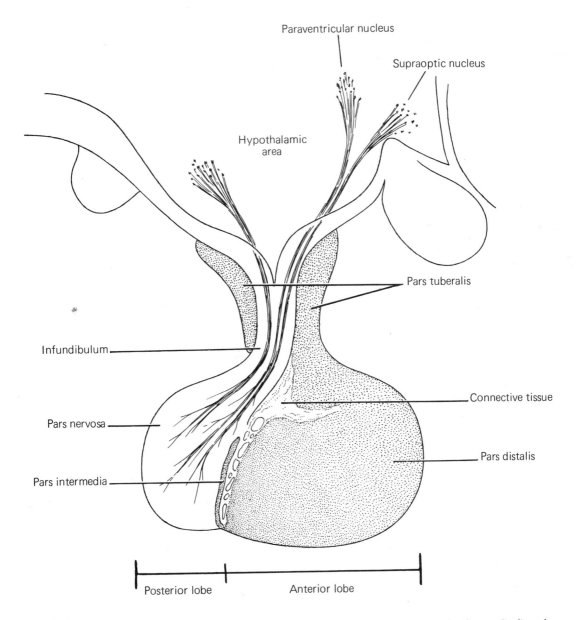

Figure 21—2. The component parts of the pituitary and their relation to the hypothalamus. The pars tuberalis, pars distalis, and pars intermedia form the adenohypophysis. The infundibulum and pars nervosa form the neurophophysis. (Modified, redrawn, and reproduced, with permission, from the *Ciba Collection of Medical Illustrations,* by Frank H. Netter, MD.)

Blood Supply

The blood supply of the pituitary derives from 2 groups of blood vessels: from above, the right and left *superior hypophyseal arteries;* and from below, the right and left *inferior hypophyseal arteries.* The anterior and posterior superior hypophyseal arteries supply mainly the more cranial portion of the pituitary stalk, where they branch. At the same time, they give branches to the hypothalamus and the caudal portion of the pituitary stalk. The capillaries thus formed join again, giving rise to venules which arborize once again in the pars distalis, forming sinusoid capillaries and constituting, in this way, a *portal system* (Fig 21–3).

This vascular disposition makes possible the transport of hormones from the cranial portion of the pituitary stalk to the cells of the pars distalis. There are 2 *lower hypophyseal arteries* running alongside the gland and supplying the posterior lobe of the pituitary. In some species, a small quantity of blood from the posterior lobe probably passes to the anterior lobe. Blood from both pituitary lobes drains into the cavernous sinus through a number of venous channels (Fig 21–3).

The nerve supply of the anterior lobe is derived

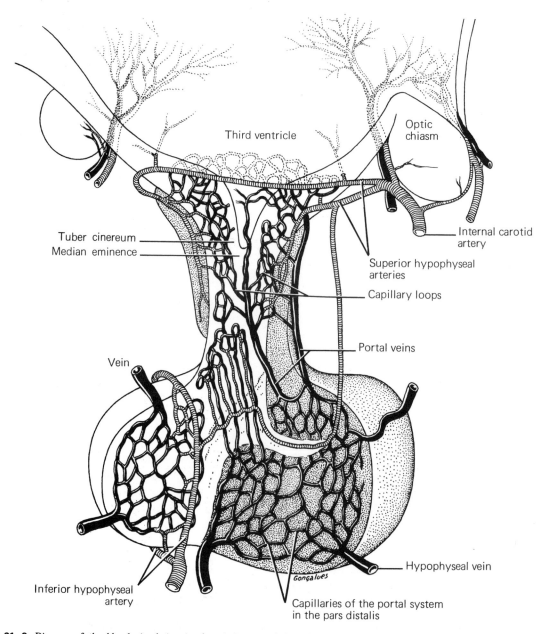

Third ventricle

Optic chiasm

Tuber cinereum

Median eminence

Internal carotid artery

Superior hypophyseal arteries

Capillary loops

Portal veins

Vein

Hypophyseal vein

Inferior hypophyseal artery

Gongalves

Capillaries of the portal system in the pars distalis

Figure 21–3. Diagram of the blood circulation in the pituitary, including the portal system. (Redrawn and reproduced, with permission, from the *Ciba Collection of Medical Illustrations,* by Frank H. Netter, MD.)

from the carotid plexus, which accompanies the arteriolar branches. These nerves appear to have a vasomotor function. Nerve fibers crossing from the posterior lobe to the anterior lobe have been described, but most investigators believe that they have no effect in regulating the function of the adenohypophysis.

ADENOHYPOPHYSIS

Pars Distalis

As opposed to the neurohypophysis, which retains some characteristics of nerve tissue, the part of the pituitary that arises from oral ectoderm presents the typical appearance of an endocrine gland composed of cells grouped in cords and follicles. Its sinusoid capillaries are classically considered to be part of the macrophage system, although it has been verified that its lining cells do not have the capacity of phagocytosis.

Three types of cells have been described in this region: follicular, chromophobe, and chromophil cells. *Follicular cells* are long, with star-shaped cytoplasmic processes that interconnect, forming a mesh that seems to constitute bridges between the capillaries. They

have been described in several species (including humans). They have a clear perinuclear cytoplasm with few organelles and few if any secretory granules seen in the electron microscope. They probably form part of the supporting stroma of the glandular cells. Their function is still uncertain.

Chromophobe cells are so called because they have no affinity for the usual dyes used in histology (Figs 21–4 and 21–8). When observed in the light microscope, these cells present no visible secretory granules and were once thought to be undifferentiated or resting cells without secretory activity. Electron microscopic examination shows, however, that most of them have small secretory granules and are therefore active glandular cells. At present, only a small percentage of chromophobe cells are considered to be undifferentiated nonsecretory cells.

Chromophil cells contain specific cytoplasmic granules which have great affinity for some dyes (Figs 21–4 and 21–8). They are generally found near the capillaries. These cells are classified as *acidophils* or *basophils* according to the affinity of their granules for acidic or basic dyes. It is known, however, that both acidophils and basophils can be classified in subgroups according to their histochemical and other staining affinities.

The gradual discovery of various hormones

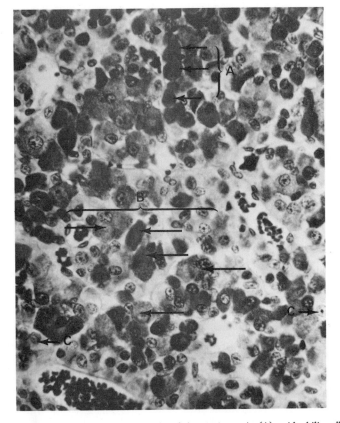

Figure 21–4. Photomicrograph of a section of the pars distalis of the pituitary. At (A), acidophilic cells stain orange-red; at (B), basophilic cells (lower arrows) stain blue. At left and right, note unstained chromophobe (C) cells. Mallory stain, reduced from × 200.

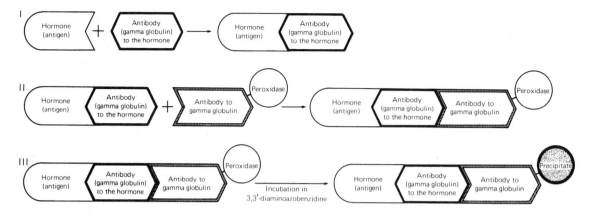

Figure 21–5. Intracellular detection of pituitary hormones by means of immunocytochemistry. *First stage:* The sections are treated by a solution containing an antibody to the hormone to be studied. The antibody binds itself to the hormone. *Second stage:* The section is incubated in a solution containing an antiantibody labeled by coupling it to peroxidase. This antiantibody binds itself to the antibody. *Third stage:* The section is incubated in an adequate substrate, 3,3′-diaminoazobenzidine, that forms a brown precipitate in the sites that contain the hormone.

synthesized by the pars distalis led investigators to try to correlate each hormone with a different cell type responsible for its production. Several staining and histochemical methods have been applied to the adenohypophysis, and the great wealth of interesting results initially obtained in the different species has tended to confuse rather than clarify the issues. Fortunately, the recent application of histochemical, immunofluorescent, and electron microscopic technics has greatly facilitated the study of the sites of hormone production in the adenohypophysis. Since these hormones are polypeptides or glycoproteins, it is possible in most cases to purify them and to produce the antibodies necessary for use in immunocytochemical studies (Fig 21–5). The human adenohypophysis contains approximately 50% chromophobes, 40% acidophils, and 10% basophils, varying within certain limits according to several factors such as age, pregnancy, thyroidectomy, hyperthyroidism, and the functional status of the gonads. The distribution of various types of cells in the gland is not homogeneous. Acidophils usually predominate at the periphery, whereas chromophobes and basophils show a preference for the most central part of the gland.

Cells of the Pituitary Gland

The cells of the pituitary can be classified on the basis of the hormone secreted (Fig 21–6):

A. Somatotropic Cells: The association of acidophilic tumors of the pituitary with acromegaly or gigantism has clearly linked these cells with growth hormone production and secretion in the normal pituitary. Immunofluorescent studies of human pituitary tissue further support this conclusion. The acidophilic granules are easily seen in the light microscope. The somatotropic cells are easily recognized in the electron microscope by their numerous dense secretory granules, 30–35 nm in diameter. The cell has a central nucleus near which is a large Golgi apparatus. Small

granules in the Golgi apparatus may represent immature secretory granules.

Mitochondria, granular endoplasmic reticulum, and some free ribosomes are found in cytoplasm between granules. A dense material, which is not bounded by a membrane and usually lies between the plasma membrane of the cell and the basal lamina, is suggested as the secretory product of the cell (growth hormone, GH; also called somatotropin, STH) by a process of reverse pinocytosis.

These cells are located predominantly in the lateral wings of the adenohypophysis and in many animals can be easily observed arranged in groups in certain parts of the pituitary.

B. Mammotropic Cells: These cells contain eosinophilic granules and can be distinguished from somatotropic cells, which also contain acidophilic granules, by their preferential affinity for erythrosin or carmine stains. They are located in a small zone in the lateral acidophilic wings of the pituitary. In the electron microscope they have large, dense secretory granules, 600–900 nm in diameter, and are of various shapes. The number and size of these cells increase during pregnancy and lactation. They are also present in increased numbers in fetal pituitary glands. These findings support the belief that they secrete *lactogenic hormone* (luteotropic hormone, LTH; also called *prolactin*). Actively secreting cells have a large juxtanuclear Golgi apparatus. The granular endoplasmic reticulum consists of long, flattened cisternae running parallel to the cell membrane. Ribosomes, mitochondria, and lysosomes are also found in the cytoplasm. Lysosomes and their derivatives are much more numerous when secretion is inhibited and are believed to function in the regulation of the secretion by degrading the unused secretory granules. The secretion of milk by nonpregnant women suffering from acromegaly as well as the increase in the number of acidophils with an affinity for erythrosin during pregnancy suggest that prolactin is also synthesized by an acidophilic cell.

C. Gonadotropic Cells: The cells that produce *follicle-stimulating hormone (FSH)* show, in both the light and the electron microscope, a large, round cell body. Dense secretory granules are seen in the cytoplasm, usually about 200 nm in diameter. The Golgi apparatus is well developed. The granular endoplasmic reticulum is composed of distended vesicular elements. Mitochondria and free ribosomes also exist. Synthesis of the protein part of the hormone takes place in the granular endoplasmic reticulum via the same process that occurs in every cell that secretes protein. However, in the case of the cells producing glycoprotein, the Golgi apparatus plays a role in the synthesis of the carbohydrate moiety as well as in concentrating the final secretory substance.

The second type of gonadotropic cells secrete *luteinizing hormone (LH)*, called also, in the male, interstitial cell–stimulating hormone (ICSH). These cells are small and round, with dense granules that are more uniform in size and larger—about 250 nm in diameter—than those that produce FSH. The Golgi complex is not as extensive, and the endoplasmic reticulum is composed of some flattened elements, in contrast to the dilated sacs of the FSH-producing cell.

At least in humans, both types of gonadotropic cells are distributed singly throughout the pituitary, and both belong to the basophilic subgroup.

D. Thyrotropic Cells: These cells produce *thyroid-stimulating hormone (TSH;* also called *thyrotropin)* and are located mainly in the central wedge of the adenohypophysis. They are large, polyhedral, and easily identified in the electron microscope by their small granules, which are only 120–200 nm in diameter. Other cytoplasmic structures are found, such as mitochondria, Golgi complexes, granular endoplasmic reticulum, and free ribosomes. The appearance of these cells depends on their functional relationship with the thyroid gland. They belong in the basophilic subgroup.

E. Corticotropic and Melanotropic Cells: The corticotropic cells produce *adrenocorticotropic hormone (corticotropin, ACTH),* and the melanotropic cells produce *melanocyte-stimulating hormone (MSH).* Human corticotropic pituitary cells can be identified by immunostaining with an antiserum which does not have immunologic determinants with α- or β-MSH and which, therefore, is specific for corticotropin. They are found mostly in the medial wedge of the pituitary, some in the lateral portion and some in the pars tuberalis. Electron microscopic examination of sections shows that they contain granules about 100–200 μm in diameter which are not as abundant as in the other cell types.

The Golgi apparatus is extensive. Free ribosomes and granular endoplasmic reticulum are found. Mitochondria are spherical to ovoid in shape.

Antisera raised against melanocyte-stimulating hormone appear to react with the cells of the pars intermedia and with the corticotropic cells of the pituitary. Secretion of both hormones by a single cell would explain why their secretion changes in parallel

in a number of diseases of the adrenal glands. They are polygonal in shape, with round eccentric nuclei, a well-developed Golgi apparatus, mitochondria, and granular endoplasmic reticulum that tends to be more elongated and at the periphery of the cell.

About one-fourth of the pituitary cells do not contain characteristic secretory granules. These cells, named chromophobes in the older classification, may participate in pituitary function. Some may represent undifferentiated precursors of the secretory cells and others hormone-producing cells which are in a temporary resting state or have been depleted of stored products. Cytologists tend to believe that these cells contain small granules, and their secretory potential has been established in corticotropin- and prolactin-secreting tumors in humans.

Histophysiology of the Pars Distalis

The hormones synthesized by this region are capable of exerting several kinds of effects. Some have a general metabolic action on the whole organism, whereas others act on specific structures known as "target organs"; the latter include nearly all of the other endocrine glands. Secretory granules appear in the human fetal pituitary at the end of the first trimester of pregnancy, and several pituitary hormones can be detected by radioimmunoassay. The time at which hormonal secretion is initiated and controlled by feedback mechanisms has not been established in man. The following are the hormones synthesized by the pars distalis (Fig 21–6):

A. Growth Hormone (Somatotropin, STH): Human growth hormone is a protein which has a molecular weight of 21,700 and 191 amino acids in its structure. It influences many metabolic processes, but its most marked effect is on the cartilage of the epiphyseal disks of long bones, stimulating their growth via somatomedin produced in the liver. An excess of somatotropin production in children and adolescents produces gigantism. If this excess occurs in adults, in whom no epiphyseal disks are present, growth of the extremities of the body (mandible, nose, fingers, etc) takes place, producing the condition known as *acromegaly.* In this disease, skin also appears to be a target organ of this hormone. Deficient secretion of growth hormone during childhood causes *hypopituitary dwarfism,* mainly as a result of incomplete growth of the long bones. This hormone also increases the plasma glucose level (diabetogenic action), plays a significant role in the metabolism of protein, lipid, and carbohydrate, and seems to potentiate the action of other hormones.

B. Prolactin (Lactogenic Hormone; Luteotropic Hormone, LTH): This protein hormone has a molecular weight of 22,500 and contains 198 amino acids. It resembles growth hormone in that it also acts directly on target tissues. It triggers the secretion of milk by the mammary glands and maintains it in association with other hormones after birth. In some species—but not in man—it acts on the corpus luteum of the ovary, and this luteotropic action elicits nesting behavior in

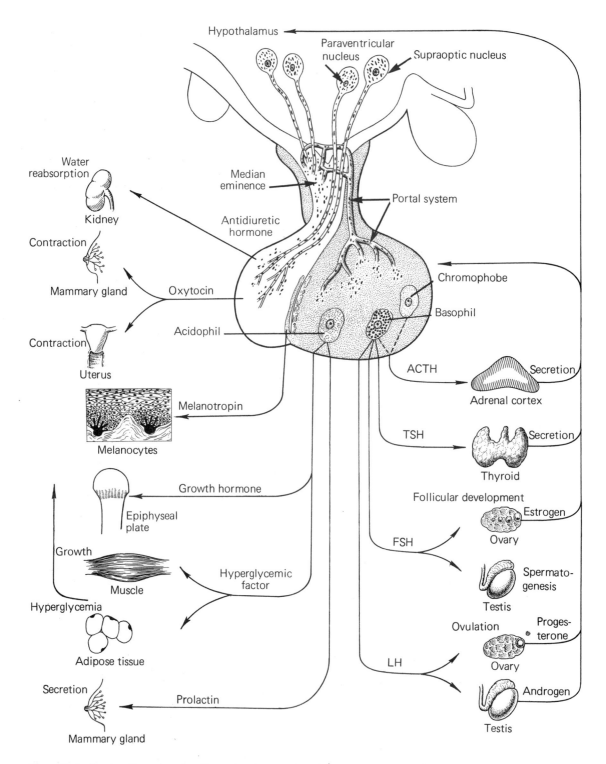

Figure 21–6. Drawing illustrating the effects of various pituitary hormones on target and organs. Observe that several of the hormones produced by the target organs can act on the pituitary or hypothalamus to regulate their activity.

some birds. The role of this hormone in males, if any, is not clearly understood.

C. Thyrotropin (Thyroid-Stimulating Hormone, TSH): This hormone is a glycoprotein with a molecular weight of 26,600. It has 2 amino acid chains, an *a* chain made up of 96 amino acids and a *β* chain with 113 amino acids, and contains 16.2% carbohydrate. Thyrotropin stimulates the synthesis of thyroid hormones as well as their liberation into the bloodstream. In experimental animals, thyrotropin preparations have a number of extrathyroidal effects.

D. Follicle-Stimulating Hormone (FSH): FSH is a glycoprotein (MW 32,000) with 236 amino acids consisting of 18.2% carbohydrate and 34% sialic acid. It stimulates follicular development in the ovary and gametogenesis in the testis.

E. Luteinizing Hormone (LH; Interstitial Cell-Stimulating Hormone, ICSH): This glycoprotein hormone has a molecular weight of about 30,000 with 2 amino acid chains: an *a* chain made up of 96 amino acids and a *β* chain with 119 amino acids. It consists of 15.7% carbohydrate. LH promotes rupture of the Graafian follicles and consequently ovulation, and the development of the corpus luteum in the ovary, maintaining the production of progesterone. It also helps to maintain the interstitial cells of the testis and stimulates the secretion of androgens.

F. Adrenocorticotropic Hormone (ACTH; Corticotropin): ACTH has a molecular weight of 4500 and is made up of 39 amino acids. It stimulates the production of corticosteroid hormones and sex hormones from the cortex of the adrenal gland. Corticotropin also has a number of actions on extra-adrenal tissues, mainly in vitro; it promotes lipolysis in fat cells, stimulates amino acid and glucose uptake in muscle cells, and stimulates pancreatic *β* cells to secrete insulin and the somatotropic cells of the pituitary to secrete growth hormone. There is no concrete evidence that the plasma levels during the normal endogenous release of corticotropin have these actions.

The positive PAS reaction of the basophilic granules of basophil cells suggests that these cells produce thyrotropin and gonadotropic hormones known to be glycoproteins. It has been observed that experimental variations or pathologic conditions that alter hormone production by the target organ or its content in the blood—surgical or functional thyroidectomy, administration of thyroxine or sex hormones, castration, etc—promote morphologic changes in the basophils, suggesting that these cells are responsible for the synthesis of thyrotropin and gonadotropins. The use of immunocytochemical technics (Fig 21–5) in the case of luteinizing hormone reveals the existence of this hormone in one type of basophil. The results of immunocytochemical tests suggest that ACTH is produced in chromophobe cells in rat pituitary and in basophils in human pituitary glands.

Study of the blood supply to the pituitary reveals that its portal system can transport to the pars distalis substances produced in the hypothalamus and accumulated in the infundibular and tuberal region of the hypothalamus. They have been called *releasing* or *inhibiting factors* according to their capacity to stimulate or inhibit release of the hormones produced by cells of the pars distalis. The following factors have been extracted to date from the mammalian hypothalamus: growth hormone-releasing factor (GRF), growth hormone-inhibiting factor (GIF), prolactin-inhibiting factor (PIF), prolactin-releasing factor (PRF), thyrotropin-releasing factor (TRF), follicle-stimulating hormone-releasing factor (FRF), luteinizing hormone-releasing factor (LRF), and corticotropin-releasing factor (CRF). It has been postulated that these hypothalamic polypeptide hormones are synthesized in the body of as yet unidentified hypothalamic or extrahypothalamic neurons and transported by their axons to a specific region of the hypothalamus—the *median emi-*

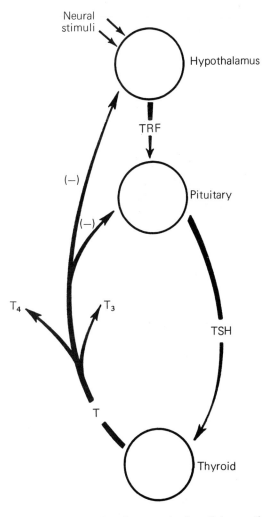

Figure 21–7. Relationships between the hypothalamus, the pituitary, and the thyroid. Thyrotropin-releasing factor (TRF) promotes secretion of thyrotropin (TSH) and acts to regulate the synthesis and secretion of the target organ hormones T_3 and T_4. These hormones, besides their effect on the peripheral tissues, regulate TSH and TRF secretion from the pituitary and the hypothalamus by a negative feedback mechanism. T, thyroid hormones.

nence (Figs 21–3 and 21–6). In this region, these factors are presumably accumulated in the form of secretory granules in bulblike dilatations at the ends of the axons (Fig 21–6). These structures are in close proximity to the blood vessels that generate the pituitary portal system. In this arrangement, a portal system is created that permits the transport of the active polypeptides released from the median eminence to the pars distalis. Control of function of the glands influenced by the hormones of the pars distalis is one of the most important facts of pituitary physiology and is accomplished by a feedback mechanism (Fig 21–7) of which an example follows:

The pars distalis is known to synthesize a hormone, *thyrotropin* (thyroid-stimulating hormone, TSH), which acts on the thyroid, stimulating the production and secretion of thyroxine and triiodothyronine. In addition to affecting the organism as a whole, thyroxine acts primarily on the pituitary, inhibiting the cells which synthesize thyrotropin. Thyroxine may also act directly on the hypothalamus, inhibiting the nerve cells encountered there which produce TRF (thyrotropin-releasing factor), a hormone that in turn stimulates the liberation of thyrotropin by the pituitary. In this way, a sensitive double control mechanism is established by which the concentration of a hormone in the blood regulates its own secretion through the secretory activity of the hypothalamus and pituitary (Fig 21–7). These control mechanisms play an important role in the adaptation of the organism to its environment. A great number of physical and psychologic stimuli that reach the central nervous system are reflected at the level of the hypothalamus, which by means of the hypothalamic factors modifies the secretions of the pituitary and consequently of the "target organs," thus enabling them to respond efficiently to stimuli.

Study of the mitotic rate in the adenohypophysis shows that cell renewal normally occurs at a slow rate. It is known that mitosis of different cell types is controlled by the same factors that influence the secretory phenomena of these cells.

Pars Tuberalis

This funnel-shaped region surrounds the infundibulum of the neurohypophysis (Fig 21–2). Microscopically, it appears highly vascularized, for it is reached by the superior hypophyseal arteries which form there in the initial part of the hypophyseal portal system. Its cells, although basophilic, differ in their structure and histochemistry from those in the pars distalis. They are arranged in cords alongside the blood vessels. Small follicles filled with an amorphous substance and lined by these cells are sometimes observed. The function of the cells of the pars tuberalis is as yet unknown.

Pars Intermedia

In man, the pars intermedia is a rudimentary region made up of weakly basophilic cells. The fissure that results from Rathke's pouch is rarely found in the adult, and follicles lined by cuboid epithelium containing colloid and known as Rathke's cysts appear in its place (Fig 21–8).

The pars intermedia synthesizes a polypeptide, *melanocyte-stimulating hormone (MSH, intermedin),*

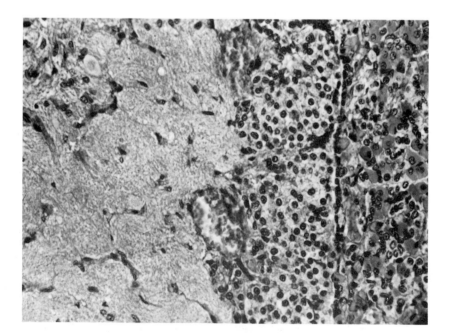

Figure 21–8. Section of pituitary showing (from left to right) the neurohypophysis, the pars intermedia, and the pars distalis. Between the pars intermedia and the pars distalis is the pituitary cleft. Chromophilic and chromophobic cells are apparent in the pars distalis. The pars intermedia consists of cords of one cell type. Mallory stain, × 340.

which in amphibia acts on the melanophores, causing dispersion of the melanin granules in this cell and, consequently, darkening of the animal's skin. The function of the pars intermedia in man is not well understood.

NEUROHYPOPHYSIS

The neurohypophysis consists of the *pars nervosa* or *neural lobe* and the *infundibulum.* The latter joins the gland with the hypothalamus. As opposed to the adenohypophysis, which presents epithelial characteristics, the neurohypophysis consists mainly of about 100,000 unmyelinated axons of *secretory nerve cells.* The cell bodies of these neurons are not in the pituitary but in the *supraoptic* and *paraventricular nuclei.*

The fibers (unmyelinated axons) of the secretory neurons converge, forming the *hypothalamohypophyseal tract.* They proceed to the neurohypophysis and appear not to form synapses with the pituicytes but terminate blindly in close relation to a rich capillary plexus. The neurosecretory material is thought to move along these axons into the neural lobe, where it is discharged or stored, possibly modified, and released into the general circulation as needed. Thus, the neural lobe per se is a depot for the storage of hormones and is not an endocrine gland since the secretions originate elsewhere.

Neurosecretory Cells

The secretory neurons and their branches have all the structural constituents typical of nerve structures in general. In addition, the axons and the cell bodies contain a granular substance which can be studied by specific technics such as staining with Gomori's chrome hematoxylin stain. The hormones of the neurohypophysis are contained in these granules.

The electron microscope reveals that these neurosecretory granules have a diameter of 100–300 nm, are surrounded by a membrane, and are more numerous in the dilated terminal parts of the axons that are closely related to fenestrated blood capillaries. Here they form accumulations visible with the light microscope and known as *Herring corpuscles.*

In addition to the secretory granules, the terminal parts of the neurohypophyseal axons contain vesicles which are morphologically similar to those of the synaptic vesicles. The function of these vesicles is still not known. These axons are not in close contact either with other nerve cells or with effector organs.

Neurosecretion is believed to be elaborated in the granular endoplasmic reticulum (Nissl corpuscles) of the cell bodies of the neurons and then to pass to the Golgi apparatus. It then moves along the axons of the hypothalamohypophyseal tract and is discharged around blood vessels in the pars nervosa.

The technic of differential centrifugation permits the isolation of these secretory granules in which the hormones of this gland are bound to proteins called *neurophysins.* There is one neurophysin for oxytocin and another for vasopressin. Neurophysin is so specific in its binding of neurohypophyseal principles that it can be utilized in separating these principles from other peptides which are present in pituitary extracts. Studies suggest that the neurohormonal peptides are bound to neurophysin within the neurosecretory cells. It is not yet clear whether these peptides exist as free peptides in the blood plasma or as peptide-protein complexes. The storage granule contains oxytocin or vasopressin, ATP, and neurophysin, and when the posterior lobe is stimulated all 3 are secreted. Neurophysins are present in the peripheral blood, where they are measurable by radioimmunoassay. There is evidence that these proteins may act as carriers and that there may be more than two. Vasopressin and oxytocin are stored in the posterior pituitary and released into the blood by impulses in the nerve fibers from the hypothalamus. Although there is some overlap, the fibers from supraoptic nuclei are concerned with vasopressin secretion, while those from the paraventricular nuclei are concerned with oxytocin secretion.

Neurohypophyseal Cells

The neurohypophysis consists mainly of axons from hypothalamic neurons. To a lesser extent, however, it also presents connective tissue cells and a specific type of cell called a *pituicyte* (Fig 21–8).

The pituicytes have an irregular shape and, at times, numerous branches. The cytoplasm of these cells may contain lipid droplets or pigment. The pituicytes do not have ultrastructural characteristics typical of secretory cells, and it is believed that their role is similar to that of neuroglia. Many of the cytoplasmic processes of the pituicytes end in perivascular spaces. However, some investigators still believe in the possibility that the pituicytes may be involved in some way either in the release mechanism or in the separation of the active peptides from the carrier substance.

Histophysiology

The neurohypophysis of all mammals except members of the pig family has 2 hormones, both cyclic peptides made up of 8 different amino acids. These hormones are *arginine vasopressin*—also called *antidiuretic hormone (ADH)*—and *oxytocin.* It is believed that these hormones are present in different secretory granules. In large doses, vasopressin promotes the contraction of smooth muscle of blood vessels, in this way raising the blood pressure. It acts mainly on the muscle layers of small arteries and arterioles. However, it is doubtful if endogenous vasopressin is ever secreted in an amount sufficient to exert any appreciable effect on blood pressure homeostasis. The main effect of vasopressin is to increase the permeability to water of the distal convoluted tubules and collecting tubules of the kidney. As a result of this action, water is reabsorbed by these tubules and urine becomes hypertonic. In this way, vasopressin helps to regulate the osmotic balance of the internal milieu. Vasopressin also increases the permeability of the collecting ducts to urea and decreases blood flow in the renal medulla. In addition, it increases the permeability to water of the toad bladder and the skin of the frog. This hormone is secreted whenever the osmotic pressure of the blood increases. In this case, the blood acts on osmoreceptor cells in the anterior hypothalamus, stimulating the secretion of this hormone from supraoptic neurons. Thus, sections of the neurohypophysis of animals previously given injections of hypertonic solutions do not contain the neurosecretory material usually present in control animals. Vasopressin secretion is increased when extracellular fluid volume is low and vice versa. A variety of stimuli in addition to these increase vasopressin secretion, eg, pain, trauma, emotional upsets, and drugs such as morphine and nicotine. Circulating vasopressin is rapidly inactivated (its half-life in humans is about 18 minutes), mainly in the liver and kidneys, and acts

on its target organ by increasing intracellular cyclic adenosine-3′,5′-monophosphate (cyclic AMP).

Lesions of the hypothalamus, which destroy the neurosecretory cells, cause diabetes insipidus, a disease in which the kidneys lose their capacity to concentrate urine. Consequently, an individual suffering from this disease may excrete up to 20 liters of urine per day (polyuria) and will drink enormous quantities of water.

Oxytocin promotes contraction of the smooth muscle of the uterine wall during copulation and childbirth and also the contraction of the myoepithelial cells which surround the alveoli and alveolar ducts of the mammary glands. The secretion of oxytocin is stimulated by distention of the vagina or of the uterine cervix and also by nursing. This always occurs via nerve tracts which act on the hypothalamus. The neurohormonal reflex triggered by nursing is called the *milk ejection reflex.*

• • •

References

Baker BL & others: Differentiation of growth hormone and prolactin-containing acidophils with peroxidase-labeled antibody. Anat Rec 164:163, 1969.

Baker BL & others: Identification of the corticotropin cell in rat hypophyses with peroxidase-labeled antibody. Anat Rec 166:557, 1970.

Bancroft FC, Tashjian AH Jr: Growth in suspension culture of rat pituitary cells which produce growth hormone and prolactin. Exper Cell Res 64:125, 1971.

Bodian D: Cytological aspects of neurosecretion in opossum neurohypophysis. Bull Johns Hopkins Hosp 113:57, 1963.

Daniel PM: The blood supply of the hypothalamus and pituitary gland. Brit M Bull 22:202, 1966.

Green JD: The comparative anatomy of the portal vascular system and of the innervation of the hypophysis. In: *The Pituitary Gland.* Vol 1. Harris GW, Donovan BT (editors). Univ of California Press, 1966.

Guillemin R: The adenohypophysis and its hypothalamic control. Ann Rev Physiol 29:313, 1967.

Guillemin R, Burgus R: The hormones of the hypothalamus. Sc Am 227:24, Nov 1972.

Harris GW, Reed M: Hypothalamic releasing factors and the control of anterior pituitary function. Brit M Bull 22:266, 1966.

Herbert DC, Hayashida T: Prolactin localization in the primate pituitary by immunofluorescence. Science 169:378, 1970.

Kurosumi K: Functional classification of cell types of the anterior pituitary gland accomplished by electron microscopy. Arch Histol Jap 29:329, 1968.

Nakane PK: Classification of anterior pituitary cell types with immunoenzyme histochemistry. J Histochem Cytochem 18:9, 1970.

Nakayama I, Nickerson PA, Skelton PR: An ultrastructural study of the adrenocorticotropic hormone-secreting cell in the rat adenohypophysis during adrenal cortical regeneration. Lab Invest 21:169, 1969.

Phifer RF, Spicer SS: Immunohistologic and immunopathologic demonstration of adrenocortocotropic hormone in the pars intermedia of the adenohypophysis. Lab Invest 23:543, 1970.

Phifer RF, Spicer SS, Orth DN: Specific demonstration of the human hypophyseal cells which produce adrenocorticotropic hormone. J Clin Endocrinol 31:347, 1970.

Siperstein ER: Identification of the adrenocorticotrophin producing cells in the rat hypophysis by autoradiography. J Cell Biol 17:521, 1963.

Smith RE, Farquhar MG: Lysosome function in the regulation of the secretory process in cells of the anterior pituitary gland. J Cell Biol 31:319, 1966.

22...
Adrenals, Islets of Langerhans, Thyroid, Parathyroids, & Pineal Body

THE ADRENAL (SUPRARENAL) GLANDS

The adrenal glands are paired organs that lie near the upper poles of the kidneys embedded in fat. They are flattened structures with a half-moon shape. In the human they are about 4–6 cm long, 1–2 cm wide, and 4–6 mm thick, and all together weigh about 15 g, but their weight and size may vary depending upon the age and physiologic condition of the individual. Examination of a fresh section of adrenal gland shows it to be covered by a capsule of collagenous connective tissue and to consist of 2 concentric layers: a yellow peripheral layer, the *adrenal cortex;* and a grayish central layer, the *adrenal medulla* (Fig 22–1).

These 2 layers may be considered as 2 morphologically and functionally distinct organs that become united during embryologic development. They derive from different tissues. The cortex arises from the celomic epithelium and therefore is of mesodermal origin. The medulla consists of cells of the neural crest from which the sympathetic ganglion cells also originate. The general histologic appearance is that of an endocrine gland with cells grouped in cords (see Chapter 4).

The collagenous connective tissue capsule which covers the gland sends thin septa to the interior of the gland as trabeculae. The stroma consists mainly of a rich network of reticular fibers that supports the cells.

Blood Supply

The adrenals are supplied by a number of arteries that enter at various points around their periphery (Fig 22–1). The 3 main groups of arteries are the *superior suprarenal* artery, arising from the inferior phrenic artery; the *middle suprarenal* artery, arising from the aorta; and the *inferior suprarenal* artery, arising from

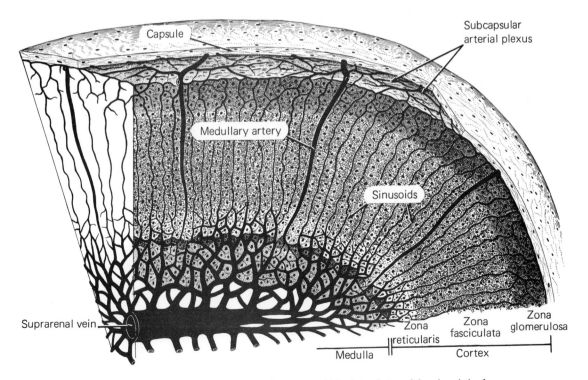

Figure 22–1. Diagram of the general architecture and blood circulation of the adrenal gland.

the renal artery. The various arterial branches that reach the organ constitute a subcapsular plexus which arborizes and forms capillaries running throughout the cortex (Fig 22–1). The cortical arteries arise from this capsular plexus and distribute blood to the anastomosing network of sinusoids surrounding the cords of cortical cells. At the corticomedullary junction, the sinusoids drain into a collecting vein, since there is no venous system in the cortex. Some branches rim the capsule—the so-called medullary arteries—and penetrate the cortex, giving off few or no branches until they reach the medulla. In the medulla they form a rich capillary network around the cords of chromaffin cells. These capillaries, together with those that supply the cortex, form the medullary veins which join to constitute the *adrenal* or *suprarenal veins* (Fig 22–1).

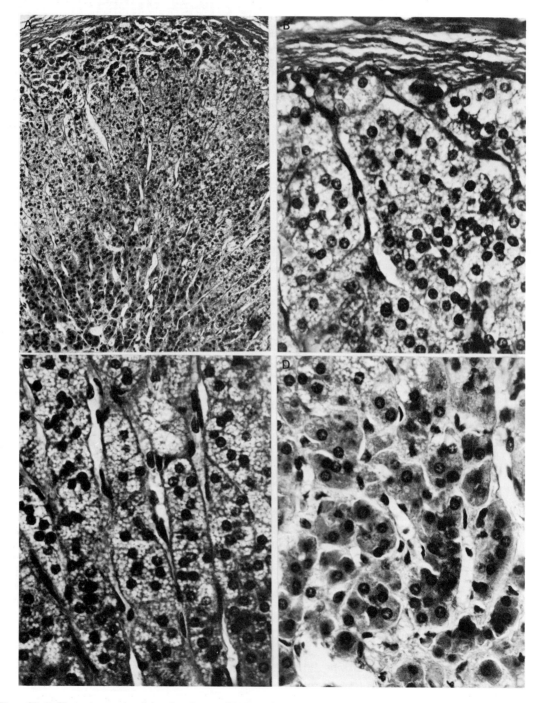

Figure 22–2. Photomicrographs of the adrenal cortex (H&E stain). *A:* A low-power general view. X 80. *B:* The capsule and the zona glomerulosa. X 330. *C:* The zona fasciculata. X 330. *D:* The zona reticularis. X 330.

The adrenal cortical capillaries are considered to be sinusoids, for their lumens are large. The endothelium is extremely attenuated and interrupted by small circular pores–fenestrae–closed by a very thin diaphragm. A continuous basal lamina is seen beneath the endothelium. The nature of the cells of these capillaries is not completely clear. It has been reported that they take up colloidal vital dyes, but more recent studies with the electron microscope have failed to reveal evidence of phagocytosis by the endothelium. Macrophages present in the subendothelial space probably are participating in phagocytosis. In the adrenal glands of some animals, including man, there is a subendothelial space between the endothelial cells of the capillaries and glandular cells in which the microvilli of the latter are observed.

The Adrenal Cortex

Because of the different disposition and appearance of its cells, the adrenal cortex can be subdivided into 3 concentric layers which, in man, are usually not sharply defined (Figs 22–1 and 22–2A): the zona glomerulosa (Fig 22–2B), the zona fasciculata (Fig 22–2C), and the zona reticularis (Fig 22–2D). The zona glomerulosa secretes the mineralocorticoids deoxycorticosterone and aldosterone, which are involved in mineral metabolism. The zona fasciculata and zona reticularis secrete the glucocorticoids cortisone and cortisol or, in some animals, corticosterone, which are concerned with the regulation of carbohydrate, protein, and fat metabolism. Estrogens and androgens appear to be produced in small amounts.

The cells of the adrenal cortex have the characteristics of steroid-synthesizing cells described in Chapter 4. The glomerulosa, fasciculata, and reticularis zones occupy, respectively, 15%, 50%, and 7% of the total volume of the adrenals.

The layer of cells immediately beneath the connective tissue capsule is the *zona glomerulosa,* where the cells are arranged in closely packed, rounded, or arched clusters surrounded by capillaries (Fig 22–2A). The cells found in this layer are cylindric and have a spherical nucleus with a well-developed nucleolus and an acidophilic cytoplasm containing basophilic granules and lipid droplets (Fig 22–2B). The cell contour is smooth except near the subendothelial space, where the plasma membrane is thrown up into folds and microvilli. A prominent feature of the cell is the extensive smooth endoplasmic reticulum (Fig 22–3). There are a few short segments of granular endoplasmic reticulum and some free cytoplasmic ribosomes. Mitochondria are spherical or ovoid and, with the smooth endoplasmic reticulum, sometimes occur in close relationship to the lipid droplets. A well-developed Golgi apparatus is present. The localization of the enzymes participating in aldosterone synthesis has been determined by the differential centrifugation technic. The synthesis of cholesterol from acetate takes place in smooth endoplasmic reticulum, whereas the conversion of cholesterol to pregnenolone takes place in the mitochondria. The enzymes associated with the synthesis of

progesterone and deoxycorticosterone from pregnenolone are found in smooth endoplasmic reticulum; those enzymes that convert deoxycorticosterone → corticosterone → 18-hydroxycorticosterone → aldosterone are located in the mitochondria.

The next layer of cells is known as the *zona fasciculata* because the cells are arranged in straight cords (Fig 22–2C) which run at right angles to the surface of the organ and have capillaries between them. The cells of the zona fasciculata are polyhedral, with a central nucleus, and their cytoplasm is slightly basophilic. Microvilli extend into the subendothelial space. The cells contain a great number of lipid droplets in their cytoplasm; therefore, they appear highly vacuolated in common histologic preparations. It is possible (eg, in the rat adrenal) to find cells containing smaller quantities of lipids in the transitional region between the zona glomerulosa and zona fasciculata (Fig 22–2C). The smooth endoplasmic reticulum is even more fully developed in the zona fasciculata than in the zona glomerulosa, and the granular endoplasmic reticulum is more abundant in this zone. Free ribosomes are also present, and the mitochondria are large and usually spherical.

The following enzymes are found in smooth endoplasmic reticulum: 3β-ol-dehydrogenase, which converts pregnenolone to progesterone; 17-hydroxylase, which converts progesterone to 17a-hydroxyprogesterone and Δ^5-pregnenolone to 17a-hydroxypregnenolone; and 21-hydroxylase, which converts 17a-hydroxyprogesterone to 11-deoxycortisol and progesterone to 11-deoxycorticosterone.

The conversion of cholesterol to pregnenolone by the 20,22-desmolase complex takes place in mitochondria, and the 11β-hydroxylase responsible for the formation of corticosterone from 11-deoxycorticosterone and cortisol from 11-deoxycortisol is in mitochondria.

The innermost layer of the cortex, between the zona fasciculata and the medulla, contains cells disposed in irregular cords forming a network and called the *zona reticularis* (Fig 22–2D). These cells are smaller than those of the other 2 layers. The cells have many of the features of the cells in the zona fasciculata, but they differ in the structure of the mitochondria, which are more often elongated, and in the number and size of their lipofuscin pigment granules. Their cytoplasm is acidophilic and contains a few lipid droplets and, at times, granules of brownish pigment and glycogen. Irregularly shaped cells with pyknotic nuclei—suggesting that they are degenerating—are often found in this layer (Fig 22–2D).

Histophysiology

The function of the adrenal cortex is to produce steroids, lipids that contain the cyclopentanoperhydrophenanthrene nucleus. Chemical radicals are added to or removed from this nucleus during the process of hormone biosynthesis, resulting in various substances with different physiologic activities. The steroids secreted by the cortex may be divided into 3 groups

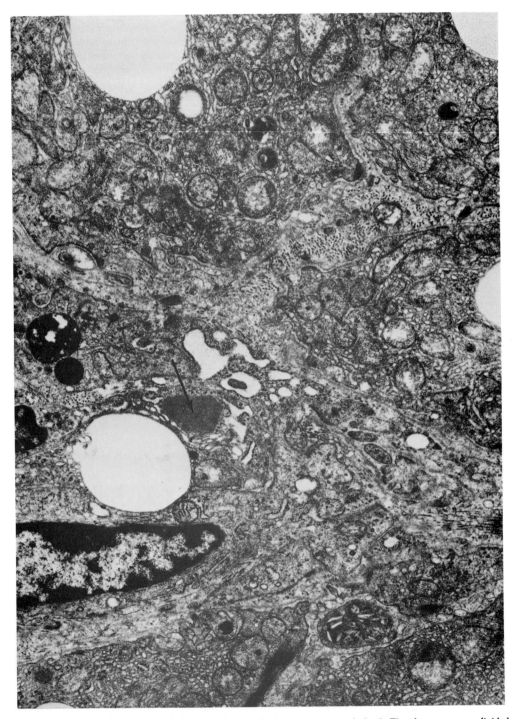

Figure 22–3. Electron micrograph of the zona glomerulosa cells of a human adrenal gland. The clear spaces are lipid droplets. Observe also the abundant mitochondria, the smooth endoplasmic reticulum, and the lysosomes. The arrow shows a crystalloid inclusion. X 15,000. (Courtesy of M Magalhães.)

according to their main physiologic actions: *glucocorticoids, mineralocorticoids,* and *sex hormones* (Fig 22–4).

The glucocorticoids—mainly cortisol and corticosterone—act predominantly on protein, lipid, and carbohydrate metabolism. They promote protein catabolism and a parallel increase in the synthesis of glycogen (glycogenesis), with an increase in the blood glucose concentration. In addition, they mobilize lipids from their normal deposits in adipose tissue.

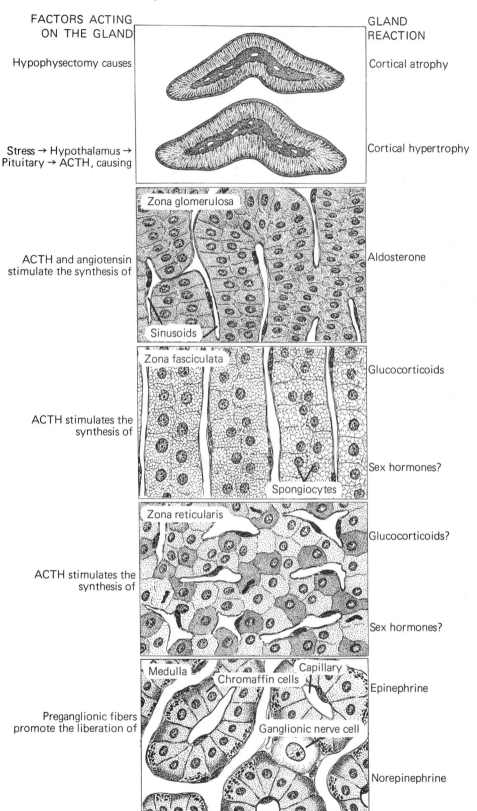

Figure 22—4. Structure and histophysiology of the adrenal gland. *Left:* Factors acting on the gland. *Right:* The effects obtained.

The mineralocorticoids, of which aldosterone is the most important, act mainly on the distal renal tubules (and perhaps also on the proximal tubules) as well as the gastric mucosa and the salivary and sweat glands, stimulating the reabsorption of sodium. They may also increase the concentration of potassium and decrease that of sodium in muscle and brain cells.

Dehydroepiandrosterone is the only sex hormone secreted in significant physiologic quantities by the adrenal cortex. It has masculinizing and anabolic effects, but it is less than one-fifth as potent as testicular androgens. For this reason, and because it is secreted in small quantities—21 mg/day in males and 16 mg/day in females—it is believed to have a negligible physiologic effect under normal conditions. When a congenital enzyme defect exists, the gland produces this hormone in abundance, and this may result in precocious puberty in males or virilism in females.

The basic function of the adrenal gland is to maintain essential homeostatic mechanisms, eg, the chemical constitution of the intercellular and extracellular fluid. This is easily understood when one considers the total effects of the hormones of this gland. A wide variety of physiologic stimuli as well as pathologic states—stress, fasting, temperature changes, infections, drugs, exercise, hemorrhage, etc—affect the central nervous system and, by stimulating hypothalamic secretion of corticotropin-releasing factor, cause an increase in the production of ACTH by the pituitary (Fig 22–5). The consequent increase in production of adrenal hormones permits the organism to counterbalance the effects of such stimuli. Since the organism is continuously receiving such stimuli, the adrenal gland and other homeostatic mechanisms are continually functioning, either in concert or in opposed balance, in order to maintain the equilibrium of the internal milieu.

Experiments on hypophysectomized animals show that the effects of glucocorticoid deficiency can be observed while their ionic equilibrium is found to be essentially normal, suggesting that the secretion of aldosterone is not greatly affected. In the morphologic study of the adrenal glands of these animals, cortical thinning is noticeable—mainly as a result of the atrophy of the zona fasciculata and zona reticularis—while the zona glomerulosa remains unaltered or may even be hypertrophic (Fig 22–4). Another argument in support of the theory that mineralocorticoid production occurs mainly in the glomerulosa is the observed fact that in sodium deficiency the glomerulosa hypertrophies considerably and that this change is accompanied by a severalfold increase in aldosterone production. The presence only in the zona glomerulosa of the 18-hydroxylating enzyme necessary for the synthesis of aldosterone is yet another piece of evidence that this hormone is synthesized in the zona glomerulosa.

The administration of ACTH to a hypophysectomized animal normalizes the secretion of glucocorticoids, demonstrating the dependence of these hormones on the pituitary hormones (Fig 22–4). The secretion of sex hormones is also controlled by ACTH. It

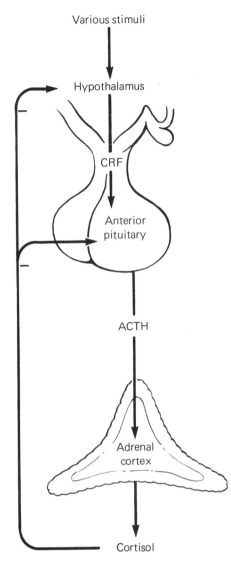

Figure 22–5. Feedback mechanism of ACTH-glucocorticoid secretion.

is now believed that ACTH does promote aldosterone secretion but that its secretion is regulated primarily via the renin-angiotensin system in a feedback fashion. Renin is produced by the juxtaglomerular cells that surround the renal afferent arterioles as they enter the glomeruli (see Chapter 20) and is liberated in response to several types of stimuli, eg, decrease of sodium concentration in the blood, decrease of the volume of circulating blood, and constriction of the renal artery. Once secreted, renin acts as an enzyme on a circulating a_2 globulin (angiotensinogen), causing the liberation of angiotensin I, a decapeptide which is converted by a "converting enzyme" which is present in abundant amounts in the lungs into angiotensin II, an octapeptide which in turn acts on the adrenal gland to stimulate the secretion of aldosterone (Fig 22–4).

The Fetal or Provisional Cortex

In man and some other animals, the adrenal gland of the newborn is more fully developed than that of the adult in terms of percentage of body weight. At this early age, a layer known as *fetal cortex* or *provisional cortex* is present between the thin adrenal cortex and the medulla. This layer is fairly thick, and its cells are disposed in cords. After birth, the provisional cortex undergoes involution, while the permanent cortex—the initially thin layer—develops, differentiating into the 3 layers described above. A major function of this fetal adrenal is secretion of sulfate conjugates of androgens, which are converted in the placenta to active androgens and estrogens that enter the maternal circulation.

There is evidence that chorionic gonadotropin may play a role in the development and maintenance of this zone, possibly by influencing the release of ACTH from the fetal pituitary.

Disorders of the adrenal gland may be classified as *hyperfunction* or *hypofunction.* Adrenal malfunction may result in undersecretion or oversecretion of only one hormone or of several hormones simultaneously.

Hyperfunction of the adrenal cortex may result in excessive production of glucocorticoids or of aldosterone. Excessive production of sex hormones by the adrenal glands causes *adrenogenital syndrome,* which may also occur with an increase of glucocorticoids. This condition is usually caused by enzymatic abnormalities in the biosynthesis of these hormones.

Hypofunction of the adrenal cortex affects mainly the glucocorticoids and may have 2 causes. The first is due to a fault in the gland itself; the other is due to reduced pituitary secretion of ACTH.

Adrenal Medulla

The adrenal medulla is composed of polyhedral epithelioid cells arranged in cords, forming a compact network surrounded by capillaries and venules, and a few sympathetic ganglion cells. They are regarded as modified postganglionic neurons (Fig 22–6). The nerve fibers which reach these cells are found on the side of the capillary. The secretory product accumulates at the cellular pole facing the vein into which it is released.

The function of the medulla is to secrete the catecholamines epinephrine and norepinephrine, and this seems to be controlled largely by neural mechanisms. Norepinephrine is the chemical mediator of the postganglionic endings of the sympathetic nervous system. On the basis of observed differences in the structure of the granules and the results of histochemical studies, it can be stated that there are 2 types of cells in the medulla: one synthesizes epinephrine and the other norepinephrine. The chromaffin cells containing epinephrine are similar in structure to those that contain norepinephrine and differ only in the structure of the granules.

In tissue fixed in glutaraldehyde and osmium, the granules of norepinephrine-containing cells are dense and a halo occurs between the granule and the enclosing membrane. The granules of the epinephrine-containing cells are opaque, and the granule is located in the center of the membrane-bound sac that encloses it. The separate liberation of these 2 hormones into the bloodstream suggests that the 2 types of cells are influenced by different factors. It appears that the enzyme phenylethanolamine-N-methyltransferase, which is required in the conversion of norepinephrine to epinephrine, is induced by glucocorticoids.

The cells of the adrenal medulla become brown when placed in contact with oxidizing agents such as chromate. This staining characteristic is known as the *chromaffin reaction* and is in fact due to the secretory

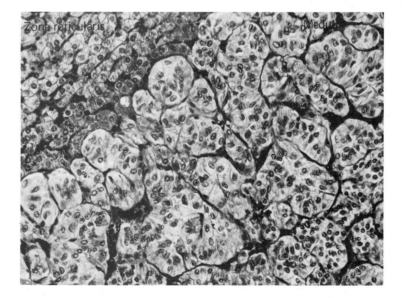

Figure 22–6. Photomicrograph of a section of adrenal medulla. H&E stain, × 200.

products of these cells stored in the cytoplasmic granules, 100—300 nm in diameter. When they are isolated and mixed with an oxidizing agent in vitro, they produce the same color. The chromaffin cells of the adrenal medulla have the following 3 characteristics: they are derived from neuroectoderm, they secrete catecholamines, and they are innervated by preganglionic sympathetic fibers.

The *paraganglia* are groups of cells found near the thoracic and abdominal sympathetic ganglia which have the same embryologic origin as the cells of the adrenal medulla and also present the *chromaffin reaction.* The chromaffin system is said to consist of the paraganglia and the cells of the adrenal medulla. Chromaffinlike cells are also found in the kidney, ovary, testis, liver, heart, and gastrointestinal tract.

Unlike the cortex, which secretes its products continuously into the bloodstream, the cells of the medulla accumulate them and store them in granules. It may be that only small quantities are continuously secreted by the medulla. Generally speaking, epinephrine and norepinephrine are secreted in large quantities only in response to intense emotional reactions (eg, fright). The secretion of these substances is mediated by the preganglionic fibers which reach the chromaffin cells of the adrenal medulla. Vasoconstriction, hypertension, changes in heart rate, and metabolic effects such as blood glucose elevation result from secretion of these substances into the bloodstream. These effects are part of the defense reaction of the organism to different kinds of stresses.

A common disorder of the adrenal medulla is the tumor known as pheochromocytoma.

THE ISLETS OF LANGERHANS

The islets of Langerhans constitute the endocrine portion of the pancreas and appear as rounded clusters of cells immersed in exocrine pancreatic tissue.

Each islet consists of polygonal or rounded cells arranged in cords separated by a network of sinusoid-like blood capillaries (Fig 22—7). A fine capsule of reticular fibers surrounds each islet, separating it from the remaining pancreatic tissue. The islets are believed to constitute about 1.5% of the total pancreatic volume, and there are about 1 million in the human pancreas.

The cells in these islets stain by hematoxylin and eosin less heavily than pancreatic acinar cells. This explains their light appearance when observed with the light microscope.

Using special staining methods, 3 different types of cells—a, β, and δ—have been described in the islets.* It is not clear whether the F (fourth) cell is another type of gastrin-secreting cell or whether gastrin is secreted by the δ cells. The β cells are most numerous

*The a, β, and δ cells are sometimes referred to as A, B, and D cells in other texts.

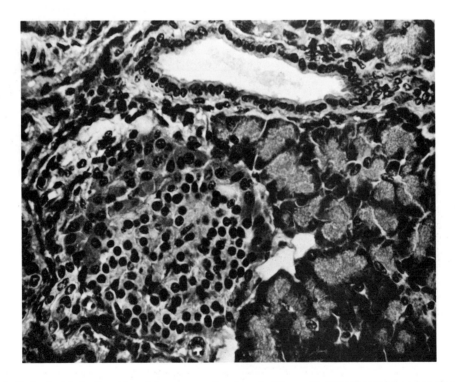

Figure 22—7. Photomicrograph of a section of the pancreas of a guinea pig. Observe the islet of Langerhans, where the a cells appear as large cells with a dark cytoplasm. The remaining cells are mostly β cells. Masson's stain, × 400.

and tend to be concentrated in the center of the islet (Fig 22–7); they constitute about 60–80% of the cells found in human pancreatic islets. These cells are small and contain in their cytoplasm granules which stain blue with Gomori's chrome hematoxylin and phloxine technic. The *a* cells are larger and less numerous (20%), are found usually at the periphery, and are characterized by the presence of secretory granules which stain red with Gomori stain. The δ cells are small and do not stain heavily. They are the least numerous cells in the islets (5%).

In addition to the granular cell types, the islets of the guinea pig pancreas also contain a nongranular cell designated the *c cell.*

The ultrastructure of the *a*, β, and δ cells is that of cells capable of synthesizing polypeptides, for they present a granular endoplasmic reticulum, Golgi apparatus, and secretory granules (Fig 22–8). However, there is much less granular endoplasmic reticulum in these cells than in the acinar cells of the exocrine pancreas. This is in accord with the less intense protein synthesis that occurs in these cells as compared to this activity in the acinar cells. In fact, the islets weigh approximately 1 g and produce about 2 mg of insulin per day. This amount is about 20% of the weight of all of the protein produced per unit weight by the acinar cells. An easy way to compare the synthesis of protein in these 2 types of cells is by radioautography after administration of a radioactive amino acid. The number of silver granules which appear over the acinar cells is much greater than that observed over the islet cells.

The secretory granules are easily observed, with a membrane usually detached from its dense core. The morphology of the granules found in the β cells varies greatly in different species (Fig 22–8).

The β cell secretory granules contained in a membrane are round, but in some species, including man, they appear to be composed of one or more crystals.

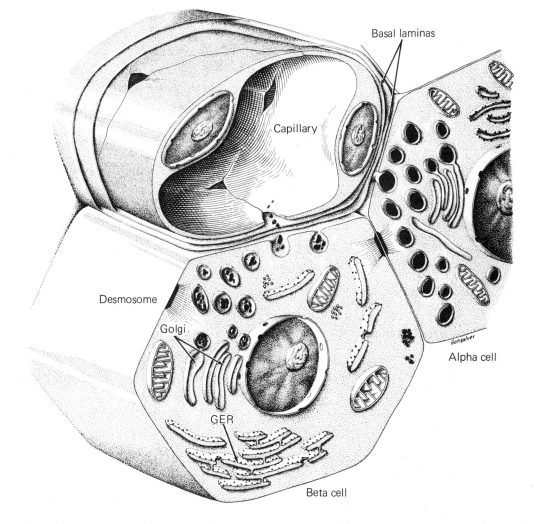

Figure 22–8. Schematic drawing of the *a* and β cells, showing the morphology of the secretory granules and their relation to blood vessels. The β cell has irregular granules, while the granules are round and uniform in the *a* cells. GER, granular endoplasmic reticulum.

They are extremely dense, and at high magnification they have a periodic internal structure.

The granules of a cells are slightly larger than those of the β cells and consist of a central spherical core and an outer halo of low density between the core and the membrane.

The β cells are the source of the hormone insulin, a polypeptide molecule (MW 6000) that decreases blood glucose and accelerates glycogenesis; the a cells are thought to secrete the hormone glucagon, a smaller polypeptide that has a glycogenolytic effect and raises blood glucose.

The existence of the δ cells as a type morphologically distinguishable from the other 2 types has been a subject of controversy. The evidence that the δ cells are altered a cells consists of reports of observations of cells with characteristics intermediate between those of the 2 types. However, the δ cells also secrete another hormone, gastrin, and their granules lack the dense core that is characteristic of the a cell.

Morphologic and biochemical data suggest that the synthesis of insulin begins on ribosomes on the surface of the granular endoplasmic reticulum of the β cells. Insulin is formed first as a single polypeptide chain, *proinsulin,* containing 81–86 residues depending on the species. The conversion of proinsulin to insulin occurs by proteolytic cleavage, giving one molecule of insulin and one of C-peptide, and takes place at the time of transport of proinsulin to the Golgi apparatus, or soon after, where it is packaged into granules. Since the granules contain insulin and C-peptide in the same amounts, it seems that the packaging occurs first and is followed by cleavage within the granules. Insulin is complexed with zinc and stored. The β cell granules also contain lipids and, in some species, monoamines.

The earliest change in the insulin release process, after a stimulus is applied, is margination of the cytoplasmic granules to the plasma membrane of the β cell. Their membranes fuse with plasma membrane of the cell and rupture, and the contents are then liberated into the extracellular space. They then rapidly disappear by a process of dissolution. With the disappearance of the granules, microvilli remain, and they have been shown to increase in number in proportion to the rate of release of the β granules. Evidence has been presented of the existence of microtubules in β cells and of their participation in transport of the secretory granules to the plasma membrane.

Although the above-described release process is perhaps the most important mechanism of β-granule release, it may not be the only one. For example, it may be that some insulin remains in soluble form, that granules dissolve in the cell—releasing insulin to the interior of the cell—or that some granules are released directly from the synthetic site without prolonged storage.

Immunofluorescent technics support the view that the a cells synthesize and accumulate a hyperglycemia-inducing polypeptide called *glucagon* (MW 3485) (Fig 22–9). Another fact in support of this hypothesis is that large doses of glucagon cause atro-

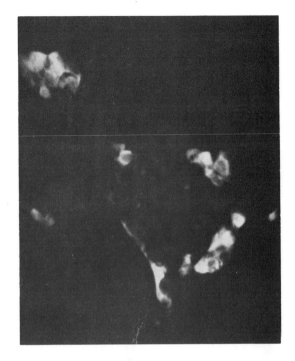

Figure 22–9. The islets of Langerhans, demonstrated by immunofluorescence microscopy to contain glucagon-producing cells. In this figure, the a cells appear fluorescent on a dark background.

phy of the a cells.

It is believed that the same synthetic sequence occurs in the a cell as in the β cell—ie, synthesis in the endoplasmic reticulum, transport to the Golgi apparatus, and packaging for release as granules.

The islets thus have a doubly sensitive regulating mechanism capable of increasing or decreasing blood glucose content. It is believed that secretion of the β cells is controlled to a large extent by the level of blood glucose because when an isolated pancreas is perfused with blood rich in glucose the secretion of insulin is increased.

Terminations of nerve fibers on islet cells can be observed by light or electron microscopy. Both sympathetic and parasympathetic nerve endings have been found in close association (synaptic?) with a, β, and δ cells. It has only recently been appreciated that these nerves function as part of the insulin and glucagon control system.

THYROID

The thyroid is an endocrine gland derived from endoderm. It develops early in embryonic life in vertebrates from the cephalic portion of the alimentary canal. Its function is to synthesize the hormones thyroxine and triiodothyronine, which stimulate the metabolic rate.

The thyroid gland is located in the cervical region, in front of the larynx, and consists of 2 lobes united by an isthmus. Thyroid tissue is usually composed of cuboid epithelium arranged in a single layer surrounding spherical spaces containing a gelatinous substance, the *colloid* (Fig 22–10). This cellular arrangement, in spheres surrounding the colloid, forms a structure known as a *thyroid follicle*. In man, this structure may reach a diameter of 0.9 mm. The gland is covered by a loose connective tissue capsule which sends septa into the parenchyma. These septa become gradually thinner and reach all of the follicles, separating one from another by fine irregular connective tissue composed mainly of reticular fibers. The thyroid is an extremely vascularized organ, presenting an extensive blood and lymphatic capillary network between the follicles. The endothelial cells of these capillaries are fenestrated, as commonly occurs in the capillaries of endocrine glands. This disposition may perhaps facilitate the passage of the hormone to the blood capillaries.

Innervation of the thyroid is via the sympathetic and parasympathetic systems. It is thought that this innervation has an essentially vasomotor function. Recent ultrastructural and radioautographic studies have shown a network of adrenergic fibers terminating near the basal membrane of the follicular cells. These findings, together with new evidence that adrenergic and other amines influence thyroid iodine metabolism in isolated thyroid cells, and in vivo, indicate that the neurogenic stimuli can influence thyroid function through a direct effect on the epithelial cells. However,

in many respects, thyroid-stimulating hormone (TSH; thyrotropin), which is secreted by the anterior pituitary, can be considered to be the major regulator of the anatomic and functional state of the thyroid gland.

The composition of the thyroid follicles varies (polymorphism) according to the region of the gland and its functional activity. Thus, in the same gland, larger follicles full of colloid and presenting a cuboid or squamous epithelium may be found alongside smaller ones formed by columnar epithelium. In spite of this variation, when the average composition of these follicles is squamous, the gland is considered hypoactive. As opposed to this, when TSH drugs capable of stimulating the synthesis of this hormone is administered to an animal, a marked increase in the height of the follicular epithelium is observed. This alteration is accompanied by a decrease in the quantity of the colloid and in the size of the follicles.

The thyroid epithelium always rests on a basement membrane. The ultrastructure of the follicular epithelium presents all of the characteristics of a cell which at the same time synthesizes, reabsorbs, and digests proteins. Thus, the basal part of these cells is rich in granular endoplasmic reticulum. The nucleus is generally round and encountered in the center of the cell. The apical pole presents a discrete Golgi apparatus and secretory granules with the staining characteristics of follicular colloid. Abundant particles, 0.5–0.6 μm in diameter, and some (usually) large vacuoles containing a clear fluid are also found in this region. These are believed to be lysosomes. The cell membrane of the apical pole contains a moderate number of microvilli. Mitochondria are dispersed throughout the cytoplasm, and some free ribosomes are found.

Small isolated clusters of light cells are frequently

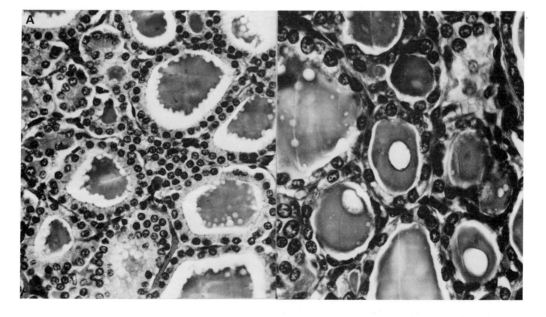

Figure 22–10. Photomicrographs of sections of thyroid glands. The higher epithelial cells and the corroded aspect of the colloid strongly indicate that the section on the left is from a more active gland. H&E stain, × 200 (A) and 400 (B).

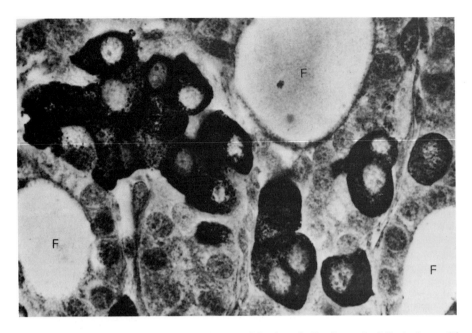

Figure 22–11. Photomicrograph of a dog's thyroid showing its parafollicular cells. F indicates the follicular lumen. Silver impregnation, × 800. (Courtesy of F Kameda.)

found between the thyroid follicles. These are known as *parafollicular cells* or *C cells (clear cells)* (Fig 22–11). Evidence has been presented that these cells are responsible for the synthesis and secretion of the polypeptide hormone *calcitonin,* a substance consisting of 32 amino acids that reduces the concentration of calcium in the blood. The following observations support this statement: (1) cytologic alterations of the parafollicular cells occur when experimental hypercalcemia is induced, and (2) there is selective binding of a fluorescent antibody (anticalcitonin) to the parafollicular cells.

The C cells have the characteristics of APUD* cells described in Chapter 4. Their ultrastructure is illustrated in Fig 22–12. Regulation of the secretion of these cells depends exclusively on the calcium blood level and is independent of thyroid, parathyroid, and pituitary functions. In man, calcitonin is found not only in the thyroid but also in the thymus and the parathyroid glands.

Histophysiology

The thyroid is the only endocrine gland whose secretory product is stored in great quantity. This accumulation occurs in the colloid. It is estimated that in man there is sufficient hormone within the follicles to supply the organism for up to 10 months. Thyroid colloid is composed mainly of a glycoprotein (thyroglobulin) of high molecular weight (680,000). The staining affinity of the follicular colloid varies greatly; it may be either acidophilic or basophilic. There is indirect proof that when the colloid is strongly baso-

philic the follicle which contains it is in a stage of intense metabolic activity—as opposed to follicles containing acidophilic colloid. It is commonly observed—mainly in active follicles of fixed and stained histologic preparations—that the colloid appears irregular and eroded in the portion alongside the follicular cells. It is believed that this is due to ingestion of thyroglobulin by these cells.

The activity of the follicular cells of the thyroid is controlled by the circulating level of thyrotropin, which acts via cyclic AMP of the cells. A rise in the circulating free thyroid hormones in turn inhibits the synthesis of thyrotropin, and when the thyroid hormone level drops the secretion of TSH is stimulated, establishing in this way a homeostatic balance which maintains an adequate quantity of thyroxine and triiodothyronine within the organism. TSH secretion is also increased by exposure to cold in animals and human infants and is depressed by heat and stressful stimuli. The negative feedback effect of thyroid hormones on TSH secretion may be exerted in part at the hypothalamus but also to a great extent upon the anterior pituitary. A tripeptide that has been isolated from the hypothalamus (thyrotropin-releasing factor, TRF) stimulates TSH secretion (Fig 22–13). Autoregulatory control of thyroid function is also shown. High concentrations of intrathyroidal iodine inhibit the rate of release of thyroidal iodine. In addition, the magnitude of the organic iodine pool inversely affects the iodide transport mechanism and the response to TSH.

Radioautographic studies performed with the electron microscope show that the synthesis of the carbohydrate fraction of thyroglobulin occurs both in the endoplasmic reticulum and the Golgi apparatus. Man-

*Amine precursor uptake and decarboxylation.

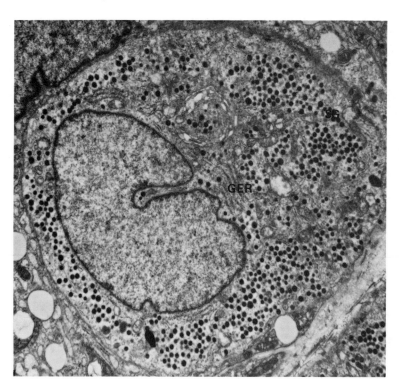

Figure 22—12. Electron micrograph of a calcitonin-producing cell. Observe the small secretory granules (SG) and the scarcity of granular endoplasmic reticulum (GER). × 5000.

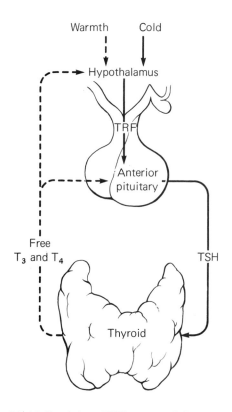

Figure 22—13. Regulation of TSH secretion. Solid arrows indicate stimulation; dashed arrows, inhibition.

nose is incorporated at the endoplasmic reticulum, whereas galactose is added to this macromolecule at the Golgi apparatus. This is another example of the way cellular organelles cooperate to synthesize a compound.

Synthesis & Accumulation of Hormones by the Follicular Cells

This process takes place in 4 stages, as follows: synthesis of thyroglobulin, uptake of iodide from the blood, activation of the iodide, and iodination of the tyrosyl radicals of thyroglobulin.

These stages are exemplified in Fig 22—14. It is thought that they take place in the following manner:

(1) Generally speaking, the *synthesis of thyroglobulin* is similar to that of protein, already described in Chapter 4. This process has been extensively studied by means of radioautographic technics with the use of tritiated leucine, an amino acid abundant in thyroglobulin (Fig 22—15). The secretory pathway is thought to be as follows: synthesis of protein in the endoplasmic reticulum, addition of polysaccharide in the Golgi apparatus and endoplasmic reticulum, and release from the formed vesicles of the apical surface of the cell into the follicles.

(2) The *uptake of circulating iodide* is accomplished in the thyroid by a mechanism of intense active transport, the iodide pump, located next to or on the cytoplasmic membrane of the basal region of the follicular cells. This pump also exists in other organs—the

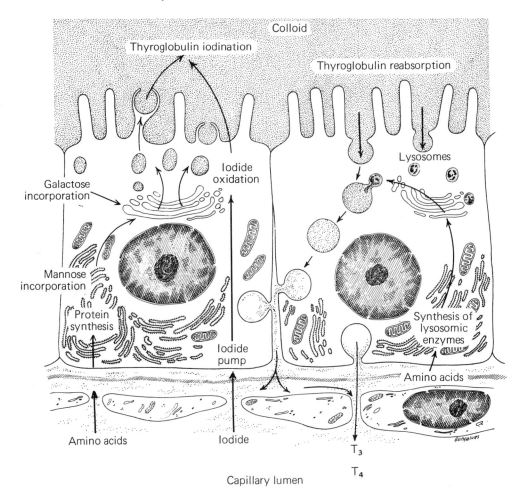

Figure 22–14. Diagram showing the processes of synthesis and iodination of thyroglobulin *(left)* and its reabsorption and digestion *(right)*. These events can occur in the same cell.

salivary and mammary glands, the stomach, etc. In these places, the synthesis of thyroid hormone does not occur and the function of the pump is obscure. This pump is readily stimulated by thyrotropin. The uptake of iodide can be inhibited by certain drugs such as perchlorate and thiocyanate which act by competing with the iodide. Another case in which the uptake of iodide is prevented is known to be a genetically determined disease in which the iodide pump does not function. In these cases, the same deficiency is observed in the above-mentioned organs, which also have an active iodide transport.

(3) During the phase of *oxidation of iodide,* iodide is transformed into iodine, which in turn combines in the colloid with the tyrosyl radicals of thyroglobulin. An enzyme, peroxidase, which has been demonstrated in the thyroid by biochemical and histochemical methods, is responsible for the oxidation of iodide inside the follicular cells. This process can be blocked by drugs (eg, propylthiouracil and carbimazole) which inactivate the peroxidase. It is now agreed that the main function of these compounds is to in-

hibit the coupling of iodotyrosines into T_3 or T_4 and that the influence on the formation of MIT and DIT is secondary. Thyroid dysfunction may also occur as a result of a genetically determined deficiency of peroxidase.

(4) In contrast to the processes described above, *iodination of the tyrosyl radicals* bound to thyroglobulin takes place not inside the follicular cells but in the portion of colloid which is in contact with the membrane of the apical region of the cells. This process has been extensively studied by means of radioautography using ^{131}I. Initially, a monoiodine compound, monoiodotyrosine (MIT), is formed, followed by the production of the diiodine compound diiodotyrosine (DIT). Two diiodotyrosine molecules are then united, releasing an amino acid, alanine, and forming the tetraiodine compound tetraiodothyronine (T_4), also known as thyroxine, which is the main thyroid hormone. Another hormone produced, although on a much smaller scale, is triiodothyronine (T_3), probably by condensation of monoiodotyrosine with diiodotyrosine. (See Fig 22–16.) The condensation reaction is an

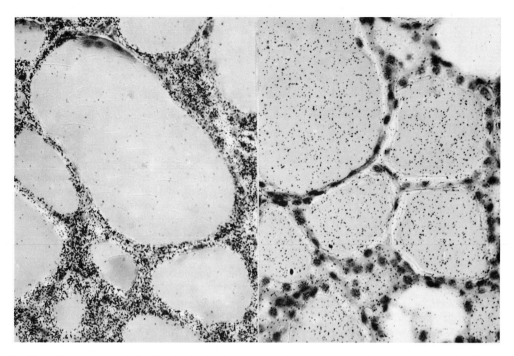

Figure 22–15. Radioautographs of the thyroid glands of rats previously injected with radioactive leucine. *Left:* The tracer was injected 30 minutes before the animal was killed. Observe the radioactivity (dark dots) concentrated mainly on the cells. *Right:* The amino acid was injected 45 days before the animal was killed, and all radioactivity is in the colloid (thyroglobulin). X 385.

aerobic, energy-requiring one. It is postulated that the union of the iodinated tyrosines is catalyzed by an enzymatic mechanism. For this process to occur normally, thyroglobulin must present the correct spatial configuration. When disease causes the production of abnormal thyroglobulin, this process is blocked, resulting in deficient synthesis of thyroid hormone.

Liberation of T_3 & T_4

The thyroid hormones remain in the bound form with thyroglobulin until secreted. The site of hydrolysis of thyroglobulin is a subject of dispute. Although some believe that proteases are secreted into the colloid, most of the evidence now supports the hypothesis that the thyroid cells ingest the colloid by pinocytosis, where the colloid merges with lysosomes. The peptide bonds between the iodinated residues and the thyroglobulin are broken by the proteases in the lysosomes, and thyroxine, triiodothyronine, diiodotyrosine, and moniodotyrosine are liberated into the cytoplasm. The

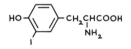

3-Monoiodotyrosine (MIT)

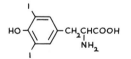

3,5-Diiodotyrosine (DIT)

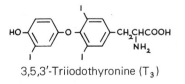

3,5,3'-Triiodothyronine (T_3)

3,5,3',5'-Tetraiodothyronine
(T_4, thyroxine)

Figure 22–16. Formulas of monoiodotyrosine (MIT) and diiodotyrosine (DIT). The condensation of 2 molecules of DIT with the elimination of an alanine residue results in the formation of tetraiodothyronine (T_4; thyroxine). The condensation of one molecule of MIT and one molecule of DIT with the elimination of one alanine residue results in the formation of triiodothyronine (T_3).

free thyroxine and triiodothyronine then cross the cells and are discharged into the capillaries. Tetraiodothyronine (thyroxine) is the most abundant of these compounds, constituting 90% of the circulating thyroid hormone, although T_3 acts more rapidly and is more potent than T_4. In man, 80 μg/day of free T_4 and 50 μg/day of T_3 are secreted by the thyroid cells into the capillaries.

Most of the effects of thyroid hormones are secondary to their calorigenic action, although they also influence body growth and especially the development of the nervous system during fetal life; increase the absorption of carbohydrates from the intestine; and help to regulate lipid metabolism. Monoiodotyrosine and diiodotyrosine are not secreted into the blood since their iodine is removed as a result of the intracellular action of a microsomal enzyme called *iodotyrosine dehalogenase.* The products of this enzymatic reaction, iodine and tyrosine, are probably reused by the follicular cells.

Factors That Affect the Synthesis of Thyroid Hormone

It is clear that a diet that contains less than 10 μg/day of iodine hinders the synthesis of thyroid hormones. Thyroid hypertrophy as a result of increased TSH secretion causes the disorder known as *iodine deficiency goiter,* which is "endemic" in some regions of the world.

The syndrome of adult hypothyroidism is called *myxedema* and may be the result of a number of diseases of the thyroid gland or may be secondary to pituitary or hypothalamic failure. Children who are hypothyroid from birth are called *cretins.*

Hyperthyroidism or thyrotoxicosis may be caused by a variety of thyroid diseases, but the most common form is *Graves' disease* or *exophthalmic goiter.* The levels of TSH are subnormal, and the thyroid hyperfunction in this disease is due to a circulating gamma globulin which exerts effects resembling those of TSH. This substance, called long-acting thyroid stimulator (LATS), is an antibody against a component of thyroid tissue.

The factor that produces exophthalmos in this disease may be of pituitary origin and is probably a derivative of TSH but is not TSH.

THE PARATHYROID GLANDS

The parathyroids are 3 or more (often 4) very small glands–3 $\times$ 6 mm–with a total weight of not more than 0.2 g. They are situated behind the thyroid gland, one at each of the upper and lower poles, usually in the capsule that covers the lobes of the thyroid. Sometimes they are found embedded in the thyroid gland. They may also be found in the mediastinum, lying beside the thymus. This is because the parathyroid glands and the thymus originate from closely contiguous pharyngeal pouch.

The parathyroid glands are derived from the third and fourth pharyngeal pouches–the superior glands from the fourth and the inferior glands from the third.

Histology

Each parathyroid gland is contained within a connective tissue capsule. These capsules send septa to the inside of the gland, where they merge with the reticular fibers supporting elongated cordlike clusters of secretory cells.

The parenchyma of the parathyroid glands consists of 2 types of cells: the chief or principal cells and the oxyphil cells (Fig 22–17). In hyperplasia, however, a third cell type, the water clear cell, is also seen. Adipose tissue cells are frequently found inside the human parathyroid gland.

The *chief cells* are the most numerous. In most mammals they are the only cells found in the parathyroid gland. They are polygonal, with a vesicular nucleus and a slightly acidophilic cytoplasm. Electron microscopy shows irregularly shaped granules 200–400 nm in diameter in the cytoplasm of the chief cells. They are believed to be secretory granules containing parathyroid hormone, which in the active form is a polypeptide with a molecular weight of 9500. These granules, the number of which varies from one cell to another, are distributed throughout the cytoplasm, but sometimes they are more numerous at the

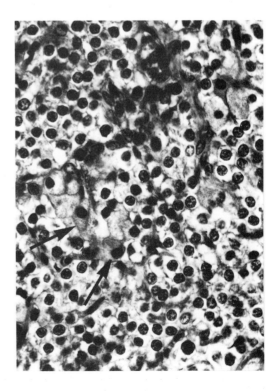

Figure 22–17. Photomicrograph of a section of the parathyroid gland. Observe the predominance of the clear (chief) cells over the dark oxyphil cells (arrows). H&E stain, $\times$ 400.

vascular pole of the cell. A prominent Golgi apparatus is situated adjacent to the nucleus. Granular endoplasmic reticulum and free ribosomes are found. Small ovoid or spherical mitochondria and lipofuscin pigment bodies are also evident. Masses of glycogen granules occur and are especially large in resting or inactive chief cells.

In man, the *oxyphil cells* begin to appear at about age 7 and increase in number with age. They too are polygonal in shape, but they are larger than chief cells and their cytoplasm contains many acidophilic granules. The electron microscope reveals that these granules are mitochondria with abundant cristae. The function and importance of such a large concentration of mitochondria in these cells are unknown.

Cells with structural characteristics intermediate between chief and oxyphil cells are also seen.

Histophysiology

Parathyroid glands are essential for life. They secrete parathyroid hormone, whose physiologic role is to control the concentration of calcium and phosphate ions in the blood.

Decrease in blood calcium stimulates the parathyroid gland to secrete its hormone. Magnesium appears to have a similar direct effect. In turn, parathyroid hormone acts on the cells of bone tissue, increasing the number of osteoclasts and bone-absorbing cells and promoting in this way the absorption of the calcified bone matrix. Increase in the concentration of calcium in the blood probably suppresses the production of this hormone. Calcitonin also acts on the osteoclasts, inhibiting their resorptive action on bone and calcium liberation, thus lowering blood calcium.

In addition to increasing the concentration of calcium, parathyroid hormone reduces the concentration of phosphate in the blood. This effect is a consequence of an increase in the excretion of phosphate in urine. Parathyroid hormone diminishes the absorption of phosphate from the glomerular filtrate at the level of the kidney tubules. There is also strong evidence that parathyroid hormone increases absorption of calcium from the gastrointestinal tract and that vitamin D is necessary for this effect. The actions of parathyroid hormone involve activation of adenylate cyclase, with consequent increased formation of cyclic AMP in the affected cells.

In hyperparathyroidism, blood phosphate is low and blood calcium is increased. This frequently promotes a pathologic deposit of calcium in several organs such as the kidneys and arteries. Bones are decalcified and become subject to fractures. The bone disease caused by hyperparathyroidism is characterized by multiple bone cysts and is known as *osteitis fibrosa cystica.*

Hypoparathyroidism causes an increase in the concentration of phosphate and a decrease in the concentration of calcium in the blood. The bones become denser and more mineralized. This condition causes spastic contractions of the skeletal muscles and generalized convulsions (also called tetany). These symptoms are due to the exaggerated excitability of the nervous system caused by the lack of calcium ions in the blood. The endogenous administration of calcium or of parathyroid hormone terminates the convulsions—the former much more rapidly.

The secretion of the parathyroid cells is regulated by the blood calcium level and apparently is not directly affected by other endocrine glands or the nervous system.

THE PINEAL BODY

The pineal body is also known as the epiphysis or pineal gland. In the adult it is a flattened, cone-shaped organ measuring approximately 5–8 mm in length and 3–5 mm in its greatest width and weighs about 120 mg. It is found in the posterior extremity of the third ventricle, above the roof of the diencephalon, to which it is connected by means of a short stalk.

The pineal is covered by pia mater. Connective tissue septa containing blood vessels and unmyelinated nerve fibers originate in the pia mater and enter the pineal tissue to surround the cellular cords and follicles, forming irregular lobules.

The pineal body consists of several types of cells but principally *pinealocytes* and interstitial cells. Pinealocytes have a slightly basophilic cytoplasm with large irregular or lobate nuclei and sharply defined nucleoli. They are also known as cells of the pineal parenchyma. When impregnated with silver salts (Del Rio Hortega's method), the pinealocytes appear to have long and tortuous branches reaching out to the vascular connective tissue septa where they end as flattened dilatations. The pineal itself is surrounded by cerebrospinal fluid. The cytoplasm of the pinealocytes contains a great number of free ribosomes and a small amount of granular endoplasmic reticulum. The Golgi apparatus and the mitochondria are poorly developed. In addition, one also finds lipid droplets and structures similar to lysosomes. Two distinctive features of the cytoplasm are the presence of large numbers of microtubules and an extensive smooth endoplasmic reticulum.

The *interstitial cells* of the pineal body are a specific type of cell characterized by elongated nuclei which stain more heavily than those of parenchymal cells. They are observed between the cords of pinealocytes and perivascular areas. These cells have long cytoplasmic processes containing a large number of fine filaments 5–6 nm in diameter and of moderate length. Interstitial cells resemble the fine structure of astrocytes, and some investigators consider them to be a type of glial cell.

In addition to the above-mentioned cell types, cells frequently encountered in the pineal body are the glia and mast cells. The mast cells are probably responsible for the high histamine content of this organ.

Age causes an increase in the amount of connective tissue in the pineal body and the formation of calcified bodies *(brain sand)* in the parenchyma of this organ. These calcified bodies are used as a reference point in skull radiology for they appear clearly in x-ray pictures.

Innervation

Silver impregnation reveals nerve fibers throughout the pineal body. When these nerve fibers penetrate the organ, they lose their myelin sheath, the unmyelinated axons ending among pinealocytes (Fig 22–18), and some actually form synapses. A great number of small vesicles 40 nm in diameter containing norepinephrine are observed in these nerve endings. Serotonin is present also, both in the pinealocytes and in sympathetic nerve terminals. The pineal body is mainly innervated by postganglionic sympathetic fibers derived from the superior cervical sympathetic ganglion. In primates, it is believed that there are also parasympathetic fibers.

Histophysiology

In spite of the great quantity of research on the pineal gland, its role as an endocrine gland is still a subject of controversy. It is thought to be capable of participating in some endocrine functions.

The pineal has been claimed at one time or another to be a source of (1) a gonadotropin-releasing hormone; (2) a gonadotropin-inhibiting principle which has a structure similar to that of arginine vasotocin; (3) a growth-inhibiting factor; (4) a thyrotropin-releasing hormone; (5) a substance that inhibits the onset of puberty; (6) melatonin, which may inhibit gonadotropin release and causes lightening of the skin; and (7) factors that antagonize the secretion of ACTH and regulate the secretion of aldosterone.

The theory that has received the widest acceptance is that the pineal acts on the gonads. Whether it secretes hormones into the blood, the cerebrospinal fluid, or both has not been clearly determined.

Melatonin

Melatonin is an indolic compound, isolated from the pineal body of mammals, that induces the aggregation of pigment granules in the melanophores of amphibia. This substance, synthesized only in the pineal, has a 100,000 times stronger effect on melanophores than norepinephrine, which has a similar effect. From this organ has been isolated an enzyme called hydroxyindole-O-methyltransferase, which is capable of methylating N-acetyl-5-hydroxytryptamine and transforming it into melatonin.

The quantity of melatonin and serotonin in the pineal body of rats undergoes rhythmic variations during the 24 hours of the day according to the alterna-

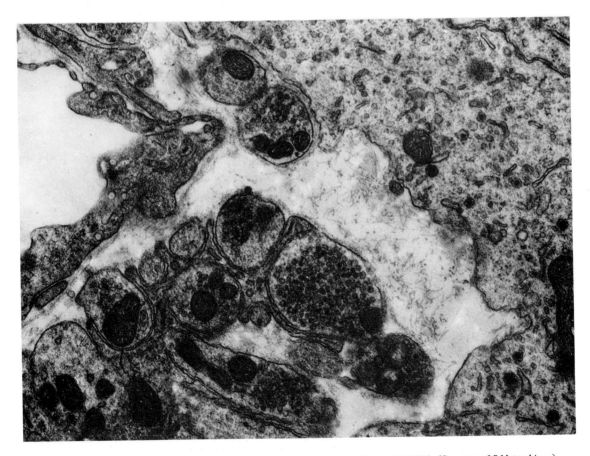

Figure 22–18. Electron micrograph of adrenergic nerve endings in the pineal body. X 32,000. (Courtesy of S Matsushima.)

tions of light and dark periods. A diminished activity of hydroxyindole-O-methyltransferase and a consequent inhibition of melatonin synthesis are observed if the rats are maintained in constant illumination.

The first evidence that the pineal body might affect the function of the gonads was the observation that an individual suffering from a destructive tumor of this organ developed precocious puberty and hyper-trophy of the gonads. However, the precise role of this organ remains an open question. We can say with some certainty, however, that the mammalian pinealocytes are neuroendocrine transducers since they respond to a neurotransmitter (ie, norepinephrine) released from their sympathetic neurons by synthesizing a group of biologically active compounds that modify the function of different endocrine organs.

● ● ●

References

Adrenal Gland

Eisenstein AB: *The Adrenal Cortex.* Little, Brown, 1967.

Giacomelli F, Wiener J, Spiro D: Cytological alterations related to stimulation of the zona glomerulosa of the adrenal gland. J Cell Biol 26:499, 1965.

Mortimore GE: The adrenal medulla. In: *Best & Taylor's Physiological Basis of Medical Practice,* 9th ed. Brobeck JR & others (editors). Williams & Wilkins, 1973.

Rhodin JAG: The ultrastructure of the adrenal cortex of the rat under normal and experimental conditions. J Ultrastruct Res 34:23, 1971.

Stachenko J, Giroud CJP: Functional zonation of the adrenal cortex: Pathways of corticosteroid biogenesis. Endocrinology 64:730, 1959.

Islets of Langerhans

Caramia F, Munger BL, Lacy PE: The ultrastructural basis for the identification of cell types in the pancreatic islets. 1. Guinea pig. Z Zellforsch Mikrosk Anat 67:533, 1965.

Falkner S, Hellman B, Taljedal IB: *The Structure and Metabolism of the Pancreatic Islets.* Pergamon Press, 1970.

Gomez-Acebo J, Parilla R, Candela JLR: Fine structure of the A and D cells of the rabbit endocrine pancreas in vivo and incubated in vitro. 1. Mechanism of secretion of the A cells. J Cell Biol 36:33, 1968.

Ichikawa A: Fine structural changes in response to hormonal stimulation of the perfused canine pancreas. J Cell Biol 24:369, 1965.

Like AA: The ultrastructure of the islets of Langerhans in man. Lab Invest 16:937, 1967.

Munger BL, Caramia F, Lacy PE: The ultrastructural basis for the identification of cell types in the pancreatic islets. 2. Rabbit, dog and opossum. Z Zellforsch Mikrosk Anat 67:776, 1965.

Thyroid Gland

Anast CS: Thyrocalcitonin: A review. Clin Orthop 47:179, 1966.

Bradley AS, Wissig SL: The anatomy of secretion in the follicular cell of the thyroid gland. 3. The acute effect in vivo of thyrotropic hormone on amino acid uptake and incorporation into protein by the mouse thyroid gland. J Cell Biol 30:433, 1966.

Bussolati G, Pearse AGE: Immunofluorescence localization of calcitonin in the C-cells of pig and dog's thyroid. J Endocrinol 37:205, 1967.

Haddad A & others: Radioautographic study of in vivo

and in vitro incorporation of fucose-^{3}H into thyroglobulin by rat thyroid follicular cells. J Cell Biol 49:856, 1971.

Heimann P: Ultrastructure of the human thyroid: A study of normal thyroid, untreated and treated toxic goiter. Acta endocrinol 53 (Suppl 110):5, 1966.

Ibrahim MS, Budd GC: An electron microscopic study of the site of iodine binding in the rat thyroid gland. Exper Cell Res 38:50, 1965.

Klinck GH, Oertel JE, Winship I: Ultrastructure of normal human thyroid. Lab Invest 22:2, 1970.

Pearse AGE: The cytochemistry of the thyroid C cells and their relationship to calcitonin. Proc Roy Soc London s.B 164:478, 1966.

Strum JM, Karnowsky MJ: Cytochemical localization of endogenous peroxidase in the thyroid follicular cells. J Cell Biol 44:655, 1970.

Wetzel BK, Spicer SS, Wollman SH: Changes in fine structure and acid phosphatase localization in rat thyroid cells following thyrotrophin administration. J Cell Biol 25:593, 1965.

Whur P, Herscovics A, Leblond CP: Radioautographic visualization of the incorporation of galactose-^{3}H and mannose-^{3}H by rat thyroid in vitro in relation to the stages of thyroglobulin synthesis. J Cell Biol 43:289, 1969.

Parathyroid Gland

Gaillard PJ, Talmage RV, Budy AM (editors): *The Parathyroid Glands.* Univ of Chicago Press, 1965.

Mecca CE, Martin GP, Goldhaber P: Alterations of bone metabolism in tissue culture in response to parathyroid extract. Proc Soc Exper Biol Med 113:538, 1963.

Tremblay G, Cartier GE: Histochemical study of oxidative enzymes in the human parathyroid. Endocrinology 60:658, 1961.

Pineal Body

Kappers JA, Schade JP: *Structure and Function of the Epiphysis Cerebri.* Elsevier, 1965.

Mamo H, Saimot G: Conceptions actuelles sur le rôle physiologique de l'épiphyse. Presse Med 75:1639, 1967.

Wurtman R, Axelrod J: The pineal gland. Sc Am 213:50, July 1965.

Wurtman R, Axelrod J, Kelly DE: *The Pineal.* Academic Press, 1968.

23...
The Male Reproductive System

The male reproductive system is composed of the testes, genital ducts, accessory glands, and penis. The *testis* is a compound tubular gland which has 2 functions— reproductive and hormonal. It is surrounded by a thick, resistant capsule of collagenous connective tissue, the *tunica albuginea*. The tunica albuginea has a thickening in its posterior region, the *mediastinum testis*, from which several fibrous septa project into the gland, dividing it into about 250 pyramidal compartments called the *testicular lobules* (Fig 23–1). These

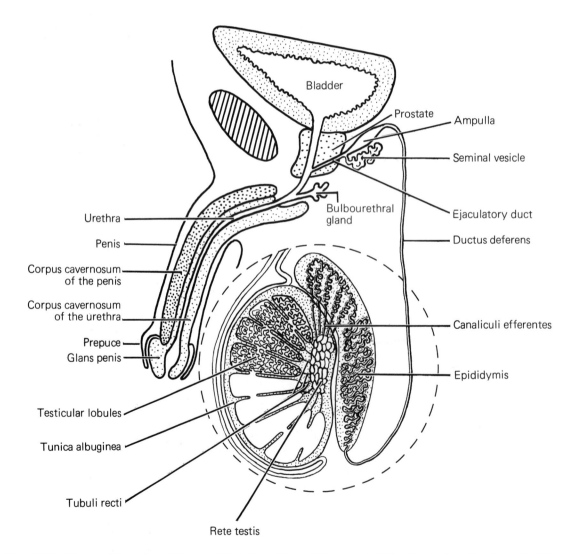

Figure 23–1. Diagram of the male genital system. The testis and the epididymis are in different scales from the other parts of the reproductive system. Observe the communication between the testicular lobules.

septa are not complete, and intercommunications frequently exist between the lobules. On the other hand, each lobule is occupied by 1–4 seminiferous tubules immersed in a web of loose connective tissue rich in vessels and nerves (Figs 23–1 and 23–2). The seminiferous tubules secrete at a low rate a fluid that flows continuously in the direction of the genital ducts. The testes develop in the dorsal wall of the peritoneal cavity and later are suspended in the scrotum outside the abdominal cavity at the ends of the spermatic cords, each carrying with it a serous sac derived from the peritoneum called the *tunica vaginalis*. This tunic consists of an outer parietal and an inner visceral layer, covering the tunica albuginea on the anterior and lateral sides of the testis. The scrotal sacs have an important role in maintaining the testicles at a temperature below intra-abdominal temperature.

Seminiferous Tubules

The seminiferous tubules are twisted tubules which end blindly and which are about 150–250 μm in diameter and 30–70 cm long. In the posterior region of the testicle, at the apex of each tubule, the seminiferous tubules open into the first part of a system of excretory ducts, the *tubuli recti,* which in turn anastomose in a network of tubules called the *rete testis.* About 8–15 *canaliculi efferentes* pass from this structure to the cephalic portion of the epididymis (Fig 23–1).

The seminiferous tubules consist of the following components (Fig 23–3): (1) a tunic of fibrous connective tissue; (2) a well-defined basal lamina; and (3) complex stratified epithelium.

In the fibrous tunic surrounding the seminiferous tubules, cells with characteristics of smooth muscle cells have been described. They are probably responsible for the contractile movements observed in isolated

seminiferous tubules. These myoid cells are bound together by membrane junctions that hinder but do not entirely prevent the passage of macromolecules from the interstitial space to the seminiferous tubules.

The epithelium consists of 2 types of cells: *Sertoli cells* and cells which constitute the *spermatogenic* or *seminal lineage.* The cells of spermatogenic lineage are stacked in 4–8 layers that occupy the space between the basal membrane and the lumen of the tubule. These cells reproduce several times and finally differentiate, producing spermatozoa. They represent various stages in the continuous process of differentiation of the male primitive germ cells. This phenomenon from start to finish is called *spermatogenesis.*

The process of spermatogenesis begins with a primitive germ cell, the *spermatogonium,* situated next to the basal lamina. It is a relatively small cell, and its nucleus contains irregular chromatin, forming rough clusters (Fig 23–3). At sexual maturity, this cell undergoes successive mitosis, and the newly formed cell can follow one of 2 paths: It can continue, after one or more mitotic divisions, in the same way as the mother cell (the spermatogonium), thus becoming a continuous source of spermatogonia; or it can divide and grow, thus becoming larger than the mother spermatogonium, in which case it is called spermatogonium B. The spermatogonia B give rise to the *primary spermatocytes.* Soon after their formation, they enter the prophase of the first step in maturation, meiotic division. At the beginning of the prophase of the first meiotic division, the primary spermatocyte has 23 pairs of homologous chromosomes, each with only one chromatid. In this prophase of the meiotic division, the cell passes through 4 stages—leptotene, zygotene, pachytene, and diplotene—and finally reaches the stage of dikinesis, resulting in the separation of the 2 chromosomes. It is during these stages of meiosis that cross-

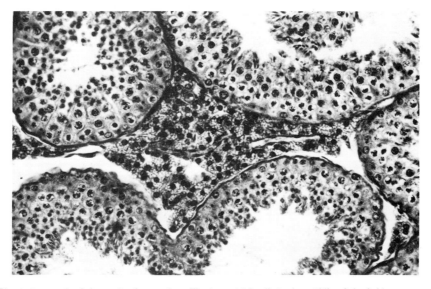

Figure 23–2. Photomicrograph of the testis of a monkey. The interstitial cells in the middle of the field present vacuoles resulting from the dissolution of lipid droplets during preparation. H&E stain, × 400.

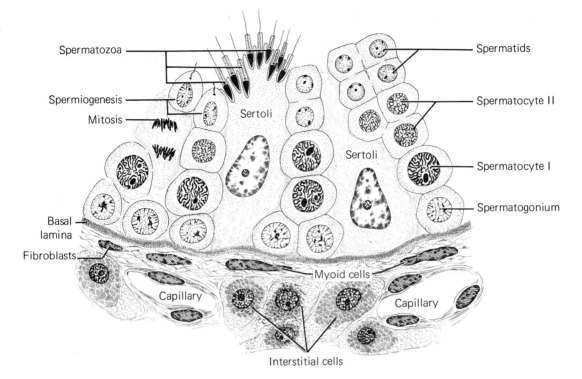

Figure 23—3. Diagram of the structure of a part of a seminiferous tubule and interstitial tissue.

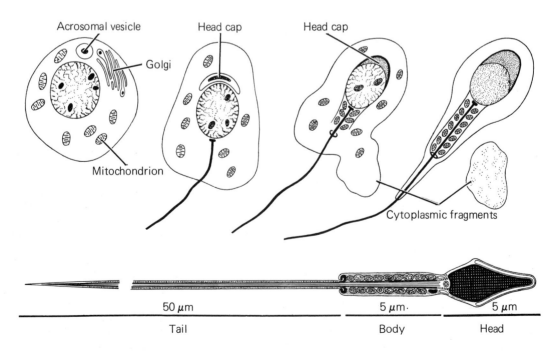

Figure 23—4. The principal changes occurring in spermatids during spermiogenesis.

ing over of genes of the chromosomes occurs. Thereafter, the cell enters the metaphase, and in the following anaphase one chromosome moves toward each pole. In the primary spermatocyte, the last duplication of DNA occurs in the S phase of the cell cycle. Since the prophase of this division takes a long time, the majority of cells seen in sections will be in this phase; consequently, their chromatin will be coiling to form the chromosomes. The primary spermatocytes are the largest cells of spermatogenic lineage and are characterized by the presence of chromosomes in different stages of the coiling process within their nuclei. From this first meiotic division there result smaller cells called *secondary spermatocytes* (Fig 23–3) which possess only 23 chromosomes, but this time with 2 chromatids each. This decrease in the number of chromosomes (from 23 pairs to 23 unpaired) is not followed by a reduction in the amount of DNA per cell because during the prophase the chromatids duplicate themselves without the duplication of the centromeres. Secondary spermatocytes are difficult to observe in sections of the testicle because they remain in interphase very briefly and enter quickly into the second meiotic division, thus being short-lived cells. From the division of the secondary spermatocytes result the so-called *spermatids,* cells which contain 23 chromosomes with one chromatid each. Therefore, the second meiotic division represents the division of the chromatids into the daughter cells. In this second division, the amount of DNA per cell is reduced by half, forming haploid cells.

The meiotic process thus results in the formation of cells with a haploid number of chromosomes. With fertilization, they return to the normal diploid number. It is the meiotic process which, because of the reductional process of cell division, guarantees a constant (fixed) number of chromosomes for the species.

The spermatids are the cells resulting from the division of the secondary spermatocytes. They can be distinguished by their small size, their nucleus with areas of condensed chromatin, and their location almost in the center of the seminiferous tubules (Figs 23–3 and 23–5). With the appearance of the spermatids, the phase of cell division known as spermatogenesis ends. Thereafter, the spermatids undergo a complex process of differentiation called *spermiogenesis* which results in the transformation of the spermatids into spermatozoa. Consequently, one can observe spermatids (Fig 23–5) with variable morphologic characteristics depending upon the phase of spermiogenesis in which they are observed. This process can be summarized in the following changes illustrated in Fig 23–4:

(1) In the Golgi apparatus, formation of proacrosomal granules rich in carbohydrates occurs first. These discrete granules coalesce into a single large granule, the acrosomal granule, contained within a membrane called the *acrosomal vesicle.* This vesicular structure, moving along with the Golgi complex in the direction of the nucleus, attaches itself to the outer part of the nuclear envelope. This is called the *Golgi phase.* The

limiting membrane of the acrosomal vesicle extends as a thick fold on the surface of the nuclear membrane. The head finally covers half or two-thirds of the nuclear membrane with a hood called the *head cap.* This is followed by a redistribution of the acrosomal substance within the head cap, thus constituting the *acrosomal cap* (or *acrosome*), rich in carbohydrates and having a different shape and size in different animal species. The spermatid elongates and passes through the final maturation phase of spermiogenesis until it assumes its final shape, ie, a dense homogeneous nuclear mass.

(2) Simultaneous changes occur in the centrioles which migrate to the opposite end of the spermatid; from one of the centrioles, which is perpendicular to the surface of the cell, a flagellum emerges which forms the tail of the spermatozoon (Fig 23–5). The other centriole migrates to form a collar around the initial part of its tail.

(3) At the same time, the cytoplasm moves in the direction of the flagellum and covers part of it. As the process evolves, parts of the cytoplasm not utilized in the formation of the spermatozoon are cast off from the cell and finally disintegrate in the form of *residual bodies.* A very thin layer of cytoplasm and the cellular membrane cover the whole site, reducing its volume considerably.

(4) Gradually and simultaneously, the mitochondria move toward the flagellum, arranging themselves as a spiral around the initial part of the tail, the so-called *body* of the spermatozoon. This disposition of the mitochondria is another example of a concentration of these organelles in sites related to cell movement and high energy consumption. The flagellum of the spermatozoon has a motor function, and the mitochondria are related to the production of energy for this movement. Carbohydrates produced by the associated glands of the male seminal system and secreted in the seminal fluid are the source of energy used. Among these carbohydrates, the most abundant is the monosaccharide fructose.

(5) The nucleus flattens and assumes the shape of an almond.

As a result of the process described above, the mature spermatozoa have the structure explained and illustrated in Fig 23–4.

Using histochemical technics, it has been shown that the acrosome possesses both protease and hyaluronidase activities. These enzymes are probably of importance in the fertilization process, for the ovum is surrounded by a glycoprotein layer containing hyaluronic acid.

The spermatocytes and the subsequent cells of spermatogenic lineage resulting from the division of the spermatogonia do not separate completely but remain held together by cytoplasmic bridges. This concept is illustrated in the upper right portion of Fig 23–3. These intercellular bridges between each cell type form a communication between the primary and secondary spermatocytes and spermatids and are probably of importance in the coordination of sperma-

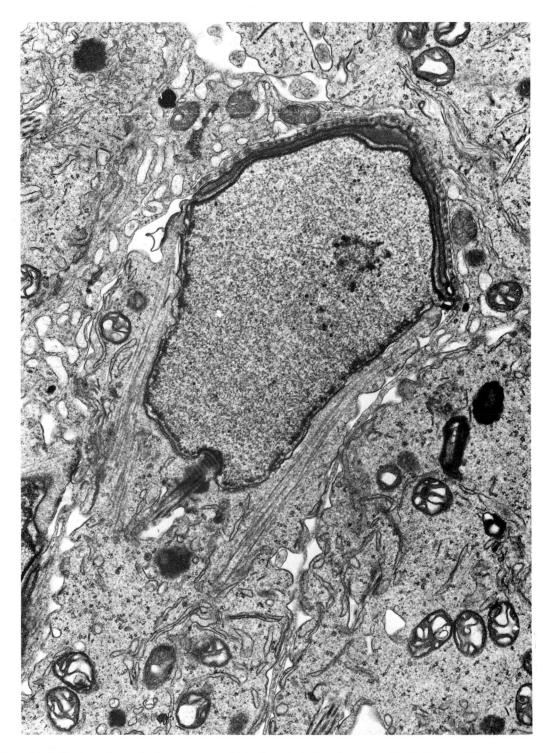

Figure 23–5. Electron micrograph of a mouse spermatid. In the center is its nucleus, covered by the head cap. The flagellum can be seen emerging in the lower region below the nucleus. Bundles of microtubules limit the cell laterally. Reduced from × 32,500. (Courtesy of KR Porter.)

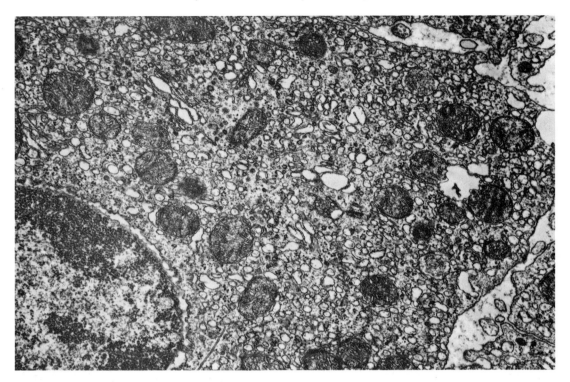

Figure 23–6. Electron micrograph of a section of an interstitial cell from the testis of a rat. There are abundant mitochondria and smooth endoplasmic reticulum. × 12,000.

togenesis, permitting the interchange of information from cell to cell. Later, when the process of spermatogenesis has been completed, these bridges disappear and the cells are separated.

Experimental injection of tritiated thymidine into the testicles of volunteers shows that in humans the processes that occur between the stage of spermatogonia and the formation of the spermatozoa take about 64 days.

Besides being a slow process, spermatogenesis is known to occur neither simultaneously nor synchronously in all of the seminiferous tubules. The process occurs in wavelike fashion, which explains the irregular appearance of the tubules, where each region is in a different phase of spermatogenesis. This is why spermatozoa are encountered in some regions of the seminiferous tubules and only spermatids in others. The *cycle of the seminiferous epithelium* is the series of maturation changes occurring in sequence in a given area of the germinal epithelium between 2 successive appearances of the same cells along the same area of the same tubule. Each cycle in the human lasts 16 ± 1 days and spermatogenesis ends 4 cycles or about 64 ± 4.5 days later.

The *nutrient* or *Sertoli cells* are elongated pyramidal cells between the seminal cells with their bases resting on the basal lamina of the seminiferous tubule. In the optical microscope, the cytoplasm is clear, poorly defined, barely visible, and quite irregular in shape (Fig 23–3). The nucleus is elongated and often triangular, with little visible chromatin and a well-defined nucleolus.

The Sertoli cells are wedged in between those of spermatogenic lineage, which probably accounts for their irregular shape. In the apical portion of these cells, groups of heads of spermatozoa can be seen nesting in a series of infoldings of its membrane (Fig 23–7). Thus, a Sertoli cell is often found with a tuft of spermatozoa which remain there until they are detached (Fig 23–8). Although no direct evidence has been presented, this intimate relation suggests a role of these cells in the support and nutrition of the spermatozoa. Electron microscopic studies suggest that transference of material from the Sertoli cell to the spermatids might occur.

The Sertoli cell in man and other species does not normally divide during the reproductive period. It is extremely resistant to adverse conditions in the testicle such as infection, malnutrition, or x-ray radiation and survives these much better than the cells of spermatogenic lineage. Indirect evidence suggests that this cell might normally produce small quantities of steroid hormones (estrogens).

The phagocytic activity of the Sertoli cells is well established. They digest the cytoplasmic fragments that detach from the spermatids during spermatogenesis. This activity explains the abundance of lysosomes observed in these cells. Careful analysis of these cells under the electron microscope reveals that their lateral walls are united by tight junctions, impermeable to

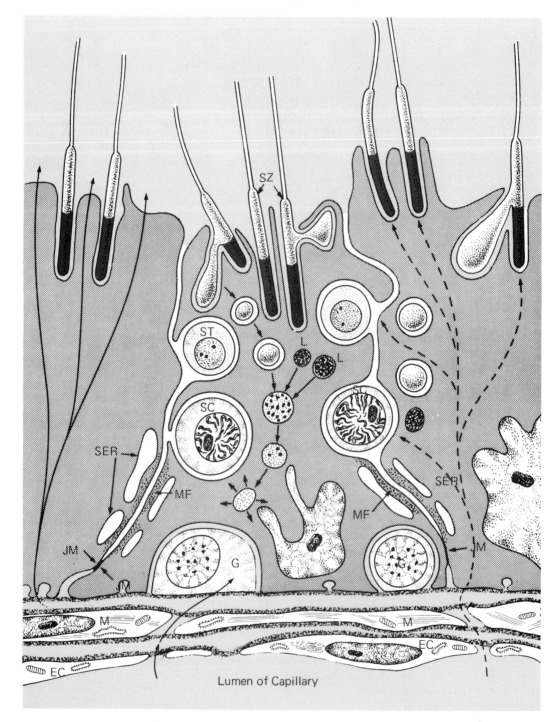

Figure 23–7. The position and functions of the Sertoli cells. These cells are bounded by their lateral walls and divide the seminiferous tubules into 3 compartments. The lower dark part is extratubular and comprises the lumen of the blood vessels, the interstitial space, and the regions occupied by the spermatogonia (G). The central part comprises the intracellular space of the Sertoli cells. The third (upper) part represents the lumen of the seminiferous tubules. The arrows pointing to the tight junctional membrane (JM) show the zones where the membranes converge and impede the passage of substances from the first to the third compartment. Above these zones appear specialized regions characterized by the presence of circularly disposed microfilaments (MF) and of cisternae of the smooth endoplasmic reticulum (SER). The 3 main functions of the Sertoli cells are also portrayed. In the cell at left, the arrows indicate secretions to the testicular fluid. In the middle cell, cytoplasmic fragments from the forming spermatids are captured and digested by lysosomes (L). In the cell at right, the dotted arrows indicate the transport of metabolites from the extracellular space to the spermatocytes (SC), the spermatids (ST), and the spermatozoa (SZ). Note also the myoid cells (M) and the endothelial cell (EC).

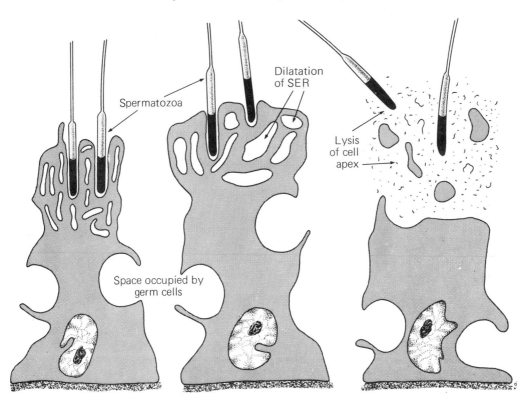

Figure 23—8. Diagram illustrating the process of liberation of spermatozoa. At left is a Sertoli cell containing mature spermatozoa. After the injection of luteinizing hormone in amphibians, the smooth endoplasmic reticulum (SER) swells (center cell) and promotes the lysis of the cell apex with liberation of the spermatozoa (right). (Redrawn and reproduced, with permission, from Vitale-Calpe R, Burgos MH: J Ultrastruc Res 31:394, 1970.)

colloidal lanthanum nitrate, forming a continuous barrier that prevents the passage of macromolecules from the interstitial space to the interior of the seminiferous tubules. It has been suggested that these junctions probably permit the passage of electrical stimuli between the Sertoli cells (Fig 23—7).

The gonadotropic hormone produced in the human placenta and eliminated in the urine of pregnant women, when injected into male frogs, stimulates the vacuolization of the apical cytoplasm of the Sertoli cells and thus liberates the spermatozoa held there. This action explains why frog spermatozoa are eliminated after the injection of urine from pregnant females—a phenomenon on which the Galli-Mainini test for the diagnosis of pregnancy was based.

Interstitial Tissue

The spaces between the seminiferous tubules in the testicle are filled with accumulations of connective tissue, nerves, blood vessels, and lymphatic vessels. The testicular capillaries are of the fenestrated type and permit the free passage of macromolecules such as the blood proteins. An extensive network of lymphatic vessels is present in the interstitial space, and this explains the similarity of composition between the interstitial fluid and lymph collected from this organ. The connective tissue consists of various cell types, includ-

ing fibroblasts, undifferentiated connective cells, mastocytes, and macrophages. In the testicle after puberty, additional cell types appear. These cells are either rounded or polygonal in shape, with a central nucleus and an eosinophilic cytoplasm rich in small lipid droplets (Figs 23—3 and 23—6). These are the *interstitial* or *Leydig cells* of the testicle which have the characteristics of steroid secretory cells described in Chapter 4. There is clear evidence that these are the cells that produce the male hormone *testosterone,* responsible for the development of the secondary male sex characteristics. Thus, a direct correlation is observed between the presence of interstitial cells and the production of androgen by the testicle. The presence in the interstitial cells of enzymes necessary for the synthesis of testosterone has already been demonstrated using histochemical methods. Among these enzymes can be named, for example, 17β-hydroxysteroid dehydrogenase, which participates in the transformation of androstenedione into testosterone. 17a-Hydroxylase is present, but 11- and 21-hydroxylase, found in the adrenal cortex, are absent. Pregnenolone is therefore hydroxylated in the 17 position, then subjected to side chain cleavage to form 17-ketosteroids. These in turn are converted to testosterone. It is also known that interstitial cell tumors can cause precocious puberty in the male.

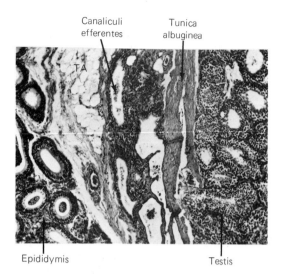

Canaliculi efferentes   Tunica albuginea

Epididymis   Testis

Figure 23–9. Photomicrograph of a section of testis and epididymis showing the canaliculi efferentes and the thick tunica albuginea (TA). H&E stain, × 80.

Small amounts of estrogen are synthesized in the testes, although it is not clear whether they are products of the Leydig cells, the Sertoli cells, or both.

The activity and the quantity of the interstitial cells depend on hormonal stimuli. Thus, during human pregnancy, placental gonadotropic hormone passes from the maternal blood to the fetus, stimulating the interstitial cells, which are abundant in the fetal testicle and which produce androgenic hormone. This hormone is important for the embryologic differentiation of the male genitalia. After birth, this stimulus disappears, returning during puberty under the stimulus of luteinizing hormone (LH) from the pituitary gland. This is the main factor that controls androgen secretion. The mechanism by which luteinizing hormone stimulates Leydig cells appears to involve increased formation of cyclic AMP and increased protein synthesis.

Intratesticular Genital Ducts

These are the *tubuli recti, the rete testis,* and the *canaliculi efferentes* (Fig 23–1). The transition from seminiferous tubules to *tubuli recti* is abrupt. The spermatogenic cells disappear, and only the Sertoli cells remain, with the appearance of a columnar epithelium supported on a dense connective tissue sheath.

Next follows the *rete testis,* which is contained within a thickening of the tunica albuginea. It is covered by cuboid or columnar epithelium (Fig 23–1).

From the rete testis extend 8–15 *canaliculi efferentes* (Fig 23–9). They have an epithelium composed of alternating groups of cuboid and columnar cells, which are often ciliated. The rapid movement of the cilia impels the spermatozoa toward the epididymis. These ducts penetrate the cranial region of the epididymis, where, after a sinuous stretch, they empty into a duct called the duct of the epididymis.

Histophysiology of the Testis

Temperature is very important in the regulation of spermatogenesis, and this process generally occurs only in temperatures below that of the human body. This is why, with rare exceptions, the testicles of mammals are located outside the abdominal cavity and in the scrotal sacs, where the temperature is lower.

Testicular temperature is controlled by several mechanisms. A rich vascular plexus in the spermatic cord forms a system of countercurrent heat exchange important in maintaining a low testicular temperature. Other factors are the evaporation of sweat from the scrotum and contraction of the muscles of the spermatic cord that pulls the testicles into the inguinal canal, raising its temperature.

Failure of descent of the testicles *(cryptorchism)* holds the testicles at a temperature of 37 °C, which inhibits spermatogenesis. In cases that are not too far advanced, spermatogenesis can occur normally if the testicle is moved surgically to the scrotum.

Malnutrition, alcoholism, and the action of certain drugs hinder spermatogenesis and lead to alterations in the cells of spermatogenic origin, with consequent decreased production of spermatozoa. Lack of vitamin E can produce—especially in the rat—total and

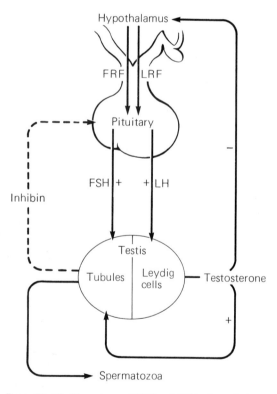

Figure 23–10. The release of FSH and LH in the male is controlled by the releasing factors of the hypothalamus (FRF, LRF) and by testosterone (LH). An ill-defined substance known as inhibin probably plays a role in the feedback of FSH and LH secretion from the pituitary gland. Small amounts of estrogens present in the circulation might also play a role in the regulation of LH secretion (inhibition) and of FSH secretion.

irreversible destruction of spermatogenic cells, including the spermatogonia, thus resulting in permanent sterility. This has not been observed in man. X-ray radiation causes destruction of spermatogonia with irreversible sterility. Cadmium salts are quite toxic to the cells of spermatogenic lineage, causing death of those cells and sterility in animals. The drug busulfan acts on the germinal cells, and when administered to pregnant female rats it promotes the death of the germinal cells of their offspring. These animals are therefore sterile, and their seminiferous tubules contain exclusively Sertoli cells.

Without doubt, however, endocrine factors have by far the most important effect on spermatogenesis. Spermatogenesis depends on the stimulus of follicle-stimulating hormone (FSH) of the pituitary and of androgenic hormones. Spermatogenesis is inhibited by estrogens and progestogens. The mechanisms of endocrine control are shown in Fig 23–10.

Blood–Seminiferous Tubule Barrier

The observation that few substances present in blood appear in the testicular fluid suggests the existence of a barrier between the blood and the interior of the seminiferous tubules. The testicular capillaries are of the fenestrated type and permit free passage of large molecules. The myoid cell layer, which sometimes contains spaces between the cells 20 nm in width, and the Sertoli cells are responsible for this barrier, which is probably of importance in protecting the seminal cells against noxious agents.

Excretory Genital Ducts

The ducts that transport the spermatozoa produced in the testis toward the surface of the body are the epididymis, the ducts deferens (vas deferens), and the urethra.

The *epididymis* consists of one long, highly tortuous tube about 4–6 meters in length. This long canal forms, with surrounding connective tissue, the body and tail of the epididymis. It is lined by pseudostratified columnar epithelium composed of rounded basal and columnar cells. These cells are supported on a basement membrane surrounded by smooth muscle fibers which probably help to move the sperms along the duct and by loose connective tissue rich in blood capillaries (Fig 23–11).

The surface of the columnar cells is covered with cytoplasmic projections forming long and irregular nonmotile microvilli, improperly called *stereocilia*. Stereocilia have neither basal bodies nor internal filaments, whereas true cilia have both. When observed with an electron microscope, the cytoplasm of these cells is seen to be filled with granules of unknown nature. A morphologic appearance similar to that of pinocytosis and digestion of the engulfed material with the presence of polymorphous vesicles, lysosomes, etc is very frequent in these cells. This aspect suggests that we are dealing with cells that have more than one function, including, probably, intracellular digestion and secretion into the lumen. Very little is really known about their function, but it is probably a major one, for it is in the interior of the epididymis that the spermatozoa from the seminiferous tubules become motile and fertile. This epithelium also participates in the reabsorption and digestion of the cytoplasmic fragments which are eliminated during spermatogenesis. Data have been presented to suggest that approximately 99% of the fluid leaving the testis is reabsorbed in the epididymis. It also has a capacity for engulfing colloidal particles

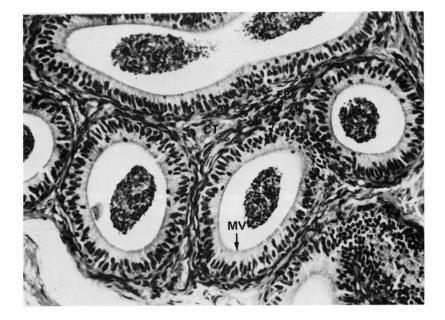

Figure 23–11. Photomicrograph of a section of epididymis showing its structure. Note the epithelium (EP), the connective tissue (CT), and the microvilli (MV) (stereocilia). H&E stain, × 200.

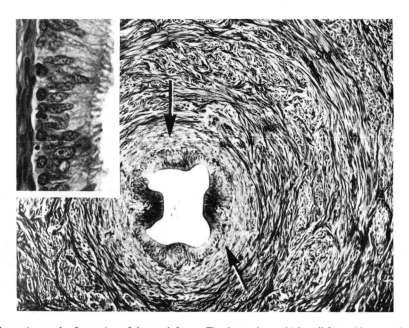

Figure 23–12. Photomicrograph of a section of ductus deferens. The ductus has a thick wall formed by smooth muscle cells (SM). The arrows point to the thin tunica propria layer. × 16. Observe in the inset the details of the pseudostratified columnar epithelium showing stereocilia. Masson's trichrome stain, × 400.

injected into the testis.

From the epididymis, a straight tube with thick walls continues toward the prostatic urethra and empties into it; this is the *ductus (vas) deferens*. It is characterized by a narrow lumen and a thick wall of smooth muscle (Fig 23–12). Its mucosa forms longitudinal folds and is covered along most of its extent by pseudostratified columnar epithelium with stereocilia. Its lamina propria is a layer of connective tissue rich in elastic fibers. The thick muscular layer consists of layers of spirally oriented smooth muscle cells. Along the ductus deferens and linked to it run the vessels and nerves which go to and come from the testicle. Before it penetrates the prostate, the ductus deferens dilates, forming a region called the *ampulla*. In this area the epithelium becomes thicker, assuming a lacelike aspect. At the final portion of the ampulla, the seminal vesicles join. From there on, the ductus deferens enters the prostate, opening into the prostatic urethra. The segment that runs in the prostate is called the *ejaculatory duct* and presents a mucous layer similar to that of the ampulla but without the muscle layer.

Accessory Male Genital Glands

These are the seminal vesicles, the prostate gland, and the bulbourethral glands.

The *seminal vesicles* consist of 2 highly tortuous tubes 15 cm in length. On sectioning the organ, the same tube can be observed sectioned in different positions. It has folded mucosa, with pseudostratified columnar epithelium which shows great individual variations depending on age and other conditions; it consists of a discontinuous layer of spherical basal cells and a layer of longer superficial cuboid or low columnar

cells, rich in secretory granules. They present an ultrastructure characteristic of protein-secreting cells (see Chapter 5). The lamina propria of the seminal vesicles is rich in elastic fibers and surrounded by a thin layer of smooth muscle (Fig 23–13). The muscular wall of the seminal vesicles contains a plexus of nerve fibers and small sympathetic ganglia. The secretion of the seminal vesicles, which accumulates in the interior of this gland, is eliminated during ejaculation by the contraction of its smooth muscle. It contains globulin and is rich in vitamin C and fructose, metabolites that are of importance in the nutrition and motility of the spermatozoa. The height of the epithelial cells of the seminal vesicles and the degree of activity of the secretory processes are testosterone-dependent. In the absence of testosterone, the epithelium of the seminal vesicles atrophies. This atrophy can be reversed by the administration of testosterone. The function of the smooth muscle of the epididymis and of the glands of the male genital system is also affected by the sex hormones.

The *prostate* is a collection of 30–50 branched tubulo-alveolar glands whose ducts empty into the prostatic urethra. The prostate not only produces prostatic fluid but also stores it in its interior for expulsion during ejaculation.

The prostate is surrounded by a fibroelastic capsule rich in smooth muscle. This capsule emits septa which penetrate the gland. Thus, an exceptionally rich fibromuscular stroma is formed which surrounds the glands (Fig 23–14). The basement membrane is indistinct, and the epithelial cells rest upon a layer of connective tissue with much smooth muscle and a dense elastic fiber network and blood capillaries. Its epithelium may be cuboid or even squamous but in most

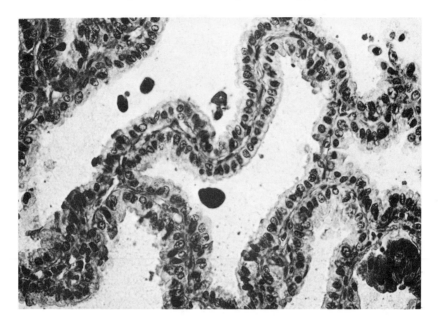

Figure 23–13. Photomicrograph of a section of human seminal vesicle. Masson's trichrome stain, × 300.

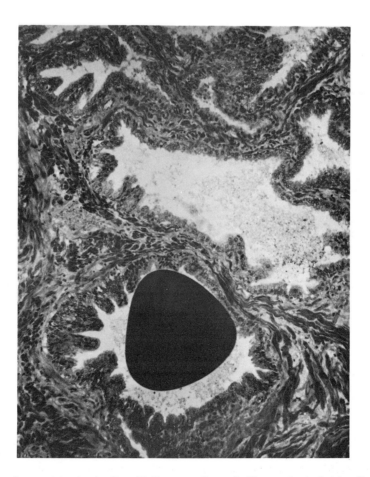

Figure 23–14. Section of a prostate, showing its epithelium, smooth muscle fibers, and a typical lamellar prostatic concretion (corpus amylaceum). H&E stain, × 300.

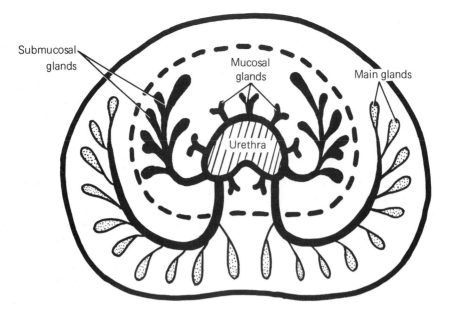

Figure 23–15. Diagram illustrating the position of the prostatic glands.

places is columnar, with a few basal cells, and its cells secrete proteins and therefore have the characteristics described for this type of cell in Chapter 4. These cells are rich in lysosomes and have intense acid phosphatase activity. This peculiarity is preserved in carcinoma of the prostate, which is characterized by the presence of this enzyme in high concentrations in the blood.

Serum acid phosphatase is measured not only in the diagnosis but also in the follow-up of patients with this tumor.

The prostatic gland is divided into 3 types of structures—mucosal, submucosal, and main glands—arranged in 3 separate areas situated concentrically around the urethra as shown in Fig 23–15. The main

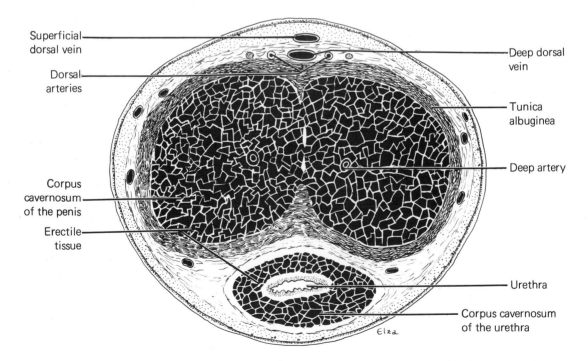

Figure 23–16. Drawing of a transverse section of the penis. (Redrawn and reproduced, with permission, from **Leeson TS**, **Leeson CR**: *Histology*, 2nd ed. Saunders, 1970.)

glands contribute most to the volume of the prostatic secretion.

For unknown reasons—often after age 40—the mucosal and submucosal glands begin to hypertrophy. This can lead to partial or total obstruction of the urethra. Carcinoma of the prostate, a frequent tumor in old men, usually starts in the main glands.

The secretory process of the prostate depends, as in the seminal vesicles, on testosterone.

Small spherical bodies of glycoprotein composition less than 0.2 mm in diameter are frequently observed in the lumen of the prostate. They are called *prostatic concretions* (Fig 23—14). These bodies often form calculi. Their significance is not understood, but their number increases with age.

The *bulbourethral glands* are pea-sized formations located behind the membranous portion of the urethra and emptying into it. They are tubulo-alveolar glands with a mucous type of epithelium. They have skeletal and smooth muscle cells in their septa which separate their lobes. Their secretion has a mucoid appearance.

PENIS

The penis consists mainly of 3 cylindric masses of erectile tissue plus the urethra, surrounded externally by skin. Two of these cylinders—the *corpora cavernosa of the penis*—are placed dorsally. The other, ventrally located, is called the *corpus cavernosum of the urethra* and surrounds the urethra. At its end it dilates, forming the *glans penis* (Fig 23—1). The corpora cavernosa are covered by a resistant membrane of hard connective tissue, the *tunica albuginea.* Orifices are often present in the area which separates the 2 corpora cavernosa of the penis, permitting communications between these 2 bodies (Fig 23—16). The corpora cavernosa of the penis and urethra are composed of a tangle of dilated blood vessels lined by endothelium.

The prepuce is a retractile fold of skin. It contains connective tissue with smooth muscle in its interior. Sebaceous glands are present in the internal fold and in the skin which covers the glans.

●　　●　　●

References

Albert A: The mammalian testis. In: *Sex and Internal Secretion,* 3rd ed. Vol 1. Young WC (editor). Williams & Wilkins, 1961.

Brökelmann J: Fine structure of germ cells and Sertoli cells during the cycle of the seminiferous epithelium in the rat. Z Zellforsch Mikrosk Anat 59:820, 1963.

Burgos MH, Vitale-Calpe R: The mechanism of spermiation in the toad. Am J Anat 120:227, 1967.

Cameron E: The effects of intratesticular injections of cadmium chloride in the rabbit. J Anat 99:907, 1965.

Christensen AK, Fawcett DW: The fine structure of the interstitial cells of the mouse testis. Am J Anat 118:551, 1966.

Clermont Y: Renewal of spermatogonia in man. Am J Anat 118:509, 1966.

Clermont Y, Leblond CP: Spermiogenesis of man, monkey, ram and other mammals as shown by the "periodic acid-Schiff" technique. Am J Anat 96:229, 1955.

Cowdry EV (editor): *Special Cytology,* 2nd ed. Hoeber, 1932.

De Kretser DM: Changes in the fine structure of the human testicular interstitial cells after treatment with human gonadotrophins. Z Zellforsch Mikrosk Anat 83:344, 1967.

De Kretser DM: Ultrastructure features of human spermiogenesis. Z Zellforsch Mikrosk Anat 98:477, 1969.

Dym M, Fawcett DW: The blood-testis barrier in the rat and physiological compartment of the seminiferous epithelium. Biol Reprod 3:308, 1970.

Fawcett DW: A comparative view of sperm ultrastructure. Biol Reprod 2 (Suppl):90, 1970.

Friend DS, Farquhar MG: Functions of coated vesicles during protein absorption in the rat vas deferens. J Cell Biol 35:357, 1967.

Hansworth BN, Jackson H: Effect of busufan on the developing gonad of the male rat. J Reprod Fertil 5:187, 1963.

Hartree EF, Srivastava PN: Chemical composition of the acrosomes of ram spermatozoa. J Reprod Fertil 9:47, 1965.

Johnson AD, Gomes WR, Van Demark NL (editors): *The Testis.* 3 vols. Academic Press, 1970.

Leeson TS, Leeson CR: The fine structure of cavernous tissue in the adult rat penis. Invest Urol 3:144, 1965.

Macklin CC, Macklin MT: The seminal vesicles, prostate and bulbourethral glands. In: *Special Cytology,* 2nd ed. Vol 3. Cowdry EV (editor). Hoeber, 1932.

Metz CW: The male germ cells. In: *Special Cytology,* 2nd ed. Vol 3. Cowdry EV (editor). Hoeber, 1932.

Murota S, Shikita M, Tamaoki B: Intracellular distribution of the enzymes related to androgen formation in mouse testes. Steroids 5:409, 1965.

Rasmussen AT: Interstitial cells of the testis. In: *Special Cytology,* 2nd ed. Vol 3. Cowdry EV (editor). Hoeber, 1932.

Ross MH: The fine structure and development of the peritubular contractile cell component in the seminiferous tubules of the mouse. Am J Anat 121:523, 1967.

Ross MH, Long JR: Contractile cells in human seminiferous tubules. Science 153:1271, 1966.

Stambough R, Buckley J: Identification and subcellular localization of the enzymes affecting penetration of the zona pellucida of rabbit spermatozoa. J Reprod Fertil 19:423, 1969.

24 . . .
The Female Reproductive System

The female reproductive system consists of 2 ovaries, 2 oviducts or Fallopian tubes, the uterus, the vagina, and the external genitalia. Between menarche and menopause, the system undergoes cyclic changes in structure and functional activity. These modifications are controlled by neurohumoral mechanisms. In this chapter we shall also study the mammary glands, though they do not belong to the genital system—being, in fact, cutaneous glands—for the reason that they undergo changes directly connected with the functional state of the reproductive system.

THE OVARY

The ovary is an almond-shaped body up to 5 cm in diameter, 1.5–3 cm in width, and 0.6–1.5 cm in thickness. It consists of a *medullary region,* containing several blood vessels and a normal amount of loose connective tissue; and a *cortical region,* where ovarian follicles, containing the oocytes, predominate. There are no sharp limits between the cortical and the medullary regions (Fig 24–1). During embryonic life, female germ cells migrate into the ovary and there are called *oogonia.* At birth, only 2 million of them are present, and this number is reduced even further in early postnatal life.

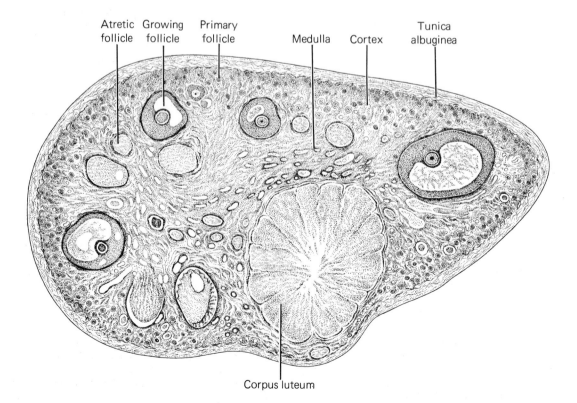

Atretic follicle Growing follicle Primary follicle Medulla Cortex Tunica albuginea

Corpus luteum

Figure 24–1. Schematic drawing showing the main components of the ovary of an adult woman. (Redrawn and reproduced, with permission, from Copenhaver WM, Bunge RP, Bunge MTS: *Bailey's Textbook of Histology,* 16th ed. Williams & Wilkins, 1972.)

The stroma of the cortical region is composed of characteristic spindle-shaped connective cells which respond in a different way to hormonal stimuli than connective cells of other organs. The surface of the ovary is lined by continuous simple squamous or cuboid epithelium called *germinal epithelium*. Under the germinal epithelium, the stroma forms a layer of thick, poorly delineated connective tissue called the *tunica albuginea* of the ovary. The tunica albuginea is responsible for the whitish color of the ovary (Fig 24—1).

Ovarian Follicles

The ovarian follicles are embedded in the stroma of the cortex. Three types can be distinguished: *primordial follicles, growing follicles,* and *mature* or *Graafian follicles.* The total number of follicles in the 2 ovaries of a normal young adult woman is estimated to be 400,000, but most of them will disappear by a degenerative process during the reproductive years. This follicular regression takes place over the entire span of reproductive life, ending after menopause, when follicles become difficult to observe. The regression may affect any type of follicle from primordial ones to those that are completely mature. Since, in general, only one oocyte is liberated by the ovaries in each menstrual cycle (average duration: 28 days) and the reproductive life of a woman lasts about 30—40 years, the total number of oocytes liberated is about 450. All of the other follicles, with their oocytes, degenerate, becoming atretic or failing to develop.

A. Primordial Follicles: The primordial follicles are the only ones present before puberty. Each consists of a primary oocyte enveloped by only one layer of flattened cells called *follicular* or *granulosa cells* (Fig 24—2).

The oocyte in the primordial follicles is a large cell measuring about 40 µm in diameter. Its nucleus is large, slightly eccentrically situated, and has finely dispersed chromatin and a large nucleolus. The electron microscope shows, in the cytoplasm of the oocytes—besides the usual elements—formations consisting of parallel lamellas and a great number of small vesicles. These 2 elements are more abundant in the oocytes of the growing and mature follicles. As soon as the oogonia are changed into primary oocytes, they enter the prophase of their first meiotic division and rest there.

B. Growing Follicles: As a practical matter, these follicles only exist between menarche and menopause. In each menstrual cycle, several follicles start to grow, but only one reaches maturity while the others degenerate.

1. Primary follicles—Follicular growth comprises mainly the follicular cells but also the oocyte and the stroma surrounding the follicle (Figs 24—1, 24—2, and 24—3). The morphology and size of the growing follicles both vary greatly since these follicles range in age from those that are only starting to grow to very large ones which have almost reached maturity. As the oocyte grows, the single layer of follicular cells becomes cuboid and then, through mitotic division, is trans-

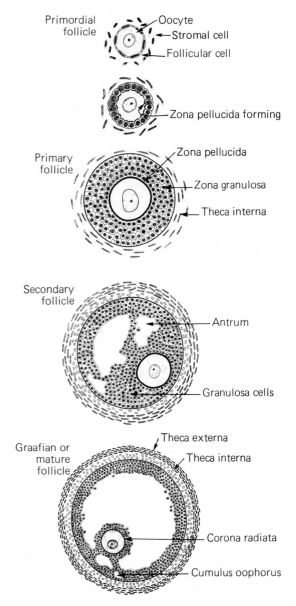

Figure 24—2. Schematic drawing of ovarian follicles, starting with the primordial follicle and ending with mature follicles.

formed into granulosa cells that form a stratified epithelium (Fig 24—4). The oocyte also becomes larger, and an acidophilic, homogeneous, and acellular layer called the *zona pellucida* appears around it (Figs 24—2 and 24—4). The zona pellucida becomes visible with the light microscope when the oocyte reaches 80 µm in diameter. With the electron microscope, its presence can be detected earlier. The zona pellucida contains glycoproteins and is PAS-positive. In its interior one can see—with the electron microscope—prolongations of the follicular cells and microvilli of the oocyte (Fig 24—4).

While these modifications are taking place, the stroma immediately around the follicle modifies itself

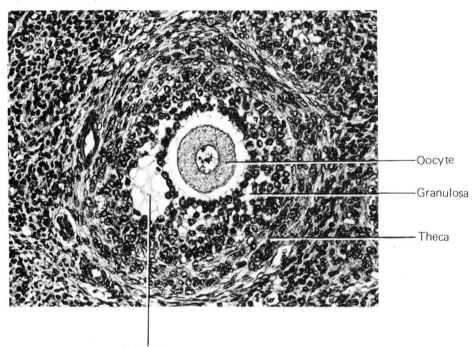

Oocyte

Granulosa

Theca

Follicle fluid

Figure 24—3. Growing ovarian follicle. In the center of the follicle is an oocyte with a lightly staining nucleus. The limits between the 2 theca layers are not clear.

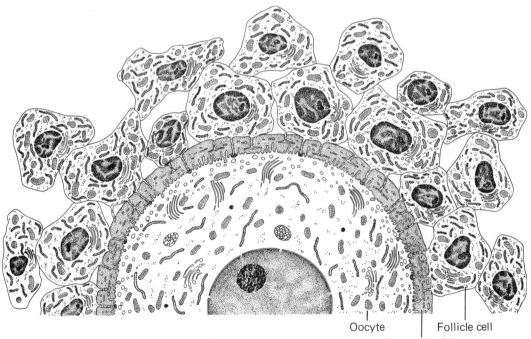

Oocyte   Follicle cell

Zona pellucida

Figure 24—4. Ultrastructure of the oocyte, zona pellucida, and follicular cells. The zona pellucida is composed of amorphous material, penetrated by oocyte microvilli and by longer processes from follicular cells. In the oocyte cytoplasm there are several arrays of parallel smooth membranes. The nucleus is the prophase of the first meiotic division.

in order to form the *theca folliculi*. This layer subsequently differentiates into the theca interna and the theca externa (Fig 24–2). The cells of the theca interna are elongated and, when completely differentiated, present the same ultrastructural characteristics of the cells that produce steroids. These cells synthesize estrogens. Like all organs of endocrine function, the theca interna is richly vascularized. The theca externa consists mainly of connective tissue. Small vessels penetrate it and supply a rich capillary plexus in the secretory cells of the theca interna. In the granulosa cell layer there are no blood vessels during the stage of follicular growth. The boundary between the 2 thecas is not clear, and the same is true of the boundary between the theca externa and the ovarian stroma. The boundary between the theca interna and the granulosa layer is well defined since their cells are morphologically different and there is a basement membrane between them. As the oocyte grows, changes occur in the distribution of its organelles. The single Golgi apparatus gives rise to multiple Golgi apparatuses dispersed in the ooplasm. The granular endoplasmic reticulum becomes more extensive, and more free ribosomes are found in the ooplasm. The number of small vesicles and multivesicular bodies also increases.

2. Secondary follicles—As the follicle grows—mainly because of the increase in number and in size of the follicular cells—some accumulations of fluid appear *(follicular liquid)*. The cavities that contain liquid converge and finally form only one cavity, the *follicular antrum* (Figs 24–2 and 24–3). The cells of the granulosa layer are more numerous at a certain point on the follicular wall, forming a thickening, the *cumulus oophorus,* which contains the oocyte. The cumulus oophorus protrudes toward the interior of the antrum (Fig 24–3). The origin of the zona pellucida is not absolutely clear; it may be formed by the oocyte, by the follicular cells, or—the most widely held current opinion—by both. The oocyte grows no more thereafter.

C. Mature Follicles: The mature follicle is about 1 cm in diameter and can be seen as a transparent vesicle which protrudes onto the surface of the ovary. As a result of the accumulation of liquid, the follicular cavity increases greatly and the oocyte adheres to the wall of the follicle through a pedicle formed by follicular cells. Since the follicular cells do not multiply in proportion to the accumulation of liquid, the granulosa layer becomes thinner.

The follicular cells of the first layer around the oocyte—and, therefore, in close contact with the zona pellucida—become elongated and form the *corona radiata,* which accompanies the oocyte when it leaves the ovary. The corona radiata is still present when the spermatozoon fertilizes the oocyte (in the oviduct) and remains for some time during the passage of the ovum through the tube.

Ovulation

Ovulation is a process that consists of rupture of the mature follicle with liberation of the oocyte which will be caught by the dilated end of the oviduct. In the human female, only one oocyte is usually liberated by the ovary at a time, but 2 or more oocytes can be expelled at the same time. In the latter case, if 2 or more of the liberated oocytes are fertilized, there will be more than one fetus (multiple pregnancy).

Ovulation takes place approximately in the middle of the menstrual cycle, ie, around the 14th day of a 28-day cycle. Under the pressure of the mature follicle, the superficial part of the ovary undergoes ischemia before ovulation, which contributes to weakening of the tissues and facilitates the exit of the oocyte.

It has been demonstrated with the electron microscope that there are smooth muscle fibers in the follicular walls of several species of mammals. It is possible that contraction of these cells participates in the process of ovulation. A number of hypotheses with supporting data have been advanced to account for ovulation. These include the above-mentioned intrafollicular increase in oncotic pressure, the enzymatic dissolution of the basal membrane, and mechanical rupture. In any event, a midcycle surge of luteinizing hormone appears to be indispensable to the occurrence of rupture.

Before ovulation, the oocyte—together with the cells of the corona radiata—detaches itself from the wall of the follicle and floats in the follicular liquid. The indication of ovulation is the appearance on the surface of the follicle of the macula pellucida or stigma, in which the flow of blood ceases, resulting in a local change in color and translucency of the follicular wall. The germinal epithelium in this area becomes discontinuous, and the stroma becomes thinner. The cone then ruptures and the oocyte is thrown out of the ovary together with the follicular liquid and blood.

The extremity of the oviduct which faces the ovary is fringed and funnel-shaped. At the moment of ovulation, this end is very close to the surface of the ovary and receives the oocyte. If the oocyte is fertilized it becomes an *ovum* and then passes through the interior of the tube toward the uterus. If it is not fertilized, it disintegrates after the first 24 hours.

Follicular Atresia

Most ovarian follicles undergo an involutional process called follicular atresia by which the follicles are said to become atretic. This is a degenerative process characterized by cessation of mitosis in the granulosa cells, separation of granulosa cells from the basement membrane, and death of the oocyte. Although the process of atresia takes place from the time of birth until a few years after the menopause, there are moments in which it is particularly intense, and these moments are linked to marked hormonal alterations. Follicular atresia is quite accentuated just after birth, when the effect of maternal hormones ceases, and also during puberty and pregnancy, ie, when marked qualitative and quantitative hormonal modifications take place.

The process of atresia may take place during any stage in the development of a follicle.

When atresia starts in a primary follicle, the out-

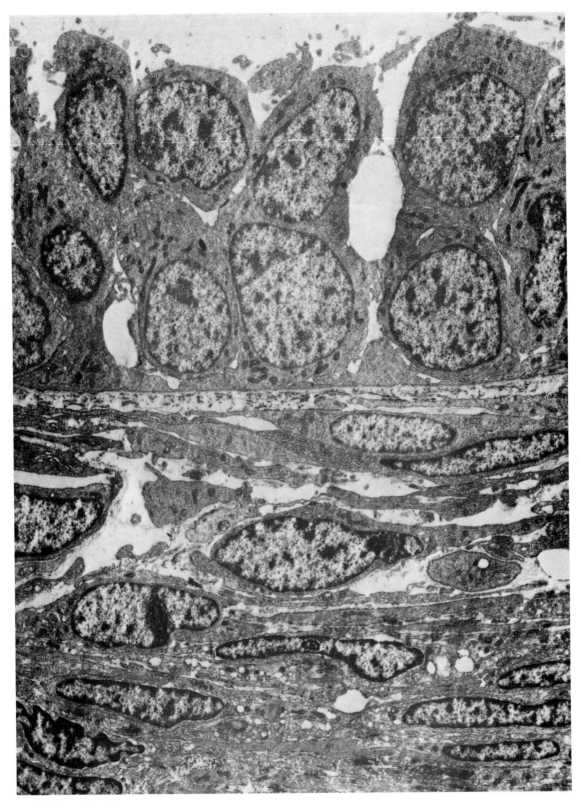

Figure 24–5. Electron micrograph of the wall of a growing ovarian follicle. In the upper part of the figure there are several cuboid follicular cells. A basement membrane separates these cells from the theca interna. × 6400.

line of the oocyte becomes irregular and the granulosa cells become smaller, separating from one another. The oocyte and the granulosa cells start to autolyze, finally leaving a space which is immediately occupied by cells of the ovarian stroma so that no vestige is left.

In growing follicles the degenerative process is basically the same. The zona pellucida is very resistant, becoming wavy and pleated at the onset of the atretic process as a result of the collapse of the follicle, but its material persists longer than the cells of the follicle.

When atresia reaches a follicle in the late stage of growth, a large quantity of degenerative material is produced which elicits the formation of macrophages from monocytes carried in the blood by vessels that invade the area of atresia and from cells of the connective tissue of the ovary. While removal of the remnants of the follicle in atresia takes place, cells of the ovarian connective tissue which invade the area produce a small amount of collagenous fiber—similar to a cicatricial process. Later, all vestiges of follicular atresia disappear since the collagen is reabsorbed and replaced by typical ovarian stroma.

Origin & Maturation of Oocytes

Oocytes are formed during intrauterine life, and their number does not increase after birth. The cells which are precursors of the oocytes are called *primordial germ cells* and originate in the endoderm of the yolk sac. Primordial germ cells migrate to the genital ridge and into the developing ovary.

Primary follicles as well as growing follicles contain primary oocytes equivalent to primary spermatocytes of the seminiferous tubules (Chapter 23). These oocytes are in the prophase of the first meiotic division.

The first meiotic division is completed just before ovulation. The chromatin is equally divided between the daughter cells, but one of the secondary oocytes has almost all of the cytoplasm. The other becomes the first polar body, a very small cell containing the nucleus and a minimal amount of cytoplasm.

Immediately after expulsion of the first polar body, and still in the cortical region of the ovary, the nucleus of the secondary oocyte starts the second meiotic division, which stops in metaphase and will only be completed when fertilization has taken place. Fertilization consists of penetration into the oocyte of the body of the spermatozoon but not the tail. The fertilized oocyte is called an *ovum.*

The secondary oocyte remains viable for an estimated maximum of 24 hours. Penetration of the sperm cell head reconstitutes the diploid number of chromosomes typical of the species and serves as a stimulus for the ovum to complete the second meiotic division and cast off the second polar body. When fertilization does not take place, the secondary oocyte undergoes autolysis in the tube without completing the second division of maturation.

Corpus Luteum

After ovulation, the follicular cells and those of the theca interna (Fig 24–5) which remain in the ovary form a temporary endocrine gland called the corpus luteum (yellow body) (Fig 24–6). The corpus luteum is localized in the cortical region of the ovary and secretes progesterone and estrogens. Progesterone prevents the development of new ovarian follicles and ovulation.

When the follicular liquid is ejected under pressure, it results in collapse of the follicle's wall so that it becomes pleated. Some blood flows out to the follicular cavity, where it coagulates and later is invaded by connective tissue cells that originate in the ovarian stroma. This connective tissue, with remnants of blood clot that are gradually removed, remains in the interior of the corpus luteum, constituting its most central part.

The follicular cells do not divide after ovulation. However, they increase greatly in volume and assume the characteristics of cells that secrete steroid hormones, thus becoming *granulosa lutein cells* (Fig 24–6). These cells contain lipid droplets in their cytoplasm, which appears little stained in common preparations. The cytoplasm of granulosa lutein cells contains *lipochrome,* a pigment that is soluble in lipids and is responsible for the yellow color of the corpus luteum when examined in the fresh ovary.

The cells of the theca interna also contribute to the formation of the corpus luteum by giving rise to the *theca lutein (paralutein) cells* (Fig 24–6). These cells are similar to the lutein cells of the granulosa layer, but they are smaller and localized in the periphery of the corpus luteum.

The granulosa lutein and the theca lutein cells show the ultrastructural organization typical of steroid-secreting cells. In humans, these cells characteristically show parallel arrays of large amounts of smooth endoplasmic reticulum and some flat cisternae of the granular endoplasmic reticulum (Fig 24–7).

The blood capillaries of the theca interna grow into the interior of the corpus luteum and form the rich vascular network of this structure.

The corpus luteum is formed by the stimulus of luteinizing hormone (LH) synthesized by the pars distalis of the pituitary under hypothalamic control. The stimulating effect of luteinizing hormone on progesterone secretion by the corpus luteum has been shown to be via increased formation of cyclic AMP. In mice and rats, it was shown that prolactin (luteotropic hormone, LTH), also secreted by the pars distalis, stimulates the secretion of progesterone by the corpus luteum, but in humans this activity has not been observed. Since the progesterone produced by the corpus luteum has an inhibiting effect on the production of luteinizing hormone, the corpus luteum will soon degenerate unless it receives a stimulus from another source. This inhibiting effect of progesterone on luteinizing hormone production is indirect and mediated through the hypothalamus (Figs 24–8 and 24–9).

It would appear that both the brain and the pituitary may be responsive to ovarian hormones and may be either stimulated or inhibited independently during

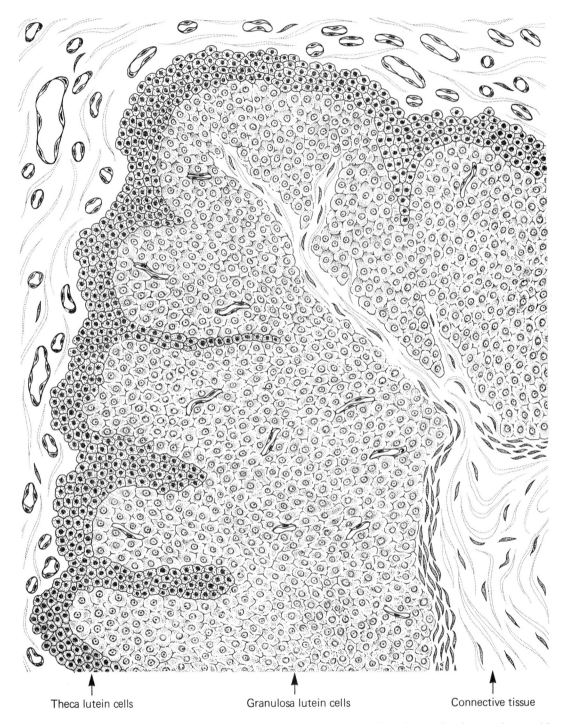

Theca lutein cells   Granulosa lutein cells   Connective tissue

Figure 24–6. Drawing of a small portion from a corpus luteum. Lutein cells derived from the granulosa layer are larger and less darkly stained than the paralutein cells, which derive from the theca interna.

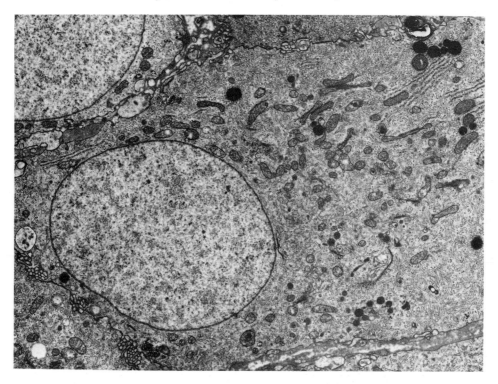

Figure 24—7. Electron micrograph of a human luteal cell. The nucleus contains finely dispersed chromatin, without a visible nucleolus in this section. Observe the marked development of the smooth endoplasmic reticulum. There are also many elongated mitochondria. (Reproduced, with permission, from Adams EC, Hertig AT: J Cell Biol 41:696, 1969.)

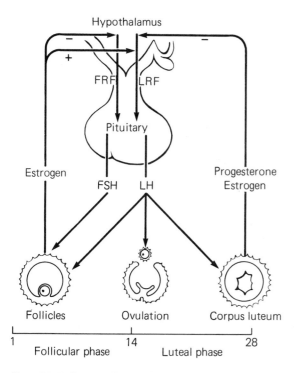

Figure 24—8. Diagram showing the relationships of the hypothalamus, pituitary, and ovaries in the feedback mechanism regulating the secretion of hormones produced during the menstrual cycle.

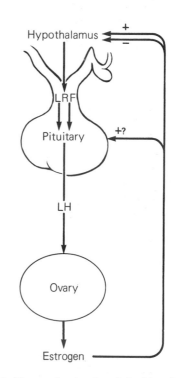

Figure 24—9. Diagram showing the relationships of the hypothalamus, pituitary, and ovaries in the feedback mechanism regulating the secretion of luteinizing hormone and estrogen.

different stages of the cycle.

When pregnancy does not occur, the corpus luteum lasts only 10–14 days, ie, it persists during the second half of the menstrual cycle. After this period, as a result of the lack of luteinizing hormone, it degenerates and disappears. This is the so-called *menstrual yellow body* or *corpus luteum spurium.*

When pregnancy occurs, the *chorionic gonadotropin* produced by the syncytiotrophoblast of the placenta will stimulate the corpus luteum, which maintains itself for about 6 months and then gradually declines but does not disappear completely and continues to secrete progesterone until the end of pregnancy. This is the *gravidic yellow body* or *corpus luteum verum.* The corpus luteum of pregnancy is larger than the corpus luteum spurium, reaching a diameter of 5 cm.

The cells of the gravidic or menstrual corpus luteum which undergo degeneration disappear by autolysis, and their cellular remnants are phagocytosed by macrophages. The site is then occupied by a scar of dense connective tissue, thus forming a *corpus albicans.* The corpus albicans remains for a variable period and is then gradually replaced by the stroma characteristic of the ovary. The absorption process of a corpus albicans may take months or even years, depending mainly on the size of the preexisting corpus luteum.

OVIDUCT
(Uterine Tube)

The oviduct (uterine tube, Fallopian tube) is a musculomembranous tube of great mobility measuring about 12 cm in length. One of its extremities opens into the peritoneal cavity next to the ovary; the other crosses the wall of the uterus and opens into the interior of this organ.

The oviduct is divided into 4 segments, some of which do not have clear limits. The first segment *(pars interstitialis)* is situated in the interior of the uterine wall. The second segment, or *isthmus,* is formed by the portion of the tube which is adjacent to the uterus. The third is the *ampulla,* which is more dilated than the isthmus. The fourth segment, the *infundibulum,* is funnel-shaped and situated near the ovary. The free (larger) extremity of the infundibulum presents fringed extensions called *fimbriae.*

Histologic Structure

The wall of the oviduct is composed of 3 layers: a mucosa, a muscular layer, and a serosa represented by the peritoneum (Fig 24–10).

The mucosa has long longitudinal folds that are numerous in the ampulla. In cross-sections, the lumen

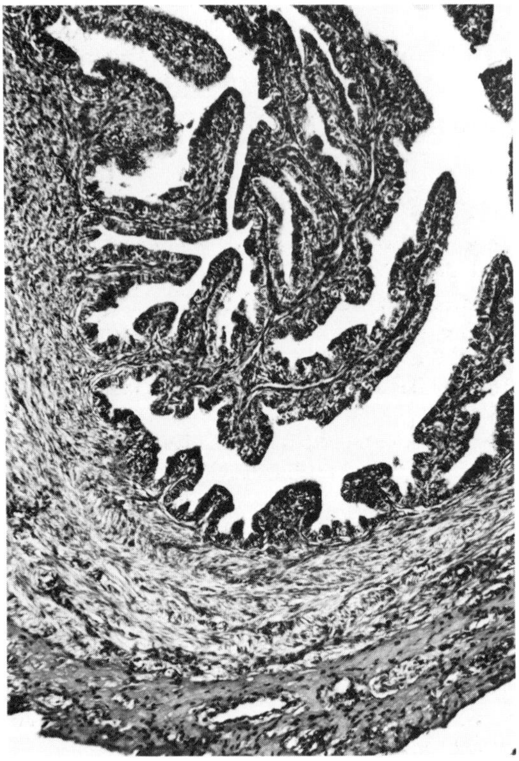

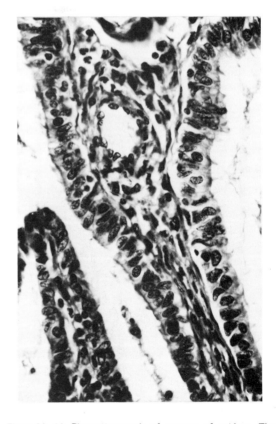

Figure 24–10. Photomicrograph of a cross-section through the ampulla of the oviduct. The mucosa projects many folds into the lumen. H&E stain, X 31.

Figure 24–11. Photomicrograph of mucosa of oviduct. The section was made at the level of the ampulla. Masson's stain, X 320.

of the ampulla resembles a labyrinth (Fig 24–10). These folds become smaller in the segments of the tube which are closer to the uterus. In the pars interstitialis, the folds are reduced to small bulges in the lumen, so that its outline is almost regular.

The epithelium lining the mucosa is simple columnar and contains 2 types of cells. One is provided with cilia and the other is devoid of cilia and appears to be secretory (Fig 24–11). The 2 types of epithelial cells are probably different functional states of a single cell type. The cilia beat toward the uterus, causing movement of the viscous liquid film that covers its surface. This liquid consists mainly of products of secretory cells interspersed between ciliated cells. Movement of the film that covers the mucosa of the tube helps to transport the oocyte or the embryo toward the uterus and hampers the passage of microorganisms from the uterus to the peritoneal cavity.

The lamina propria of the mucosa is composed of loose connective tissue. In cases of abnormal nidation, in which the embryo implants itself in the tube (ectopic pregnancy), the lamina propria reacts as the endometrium, forming numerous decidual cells.

The muscle layer is composed of smooth muscle fibers disposed in groups separated by abundant loose connective tissue.

Histophysiology

The oviduct receives the oocyte expelled by the ovary and carries it toward the uterus. Its lumen represents an environment adequate for fertilization, and the secretion contained there contributes to the nutrition of the embryo during the earlier phases of development.

At the time of ovulation, the oviduct exhibits active movement. The fimbriae of the infundibulum move closer to the surface of the ovary, and the funnel shape of the oviduct facilitates the recovery of the liberated oocyte.

The oviduct also presents waves of rhythmic contractions starting at the infundibulum and directed toward the uterus. These waves seem to be important in the movement of the ovum toward the uterus.

The wall of the oviduct is richly vascularized, and its vessels become dilated at the time of ovulation. This gives a certain rigidity and distention to the organ, facilitating its approximation to the ovary.

UTERUS

The uterus is a pear-shaped organ with a dilated portion, the *body,* whose upper part is the *fundus of the uterus;* and a lower cylindric part which opens into the vagina–*cervix* or *uterine neck.* The cervix bulges into the lumen of the vagina.

The wall of the uterus is relatively thick and is formed by 3 coats: in different parts of the uterus either the outer *serosa* (connective tissue and mesothe-

lium) or *adventitia* (connective tissue); the *myometrium,* a tunic of smooth muscle; and the *endometrium,* or mucosa of the uterus.

Myometrium

Myometrium is the thickest tunic of the uterus, being composed of bundles of smooth muscle fibers separated by connective tissue. The bundles of smooth muscle form 4 layers which are not well defined: the *stratum submucosum,* the *stratum vasculare,* the *stratum supravasculare,* and the *stratum subserosum.* The first and the fourth are composed mainly of fibers disposed longitudinally, ie, parallel to the long axis of the organ. The stratum vasculare is so named because of its many large blood vessels. In this layer, muscle bundles with a circular structure predominate.

During pregnancy, the myometrium goes through a period of great growth; after childbirth, it regresses to its former size. The growth is due to an increase in the number of smooth muscle fibers through division and through transformation of embryonic intercellular connective tissue cells into new muscle fibers as well as to hypertrophy of existing smooth muscle fibers. Electron microscopic studies have shown that, during pregnancy, many smooth muscle fibers have ultrastructural characteristics of protein-secreting cells and actively incorporate collagen precursors (^{3}H-proline).

After pregnancy, there is destruction of some smooth muscle fibers, reduction in size of others, and enzymatic degradation of the collagen. The uterus is reduced in size almost to its prepregnancy dimensions. The connective tissue consists of collagenous fibers, fibroblasts, embryonic connective tissue cells, macrophages, and mast cells. An elastic network and some reticular fibers are also present.

Endometrium

The endometrium consists of epithelium and lamina propria containing simple tubular glands which sometimes branch in their deeper portions (near the myometrium). Its epithelial cells are simple columnar and are a mixture of ciliated and secretory cells. The epithelium of the uterine glands is similar to the superficial epithelium, but ciliated cells are more rare in the glands.

The connective tissue of the lamina propria is rich in cells and contains abundant amorphous intercellular material. Connective tissue fibers are rare, which makes this tissue somewhat similar to mesenchyme.

The Menstrual Cycle

The action of ovarian hormones (estrogens and progesterone) under the stimulus of the anterior lobe of the pituitary causes the endometrium to undergo cyclic structural modifications which constitute the menstrual cycle. The duration of the menstrual cycle is variable but averages 28 days.

Menstrual cycles start usually between 12 and 15 years of age and continue until about age 45–50. Since menstrual cycles are a consequence of ovarian modifications related to the production of ova, the female is

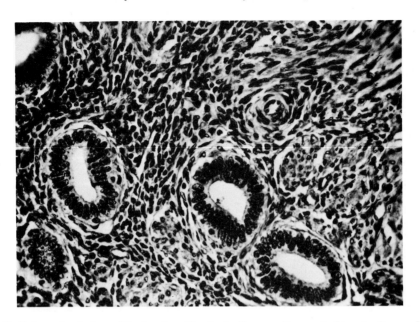

Figure 24–12. Endometrium in the proliferative phase. The gland cells are usually organized in a simple array. H&E stain, × 320.

fertile only during the years when she is having menstrual cycles. This does not mean that sexual activity is terminated by menopause—only that fertility ceases.

For practical purposes, the beginning of the menstrual cycle is taken as the day when menstrual bleeding appears. The menstrual discharge consists of endometrium that is partially destroyed and desquamated mixed with blood from the torn vessels. The *menstrual phase* is defined as the first to the fourth days of the cycle; the *proliferative phase* is the fifth to the 14th days; and the *secretory phase* is the 15th to the 28th days. The duration of each phase is variable, and the intervals given are only estimates.

The functional sequence of the menstrual cycle will be described in the following order: proliferative phase, secretory or luteal phase, and menstrual phase.*

A. Proliferative Phase: After the menstrual phase, the uterine mucosa becomes reduced to a small band of connective tissue containing the basal portion of the glands but without their upper part and the epithelial lining. This deep part of the endometrium which does not peel off during menstruation is called the *basal layer;* the portion that is destroyed and renewed in each cycle is called the *functional layer.*

The proliferative phase is also called the *estrogenic phase* because it coincides with the development of the ovarian follicles and with the production of estrogens.

The cells in the fundi of the glands proliferate, migrate to the surface of the mucosa, and reconstitute the glands and the epithelial lining of the endome-

trium. Cellular proliferation continues during the entire proliferative phase, and mitoses are observed both in the cells of the epithelial lining and in the glands (Fig 24–12). Proliferation of the connective cells of the lamina propria also occurs, and there is consequently a growth of the endometrium as a whole.

At the end of the proliferative phase, the glands appear straight, with narrow lumens, and their cells begin to accumulate glycogen. The coiled arteries are elongated and convoluted.

B. Secretory or Luteal Phase: This phase starts after ovulation and depends upon the formation of corpus luteum, which secretes progesterone. Acting upon the glands already developed by the action of the estrogens, the progesterone stimulates the gland cells to secrete.

The glands become tortuous as the lumens are dilated by the secretion which accumulates in their interiors. In this phase, the endometrium reaches its maximum thickness (5 mm) as a result of the accumulation of secretions and edema of the stroma. Mitoses are rare during the secretory phase (Fig 24–13). The elongation and convolution of the coiled arteries continue and extend into the superficial portion of the endometrium.

C. Menstrual Phase: When fertilization of the ovum expelled by the ovary fails to occur, nidation does not occur and the levels of estrogens and progesterone in the blood fall suddenly. The endometrium which was developed in response to the stimulus of these hormones collapses and is then partially destroyed.

At the end of the secretory phase, the walls of the coiled arteries contract, closing off blood flow and producing ischemia, which leads to death (necrosis) of the endothelium. At this stage, desquamation of the endo-

*The structural changes that occur during the menstrual cycle are gradual; the clear division of the phases implied in the text has mainly teaching value.

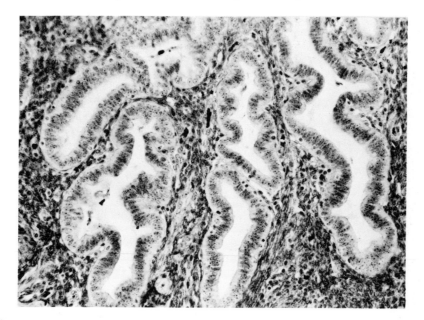

Figure 24—13. Endometrium in the secretory phase (21st day of the menstrual cycle). Uterine glands are tortuous, with lumens dilated by accumulation of secretory material. H&E stain, × 224.

metrium and rupture of blood vessels take place and bleeding begins.

The endometrium becomes partially detached. The amount lost is variable in different women and even in the same woman at different times. At the end of the menstrual phase, the endometrium is almost always reduced to nothing but the basal layer, containing the blind ends of the endometrial glands. At that time, the surface of the endometrium is entirely deprived of its lining. Proliferation of the gland cells and their migration to the surface begin the proliferative phase, restarting the cycle.

Uterine Cervix

As previously noted, the *cervix* or *collum* is the lower, cylindric part of the uterus. This portion differs in histologic structure from the rest of the uterus. It has few smooth muscle fibers and a large quantity of connective tissue.

The mucosa of the cervix contains the mucous *cervical glands,* which are extensively branched. This mucosa does not desquamate during menstruation, although its glands undergo small variations in their structure during the menstrual cycle. When blocking of the ducts of these glands occurs, the retained secretion causes a dilatation which gives rise to the *Nabothian cyst.*

During pregnancy, the cervical mucous glands proliferate and secrete a more viscous and more abundant mucus.

The external aspect of the cervix which bulges into the lumen of the vagina is lined by stratified squamous epithelium.

IMPLANTATION

The human oocyte is fertilized at the upper portion of the oviduct, and segmentation of the corona radiata occurs as the oocyte moves passively toward the uterus. Through successive mitoses, a compact collection of cells covered by the zona pellucida and called a *morula* is formed (Fig 24—14). Formation of this structure is followed by the appearance on the surface of special regions where the cells come into contact with each other. These regions are smoother than the rest of the surface, which continues to be covered with microvilli. During this period, the fertilized ovum does not increase in size (Fig 24—14) and is contained by the zona pellucida. The cells that result from segmentation of the fertilized ovum are called *blastomeres.*

A cavity at the central part of the morula appears as a result of the gradual accumulation of liquid transferred from the lumen of the oviduct; the cells form a fluid-filled sphere called the *blastocyst.* The blastomeres separated by this liquid arrange themselves in a peripheral layer *(trophoblast)* which is thickened at one point where a collection of cells remains *(inner cell mass)* and bulges into the cavity. This is the phase of the blastocyst and corresponds approximately to the fourth or fifth day after ovulation. At this time, the embryo reaches the uterus. For 1 or 2 days, the blastocyst remains in the uterine lumen and finally comes into contact with the surface of the endometrium, immersed in the secretion of the endometrial glands.

In the blastocyst phase, the zona pellucida becomes thinner and disappears, allowing the cells of the trophoblast, which have the capacity to invade the

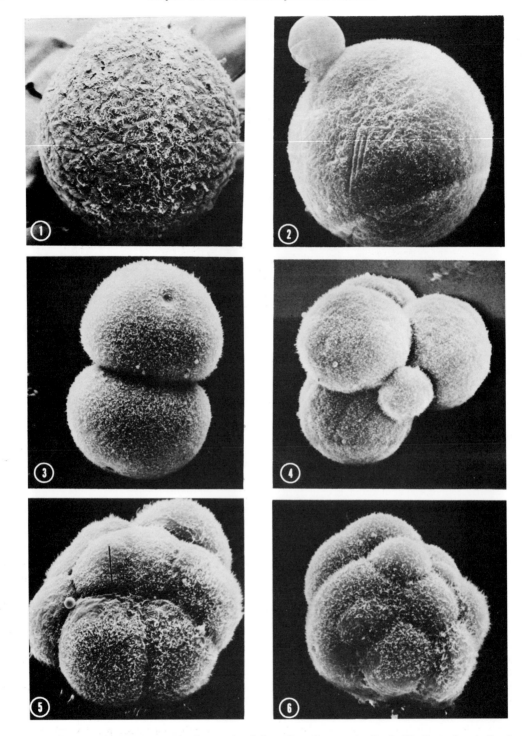

Figure 24–14. Scanning electron microscopic photographs of the surface of an oocyte after fertilization and up to the stage of a morula. The zona pellucida has been digested with pronase. *(1)* The primary oocyte of the mouse shortly after its release from an ovarian follicle. The oocyte has an intact germinal vesicle at this stage. × 1380. *(2)* Fertilized egg. Note the microvillous surface of the egg and the smooth surface of the first polar body. × 1300. *(3)* Two-cell stage evenly covered with microvilli. × 1320. *(4)* Four-cell stage with microvillous second polar body. × 1870. *(5)* Eight-cell stage. Note smoother regions of membrane where cells come into contact (arrow). × 1400. *(6)* Morula of the mouse. Microvilli are quite numerous, particularly in the area of cell contact. × 1540. (Reproduced, with permission, from Calarco P: Mammalian preimplantation development. In: *Scanning Electron Microscopy Atlas of Mammalian Reproduction.* Hafez ESE [editor] . Igaku Shoin Ltd, 1975.)

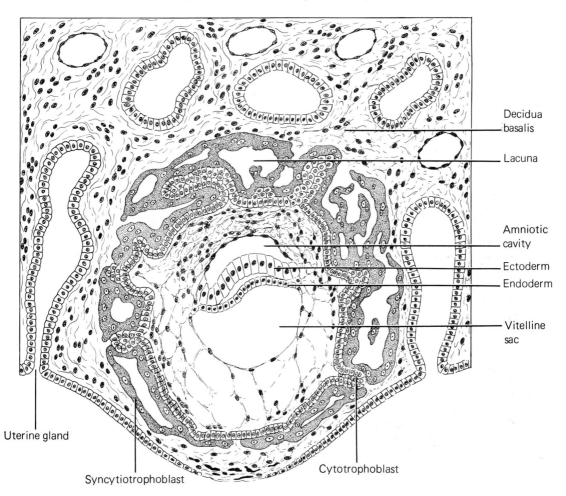

Decidua basalis

Lacuna

Amniotic cavity

Ectoderm

Endoderm

Vitelline sac

Uterine gland

Syncytiotrophoblast

Cytotrophoblast

Figure 24–15. Schematic drawing of a human embryo at 12 days, showing the relationships between the embryo and the endometrium (which after implantation is called the decidua).

mucosa, to come into direct contact with the endometrium. Immediately thereafter, the cells of the trophoblast begin to multiply, thus ensuring, with the help of the endometrium, the nourishment of the embryo. The inner cell mass, from which the body of the embryo will originate, grows very little during this phase.

The trophoblast also secretes enzymes which destroy the epithelium of the endometrium, allowing *implantation* or *nidation* of the embryo in the interior of the uterine mucosa (Fig 24–15). This type of *interstitial* implantation occurs exclusively in humans and some other animals. The process starts around the sixth day, and on about the ninth day after ovulation the embryo is totally submerged in the endometrium from which it will receive protection and nourishment for as long as the pregnancy lasts.

Implantation takes place only when the endometrium is in the secretory phase. The uterine glands contain glycoproteins and glycogen. The vessels are dilated and the lamina propria slightly swollen. The endometrium at that point is 5 mm thick.

During implantation, the trophoblast differentiates into 2 layers, the *syncytiotrophoblast* and the *cytotrophoblast* (Figs 24–15 and 24–16). The former is external and has many large nuclei; and its cytoplasm is continuous, forming a syncytium. The cytotrophoblast consists of an irregular layer of ovoid cells immediately under the syncytiotrophoblast.

Electron microscopic study shows that the surface of the syncytiotrophoblast contains irregular microvilli and the superficial cytoplasm contains several vesicles delimited by smooth membranes. This suggests the existence of an intense process of pinocytosis in the syncytiotrophoblast, possibly related to the transference of material from the maternal circulation to the fetus. More deeply, the cytoplasm of the syncytiotrophoblast shows an abundance of both granular and smooth endoplasmic reticulum, a developed Golgi apparatus, and numerous mitochondria. These ultrastructural characteristics are consistent with the role presently attributed to the syncytiotrophoblast in the secretion of chorionic gonadotropin (a glycoprotein hormone), placental lactogen (a protein hormone),

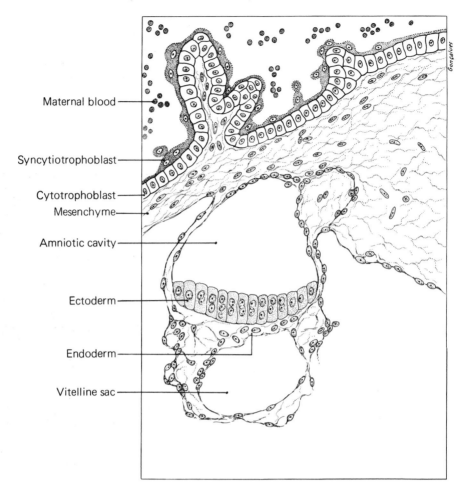

Figure 24—16. Human embryo at 15 days. At upper left is shown a chorionic villus protruding into a lacuna containing maternal blood.

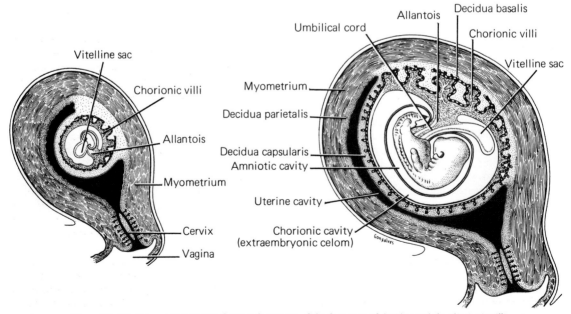

Figure 24—17. Schematic drawings showing formation of the 3 regions of decidua and the chorionic villi.

and estrogen and progesterone (steroids). The syncytiotrophoblast contains lipid droplets whose composition (as determined by cytochemical methods) is compatible with the presence of steroids.

In the syncytiotrophoblast, extracytoplasmic cavities appear; they grow and communicate with one another, conferring a spongy structure on this layer (Fig 24–15). Thus, *lacunae* are formed, lined with syncytiotrophoblast. On the other hand, the lytic activity of the syncytiotrophoblast causes the rupture of both arterial and venous blood vessels, with overflow of blood to these lacunar spaces. The direction of blood flow in the lacunar spaces is due to the difference in pressure between arterial and venous vessels. Consequently, the blood flows from the arterial vessels to these spaces and from there to the veins.

After implantation of the embryo, the endometrium goes through profound changes and is then called *decidua;* and the cells of the stroma become enlarged and polygonal. The decidua can be divided into *decidua basalis,* situated between the embryo and the myometrium; *decidua capsularis,* between the embryo and the lumen of the uterus; and *decidua parietalis,* which is the remainder of the decidua (Fig 24–17).

The trophoblast in contact with the decidua capsularis develops only to a slight extent since its nutrition is deficient. Growth of the trophoblast in the part of the embryo facing the myometrium is, however, assured by the maternal blood, and its growth is exuberant. From this part of the trophoblast, elongated expansions called *primary villi* are formed. Their main characteristic is that they are composed only of cytotrophoblast and syncytiotrophoblast early in pregnancy. During this stage of embryonic development, an extraembryonic mesenchyme appears before the intraembryonic one and contributes to the formation of the fetal membranes and placenta. The extraembryonic mesenchyme plus the trophoblast form the *chorion.* On the side of the *decidua capsularis,* the chorion does not develop *(smooth chorion* or *chorion laeve);* on the side of the decidua basalis, the chorion grows extensively and forms the *chorion frondosum.* The layers of the chorion (beginning at the surface) are (1) syncytiotrophoblast, (2) cytotrophoblast, and (3) extraembryonic mesenchyme.

The mesenchyme, when it penetrates into the primary villi, transforms them into *secondary villi* (Fig 24–18). Vessels are formed gradually in situ in this mesenchyme and later will join those formed in the body of the embryo, establishing a circulation and thus allowing exchange of substances and gases between the fetal and maternal blood (Fig 24–18).

PLACENTA

The placenta is a temporary organ found only in eutherian mammals at the site where the physiologic exchanges between the mother and the fetus occur. It consists of a fetal part (chorion) and a maternal part (decidua basalis).

The placenta is the only organ composed of cells derived from 2 different individuals.

Fetal Part

The fetal part of the placenta consists of the chorion. It has a *chorionic plate* at the point where the *chorionic villi* start–the secondary villi already described. These villi consist of a connective core derived from the extraembryonic mesenchyme surrounded by the syncytiotrophoblast and the cytotrophoblast (Fig 24–19). The syncytiotrophoblast remains until the end of pregnancy, but the cytotrophoblast disappears gradually during the second half of pregnancy.

The chorionic villi can be either free or anchored. Both have the same structure, but the free ones do not reach the decidua, whereas the anchored chorionic villi become attached to the decidua basalis. The surface of the villi is bathed with blood from the lacunae of the basal decidua and is the site where the exchange of substances between fetal and maternal blood occurs.

Maternal Part

The maternal part of the placenta–the decidua basalis–supplies arterial blood for the lacunae situated between the secondary villi and receives venous blood from these lacunae. Although the maternal blood vessels are opened during implantation, the fetal vessels contained in the secondary villi remain intact. Fetal blood and maternal blood do not mix except occasionally at the end of pregnancy, when the cytotrophoblast is no longer continuous, the capillaries of the villi are close to the surface, and a very slight exchange of blood cells may occur. At that time, the walls of the fetal capillaries are separated from the maternal blood only by the syncytiotrophoblast. Ruptures of the capillaries are not rare at this time, with a consequent mixture of fetal and maternal blood.

In the borderlines of the placenta, the decidua basalis is firmly united to the chorion by the *marginal zone.* This zone follows the outline of the placenta.

During pregnancy, cells from the connective tissue of the decidua basalis and a lesser number of cells from the decidua parietalis form the *decidual cells.* These large cells have a vacuolated cytoplasm that contains glycogen and lipids and a clear nucleus with a prominent nucleolus. Decidual cells are more numerous during the first half of pregnancy. Their function is not well established.

At the end of pregnancy, the placenta has the shape of a disk. The umbilical cord usually starts from the center of the placenta and forms a communication between the fetal and placental circulations.

Histophysiology

Fetal venous blood reaches the placenta through the 2 umbilical arteries, which branch and continue with the vessels of the chorionic villi. In these villi, the fetal blood is oxygenated, loses its CO_2, and returns to

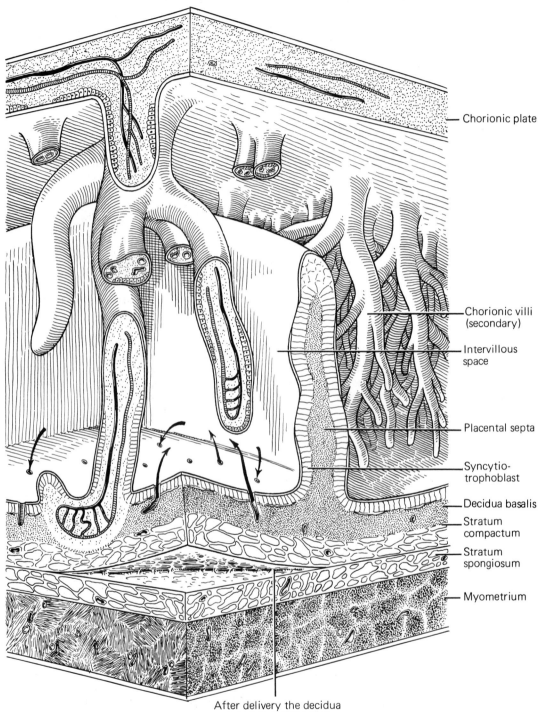

Chorionic plate

Chorionic villi (secondary)

Intervillous space

Placental septa

Syncytio- trophoblast

Decidua basalis

Stratum compactum

Stratum spongiosum

Myometrium

After delivery the decidua detaches at this point

Figure 24–18. Schematic drawing of placental structure. Arrows indicate the blood flow from decidual arteries to intervillous space and back to decidual veins. This direction is determined by the difference in pressure between arterial and venous blood. (Redrawn and reproduced, with permission, from Duplessis GDT, Haegel P: *Embryologie.* Masson, 1971. [English edition © Springer Verlag, 1972; Chapman & Hall, 1972; Masson, 1972.])

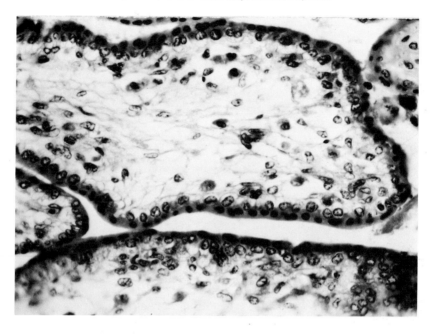

Figure 24–19. Photomicrograph of a chorionic villus in the second half of pregnancy. The syncytiotrophoblast is continuous, but most of the cytotrophoblast has disappeared. H&E stain, X 320.

the fetus through the umbilical vein.

Since the chorionic villi are submerged in maternal blood, the fetal blood remains isolated by the following structures which form the *placental barrier:* (1) the walls of the fetal capillaries, (2) the basal lamina of the capillaries and of the trophoblast, (3) the mesenchyme in the interior of the villus, (4) the cytotrophoblast (mainly during the first half of pregnancy), and (5) the syncytiotrophoblast.

The placenta is permeable to several substances, and normally it transfers oxygen, water, electrolytes, carbohydrates, lipids, proteins, vitamins, hormones, antibodies, and some drugs from maternal blood to fetal blood. From the fetal blood to the maternal blood it transfers CO_2, water, hormones, and residual products of metabolism.

The placenta is also an endocrine organ which elaborates chorionic gonadotropin, estrogen, progesterone, one or possibly 2 substances with thyrotropic activity, renin, and relaxin. It also secretes a protein hormone called human placental lactogen (HPL) which has lactogenic and growth-stimulating activity. All of these hormones seem to be synthesized by the syncytiotrophoblast. Even the gonadotropin, whose synthesis was attributed to the cytotrophoblast—because at the end of pregnancy the level of gonadotropin decreases when the cells of the cytotrophoblast almost disappear—is today considered to be a product of the syncytiotrophoblast. Examination of sections of placenta treated with fluorescent antigonadotropin antibody shows fluorescence in the whole trophoblast but especially in the syncytiotrophoblast.

Radioautographic studies after injection of radioactive thymidine show that the cells of the cytotrophoblast multiply actively and incorporate themselves into the syncytiotrophoblast. This indicates that the syncytiotrophoblast grows as a result of mitotic activity of the cytotrophoblast.

VAGINA

The wall of the vagina is devoid of glands and presents 3 layers: a *mucosa,* a *muscular layer,* and a *fibrous layer.* The mucus found in the lumen of the vagina comes from the glands of the uterine cervix.

The epithelium of the mucous layer is stratified squamous and has a thickness of 150–200 μm. Its cells may contain a certain amount of keratohyalin. However, intense keratinization with change of the cells into keratin plates, as in typical keratinized epithelia, does not occur (Fig 24–20). Under the stimulus of estrogen, the vaginal epithelium synthesizes and accumulates a large quantity of glycogen which is thrown into the lumen of the vagina when the vaginal cells desquamate or peel off. Bacteria in the vagina metabolize glycogen and form lactic acid, which is responsible for the usually low pH of the vagina.

The lamina propria of the vaginal mucosa is composed of loose connective tissue which is very rich in elastic fibers. Among the cells present, one can find lymphocytes and neutrophils in relatively large quantities. During certain phases of the menstrual cycle, these 2 types of leukocytes usually invade the epithelium and pass into the lumen of the vagina.

The muscular layer of the vagina is composed

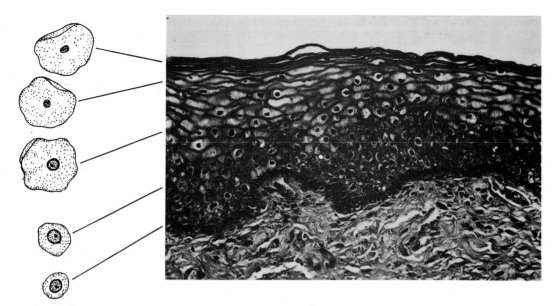

Figure 24—20. Photomicrograph of a section of vaginal mucosa and drawings of the cells found in various epithelial layers. Masson's stain, X 250.

mainly of longitudinal bundles of smooth muscle fibers. There are some circular bundles, especially in the innermost part (next to the mucosa).

Outside the muscular layer, a coat of dense connective tissue, the *adventitial coat,* rich in thick elastic fibers, unites the vagina with the surrounding tissues. The great elasticity of the vagina is related to the large number of elastic fibers in the connective tissues of its wall. In this connective tissue there are an extensive venous plexus, nerve bundles, and groups of nerve cells.

Near the external orifice of the vagina is a circular fold of mucosa, the *hymen.*

EXTERNAL GENITALIA

The female external genitalia or vulvae consist of the *clitoris, labia minora, labia majora,* and certain glands that open into the vestibulum, a space enclosed by the labia minora.

The urethra and the ducts of the vestibular glands open into this portion of the vagina. The 2 *glandulae vestibulares majores,* or *glands of Bartholin,* are situated one on each side of the vestibulum; the *glandulae vestibulares minores* are more numerous and scattered, occurring with greater frequency around the urethra and clitoris. All of the glandulae vestibulares are of the mucous type.

Both in embryonic origin and in histologic structure, the clitoris can be thought of as a rudimentary and incomplete penis. It is formed by 2 erectile bodies with rudimentary glands and a prepuce. The clitoris is lined by stratified squamous epithelium.

The labia minora are folds of skin with a core of spongy connective tissue permeated by elastic fibers. The stratified squamous epithelium which lines them has cells rich in melanin and has a thin keratinized layer on the surface. It resembles mucosa, and sebaceous and sweat glands occur on both surfaces.

The labia majora are folds of skin and contain a large quantity of adipose tissue and a thin layer of smooth muscle. Their inner aspect has a histologic structure similar to that of the labia minora. The external surface is covered by skin and coarse, curly hair. Sebaceous and sweat glands are numerous on both surfaces.

The external genitalia are supplied with sensory nerve endings. Meissner and Pacini corpuscles have also been found.

ENDOCRINE INTERRELATIONSHIPS

Female reproductive function is regulated through certain nuclei of the hypothalamus. Nerve cells in the hypothalamus produce and introduce into the blood specific polypeptides that act on the anterior lobe of the pituitary and liberate gonadotropins; these gonadotropins in turn stimulate the secretion of ovarian hormones (estrogens and progesterone) (Fig 24—21). The hypothalamic localization of the ovarian hormone control mechanism might explain why strong nonspecific cerebral stimuli occasionally affect reproductive function—"boarding school amenorrhea," pseudocyesis, etc. Similar results have been obtained experimentally.

The developing ovarian follicle synthesizes *estrogens* and the corpus luteum synthesizes estrogens and *progesterone*. The main source of the estrogens in the developing follicle seems to be the cells of the theca interna.

The principal estrogen isolated from the ovary is *estradiol-17β*; in the blood, however, *estrone* is the predominant circulating hormone, secreted directly in small amounts by the ovary and accumulated in the circulation by metabolism of estradiol and androstenedione. Estrone is further metabolized to *estriol*, probably in the liver. Estradiol is the most potent estrogen of the three.

The pituitary gonadotropins, follicle-stimulating hormone (FSH) and luteinizing hormone (LH), are produced under the control of "releasing factors" liberated by the hypothalamus. Follicle-stimulating hormone stimulates the growth of the ovarian follicles and the formation of estrogens. Luteinizing hormone promotes the formation of the corpus luteum through differentiation of granulosa cells which remain in the follicle after expulsion of the oocyte (Fig 24–21).

The ovary also acts on the pituitary directly and through the hypothalamus. Estrogens inhibit the secretion of follicle-stimulating hormone and stimulate the secretion of luteinizing hormone. The production of luteinizing hormone is inhibited by progesterone. When the follicle matures and secretes great quantities of estrogen, there is a fall in follicle-stimulating hormone and an increase in the level of luteinizing hormone in blood. Luteinizing hormone promotes ovulation, formation, and maintenance of the corpus luteum. In other species, *prolactin (luteotropic hormone, LTH)* is necessary for the maintenance of corpus luteum. As the secretion of luteinizing hormone is inhibited by progesterone produced by the corpus luteum, this structure is soon deprived of the pituitary stimulus (LH) necessary for its functioning and consequently degenerates.

When fecundation and nidation occur, the chorion synthesizes the chorionic gonadotropins which stimulate and maintain the function of the corpus luteum during pregnancy.

In rats and mice, the corpus luteum is sensitive also to prolactin. In these species, prolactin stimulates the secretion of an already formed corpus luteum. However, there is no evidence that prolactin has any influence on human corpus luteum. In humans, prolactin initiates and maintains milk secretion by mammary glands already stimulated by estrogen, progesterone, corticosteroids, and insulin.

The Menstrual Cycle

The menstrual cycle is under the control of ovarian and pituitary hormones. The proliferative phase corresponds to the period during which—under the action of follicle-stimulating hormone—the developing follicle is synthesizing estrogens which stimulate the growth of the uterine mucosa. On the other hand, the secretory phase of the menstrual cycle occurs when the ovary is secreting both estrogens and progesterone (Fig 24–21).

Although more complete studies must be performed before a definitive statement can be made, the data now available allow us to assume that menstruation is a consequence of the decline of estrogens and progesterone. There are 2 peaks in the production of estrogens during the menstrual cycle: on the 13th and on the 21st days of the cycle. The former, which is reached after a gradual elevation in the level of estrogen, can be explained by the growth of the follicle that reaches its maximum on the 13th day. The latter is due to the production of estrogens by the corpus luteum. The production of progesterone increases gradually after ovulation as a consequence of formation of the corpus luteum; it then declines around the 26th day of the cycle.

EXFOLIATIVE CYTOLOGY

Exfoliative cytology is the study of the characteristics of cells that normally desquamate from various surfaces of the body. Cytologic examination of vaginal mucosa gives important data on hormonal balance and allows early detection of some types of cancer of the female genital system.

The cells to be examined are taken from the vagina with the secretion contained there; they are then spread on a slide, fixed, and stained by special technics such as the Shorr trichrome technic, acridine orange, etc. Cells from the epithelium of the vagina predominate in this type of preparation.

In the fully mature vaginal mucosa, 5 types of cells are easily identifiable: (1) cells of the internal portion of the basal layer (basal cells), (2) cells of the external portion of the basal layer (parabasal cells), (3) cells of the intermediate layers, (4) precornified cells, and (5) cornified cells (Figs 24–20 and 24–21).

Under the stimulus of estrogens, the vaginal epithelium becomes thicker, with a larger number of cellular layers. Partial keratinization of the most superficial cells also occurs. The superficial keratinized cells are characterized by a dense, shrunken (pyknotic) nucleus and an acidophilic cytoplasm (keratin is an acidophilic protein). These cells predominate in the smears of estrogen-stimulated vaginal secretions. They have the shape of a plate since they represent the most superficial elements of stratified squamous epithelium. This aspect is so characteristic of the action of the estrogens that the percentage of acidophilic cells in a smear is considered to be a reliable index of estrogenic stimulation and is therefore much used in clinical practice. Cytologic smears reveal not only the quantitative changes in estrogen but also the effect of progesterone. In the normal menstrual cycle, by day 6 most of the cells are from the intermediate layer, polygonal in shape, and contain basophilic cytoplasm. At the time of ovulation, under the influence of estrogen, most of the cells are from the precornified layer but 20% or more are fully cornified cells. By day 20, the influence of progesterone in addition to estrogen can be clearly

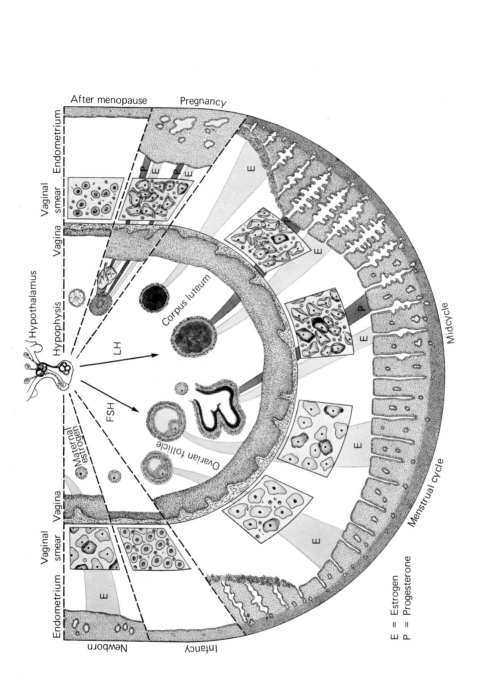

Figure 24–21. Functional changes relating to the hypothalamus, pituitary, ovary, vaginal epithelium, and endometrium. E, estrogen; P, progesterone. (Modified and redrawn from FH Netter, MD.)

noted. There is an increased number of desquamated cells which are of the intermediate type. In contrast to the clearly outlined and separated cells of the proliferative phase, during the secretory phase a loss of cellular outline and clumping can be seen. Almost all of the cells have again become basophilic.

The above characteristics of the progesterone effect are more prominent during pregnancy.

Hormonal deficiency during menopause causes the vaginal epithelium to be thin, with no keratinized cells. The vaginal smear cells are mainly spherical, basal or parabasal cells with basophilic cytoplasm whose large nuclei present dispersed chromatin. The same type of vaginal smear is obtained during the prepubertal state.

The internal basal cells—those from the deepest layer of the vaginal epithelium—only rarely peel off. This happens after childbirth but is not due to the trauma caused by expulsion of the fetus, as one might suppose, because it also occurs in women who have had abdominal deliveries (cesarean operation). The internal basal cells appear on the smear as a result of the intense peeling off of the vaginal epithelium that occurs after delivery, which in turn is a consequence of the sudden decline of the hormonal levels of the placenta and ovaries. These cells are small, spherical, and basophilic and present large nuclei with dispersed chromatin (Fig 24—20).

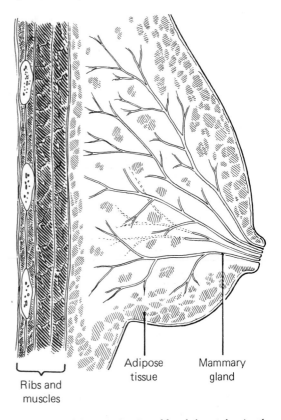

Ribs and muscles

Adipose tissue

Mammary gland

Figure 24—22. Schematic drawing of female breast showing the mammary glands with ducts that open in the nipple.

MAMMARY GLANDS

Each mammary gland comprises 15—25 irregular lobes of the compound tubulo-alveolar type whose function is to secrete milk to nourish newborns (Fig 24—22). Each lobe is separated from the others by dense connective tissue and much adipose tissue and is really a gland in itself with its own excretory duct. These excretory *lactiferous ducts,* 2—4.5 cm long, emerge independently in the *mammary papilla,* or nipple, which has 15—25 openings, each about 0.5 mm in diameter.

The interlobar connective tissue penetrates each lobe, dividing it into lobules by the interlobular connective tissue that surrounds each secretory unit.

The histologic structure of the mammary glands varies according to sex, age, and the physiologic conditions of the body.

Embryonic Breast Development

The mammary gland appears in a human embryo of 8 mm as a thickening of the epidermis, the "milk line." It continues to thicken and becomes the mammary fold. In the course of time, these epithelial thickenings become spherical or club-shaped, with cylindric and polyhedral cells. By continuing to multiply, they form projections with swellings at their ends. These projections gradually grow in the direction of the connective tissue and become the mammary ducts.

In newborns of both sexes, the glands have a diameter of 3.5—9 mm and contain distinct alveoli. In females, the development continues and, with the onset of sexual maturity, increases in intensity and quantity.

Breast Development During Puberty

Before puberty, the mammary glands are composed of lactiferous sinuses and ramified lactiferous ducts which have small cellular aggregates in their extremities.

The development of mammary glands in females during puberty constitutes one of the secondary sex characteristics. During this period, the mammary glands increase in size and develop a prominent nipple. In males, they remain flattened.

Breast enlargement during puberty is the result of 2 growth processes: (1) increase in the volume of the lactiferous ducts, promoted by cell proliferation; and (2) accumulation of adipose tissue in both the interlobar and the interlobular connective tissue. Proliferation of the lactiferous ducts and accumulation of fat are due to an increase in the amount of ovarian hormones during puberty. During this stage, the formation of small tubulo-alveolar structures can be observed in the extremities of the ducts.

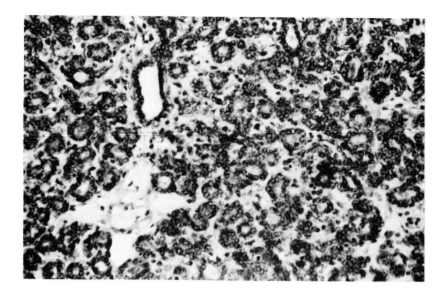

Figure 24–23. Photomicrograph of a mammary gland during pregnancy. There is intense proliferation of the gland alveoli. No secretion is seen. H&E stain,✕ 200.

Breast Development in Adult Women

The adult mammary glands are composed of *lactiferous ducts* and tubulo-alveolar secretory glands. Near the opening of the papilla, the lactiferous ducts dilate to form the *lactiferous sinuses* or *ampullae*.

The lactiferous ducts are lined by squamous stratified epithelium near their external openings. Deeper in the gland the epithelium becomes progressively thinner, with fewer cell layers, until there are only 2 layers of cuboid or low columnar cells. Closer to the secretory portions of the gland—the alveolar ducts and alveoli—the epithelium becomes simple cuboid, resting on a basement membrane and a discontinuous layer of myoepithelial cell processes.

During the menstrual cycle, small alterations in the histologic structure of these glands are observed, ie, proliferation of the ducts and the secretory parts at about the time of ovulation. This coincides with the period during which circulating estrogen is at its peak. Greater accumulation of adipose tissue and greater hydration of connective tissue in the premenstrual phase produce breast enlargement. During this phase, division of the mammary glands into lobules becomes accentuated.

The mammary papilla or nipple has a cylindro-conical shape. In color it may be light brown, dark brown, or black. Externally, it is covered by keratinized stratified squamous epithelium which is continuous with that of the adjacent skin. This epithelium—like that of the vagina—is sensitive to the action of estrogen.

The epithelium of the mammary papilla rests on a layer of connective tissue rich in smooth muscle fibers. These fibers are disposed in circles around the lactiferous ducts and parallel to them where they cross the papilla and open separately in the apex of the papilla.

During puberty, the mammary papillae become more prominent.

The skin around the papilla constitutes the areola. The color of the areola changes from rose to dark brown during pregnancy owing to a local accumulation of melanin. After delivery, it may become lighter in color but never returns to its original shade.

The Breasts During Pregnancy

The mammary glands undergo intense growth during pregnancy as a result of proliferation and ramification of the lactiferous ducts with a consequent active production of secretory tubules and alveoli. The connective stroma and the adipose tissue decrease considerably. Despite this great growth process, there are no visible signs of secretion until late in pregnancy (Fig 24–23).

Growth of the mammary glands during pregnancy occurs as a result of the synergistic action of several hormones, mainly estrogen, progesterone, prolactin, and placental mammotropic hormone. The estrogen acts upon the lactiferous ducts, stimulating their growth by increasing the number of mitoses and causing ramification to occur. Progesterone stimulates the growth of the secretory parts of the mammary glands.

During pregnancy, the quantity of estrogen increases since this hormone is also produced by the placenta. The amount of progesterone also increases, as this steroid is produced first by the corpus luteum (which remains during pregnancy) and later by the placenta.

In hypophysectomized animals, estrogen and progesterone have no effect upon the mammary glands. Other experiments show that the pituitary glands of animals can be removed when pregnancy is advanced without any impairment of growth of the mammary

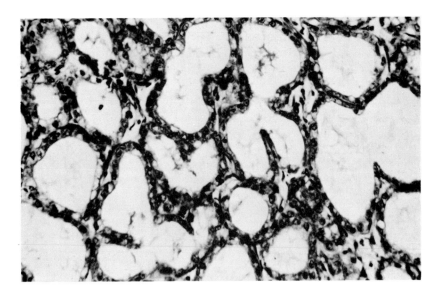

Figure 24—24. Photomicrograph of a lactating mammary gland. The alveoli are distended by the secretion (milk) accumulated in their lumens. H&E stain, × 200.

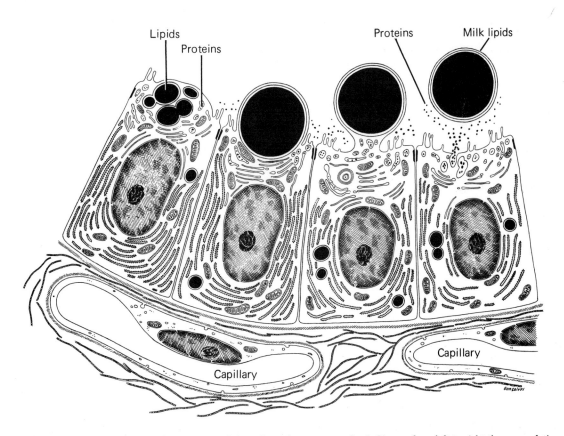

Figure 24—25. Schematic drawing of secretory epithelium from the mammary gland. Observe from left to right the accumulation and extrusion of milk lipids and proteins.

glands, which continue to enlarge as long as the placenta remains functioning. These experiments suggest that prolactin is essential for the early phase of growth of the mammary glands but not for continuation of growth.

Although estrogen, progesterone, and prolactin are the main hormones responsible for the growth of mammary glands during pregnancy, other hormones such as thyroxine, corticosteroids, and growth hormone also play a role in this process.

The Breasts During Lactation

Milk is produced inside the epithelial cells of the secretory portions of the glands and accumulates in their lumens and inside the lactiferous ducts (Fig 24–24). The secretory cells become small and cuboid or squamous. Their cytoplasm becomes a greatly enlarged smooth endoplasmic reticulum with abundant spherical vacuoles of various sizes containing lipids. These vacuoles have a continuous smooth surface membrane. They pass out of the cells into the lumen with this membrane intact (Fig 24–25). The lipids constitute 4% of human milk.

Besides the lipid vacuoles, which are at the apical pole of the secretory cells, one can see protein granules similar to those in the zymogenic cells discussed in Chapter 4. Therefore, the synthesis of milk proteins occurs at the level of the granular endoplasmic reticulum, which is abundant in the basal part of this cell, passing then through the Golgi apparatus and accumulating at the apical portion. Contrary to what occurs with the vacuoles of lipids, the smooth membrane which involves the granules of protein is not eliminated with the protein that appears free in the lumen of the secretory portions (Fig 24–25). Proteins constitute approximately 1.5% of human milk.

Lactose, the third important component of milk, is synthesized from glucose. Lactose constitutes about 7% of human milk.

Sections of mammary gland from a lactating woman show several alveoli in different phases of secretion. Large cells filled with secretion and small cuboid cells with almost no secretion in their interiors can be seen.

When a woman is breast feeding, the suction of the child stimulates tactile receptors, which are abundant around the nipple, resulting in liberation of the posterior pituitary hormone oxytocin. This hormone causes contraction of myoepithelial cells in the gland and ejection of milk occurs. Emotional and genital stimuli also can result in the liberation of oxytocin, forcing milk to appear in the nipples.

Senile Involution of the Breasts

After menopause, involution of the mammary gland is characterized by reduction in size and atrophy of its secretory portion and partly also of the excretory ducts. Striking atrophic changes occur also in the interstitial connective tissue.

●   ●   ●

References

Adams EC, Hertig AT: Studies on guinea pig oocytes. 1. Electron microscopic observations on the development of cytoplasmic organelles in oocytes of primordial and primary follicles. J Cell Biol 21:397, 1964.

Adams EC, Hertig AT: Studies on the human corpus luteum. J Cell Biol 41:696, 1969.

Anderson E, Beams HW: Cytological observations on the fine structure of the guinea pig ovary with special reference to the oogonium, primary oocyte and associated follicle cells. J Ultrastruct Res 3:432, 1960.

Baker TG: A quantitative and cytological study of oogenesis in the rhesus monkey. J Anat 100:761, 1966.

Blanchette EJ: Ovarian steroid cells. 2. The lutein cell. J Cell Biol 31:517, 1966.

Boyd JD, Hamilton WJ: Electron microscopic observations on the cytotrophoblast contribution to the syncytium in the human placenta. J Anat 100:535, 1966.

Brandes D, Anton E: An electron microscopic cytochemical study of macrophages during uterine involution. J Cell Biol 41:50, 1969.

Dirksen ER, Satir P: Ciliary activity in the mouse oviduct as studied by transmission and scanning electron microscopy. Tissue & Cell 4:389, 1972.

Enders AC, Lyon WR: Observations on the fine structure of lutein cells. 2. The effects of hypophysectomy and mammotrophic hormones in the rat. J Cell Biol 22:127, 1964.

Ferenczy A & others: Scanning electron microscopy of the human Fallopian tube. Science 175:783, 1972.

Fredricsson B, Björkman N: Studies on the ultrastructure of the human oviduct epithelium in different functional states. Z Zellforsch Mikrosk Anat 58:387, 1962.

Hertig AT, Adams EC: Studies on the human oocyte and its follicle. 1. Ultrastructural and histochemical observations on the primordial follicle stage. J Cell Biol 34:647, 1967.

Nemanic MK, Pitelka DR: A scanning electron microscope study of the lactating mammary gland. J Cell Biol 48:410, 1971.

Ross R, Klebanoff SJ: Fine structural changes in uterine smooth muscle and fibroblasts in response to estrogen. J Cell Biol 32:27, 1967.

Tersakis J: The ultrastructure of normal human first trimester placenta. J Ultrastruct Res 9:268, 1963.

Wellings SR, Phelp JR: The function of the Golgi apparatus in lactating cells of the BALB/c Crgl mouse: An electron microscopic and autoradiographic study. Z Zellforsch Mikrosk Anat 61:871, 1964.

Yoshida Y: Ultrastructure and secretory function of the syncytial trophoblast of human placenta in early pregnancy. Exp Cell Res 34:305, 1964.

Index